An Introduction to Programming and Object-Oriented Design Using Java 5.0™

An Introduction to Programming and Object-Oriented Design Using Java 5.0™

Second Edition

Jaime Niño and Frederick A. Hosch
University of New Orleans

WILEY

John Wiley & Sons, Inc.

EXECUTIVE EDITOR	Bill Zobrist
SENIOR EDITORIAL ASSISTANT	Simon Durkin
SENIOR PRODUCTION EDITOR	Ken Santor
SENIOR MARKETING MANAGER	Jennifer Powers
COVER DESIGN	Madelyn Lesure
COVER PHOTO	© Johner Bildbyra/Photonica

This book was set in Adobe Framemaker by the authors and Publication Services and printed and bound by R.R. Donnelley Crawfordsville. The cover was printed by Phoenix Color Corporation.

This book is printed on acid free paper.

ISBN   0-471-71227-2

Printed in the United States of America

10 9 8 7 6 5 4 3 2 1

In memory of my mother, Maria del C. Salcedo, a most unselfish being.

—*J. N.*

To Katherine and the rest, Andrew, Laura, Spike, Mary.

—*F. A. H.*

PREFACE

Purpose and approach

This book is an introductory text on programming using Java™. It is intended for first-year undergraduates in computer science, software engineering, or computer engineering. We assume no previous programming experience, and no more mathematics than elementary algebra. The approach is object-oriented, sometimes called "objects first." We hope that more advanced students or more experienced programmers might also find some benefit in the text. In particular, it should serve as a suitable introduction to object-oriented techniques and Java programming for programmers with limited experience in these areas. For introductory students, we assume topics will be further explained in lectures, discussions, or tutorials. Ideally, concepts should also be reinforced by regular laboratories, where they can be reviewed and practiced.

While traditional introductory programming texts approach the subject in a syntax and example driven format, we stress design and the discipline needed for developing complex software systems. The emphasis throughout the book is on problem modeling using sound software engineering principles and concepts. It takes considerable experience, of course, to acquire real proficiency in the design and construction of software systems. We hope to develop a set of fundamental skills in constructing system components and to introduce a point of view regarding system design that will be as useful in the construction of large systems as it is in the building of small components.

The programming language used is Sun Microsystem's Java. We should be clear that this is not just a text about Java. We are more concerned with the design and construction of software systems than with fluency in a particular programming language. Nevertheless as we assume our readers have no previous programming experience, we spend quite a bit of time covering Java syntax and semantics. In fact, we cover all but a few obscure features of the language. We chose Java because it offers a good compromise between viability and semantic coherence. As the language is quite popular, adequate tools and libraries are readily available. At the core, Java is a relatively clean and small language: one that supports the concepts we present without "getting in the way." We do not need to spend much time explaining language peculiarities that have little to do with the fundamentals of software design. We informally adopt a notation called the Unified Modeling Language (UML) for graphically denoting objects, object relationships, and system dynamics.

We use version 5.0 of the Java 2 SE. This version supports generic features useful in developing lists and other container classes. It also includes the class *java.uitl.Scanner*, which is handy for simple textual input. As this is written, version 5.0 is available only in beta release, and Java Language Specification defining the new 5.0 features has not been published. Thus it is possible that there will be some changes from what is described here. Any discrepancies with the final version, however, should be minima.

Finally, the text includes optional interactive exercises to be done using the DrJava software development environment. DrJava is designed primarily for students and includes an easy to use facility for interactively evaluating Java code. It is freely available under an open source license from

```
http://drjava.sourceforge.net/
```

and it is under active development by the JavaPLT group at Rice University. While these exercises are not intended as a substitute for a structured laboratory component, they will help students understand, through direct experience, the implications of the concepts discussed in the text. They should be particularly valuable to the reader who is not using the text in a class.

Overview

Chapter 0 presents an introduction to object-oriented software development. The two fundamental problems we face in building software systems—that they are complex and dynamic—are introduced, along with the concepts of composition and abstraction. Virtually everything we do in the remainder of the text centers on using abstraction and composition to address the complexity and evolutionary nature of software.

The actual study of software design and the programming language Java begins in Chapter 1. A reader who has little or no experience with computers may want to read the supplements on *Systems and software* and *Programming errors* before beginning this chapter. Chapter 1 introduces the fundamental concepts of *object* and *class*, and relates them to the notions of *value* and *type*. Examples of a class definition and of a complete program to test the class offer a "preview" of Java syntax.

Chapters 2 through 8 progress from specifying, implementing, and testing simple, well-defined classes, through designing and building small collections of interacting classes. Very simple classes are defined in Chapters 2 and 3. Elementary Java expressions and statements, including arithmetic expressions, assignments, and method invocations, are explained. Chapter 3 includes the development of a complete system for testing a class. Boolean expressions and conditional statements are added in Chapter 4, while the important notion of component correctness is introduced in Chapter 5. Chapter 6 deals with testing, with particular emphasis given to "test driven" implementation. A DrJava exercise in Chapter 6 introduces the JUnit testing framework. A text-based user interface is developed in Chapter 7, and this first part of the text concludes with the design and implementation of a complete system of moderate complexity in Chapter 8.

Much of this early material of necessity deals with elementary algorithmic concepts. However the context in which topics are presented is one of class development. Classes are specified and designed with the assumption that they are to be incorporated into a larger whole. Fundamental notions such as the distinction between specification and implementation, and the architectural distinction between model and user interface are emphasized. The basic structuring mechanism of composition is also introduced in this part.

The next three chapters deal with abstraction. Interfaces and subtypes are introduced in Chapter 9, while class extension and polymorphism are treated in Chapter 10. The discussion of inheritance and polymorphism necessitates a presentation of some of the more baroque aspects of Java's scoping and accessibility semantics. While it is tempting to skip much of the detail, enough must be presented to enable readers to understand otherwise incomprehensible program behavior. Chapter 11 introduces abstract classes, and compares the fundamental structuring techniques of composition and extension.

Chapter 12 presents the sequential list as the paradigmatic container class. ("List" is simply a more fundamental and abstract notion than "array." Arrays are hardware architectural features—see the IBM 704—bubbling up into the language syntax.) Iteration is discussed extensively in Chapter 12.

The remaining chapters are much less sequentially dependent on each other. Chapter 13 introduces arrays and considers the use of arrays to implement lists. Basic sorting and searching algorithms are presented in Chapter 14. Chapter 15 expands on the programming by contract methodology, addressing the complex problem of error handling. Java's exception mechanism is introduced here. Chapter 16 discusses stream i/o, and surveys the fundamental `java.io` classes.

Chapters 17 and 18 provide an overview of the Java Swing library and the *model-view-controller* architecture. The discussions of MVC and Swing allow us to examine specific examples of additional fundamental design patterns such as *composite* and *observer*.

The algorithmic topic of recursion is the topic of Chapter 19. Backtracking and object recursion are also covered here. Finally, Chapter 20 investigates linked list implementations, while Chapter 21 presents iterators as an efficient means of accessing list elements.

The following are key points of presentation.

- Methods are categorized as commands that change state or queries that return some aspect of an object's state.

- Class specification is clearly distinguished from class implementation.

- System and class design are distinguished from algorithm design.

- Design by contract, with preconditions and postconditions, is employed throughout.

- Assertions, in particular invariants, are used to design, document, and test classes.

- The fundamental role of testing in the design-specify-implement cycle is emphasized.

- An architecture that distinguishes the model from the user interface is employed regardless of system size.

- The class *List* is used to provide a basic container abstraction, and several implementations are developed including implementations based on arrays.

Optional material, DrJava

Some sections in the text are marked with a blue asterisk (✳) and a gray bar similar to that shown at the left. These sections are optional, and can be skipped without affecting the general flow of the presentation. Subsequent material does not depend on these sections. Some contain less commonly used material included "for completeness." Others include topics that might require a bit more background than can be generally assumed of introductory students. (Exercises that depend on optional material are also marked with a blue asterisk.)

There are also DrJava exercises throughout the text marked with [image] and a blue bar as shown to the left. Though we encourage readers to do these exercises, subsequent topics are not dependent on them and they can be skipped without loss of continuity.

Supporting material

Supporting material can be accessed through the Wiley server at

```
http://www.wiley.com/college/nino/
```

or through our servers at

```
http://www.cs.uno.edu/~fred/nhText or
http://wakko.cs.uno.edu/nhText
```

For students

The following material is available on line: libraries used in the text, including source and documentation; supporting code for DrJava exercises; source code for examples used in the text.

For instructors

Slides to accompany the text are available through the Wiley site listed above. Solutions to the exercises are available to adopting instructors. To obtain the exercise solutions, instructors should contact their local Wiley sales representative. Finally, laboratory material used in our courses is generally available through the UNO sites listed above. Instructors should feel free to contact the authors if necessary.

Tools and documentation

Software tools and documentation can be found at these sites.

- The Java Software Development Kit

```
http://java.sun.com/j2se/
```

- The DrJava development environment

    `http://drjava.sourceforge.net/`

- Documentation for the standard Java libraries

    `http://java.sun.com/j2se/1.5.0/docs/api/`[1]

- Documentation for local libraries used in the text

    `http://www.cs.uno.edu/~fred/nhText/nhUtilities/docs/`
    `http://wakko.cs.uno.edu/nhText/nhUtilities/docs/`

    If you have difficulty accessing these sites, check the Wiley site at

    `http://www.wiley.com/college/nino/`,

the Sun sites

    `http://java.sun.com/products/`, and
    `http://java.sun.com/`,

or contact the authors directly.

Readers interested in learning more about Java *per se* should investigate the Sun Java tutorial at

    `http://java.sun.com/docs/books/tutorial/`.

For specifics on the language syntax and semantics, consult the *The Java language Specification*, available at `http://java.sun.com/docs/books/jls`.

Comments, suggestions, corrections, contributions, *etc.* can be forwarded through the above sites, or to the authors directly at

    `fred@cs.uno.edu`
    `jaime@cs.uno.edu`.

To the instructor

As mentioned above, the text is intended for beginning undergraduates in computer science, software engineering, or computer engineering. No previous programming experience is assumed, and the only mathematics required is elementary college algebra.

We believe there is considerable benefit in beginning with the same fundamental methodology we expect students to be using when they complete the curriculum. This creates far fewer problems than starting with a procedural approach and asking students to "shift paradigms" (apologies, Thomas Kuhn) after they've experienced some initial success. With the approach we've used in the past, students started by developing complete, self-contained solutions to simple, well-defined problems. This had the advantage of introducing fundamental algorithmic constructs and providing a grounding in the specifics of

---

1. As this is written, the 5.0 version of the Java SDK is available as a 1.5 Beta release.

some programming language in a nicely confined context. The difficulty was that students found that these problems yield to an undisciplined, *ad hoc* approach. When later confronted with more substantial, less well-defined problems—problems for which design issues involving complex structural relations between components must be effectively addressed—they floundered, unwilling to abandon the "code now, think later" approach that had served them so well. We will go so far as to say that having students start by writing small, complete, self-contained programs is detrimental to their later development as competent programmers.[1,2]

We must, of course, begin with small well-defined components, even though the payoff will be in the construction of large, evolving systems. But the software elements we ask students to construct are carefully specified components of a conceptually large system. (We note that instruction in many other disciplines, from architecture to automotive technology, proceeds in exactly this way.)

We have taught the material for more than six years as part of an introductory sequence in programming and software design. Our students are first and second year computer science majors with no previous computer science coursework. We are not a selective university, and our students can best be described as "average." Our experience has been that students do not find fundamental object-oriented concepts difficult, and have no more trouble than with a traditional procedural approach to programming. On the other hand, they develop a higher degree of facility with abstract design, and generally produce better structured programs in upper-level courses.

We enjoy two advantages, however, that are not available to every instructor. First, our introductory software design sequence—essentially CS1 and CS2—has always been composed of three semester-long courses and has included a substantial "software engineering" component. Thus there were few logistical difficulties in incorporating an objects first approach into the curriculum, and we are able to proceed at a somewhat more leisurely pace than if we had, say, only a quarter or two to work with. Second, since the sequence is intended for computer science majors, we can define performance goals in terms of the complete sequence. There is no pressure for students to acquire a complete, self-contained set of "useful" skills after a single semester.

The role of the text

We should make clear our view that the text is only one part of an introductory student's learning environment. Many of the ideas presented are not easy to grasp on a casual first reading. (Though certainly not so difficult as concepts found in freshman calculus or mechanics!) Regular lectures, discussions, or tutorials in which topics are elaborated and examples developed are essential.

---

1. See, for instance, Duane Buck and David J. Stucki, "Design Early Considered Harmful: Graduated Exposure to Complexity and Structure Based on Levels of Cognitive Development," *31st SIGCSE Technical Symposium*, Austin, March, 2000.

2. Another point of view is that this is complete hokum; the only useful programs are written by very clever people, and there's not much we can do to ruin them.

Furthermore, it is fundamental that students, particularly at the introductory level, be "immersed in code." Regular homework assignments and laboratory work are indispensable to a student's progress. And it is as important for the novice programmer to read well-organized code as to write his or her own. Thus some exercises should involve reading and understanding, and then modifying or extending, existing code. To this end, a substantial number of exercises are included in the text, and source and supporting code for examples and exercises used in the text are available on line. But here, clearly, the role of the text is ancillary. Much of the work and all of the feedback, alas, falls to the instructor.

Laboratories and DrJava

We are of the opinion that learning to program at the introductory level is best supported by regular participation in structured laboratories. Detailed explanation of syntactic issues, for instance, can take place in the laboratories, leaving the lecturer free to concentrate on fundamental concepts, design issues, and case studies.

We employ the DrJava software development environment in our labs. There are several advantages to this tool. First, it is relatively intuitive and easy to learn. Second, it incorporates an "interactions pane" in which arbitrary Java expressions can be evaluated. This greatly simplifies class development and initial unit testing. A student will write a method and then immediately test and experiment with it without having to construct a test driver. Finally, the JUnit testing framework is incorporated into the DrJava environment. From the beginning we insist that a unit "test plan," expressed as a set of JUnit tests, is an essential part of the "programming product" developed in an exercise.

To give some of the flavor of a laboratory, we have incorporated a number of DrJava exercises in the text. These exercises should be of particular value to the reader who is not participating in a structured, scheduled laboratory. However, as many instructors prefer other development environments, we have included these exercises in an inessential way. They can be ignored completely without affecting the thread of topic development. The price we pay is that the DrJava material seems "pasted on" rather than integrated into the text.

Topic organization

Chapters 0 through 8 comprise the basic topics covered in the text. Students with little familiarity with computers should probably start by reading the supplements *Systems and software* and *Programming errors*. These early chapters present fundamental algorithmic constructs from an object-oriented perspective. While many students will be familiar with the elementary algorithmics, the object-oriented slant will be new. In our experience, students find the approach natural and have far fewer problems with the object-oriented concepts than one might expect. A substantial system involving a number of interacting objects, with a separately identifiable model and user interface, is put together in Chapter 8.

Chapters 9, 10, and 11 cover abstraction. These chapters are a bit more conceptually advanced than the previous ones, and are the first in which more general design issues are addressed in a substantial way.

Chapter 12 introduces the "list" as the basic manifestation of "container." The notion of a list is easy to understand, and is more fundamental and general than the notion of an array. We do the same algorithmic development with indexed lists as is conventionally done with arrays.

The remaining chapters exhibit fewer mutual dependencies. Chapter 13 introduces arrays and shows how to use arrays to implement lists. (In our course, we postpone this material until after Chapter 19.) Chapter 14 consists of the traditional algorithmic topics of searching and sorting.

Chapter 15, *Exceptions*, and Chapter 16, *Stream i/o*, are mostly self-contained. Chapter 15 can be presented after Chapter 10, for instance. Chapter 16 is included mostly for completeness, and can be treated as a reference.

Chapters 17 and 18 deal with event-driven graphical user interfaces. A large part of Chapter 17 consists of "nuts and bolts" regarding Swing. Much of this material shows how to handle specific Swing components, and can be omitted or treated as a reference. Chapter 18 discusses the architecture of an event-driven system.

Chapter 19, on recursion, is again algorithmic in content. It can be presented after Chapter 14, on iterative sorting and searching algorithms.

Chapters 20 and 21 again deal with lists. Chapter 20 covers linked implementations and Chapter 21 iterators. In our course, we present Chapters 13 and 20 as a package illustrating "alternative list implementations."

The basic dependencies between chapters is shown in the graph below. A few minor, non conceptual dependencies are not illustrated in the graph. To whit,

- Chapters 17 and 18 each include an example in which a try statement is used to catch a *NumberFormatException*; Chapter 18 also uses a throws clause in an example, and Chapter 20 refers to an exception in an exercise. Exceptions are introduced in Chapter 15.

- Chapters 17 and 18 use "anonymous classes" to implement *WindowListeners*. Anonymous classes are introduced in Chapter 14.

- Chapter 19 uses the observer pattern in the tower puzzle example. Observer is introduced in Chapter 18.

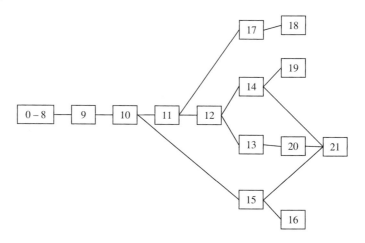

Sections marked with a blue asterisk (✳) and gray bar are optional. They can be omitted without affecting the flow of the presentation. In some case, they are included "for completeness" and can be treated as references. In other cases, they contain topics that might require a bit more background or mathematical maturity than can be generally assumed of introductory students.

Coding conventions

We have, for the most part, adopted the conventions of *The Java Language Specification* [Joy 00]. However, we have generally avoided names get*A* and set*A* to retrieve and modify the value of an attribute *A*. Rather, we use the older convention of using nouns or adjectival predicates to name value-returning methods (size, isEmpty), and imperative verb phases to name state-modifying methods (resetCount). The reason is that we want to discourage the view of an object as a "data record" that simply holds a collection of related values. We try to emphasize the point of view that an object's data is there *solely to support its functionality*. If an object is simply making data available to clients via gets and sets, there is likely something seriously wrong with the coherence of the object.

For the same reason, in the previous edition we adopted the convention of declaring instance variables at the end of the class declaration, along with other private, auxiliary, implementation-related members. In this edition, we have yielded to convention and moved instance variable declarations to the top.

We have also eschewed HTML tags and character names in doc comments. Specifically, in doc comments Java identifiers and key words and Java expressions should be wrapped in <code>...</code> or <tt>...</tt> tags, and the characters '<', '>', and '&' should be written '<', '>' and '&'. However, as this 'severely hinders the readability of the source code, we have chosen to write doc comments as plain text.

Changes since the first edition

We have made many changes in this edition. Among the most substantial are the following.

- Introductory material on computers and software has been moved to a supplement. Almost all of our students have had a high school course in computing and are familiar with these fundamental concepts.

- Implementing code is introduced much earlier. In Chapter 1, we preview a class definition and a complete system to test a class. In Chapters 2 and 3, we specify and implement as we go rather than writing a specification in one chapter and postponing the implementation to the next.

- Test-driven implementation is emphasized, and a complete test system is developed in Chapter 3.

- Interfaces are presented before class extension.

- Lists are defined using generic interfaces and classes. (Generic constructs were added to the language with J2SE version 5.0.)

- Arrays have been moved to a much earlier point in the text. They are now introduced immediately after lists.

- A chapter on stream i/o and the java.io library has been added.

- Optional exercises have been incorporated into the text using the DrJava development environment.

- Substantially more exercises have been added, including "self-study" exercises with answers.

  Chapters from the first edition on software quality, computational complexity, and dispensers are not included in this edition.

Changes in the revised edition

The second edition made use of generic classes and interfaces to develop lists. Other J2SE 5.0 features were introduced in a supplement. Now that the specification of these features appears to be stable, this revised edition integrates 5.0 features into the text. Specifically,

- automatic boxing and unboxing are discussed in Section 1.7;

- static import is presented in Section 3.7.3;

- enumeration types are introduced in Section 5.4;

- *java.util.Scanner* is used for simple input in Chapter 7, replacing our local library class *BasicFileReader*;

- the "for each" variant of the for statement is discussed in Section 12.1 and Section 21.4.1.

Finally

We could not, of course, have completed this text without the help and support of many people. We are indebted to our colleagues for the confidence they showed in us by allowing us to overhaul the introductory programming curriculum and install an unproven approach. We are also indebted to the first few classes of students who endured our trials and errors—getting a first hand view of the design-implement-test cycle. They seem no worse for the experience, and didn't have much of a choice anyway.

We are grateful for the conscientious efforts of our reviewers, Hal Perkins, Dwight Barnette, Kevin O'Gorman, Elizabeth Boese, Stan Kwasny, Peter Dobbins, Christopher Elio, Deborah Trytten, Oliver Grillmeyer, and Michael Eisenberg. The book is much better than it ought to be because of their many helpful suggestions.

Thanks to Martin Dickey, Rob Duisberg, Laurie Poulsen, and Jonathan Pool at the University of Washington for logging errors in preliminary drafts and offering a number of helpful suggestions.

We'd like particularly to thank our colleague Bill Greene who has labored through several versions of the text and notes on which this text was based. His observations are always constructive.

Special thanks again to Robert Burton, for his many insightful suggestions, and his careful reading of the both editions of the text.

We are grateful for the help and guidance of the folks at Wiley, particularly Bruce Spatz and our editor, Paul Crockett; editorial assistant Simon Durkin; Ken Santor, who put up with us through production; Jeri Warner, our copy editor; and Madelyn Lesure who did a splendid cover.

Thanks to Gilad Bracha at Sun for patiently answering our continuous questions regarding J2SE 5.0, and to Robert Cartwright, James Hsia, and the DrJava team at Rice for the exceptional development tool.

Finally, we are grateful for the support of our family and friends, and for Bill Joy, James Joyce, Thomas Kuhn, George Eliot, John Reynolds, Ray Witham, Stephen Kleene, Larry Landweber, Dana Scott, John Adams, Jacques Barzun, Arnold Schoenberg, Jacqueline Du Pré, Immanuel Kant, and Karl Hoffman.

I should without hesitation split the infinitive and write *to calmly consider.*
—*Jacques Barzun*

They lard their lean book with the fat of others' works.
—*Robert Burton (1576-1640)*[1]

---

1. Borrowed from the preface of [Joy 00].

CONTENTS

CHAPTER 0 Introduction to object-oriented software design

computer science *n.*   A study akin to numerology and astrology, but lacking the precision of the former and the success of the latter.

— *Stan Kelly-Bootle*

But fundamentally, computer science is a science of abstraction—creating the right model for a problem and devising the appropriate mechanizable techniques to solve it.

— *A. Aho and J. Ullman*

This book is about building software. In particular, we study fundamental tools and techniques proven successful in building a wide variety of software, from small programs to incredibly large systems. Surely, to build software, you must know a programming language. But owning a hammer doesn't make you an architect. You need more than fluency in a programming language. Read Aho and Ullman's definition of computer science again. It is particularly insightful. Before you can implement a solution, you must *model* the problem: that is, describe the problem in suitably abstract terms. For instance, if you want to explain to someone how an internal combustion engine works, you might use a set of diagrams or even a cardboard cutaway. The diagrams or cutaway are *abstract models* of the engine: abstract in that they omit many of the details of an actual engine, but concrete enough to capture the critical points of the operation.

A programming language is one of our basic software modeling tools. It is the formal notation we use both to model the problem and describe the solution. Thus much of this text is devoted to explaining the programming language Java. But we want to do more than wield a hammer. We want to build things, including very large, complex things. It is the product, the software system, and how it is structured, that we are ultimately interested in. And it is the system and its structure that provides the underlying organization of the text and the context in which you will learn to program in Java.

In subsequent chapters, we'll see how to design, specify, implement and test a system. In this introductory chapter, we analyze the important properties of large software systems, noting in particular that such systems

1

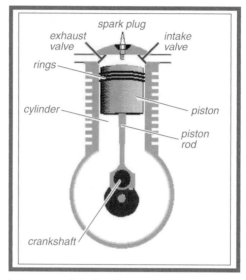

Figure 0.1 **An abstract model of an internal combustion engine.**

- are inherently complex, and
- require constant modification.

  These observations lead us to a data-oriented software development strategy based on *composition* and *abstraction*. This approach, referred to as "object-oriented," has proven to produce software systems of high quality. It is the one we follow throughout the text.

Objectives

After studying this chapter you should understand the following:

- the nature of software systems;
- how abstraction and decomposition are used to deal with complexity in problems;
- the fundamental components of a program, data, and functionality;
- objects, and object-oriented systems and their relationship to software systems in general.

  Also, you should be able to:

- identify basic components in complex structures;
- provide examples of abstraction levels from least abstract to more abstract;
- explain how composition and abstraction simplify the organization of a system;
- provide informal algorithms for common activities.

0.1   What is a software system?

You may ask why we say "software system" when we could get by with a smaller mouthful by simply saying "program." Basically, the term "program" has connotations we wish to avoid. A program is usually considered to be a self-contained piece of software that solves a particular, fixed, clearly-defined problem. In actuality, problems are seldom fixed and clearly-defined, and the software built to address them is rarely simple or self-contained. (Having said this, we'll proceed to use the terms "program" and "software system" more or less interchangeably throughout the text, much to the distress of one of the authors. We also use the term "application" as essentially synonymous with "software system.")

A key aspect of real systems is that the problems they solve are rarely stable over time. The environment in which a system is used, the needs of the users, and therefore what is required of the system, changes constantly. A software system is at best a temporary solution to a changing problem. This is true even when the problem appears completely straightforward. For example, the basic text editor installed on the system being used to write this book is version 21.1 (patch 12). Without getting into version numbering details, it should be evident that there have been dozens of modifications to this piece of software, even though it is hard to imagine a more well-defined problem than editing text.

The dynamic nature of problems and the inherent complexity of software solutions unequivocally constrain the strategies we can use when developing a system. The approach we adopt in this text and the mind-set we hope to develop is largely driven by these two aspects of real-world systems, *i.e.*,

- they are *dynamic*: the demands made of a software system, and hence the software system itself, constantly change; and

- they are *complex.*

0.1.1   Dealing with complexity: composition and abstraction

The difference in size and complexity between a small program and a large application can be compared to the difference in size and complexity between a plank footbridge across a ditch and cantilever highway bridge across a river. It would be rash indeed to assume that techniques adequate for constructing one are also suitable for building the other. If we only want to build small programs, almost any approach will do. We don't need to be structural engineers, after all, to build a footbridge. But real problems are another matter entirely. To manage the complexity of both problems and their solutions, we depend on *composition* and *abstraction*.

Composition

The size of a typical software system implies that it must be broken down into manageable pieces—that it be dealt with as a *composite structure*. The smaller a component is, the easier it is to build and understand. On the other hand, the smaller the parts, the more parts one has to deal with. The more parts, the more possible interactions there are between the parts and the more complex the resulting structure. Thus a critical balance must be achieved in a design. The parts must be simple enough to be understood and managed, but the interaction between them must be minimized to keep the complexity of the entire system under control. The quality of a design, and hence of the resulting system, is directly related to how successfully the problem has been decomposed into relatively independent parts.

To get an idea of what we mean, consider a home entertainment system. The system is composed of a number of components—TV monitor, tuner, speakers, DVD player, amplifier, and so on—wired together. Each component has a carefully specified function that can be understood independently of the entire system. Their interaction is through connecting wires, each carrying a precisely specified signal with a clearly defined purpose. It is a simple matter to improve the system by replacing or adding components. Speakers, for instance, can be easily replaced with ones of better quality. Furthermore, each component is itself constructed of smaller parts. But how these smaller pieces fit together inside a speaker or amplifier is not relevant to understanding how the speaker connects to the amplifier.

Figure 0.2 **A home entertainment system: clearly defined interacting components.**

At the other extreme, consider a "Rube Goldberg" device or a house of cards. In a Rube Goldberg device (see Figure 0.3 for an example), the parts are unusual and connected in intricate, clever, and unexpected ways. The functioning of the device is not obvious, and modification almost unthinkable. Understanding the parts independently is of little help in understanding the system as a whole, since the parts themselves are in no intrinsic way related to the problem the device solves. Though the number of parts might be relatively small, the complexity is considerable due to their elaborate and unexpected interactions. With a house of cards, the components themselves are trivially simple. But the stability of each card is dependent on all the others: each component is related in a critical way to every other component. The slight movement of any card will cause the entire structure to collapse.

> **composition:** the process of building a system using simpler parts or components.

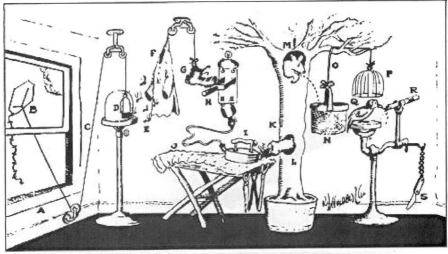

Pencil Sharpener   RUBE GOLDBERG (tm) RGI 038

Open window (A) and fly kite (B). String (C) lifts small door (D) allowing moths (E) to escape and eat red flannel shirt (F). As weight of shirt becomes less, shoe (G) steps on switch (H) which heats electric iron (I) and burns hole in pants (J). Smoke (K) enters hole in tree (L), smoking out opossum (M) which jumps into basket (N), pulling rope (O) and lifting cage (P), allowing woodpecker (Q) to chew wood from pencil (R), exposing lead. Emergency knife (S) is always handy in case the opossum or the woodpecker gets sick and can't work.

Figure 0.3 A "Rube Goldberg" device. (*Rube Goldberg* is the ® and © of Rube Goldberg Inc.)

Abstraction

The process of abstraction allows us to deal with system components and their interactions without worrying about the details of how each component is constructed. Suppose we are designing an automobile, certainly a complex system composed of many parts. In our initial design, we decompose the system into a few high-level components, engine, transmission, frame, *etc.* We can describe, rather precisely, what each component does and how they interact without giving construction details of the individual components. We are dealing with *abstractions* of the components. As we elaborate the design of one component, we view the others only as they relate to the one we're working on. For instance, when we design the transmission, we probably need to know the power specifications of the engine, but its size and shape are irrelevant. When we design the body panels, we need to know the size and shape of the engine, but are not concerned with power. In neither case do we care about the internal components of the engine and exactly how it is put together. That is, in each case we have a distinct abstract view of the engine, a representation in which most details are not relevant to the task at hand and can be ignored. Note that "abstract" does not mean "vague" or "imprecise." It simply means that we limit our view of an object to a few of its properties. Imagine, for example, that two different kinds of engine happen to have the same power specifications. These two engines would be identical to the transmission designer. At the level of abstraction from which the transmission designer views the engine, they are equivalent. But whatever kind of engine we build, we must make sure that those properties used to specify its interaction with other components are maintained. If we use an engine with twice the power assumed when designing the transmission, we will not have a reliable vehicle. And of course, components like engines or transmissions are complicated systems constructed of their own component subsystems.

Now in reality an automobile isn't designed in the simple manner implied above. The various components are designed simultaneously by teams composed of many individuals. Furthermore, the use of parts directly "off the shelf" with little or no modification greatly simplifies and speeds the process. The same is true of large software systems, which are often more complex and have a less standardized "parts catalogue" than an automobile. But the notions of a *composite* system comprised of clearly identifiable interacting parts each of which can be dealt with independently, and of an *abstraction* in which only a few details need to be considered, are the two principal means the system designer has for coping with the complexity of large systems.

To summarize, abstraction can be defined as ignoring irrelevant details and emphasizing the essential ones. (See Figure 0.4.) To abstract is to eliminate details from consideration, and thus eliminate distinctions. Things that are different from one point of view become "equivalent" when viewed from a sufficiently abstract perspective. In this sense, we often consider abstraction as capturing the "commonality" between different things.

> **abstraction:** the process of ignoring details irrelevant to the problem at hand and emphasizing essential ones. To abstract is to disregard certain differentiating details.

0.1.2 Two aspects of a system: data and functionality

Two aspects of any program or software system are *data*, the information the program deals with, and *functionality*, what the program does with this data. ("Functionality" means the same thing as "function," but has more letters and so is preferred.) Data for an income tax program, for instance, is the information entered on a tax form, number of dependents, gross wages, taxable income, gross tax, *etc.* The function of the program is to compute the amount of tax owed. The data for a student records system relates to students and courses, names and addresses of students, courses taken, grades, credits earned, and so

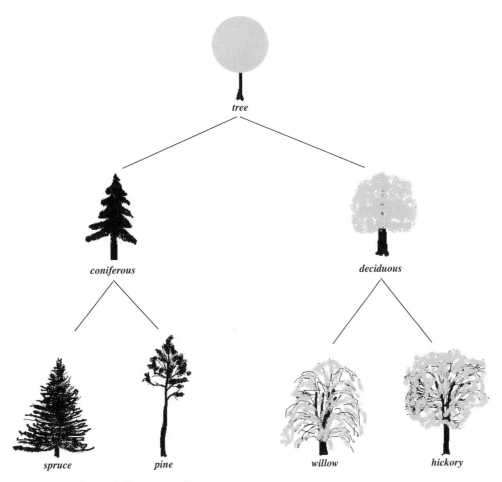

Figure 0.4 **Abstracting trees.**

on. Functions of such a system might include producing transcripts and grade reports, determining if a student should be placed on probation, determining which students have completed degree requirements, *etc*. The data for the document processing software used to prepare this book are text and graphics, and the functionality provided by the software includes facilities for displaying, printing, adding, deleting, modifying, rearranging text and graphics.

If we consider the data for a moment, it should be clear that the *data descriptions* for a program are fixed, while the individual *data values* change each time the program is run. Taking the tax program as an example, "number of dependents" is the *description* of a particular data item. The data *value* associated with this item is some integer number, like 3 or 12. We can imagine running the tax program many times to compute taxes for many different individuals. Each time we run the program, the number of dependents must be provided. But the *specific number* will be different for different individuals, 4 for me, 2 for you, and so on. The same is true for the other data items mentioned above. In the student record system, the same kind of information is kept for each student, name, address, credits earned, *etc*. But the particular values of these data items are, of course, different for different students. An important part of designing and constructing a software system is determining and describing the data items that the system will use.

Now let us briefly turn our attention to the system's functionality. To solve a problem, the system must perform some sequence of actions with a set of data values. For instance, the tax system must perform the calculations required to compute a person's tax. We'll use the term *processor* to refer to whatever it is, person or electronic computer, that actually performs the actions. (If I fill out my tax return manually, I'm the processor.) The *sequence of actions* the processor performs to accomplish some end is a *computation*. Clearly the particular actions the processor performs depend on the data values. If I complete my tax return and then do yours, the same processor (me) performs two computations with the same goal, *i.e.*, to determine someone's income tax. But the particular actions I perform in each case—the numbers I manipulate, the sections of the form I fill in—differ because the data values I start with differ. Nevertheless there is an identifiable, common *pattern* to each of the two computations. This pattern is described by the *instructions* provided in the IRS booklet I follow. That is, in each case I follow the same instructions but in fact perform different actions. The instructions define the *pattern* each computation will follow; the instructions plus specific data values determine the exact *actions* I perform. A precise set of instructions that describe a pattern of behavior guaranteed to achieve some goal is an *algorithm*. In addition to defining the data items, the software builder must also construct the algorithms that provide the functionality of the system.

> **computation:** a goal-directed sequence of actions performed by a processor.
>
> **algorithm:** a set of instructions describing a pattern of behavior guaranteed to achieve some goal.

0.2   Object-oriented systems

We now have the following general picture of a software system. (See Figure 0.5) The definition of the system includes a description of the data items that will be manipulated and a collection of algorithms that provide the system's functionality. Both are expressed in the formal notation of a programming language. A processor, given a particular set of initial data values, follows an algorithm and performs a sequence of actions, a computation, that produces a result. We also know that in the design of a system we must manage complexity (abstraction and composition are relevant tools here) and address the inevitability that the system will change.

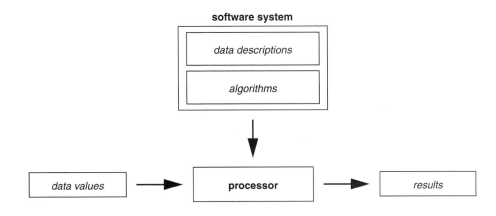

Figure 0.5 **Components of a computation.**

Several fundamentally different methods for structuring software systems have been developed during the past thirty or so years. The approach we take here is called *object-oriented*. It is intended to produce systems that are composite, modular constructions, built using abstraction, and organized around the data. It is generally accepted that this is the best strategy for designing and implementing large, evolving software systems.

Before we can devise an automated solution to a problem, we need to design the right *model*—that is, create *abstractions* of the real-world problem that can be represented and manipulated with a computing system. A *software system* is a collection of such abstractions that work together to solve a problem or set of related problems. In the object-oriented approach, the abstractions used to describe the problem are called *objects*, and are often abstractions of the real-world entities. For example, if we're building a student record system, we will have objects representing students, courses, and so on. For each student there will be a component of the student record system—a software *object*—that represents the student. The component will contain only information about the student that is relevant to the student record system. It will include the student's name, address, list of courses, *etc.*, but will not include the student's shoe size. In this sense, it is an "abstraction" of the student. The aspects of a student that we choose to represent with a student object are the *properties* of the object.

The functionality of the system is distributed to the objects: the tasks the system is required to perform are allocated to objects that perform them. A student record system, for instance, must be able to determine whether a student should be placed on probation. Some object will be assigned the responsibility for performing this job: perhaps it will be the responsibility of the object representing a particular student to determine if that student should be placed on probation. The algorithm for accomplishing this task will be incorporated as part of the student object. In this sense, the system is structured on the *objects* rather than on the *functions* that it will perform. This is not to say that the functions are unimportant: the objects themselves are created to support the basic functionality required of the system. But the fundamental organizational structure of the system is based on the

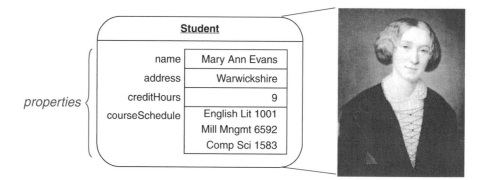

Figure 0.6 **An object *models* a student.**

objects. Objects provide the basic abstractions with which we model the problem, and are the elementary components from which we structure the solution.

0.3   Summary

By now, you should begin to have an appreciation for the challenges involved in building a software system, and how the methodology adopted in this book applies. Specifically,

- software systems are complex; and
- systems change over time.

    To address these difficulties, we adopt a methodology that allows us to

- make extensive use of abstraction;
- build systems that are modular, composite construction.

    To define a software system, we must include a description of the data items to be manipulated by the system and a collection of algorithms that provide the system's functionality. The object-based methodology we adopt structures the system around the data.

SELF-STUDY EXERCISES

0.1   What two properties of large software systems make their design difficult?

0.2   The adage "divide and conquer" implies that a problem can more easily be solved if it is broken down into simpler subproblems. How does this apply to software systems?

0.3   What difficulty must be managed when building a system from many simple parts?

0.4   Which of the following is the most abstract description of a 1962 Datsun Fairlady? Which is the least abstract?

  a.   a roadster;

  b.   a vehicle;

  c.   an automobile.

0.5   Consider modeling an aircraft for a video game and for an airline scheduling system. List some properties that might be modeled in the first case that would not be relevant in the second.

0.6   The more abstract the view, the fewer the distinctions. Name an abstract view that would capture the commonality between "student" and "instructor."

0.7   The following data values are included with an object modeling an author in a library system:

   William Faulkner
   New Albany, Mississippi
   September 25, 1897

   What data descriptions are likely associated with these items?

0.8   Jacqueline Du Pré performs Bach's *Suite for Cello solo no 2 in D minor*. What is the algorithm? The processor? The computation?

0.9   Consider the following algorithm:

   1.   Pick a number between 1 and 10.

   2.   Multiply it by 9.

   3.   If the result has more than one digit, add the digits together.

   4.   If the number is greater than 5, subtract five.

   5.   Find the corresponding letter of the alphabet: 1 = "a", 2 = 'b', *etc.*

   6.   Think of a country that begins with that letter.

   7.   Get the last letter of that country.

   8.   Think of an animal that begins with that letter.

   9.   Get the last letter of that animal.

   10. Think of a fruit that begins with that letter.

   11. Read footnote[1] at the bottom of the page.

   What are some of the data descriptions associated with this algorithm? What are possible data values associated with these data description?

0.10   What is the most abstract description of a basic component of an object-oriented system?

---

1. You're thinking of an orange.

EXERCISES

0.1   Find the jargon file (a.k.a. *The New Hacker's Dictionary*) on the net. Find the definitions of all the terms you need to know that weren't defined in this chapter.

0.2   Go to the site *http://java.sun.com/docs/index.html*. For how many versions of the Java SDK (Software Development Kit) is documentation available?

Go to the documentation page for the most recent version, scroll down until you see a "Summary of new features" link. Scan the list of enhancements and changes. What does this tell you about the stability of a large software system like the Java SDK?

0.3   What operating system version are you using on your home or lab computer? Do you know when this version was produced? Can you speculate on when it will be outdated?

0.4   A university is a composite organization. What are some of the components?

0.5   Develop a sequence of abstractions starting with "cocker spaniel" (least abstract) and ending with "animal" (most abstract). You don't need to be scientifically accurate.

0.6   For each of the following systems, identify two parts (components) that interact with each other, and two that do not.

a.   an automobile;

b.   a home entertainment system;

c.   a refrigerator;

d.   a desk lamp.

0.7   Illustrate composition and abstraction using a computer system as an example.

0.8   Assume that you are going to cook chicken stew. Determine the following:

a.   the algorithm;

b.   the data description;

c.   the data values;

d.   the computation.

0.9   Describe an algorithm to register for classes at your school. What is the data for this algorithm?

0.10   Suppose you want to write a program to play chess. What are some of the objects you might use to model the game? Suggest some properties and responsibilities these objects might have.

0.11   Read Thomas S. Kuhn's *The Structure of Scientific Revolutions*. Is it reasonable to call the object-oriented approach to software development a "paradigm"?

SELF-STUDY EXERCISE SOLUTIONS

0.1   They are complex and they change over time.

0.2   Software systems are designed as composite structures, built from simpler parts.

0.3   With many parts, there are many possible interactions between the parts. The interactions between parts must be minimized to keep system complexity under control.

0.4   "Roadster" is the least abstract, "vehicle" the most abstract.

0.5   Things like current air speed, altitude, heading, *etc.* would likely be modeled in the video game, but are not relevant to scheduling flights.

0.6   Perhaps "person."

0.7   Name, place of birth, date of birth.

0.8   The algorithm is the score, the processor is the performer, and the computation is the performance.

0.9   Data descriptions are things like "a number between 1 and 10," "a country that begins with that letter," "the last letter of that country," "a fruit that begins with that letter," *etc.*

Possible values for these data descriptions are: 2, Denmark, k, orange; or 3, Dominica, a, kiwi.

0.10   An object!

CHAPTER 1

Data abstraction: introductory concepts

We now begin considering, in detail, how to build components of a software system. In this chapter, we introduce the foundational notions of value and type, and of object and class. *Values* are the basic items of data we manipulate with a program, and are grouped into *types*. *Objects* are the fundamental abstractions from which we build our systems, and are grouped into *classes*.

Objects maintain a set of data values and carry out operations with the data. We refer to the set of data maintained by an object at any given time as the *state* of the object. The set of operations an object performs is its *functionality*. We'll see how data is stored in an object, and the kinds of operations an object can perform. We also introduce *reference values*, an elementary mechanism by which objects can be related to each other. If objects are to function cooperatively in solving a problem, they must certainly know about each other. A reference value denotes a particular object, and so provides a "handle" that other objects can use to interact with it.

Finally, we initiate our study of the programming language Java. We take a quick overview of how objects are defined in Java and see what a complete software system looks like. We examine the primitive values and types provided by the language in some detail, and review the lexical structure of the language.

Objectives

After studying this chapter you should understand the following:

- the nature of a software object—its properties, functionality, data, and state;
- the notions of query and command;
- values and collection of values called types;
- Java's built-in types;
- variables, and the relationship between values, variables, and types;
- classes as collections of related objects;

- the syntactic layout of a class as defined in Java;
- reference values and reference types.

  Also, you should be able to:

- classify an object as immutable or mutable;
- describe the components of a system developed using objects;
- describe the values comprising the built-in Java types;
- describe literals of the built-in Java types;
- form legal Java identifiers and name the role of identifiers in programming.

1.1   Objects

As we mentioned in the previous chapter, *objects* are the fundamental abstractions from which we build software systems. Objects are often abstractions of real-world entities: students, employees, rooms, passageways, chess pieces, *etc.* Any system we design has a set of tasks that it must perform. We refer to this collection of tasks as the *functionality* of the system. Objects are designed to support this functionality. That is, the tasks the system must perform are allocated to software objects that perform them. We say an object has the *responsibility* for performing certain specific tasks. An extremely critical part of system design is allocating responsibilities to objects.

For example, in designing a university registration system, we may decide to model students and courses with objects. Each student and each course will be represented by a separate software object. (We say "course" rather than "class" to avoid confusion with the technical term "class" introduced later.) Among the functions this system must perform are enrolling students in courses and producing course rolls. The responsibility for enrolling a student in a course might be given to the object representing the student, and the responsibility for producing a course roll given to the object denoting the course. In this way the functionality required of the system is distributed to the objects that comprise the system. Now to enroll a student in a course, the student object almost certainly needs to interact with the object representing the course. The software system is composed of a collection of objects that *cooperate* to solve a problem.

1.1.1 Data and state

The importance of an object is the set of functions it is responsible for performing, that is, the role it plays in contributing to the problem solution. But typically an object models some "real-world entity"—some aspect of the problem that actually exists. As such, the object is responsible for maintaining relevant data about the thing it models. Consider an object that models a student in the registration system. Characteristics of a student relevant to the registration system include the student's name and address, the number of credit hours the student is enrolled in, the student's course schedule, whether or not the student has paid fees, *etc*. It is the responsibility of the object modeling a particular student to maintain this information about the student. The object is an abstraction of the student. There are many other characteristics of the student that are not relevant for the registration system and won't be represented in the object: shoe size, eye color, the amount of change in the student's pocket, and so on.

An object contains a number of *data items*, each consisting of a *data description* and an *associated value*. The data descriptions are the *properties* of the object. Properties of a student object include name, address, *etc*. If we are modeling a playing card, object properties will include suit and rank. If we are modeling a window on a computer screen, properties might include location, width, height, whether the window is iconified, whether it is active. When we design the object, we decide which properties it will have depending on its function in the system. Is the manufacturer's suggested retail price, for instance, an important property of an object modeling an automobile? Probably so if the object is part of an automobile dealership inventory system; probably not if the object is modeling an automobile in a video game.

Instance variables

At any given time, each property of an object has an *associated value*. The student's name is Stephen Dadelus, the playing card's rank is Jack, the window's width is 100 pixels[1]. These data values are stored in chunks of computer memory called *variables*. A variable is simply a portion of computer memory reserved for storing a particular value. Of course, the particular value stored in a variable can be changed—hence the name "variable."

The memory space used to store an object's data is allocated to the object when the object is created. These variables are called *instance variables*. Essentially, an instance variable is allocated for each property of the object. The instance variable contains the data value associated with that property. (We sometimes refer to instance variables as *components* of the object.)

---

variable: a portion of memory reserved to hold a single value.

instance variable: a variable that is a permanent part of an object; memory space for the variable is allocated when the object is created.

State

While the set of properties an object has is fixed when the object is designed, the associated values can often change over time: a student can change address or even name; a computer user can change the width and height of a window on the screen. The set of an objects's instance variables and associated values at a given time is called the *state* of the object.

---

1. A *pixel* is the smallest dot that can be independently colored on a display screen.

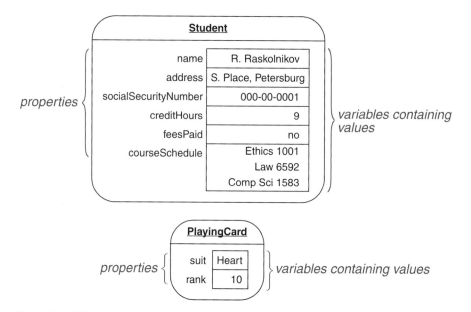

Figure 1.1 **Objects, showing their state.**

We use a rounded box to represent an object graphically. In Figure 1.1, the state of the object, as a set of variables and their current values, is given below the horizontal line. The rectangular boxes represent the variables.

> **state:** the set of an object's instance variables and associated values at any given time.

Mutable and immutable objects

An object whose state cannot be changed is called *immutable*. Conversely, an object whose state can be changed is *mutable*. Our student object, for instance, is mutable. We expect the values associated with properties such as the number of credit hours the student is enrolled in to change as the student enrolls in or drops courses. On the other hand, a playing card is immutable. We don't expect a playing card to change suit or rank over time. Other examples of objects that might be immutable are objects representing calendar dates or colors. We can model a date with an object having three properties: month, day of the month, and year. Modeling colors is in fact quite complicated. One approach uses three integers representing the amount of red, green, and blue in the color.

Whether an object is immutable or not is to some degree determined by the role the object plays in the problem. For instance, if we are writing a program to play solitaire, we might decide that it is the responsibility of a playing card to know whether it is face up or face down. In this case, we would build mutable playing card objects: objects whose state can change from "face up" to "face down" and *vice versa*.

1.1.2 Functionality: queries and commands

An object-oriented system is a collection of objects that cooperate to solve a problem. If we're building a program to allow a person to play chess against "the computer," we might have objects representing the players (person and computer), the chess pieces, and the board. Player objects move the pieces, and each piece is responsible for knowing its board location. Of course, at some point the system must interact with the outside world—with the human player, in particular. But that's the responsibility of a separate part of the system called the user interface. For the moment, we can ignore the user and think of the system as nothing more than a collection of interacting objects.

An object maintains data in order to support its functionality. Exactly what does this mean? By *functionality* we mean the actions the object will perform in response to requests from other objects in the system. There are two kinds of requests an object can serve:

- a request for data, called a *query*;
- a request to change state, called a *command*.

The collection of queries and commands a given object will respond to are called the object's *features*, and are determined when the object is designed.

Queries

Queries often simply request data maintained by the object. For instance, a student object might be queried for the student's name, a playing card object for the card's suit, a chess piece for its position, and so on. When an object is queried, it responds by providing a value.

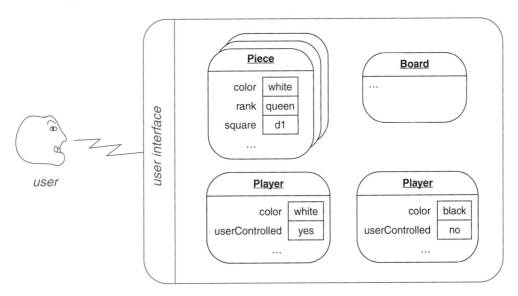

Figure 1.2 Objects in a chess-playing program.

Do not assume that there is a "one-to-one" correspondence between the set of queries defined for an object and data items the object maintains. An object might support queries for information it does not explicitly store. Suppose an object modeling a window maintains the length and width of the window. The object could be designed to respond to a query for the window's area. Even though this value is not explicitly stored in one of the object's instance variables, it can easily be computed on demand. Note that from the point of view of the object requesting the data (the *client* object), it doesn't matter that the area is computed when needed and not explicitly stored in the object. The client requests the area which is delivered by the window object.

Also, an object might not be able to be queried for data that it does store. Suppose an object representing a computer user contains the user's password. The object is not likely to support a query for the password. Rather, it will allow another object to ask if some particular string of characters *is* the password. The client object must ask "Is 'foobar' the password?" rather than "What is the password?"

Commands

Queries provide information about an object's state. But querying an object does not change its state. (As Bertrand Meyer put it, "Asking a question doesn't change the answer."[1]) An object changes state in response to a *command* from some other object. A command instructs the object to perform some action which typically results in the value stored in one or more of the object's instance variables to be changed. For instance, a student object might be instructed to drop a course, changing the credit hours and course schedule properties of the object; a chess piece might be told to move to a different square; or a solitaire playing card object might be instructed to turn over, changing its "is face up" property. The only way that an object's state changes is as a result of some action by the object itself. (Clearly, an immutable object supports no commands that change its state.)

> An object is characterized by the **features** it offers, including:
> **queries**, by which data associated with the object's state are obtained; and
> **commands**, which can change the object's state.

1.1.3 Some cautions

We should be careful to note that software objects do not behave exactly like the real entities they are modeling. Real things might change even though they are completely passive; software objects will not. People age, light bulbs burn out, switches are turned off and on. All this happens without any obvious active participation required of the people, light bulbs, or switches. If Sally is now 25 years old, she does not need to perform any specific action to turn 26. She will be 26 one year from now regardless of what she does or doesn't do. On the other hand, suppose a software object representing Sally stores the property age

---

1. This is, after all, software engineering and not quantum physics.

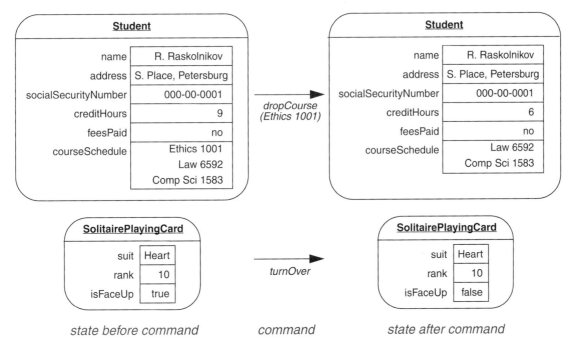

state before command   command   state after command

Figure 1.3 **Objects change state in response to a command.**

in an instance variable. The only way this object will change state is in response to an explicit command. If we want the software object Sally to change age, it must be a responsibility of the object: for instance, a command "update age" might be included in the object's features.[1]

Or suppose an object models a lamp. Two properties we might be interested in are whether the lamp is on and whether the lamp is burned out. To determine if an actual lamp is on, we simply look at it. But we can't just "look at" a software object. We must query the object to determine its state. To be specific, let's assume that variables are associated with the properties "lamp is on" and "lamp is burned out." We query the lamp object to determine if it is on, and get a response of "yes" if the lamp is on, "no" if it is off; and we query it to determine if it burned out in a similar way. The only way the lamp object changes state is in response to a command. Thus we might have commands like "turn on" and "turn off." How does the lamp burn out? Again, as with any state change, it must be the result of some specific action by the object itself. We might have a command "burn out" that explicitly changes the state of the lamp. Or the lamp might remember how many times it was turned on, and burn out when it is turned on for the 100th time. How the lamp object works is a matter of design. The important thing to remember is that an object will

---

1. A more reasonable approach would be to store Sally's birth date. Then Sally's age could be computed on demand from her birth date and the current date.

only change state in response to an explicit command. It is the object's responsibility to change its state.

1.2   Values and types

In the previous section, we encountered *values* in several contexts: an object stores *values* in its instance variables; an object returns a *value* in response to a query; an object changes one or more *values* stored in its instance variables in response to a command.

Values are the fundamental pieces of information manipulated by a program. The most obvious examples of values are numbers. Other examples are characters (letters, digits, and punctuation marks), colors, points in a plane. Exactly what kind of values are available to a programmer depends on the programming language used.

Values are abstractions used to represent, or *model*, various aspects of an object. We use an integer, for instance, to denote the number of students in a class or the number of words on a page. Integers model problem features we count. We use real numbers to represent problem features we measure: the width of a table, the voltage drop across a line. Representing problem characteristics with numeric values and then manipulating the values to solve the problem is exactly what we do when we solve an exercise in physics or a "word problem" in mathematics.

Values are grouped together according to how we use them and according to the *operations* we perform with them. A set of values along with the operations that can be performed with them is called a *type*. The idea is to collect values that can be used in the same way in a type. We use integer numbers to model things we can count, for instance, and perform operations such as addition, subtraction, and multiplication with them. The operations we can perform with one integer (double it, subtract it from 10, *etc.*) we can perform with any other integer. Hence a set of integers along with the operations of arithmetic comprise a type. The values are said to be "of the same type." A color, on the other hand, is a completely different kind of value. It wouldn't make much sense to use a color to denote the number of students in a class, or to multiply two colors. Operations we might want to perform with colors include combining, complementing, and so on. A set of colors along with a collection of appropriate operations can also form a type, but a color and an integer would not be of the same type.

> **value:** a fundamental piece of information that can be manipulated in a program.
>
> **type:** a set of related values along with the operations that can be performed with them.

1.2.1   Values and types in Java

A programming language provides some *built-in* types that are an integral part of the language. Most programming languages also include facilities that allow programmers to define their own types. There are two kinds of types in Java, built-in *primitive* types and *reference* types. We describe Java's primitive types here. Reference values denote objects, and we must postpone a discussion of reference values and reference types until we've had a look at classes later in the chapter.

Java's built-in types include **byte**, **short**, **int**, **long**, **float**, **double**, **char**, and **boolean**. (Note that we use a recognizably distinct type font when we write something that has a specific meaning in the programming language.) The types **byte**, **short**, **int**, and **long** are all sets of integer values. The operations that can be performed with these values include the usual arithmetic operations of addition, subtraction, multiplication, and division. The only difference in these types is the size of the sets they denote. For instance, as shown in Figure 1.4, the type **int** contains the integers from –2,147,483,648 through 2,147,483,647, while the type **short** contains the integers from –32,768 through 32,767.

Type	Smallest value	Largest value
byte	–128	127
short	–32,768	32,767
int	–2,147,483,648	2,147,483,647
long	–9,223,372,036,854,775,808	9,223,372,036,854,775,807

Figure 1.4   **Value ranges for integer types.**

As is the case with most languages, Java distinguishes real numbers from integers. The types **float** and **double** are sets of real (in fact, rational) numbers. These values are sometimes called "floating point" numbers because of how they're encoded in the computer's memory. Computers represent integer numbers and floating point numbers with quite different encodings, and have different machine instructions for manipulating them.

An important distinction is that integer numbers are represented exactly while real numbers are approximated. Values of type **float** are stored to about seven places[1] of accuracy, and values of type **double** to about sixteen. If the **float** representation of the number 0.01 were summed 100 times, for instance, the sum would be very close to, but not exactly equal, 1.0. The reason is that the computer's representation of 0.01 is not exact: it's an approximation, in much the same way that 0.33333 is an approximation of 1/3. For the same reason, the **float** representations of the numbers 17,000,000 and 17,000,001 are identical. The numbers differ in the eighth place, but are represented in the machine to only about seven places of accuracy. On the other hand, these numbers would be distinguishable if encoded as integers, since each would be represented exactly.

As mentioned above, we use integer values to represent things we count: the number of students in a class, the number of angels dancing on the head of a pin, the number of

---

1. We say "*about* seven places" because these numbers are stored using a *binary* representation which does not translate into an exact number of *decimal* places.

banking transactions this month, the number of pixels on a computer screen. We use floating point values to represent things we measure: the width of a desk top, the voltage drop across a battery, the luminescence of a light bulb. Generally we use the type **int** for integer values and the type **double** for floating point values.

The type **char** is a set of values representing *Unicode* characters. Characters are the upper and lower case letters, digits, punctuation marks, and spaces that constitute text. Unicode is a standard system of encoding the characters of virtually every written language. You might be familiar with the ASCII (*A*merican *S*tandard *C*ode for *I*nformation *I*nterchange) character set, commonly used to store text on personal computers. The ASCII character set is shown in Appendix iii. The Unicode standard extends the ASCII character set: the first 128 Unicode charters are the ASCII characters.

Note that the integer value 2, the floating point value 2.0, and the character '2', for instance, are distinct values, and are encoded differently in the computer's memory. Only the first two are used for arithmetic.

The type **boolean** contains only the two values *true* and *false*.

1.2.2 Types and variables

We've seen that instance variables contain an object's data. Though different values can be stored in a variable at different times, any given variable can contain values of only one type. An **int** variable contains a single **int** value, a **double** variable contains a **double** value, and so on. An **int** variable cannot contain a **double** value, and *vice versa*. We refer to the type of value a variable contains as the "type of the variable."

An instance variable contains the value associated with a property of an object. The *type* of the value, and so the type of the variable, is fixed when the object is designed. The width of a window might be 100 pixels at one time, and 150 pixels some time later, but the value will always be an integer.

So far the only types we know about are the integer, floating point, boolean, and character types discussed in the previous section. If we are modeling something simple like a solitaire card or date, these types are adequate. We can use integers to denote month, day, and year, for instance, and we might use integers to represent the suit and rank of a card. Perhaps we encode suits as 1 = clubs, 2 = diamonds, 3 = hearts, and 4 = spades, and use 11 to denote jack, 12 to denote queen, and 13 to denote king. We can use a boolean value to indicate whether the card is face up or face down. Then objects representing the date June 16, 1904 and the ace of hearts might appear as shown in Figure 1.5.

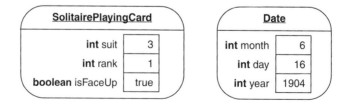

Figure 1.5 **Objects, showing variable types.**

But what about the values in the student object? Here we have names, addresses, lists of courses, and so on. Clearly simple numbers or boolean values won't do. We need reference types for these values, as we'll see in Section 1.5.

 ### DrJava: variables and types

Let's create an **int** variable. In the DrJava *Interactions* pane, key

```
> int i;
```

Be sure that you are keying next to the last ">   " prompt in the window. Key the line exactly as shown, including the semicolon at the end. Press the "Return" or "Enter" key at the end of each line.

This creates an **int** variable named i in the DrJava environment:

i ▢

Next, we'll store a value in the variable:

```
> i = 17;          i  17
```

(Here, the equals sign "=" doesn't mean "equals." It means "store the value given on the right into the variable named on the left.") We can see the value stored in the variable by keying the name of the variable:

```
> i
17
```

Note there is no semicolon at the end of the line. (We show DrJava's response in slanted font.)

We can change the value stored in the variable:

```
> i = 18;          i  18
> i
18
```

Now do the following:

```
> i+1
19
> i*2
36
```

Keying the expression i+1 gives us the value stored in i plus 1. What does i*2 produce?

Next, let's create a **float** variable and give it a value:

```
> float f;
> f = 17000000;
> f
1.7E7
```

The expression $1.7E7$ is a way of saying 1.7×10^7, that is, seventeen million.
Now key

> f+1

and note the result. Keying

> f == f+1

says "f is equal to f+1." Can you explain the answer? What result do you get when you key

> i = 17000000;
> i == i+1

Create a new **int** variable named i2:

> int i2;

What happens if we ask for the value of i2

> i2

before we have stored a value in the variable?
What happens if we attempt to store the value of f into i2?

> i2 = f;

1.3   Classes

Just as we collect values and operations into types, we categorize objects according to their features. Objects representing students *me*, *you*, *him*, *her* are likely to have the same set of properties (though different values associated with these properties) and respond to the same commands (though perhaps in different ways). A collection of similar objects, objects with the same set of features and properties, is called a *class*. Every object is an element of some class: we say an object is an *instance* of the *class*. The student objects *me*, *you*, *him*, *her* all belong to the same class; the objects representing the playing cards in a deck of cards are also instances of a common class. Again, a class specifies the features of a group of similar objects. If two objects (two instances) are of the same class, they will support the same set of queries and the same set of commands. They are the same kind of object, having the same functionality and properties, though of course they will likely have different values associated with their properties.

> **class:** a set of objects having the same features and properties; *i.e.*, supporting the same queries and commands.
>
> Every object is an **instance** of some class, which determines the object's features.

A critical part of designing a software system is defining classes appropriate for modeling the various entities involved in the problem solution. When we define a class, we specify the features—queries and commands—and properties for members of the class. The objects—the instances of the class—are created dynamically as the system runs. For example, when we design a registration system, we decide what aspects of a student we want to model and what functionality an object representing a student should have. This is reflected in the design of the class *Student*. However, we have no idea who the actual students will be when we design the system. When the system is running, as each student is enrolled, a new instance of class *Student* is created to represent that student. The class definition determines what the newly created *Student* object will look like: what its features and properties will be. Thus we can think of a class definition as a *pattern* or *blueprint* for creating instances of the class.

As illustrated in Figure 1.6, we use a box to denote a class and a rounded box to denote an object.

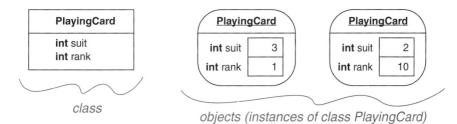

Figure 1.6 **Class and instances.**

1.4   An example

Before we go further, let's take a brief look at a class definition written in Java. We'll fill in the details later, but it will help at this point to see a concrete picture of how the things we've been talking about are expressed in the programming language.

When we write a program, we write a collection of class definitions. As mentioned above, these class definitions serve as templates or blueprints for constructing objects when the program is run. A class definition describes a class instance. It specifies both the data maintained by an object that is an instance of the class, and the functionality—the queries and commands—supported by the object. Specifically, a class definition includes

- instance variable definitions, and
- query and command definitions.

A variable definition specifies the type and name of the variable. Queries and commands are collectively called *methods*. A method definition includes a name for the method, the type of the value returned in the case of a query, and an algorithm for carrying out the method. The algorithm defines the sequence of actions that must be performed by the object in order to accomplish the query or command.

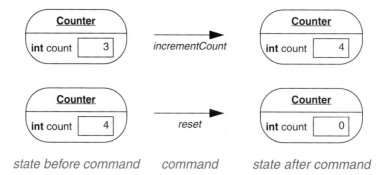

state before command   command   state after command

Figure 1.7 **Counter** **changes state in response to commands.**

Suppose we want an object that models a very simple counter. What we have in mind is a hand counter such as a ticket-taker might use, or a device that counts cars as they pass a particular spot on a road. The functioning of a counter is very straightforward. The only data value that the object needs to maintain is the count. The object should be able to be queried for its count, and should respond to two commands: one to increment the count, and one to reset the count to zero. The change in state resulting from these commands is illustrated in Figure 1.7.

The class definition, written in Java, is shown in Listing 1.1. The blue numbers to the left are not part of the class definition, but are included so that we can easily call your attention to specific lines in the definition. Note that the grammatical and punctuation rules for a programming language—the language *syntax*—are very rigid. Whether we punctuate an English sentence with a comma or semicolon isn't likely to affect its understandability. In a programming language, however, using a comma rather than a semicolon may make a construct invalid or completely change its meaning. We'll examine Java's specific syntax rules as we go.

The words written in boldface, such as **public**, are *keywords*: they have very specific meanings in Java. The names of the primitive types—**int**, **double**, *etc.*—are keywords that we've already encountered. We'll learn the meaning of other keywords, such as **public** and **private**, in subsequent chapters when we study Java constructs in detail.

Words such as Counter, incrementCount, count, are *identifiers*. Identifiers are used to name things: classes, variables, queries, commands, and so on. In general, it does not matter what identifiers we use to name things. But we should choose names that convey something of our intention. A detailed discussion of identifiers and their use appears later in this chapter.

- Sections of text that begin "/∗∗" and end "∗/" are called *comments*. For instance, lines 1 though 3 contain a comment. Comments are intended for the human reader and are ignored by the computer. We can write anything we want in a comment. Comments are extremely important since they are used to generate documentation for programmers who need to use the class.

- The definition of the class proper begins on line 4 and extends through line 31. Note that the closing brace "}" on line 31 matches the opening brace "{" on line 4. "Counter" is

Listing 1.1   The class *Counter*

```
1.    /**
2.     * A simple integer counter.
3.     */
4.    public class Counter {

5.        private int count;

6.        /**
7.         * Create a new Counter, with the count initialized
8.         * to 0.
9.         */
10.       public Counter () {
11.           count = 0;
12.       }

13.       /**
14.        * The number of items counted.
15.        */
16.       public int currentCount () {
17.           return count;
18.       }

19.       /**
20.        * Increment the count by 1.
21.        */
22.       public void incrementCount () {
23.           count = count + 1;
24.       }

25.       /**
26.        * Reset the count to 0.
27.        */
28.       public void reset () {
29.           count = 0;
30.       }

31.   }
```

the name of the class being defined. As mentioned above, we could have named the class anything we wanted. But "Counter" is simple and descriptive of an object that is an instance of this class.

- Line 5 is an instance variable definition. It specifies that every instance of the class *Counter* will have an **int** instance variable named count. Again, we can choose any name for the variable, but we should pick something descriptive. Since a *Counter* object needs to maintain only one data value, we need to define only one instance variable.

- Lines 6 through 12 define a *constructor*. A constructor specifies actions to be taken when a new class instance is created. In this case, there is only one step required, specified by line 11:

```
count = 0;
```

This is an example of an *assignment statement*. The character "=" is called the *assignment operator*; it does not mean "equals" in this context. An assignment statement is used to store a value in a variable. The variable is named on the left of the "=" and the value to be stored is described on the right. This assignment says "store the value 0 into the variable named count." Thus we insure that every newly created *Counter* object will have a count of 0.

- Lines 13 through 18 define a query. Note that the query is named with an identifier, in this case currentCount. (We could have used the same identifier to name both the query and the instance variable, and often do so. We have chosen different names in this example to reduce the possibility of confusion.) The definition of the query indicates an **int** will be returned in response to the query. A given query always returns values of the same type. If a *Counter* object is queried for its count, it will respond by providing the value stored in the variable count.

- Lines 19 through 24 define the command incrementCount. The keyword **void** indicates that this is a command and not a query. There is only one action to be performed in response to this command, and that action is described by the assignment

```
count = count + 1;
```

The variable that will get the value is, as before, count. The value to be stored is described by the expression "count + 1." This expression says "compute a value by taking the value currently stored in count and adding one to it." The assignment has the effect of incrementing the value stored in count by one.

- Finally, lines 25 through 30 define the command reset. Executing this command results in a zero being stored in count.

Do not be concerned if all this is a little fuzzy. Our purpose here is just to get a general idea of what a class definition looks like. We'll see all this again, in much more detail, in the following chapters.

DrJava: exercising an object

The class Counter

Open the file Counter.java in DrJava. (*Open* is an option on the tool bar, and in the *File* pull-down menu. Counter.java is located in the folder (directory) ch1, which is located in the folder (directory) nhText. See Appendix ii for details.) You will see text similar to that of Listing 1.1 in the main window.

Let's create a *Counter* instance named c. In the *Interactions* pane, key

```
> Counter c = new Counter();
```

(Java is "case sensitive." You must key uppercase and lowercase letters exactly as shown.)

We can query c to determine what the current count is:

```
> c.currentCount()
0
```

Give c the command incrementCount twice, and query again:

```
> c.incrementCount();
> c.incrementCount();
> c.currentCount()
2
```

Finally, give c the reset command, and query for count:

```
> c.reset();
> c.currentCount()
0
```

Now in the main window, edit the assignment statement in the method increment-Count replacing the 1 with a 2. That is, the statement should now read

```
count = count + 2;
```

Save your modification (there is a *Save* button on the tool bar), and recompile the class definition (use the *Compile All* button on the tool bar).

Go back to the *Interactions* pane (you'll need to click the *Interactions* tab). The interaction environment has been reset because of the compilation. Again, create a Counter instance by keying

```
> Counter c = new Counter();
```

How do you think this *Counter*'s behavior will differ from the original version? Verify your assumption by exercising the *Counter*.

The class Rectangle

Open the file Rectangle.java, which is also located in folder ch1. This class is a bit more complicated than the previous. Do not expect to understand everything in the class definition at this point.

A *Rectangle* can be queried for its length, width, and area, and has commands for changing length and width. Create a Rectangle instance named r1:

```
> Rectangle r1 = new Rectangle();
```

What should the initial length and width of the *Rectangle* be? Verify this with queries

```
> r1.length()
> r1.width()
```

Change the length of `r1` with the `setLength` command. The new length must by written inside the parentheses when invoking the command:

```
> r1.setLength(3);
```

Query the `r1` for its length and area.

Rectangle has a query `toString`. Invoke this query and note the result:

```
> r1.toString()
```

The definition of the class *Rectangle* should be in the main editing window. Scroll down and find the definition of `toString`. Do you think the plus sign "+" denotes addition in this method?

Now key `r1` on a line by itself:

```
> r1
```

and compare the result to the previous.

Create another *Rectangle* named `r2`:

```
> Rectangle r2 = new Rectangle();
```

What are the length and width of `r2`?

The class *Rectangle* also defines a query `hasEqualDimensions`. Key

```
> r1.hasEqualDimensions(r2)
```

What type of value does this query return?

1.5   Reference values: objects as properties of objects

We've seen that an object has a number of properties, with instance variables containing the data values associated with these properties. While the value stored in a variable can change, the type of the value stored in a particular variable is fixed. Furthermore, we've seen examples in which the type is a primitive Java type: **int** for the suit of a playing card, for example. But what about properties like the name, address, and course schedule of a student? As we've mentioned above, simple values won't do. The solution is to associate an *object* with the property.

To start with a simple example, suppose we want a *Student* object to keep track of the student's birthday. The *Student* object will have a property "birthday", which will have a date as its value:

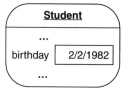

How do we model a date, and what kind of value do we associate with the "birthday" property? We've already suggested that a date can be modeled with an object containing day, month and year:

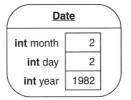

The value associated with the property "birthday" should be a value that *denotes* or *refers to* a *Date* object. Such a value is called a *reference* value. Its type, in this case, is *reference-to-Date*, since the object it refers to is an instance of the class *Date*. A value that refers to a *Student* object would be of type *reference-to-Student*, and so on. The variable storing the value is a *reference-to-Date* variable (or simply a *Date* variable). We illustrate a reference value with an arrow, as shown in Figure 1.8. (You can think of a reference value as data, such as a memory address, that allows the object to be located in memory.)

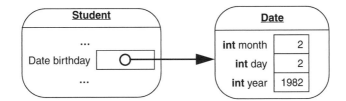

Figure 1.8 **A property of one object references another.**

We repeat for emphasis. *Date* is a *class*. A class specifies the features that instances of the class will have. We can think of a class definition as providing a pattern or template for creating objects. The entity representing February 2, 1982 is an *object* – an instance of the class *Date*. Associated with each object is a reference *value* that identifies the object. The *type* of this value is *reference-to-x*, where *x* is the class of the object. The value that denotes the "February 2, 1982" object is of type *reference-to-Date*, since the object it denotes is an instance of class *Date*. In Figure 1.8, this value is stored in the variable "birthday" of the *Student* object.

---
reference value: a value that denotes an object.

Now let's look at the name and address properties. Again, there is no obvious primitive type to use for these properties, so we model them with a class. But what class specifically? Java provides a substantial library of predefined classes, many of which we'll encounter in subsequent chapters. Of interest at the moment is the predefined class *String*. A *String* instance is an immutable object that contains a sequence of characters: that is, a sequence of primitive values of type **char**. A *String* can be queried for its length and for the individual characters that comprise the sequence. Since *Strings* are immutable, the

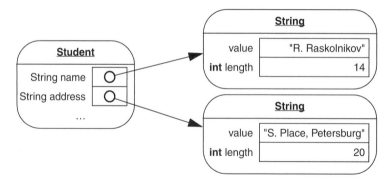

Figure 1.9 **Properties modeled as Strings.**

class contains no state-changing commands. Once an instance is created, it cannot be modified.

We can associate *String* references with the name and address properties, as illustrated in Figure 1.9. (The alert reader might wonder about the type of the *String* instance variable labeled "value." Since the class is already defined, we can ignore this point and simply consider it a "sequence of **char** values.")

Be sure you understand the difference between a string and a character. A string is an *object*, an instance of the class *String*. A character is a *value*, an element of the type **char**. A **char** value denotes a single character. A *String* instance includes a sequence containing any number of characters.

The fact that a *String* is immutable doesn't mean that a student's name or address can't change. To change address, for instance, the value stored in the address variable is replaced with a reference to a different *String* containing the new address.

In actuality, *Strings* are not the best way to model names and addresses. We are likely to want more functionality from the classes used for name and address. For instance, we might want to query for last name or for zip code. Thus we might define a class *Name* with properties first name, last name, *etc.*, and a class *Address* with properties number, street, city, and so on. We won't pursue this thought further, though. (See Exercise 1.1.)

A particular reference value can be used in many different places, just as a particular integer value can be used in many different places. For example, suppose a *Student* object stores more than one address: a home address and a mailing address perhaps. Both variables can have the same value stored in them, that is, they can both reference the same object, as shown in Figure 1.10.

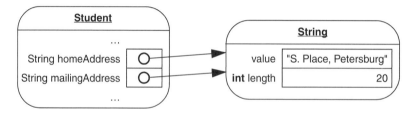

Figure 1.10 **Two references to the same object.**

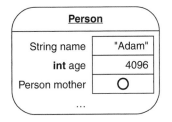

Figure 1.11 **The null reference: a *Person* with no mother.**

The null reference

Suppose a class *BoardSquare* models a square on a chess board. A *BoardSquare* has a variable *occupyingPiece* that references the piece that is on the square. What value should this variable contain if the square is not occupied? There is a unique value called the *null* reference that doesn't denote any object. The null reference essentially says "no object." We picture it as a circle with no arrow, as shown in Figure 1.11.

We must be careful to distinguish the null reference from an object such as an empty *String*. An empty *String* is a string of 0 characters. It is a perfectly good object, in much the same way that 0 is a perfectly good integer. The null reference is a special value that doesn't refer to any object. Figure 1.12 shows a *Student* with the empty *String* as nickname.

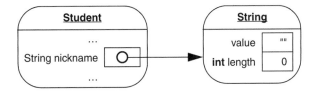

Figure 1.12 **The empty *String*.**

DrJava: Strings and reference values

Strings are objects and respond to a number of queries. Since *Strings* are immutable, there are no state-changing commands.

Start by creating a *String* named s1 in the *Interactions* pane. When creating a *String*, the sequence of characters that comprise the *String* must be given:

```
> String s1 = new String("Adam");
```

Note that the characters are enclosed in quotation marks ("). You must use quotation marks and not apostrophes.

Now try a few queries and note the results:

```
> s1.length()
> s1.charAt(0)
```

```
> s1.charAt(1)
> s1.indexOf('A')
> s1.indexOf('a')
```

In the last two queries, the characters in parentheses are enclosed in apostrophes, or single quotes.

Key the following and explain the result

```
> s1.indexOf('z')
```

Now define *String* s2 as follows:

```
> String s2 = "Dot";
```

and query s2:

```
> s2.length()
> s2.charAt(0)
> s2.charAt(1)
```

What do you think is the relationship between the expressions "Dot" and new String("Dot")?

Open the file Person.java, also located in ch1. What properties of a person are modeled in this class? What instance variables will a *Person* object have, and what are their types? What commands and queries will it have?

When a *Person* is created, a name must be specified. Create two *Persons* as follows:

```
> Person p1 = new Person(s1);
> Person p2 = new Person(s2);
```

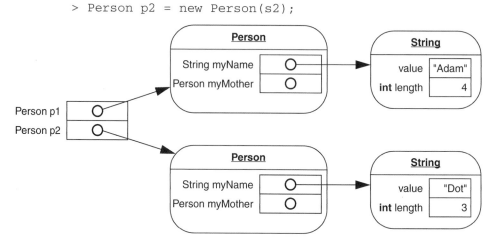

What do you expect to get when you query p1 for its name? Verify your assumption. What do you get if you query p1 for its mother?

Next, let's use the setMother command to give p1 a mother:

```
> p1.setMother(p2);
```

This command copies the value stored in p2 (a reference to the *Person* named "Dot")
into p1's myMother instance variable:

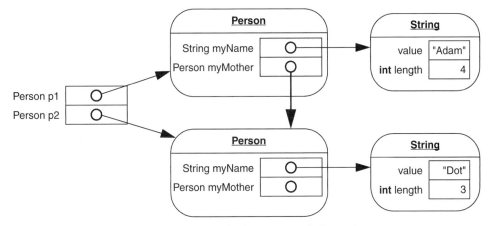

If we query p1 for its mother, we don't get a very informative answer:

```
> p1.mother()
Person@5093f1
```

(The result you get may not be exactly what we have shown, but will be similar.) That's
because the query mother returns a reference value: specifically, a value of type *refer-
ence-to-Person*. Remember that a reference value denotes an object, and contains sufficient data for the object to be located in memory.[1]

Let's define a variable p3, and store a reference to p1's mother in p3:

```
> Person p3 = p1.mother();
```

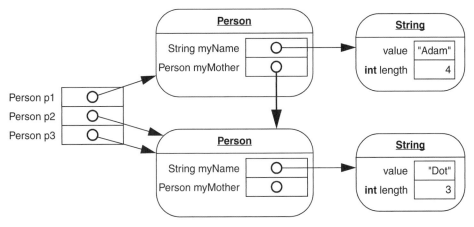

---

1. The value displayed by DrJava is typically obtained by converting the internal address of the
   object into an integer.

We now have defined three *Person* variables, p1, p2, and p3. When we defined p3, we copied this same value stored in Adam's myMother instance variable into p3. Notice that variables p2, p3, and Adam's instance variable myMother all contain the same value.

Key the following and note the results.

```
> p3.name()
> p1.mother().name()
```

1.6   Overview of a complete system

As we've seen, an object-oriented system is a collection of cooperating objects. The set of objects that comprise the system can generally be divided into three basic subsystems: *model*, *external interface*, and *data management*.

The problem at hand is expressed in terms of entities represented by objects that make up the model, or the *problem domain*, subsystem. These are the objects that cooperate to actually solve the problem. For example, if we consider the chess-playing program mentioned previously, the model will include objects representing the players, the chess pieces, and the chess board. Knowledge of rules of the game, how pieces move, move strategies, and so on, will reside in these objects.

Every system must communicate in some way with the external world. Managing this interaction is the job of the external interface. Since the "external world" is a human user for the systems we consider, we refer to the external interface as the *user interface*. In the chess-playing program, the user interface is responsible for displaying the model state to the user and for getting input from the user. Note that the model is relatively independent of the user interface. The user interface might communicate with the user with simple text output or might include a three-dimensional animated display. The model is the same in either case: the rules, moves, strategies it contains remain the same regardless of how we display the board.

Systems must often maintain *persistent* data: data that must be kept whether the system is running or not. This data is typically kept in a set of files or in a database. For instance, we might want the chess-playing program to keep won-lost statistics or to allow a user to suspend a game and resume play at a later time. These functions involve storing and retrieving data from the file system. Such functions are the responsibility of the *data management subsystem*.

In this text, particularly in the early chapters, we concentrate on the model. This is where fundamental problem solving techniques are most easily learned. User interface and data management are specialized subsystems, built with elaborate sets of specialized software tools. For instance, the standard Java graphical user interface libraries include over a thousand classes. Our early examples will employ a simple text-based user interface. We'll take a look at designing a graphical user interface and interacting with the file system in later chapters.

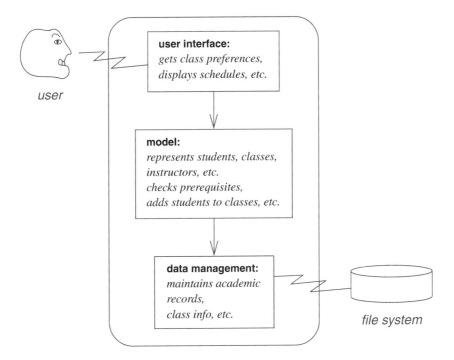

Figure 1.13 Subsystems in a student registration system.

✳ 1.6.1 An example: testing a *Counter*

A simple user interface

Let's see what a complete system looks like when written in Java. As with the *Counter* class, we'll skip lightly over the details. We build a very simple system to test a *Counter*. The model and user interface will each consist of a single object. We need no data management component.

Suppose we want to test that the *Counter* class has been implemented correctly. What should we do? We should create an instance of the class, exercise it by giving it commands and queries, and make sure that it behaves as expected. We must make sure that the initial state of the newly created object is correct, that the command `incrementCount` properly modifies the count, and that the command `reset` sets the count back to 0. A minimal test might look something like this:

action:	expected result:
create *Counter*	
query for `currentCount`:	0
`incrementCount`	
`incrementCount`	

Listing 1.2   The class *CounterTester*

```
1.     /**
2.      * A simple tester for the class Counter.
3.      */
4.     public class CounterTester {

5.         private Counter counter;

6.         /**
7.          * Create a new CounterTester.
8.          */
9.         public CounterTester () {
10.            counter = new Counter();
11.        }

12.        /**
13.         * Run the test.
14.         */
15.        public void start () {
16.            System.out.println("Starting count:");
17.            System.out.println(counter.currentCount());
18.            counter.incrementCount();
19.            counter.incrementCount();
20.            counter.incrementCount();
21.            System.out.println("After 3 increments:");
22.            System.out.println(counter.currentCount());
23.            counter.reset();
24.            System.out.println("After reset:");
25.            System.out.println(counter.currentCount());
26.        }

27.    }
```

```
incrementCount
query for currentCount:      3
reset
query for currentCount:      0
```

The user interface object, which we'll call a *CounterTester*, will create a *Counter* instance, exercise it by invoking its commands, and write the results to the display screen. The definition of the class is given in Listing 1.2. The class includes the definition of a sin-

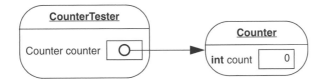

Figure 1.14 *CounterTester* and *Counter*

gle instance variable (line 5), a constructor (lines 6 through 11), and a single command (lines 12 through 26).

The instance variable, named `counter`, is of type *Counter*. That is, it will contain a reference to a *Counter* object. Recall that the constructor specifies actions to be performed when a *CounterTester* instance is created. In this case, a new *Counter* instance is created and a reference to the newly created *Counter* is stored in the variable `counter`. Thus creating a *CounterTester* results in a *Counter* also being created. A newly created *CounterTester* is shown in Figure 1.14.

Lines 12 through 26 define the command `start`. They specify a sequence of actions the *CounterTester* must carry out in response to the command. `System.out` is a predefined object that can write to the display screen. Line 16 instructs `System.out` to write the line

```
Starting count:
```

to the screen. Recall that a *Counter* supports a query `currentCount`, and commands `incrementCount` and `reset`. In line 17, the *Counter* object `counter` is queried, `counter.currentCount()`, and the resulting value written to the screen. Thus lines 16 and 17 write the following two lines to the display screen:

```
Starting count:
0
```

In lines 18, 19, and 20, `counter` is given the command `incrementCount` three times. Lines 21 and 22 write out:

```
After 3 increments:
3
```

Finally, `counter` is given the command `reset`, and lines 24 and 25 write out:

```
After reset:
0
```

Getting it all started

We've defined a model class *Counter* and a user interface class *CounterTester*. The *CounterTester* creates a *Counter* to test. But where does the *CounterTester* come from? How do we get the system started? We need one more class containing a method named `main`, as shown in Listing 1.3.

Listing 1.3   **The class *Test***

```
1.      /**
2.       * Test the class Counter.
3.       */
4.      public class Test {

5.          /**
6.           * Run a Counter test.
7.           */
8.          public static void main (String[] args) {
9.              CounterTester tester = new CounterTester();
10.             tester.start();
11.         }

12.     }
```

Although the `main` method is defined in a class, it is really outside the object-oriented paradigm. Its only purpose should be to create the top-level objects and get the system started. Our convention is that the class containing `main` contains no other methods, and is not used to model any other part of the system. In the example shown here, `main` creates a *CounterTester* and gives it the command `start`.

How we run a program depends on the computing system and environment we are using. (See Appendix i.) But in any case, we must identify the class containing the method `main` to the Java run-time system. For instance, we might key something like

```
$ java Test
```

Running the program will produce six lines of output:

```
Starting count:
0
After 3 increments:
3
After reset:
0
```

DrJava: running a program

It is possible to run a program from DrJava. Open the file `CounterTester.java` (located in folder `ch1`, which is in folder `nhText`).

In the *Interactions* pane, key

```
> java Test
```

Output will appear in the *Interactions* pane.

Is the output correct? If not, did you modify the assignment statement of the `incre-mentCount` method to read

```
count = count + 2;
```

and not change it back? Open `Counter.java`, change the assignment now to read

```
count = count + 1;
```

Save and compile. Run the program again.

✴ 1.7   Objects that "wrap" primitive values

At this point, you should understand the difference between values and objects. Sometimes, however, we want to use a primitive value as if it were an object. For each primitive type, Java provides a corresponding class that allows us to do just that. An instance of the predefined classes *Boolean*, *Character*, *Byte*, *Short*, *Integer*, *Long*, *Float*, and *Double* is an immutable object that "wraps" a primitive value in an object.

As an example, consider the class *Integer*. An *Integer* is an immutable object with a single **int** property:

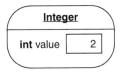

The **int** value is specified when the object is created, and can be accessed with the query `intValue`. If `anInt` is an **int** variable and `anInteger` an *Integer* variable, the following statements create an *Integer* object wrapping the **int** value 2, and then assign its value to the **int** variable:

```
Integer anInteger = new Integer(2);
int anInt = anInteger.intValue();
```

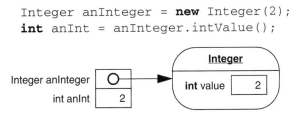

Note that the variable `anInt` contains a *primitive value*, while the variable `anInteger` contains a *reference value*.

Boxing and unboxing

When required by the context, Java automatically converts a primitive value to an object or retrieves the primitive value wrapped in a an object. For instance, suppose we write

```
anInteger = 3;
```

where, as above, `anInteger` is an *Integer* variable. The variable `anInteger` cannot contain a primitive value: it can only contain a value that references an *Integer* object. The value to be stored in the variable, that is, the value given by the expression to the right of the equal sign, must be a reference to an *Integer*. Java automatically translates this statement into

```
anInteger = new Integer(3);
```

wrapping the **int** value in an *Integer* object, and storing a reference to that object in the variable `anInteger`.

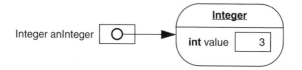

This operation is referred to as *boxing*.

Similarly, we can also write a statement like

```
anInt = anInteger + 1;
```

This addition operation requires two **int** values as operands. Java automatically converts the *Integer* object to a primitive value by invoking its `intValue` method. That is, Java automatically translates the statement into

```
anInt = anInteger.intValue() + 1;
```

This is referred to as *unboxing*.

Values and objects are distinct semantic notions in Java. To avoid blurring the distinction, we'll explicitly do the conversions and not depend on automatic boxing and unboxing.

✳ 1.8   Java in detail: primitive types

The primitive Java types **byte**, **short**, **int**, **long**, **float**, **double**, and **char** are called *numeric types*. (It might surprise you to see **char** included in the numeric types.) **float** and **double** are *floating point* types, the others *integral* types. Arithmetic operations such as addition, subtraction, multiplication, and division can be performed with numeric values. But values of integral and floating point types are encoded quite differently in the computer's memory.

All of the values the processor manipulates are encoded as sequences of *bits*, that is, sequences of binary digits, 0's and 1's. The basic difference between the types **byte**, **short**, **int**, and **long** is the number of bits used to encode values. Specifically, a **byte** value is 8 bits long, a **short** value 16, an **int** 32, and a **long** 64. Note, for instance, that there are 2^8, or 256, different 8-bit patterns comprising the type **byte**. Half these patterns represent negative integers, and half represent non-negative integers. Thus the type **byte** consists of the set of values –128 through 127:

$$
\begin{array}{ll}
-128: & 10000000 \\
-127: & 10000001 \\
-126: & 10000010 \\
& \cdots \\
-1: & 11111111 \\
0: & 00000000 \\
1: & 00000001 \\
2: & 00000010 \\
& \cdots \\
126: & 01111110 \\
127: & 01111111
\end{array}
$$

The difference between **float** and **double** is also in the number of bits used to encode values: a **float** is 32 bits long, while a **double** is 64 bits long. However, the scheme used to encode floating point numbers is quite different from that used to encode integers. The 32-bit encoding of the number 1 as a **float**, for example, is

00111111100000000000000000000000

while the 32-bit encoding of the number 1 as an **int** is

00000000000000000000000000000001

A discussion of how floating point numbers are encoded is beyond the scope of our discussion.

The type **char** is also, somewhat surprisingly, an integral type. That means that arithmetic operations such as addition and subtraction can be performed with values of type

Integral types

Type	Bits	Smallest value	Largest value
byte	8	–128	127
short	16	–32,768	32,767
int	32	–2,147,483,648	2,147,483,647
long	64	–9,223,372,036,854,775,808	9,223,372,036,854,775,807
char	16	0	65,535

Floating point types

Type	Bits	Largest value	Smallest positive non-zero value
float	32	$(2-2^{-23})\cdot 2^{127}$	2^{-149}
double	64	$(2-2^{-52})\cdot 2^{1023}$	2^{-1074}

Figure 1.15 **Numeric types.**

char. Values of type **char** are 16 bits, interpreted as integers in the range $0 - 65,535$. But these values are intended to be used to represent Unicode characters, and it would be misleading to use them for arithmetic. Unicode is a universal character encoding standard that assigns a unique number to every character used in the world's major written languages, including European alphabetic scripts, Middle Eastern right-to-left scripts, and many scripts of Asia. The majority of common characters can be encoded as 16-bit numbers.

The first 128 Unicode characters are the same as the widely used ASCII (American Standard Code for Information Interchange) character set. This character set includes familiar uppercase and lowercase letters of the Latin alphabet, digits, punctuation marks, space, and a number of special "control characters." (See Appendix iii.)

1.9   Java in detail: identifiers and literals

1.9.1   Identifiers

When we write a program in Java, we need to name classes, objects, properties, features, *etc.* We use *identifiers* to name things in Java. In the example shown in Listing 1.1, `Counter`, `currentCount`, `incrementCount`, `reset`, and `count` are identifiers. A Java identifier is a sequence of characters consisting of letters, digits, dollar signs($), and/or underscores(_). An identifier can be of any length, and cannot begin with a digit. The following are examples of Java identifiers. (Recall we use a distinct type font when we write in the language.)

```
X       Abc     aVeryLongIdentifier      b29     a2b     A_a_x
b$2     $_      $$$     IXLR8
```

The following are not legal Java identifiers. (Why not?)

```
✗       2BRnot2B        a.b     Hello!      A-a     Test.java
```

The $ character is used in computer generated source code, and should be avoided in your programs. Also, we follow a convention that rarely uses underscores. Our identifiers, therefore, will be made up of letters and digits.

Java identifiers are *case sensitive*. This means that uppercase and lowercase characters are different. For example, the following are all different identifiers.

```
total       Total       TOTAL       tOtAl
```

Though it may be obvious, identifiers can't contain spaces, and the digits 1 and 0 (one and zero) are different from the letters l and O (el and oh). (Though the difference is not always easy to see in print.).

> **identifier:** a sequence of characters that can be used as a name in a Java program.

abstract	default	goto	package	this
assert	do	if	private	throw
boolean	double	implements	protected	throws
break	else	import	public	transient
byte	enum	instanceof	return	true
case	extends	int	short	try
catch	false	interface	static	void
char	final	long	strictfp	volatile
class	finally	native	super	while
const	float	new	switch	
continue	for	null	synchronized	

Figure 1.16 **Identifier literals and keywords.**

There are a number of *keywords* and *identifier literals*[1] reserved for special purposes. These cannot be used as identifiers, and are given in Figure 1.16. In the text, we use a bold face font to distinguish keywords and identifier literals.

Guidelines in choosing identifiers

The compiler insists only that we use legal identifiers when naming entities in a Java program; it does not matter to the compiler which specific identifiers we use. However, following standard conventions and intelligently choosing identifiers are crucial factors in producing a readable program. If we are defining a class to model a student, it is sensible to give the class a name like "Student" rather than "S" or "X" or "Foo." It is just as essential that your code be comprehensible to a human reader, not just to the compiler.

We adopt the following two conventions.

- Use lowercase characters, with uppercase characters inserted for readability. (This convention is sometimes called "camel case.") For instance,

        addCourse

rather than

        addcourse or add_course

- Capitalize class names. For instance,

        Student and PlayingCard

are class names, but

        homeAddress and suit

are not.

Note that these are only conventions—commonly adopted practices. The rules of the language put no restrictions on identifier usage.

1. **true**, **false**, and **null** are identifier literals; the rest are keywords.

Here are a few general, common-sense guidelines in choosing identifiers.

1. Choose descriptive identifiers, that is, choose identifiers that reveal the purpose of the named entity. Single-letter identifiers are seldom appropriate. Avoid unnecessary, cryptic, or unintelligible abbreviations, and cuteness.

   Use

   ```
   Student       addCourse    ExpressionTree
   ```

   not

   ```
   X1            Vodka        XpsnTr
   ```

2. Avoid overly long identifiers. Generally, one or two words will suffice. In particular, don't use "noise words" in identifiers.

   Use

   ```
   ExpressionTree
   ```

   not

   ```
   TheParseTreeForAnExpression
   ```

3. Avoid abbreviations. If you abbreviate, be consistent. In particular, if a word is abbreviated as part of one identifier, its occurrence in any other identifier should be similarly abbreviated.

   Use

   `employeeRecord` and `masterRecord`

   or

   `employeeRec` and `masterRec`

   not

   `employeeRec` and `masterRecord`

   There are two common methods for choosing abbreviations: using the first few letters of a word or deleting vowels. Be consistent in your method of choosing abbreviations. If `msg` abbreviates "message" then `opr`, not `oper`, should abbreviate "operator."

4. Be as specific as possible. Identifiers like `computeResults`, `processData`, *etc.* are virtually contentless, and rarely satisfactory choices.

5. Take particular care to distinguish closely related entities. Names should be as descriptive as you can make them, and differences in entities should be mirrored by differences in their names.

   Use

   `newMasterRecord` and `oldMasterRecord`

   not

   `masterRecord1` and `masterRecord2`

or worse

masterRec and masRec

6. Don't incorporate the name of its syntactic category in the name of an entity.

Use

Student

not

StudentClass

1.9.2 Literals

Sometimes we need to denote a specific value in a program. A *literal* is a representation of a value in a programming language. In the example shown in Listing 1.1, the 0 occurring in lines 11 and 29,

count = 0;

and the 1 in line 23,

count = count + 1;

are literals. Java defines literals for the primitive types **int**, **double**, **boolean**, and **char**, and for the reference type *reference-to-String*.

Integer literals

Integer literals look like ordinary decimal numbers, and denote values of the type **int**. The following all denote **int** values:

25   0   1233456   289765   7

Integer literals can't contain commas and shouldn't have leading zeros. For instance,

✗   123,456

is not a legal literal, and

0123

doesn't represent the value that it appears to.[1]

Floating point literals

Numbers that include a decimal point denote values of type **double**. For instance,

0.5   2.67   0.00123   12.0   2.   .6

---

1. The leading zero means the number is given in *octal*, or *radix 8*, notation.

all denote values of type **double**. Even though the last two numbers on the above line are legal, we prefer to always write digits before and after the decimal point. This makes the numbers a bit easier to read. Thus, we'll write

```
2.0    0.6
```

to represent these values.

Exponential notation can also be used for **double** literals. The following are legal **double** literals:

```
0.5e+3    0.5e-3    0.5E3    5e4    2.0E-27
```

They represent the values

0.5×10^3 (=500.0), 0.5×10^{-3} (=0.0005), 0.5×10^3, 5.0×10^4, and 2.0×10^{-27}

Note that the "e" can be upper or lower case, and that the mantissa (the number before the "e") need not contain a decimal point. The exponent (after the "e") is an optionally-signed integer.

Character literals

Character literals (denoting values of type **char**) consist of a single character between apostrophes. For instance:

```
'A'    'a'    '2'    ';'    '.'    ' '
```

The last example on the previous line represents the "space" or "blank" character, the character that is generated by pressing the space bar on the keyboard. Note that uppercase letters are distinct from lower case letters. Thus the first two literals on the line above represent different characters. Also note that the following three literals

```
2    2.0    '2'
```

denote values of *different types*. The first denotes an **int**, the second a **double**, and the third a **char**. These three values are encoded quite differently in the computer's memory, and are manipulated with different instructions.

The apostrophe, quotation mark, and backslash must be preceded by a backslash in a character literal. Thus these characters are represented as

```
'\''    '\"'    '\\'
```

and not as

✗   '''   '"'   '\'

Certain special characters are also represented by using a backslash. In particular, the "tab" character is represented `'\t'`, and the "end of line" character ("linefeed") is denoted `'\n'`.

Except for the space character, character literals shouldn't include spaces. Thus

✗   ' A '

is not legal, where there are spaces before and after the letter 'A'.

Boolean literals

The two values of type **boolean** are written as follows:

`true`   `false`

Since Java is case sensitive, we must use lowercase letters when writing these boolean values. We can't write **true** as **TRUE** or **True**.

String literals

A string literal is a possibly empty sequence of characters enclosed in quotations:

`"ABC"`   `"123"`   `"A"`   `" "`

String literals are a little different from those literals discussed above. As mentioned previously, *String* is a class defined in a standard Java library. A string literal denotes a reference value: a reference to an instance of this class.

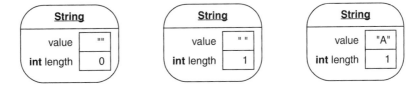

Figure 1.17 The empty *String*, and two *Strings* of length 1.

The third example on the line above, `"A"`, denotes a (reference to a) string of length 1, consisting of the single character 'A'. This is quite different from the character literal `'A'`. In particular, the string is an object, while the character value is not. The fourth example on the line above, `" "`, denotes the empty string, a string with 0 characters. This is different from a string containing a single space character, for instance.

A string literal cannot extend past the end of a line. And the quotation mark and backslash must be preceded by a backslash in a string literal:

```
"He said, \"Let's go!\""
"The business plan is C:\\msn\\EvilMonkeys.doc."
```

Null literal

The *null* reference, introduced at the end of Section 1.5, is denoted by the literal **null**.

> **literal:** a sequence of characters that denotes a particular value in a Java program.

✳ 1.9.3 Java in detail: literals, the rest of the story

Though not commonly used, values of type **long** can be denoted by suffixing an integer literal with the letter L or l:

        21   2L

Similarly, values of type **float** can be represented by suffixing the letter F or f to a floating point literal:

        2.0f 2e2F

Integer literals can be expressed in octal (radix 8) or hexadecimal (radix 16) as well as in decimal. A sequence of digits beginning with 0 is an octal representation. An octal representation can contain only the digits 0 through 7. For example,

        07   012   0123

denote the values 7, 10 ($= 1 \times 8 + 2$), and 83 ($= 1 \times 64 + 2 \times 8 + 3$) respectively.

A sequence of digits beginning with 0x or 0X is a hexadecimal representation. A hexadecimal representation can contain the digits 0 through 9 and the letters a through f, uppercase or lowercase. The letter a (or A) has value 10, b (or B) value 11, *etc.* For example,

        0xAF   0xff   0X123

denote the values 175 ($= 10 \times 16 + 15$), 255 ($= 15 \times 16 + 15$), and 291 ($= 1 \times 256 + 2 \times 16 + 3$).

A character literal is any single character (except \ or ') enclosed in single quotes, such as

        'a'   '2'   ' ' (the space character)

or an *escape sequence* enclosed in single quotes. An escape sequence is a character sequence preceded by a backslash. Escape sequences include:

\b	backspace
\t	horizontal tab
\n	linefeed
\f	formfeed
\r	carriage return
\"	quotation (double quote)
\'	apostrophe (single quote)
\\	backslash

For example, '\n' and '\t' denote the linefeed (or "newline") and tab characters respectively.

A character can also be denoted by prefixing \u to its four digit Unicode value, expressed in hexadecimal. For instance, the character with Unicode hex value 0x03a9 can be denoted by the character literal '\u0x03a9'.

You must exercise some caution when using Unicode escapes. Since Unicode escapes are processed very early in the compilation process, it is not correct to write '\u000a' for the linefeed character or `'\u000d'` for the carriage return character. The escapes \u000a and \u000d become line terminators, making the character literal invalid. That is, `'\u000a'` appears to the compiler as a single quote, followed by the end of line, followed by a single quote at the start of the next line. See [Joy 00] for details.

Escape sequences can also be used in *String* literals, and, as mentioned above, are required for quotation marks (`"`) and backslash (`\`). For instance, the following *String* literal contains quotation marks and a linefeed character:

```
"He said, \"Hello\nI must be going.\""
```

1.10   Java in detail: lexical structure

A class definition is made up of *tokens* – identifiers, keywords, literals, punctuation marks. How things are spaced and where a line ends are somewhat arbitrary. Spaces are required to separate words, but are otherwise irrelevant. For instance, the line

```
public class Student
```

contains two keywords followed by an identifier, while the line

```
publicclass Student
```

contains two identifiers.

Spaces are not required but are usually permitted around punctuation. For instance, the following two lines are equivalent:

```
class Student{
class Student {
```

In a few cases, spaces are not allowed around punctuation marks. In particular, spaces are not allowed around a period. For example, there can be no spaces in the expressions

```
c.reset
1.0
TrafficSignal.RED
```

Finally, several spaces can generally appear, and a line can end, wherever one space can appear. The following two lines are equivalent:

```
public class Student{
public      class      Student {
```

and are each equivalent to the following four lines:

```
public
           class
  Student
  {
```

However, in order to make our programs easier to read we adhere to rather rigid rules for spacing. We'll illustrate these conventions as specific syntactic constructs are introduced.

Comments

Comments are explanatory remarks included in a program solely for the benefit of a human reader. They are completely ignored by the compiler. There are three kinds of comments in Java. We'll see them used throughout the text. The first begins with a pair of "slash" characters, and extends to the end of the line:

```
// This is a one-line comment.
```

The second form of comment, a "multiline comment," begins with the character pair "/*" and extends to the character pair "*/". This form of comment may extend across several lines:

```
/* This is a comment that
extends across more than one line. */
```

The final form is called a "doc comment." It is similar to the multiline comment but starts with the three characters "/**". Doc comments are recognized by *javadoc* and other software tools that produce specification documentation.[1]

```
/** This is a doc comment. Like the above,
it can continue for more than one line. */
```

We use a convention of starting each line in a doc comment with an aligned "*", and putting the starting "/**" and ending "*/" on lines by themselves.

```
/**
 * This is a doc comment.
 * By convention, each line starts with a "*" and
 * the starting and terminating characters are put on
 * lines by themselves.
 */
```

Again, although comments are very important for programmers who need to use or understand our code, they have nothing to do with how the program behaves when it is run.

> **comment:** explanatory remarks that are included in a program for the benefit of a human reader and are ignored by the compiler.

---

1. Doc comments are written in HTML: *Hypertext Markup Language*.

1.11   Summary

This chapter introduced the fundamental notions of value, type, object, and class. We also saw Java identifiers and literals.

Values are the fundamental pieces of information manipulated in a program. Values are grouped, along with their operations, into types. Java has two kinds of types: primitive types and reference types. Java provides as primitive:

- several integer types (**byte**, **short**, **int**, **long**);
- two real or floating types (**float** and **double**);
- the character type **char**, and
- the type **boolean** which contains two values, *true* and *false*.

A reference value denotes, or refers to, an object. Objects are the fundamental abstractions from which software systems are built. Objects are often abstractions of real-world entities, and are designed to support the functionality of the system. An object's role in the system determines the set of features the object is responsible for supporting. These features include

- queries, by which data values are obtained from the object; and
- commands, which cause the object to perform some actions that typically change the state of the object.

An object must contain adequate data to carry out its responsibilities. Data maintained by the object are stored in the object's instance variables. These variables and their values at any given point in the computation make up the state of the object. Thus a query reports information obtained from the state of the object, while a command usually causes the object to change state. The only way an object can change state is if the object itself performs some command. Some objects are immutable. The state of an immutable object cannot change after the object is created.

Objects are grouped into classes. A class defines the features of, and data items maintained by, its members. All objects in a particular class have the same features. An object that is a member of a particular class is called an instance of the class. When we define a class, we define instance variables that each member of the class will have, and algorithms for carrying out queries and commands. These algorithms are collectively called methods.

For every object there is a value that denotes or refers to the object. Such a value is called a *reference value*; its type is *reference-to-x*, where *x* is the class of the object. It is common for a data item of one object to reference another object. In this way, relationships between objects are created.

The collection of objects that comprise a system can be divided into three basic subsystems: model, external interface, and data management. The model objects represent the problem and cooperate to provide the solution. The external interface, or user interface, controls the interaction between the model and the user. The data management component is responsible for storing and retrieving persistent data in a file system or data base.

In a Java program, we name things—classes, objects, properties, features—with identifiers. An identifier is a sequence of characters consisting of letters, digits, dollar signs, and/or underscores. If we need to denote a particular value in a program, we use a literal. Literals can be used to denote integer and floating point values, character values, boolean values, and *Strings*.

SELF-STUDY EXERCISES

1.1   Why would the value 1 and the value *true* not be in the same type?

1.2   Suggest an appropriate type for each of the following data items.

    a.   The number of siblings a person has.

    b.   Whether a switch is off or on.

    c.   The current temperature.

    d.   The number of students at a large state university.

    e.   The population of the world.

    f.   The wave length of a radio signal.

    g.   The amount of interest paid by your bank today.

    h.   Whether you are a World War II veteran.

    i.   The population of a city.

    j.   The first line of your favorite sonnet.

    k.   What you write in a single crossword puzzle square.

1.3   Consider an object that represents a complex number. What are the properties of such an object? What are the types of the properties?

1.4   What properties would be appropriate for an object modeling a telephone number? Is this likely to be an immutable object?

1.5   An object modeling a music CD has the following properties: title, composer, performer, playing time. Suggest appropriate types for each of these properties.

1.6   An object modeling the destination of an airline flight includes the following properties: airport, gate, arrival time. Suggest a command appropriate to this object.

1.7   Explain the statement: values are to types as objects are to classes.

1.8   In a library system, which of the following objects are likely to be in the same class?

    a.   An object modeling *Absalom, Absalom!* by William Faulkner.

    b.   An object modeling William Faulkner, the author.

    c.   An object modeling *Finnegans Wake*, by James Joyce.

    d.   An object modeling William Faulkner, a library patron.

1.9   Stylistically, how is an identifier used to name a class different from an identifier used to name a query or command?

1.10   What is the maximum length of a Java identifier?

1.11   For each of the following, indicate whether or not it is a legal Java identifier.

      (a) `Foo`   *(b)* `x`   *(c)* `2E2`   *(d)* `ver2.1` *(e)* `class`
      (f) `"Foo"`   *(g)* `True` *(h)* `$2`   *(i)* `Class`

1.12   For each of the following, indicate whether or not it is a legal Java literal. If it is, give the type of the value denoted.

      (a) `1000`   *(b)* `10x5`   *(c)* `2E2`   *(d)* `2.e.2`   *(e)* `'0'`
      (f) `'abc'`   *(g)* `True`   *(h)* `"0"`

EXERCISES

1.1   An object is to be used to model a street address. What are some properties such an object would contain? Write instance variable definitions for these properties.

1.2   An object models a three-way lamp. (That is, the lamp has off, low, medium, and high settings.) The lamp has only one property, its setting. What type is associated with this property? What query (or queries) should the object support? What command(s)?

1.3   An object models a combination lock. What properties should this object have? What types are associated with these properties? What queries should the object support? What commands?

1.4   A university course scheduling system has classes representing faculty members, courses, and classrooms. Suggest properties that a course object might have, including properties whose associated values are of primitive types, and properties whose associated values are of reference types.

1.5   For each of the following objects, list some possible properties that the object might contain.

    a.   An object modeling a classroom in a class scheduling program.

    b.   An object modeling a book in a library catalogue.

    c.   An object modeling a back pack in a retail store inventory system.

    d.   An object modeling a player's back pack in a video game.

    e.   An object modeling an elevator in a simulation.

1.6   For each of the objects described in Exercise 1.5, give an example of an applicable query and the type of the value returned by the query.

1.7   For each of the objects described in Exercise 1.5, if the object is mutable give an example of a command and indicate which properties the command will modify.

1.8   For each of the following classes, give examples of at least two instances of the class.

    a.   A class used to model automobile manufacturers.

    b.   A class used to model automobiles in a dealer's inventory.

    c.   A class used to model videos in a video rental store.

    d.   A class used to model customers of a video rental store.

1.9   For each class described in Exercise 1.8, give an example of a property whose associated value is of a primitive type, and a property whose associated value is of a reference type.

1.10   For each of the following applications, suggest some objects that might be included in the system design. Give one or two responsibilities that might be assigned to each object.

    a.   Your favorite computer game.

    b.   A program modeling traffic flow on major thoroughfares in a city.

    c.   An inventory control system for a hardware store.

    d.   A program controlling a vending machine.

    e.   A university registration system.

    f.   A program that translates English into French.

    g.   A program for recording and manipulating genealogical data.

1.11   Consider classes modeling students in a university registration system and modeling students as users of the university library. What properties will these classes have in common? Would it make sense to have a single object represent a student for both purposes?

1.12   When a student user of the library borrows a book, the system must have a record that, among other things, associates the book borrowed with the student borrowing it. Suppose an object is to be used to represent such a transaction. What information should it contain?

1.13   A class is being designed to model an item of inventory in a retail store. An instance of the class will have the following properties: item number, item description, price, and quantity on hand. It will have commands to modify or set each of its properties. Suggest reasonable identifiers for naming the class and its features. Give some examples of inappropriate identifiers, and indicate why they are inappropriate.

SELF-STUDY EXERCISE SOLUTIONS

1.1   The operations that can be performed with the value 1 (arithmetic) are meaningless when applied to the value *true*.

1.2   *a.*   **byte**, **short**, or **int**.

    b.   **boolean**.

    c.   **double** (or **float**).

    d.   **int**.

    e.   **long**.

    f.   **double** (or **float**).

    g.   Money is tricky since approximations can get you into trouble. **int** or **double**, depending on whether the fractions of a cent matter.

    h.   **boolean**.

    i.   **int**.

    j.   *String*.

    k.   **char**.

1.3   Real part and imaginary part. **double** (or **float**).

1.4   Area code, exchange, last four digits. Yes, likely to be immutable.

1.5   Title: *String*; composer: *String* or reference to a *Composer* object; performer: *String* or reference to a *Performer* object; playing time: **double** or **int**.

1.6   Change gate or change arrival time.

1.7   A value is a member of a type and an object is a member of a class.

1.8   *(a)* and *(c)*.

1.9   Names of classes, by convention, begin with uppercase letters.

1.10   There is no maximum length.

1.11   *(a) yes*   *(b)* yes   *(c)* no   *(d)* no   *(e)* no (key word)
        (f) no (*String* literal)   *(g)* yes   *(h)* yes   *(i)* yes

1.12   *(a)* **int**   *(b)* not a literal   *(c)* **double**   *(d)* not a literal   *(e)* **char**
        (f) not a literal   *(g)* not a literal (an identifier, because of the upper case 'T')
        (h) String

CHAPTER 2

Defining a simple class

In this chapter, we build some simple classes. Our goal is to see how to write a specification for a class, that is, a precise description of the features common to all instances of the class, and how to implement basic features.

We start by explaining what it means for one object to "use" another. This is the *client-server* relationship between two objects. The features offered by the server object to the client comprise the *specification* of the server object. The object specification is distinct from the *implementation* of the object. The specification defines the object's behavior as seen by its client objects. The implementation, on the other hand, provides the internals that enable the object to behave according to its specifications.

We construct several simple classes in Java: counters, traffic signals, playing cards. Our initial examples are, of necessity, simplified and incomplete. We settle for vague descriptions of the general problem, and assume our object design is "right" without justification based on a careful analysis of the problem statement. This is adequate for our exposition, since we're more concerned here with illustrating various design and language constructs than with demonstrating a comprehensive design methodology. While this degree of *nonchalance* about the problem statement would hardly be suitable in "real life," the situation we present isn't too far from reality. We never create a "perfect" design on first try, and rarely, in fact, work from a complete and comprehensive problem statement.

As we go, we see how to store data in an object and how to write method bodies. We learn the basics of statements and expressions—two fundamental Java syntactic constructs. We conclude by considering arithmetic expressions in some detail, and by examining the overall structure of a Java program.

Objectives

After studying this chapter you should understand the following:

- the client-server relationship;
- the purpose of a class specification;
- the purpose of a class implementation;
- the function of statements in a program;

- the function of arithmetic expressions in a program;
- the meaning and use of an assignment statement;
- the role of parameters in the specification of a method;
- the role of comments in programs.

  Also, you should be able to:
- write the specification of a simple class;
- implement a simple class;
- invoke an object's methods;
- construct a simple static diagram;
- construct a simple interaction diagram describing the interaction of two objects;
- write and evaluate arithmetic expressions;
- write legal return statements;
- write legal assignment statements;
- develop a javadoc document for the client.

2.1   Object interaction: clients and servers

An object has a set of *features*: queries and commands. An object can be queried to ascertain values based on its state, and given commands that change its state. We have also noted that objects cooperate to produce a problem solution. An important structuring relation that can exist between two objects is that one object (object *A*) *uses* another object (object *B*) by querying and commanding it, that is, by using its features. In this relationship, object *A* is termed the *client*, and object *B* is the *server* or *supplier*. In the overall system design, a given object will sometimes play the role of client and sometimes the role of server.

> A **client** queries and commands a **server**.

If we consider the chess playing program introduced in Section 1.1.2, a *Player* object might query a *Piece* object to determine its location, or command the *Piece* to move, that is, to change its location. The *Player* object is the client, the *Piece* is the server. This is illustrated in Figure 2.1.

As another example, suppose a *Student* object and a *Course* object are part of a registration system. We can imagine that the *Course* object might have a list of enrolled students as part of its state. To enroll in the course, the *Student* object instructs the *Course* object to add it (the *Student*) to the list of enrollees. The *Student* object gives the *Course* object a command that changes the *Course*'s state. The *Student* object is the client, the *Course* object the server. At some later time, the *Student* object might be queried for the

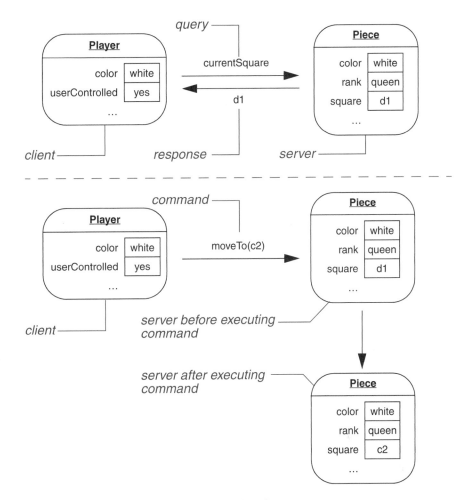

Figure 2.1 *Player* **object is client,** *Piece* **object is server.**

name and address of the student it represents, or instructed to change the student's address. In this case, the *Student* object is acting as server.

The relation of client to server is described as the *"uses"* relation. The client object (for instance, the *Player*) *uses* the server object (the *Piece*).

2.1.1 Specification and implementation

In the introductory chapter, we noted that the interaction between system components must be minimized to keep the complexity of the entire system under control. A question in a client-server relationship is to what extent should a client know about a server to be able to use its features? A client need only know the server's features and their proper use. A client should not depend on how the server is built.

The collection of an object's features as seen by its clients is called the object's *interface*[1] or *specification*. The *implementation* provides the "internals" that actually make up the features. We see this distinction often in everyday life. Consider a standard 110 volt wall receptacle. The *specification* guarantees that if you plug an appliance into the receptacle, you will get alternating current with certain well-defined characteristics. How the current is produced and how it gets to the receptacle—the *implementation*—you neither need to know nor care about. The specification *isolates* you from the details of the implementation. If the nuclear power plant that is supplying current to the receptacle begins to glow and the power company switches the feed to a coal-burning station, it makes no difference to the toaster plugged into the receptacle. Your toaster is content as long as it gets the expected kind of current, that is, as long as the receptacle's *specifications* are met. The toaster's operation is independent of *how* the current is created or delivered. Similarly, we drive automobiles, operate television sets, use computers by means of well-defined interfaces: to use these products, we don't know or care what goes on "under the hood."

> **specification (interface):** definition of an object's features, as seen by its clients.

The situation with software objects is analogous. A client object knows only the queries and commands a server object will respond to. The server object's features are well-defined and completely specified. This is the *specification* of the server object. How the features are actually implemented is of no concern to the client. For instance, suppose a

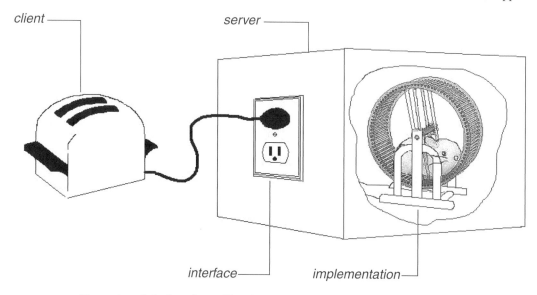

client   *server*

interface   *implementation*

Figure 2.2 *Interface* (*specification*) and *implementation*.

---

1. There is also a Java construct called an *interface* that we'll see later.

Course object in the registration system can be queried for a list of enrolled students either in alphabetical order or in the order in which they enrolled. These queries are part of the specification of the *Course* object, and are relevant to a client. *How* the ordering is actually accomplished is part of the object's implementation; it is not information available to the client.

The importance of this simple distinction cannot be overemphasized. Understanding and preserving the distinction between specification and implementation is absolutely essential to good system design.

2.2   Defining a class: a simple counter

We next give a few examples of writing classes. A warning, though: in describing an object, we first enumerate the object's responsibilities, and then give the properties of the object for which we can query and the commands. In reality, the responsibilities of an object are determined by the *system's functionality*, and by the object's *relationships* with other objects in the system. That is, we first need a good idea of what we want an object to do in support of system requirements before we can enumerate its responsibilities and specify its features. Indeed, even the fact that a particular aspect of a system is to be modeled as an object requires some analysis of the system's required behavior.

To start with, let's revisit the simple counter of the previous chapter and take a more careful look at the definition. The only property we are interested in is the count. A counter's responsibilities are simply to know the count, and to increment and reset the count. Our object responds to one query and two commands. We can query the object for the current count, and command the object to increment the count or reset the count to 0. We summarize:

Class: *Counter*

queries:
> *currentCount*   the value of the count, a non-negative integer

commands:
> *reset*   set the value of count to 0
> *incrementCount*   increment the value of count by 1

Note that we're actually defining a *class*. An object that represents a counter will be an instance of this class. The class definition determines the features of its instances. To define the class completely, we must provide both the *specification* and *implementation* of each feature. As explained above, the specifications describe the features that every object of the class will have, that is, the features seen by other (client) objects.

Let's start writing the class definition in Java. We name the class with the identifier `Counter`. (Recall that by convention we capitalize class names.) Classes are grouped together into *packages*. A package is simply a collection of one or more related classes. How we decide which classes to group together into a package need not concern us now. (See more about packages in Section 2.8.) We'll name the package containing our class `counters`.

The class definition will be in a text file (called a *source file*) named `Counter.java`. The file begins with a *package statement* that identifies the package the class is part of. Any class defined in the file is included in the package named in the package statement. The format for a package statement is the keyword **package**, followed by the name of the package (an identifier), followed by a semicolon:

> **package** *PackageName*;

For instance,

> **package** counters;

(Recall that we show keywords in boldface to distinguish them from identifiers.)

Unfortunately, the Java syntax does not permit us to separate the class specification from its implementation. The class is defined with a *class declaration* or *definition*, which contains both the specification and implementation of the features of the class. A class declaration looks like this:

```
/**
 * A simple integer counter.
 */
public class Counter {
    ...                                          definitions of
}                                                features go here
```

(The ellipsis (…) is not part of the class definition. We use it to indicate that something is missing and remains to be filled it.) The keyword **public** indicates that this is a public class: objects of this class will be accessible throughout the system. The definitions of the features will be contained between the braces. Note that braces, { and }, *must* be used; parentheses or brackets are not equivalent.

The text included between the character sequence "/**" and the sequence "*/" is a *comment*. Comments can include any text at all, and are solely for the benefit of a human reader. They are completely ignored by the computer when the program is run. This specific kind of comment is a *doc comment*. Doc comments are used to create specification documentation as described below. It is important that these comments be precise and concise. Someone who needs to use what you have written should be able to locate the class definition easily and quickly by scanning these doc comments. A doc comment precisely describes what the class models, and should precede every class that you define. (See more about comments in Section 1.10.)

2.2.1 Specifying the class features

Specifying a method for a query

We have determined that *Counter* objects have only one property: the current count. The value associated with this property is an integer. That is, when a client queries a *Counter* for the count, it will get an integer in response. (We can be more precise in specifying the result of the query: the integer result is non-negative, and there might be an upper limit as well. We'll return to this issue later.) As we saw in Section 1.2.1, Java has four built-in integer types: **byte**, **short**, **int**, and **long**. With no compelling reason to do otherwise, we'll choose the built-in type **int**.[1] The value associated with the property count will be of type **int**.

To enable a client to query a *Counter* object for this value, we define a *method*. To define the method, we write:

```
/**
 * The number of items counted.
 */
public int currentCount () {
    ...
}
```

the implementation of the method goes here

type of value returned by query

name of method

The keyword **public** stipulates that this method is part of the class specification, that is, it is a feature available to clients of *Counter* objects. The keyword **int** indicates the type of value the method will provide to the client. (The method implements a query, so it must provide a value when invoked.) The name of the method, currentCount, is simply an identifier. We could have chosen any identifier at all, but it makes sense to use the name of the property we are querying for. As mentioned previously, by convention we use lowercase letters for methods.

What we have so far is the *specification* of the method. This is all a client needs to use the method. To complete the method definition, we must yet provide an *implementation*.

Specifying methods for commands

Next, let's specify the commands for a *Counter* object. Recall that there were two: *incrementCount* and *reset*. Here's the specification for these features:

```
/**
 * Increment the count by 1.
 */
public void incrementCount () {
    ...
}
```

the implementations of the method goes here

---

1. When we do this, we are implicitly asserting that the value of the count will not exceed the maximum **int** value, 2,147,483,647.

```
/**
 * Reset the count to 0.
 */
public void reset () {
    ...                                              the implementations of the
}                                                    method goes here
```

Both of these methods have the keyword **void** in place of the type name used in the query. This is because these methods are *commands*: they change the state of the object but do not provide the client with a value.

By convention we use imperative verbs (*e.g.*, incrementCount, reset) for commands, and nouns (or adjectives) descriptive of the value returned (*e.g.*, currentCount) for queries.

> **method:** a language construct that defines and implements a query or command.

Constructors

A class must provide a means for creating instances. A mechanism for creating a new object is called a *constructor*. Invoking a constructor creates a new instance of the class and gives initial values to the data maintained by the instance.

The name of the constructor is the same as the name of the class. The specification for a *Counter* constructor is as follows:

```
/**
 * Create a new Counter, with the count initialized
 * to 0.
 */
public Counter () {
    ...
}
```

The constructor is part of the class definition but is not a feature of an object. Invoking the constructor will create a new instance of the class and initialize the count to 0.

> **constructor:** a language construct used to create and initialize an object.

We now have a complete specification for the class *Counter*. Listing 2.1 shows the specification as a class declaration with the method implementations omitted. The lines beginning "//" are comments. (See page 54.) The constructor and method definitions can appear in any order. We sometimes separate the definitions into labeled sections for the convenience of a human reader, and write constructors first, followed by queries and commands. Of course, the class definition is not yet complete. We must include implementations of the methods before we have a legal Java class definition.

Listing 2.1 **The class *Counter***

```
package counters;

/**
 * A simple integer counter.
 */
public class Counter {

    // Constructors:

    /**
     * Create a new Counter, with the count initialized
     * to 0.
     */
    public Counter () {
        ...
    }

    // Queries:

    /**
     * The number of items counted.
     */
    public int currentCount () {
        ...
    }

    // Commands:

    /**
     * Increment the count by 1.
     */
    public void incrementCount () {
        ...
    }

    /**
     * Reset the count to 0.
     */
    public void reset () {
        ...
    }

} // end of class Counter
```

2.2.2 Static diagrams

As we mentioned in the previous chapter, we use a rectangle to denote a class in our diagrams. Diagrams showing classes are referred to as *static diagrams*. We sometimes show a class's features, as illustrated in Figure 2.3. By convention, the "+" preceding the feature indicates that the feature is public, and part of the class specification.

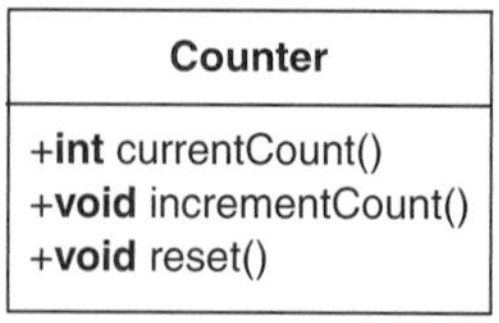

Counter
+**int** currentCount() +**void** incrementCount() +**void** reset()

Figure 2.3 **Static diagram of the class** *Counter.*

DrJava: specifying a class

Create a directory (folder) named `counters` in your Java working directory. In the large DrJava edit panel, start the definition of the class *Counter*.

1. Key Listing 2.1 as shown above. Don't include the ellipses! Leave the bodies of the commands and constructor empty. (The body of a method or constructor is the stuff between the braces.) Note that DrJava helps with indenting commenting.

2. Write the following single line as the body of the query:

    ```
    return 0;
    ```

    What we're doing is sometimes referred to as *stubbing*. A *stub* is a "dummy" method or constructor. Stubs don't actually do anything useful. They are "place holders" that satisfy the compiler so that a class can be compiled and tested before it is completely implemented. Since we develop by "specifying a bit, implementing a bit, testing a bit," stubs can be quite useful. Of course, a stub will ultimately be replaced with an actual implementation.

    Constructors and commands can be stubbed by simply leaving the body empty. Queries are stubbed with a simple return as follows.

    If the query returns: stub with:
        a numeric value   `return 0;`
        a boolean value   `return true;`
        a reference value   `return null;`

3. Save the definition in a file named `Counter.java`, in the directory `counters`. (Use the *Save* button on the tool bar.)

4. Compile the class. (Use the *Compile All* button on the tool bar.)

    Since you have written a syntactically correct class definition, the compilation should succeed. (Of course, the class does nothing at all.) If there are compilation errors, look carefully at the highlighted text and compare what you have written to what appears in the book. Check spelling and capitalization. Make corrections if necessary, save, and recompile until the compilation is successful.

Now let's create an instance and try it out.

5.   In the *Interactions* pane, key

```
> import counters.*;
> Counter c = new Counter();
```

The *import* statement allows us to refer to classes in the package `counters` by class name.

6.   Query `c` to determine what the current count is:

```
> c.currentCount()
```

7.   Give `c` the command `incrementCount` and query again:

```
> c.incrementCount();
> c.currentCount()
```

Are you surprised by the results? You shouldn't be!

2.2.3 Invoking a method or constructor

Before we complete the *Counter* implementation, let's take a quick look at how one object (a client) invokes another object's (a server's) methods.

Before a client can use a server, the client must somehow know about the server object. As we've seen in Section 1.5, reference values denote objects. A reference value provides a "handle" by which one object can know about another. We'll see how an object can get a reference to another object in the next chapter. For the moment, assume that `myCounter` is a reference to a *Counter* object available to a client.

To query the object `myCounter` for the current value of its count, we write

```
myCounter.currentCount()
```

This construct is called a *method invocation*. (This is exactly what we've been writing in the DrJava exercises.) A method invocation causes the object (`myCounter` in this case) to perform actions prescribed by the method implementation: actions determined by what we write between the braces in the definition of the method. In this case, the call results in the server object `myCounter` delivering the current value of its current count to the client.

The method invocation for a command is similar. For instance, to invoke the command `reset` for the object `myCounter`, we write

```
myCounter.reset();
```

Note the semicolon is part of the command invocation syntax. Again, the object `myCounter` performs actions as specified by the implementation of the method. The difference here is that the actions result in the state of the object `myCounter` being changed, rather than a value being delivered to the client. This is illustrated in Figure 2.5.

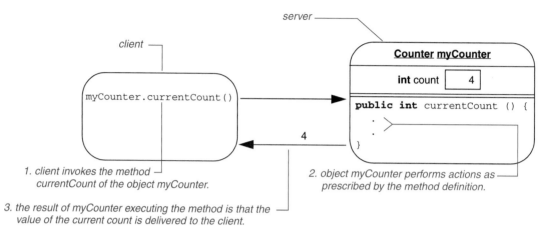

Figure 2.4 **Steps in a query and response.**

To invoke a constructor and create an object, the key word **new** is used:

> **new** *constructorName*()

Invoking the constructor to create a new *Counter* object would look like this:

> **new** Counter()

We'll see examples of method and constructor invocations in the next chapter.

2.2.4 Interaction diagrams

A common means of illustrating the order in which objects interact is an *interaction diagram*, as shown in Figure 2.6. Time advances from top to bottom in the diagram. Each vertical line or bar represents an object. A vertical rectangle signifies that the object is active, that is, it is executing one of its methods. A labeled horizontal arrow indicates that one object is invoking one of the features of another object. The object at the arrow point is acting as server; the object at the arrow tail is client. Sometimes we show the value being returned from a query as a horizontal dashed arrow.

Figure 2.6, for instance, shows some client object interacting with a *Counter*. The object first queries the *Counter* for its current count, and then gives the *Counter* the command reset.

2.3   Implementing the class *Counter*

To complete the definition, we must define *instance variables* for the data values an object will contain, and develop *algorithms* that will manipulate these data values, providing the object's functionality.

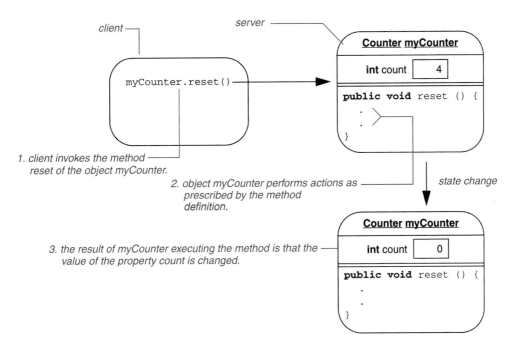

Figure 2.5 **Steps in a command execution.**

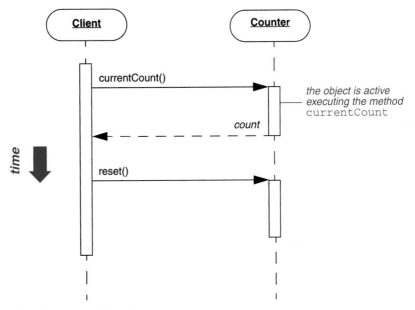

Figure 2.6 **An *interaction diagram.***

2.3.1 Implementing data

Recall from the previous chapter that a variable is simply a portion of memory reserved for storing a value. An instance variable is a variable that is part of an object: the memory space is allocated when the object is created, and the variable is used to store data maintained by the object. Though different values can be stored in a variable at different times, any given variable can contain values of only one type. The type of the variable is specified in the variable's definition.

A *Counter* needs only to know the current value of the count. Thus we define only one instance variable, an **int** variable named count. As we mentioned in the previous chapter, we can name the variable anything we want. But we should choose a name that has some meaning for anyone who must read the program.

Since the variable is part of the *implementation*, and *not directly accessible* by the object's clients, it is labeled **private**. The syntax for a private instance variable definition or *declaration* is

```
private variableType variableName;
```

The variable definition is included in the definition of the class:

```
public class Counter {

    private int count;      // current count
    ...


}
```

Every *Counter* object will now have a component that is an **int** variable named count, containing some **int** value. This is illustrated in Figure 2.7, where, as before, the box denotes the variable.

When illustrating a class with a static diagram, conventional practice is to list the instance variables in a box below the class name. The minus sign preceding the variable name emphasizes that the variable is private, part of the implementation, and not accessible by clients. Figure 2.8 shows how the class *Counter* might be illustrated.

At the risk of belaboring the point, we note again that a *Counter* object has a property whose associated value (an **int**) can be obtained with the query currentCount. This is part of the object's *specification*. It is included in the view a client has of a *Counter* object. As part of the *implementation* of a *Counter* object, we have decided to store the

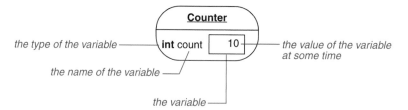

Figure 2.7 A *Counter* object, showing its instance variable.

Counter
-**int** count
+**int** currentCount() +**void** incrementCount() +**void** reset()

Figure 2.8 **Static diagram of the class *Counter*, showing its instance variable.**

value of this property in a variable named count. The name of the variable and its associated type (and even the fact that the value is stored in a variable) are part of the object's *implementation* and not part of the *specification*. This information is not directly available to clients. Clients interact with the object only through its queries and commands.

In our early examples, there is a close correspondence between instance variables and queries: values that an object provides to a client through a query are values stored in the object's instance variables. But these are distinct issues. Instance variables store the data necessary to support an object's functionality. This is essentially an implementation issue. Queries support the object's responsibilities with regard to its clients. This is a specification issue. Queries can be categorized as returning

- values that are not computed by the object and are maintained in instance variables; or
- values that are computed using other values stored in instance variables.

While it is often the case that a query returns a value stored in an instance variable, we must remember that the decision to provide a query and the decision to define an instance variable are separate design decisions. One is made when we are specifying the object, the other when we are implementing the class.

2.3.2 Implementing functionality

The instance variables of an object comprise the object's *data*. We must now see how to provide the object's *functionality* by attaching algorithms to the features of the object.

As we know, an object's features include queries and commands. The object responds to a query by providing a value determined by its state. It responds to a command by performing an action that might change its state. In each case, we must provide an algorithm, a set of instructions, that describes how the processor is to carry out the operation.

Method implementation: simple queries

We've seen that a method implements a feature. The method definition includes both the method specification as seen by the client, and the algorithm that implements the method. The definition specifies the name of the method, whether it is a query or command, and the type of value returned in the case of a query. In Section 2.2.1, we specified the method currentCount for the class *Counter* as

```
public int currentCount () {
    ...
}
```

The keyword **public** indicates that this method is part of the specification: it is available to clients of a *Counter* object. The type name **int** indicates that it is a query and returns a value of type **int** when invoked. The identifier currentCount is the name of the method.

The method definition must also provide an implementation, an *algorithm* that specifies the actions the processor is to perform when the method is invoked. The algorithm, or *method body*, is included between the braces in the definition, where we've written the ellipsis.

A method body consists of a sequence of one or more *statements*:

```
{
    statement₁
    statement₂
    statement₃
    ...
    statementₙ
}
```

For readability, we usually start each statement on a separate line. A statement describes an *action* that the processor is to carry out. When the method is invoked, the processor performs the actions specified by the statements that make up the method body. These actions are performed one at a time, in the order in which the statements are written. The statements that comprise the body of the method express an algorithm that implements the method. Thus implementing the method consists of designing an algorithm.

---

statement: a language construct that describes an action for the processor to perform.

What actions must the processor perform to execute the query currentCount? It must simply deliver the value stored in the variable count to the client. This is done by using a *return* statement:

```
return count;
```

The return statement tells the processor to furnish a particular value to the client. It is the final action the processor performs in executing the method. When the processor executes the return statement, it is finished with the method and delivers the specified value to the client. Every query ends with the execution of a return statement. If our code does not end with a return statement, the compiler will detect and report the error.

In our example, this is the only action the processor needs to perform. Thus the method body consists of only a single statement. The implementation looks like this:

```
/**
 * The number of items counted.
 */
public int currentCount () {
    return count;
}
```

It is important to realize that while a client can get the value of the instance variable count by calling the method, the client cannot *directly* access or modify the variable. Only the object itself can directly reference or change its private instance variables. If we write client code that attempts to access a private instance variable, the compiler will detect and report an error.

The general form of a return statement is

```
return expression;
```

where *expression* is a language construct that describes how to compute a particular value. An expression is *evaluated* to produce a value. The expression in this case is very simple: the name of an instance variable. We'll encounter more complex expressions as we go.

---

expression: a language construct that describes how to compute a particular value. Evaluation of an expression produces a value.

Method implementation: simple commands

Next let's look at the commands reset and incrementCount. A client invokes the command reset to change the count to 0, and calls the command incrementCount to increment the count by 1. The value of this property is stored in the instance variable count; hence, each of these commands changes the value stored in count. Modifying the value stored in a variable is accomplished by an *assignment* statement which has the following general form:

```
variableName = expression;
```

The processor executes an assignment statement in two steps:

1.   first it computes the value denoted by the expression on the right;
2.   then it stores that value into the variable named on the left, replacing the previous value of the variable.

The equal sign "=" should be thought of as indicating a "store" operation and ***not*** denoting mathematical equality. The type of the value produced by the expression must, in general, be the same as the type of the variable. For instance, it would not be legal if the expression produced a **double** and the variable was of type **int**. One cannot put a **double** value into an **int** variable.

In the case of the command reset, we want to store 0 in the variable count. Thus we write the assignment:

```
count = 0;
```

> **assignment:** a statement that instructs the processor to compute a value and store it in a variable.

Again, we see a very simple form of expression: in this case, the **int** literal 0. When the processor performs the assignment, the value 0 is put into the instance variable count, replacing whatever value was previously stored in the variable. Since this is the only action the processor need take, the implementation of the method reset consists of one assignment statement:

```
/**
 * Reset the count to 0.
 */
public void reset () {
    count = 0;
}
```

Note that there is no return statement. This method implements a command, and does not return a value to the client.

When the command incrementCount is carried out, we want the value of count to be changed. We again use an assignment statement. What value do we want to put in the variable? Well, we want the value currently in the variable count plus one. This computation is described by the expression

```
count + 1
```

To evaluate this expression, the processor gets the value stored in count and adds one to it. If count contains the value 3, evaluating the expression gives the value 4; if count contains 4, the expression evaluates to 5, and so on. Note that evaluating the expression *does not effect* the value stored in the variable. Evaluating an expression does not change the object's state.

The assignment statement instructs the processor to compute this value, and then store it into count, replacing the previous value:

```
count = count + 1;
```

In performing the assignment statement, the processor changes the state of the object.

It should be clear from this example that the equal sign "=" does not denote mathematical equality. The assignment statement instructs the processor to compute a value as described by the expression on the right, and then store the value into the variable named on the left.

The action described by the assignment statement is all the processor needs to do to execute the command incrementCount.

```
/**
 * Increment the count by 1.
 */
public void incrementCount () {
    count = count + 1;
}
```

Implementing the constructor

We have only to implement the constructor to complete the definition of the class *Counter*. Invoking the constructor creates a new instance of the class and initializes instance variables. All the hard work of actually creating the object is done automatically when the constructor is invoked. The critical thing we need to worry about is that the newly created object has a proper initial state. In the present case, we want the instance variable count of the newly created object to have a value of 0. We already know how to use an assignment statement to do this:

```
/**
 * Create a new Counter, with the count initialized
 * to 0.
 */
public Counter () {
    count = 0;
}
```

Since the count is the only instance variable, the constructor's responsibilities are satisfied by initializing this variable. The complete definition of the class *Counter* is given in Listing 2.2. Methods, constructors, and variable declarations can appear in any order in a class definition. Our convention is to start with instance variable declarations, followed by constructors, queries, and commands.

DrJava: implementing a class

Open the file Counter.java in the directory counters, that you created previously.
1. Add the definition of the instance variable count, and modify the query so that it returns the value of count. Leave the constructor and command bodies empty.
2. Save and compile.
3. In the *Interactions* pane, create a *Counter* instance by keying

```
> import counters.*;
> Counter c = new Counter();
```

and then query c to determine the value stored in count:

```
> c.currentCount()
```

Where did the value come from? If an instance variable is not initialized in a constructor, it will be given a default initial value by Java. However explicitly initializing each instance variable insures that a variable will not be accidentally initialized incorrectly and unequivocally expresses the implementor's intention.

4. Add the body statements of the constructor and of the commands. Save and recompile.
5. In the *Interactions* pane, create a *Counter* instance.

Listing 2.2   The class *Counter*

```
package counters;

/**
 * A simple integer counter.
 */
public class Counter {

    private int count;    // current count

    // Constructors:

    /**
     * Create a new Counter, with the count initialized
     * to 0.
     */
    public Counter () {
       count = 0;
    }

    // Queries:

    /**
     * The number of items counted.
     */
    public int currentCount () {
       return count;
    }

    // Commands:

    /**
     * Increment the count by 1.
     */
    public void incrementCount () {
       count = count + 1;
    }

    /**
     * Reset the count to 0.
     */
    public void reset () {
       count = 0;
    }

}
```

```
> import counters.*;
> Counter c = new Counter();
```

6. Test the *Counter*, by invoking the commands `incrementCount` and `reset`, and verifying the results with the query `currentCount`.

```
> c.currentCount()
0
> c.incrementCount();
> c.currentCount()
1
> c.incrementCount();
> c.currentCount()
2
> c.reset();
> c.currentCount()
0
> c.reset();
> c.currentCount()
0
c.incrementCount();
> c.currentCount()
1
...
```

2.3.3 Documenting specification

Even though they are logically distinct, the Java syntax does not separate a class's specification from its implementation. There are, however, software tools such as Sun's *javadoc* tool that generate documents containing class specifications. *javadoc* extracts specification information from a collection of source files containing class definitions, and generates the specifications as a set of HTML[1] documents. For instance, the documentation produced for the class *Counter* is shown in Figure 2.9. We'll use a similar format when we want to specify a class or method in the text.

We should assume that a programmer who needs to use a class will only have access to the generated specification documents and not to the actual source file containing the entire class definition. Since these documents include doc comment text, it is critically important to write doc comments that are complete and comprehensible. A programmer should be able to use a class correctly by reading nothing more than the specification documents. Correspondingly, we should avoid verboseness and "noise" in doc comments. In particular, doc comments should never refer to implementation details.

---

1. HTML is *Hypertext Markup Language*, a standard notation for Web documents. Doc comments should be written in HTML. However, since the inclusion of HTML tags and named characters hinders readability of the source code, we will not use them in the text examples.

public class **Counter**
extends java.lang.Object

A simple integer counter.

Constructor Summary	
Counter()	
Create a new Counter, with the count initialized to 0.	
Method Summary	
int	currentCount()
	The number of items counted.
void	incrementCount()
	Increment the count by 1.
void	reset()
	Reset the count to 0.

Constructor Detail

Counter

public **Counter**()

Create a new Counter, with the count initialized to 0.

Method Detail

currentCount

public int **currentCount**()

The number of items counted.

incrementCount

public void **incrementCount**()

Increment the count by 1.

reset

public void reset()

Reset the count to 0.

Figure 2.9 Specification documentation, generated from the class _Counter_.

★ *DrJava: generating documentation*

In the directory `counters`, created in the previous exercise, create a subdirectory named doc. Close any open files (*Close All*, option from the *File* pull-down menu). Open the file `Counter.java` that you have created previously.

1. Press the *Javadoc* button on the tool bar. This opens a window in which you select the directory in which the specification documents will be created.

2. Click on the directory `doc` that you created above, and press *Select*. The *javadoc* utility will be run, and documentation for all open packages will be generated into the doc directory.

3. If the process is successful, a documentation viewer will be opened. (You can also view the documentation with your web browser.) Click the link `Counter` under *All Classes*, and compare with the specifications shown in Figure 2.9.

2.4   Simple arithmetic expressions

Both the return statement and the assignment statement are built from expressions. The expressions that we have seen so far have been very simple: the name of an instance variable, an integer literal, a simple addition. Expressions can be considerably more complex. For example, we might have an object representing a rectangle with instance variables `length` and `width`. If we want a query to return the area of the rectangle, the query must compute the product of `length` and `width`. An expression to compute the area of a rectangle indicates that a multiplication is to be performed. The return statement for a query providing the area of a rectangle looks like this

```
return length*width;
```

where `length` and `width` are instance variables. The expression `length*width` states that the values stored in the two variables are to be multiplied.

When the processor encounters an expression in a statement, the processor evaluates the expression. Evaluating the expression produces a value. The type of value produced by a given expression is fixed. That is, one expression might deliver an **int** value and another might deliver a **double**, but a single expression cannot evaluate to an **int** at one time and a **double** later on.

Expressions that evaluate to integer and floating point values, that is, expressions of type **byte**, **short**, **int**, **long**, **float**, and **double**, are collectively called *arithmetic expressions*. Arithmetic expressions can be built by combining literals and variable names with *arithmetic operators* "+", "–", "*", "/", and "%". In the following, assume that `i1`, `i2`, and `i3` are **int** variables containing values 10, -20, and 30, respectively, and that `d1` and `d2` are **double** variables containing values 2.5 and 0.5.

Unary or *monadic* operators "+" and "–" can be prefixed to an arithmetic expression. Prefixing a "+" has no effect on the expression's value. (We use the symbol "⇒" to represent expression evaluation.)

$$+7 \Rightarrow 7 \qquad -0.5 \Rightarrow -0.5 \qquad -\texttt{i1} \Rightarrow -10$$
$$-\texttt{i2} \Rightarrow 20 \qquad -\texttt{d1} \Rightarrow -2.5 \qquad +\texttt{d2} \Rightarrow 0.5$$

Two arithmetic expressions can be combined with *binary* or *dyadic* operators "+", "–", "*", "/", and "%". These operations denote addition, subtraction, multiplication, division, and remainder, respectively. The behavior of the first three operators is straightforward:

$$1 + 2 \Rightarrow 3 \qquad \texttt{i1} + 10 \Rightarrow 20 \qquad \texttt{i1} + \texttt{i2} \Rightarrow -10$$
$$\texttt{d1} + \texttt{d2} \Rightarrow 3.0 \qquad \texttt{i3} - \texttt{i1} \Rightarrow 20 \qquad \texttt{i3} - \texttt{i2} \Rightarrow 50$$
$$\texttt{i1} * 2 \Rightarrow 20 \qquad \texttt{d2} * 0.5 \Rightarrow 0.25$$

The division operator "/" denotes division when applied to two **double** operands, but *integer quotient* when applied to two integer operands. For instance

$$\texttt{d1} / 2.0 \Rightarrow 1.25$$

but

$$\texttt{i1} / 5 \Rightarrow 2 \qquad \texttt{i1} / 3 \Rightarrow 3 \qquad \texttt{i1} / 6 \Rightarrow 1$$
$$\texttt{i1} / 11 \Rightarrow 0$$

The operator "%" denotes the *remainder* of the first operand divided by the second.

$$\texttt{i1} \% 5 \Rightarrow 0 \qquad \texttt{i1} \% 3 \Rightarrow 1 \qquad \texttt{i1} \% 6 \Rightarrow 4$$
$$\texttt{i1} \% 11 \Rightarrow 10$$

Although this operator is also defined for floating point operands, we'll use it only with integers.

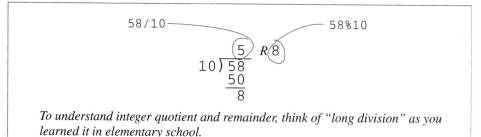

To understand integer quotient and remainder, think of "long division" as you learned it in elementary school.

A more complete description of arithmetic expression evaluation is given in Section 2.7.

2.5   The class *TrafficSignal*

As a second example, suppose we want to model a simple green-yellow-red traffic signal as part of a traffic simulation. What is the function of such an object? As we know, we can't give a definitive answer without a more complete description of the application. Let's assume that all we'll ever ask the object is which light is on: green, yellow, or red.

(We also assume that only one light will be on at any time.) What should a *TrafficSignal* be able to do? The only property we can access is the current light, so the only obvious action is to change to the next light. It is reasonable to give the *TrafficSignal* the responsibility for knowing the order in which the lights are sequenced. Thus the class will have two features:

- a query to determine the current light; and
- a command to change to the next light.

The only data that needs to be maintained is the current light. What type should we use to model this property? We could define a class *Light*, with instances representing the possible lights. We could use *Strings* naming the lights. But for simplicity, let's use an **int** for this property, and represent the possible lights with integers: 0 for green, 1 for yellow, 2 for red.

The class definition will have the same basic structure we've seen with the class *Counter*. The only remaining issue to be decided is the initial state of a *TrafficSignal*, that is, which light will be on when a *TrafficSignal* instance is created. It does not particularly matter what we choose, but we must clearly specify our choice. We summarize the specification as follows:

public class TrafficSignal
    A simple green-yellow-red traffic signal.

public TrafficSignal ()
    Create a new TrafficSignal, initially green.

public int light ()
    The light currently on.

public void change ()
    Change to the next light.

We can see that light is a query that returns a value of type **int**, and change, specified as **void**, is a command.

2.5.1 Named constants

There is one flaw in our specification, however. We have indicated that the query light will return an **int** value, but we have given no indication as to how this value should be interpreted. We could simply describe the encoding that we used in the method's doc comment:

```
/**
 * The light currently on.
 * 0 = green, 1 = yellow, 2 = red.
 */
public int light () { ...
```

But this is not entirely satisfactory. Specifically, the numbers we choose to represent the lights are completely arbitrary. A client should not care about, and should not depend on, the particular values that we choose. That is, a decision to use 2, 3, and 5 rather than 0, 1, and 2 should have no effect on a client.

We can isolate the client from the specific values we use by *giving a name* to each value with a *constant definition*. A simple constant definition looks like this:

```
public static final type identifier = literal;
```

(We can write the keyword **static** and **final** in any order, that is, we can write either **static final** or **final static**.) For example, the definition

```
public static final int GREEN = 0;
```

makes the identifier GREEN a name for the value 0. (By convention, uppercase letters are used for named constants.) A client uses the name by prefixing it with the class name followed by a period: TrafficSignal.GREEN. Writing TrafficSignal.GREEN in the program has the same effect as writing the literal 0. They both denote the value 0.

Unfortunately, there is nothing in the language syntax or semantics to *prevent* a client from using the literal 0 rather than the named constant TrafficSignal.GREEN. We can depend only on good programming practice. With the exception of occasional occurrences of 0 and 1, literals in a program invariably represent some describable concept: the maximum number of students in a class, the speed of light in kilometers per second, the text of a message to be delivered to the user if a file does not exist, the number of shillings in a pound, *etc*. Good programming practice requires that such literals be named, and that the named constants be used in the program rather than the literals. Except for literals like 1 and 0 simply standing for themselves, literals should only appear in constant definitions.

We include three constant definitions in the class, documenting them appropriately:

```
public class TrafficSignal {

    /**
     * The green signal light.
     */
    public static final int GREEN = 0;

    /**
     * The yellow signal light.
     */
    public static final int YELLOW = 1;

    /**
     * The red signal light.
     */
    public static final int RED = 2;
    ...

}
```

The complete specification for this class is shown in Listing 2.3. The package containing the class is trafficSimulation. The specification includes the names and types of the named constants, but not the actual values. A client should always refer to these values by name, and not depend on the specific values used to encode the lights.

> **named constant:** a value that has an identifier (a name) associated with it; the associated identifier can be used to denote the value.

2.5.2 Implementing the class *TrafficSignal*

A *TrafficSignal* needs a single instance variable storing the current light:

```
private int light;
```

Notice that we have named both the query and the instance variable with the same identifier, light.

The query simply returns the value stored in this variable:

```
public int light () {
    return light;
}
```

Implementing the constructor for *TrafficSignal* is straightforward. We must initialize the instance variable light to the value denoting "green." Recall that we have given this value a name with a constant definition:

```
public static final int GREEN = 0;
```

We should use it. We write:

```
/**
 * Create a new TrafficSignal, initially green.
 */
public TrafficSignal () {
    light = TrafficSignal.GREEN;
}
```

There are a few things to note. First, the constructor is independent of the specific value we have chosen to represent "green." The assignment statement we have written is preferable to

```
light = 0;
```

even though, in this case, both have the same effect. The former is easier to understand and does not need to be changed if we decide to use a different value to represent "green."

Second, a named constant is not a variable and can not be changed with an assignment. For instance, the following would be meaningless:

✘   `TrafficSignal.GREEN = 2;   // this is not legal!`

Listing 2.3   **Specification for the class *TrafficSignal***

===

`trafficSimulation`
Class TrafficSignal

> **public class** `TrafficSignal`
> A simple green-yellow-red traffic signal.

Named Constants

> **public static final int** `GREEN`
> The green signal light.

> **public static final int** `YELLOW`
> The yellow signal light.

> **public static final int** `RED`
> The red signal light.

Constructors

> **public** `TrafficSignal ()`
> Create a new *TrafficSignal*, initially green.

Queries

> **public int** `light ()`
> The light currently on.
> Returns `TrafficSignal.GREEN`, `TrafficSignal.YELLOW`, or
> `TrafficSignal.RED`.

Commands

> **public void** `change ()`
> Change to the next light.

===

Finally, when we are writing code that is part of the definition of a class, we need not prefix the class name to named constants defined in the class. That is, since we are writing code that is part of the class *TrafficSignal*, we can write

```
light = GREEN;
```

rather than

```
light = TrafficSignal.GREEN;
```

Continuing with the implementation, we must next implement the command `change`. This command should change the value stored in `light` from 0 to 1, or from 1 to 2, or from 2 to 0. For instance, if the light is green (`light` is 0), and the command `change` is executed, the light becomes yellow (`light` is 1). Our first attempt might be to add 1 to `light`:

```
public void change () {
    light = light + 1;
}
```

This works fine if `light` is 0 or 1. But if `light` is 2, it is changed to 3 which is not a legitimate value. Can we find another operation that will give us 0 when applied to 3? Specifically, we need an operation that produces 1 when applied to 1, 2 when applied to 2, and 0 when applied to 3:

$$op(0+1) \Rightarrow op(1) \Rightarrow 1$$
$$op(1+1) \Rightarrow op(2) \Rightarrow 2$$
$$op(2+1) \Rightarrow op(3) \Rightarrow 0$$

If we look over the arithmetic operators we've seen, the only one that could be of possible use is remainder, "`%`". In fact, the remainder of the number divided by 3 is exactly what we want:

$$1\%3 \Rightarrow 1$$
$$2\%3 \Rightarrow 2$$
$$3\%3 \Rightarrow 0$$

We can now complete the definition of the method `change`:

```
/**
 * Change to the next light.
 */
public void change () {
    light = (light + 1) % 3;
}
```

The parenthesis are essential in this expression. Without the parenthesis, the subexpression `1%3` would be evaluated first, and the result (which is always 1) added to `light`. (See Section 2.7 for details.)

This method clearly depends on the fact that we used the values 0, 1, and 2 to represent the lights. If we chose 3, 5, and 7 for instance, it would not work at all. But it does not depend on which value we use for green. We could have chosen 1 for green, 2 for yellow, and 0 for red. The complete definition is given in Listing 2.4.

Listing 2.4   The class *TrafficSignal*

```
package trafficSimulation;

/**
 * A simple green-yellow-red traffic signal.
 */

public class TrafficSignal {

    // Named constants

    /**
     * The green signal light.
     */
    public static final int GREEN = 0;

    /**
     * The yellow signal light.
     */
    public static final int YELLOW = 1;

    /**
     * The red signal light.
     */
    public static final int RED = 2;

    // Private components:

    private int light;// current light

    // Constructor

    /**
     * Create a new TrafficSignal, initially green.
     */
    public TrafficSignal () {
       light = GREEN;
    }
```

continued

Listing 2.4   **The class *TrafficSignal* (cont'd)**

===

```
/**
 * The current light that is on.
 * Returns TrafficSignal.GREEN,
 * TrafficSignal.YELLOW, or TrafficSignal.RED.
 */
public int light () {
    return light;
}

/**
 * Change to the next light.
 */
public void change () {
    light = (light + 1) % 3;
}

}
```

===

DrJava: exercising a TrafficSignal

Open the file `TrafficSignal.java`. It is located in folder named `trafficSimu-lation`, in folder `ch2`, in folder `nhText`.

1. In the *Interactions* pane, create a *TrafficSignal* instance:

    ```
    > import trafficSimulation.*;
    > TrafficSignal myLight = new TrafficSignal();
    ```

    As above, the import statement allows us to refer to classes in the package by class name.

2. Query `myLight`

    ```
    > myLight.light()
    ```

    and note that the value returned is 0, the value that represents green.

    To determine whether two values are equal in Java, we use the operator ==, two equal signs with no space between them.

3. Key the following two lines and note the results:

    ```
    > myLight.light() == TrafficSignal.GREEN
    > myLight.light() == TrafficSignal.RED
    ```

4. Verify that the *TrafficSignal* cycles through all three values by giving `myLight` the command `change` three times, and querying for `light` after each command, as follows:

```
> myLight.change();
> myLight.light() == TrafficSignal.YELLOW
true
> myLight.change();
> myLight.light() == TrafficSignal.RED
true
> myLight.change();
> myLight.light() == TrafficSignal.GREEN
true
```

5. In the edit window, change the definitions of the named constants so that GREEN is 1, YELLOW is 2, and RED is 0. Save and recompile.

6. Return to the *Interactions* pane. Create a new *TrafficSignal* and test:

```
> import trafficSimulation.*;
> TrafficSignal myLight = new TrafficSignal();
> myLight.light() == TrafficSignal.GREEN
> myLight.change();
> myLight.light() == TrafficSignal.YELLOW
> myLight.change();
> myLight.light() == TrafficSignal.RED
> myLight.change();
> myLight.light() == TrafficSignal.GREEN
```

Are you surprised that the class is still correct? (You shouldn't be.) What would happen if you defined GREEN as 2, YELLOW as 1, and RED as 0?

2.6   The class *PlayingCard*

As a final example, we'll define a simple class modeling playing cards, as introduced in Section 1.2.2. For this example, we assume playing cards are immutable and have two properties, suit and rank. As explained in the previous chapter, we model both these properties with integers. Perhaps we encode suits as 1 for clubs, 2 for diamonds, 3 for hearts, and 4 for spades, and use 11 to denote jack, 12 to denote queen, and 13 to denote king.

As we did with the traffic signal lights, we use named constants for suits and honors. Omitting the obvious comments, the definitions are

```
public static final int CLUB = 1;
public static final int HEART = 2;
public static final int DIAMOND = 3;
public static final int SPADE = 4;
```

```
public static final int ACE = 1;
public static final int JACK = 11;
public static final int QUEEN = 12;
public static final int KING = 13;
```

Note again that the specific values are *not part of the specification*. For instance, the client is not told whether an ace is represented by 1, 14, or some other number entirely. (See Listing 2.5, which shows the class specification in a format similar to that produced by *javadoc*.)

A *PlayingCard* needs two instance variables, one for storing the suit and one for storing the rank

```
private int suit;
private int rank;
```

and queries for both these values:

```
/**
 * The suit of this PlayingCard.
 */
public int suit () {
    return suit;
}

/**
 * The rank of this PlayingCard.
 */
public int rank () {
    return rank;
}
```

Since a *PlayingCard* instance is immutable, there are no commands. But the constructor must do a bit of work. A *PlayingCard*'s properties are determined when it is created. Therefore, when a client invokes the constructor, the client must indicate what card is to be created. In particular, the client must specify suit and rank.

2.6.1 Constructor with parameters

It is often the case that a client must provide additional information when invoking a constructor or method. The elements of information that must be provided are called *parameters* (or sometimes *formal parameters*) of the constructor or method. In this case, there are two parameters: the suit and rank of the card to be created. The parameter definitions are written inside the parentheses in the constructor specification, and consist of a type and name for each parameter. The type is the type of the value a client must provide when invoking the constructor. The name is an arbitrary identifier chosen to name the parameter. Parameter definitions are separated by commas.

```
public PlayingCard (int suit, int rank) {
    ...
}
```

      parameter type ———┘   └——— *parameter name*

The actual values provided by the client when invoking the constructor are called *arguments* (or sometimes *actual parameters*). In this case, the client must provide two arguments of type **int**. The client puts the arguments, separated by commas, inside the parentheses in the constructor invocation:

```
new className(arguments)
```

Invoking the constructor to create a new *PlayingCard* object looks like this:

```
new PlayingCard(PlayingCard.SPADE,3)
```

This invocation creates a new three of spades: that is, a new *PlayingCard* instance with a suit value `PlayingCard.SPADE`, and a rank value 3.

Note that we use a named constant rather than a literal in the example. Since `PlayingCard.SPADE` is defined to be 4, we could have written

```
new PlayingCard(4,3)
```

But a client should not make use of, and should not be dependent on, the particular value chosen to represent the spade suit. The class specification does not include the specific value used, and this value can be changed without changing the class specification.

The complete specification of the class in given in Listing 2.5.

Method variables: parameters

Let's take a closer look at what happens when the constructor is executed. A client invokes the constructor, providing two **int** values as arguments, for example,

```
new PlayingCard(PlayingCard.SPADE,3)
```

When the constructor is invoked, variables are created for each of the parameters. In this case, two **int** variables are created named `suit` and `rank`. These variables are called *method* variables. They are created when the constructor is invoked, and deallocated when execution of the constructor is completed. When a variable is created, memory space is allocated for it. When the variable is deallocated, the memory space is reclaimed and available for other uses. The lifetime of the method variable is the execution of the constructor body. This is substantially different from an instance variable, whose lifetime is the lifetime of the object.

> **method variable:** a variable that is created when a method is invoked, and de-
> allocated when the processor finishes executing the method.

Listing 2.5   **Specification for the class *PlayingCard***

`cardGame`
Class PlayingCard

> **public class** `PlayingCard`
> A playing card used in a card game.

Named Constants

> **public static final int** CLUB
> The club suit.

> **public static final int** DIAMOND
> The diamond suit.

> **public static final int** HEART
> The heart suit.

> **public static final int** SPADE
> The spade suit.

> **public static final int** ACE
> The ace rank.

> **public static final int** JACK
> The jack rank.

> **public static final int** QUEEN
> The queen rank.

> **public static final int** KING
> The king rank.

Constructors

> **public** `PlayingCard` (**int** suit, **int** rank)
> Create a new *PlayingCard* with the specified suit and rank.
> `suit` must be one of `PlayingCard.CLUB`, `PlayingCard.DIAMOND`,
> `PlayingCard.HEART`, or `PlayingCard.SPADE`.
> `rank` must be `PlayingCard.ACE`, `PlayingCard.JACK`,
> `PlayingCard.QUEEN`, `PlayingCard.KING`, or a value from 2
> through 10.

continued

Listing 2.5   Specification for the class *PlayingCard* (cont'd)

Queries

---

public int suit ()

The suit of this *PlayingCard*.

Returns `PlayingCard.CLUB`, `PlayingCard.DIAMOND`, `PlayingCard.HEART`, or `PlayingCard.SPADE`.

public int rank ()

The rank of this *PlayingCard*.

Returns `PlayingCard.ACE`, `PlayingCard.JACK`, `PlayingCard.QUEEN`, `PlayingCard.KING`, or a value from 2 through 10.

The parameter method variables are initialized with the arguments provided by the client. Thus when the processor executes the body of the constructor, available variables include the instance variables of the newly created object and the method variables. This is illustrated in Figure 2.10.

Note that we now have three distinct things named `suit`, and three distinct things named `rank`: an instance variable, a method, and a method variable. This is not uncommon. The context in which the identifier is used determines which item is referred to. For example, an identifier followed by a parentheses pair, `suit()`, is a method invocation.

What should the constructor do? It should copy the values from the parameters into the instance variables. That is, it should assign the value from the parameter `suit` to the instance variable `suit`, and the value from the parameter `rank` to the instance variable `rank`. But how do we do this? Inside the body of the constructor, the identifiers `suit` and `rank` refer to the parameters, and not the instance variables. Thus if we were to write

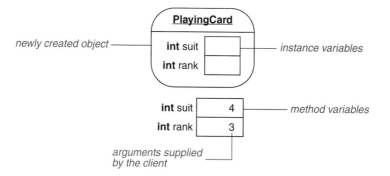

Figure 2.10 Available variables when *PlayingCard* constructor is executed.

```
     public PlayingCard (int suit, int rank) {
✗        suit = suit;
✗        rank = rank;
     }
```

the assignments would simply copy the values stored in the parameters into the parameters themselves. That is, the first assignment says "get the value stored in the parameter `suit` and store it into the parameter `suit`." This is nonsense. It has no effect at all. The value of the parameter is not changed, and, more to the point, the instance variable is not properly initialized.

How can we distinguish between the instance variable and the parameter when both have the same name? The keyword **this** refers to the "current" object. In the body of a constructor, it refers to the object being initialized. In the body of a method, it refers to the object performing the method. Writing

　　　　this.suit

in the body of the constructor denotes the instance variable of the newly created object, while writing `suit` without the prefix refers to the parameter. (Some programmers adopt the convention of always using the keyword **this** when referring to instance variables.)

We can implement the constructor as

```
     public PlayingCard (int suit, int rank) {
         this.suit = suit;
         this.rank = rank;
     }
```

Each assignment statement copies a value from a parameter and stores it in an instance variable. Upon completion of constructor execution, the object will appear as shown in Figure 2.11.

Figure 2.11 *PlayingCard after constructor is executed.*

DrJava: building a SolitairePlayingCard

Open the file `PlayingCard.java`, located in the folder `cardGame`, in `ch2`, in `nhText`. We will modify this class to build a class *SolitairePlayingCard*, as described in Chapter 1.

1. In the edit window, change the name of the class and of the constructor to `SolitairePlayingCard`.

2. A *SolitairePlayingCard* has an additional property: *isFaceUp*. Add the definition of a boolean instance variable named `isFaceUp`. This definition looks exactly like the definitions of `suit` and `rank`, except that its type is **boolean**.

3. Save the modified definition in a file named `SolitairePlayingCard.java`, in the folder `cardGame`. To do this, use the *Save as …* option from the *File* pull-down menu. Compile and make sure there are no compilation errors.

4. The constructor must initialize the new instance variable. You can initialize it to either true or false. Add an assignment statement to the constructor that initializes the instance variable `isFaceUp`. For instance,

    ```
    isFaceUp = true;
    ```

    Save and recompile.

5. Add a query `isFaceUp` that returns the value of the instance variable `isFaceUp`. What type is the query? Save and recompile.

6. Let's test the implementation before we go any further. In the *Interactions* pane, create a *SolitairePlayingCard*:

    ```
    > import cardGame.*;
    > SolitairePlayingCard myCard =
        new SolitairePlayingCard(
          SolitairePlayingCard.HEART, 2);
    ```

    (To continue a statement on the next line in the *Interactions* pane, hold the *Shift* key while pressing *Enter* or *Return*.)

    Verify that the initial state is correct by querying the object:

    ```
    > myCard.isFaceUp()
    ```

    To implement the command `turnOver`, we need an operator that inverts true and false:

    $$op(\text{true}) \Rightarrow \text{false}$$
    $$op(\text{false}) \Rightarrow \text{true}$$

    We haven't yet seen operators for boolean values. We'll meet them formally in Chapter 4. But the "not" operator, written as an exclamation mark !, is what we want. With this operator, we can write an assignment statement that inverts the value of the variable `isFaceUp`:

    ```
    isFaceUp = !isFaceUp;
    ```

7. Using the above assignment statement, define the command `turnOver`. Save and recompile.

8. In the *Interactions* pane, create a *SolitairePlayingCard* as above. Test the object to make sure that your implementation is correct.

9. Have you modified the documentation in the new class? In particular, does the doc comment for the constructor specify whether a newly created *SolitairePlayingCard* is

face up or not? Make sure the doc comments are accurate and complete. Remember that someone who uses your class will see only the specification.

2.7   Java in detail: arithmetic expressions

We introduced arithmetic expressions in Section 2.4. Here we take a more comprehensive look.

Simple expressions

Literals are the simplest form of expressions. (We encountered literals in Section 1.9.2.) Some **int** and **double** literals are shown below. The values they denote should be obvious from our previous discussion:

```
0     7     23     0.5     2.0     3.14159     2.4e-23
```

Variable names are a second simple form of expression. A variable name denotes the value currently stored in the variable. Suppose i1, i2, and i3 are variables of type **int** containing values 10, –20 and 30, respectively; suppose d1 and d2 are variables of type **double** containing values 2.5 and 0.5. Then evaluating these simple expressions produce the values shown. (As before, we use the symbol "⟹" to represent expression evaluation.)

```
i1  ⟹  10      i2  ⟹  -20      i3  ⟹  30
d1  ⟹  2.5     d2  ⟹  0.5
```

Operators

Expressions can be combined with *operators* to form more complicated expressions. We've already seen the *unary* or *monadic* operators "+" and "−" and the *binary* or *dyadic* operators "+", "−", "*", "/", and "%". A couple of notes for completeness: integer quotient is "truncated toward 0." So

```
i1 / -3  ⟹  -3          -7 / 2  ⟹  -3
```

and since the remainder should satisfy the equation
(*divisor* × *quotient*) + *remainder* = *dividend*,

```
i1 % -3  ⟹  1           -7 % 2  ⟹  -1
```

Numeric promotion

In all the above examples, both operands of a binary operator have been **int**, producing a result of type **int**, or both operands have been **double**, producing a result of type **double**. We might reasonably ask what happens if one operand is **int** and the other **double**, as in the expression

```
7 / 2.0
```

In this case, the **int** operand is converted to a **double** representing the same mathematical number, and the operation is performed with the two **double** values.

```
7 / 2.0  ⇒  7.0 / 2.0  ⇒  3.5
i1 * 0.5  ⇒   10 * 0.5  ⇒  10.0 * 0.5  ⇒  5.0
```

This is an example of *numeric promotion*. The conversion of an **int** to a **double** is by far the most commonly occurring case of numeric promotion. Additional cases are given in Section 2.10. In general, numeric operands of binary and unary operators are automatically converted to similar values of a different type when necessary.

Operator precedence

We've implied that we can combine two arbitrary arithmetic expressions with a binary operator to build a new expression. If we use the operator "*" to combine the expressions i1 + 10 and 2, we get

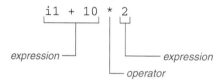

A question arises as to how we are to interpret the above line, given that putting together i1 and 10 * 2 with the "+" operator yields the same expression:

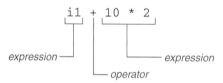

That is, should

```
i1 + 10 * 2
```

be interpreted as

```
(i1 + 10) * 2  ⇒   20 * 2  ⇒  40
```

or as

```
i1 + (10 * 2)  ⇒  10 + 20  ⇒  30
```

Java's *operator precedence* rules give the second interpretation. Java evaluates the expression by first performing the multiplication and then the addition. We say the operators *, /, and % have *higher precedence* than the binary operators + and −. In particular, the multiplication is done before the addition in an unparenthesized expression like that shown above:

$$i1 + \boxed{10\ *\ 2} \Rightarrow\ i1\ +\ 20\ \Rightarrow\ 30$$

— multiply before adding

A few more examples:

```
i1 * 10 + 2  ⇒  100 + 2  ⇒  102
 10 / 2 + 1  ⇒    5 + 1  ⇒  6
 5 + 6 / 10  ⇒    5 + 0  ⇒  5
```

Unary + and − have higher precedence than the binary operators. Thus

```
- 5 + i1  ⇒  (-5) + 10  ⇒  5
```

and *not*

✗   `- 5 + i1  ⇒  -(5 + 10)  ⇒  -15`

Associativity

Suppose our expression contains two operators with equal precedence, such as

```
i1 / 5 * 2
```

or

```
10 - 4 - 3
```

The binary operators in Java are *left associative*. This means that, in cases like the one above, the operations are performed left to right. Thus

$$\boxed{i1\ /\ 5}\ *\ 2\ \Rightarrow\ 2\ *\ 2\ \Rightarrow\ 4$$

— left operator before right

```
10 - 4 - 3  ⇒  6 - 3  ⇒  3
```

```
high

unary +    unary −
*   /   %
+   −

low
```

Figure 2.12 Precedence of common arithmetic operators.

The combination of left associativity and integer division can sometimes be confusing. Note the following examples:

```
i1/20 * 2    ⇒  10/20 * 2    ⇒  0*2    ⇒  0
2*i1/20      ⇒  2*10/20      ⇒  20/20 ⇒  1
20 / i1*2    ⇒  20 / 10*2    ⇒  2*2    ⇒  4
```

Expression evaluation can involve both the precedence and associativity rules. For instance

```
i1 - 2 * 5 - i3  ⇒  i1 - 10 - i3  ⇒  0 - i3  ⇒  -30
```

Finally, we can parenthesize expressions to explicitly specify the order in which we want the operations to be performed. For instance,

```
(i1 + 10) * 2  ⇒    20 * 2 ⇒ 40
     -(5 + i1)  ⇒  -15
i1 / (5 * 2)  ⇒    i1 / 10  ⇒ 1
```

Concatenation

When its operands are *Strings*, the binary operator "+" denotes string *concatenation*. That is, if *string1* and *string2* are *String* instances, the expression

```
string1 + string2
```

evaluates to a *String* containing the characters of *string1* with the characters of *string2* appended. Thus

```
"abc" + "def"    ⇒    "abcdef"
```

Furthermore, if one of the operands of "+" is a *String* and the other isn't, the non-*String* operand will be converted to a *String*, and concatenation performed. For instance, given

```
int i = 23;
```

the expression "abc" + i evaluates to the *String* "abc23":

```
"abc" + i      ⇒    "abc23"
```

The left operand in this case is a *String* and the right operand is an **int**. The **int** value is automatically converted to a *String* before being appended to the left operand.

The operator is still left associative. The following expressions evaluate as indicated:

```
i + " "        ⇒    "23 "
"2*i=" + 2*i    ⇒    "2*i=46"
2+i+"!"        ⇒    "25!"    remember "+" is left associative!
"!"+2+i        ⇒    "!223"
```

Casting

Occasionally we must explicitly convert an **int** value to a **double** or a **double** to an **int**. For instance, if we divide i1 by i3, the result will be the integer quotient 0:

i1 / i3 ⟹ 10 / 30 ⟹ 0

If we want the result to be a **double**, we can convert either (or both) **int** operand to a **double** by a *cast operation*. To cast the result of an expression to a different type, we prefix the expression with the new type, in parentheses:

(*type*) *expression*

For example.

(**double**) i1 ⟹ (**double**) 10 ⟹ 10.0

and so

(**double**) i1 / i3 ⟹ 10.0 / 30 ⟹ 0.333…

(Note that the value *stored in the variable* i1 remains the **int** 10.)

We can also cast a **double** to an **int**. The **double** value is truncated to produce the **int**: that is, the fractional part is discarded. If d3 and d4 are **double** variables containing the values 2.9 and –2.9 respectively, then

(**int**) d3 ⟹ 2
(**int**) d4 ⟹ -2

Finally, note that the cast operation has higher precedence than the arithmetic operators, so that

(**double**) i1/i3 ⟹ 10.0/30 ⟹ 0.333…

is not the same as

(**double**) (i1/i3) ⟹ (**double**) 0 ⟹ 0.0

DrJava: evaluating arithmetic expressions

In the *Interactions* pane, create several **int** and **double** variables and initialize them:

```
> int i1 = 10;
> int i2 = 20;
> double d1 = 0.5;
```

Evaluate the following expressions. In each case, determine what the result should be before keying the expression.

```
> i1+1*2          > i2/2*i1          > 2*d1
> 2*(i1/i2)       > d1*(i1/i2)       > (d1*i1)/i2
> i1%3            > i1+1 % 3         > ""+i1+2
```

2.8   Java in detail: basic organizational structure

As we have explained, a software system consists of a collection of software objects that cooperate to solve a problem. To create a system, we define the classes to which the objects belong. What we write—what the "program source" consists of—is a *collection of class definitions*. At this point, we want to see how the class definitions are organized into a program.

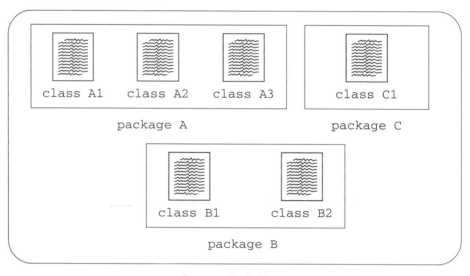

System Definition

Figure 2.13 **Class definitions are grouped into packages.**

Packages

A system definition is composed of a number of modules called *packages*. Each package contains the definition of one or more closely related classes. Suppose we have a class *Room* that models rooms in an architectural plan. We might well have a collection of classes closely related to *Room*, maybe *Door* and *Wall*, that would be conveniently grouped in the same package as *Room*.

A class defined in a particular package can make use of other classes defined in the package. In the above example, a *Room* object could reference a *Door* object and *vice versa*. By default, classes defined in one package are not accessible (not visible) to classes defined in another package. (Such classes are sometimes called "package private.") We make a class accessible throughout the entire system by explicitly marking the class *public*. For example, if we wanted *Room* objects to be visible throughout the entire system but wanted *Wall* objects to be visible only within their package, we would define the classes as follows:

```
public class Room {
    ...
}

class Wall {
    ...
}
```

Looking at Figure 2.13, an object of class *A1* can access other objects of class *A1* as well as objects of classes *A2* and *A3*. Classes *A1*, *A2*, and *A3* are all defined in the same package. However, if we want an object of class *A1* to access an object of class *B1*, then we must mark *B1* public. Otherwise, only instances of classes defined in package *B* will be able to access objects of class *B1*. In our initial examples, each class will be public.

Finally, we should mention that one package can contain another package as a member. There is no semantic significance to this structure. A package's classes are not more or less visible because the package is contained in another. However, the name of a package includes the name of a package of which it is a member. For example, the standard package `javax` includes as a member the package `swing`, which includes the package `border`. The actual name of this last package is `javax.swing.border`. This package contains a class *LineBorder*. So the fully qualified name of this class is

```
javax.swing.border.LineBorder.
```

Compilation units

The class definitions that make up a package are written in a set of source files called *compilation units*. A package is made up of one or more files (compilation units), each containing the definition of one or more classes. The **package** statement at the beginning of the file determines the package that classes belong to. If the file does not contain a **package** statement, the classes belong to an "unnamed package."

At most one class in a compilation unit can be public. (In fact, at most one class in a compilation unit can be referenced from outside the compilation unit.) For instance, looking at Figure 2.13 again, if *A1* and *A2* are both public classes then the definition of class *A1* and the definition of class *A2* must be in different files. The file name is the name of the public class with ".java" appended. A possible organization of the packages of Figure 2.13 into compilation units is shown in Figure 2.14. Details concerning the naming and organization of compilation units can be found in Appendix i.

---

package: a collection of closely related classes.

compilation unit: a file containing the definition of one or more classes of a package.

```
package A;

public class A1 {
   ...
} // end of class A1

class A3 {
   ...
} // end of class A3
```

A1.java

```
package B;

public class B1 {
   ...
} // end of class B1

class B2 {
   ...
} // end of class B2
```

B1.java

```
package A;

public class A2 {
   ...
} // end of class A2
```

A2.java

```
package C;

public class C1 {
   ...
} // end of class C1
```

C1.java

Figure 2.14 **Four compilation units.**

2.9   Java in detail: referring to classes in a different package, *import* statements, and the class *java.lang*

In our examples so far, we have assumed that all the classes are in the same package. But suppose a class in one package must refer to a class defined in a different package. For instance, suppose class *A2* in Figure 2.14 defined a variable of type *B1*. To reference a class defined in another package we must use a fully qualified class name. That is, we prefix the package name to the class name, as

> *PackageName.ClassName*

The fully qualified name of the class *B1* is B.B1; the fully qualified name of the class *LineBorder* in the package javax.swing.border is javax.swing.border.LineBorder.

The definition of a variable of type *B1* in class *A2* would look something like this

> **private** B.B1 myB1;

and an initialization statement like this:

> myB1 = **new** B.B1();

The import statement

By using an *import* statement, we can refer to a class in another package with its simple name rather than with its fully qualified name. Import statements are placed at the beginning of a compilation unit (file), after the package statement, and apply to all classes defined in the compilation unit.

The are two formats for an importing a class name:

```
import packageName.className;
import packageName.*;
```

For example,

```
import javax.swing.border.LineBorder;
import javax.swing.border.*;
```

The first format allows the simple name of the specified class to be written in the compilation unit in place of the fully qualified name. We can write

```
LineBorder myBorder;
```

and

```
myBorder = new LineBorder(myColor);
```

rather than

```
javax.swing.border.LineBorder myBorder;
```

and

```
myBorder = new javax.swing.border.LineBorder(myColor);
```

The second format allows the simple name of any class in the specified package to be written in place of the fully qualified name.

Note that import statements do not affect which classes are "visible" in a compilation unit. They simply permit simple names to be written in place of fully qualified names.

To what extent should we use import statements? The general rule is to use import statements for common packages, where there is no doubt as to the source of a class. (For instance, any experienced Java programmer can guess the source of the class *LineBorder*.) But if there is likely to be any confusion, use the fully qualified name.

The package java.lang

The predefined package `java.lang` contains the definitions of a number of commonly used classes, such as *String*. Since use of these classes is so commonplace, Java allows them to be referenced by their simple names without an import statement. That is, you can imagine that every compilation unit implicitly contains the statement

```
import java.lang.*;
```

immediately after the package statement.

✳ 2.10   Java in detail: arithmetic expressions, the rest of the story

The expression formats introduced in this section are less commonly used. We include them for completeness. Figure 2.15 provides a complete table of operator precedence and associativity.

Assignment expressions

We've seen assignment statements in Section 2.3.2. Technically, an assignment statement is an *assignment expression* followed by a semicolon. An assignment expression consists of a variable (left-hand side), assignment operator (=), and expression (right-hand side). For instance, if i1 is an **int** variable,

```
i1 = 2*i1
```

is an assignment expression. The value of the assignment is the value of the right hand side. Evaluating an assignment has the side effect of changing the value of the left hand side variable. If i1 has value 10, evaluating the above expression produces the value 20 and also changes the value of i1 to 20.

An assignment statement is an assignment expression followed by a semicolon:

```
i1 = 2*i1;
```

An assignment statement is executed for the side effect: that is, it is executed to change the value of the left hand side variable. The value returned is ignored. But note that the following is legal, if not necessarily recommended style:

```
i2 = (i1 = 2*i1) + 3;
```

If i1 is 10, the statement assigns 20 to i1 and 23 to i2.

Unlike the binary operators we've seen previously, assignment is *right associative*. That means that an expression like

```
i2 = i1 = 3
```

is equivalent to

```
i2 = (i1 = 3)
```

The value 3 is assigned to i1 and is the result of the right assignment expression. The value 3 is then assigned to i2.

There are eleven other assignment operators that incorporate binary operators. They are:

```
*=    /=    %=    +=    -=    <<=    >>=    >>>=    &=    ^=    |=
```

The effect of executing

```
i1 *= 2
```

is essentially the same as executing

```
i1 = i1*2
```

Other assignment operators work in a similar way. If *expr1* and *expr2* are expressions, then

> *expr1 op= expr2*

is equivalent to

> *expr1 = (expr1) op (expr2)*

except that *expr1* is evaluated only once.

We strongly recommend that assignment expressions be used only in simple assignment statements.

Increment and decrement expressions

A numeric variable can be prefixed with or followed by the increment operator `++` or the decrement operator `--`. If `i1` is an **int** variable, `i1++` and `++i1` are increment expressions, and `i1--` and `--i1` are decrement expressions.

Increment and decrement expressions are unusual in that their evaluation causes the value of the variable to change. ("Asking the question changes the answer.") The expression `i1++` delivers the value of `i1` and then increments `i1` by 1. The expression `++i1` increments `i1` by one, and then delivers the resulting value. The decrement operator works analogously.

If `i1` is an **int** variable with value 10 in each of the following expressions,

> `i1++`   ⇒   delivers `10` and changes `i1` to `11`;
> `++i1`   ⇒   changes `i1` to `11` and delivers `11`;
> `i1--`   ⇒   delivers `10` and changes `i1` to `9`;
> `--i1`   ⇒   changes `i1` to `9` and delivers `9`.

Increment and decrement expressions can be made into statements by appending a semicolon. Thus

> `i1++;`

and

> `++i1;`

are statements that increment `i1` by 1. Since the value produced by the expression is ignored in each case, these statements are equivalent.

The operand of an increment or decrement operator must be a variable. Expressions such as `++3` or `(i*2)++` are not legal.

Unlike many programming languages, Java guarantees that an operator's operands appear to be evaluated from left to right. Note that this is not a matter of operator associativity. Associativity insures that in an expression such as

> `operand1 * operand2 / operand2`

the multiplication is performed before the division. Left to right operand evaluation guarantees that in an expression such as

```
operand1 * operand2
```

`operand1` is evaluated before `operand2`. Both operands, of course, must be evaluated before the multiplication can be performed. Thus if `i1` is initially 10, the expression `(i1++)*i1` evaluates as follows:

$$(i1{+}{+}){*}i1 \;\Rightarrow\; 10{*}i1 \text{ (and changes i1 to 11)} \;\Rightarrow\; 10{*}11 \Rightarrow 110$$

We strongly recommend against writing expressions whose evaluation changes the values of variables in the expression. We particularly suggest that you avoid writing expressions that depend on left to right operand evaluation.

Bitwise operators

Bitwise operators allow the bit patterns of integral values to be manipulated. They are not commonly used. Operands of bitwise expressions must be integral values. To more clearly illustrate the result of bitwise operations, we will use hexadecimal literals in the examples.

Shift operators, `<<`, `>>`, and `>>>`, shift the left operand left or right the number of bits specified by the right operand. Left shifts fill the low-order bits with 0. For example,

```
0x12345678<<4
```

shifts the **int** value `0x12345678` four bits to the left, filling in with 0's. Thus,

$$0x12345678{<}{<}4 \;\Rightarrow\; 0x23456780$$

(Each hexadecimal digit represents four bits.)

The right-shift operator `>>>` fills in the high-order bits with 0's. Thus,

$$0x12345678{>}{>}{>}4 \;\Rightarrow\; 0x01234567$$

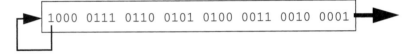

The right-shift operator `>>` "sign extends." That is, it fills with the high-order bit of the left operand. Thus,

$$0x12345678{>}{>}4 \;\Rightarrow\; 0x01234567$$

but

$$0x87654321{>}{>}4 \;\Rightarrow\; 0xF8765432$$

The unary operator ~ is bit complement. 0 bits in the operand become 1's in the result, and vice versa. For example,

```
~0xFFFF0000   ⇒   0x0000FFFF
```

The binary operators &, |, and ^ are bit-by-bit *and*, *or*, and *exclusive or*. A bit in the result of an & operation is 1 when the corresponding bits in both operands are 1's:

```
0x00FF00FF & 0x0F0F0F0F     ⇒   0x000F000F

0000 0000 1111 1111 0000 0000 1111 1111
0000 1111 0000 1111 0000 1111 0000 1111

0000 0000 0000 1111 0000 0000 0000 1111
```

A bit in the result of a | operation is 1 when the corresponding bit in either or both operands is 1:

```
0x00FF00FF | 0x0F0F0F0F     ⇒   0x0FFF0FFF

0000 0000 1111 1111 0000 0000 1111 1111
0000 1111 0000 1111 0000 1111 0000 1111

0000 1111 1111 1111 0000 1111 1111 1111
```

A bit in the result of a ^ operation is 1 when the corresponding bit in one of the operands, but not both, is 1:

```
0x00FF00FF ^ 0x0F0F0F0F     ⇒   0x0FF00FF0

0000 0000 1111 1111 0000 0000 1111 1111
0000 1111 0000 1111 0000 1111 0000 1111

0000 1111 1111 0000 0000 1111 1111 0000
```

The operator & is often used to "mask" bits. For instance if n is an **int**, the assignment

```
n = n & 0x0000000F;
```

sets all but the low order 4 bits of n to 0. The low-order 4 bits remain unchanged.

The operator | is often used to "set" bits. For instance, the assignment

```
n = n | 0xC0000000;
```

sets the high-order 2 bits of n to 1. The remaining bits remain unchanged.

Numeric promotion

Numeric operands of binary and unary operators are automatically converted to similar values of a different type when necessary. In particular:

- **byte**, **short**, or **char** operands of a unary operator are converted to **int**;
- if either operand of a binary operator is **double**, the other is converted to **double**;

- otherwise, if either operand of a binary operator is **float**, the other is converted to **float**;
- otherwise, if either operand of a binary operator is **long**, the other is converted to **long**;
- otherwise, both operands of a binary operator are converted to **int**.

For example, if b is a **byte**, 1 a **long**, and f a **float**, then

```
-b is an int;
f + 2 is a float;
1 + 2 is a long;
1 * f is a float.
```

Casting numeric values

A value of one numeric type can be explicitly converted to a value of another numeric type by *casting*. To do this, the target type is written in parentheses in front of the expression. For instance, if length is an **int**, the following evaluates to an equivalent **double**:

```
(double) length
```

Converting a value of one numeric type to another may result in loss of information regarding the magnitude of the number or its precision. For instance, a value of type **int** (32 bits) is converted to a value of type **short** (16 bits) by discarding the high-order 16 bits. Converting an **int** or **long** to **float** or a **long** to **double** may result in the loss of precision, that is, may loose some of the least significant bits of the value. Also note that floating point values are truncated toward 0 when being converted to integer values. The following examples illustrate some of these points.

Given:

```
int i = 0x12345678;
double d = 1.9;

(short)i           ⇒  0x5678;
(int)((float)i)    ⇒  0x12345680;
(int)d             ⇒  1
```

2.11   Summary

In this chapter, we saw how to specify and implement a simple class using the programming language Java. Two objects are related in a fundamental way when one object *uses* the other, that is, one object queries and commands the other. This relation is termed the *client-server* relationship. The client object queries and commands the server object.

The definition of an object, or more properly, the definition of the class of which the object is an instance, consists of two parts:

- a *specification*, a precise description of the object's features *as seen by a client*; and

precedence (high to low))							associativity
!	~	++	−−	unary +	unary −	cast ( )	right to left
*	/	%					left to right
+	−						left to right
<<	>>	>>>					left to right
&							left to right
^							left to right
|							left to right
=	*=	/=	%=	+=	−=	<<= >>=	right to left
	>>>=	&=	^=	|=			

Figure 2.15 **Precedence and associativity of arithmetic operators.**

- an *implementation*, the internal mechanisms that enable an object to behave according to its specification.

It is important to appreciate that the client can use only the specification of a server object. Details of the implementation are not available to the client.

A class specification is made up of method specifications and constructor specifications. Methods define both the specifications and implementation of an object's features. A method that defines a query returns a value of a given type. A method that defines a command typically causes the object to change state when it is invoked. Constructors are used to create objects and initialize their states.

Implementing a class involves

- writing data descriptions for data stored in class instances, and
- writing method bodies that define the actions the processor performs when the methods are invoked.

An object's data are stored in instance variables. Instance variables, created when the object is created, are part of the object's implementation, and are not generally accessible by the object's clients. An instance variable is created with a variable declaration, having the form:

```
private variableType variableName;
```

A method body is made up of a sequence of statements that implements the method algorithm. Statements describe actions the processor performs when executing the method. When the method is invoked, the processor executes the statements one after the other, in the order in which they appear in the method body.

Two elementary kinds of statements are *return* statements and *assignment* statements. A return statement is the last statement executed in a query, and specifies the value to be delivered to the client. It has the form:

```
return expression;
```

An assignment statement stores a value in a variable. Its format is:

```
variable = expression;
```

Both return statements and assignment statements include expressions. An expression describes how a value is to be computed. Arithmetic expressions, in particular, produce numeric values when they are evaluated.

Some methods and constructors require that the client provide information when the method or constructor is invoked. This is indicated by parameters in the method or constructor definition. The values the client supplies when invoking the method or constructor are called arguments. When a method or constructor with parameters is invoked, a variable is allocated for each parameter and initialized with the argument provided by the client. These variables are method variables. They are created when the method is invoked, and deallocated when execution of the method is complete. Method variables are substantially different from instance variables. Instance variables contain data that is permanently maintained as part of the object's state. Method variables contain values that are used only for a specific computation.

In the examples in this chapter, methods generally contained only a single statement. The algorithms required were very simple, and could generally be expressed with a single *assignment* or *return*. In subsequent chapters, we will see other forms of statements which allow us to write more complex algorithms.

Looking at the overall organization, we learned that the class definitions that make up a program are grouped together into packages. Classes defined in the same package are closely related to each other: instances of these classes can access each other by default. On the other hand, if a class is to be visible throughout the entire system, it must be explicitly labeled as public.

Class definitions are written in source files called compilation units. Each compilation can contain the definition of at most one public class. All the classes defined in a given compilation unit are part of the same package.

SELF-STUDY EXERCISES

2.1 Identify the client and the server in the following interactions.

   a. Mr. Joy asks the desk clerk, Mr. Steele, for his bill.

   b. Mr. Steele asks Mr. Joy for his room number.

   c. Mr. Steele tells the intern, Mr. Gosling, to prepare Mr. Joy's bill.

   d. Mr. Joy tells Mr. Steele to charge his bill to his credit card.

   e. Mr. Steele verifies the amount with the credit card company.

   f. Mr. Steele tells Mr. Joy to sign the invoice.

2.2 One of each pair of phrases below refers to the specification, and one to the implementation. Identify each.

   a. how it does it; what it does.

     b.   description of services; details, details.

     c.   steps it takes to get it done; how to request it.

     d.   nothing but promises; the devil is in the details.

2.3   Classify each of the following as a query, command, or constructor.

     a. **public int** length ()

     b. **public** Date next ()

     c. **public void** empty ()

     d. **public** Date (**int** day, **int** month, **int** year)

2.4   Fill in the blanks in the following statements.

     a.   A variable has a(n) _____, a(n) _____, and a(n) _____.

     b.   A variable that is a permanent part of an object and stores an object property is a(n) _____ variable.

     c.   The specification that an instance variable is "private" means that it is part of the _____ and not available to the _____.

     d.   Instance variables should be initialized in a(n) ___.

     e.   A language construct that describes an action is a(n) _____.

     f.   Every query must end with a(n) _____.

     g.   A language construct that describes computation of a value is a(n) _____.

     h.   A statement that changes the value of a variable is a(n) _____.

2.5   Given that i and j are variables of type **int** containing the values 2 and 3 respectively, and that x and y are variables of type **double** containing the values 4.0 and 5.0 respectively, evaluate the following expressions and state the type for each resulting value.

     (a) i*j   *(b)* i/j   *(c)* j/i   *(d)* x/y

     (e) j/x   *(f)* i%j   *(g)* 12/i+j   *(h)* j+12/i

     (i) 12/(i+j)   *(j)* -i+2   *(k)* x+y*3   *(l)* x+j/i

     (m) i-j-2   *(n)* 12/i*j   *(o)* 12/i%j   *(p)* 12/i/j

     (q) (x-y)*(i+j)/10   *(r)* (3+i)+(2-j)*(25%i)

     (s) (**double**)(j/i)

2.6   Given that i and j are **int**'s greater than 0, what is the minimum value of i % j? What is the maximum value?

2.7   What steps does the processor take in executing the statement

```
size = (length+width)/16;
```

2.8   Given that i is an **int** variable, write the following in Java:

     a.   an expression that evaluates to twice the value stored in i;

     b.   a return statement that delivers to the client twice the value stored in i;

     c.   an assignment statement that doubles the value stored in i.

2.9   Given that i, j, and k are **int** variables containing the values 2, 4, and 6, respectively, indicate what values i and j will have after each of the following statement sequences:

    (a) i = j;   *(b)* i = j;   *(c)* k = i;   *(d)* i = i - j;
        j = 5;   j = i;   i = j;   j = j + i;
                                    j = k;   i = j - i;

2.10   Assume that day, month, and year are **int** variables containing the values 4, 7, 1776 respectively. What do each of the following expressions evaluate to?

    a.   day+month+year

    b.   "day:"+day+"month:"+month+"year:"+year

    c.   "date:"+day+month+year

    d.   day+month+year+"is the date"

2.11   Consider a class intended to model rectangles. Write declarations for instance variables storing a rectangle's width and length. Assume dimensions are **double**.

2.12   Write queries that return a rectangle's length and width. Assume the instance variables defined in the previous question.

2.13   Given that spongeBob is a rectangle, write an invocation of the query that returns spongeBob's length. Assume the methods specified in the previous question.

2.14   Write a Java definition for a constructor for the class *Rectangle*. The client must provide the length and width of the *Rectangle*. Assume dimensions are **double**.

2.15   Write a constructor invocation that creates a *Rectangle* with length and width 10.0. Assume the constructor specified in the previous question.

2.16   A *Date* object has day, month, and year properties. Write declarations for instance variables storing the values of these properties.

2.17   The *Date* constructor,

        public Date (**int** day, **int** month, **int** year)

must initialize instance variables day, month, and year with argument values. Write statements to do this.

2.18   The following line of code is written as part of the class *TrafficSignal*, to change the green light to yellow:

        TrafficSignal.GREEN = TrafficSignal.GREEN + 1;

What's wrong with the line?

2.19   Suppose that in addition to red, green, and yellow lights, a *TrafficSignal* has a left-turn light. Write a constant definition for the left-turn light. Assume that the integer 4 will represent the left-turn light.

2.20   The class *PlayingCard* is defined in the package cardGame. In a package other than cardGame, how would you refer to the named constant representing an ace?

2.21   What determines the package that a class belongs to?

2.22   Suppose that a system is built from the classes shown in Figure 2.13, and that classes A1, B1, and C1 are the only public classes. What is the minimum number of compilation units that can be used to define the system? What is the maximum number?

✳ 2.23   Given that i and j are **int** variables containing the values 2 and 3 respectively, and that x and y are **int** variables containing the values 0xF0F0F0F0 and 0x00FF0000 respectively, evaluate the following expressions and state the type for each resulting value. For (a) through (e), also give the final value of i.

(a) i=j	(b) i+=2	(c) i++	(d) ++i
(e) (++i)*(i++)	(f) x<<4	(g) x>>4	(h) x>>>4
(i) ~x	(j) x&y	(k) x|y	(l) x^y

EXERCISES

2.1   Write a Java specification for a counter that counts balls and strikes in a baseball game. The counter should automatically reset when the third strike or fourth ball is counted. Be sure to include doc comments.

2.2   Write a Java specification for a "modulus" counter. When a counter is created, the maximum value of the count is specified. If the count is at the maximum value and the counter is given a command to increment count, the counter resets to 0.

2.3   Write a Java specification for a street address. Instances of this class are immutable. Assume that a street address contains number, street, city, state, and zip.

2.4   Exercise 1.2 on page 57 describes an object modeling a three-way lamp: a lamp with off, low, medium, and high settings. Write a Java specification for a three-way lamp.

2.5   For any of the classes specified in Exercise 2.1 through Exercise 2.4 above, write a stubbed implementation and compile the class. Use *javadoc* to generate HTML specifications.

2.6   Suppose that i is an **int** variable containing a two-digit number, that is, a number in the range 0 through 99. Write assignment statements that will store the low-order digit in the **int** variable ones, and the high-order digit in the **int** variable tens. For instance, if i contains 23, the statements should assign 3 to ones, and 2 to tens.

2.7   Write statements as in Exercise 2.6, but assuming that i contains a three-digit number. Store the low order digit in ones, the next digit in tens, and the high order digit in hundreds.

2.8   Assume that pennies, dollars, and cents are **int** variables. The variable pennies contains a value representing a number of pennies. Write assignment statements that will represent this value as dollars and cents by assigning the dollars to dollars and the cents to cents. For instance, if pennies contains 298, the statements should assign 2 to dollars, and 98 to cents.

2.9   Write statements as in Exercise 2.8, but using the variable `nickels` rather than `pen-nies`. Assume that `nickels` represents a number of nickels. For instance, if `nickels` contains 23, the statements should assign 1 to `dollars` and 15 to `cents`.

2.10   Write statements as in Exercise 2.8, but using both variables `nickels` and `pennies`. For instance, if `pennies` contains 298 and `nickels` contains 23, the statements should assign 4 to `dollars` and 13 to `cents`.

2.11   Add a method to the class *Counter* that will double the *count* of a *Counter*.

2.12   We want to add to the *Counter* class, a command `unReset` that restores the *count* to what it was before the most recent `reset`. For instance, if the *count* is 10 and the command `reset` is performed, the count will be 0. If `unReset` is done, the *count* will again be 10.

Implement `unReset`. This will involve adding an additional instance variable and modifying the `reset` command as well. Test and verify that your implementation is correct.

2.13   Implement and test the modulus counter described in Exercise 2.2. Since the constructor for a modulus counter has a parameter, you will want to test several different modulus counters with different constructor arguments.

2.14   Implement and test a class modeling a three-way lamp, as described in Exercise 2.4.

2.15   Implement and test a class modeling rectangles. The constructor should specify the length and width of the rectangle. The class has queries for length, width, perimeter, and area.

2.16   Using a Web browser, access the Java API documentation for the predefined class *String*. (If you don't have the documentation locally, it can be accessed through the document *http://java.sun.com/apis.html*.) Scan the class definition. What package contains this class?

Note that there are several constructors for the class. How many constructors are there?

Note that there are several methods (such as `concat`) that build new *String* instances. Such methods are sometimes called factory methods. How many such methods do you see?

SELF-STUDY EXERCISE SOLUTIONS

2.1   Client: Server:
  a.   Mr. Joy   Mr. Steele
  b.   Mr. Steele   Mr. Joy
  c.   Mr. Steele   Mr. Gosling
  d.   Mr. Joy   Mr. Steele
  e.   Mr. Steele   The credit card company
  f.   Mr. Steele   Mr. Joy

2.2   *a.*   implementation; specification

        b.   specification; implementation

    c.   implementation; specification

    d.   specification; implementation

2.3   *a.*   query

    b.   query

    c.   command

    d.   constructor

2.4   *a.*   name, type, value.

    b.   instance

    c.   implementation, client

    d.   constructor

    e.   statement

    f.   return statement

    g.   expression

    h.   assignment

2.5   *(a)* 6 (**int**)   *(b)* 0 (**int**)   *(c)* 1 (**int**)   *(d)* 0.8 (**double**)

    (e) 0.75 (**double**)   *(f)* 2 (**int**)   *(g)* 9 (**int**)   *(h)* 9 (**int**)

    (i) 2 (**int**)   *(j)* 0 (**int**)   *(k)* 19.0 (**double**)   *(l)* 5.0 (**double**)

    (m) -3 (**int**)   *(n)* 18 (**int**)   *(o)* 0 (**int**)   *(p)* 2(**int**)

    (q) -0.5 (**double**)   *(r)* 4 (**int**)   *(s)* 1.0 (**double**)

2.6   Minimum is 0, maximum is `j`-1,

2.7   The processor evaluates the expression `(length+width)/16`, and then stores the result in the variable `size`.

2.8   `2*i`

    `return 2*i;`

    `i = 2*i;`

2.9   *(a)* `i: 4; j: 5`   *(b)* `i: 4; j: 4`   *(c)* `i: 4; j: 2`   *(d)* `i: 4; j: 2`

2.10 *a.*   1787

    b.   `"day:4month:7year:1776"`

    c.   `"date:471776"`

    d.   `"1787is the date"`

2.11 `**private double** length;`

    `**private double** width;`

2.12
```
/**
 * The length of this Rectangle.
 */
public double length () {
   return length;
}
```

```
/**
 * The width of this Rectangle.
 */
public double width () {
    return width;
}
```

2.13 `spongeBob.length()`

2.14
```
/**
 * Create a new Rectangle with the specified length and
 * width.
 */
public Rectangle (double length, double width) {
    this.width = width;
    this.length = length;
}
```

2.15 `new Rectangle(10.0,10.0)`

2.16
```
private int day;
private int month;
private int year;
```

2.17
```
this.day = day;
this.month = month;
this.year = year;
```

2.18 `TrafficSignal.GREEN` is a named constant, not a variable. It cannot appear on the left side of an assignment statement.

2.19
```
/**
 * The left-turn signal light.
 */
public static final int LEFT_TURN = 4;
```

(Of course, it does not matter what identifier you use. By convention, underscores are used to separate words in all uppercase identifiers.)

2.20 `cardGame.PlayingCard.ACE`

2.21 The **package** statement at the beginning of the file (compilation unit) containing the class definition.

2.22 Minimum of three compilation units: one containing A1, A2, and A3; one containing B1 and B2; one containing C1. Maximum of six: each class definition in its own compilation unit.

✳ 2.23 (a) 3 (i is 3)   (b) 4 (i is 4)   (c) 2 (i is 3)   (d) 3 (i is 3)
         (e) 9 (i is 4)   (f) 0x0F0F0F00   (g) 0xFF0F0F0F   (h) 0x0F0F0F0F
         (i) 0x0F0F0F0F   (j) 0x000F0000   (k) 0xF0FFF0F0   (l) 0xF00FF0F0

CHAPTER 3 Designing interacting classes

In the previous chapter, we introduced the client-server relation—the "uses" relation—between objects, and saw how to construct simple objects. In this chapter, we encounter objects that interact in the client-server relation.

We begin with a discussion of object design by considering the responsibilities an object should have in the problem solution. Enumerating what an object should know and what it should do leads to a specification of the object's features and a determination of its role with regard to other objects in the system.

We then consider simple examples in which two or more objects cooperate. We see how an object can get a "handle" on another by means of a method argument, and how one object acts as client to another by invoking queries and commands in the second object. We put together a simple but complete system, consisting of a model object and user interface object. We see how program execution is started, and how objects are created. Finally, we build a system to test an object. This gives us a further example of interacting objects in a complete system, and introduces the basic strategy of test-driven implementation.

Objectives

After studying this chapter you should understand the following:

- the role of responsibilities in the design of an object;
- the categorization of an object's responsibilities as knowing responsibilities or doing responsibilities;
- the difference between local variables and instance variables;
- the structure of a complete program in Java;
- the structure of a test system;
- the purpose of named constants.

Also, you should be able to:

- analyze the role a simple object plays in a given problem and list its responsibilities;
- use Java to specify the features of an object based on its responsibilities;

- use Java to implement a simple class that has been specified;
- implement a complete Java program using a simple text-based interface for an object;
- implement a simple tester for testing a class implementation;
- define named constants.

3.1   Designing with objects

When we design a system with an object-oriented methodology, there are two fundamental questions that we must address:

- what are the objects? that is, what aspects of the problem should be represented as objects? and
- what features should these objects have?

Several techniques of varying degrees of sophistication have been proposed for identifying potential objects. In many cases, however, there are rather conspicuous candidates. Certain aspects of the problem lend themselves to being modeled with objects in an obvious way. If we're designing a university registration system, for instance, it doesn't take a great leap of imagination to start by modeling students and courses as objects. Such objects are sometimes said to be "there for the picking."

Of course, it takes some experience to identify a suitable collection of objects for modeling a complete system. As we'll see, many objects serve to structure the solution and do not directly model real entities. Since our immediate goal is to learn how to design and implement simple objects, we assume, for now, that the decomposition of the system into objects is rather obvious. That is, we limit our attention to objects that are there for the picking.

Having identified a number of objects that can be used to build the system, we must determine what features each of these objects will have. Objects are designed to support the functionality of the system. We determine a set of requirements from the system specification and distribute these requirements as *responsibilities* to the objects. The functionality required of the system is *decomposed* or *partitioned* into responsibilities of the objects that will comprise the system. In the view of some experts, the ability to skillfully assign responsibilities to objects is the most critical skill an object-oriented designer must have.

In determining the responsibilities a particular object should have, it is useful to think in terms of what the object must *know* and what the object must *do*.

Knowing responsibilities include:

- knowing the properties of the entity the object is modeling;
- knowing about other objects with which it needs to cooperate.

    Doing responsibilities include:

- computing particular values;
- performing actions that modify its state;

- creating and initializing other objects;
- controlling and coordinating the activities of other objects.

"Knowing responsibilities" generally translate into data the object must maintain and sometimes into queries. If we want some particular piece of information about the entity being modeled, we query the object. "Doing responsibilities" translate into commands and sometimes queries. If we want some particular piece of information that the object knows how to compute, we query the object. If we want the object to perform some action that will change its state, we give the object a command.

Often a particular responsibility can be categorized as either a "knowing" responsibility or a "doing" responsibility. For instance, we can think of the student object as knowing the number of credit hours the student is enrolled in, or as computing the value from the student's schedule. It really does not matter at this point in the design. What we are determining here is that the object will support a query for number of credit hours. The decision as to whether this value will be explicitly maintained as a data item by the object or be computed from the schedule as needed is a separate, subsequent decision. It is a decision about *how* the query will work, given that the object will support the query.

An object's responsibilities are determined by the object's role in supporting the functionality of the system. Suppose, for instance, we are designing an object to model a simple wall switch. What information should the object know about the switch? Should it know the position of the switch, whether it's on or off? Should it know the color? If we're modeling electrical circuits, we would surely answer "yes" to the first and "no" to the second. On the other hand, if we're building an inventory system for a hardware store, the position of the switch is irrelevant, but color might be important to know.

In our early examples, we consider objects more or less in isolation and simply assume a set of responsibilities *a priori*. As our examples become more comprehensive, we will get a better idea of how an object's features are determined by the requirements of the system.

> To design a class, determine an object's responsibilities and classify them as knowing responsibilities or doing responsibilities.

3.2   A nim game example

For a little more complex example, let's look at two classes that might be part of a program to play a game of "simple nim." In this game, players take turns removing sticks from a pile. Each player in turn removes one, two, or three sticks. The player who removes the last stick loses.

Let's assume that each player and the pile of sticks will be modeled by distinct objects. The players have a set of common features, and will be instances of the same class that we'll call *Player*. The object representing the pile of sticks will be an instance of the class *Pile*. In Section 1.6, we distinguished model and user interface subsystems. The classes *Pile* and *Player* are part of the model: they model aspects of the game independently of how the game is presented to a user or how a user interacts with the game.

A *Pile* is a very simple object: it only needs to keep track of how many sticks remain. Since the number of sticks remaining will be maintained in the *Pile*'s state, the *Pile* must provide commands for modifying this data. We assign the *Pile* the following minimal responsibilities:

Pile responsibilities:

know:

> the number of sticks remaining

do:

> reduce the number of sticks (remove sticks)

The basic function of a *Player* is to take a turn in the game, that is, to remove sticks from the *Pile*. Without doing any analysis to justify our design, we also give a *Player* a name and make the *Player* responsible for remembering how many sticks were taken on the *Player*'s most recent turn. This is for the benefit of the user interface. The user interface reports the play of the game to the user, and a name is an easy way of identifying *Players* to the user. We assign the following responsibilities to a *Player*:

Player responsibilities:

know:

> this *Player*'s name
> how many sticks this *Player* removed on his/her most recent turn

do:

> take a turn by removing sticks from the *Pile*

The knowing responsibilities translate rather directly into queries.

Class: *Player*

queries:

name	this *Player*'s name, a *String*
sticksTaken	the number of sticks this *Player* removed on his/her most recent turn, 1, 2, or 3.

Class: *Pile*

queries:

sticks	the number of sticks remaining in this *Pile*, a non-negative integer

Commands are not quite as simple. For instance, we want the *Pile* to have a command to remove sticks. But we must tell it how many. In Section 2.6.1, we saw that a client provides additional information when invoking a constructor or method by means of parameters. This command has a parameter: the number of sticks to be removed from the pile. We include parameters in parenthesis when describing the command, for example,

Class: *Pile*

commands:

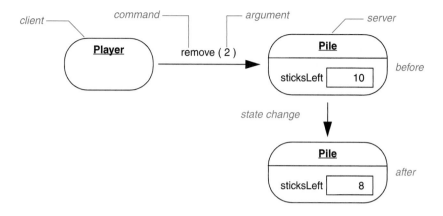

Figure 3.1 **Player commands the Pile.**

remove   reduce the number of sticks by the specified amount
                    (*number*)

When a client invokes the command, the client will provide an argument value. If a client commands a *Pile* to remove 2 sticks, then the value 2 is the argument associated with the command parameter (number).

Considering the class *Player*, we want a *Player* to have a command to take a turn and remove sticks from the *Pile*, as illustrated in Figure 3.1. That is, a *Player* is a *client* of the *Pile*. The relationship between *Player* and *Pile* can be shown in a static diagram, Figure 3.2, where the relation is represented by a labeled arrow.

Figure 3.2 **Player is client to Pile.**

To give the *Pile* a command, the *Player* must somehow get access to the *Pile*. One way to do this is make the *Pile* a parameter to the *Player* command *takeTurn*:

Class: *Player*

commands:

takeTurn   remove 1, 2, or 3 sticks from the specified *Pile* (*pile*)

Note that in this case, the argument, the value provided by a client when invoking the command, will be a *reference value*, in particular, a *reference-to-Pile* value.

Of course, some *Player* client must command a *Player* to take a turn and provide the *Pile* as argument. What kind of object this might be we won't yet consider. We can illustrate the sequence of interaction in an interaction diagram. In Figure 3.3, some client object gives a *Player* a command to take a turn. In the process of executing this command, the *Player* gives the *Pile* a command to remove sticks.

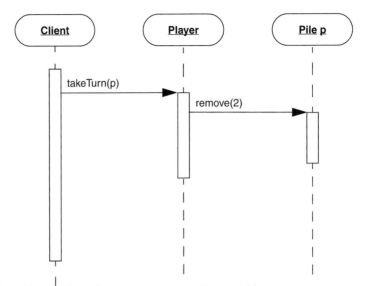

Figure 3.3 **An *interaction diagram* showing a *Player* taking a turn.**

There are still two issues to be resolved. How are the *Player*'s name and the number of sticks initially in the *Pile* determined? It seems reasonable to set these values when the objects are created. Constructors can have parameters, so we'll make a *Player*'s name and the initial number of sticks in the *Pile* constructor parameters.

Preliminary specifications for the classes *Pile* and *Player* are given in Listing 3.1. In order to elucidate the problem at hand, we often give rather complete specifications for a class before beginning the implementation. In practice, design, specification, implementation, and testing are generally carried out concurrently in rather small steps. In particular, we rarely complete the specification of a substantial class before beginning implementation and testing.

Listing 3.1   **Preliminary specifications for *Pile* and *Player***

===

`nimGame`
Class Pile

> **public class** `Pile`
>> A pile of sticks for playing simple nim.

Constructors

> **public** `Pile` (**int** `sticks`)
>> Create a new *Pile*, with the specified number of sticks. `sticks` must be non-negative.

continued

Listing 3.1   **Preliminary specifications for *Pile* and *Player* (cont'd)**

Queries

---

public int sticks ()
>   The number of sticks remaining in this *Pile*.

Commands

---

public void remove (**int** number)
>   Reduce the number of sticks by the specified amount. number must be non-negative and not greater than the number of sticks remaining.

===

nimGame
Class Player

public class Player
>   A player in the game simple nim.

Constructors

---

public Player (String name)
>   Create a new *Player* with the specified name.

Queries

---

public String name ()
>   The name of this *Player*.

public int sticksTaken ()
>   The number of sticks this *Player* removed on this *Player*'s most recent turn: 1, 2, or 3.

Commands

---

public void takeTurn (Pile pile)
>   Remove 1, 2, or 3 sticks from the specified *Pile*.

3.2.1 Implementing the class *Pile*

Our classes must be in some package, and with no good reason to do otherwise, we'll assume that both *Player* and *Pile* are in the same package, nimGame. Let's start writing the definition for the class *Pile* in Java.

The only data to be maintained by a *Pile* is the number of sticks remaining. A single instance variable is sufficient:

```
private int sticksLeft;   // sticks left in the Pile
```

This variable is initialized in the constructor and its value is returned by the query sticks:

```
/**
 * Create a new Pile, with the specified number of
 * sticks. sticks must be non-negative.
 */
public Pile (int sticks) {
   sticksLeft = sticks;
}


/**
 * The number of sticks remaining in this Pile.
 */
public int sticks () {
   return sticksLeft;
}
```

Note that since the constructor parameter and instance variable have different names, we do not need to use the keyword **this** in the constructor. Of course, there is nothing wrong with writing the constructor assignment statement as

```
this.sticksLeft = sticks;
```

Also note that the constructor specification places an additional restriction on the values that can be supplied as argument. Though the specification stipulates that the argument sticks must be non-negative, there is nothing to prevent the constructor from being invoked with a negative argument. We consider this issue in detail in subsequent chapters.

The command remove is specified with an **int** parameter:

```
public void remove (int number) { ...
```

The client provides an argument indicating the number of sticks to be removed. Executing the command should reduce the instance variable sticksLeft by whatever argument value the client supplies. Just as with a constructor, a method variable is created for the parameter when the method is invoked. This variable is initialized with the argument provided by the client. Figure 3.4 illustrates the situation when the remove method has been invoked with an argument 2. When the method finishes executing, the method variable is deallocated, and the memory space is reclaimed for other uses.

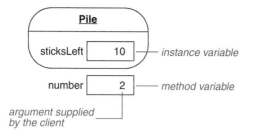

Figure 3.4 **Available variables when *remove* is executed.**

Clearly we need an assignment statement to store a new value into `sticksLeft`. The expression denoting the value to be stored is

```
sticksLeft - number
```

and the complete assignment statement is

```
sticksLeft = sticksLeft - number;
```

The method body consists of the single assignment statement:

```
/**
 * Reduce the number of sticks by the specified
 * amount. number must be non-negative and not greater
 * than the number of sticks remaining.
 */
public void remove (int number)
    sticksLeft = sticksLeft - number;
}
```

At the risk of beating the point into submission, let's review what happens when the method is invoked. When invoking the method, the client provides an **int** value as argument. A method variable is created for the parameter `number` and is initialized with the argument provided by the client. To execute the method, the processor evaluates the expression "`sticksLeft - number`" and stores the result in the instance variable `sticksLeft`. When execution of the method is complete, the space allocated for the variable `number` is released. This variable effectively no longer exists.

As before, there is nothing but the comment to prevent the value of `sticksLeft` from becoming negative. If the value of `sticksLeft` is 1 and the method is invoked with an argument of 2, the assignment will store –1 into the variable `sticksLeft`.

DrJava: exercising the Pile

Open the file `Pile.java`, located in folder `nimGame`, in `ch3`, in `nhText`. Note that this file contains only a stubbed implementation of the class *Pile*.

1. Compile the class, and make sure that it compiles successfully.

2. Write the implementation presented in the above section. Save and recompile.

3. In the *Interactions* pane, create a *Pile* instance. Note that you must supply an integer argument to the constructor.

```
> import nimGame.*;
> Pile thePile = new Pile(5);
```

4. Verify the correctness of the initial state.

```
> thePile.sticks()
5
```

5. Give the *Pile* several `remove` commands, verifying the state after each.

```
> thePile.remove(1);
> thePile.sticks()
4
> thePile.remove(2);
> thePile.sticks()
2
```

6. What happens if you try to remove more sticks than are in the *Pile*? What happens if you try to remove a negative number of sticks?

3.2.2 Implementing the class *Player*

A *Player* needs to know its name and the number of sticks taken on the *Player*'s most recent turn. Thus two instance variables are appropriate:

```
private String name;      // this Player's name
private int sticksTaken;   // sticks taken on this
                           // Player's most recent turn
```

These variables should be initialized in the constructor. The *Player*'s name is provided as a constructor argument. But to what should we initialize `sticksTaken` before the *Player* has taken a turn? We should use some value that can be interpreted as meaning "this *Player* has not taken a turn." Zero seems an appropriate choice.

```
/**
 * Create a new Player with the specified name.
 */
public Player (String name) {
    this.name = name;
    this.sticksTaken = 0;
}
```

Note that as with the *PlayingCard* constructor in Section 2.6.1, we must use the keyword **this** to distinguish the instance variable name from the parameter.

Queries simply return the values of the instance variables:

```
/**
 * Create a new Player with the specified name.
 */
public String name () {
   return name;
}


/**
 * The number of sticks this Player removed on his/her
 * most recent turn: 1, 2, or 3. Returns 0 if this
 * Player has not yet taken a turn.
 */
public int sticksTaken () {
   return sticksTaken;
}
```

Note that the value returned by the query name is a reference value of type *reference-to-String*. This type is denoted in Java simply by using the class name. Thus we write String for the type of value returned by the method name.

Our original specification of takeTurn states that the method will return 1, 2, or 3. We have now introduced the possibility that the method will return 0, and this should be clearly documented in the doc comment.

Invoking a method: acting as client

We've talked quite a bit about a client accessing the features of a server object by invoking the server's methods, but we have yet to see this done. We see an object acting as client in the implementation of the *Player* command takeTurn. This command is specified as

```
/**
 * Remove 1, 2, or 3 sticks from the specified Pile.
 * The Pile must not be empty.
 */
public void takeTurn (Pile pile) { ...
```

The command instructs the *Player* to remove sticks from the *Pile* provided as argument. We know that in order for this command to be executed, some other object must invoke it. That is, some object must instruct the *Player* to perform the command. In this relationship, the other object is client and the *Player* object is server: the other object is accessing a feature of the *Player*. When the client invokes the *Player*'s method takeTurn, it must provide (a reference to) a *Pile* object as argument.

Assume that firstPlayer is a *Player* object, and thePile is a *Pile*. If a client wants to call firstPlayer's method takeTurn, the call would look something like this:

```
firstPlayer.takeTurn(thePile);
```

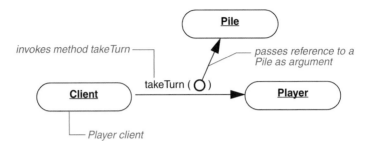

This argument value is stored in the method variable `pile`. Now the *Player* "knows about" the *Pile*: there is a reference to the *Pile* in the variable `pile`, as shown in Figure 3.5.

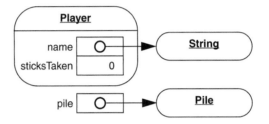

Figure 3.5 Variables when *Player*'s method *takeTurn* is being executed.

The general form for invoking a method for a query is

> *objectReference.queryName(arguments)*

and the general form for a command is

> *objectReference.commandName(arguments)*;

Returning to the `takeTurn` method, it must

- determine how many sticks to take;
- remove them from the *Pile*;
- store the number removed in the `sticksTaken` instance variable.

For the moment, let's give our *Player* the trivial move strategy of always removing just one stick. This certainly conforms to the specifications, even though it does not make a particularly interesting game.

To change the *Pile*'s state, the *Player* invokes the *Pile*'s `remove` command. When the *Pile*'s `remove` command is invoked, an integer argument must be supplied. An invocation looks like this:

A command invocation is another form of statement. The body of the `takeTurn` method consists of two statements, a command invocation to modify the state of the *Pile* and an assignment to store the number taken in the instance variable `sticksTaken`. When the method is executed, these statements are done in the order in which they are written.

```
public void takeTurn (Pile pile) {
    pile.remove(1);
    sticksTaken = 1;
}
```

(You might think that the methods we are building are unrealistically small. This is not the case. It is not uncommon for the methods implementing a substantial class to average less than two statements each.)

Note that in executing the command `takeTurn` the *Player* acts both as server and client. The *Player* is a server for whatever object invoked its `takeTurn` command. To perform the command `takeTurn`, the *Player* invokes the feature `remove` of the *Pile* object. Here the *Player* is client of the *Pile*, and the *Pile* is server to the *Player*.

Even though there are several objects involved in this interaction, remember that there is only a *single thread of execution*, that is, there is one processor executing a sequence of instructions. We repeat Figure 3.3, suggesting "processor activity" by blue checks (✓).

Summarizing, when a client invokes the *Player*'s method `takeTurn`, the client supplies a (reference to a) *Pile* object as argument. This reference value is stored in a newly created method variable named `pile`. The first statement of the method body is a call to the *Pile* object's `remove` command. This method requires an **int** argument. The complete definition of the class *Player* is given in Listing 3.2.

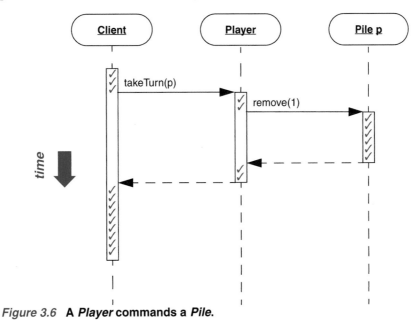

Figure 3.6 **A *Player* commands a *Pile*.**

Listing 3.2   **The class *Player***

```
package nimGame;

/**
 * A player in the game simple nim.
 */
public class Player {

   // Private components:

   private String name;          // this Player's name
   private int sticksTaken;      // sticks taken on this
                                 // Player's most recent
                                 // turn; 0 if this Player
                                 // has not taken a turn.

   // Constructors:

   /**
    * Create a new Player with the specified name.
    */
   public Player (String name) {
      this.name = name;
      this.sticksTaken = 0;
   }

   // Queries:

   /**
    * The name of this Player.
    */
   public String name () {
      return name;
   }

   /**
    * The number of sticks this Player removed on this
    * Player's most recent turn: 1, 2, or 3. Returns 0
    * if this Player has not yet taken a turn.
    */
   public int sticksTaken () {
      return sticksTaken;
   }
```

continued

Listing 3.2   **The class *Player* (cont'd)**

```
// Commands:

/**
 * Remove 1, 2, or 3 sticks from the specified Pile.
 * The Pile must not be empty.
 */
public void takeTurn (Pile pile) {
    pile.remove(1);
    sticksTaken = 1;
}


}
```

A few observations are in order before we conclude this section. First, arguments are provided in a method invocation by *expressions*. Thus we could write something like

```
pile.remove(sticksTaken + 1);
```

or even

```
pile.remove(2*sticksTaken+2);
```

However, these invocations would not conform to the specifications unless we could guarantee that the value of the argument expressions would always be either 1, 2, or 3, and would never be more than the number of sticks remaining in the *Pile*.

Second, a method invocation must provide an argument of the appropriate type for each parameter. For instance, if a method were specified as

```
public void move (int direction, double distance) {
    ...
}
```

an invocation of that method would provide two arguments, an **int** and a **double**, in that order. For example,

```
object.move(90, 2.5);
```

Finally, while a command invocation is a form of *statement*, a query, which produces a value, is a form of *expression*. Recall that the general form of a query is

```
objectReference.queryName (arguments)
```

If myCounter is a *Counter* object and i an **int** variable, assignment statements such as the following, which use the value of myCounter's method currentCount, are legal.

```
i = myCounter.currentCount();
i = myCounter.currentCount()+10;
```

DrJava: Pile and Player

Open the file `Player.java`, located in folder `nimGame`, in `ch3`, in `nhText`. `Player.java` contains an implementation of *Player*, as shown in Listing 3.2.

1. Compile the class *Player*.

2. In the *Interactions* pane, create a *Player* and a *Pile*. Note that you must provide a *String* as argument to the *Player* constructor.

```
> import nimGame.*;
> Player myPlayer = new Player("Spike");
> Pile thePile = new Pile(5);
```

3. Command the *Player* to take a turn, and note the state changes in *Player* and *Pile*.

```
> myPlayer.takeTurn(thePile);
> myPlayer.sticksTaken()
1
> thePile.sticks()
4
> myPlayer.takeTurn(thePile);
> myPlayer.sticksTaken()
1
> thePile.sticks()
3
```

4. Modify the *Player* so that 2 sticks are taken on a turn rather than 1. Save and recompile.

5. Again create a *Player* and *Pile*, and test. Note that there is nothing to prevent the *Player* from "removing" more sticks than are left in the *Pile*.

6. Modify the *Player* so that all the sticks in the *Pile* are taken on a turn. That is, modify the `takeTurn` method so that its body is

```
pile.remove(pile.sticks());
sticksTaken = pile.sticks();
```

Save and recompile.

7. Create a *Player* and *Pile*, and test. Something is wrong with this method. Can you determine what it is?

The query `pile.sticks()` is invoked twice, but the state of the *Pile* changes between the two invocations. It is rather easy to fix the problem. Do you see how?

3.3   A maze game example

As another example, consider a maze game: a game in which a player must find his way through a set of connected rooms to reach some goal. We can imagine that there will be tricks the player must figure out and creatures of various kinds ("maze denizens") to be defeated along the way. Even from this minimal description, it seems clear that among the things we should model are the player, maze denizens, and rooms.

There will be a number of rooms and denizens in our maze, but perhaps only one player. The player, each room, and each maze denizen will be modeled by distinct objects. Denizen objects will have a set of common features and will be entities of the same class, which we'll call *Denizen*. Similarly, room objects will be members of the class *Room*. The player object will be an element of the class *Explorer*.

Queries for class Explorer

Let's consider some responsibilities we might expect an *Explorer* to have. We'll give the *Explorer* a name and want to know where he or she is in the maze. For location, we'll simply note the room in which the *Explorer* is located. We might decide later that we want to be more specific about location—exactly where the *Explorer* is in the room. But for now, we'll be satisfied with just the room. Since we expect the *Explorer* to defeat denizens, we need to model fighting ability. In our initial view, an *Explorer* can relate to a *Denizen* in two ways: the *Explorer* can poke the *Denizen*, and the *Explorer* can be poked by the *Denizen*. (We don't want the game to get too violent, so we'll just let the *Explorer* and *Denizen* annoy each other.) As a first cut, we'll include two properties, one describing how much the *Explorer* annoys a *Denizen* when poking it, and a second measuring how much annoyance the *Explorer* can endure before being defeated. Thus we expect the *Explorer* object to know the following:

Explorer responsibilities:

know:

    his/her name

    location in the maze

    amount of annoyance done when poking an opponent

    amount of annoyance he/she can endure before being defeated.

These responsibilities translate into properties in a rather straightforward manner:

name	the name of the *Explorer*
location	the room in which the *Explorer* is currently located
strength	a measure of the *Explorer*'s offensive ability: how much annoyance the *Explorer* causes when poking a denizen
tolerance	a measure of what it takes to defeat the *Explorer*

Before we go further, let's see what type of value will be associated with each property. For name, we'll use a *String* as before. For location, we could use a description or some identifying room number. But as suggested above, we also want to model rooms as objects. That is, we will have a class *Room* whose objects will be the rooms of the maze. The *Explorer* object is related to a *Room* object by a relation we might call *is in*: the *Explorer is in* the *Room*. So we associate a reference to a *Room* object—a reference to the room containing the player—with the *Explorer*'s property *location*. The *type* of the value associated with the property *location* is *reference-to-Room*.

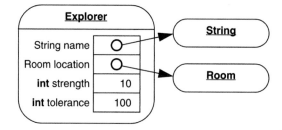

Figure 3.7 **An *Explorer*.**

Finally, we'll simply model strength and tolerance with integers. The general idea is that it will take ten pokes of strength 10 or five pokes of strength 20 to defeat a player (or denizen) with tolerance 100. An *Explorer* object is pictured in Figure 3.7

Commands for class Explorer

What should an *Explorer* be able to do? We need a general idea of how the object behaves in the system before we can even make a reasonable guess. The *Explorer* will move from room to room in response to input from the user, changing location, and sometimes encountering denizens. So the *Explorer* must be able to move and fight.

Explorer responsibilities *(continued)*:

do:

>   change location in the maze (move from room to room)
>   fight a maze *Denizen*

We need commands to tell the *Explorer* to perform these actions. We include a command *move* that changes the *Explorer's* location, and a command *poke* that instructs the *Explorer* to poke a *Denizen*:

>   *move*   change location
>   *poke*   poke a *Denizen*

As in the previous example, the object must be provided with additional information in order to carry out these commands. If we want the *Explorer* to change location, it must be provided with a new location, or some other information like direction of movement from which the new location can be determined. If we want the *Explorer* to poke a *Denizen*, the *Explorer* must be told which *Denizen* to poke. Thus both commands will have parameters:

>   *move*   change location (new *location*)
>   *poke*   poke a *Denizen* (*denizen* to poke)

Note that performing the *poke* command doesn't change the state of the *Explorer*. Rather, we expect the *Denizen* provided as argument to be changed as a result of being poked. But how does the state of the *Denizen* change? It is the *Denizen's* responsibility to change its state, and in order to change its state, the *Denizen* must execute a command. So we have the *Explorer* acting as client in poking the *Denizen*, and the *Denizen* acting as server. The *Explorer* gives the *Denizen* a command that causes the *Denizen* to change state. *The only way an object's state can change is by means of an action of the object itself in response to a command.*

Assuming that the *Denizen* command is called *takeThat*, we illustrate the action in Figure 3.8. Some client commands the *Explorer* to poke a *Denizen*, and provides the *Denizen* as argument. The *Explorer*, acting as client, invokes the *takeThat* method of the *Denizen*. (Note the similarity of Figure 3.8 to Figure 3.3.)

We expect *Explorers* and *Denizens* to be somewhat symmetric: an *Explorer* can poke a *Denizen*, and a *Denizen* can poke an *Explorer*. Thus *Explorer* must also have a method *takeThat*, in which the strength of the poke is provided as an argument.

    takeThat   receive a poke of the specified strength (*strength*)

The *Explore*'s tolerance is reduced by the strength of the poke. If the *Explorer* has a tolerance of 100 for instance and takes a poke of strength 5, the tolerance is reduced to 95, as illustrated in Figure 3.9.

A few questions may have occurred to you at this point. There is no command to increase or restore *tolerance*—perhaps we should add *meditate*. There is no obvious way to change *strength*. There are in fact many additional properties and commands that could be part of the specification of an *Explorer*. What we have is adequate for our exposition, and we'll be content without these for now.

It may also seem that the *strength* property should in some way be dependent on *tolerance*. As *tolerance* decreases, so might *strength*. This is a detail of implementation that should not concern us at this point. And if the relationship between *strength* and *tolerance* can be dismissed as part of the implementation, an astute reader might ask if *strength* and *tolerance* should be part of the specification at all. That is, should a client be able to query for specific *strength* and *tolerance* values, or should these simply be implementation details of no concern to the client? We'll leave them as part of the specification, since we can imagine, at least, that we might want to display these values to the user.

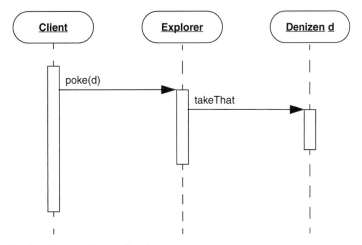

Figure 3.8 **An *Explorer* pokes a *Denizen*.**

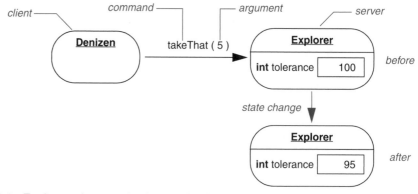

Figure 3.9 *Explorer* takes a poke from a *Denizen*.

A constructor for the class Explorer

Finally, we need a constructor for creating instances of the *Explorer* class. When a new *Explorer* is created, initial values must be given to the object's properties. We can require that these initial values be provided as constructor arguments, as we did with the name of a player in the nim game, or we could assign predetermined values as we did with the counter. To keep our example simple, we'll require that values for name, location, strength, and tolerance be provided as argument. Thus the constructor for an *Explorer* will have four parameters:

> *create new Explorer*   *(name, location, strength, tolerance)*

Preliminary specification for the class Explorer

Assume that all the relevant classes are in the package `mazeGame`. The specification of the features of the class *Explorer* is straightforward and is given in Listing 3.3.

Note that the value returned by the query `location` is a *reference-to-Room*, and that the commands `move` and `poke` require reference values as arguments. The method `takeThat` requires an **int** argument. If `myHero` is an *Explorer* and `hall` is a Room, calls of `myHero`'s methods `takeThat` and `move` would look something like this:

```
myHero.takeThat(10);
myHero.move(hall);
```

The constructor has four parameters. When the constructor is invoked, a *String*, *Room*, and two **int**s must be provided as arguments, in that order. Invoking the constructor to create a new object would look like this:

```
new Explorer("Marjorie",entry,10,100)
```

where we assume that `entry` is a *Room*.

Listing 3.3   **Specification for the class *Explorer***

`mazeGame`
Class Explorer

> **public class** Explorer
> A maze game player.

Constructors

> **public** Explorer (String name, Room location,
>   **int** strength, **int** tolerance)
> Create a new *Explorer* with the specified name, initial location, strength,
> and tolerance.

Queries

> **public** String name ()
> Name of this *Explorer*.

> **public** Room location ()
> *Room* in which this *Explorer* is currently located.

> **public int** strength ()
> Annoyance (hit points) this *Explorer* causes when poking an opponent.

> **public int** tolerance ()
> Annoyance (hit points) required to defeat this *Explorer*.

Commands

> **public void** move (Room newRoom)
> Move to the specified *Room*.

> **public void** takeThat (**int** hitStrength)
> Receive a poke of the specified number of hit points.

> **public void** poke (Denizen opponent)
> Poke the specified *Denizen*.

3.3.1 Implementing the class *Explorer*

Objects of this class have four properties: *name*, *location*, *strength*, and *tolerance*. We use instance variables to store the values of these variables.

```
private String name;         // name
private Room location;       // current location
private int strength;        // current strength
                             // (hit points)
private int tolerance;       // current tolerance
                             // (hit points)
```

These variables are initialized in the constructor, and their values returned by the queries. The query `location`, for instance, returns the value stored in the instance variable `location`, which happens to be a reference value:

```
public Room location () {
    return location;
}
```

To Implement the method `move`, the argument value provided by the client (a reference value in this case) is stored in the instance variable `location`:

```
public void move (Room newRoom) {
    location = newRoom;
}
```

The method `takeThat` is similar to the *Pile* method remove. The argument value, provided by the client and stored in the method variable `hitStrength`, is subtracted from the instance variable `tolerance`. The result is stored in `tolerance`:

```
public void takeThat (int hitStrength) {
    tolerance = tolerance - hitStrength;
}
```

The command `poke`, specified as

```
public void poke (Denizen opponent)
```

instructs the *Explorer* to poke the *Denizen* provided as argument. This argument value is stored in the method variable `opponent`, as shown in Figure 3.10.

To change the *Denizen*'s state, the *Explorer* must give the object `opponent` a command. As we mentioned above, we assume the class *Denizen* has the command `takeThat`, specified as follows:

```
public void takeThat (int hitStrength)
```
          Receive a poke of the specified number of hit points.

An invocation of this command must include an integer argument: the strength of the blow. This is just the value of our *Explorer*'s `strength` variable. The only action that the

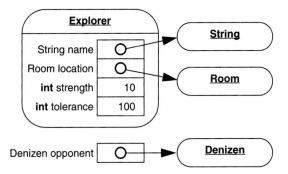

Figure 3.10 **Variables when *Explorer*'s method *poke* is being executed.**

Explorer needs to take in responding to a `poke` command is to call the *Denizen*'s `takeThat` command. The method contains only one statement.

```
public void poke (Denizen opponent) {
    opponent.takeThat(strength);
}
```

DrJava: the Explorer class

Open the file `Explorer.java`, located in folder `mazeGame`, in `ch3`, in `nhText`. This file contains a stubbed implementation of the class *Explorer*.

1. Complete the implementation of the class *Explorer* as described above. Save and compile.

2. The files `Room.java` and `Denizen.java` contain minimal implementations of the classes *Room* and *Denizen*. Open these files and take a look at them.

3. In the *Interactions* pane, create a *Room*, *Denizen*, and *Explorer*.

```
> import mazeGame.*;
> Room entry = new Room("Entry way");
> Denizen oldBat = new Denizen();
> Explorer myHero = new Explorer(
    "Buffy",entry,10,100);
```

4. Exercise the *Explorer*.

```
> myHero.location()
Room: Entry way
> myHero.name()
"Buffy"
> myHero.tolerance()
100
> myHero.takeThat(10);
```

```
> myHero.tolerance()
90
> oldBat.tolerance()
100
> myHero.poke(oldBat);
> oldBat.tolerance()
90
```

Note in particular the response to the query `location`. This query returns a reference value. Where did DrJava's output come from?

3.4   Local variables: another kind of method variable

We were introduced to method variables in Section 2.6.1. When a method or constructor is invoked, a method variable is allocated for each parameter and initialized with the argument value provided by the client. When we implement a method, it is often handy to have additional method variables available for storing intermediate results. These are called *local variables*. Their lifetime is the same as the method variables seen previously. They are created when the method is invoked, and deallocated when the method completes. However, they are not initialized by client-provided arguments. When a local variable is created, it is *undefined*, that is, it does not contain a predetermined value. It must be assigned a value before it can be meaningfully used. Use of a potentially undefined local variable will be treated as an error by the compiler.

A local variable is created with a variable declaration of the form:

```
type identifier;
```

The declaration is simply written as one of the statements in the method body.

> **local variable:** a method variable created as part of a method execution, used to hold intermediate results needed during the computation.

While we can't give a completely meaningful example at this point, the following should illustrate the mechanism. Suppose we are modeling items in a retail sales system. Assume that a *RetailItem* includes the following instance variables, with the obvious meanings:

```
private double basePrice;
private double discountRate;
private double taxRate;
```

We want to implement a *RetailItem* method `netPrice`:

public double netPrice ()
>   The cost of this *RetailItem* after discount, and including tax.

Since the expression needed to compute the net price is rather complex, we might find it useful to compute the tax and discount amounts separately, and then apply them to the base price to determine net price. We can use local variables to store these intermediate values.

```
public double netPrice () {
    double discount;
    double subtotal;
    double tax;
    discount = basePrice * discountRate;
    subtotal = basePrice - discount;
    tax = subtotal * taxRate;
    return subtotal + tax;
}
```

In the above, subtotal, discount, and tax are local method variables. They are created whenever the method is invoked, and are deallocated when the method completes. They contain "undefined" values when created, and are used only to hold the discount, subtotal, and tax amounts until they are needed in subsequent statements. For example, suppose the method is invoked for an item with basePrice, discountRate, and taxRate of 10.00, 0.10, and 0.08 respectively. Three method variables will be created:

discount	???
subtotal	???
tax	???

These local variables are undefined after creation.

The first assignment statement,

```
discount = basePrice * discountRate;
```

assigns a value to the local variable discount:

discount	1.00
subtotal	???
tax	???

The next assignment,

```
subtotal = basePrice - discount;
```

assigns a value to subtotal:

discount	1.00
subtotal	9.00
tax	???

The final assignment,

```
tax = subtotal * taxRate;
```

assigns a value to `tax`:

discount	1.00
subtotal	9.00
tax	0.72

Now the values stored in `subtotal` and `tax` can be used to compute the return value. When the method completes execution, space for these three variables is deallocated.

Note that local variables and instance variables are fundamentally different. An instance variable contains an element of the object's state. It must always contain a meaningful value whether a method of the object is executing or not. A local variable, on the other hand, contains some intermediate value needed only during a particular computation. You should never use an instance variable for this purpose.

Local Variable:

- Defined inside a method.
- Exists only while the method is being executed.
- Must be initialized before being used; otherwise, a compiler error occurs.
- Can be accessed only from the method.
- Is only meaningful during execution of the method.
- Contains some intermediate value needed only during execution of the method; its value is not part of the object's state.

Instance Variable:

- Defined outside any method.
- Exists as long as the object exists.
- Initialized in a constructor.
- Can be accessed from any method in the class.
- Has a meaningful value at any time during the life of the object, whether the object is actively doing something or not.
- Represents a property of the object; its value is part of the object's state.

Figure 3.11 **Local variables are not components.**

Initializing variables

A variable can be initialized by including an expression in its declaration:

```
type identifier = expression;
```

For example, we could have written the declaration of the variable tax above as

```
double tax = basePrice * taxRate;
```

This form of declaration effectively combines a declaration and assignment statement. The variable is allocated, the expression evaluated, and the resulting value assigned to the variable.

Though initializing expressions can be used in both local variable and instance variable declarations, we use them only for local variables. Instance variable initialization should take place in the constructors and only in the constructors.

A common error is to confuse an initializing declaration with an initializing assignment in a constructor. For instance, suppose we wrote the *TrafficSignal* constructor as follows:

```
        public TrafficSignal () {
✗           int light = TrafficSignal.GREEN;
        }
```

The single line that makes up the body of the constructor is a *local variable declaration* and does *not* assign a value to the instance variable light. The effect of executing the constructor is to create a new local variable named light, initialize it with the value TrafficSignal.GREEN, and then immediately dispose of the variable. The instance variable light is not affected at all.

DrJava: local variables

Open RetailItem.java, located in folder retailItems, in ch3, in nhText. Read the specification carefully. This is a partial implementation of the class *RetailItem*.

1. Key in the implementation of netPrice as given above. Save and compile.

2. In the *Interactions* pane, create a *RetailItem* and exercise it.

```
> import retailItems.*;
> RetailItem item = new RetailItem(10.0, 0.05, 0.1);
> item.netPrice()
```

3. Verify the net price for the data entered in the constructor by hand.

4. Implement the method taxCharged by entering the statement below, where tax is the variable declared in netPrice:

```
return tax;
```

Now implement the query discountedPrice by entering the statement below, where subtotal is the variable declared in netPrice:

```
return subtotal;
```

5. Save and compile. Why does the compilation fail?

There are two approaches to correcting the problem: *(1)* taxCharged and discountedPrice can compute these values as needed, or *(2)* these values can be maintained in instance variables as part of the object's state.

6. Let's try a simple fix. Make `tax` and `subtotal` instance variables rather than local variables. That is, declare instance variables

```
private double tax;
private double subtotal;
```

and remove the corresponding local variable declarations from netPrice. Save and compile. The compilation should now succeed

7. But is the fix correct? In the *Interactions* pane, create a *RetailItem* as before.

```
> import retailItems.*;
> RetailItem item = new RetailItem(10.0, 0.05, 0.1);
```

Query the item for tax charged:

```
> item.taxCharged()
```

What's wrong? If `tax` and `subtotal` are to store properties of the object, they must *always contain meaningful values*. Correct the problem, save, compile, and test.

8. Add commands to change the tax rate and discount rate.

3.5   Putting together a complete system

In Section 1.6, we learned that a complete system includes a user interface and model. Next, we'll put together a very simple system consisting of a single model object and a single user interface object, just to get an idea of how the parts fit together. The model object will be a *Rectangle* instance, as specified in Listing 3.4. Since we have a rectangle on a computer screen measured in pixels in mind, we make its dimensions **int** rather than **double**.

The user interface object will be an instance of the class *RectangleViewer*. It will have only a single feature, a command displayRectangle that writes a *Rectangle*'s length, width, area, and perimeter to the user's display screen. The *RectangleViewer* will query the *Rectangle* for the data to be displayed, and will be a client of the *Rectangle* as shown in Figure 3.12.

Figure 3.12   RectangleViewer is client to Rectangle.

Listing 3.4   **Specification for the class *Rectangle***

===

```
figures
```
Class Rectangle

> **public class** Rectangle

Constructors

> **public** Rectangle (**int** length, **int** width)
> > Create a new *Rectangle* with the specified length and width. Length and width must be non-negative.

Queries

> **public int** length ()
> > The length of this *Rectangle*.
>
> **public int** width ()
> > The width of this *Rectangle*.
>
> **public int** area ()
> > The area of this *Rectangle*.
>
> **public int** perimeter ()
> > The perimeter of this *Rectangle*.

===

How does the *RectangleViewer* get a *Rectangle* instance to display? There are several possibilities:

- the instance could be provided as an argument, either to the *RectangleViewer* constructor or to the method displayRectangle, that is, we could specify the constructor as

> **public** RectangleViewer (Rectangle rectangle) ...

or the method displayRectangle as

> **public void** displayRectangle (Rectangle rectangle) ...

- the instance could be created by the *RectangleViewer*, either in its constructor or in the method displayRectangle, that is, either the constructor or the method displayRectangle could contain a statement like

> rectangle = **new** Rectangle(50,100);

Any of these approaches will work, but creating *Rectangles* doesn't really sound like the business of a *RectangleViewer*. We'll provide the *Rectangle* to the *RectangleViewer* as an argument to the method `displayRectangle`. In this way, we can use a single *RectangleViewer* to display any number of different *Rectangles* if we so choose. The specification of `displayRectangle` looks like this:

> **public void** displayRectangle (Rectangle rectangle)
> Write the length, width, area, and perimeter of the specified *Rectangle* to standard output.

System.out.println

We consider input and output in some detail in later chapters. For now we need a simple way to write output to the user's display. The predefined object `System.out` has a method `println`, specified as

> **public void** println (String s)
> Write a line containing the specified *String* to standard output.

Executing the method results in its argument being written, typically to the window from which the program is run. ("Standard output" is generally written to this window.)

Using this method, we can write `displayRectangle` so that it displays the results obtained from the querying the *Rectangle* provided as argument.

Implementing displayRectangle

The implementation of `displayRectangle` is straightforward. We must query the argument *Rectangle*, and use `System.out.println` to display the results. Recall that the operator + denotes concatenation when either or both operands is a *String*.

```
public void displayRectangle (Rectangle rectangle) {
    int outputValue;
    outputValue = rectangle.length();
    System.out.println("length: " + outputValue);
    outputValue = rectangle.width();
    System.out.println("width: " + outputValue);
    outputValue = rectangle.area();
    System.out.println("area: " + outputValue);
    outputValue = rectangle.perimeter();
    System.out.println("perimeter: " + outputValue);
}
```

When we run the program, we expect the output to look like this, depending, of course, on the dimensions of the *Rectangle*:

```
length: 100
width: 50
area: 5000
perimeter: 300
```

The use of a local variable is not necessary. Each query produces an **int** and could be incorporated into the println argument expression. For instance, we could write the method as:

```
public void displayRectangle (Rectangle rectangle) {
    System.out.println(
        "length: " + rectangle.length());
    System.out.println(
        "width: " + rectangle.width());
    System.out.println(
        "area: " + rectangle.area());
    System.out.println(
        "perimeter: " + rectangle.perimeter());
}
```

3.5.1 Getting it started

We've defined the classes *Rectangle* and *RectangleViewer*, but where do the instances come from? How do we get the system started? We need one more public class, containing a method main specified as:

```
public static void main (String[] argv)
```

We'll ignore the details of this specification for now. This is the method that is executed when you run the program. Although the main method is defined in a class, it is really outside the object-oriented paradigm. Its only purpose should be to create the top-level objects and get the system started.

> ***main* method:** the top-level method that initiates execution of a system.

Though it's not absolutely essential to do things this way, our convention is that the class containing main contains no other method, and is not used to model any other part of the system.

What must the method main do in our program? It simply creates a *Rectangle* and *RectangleViewer*, and commands the *RectangleViewer* to display the *Rectangle*.

To create a *Rectangle* instance, we invoke the constructor providing two **int** arguments:

```
new Rectangle(100,50)
```

This constructor invocation is an expression that creates a new instance of the class, and returns a reference to the newly created instance. What should we do with the reference value? Store it in a variable with an assignment statement:

```
theModel = new Rectangle(100,50);
```

We make this a local variable of the method `main`. Since the method `main` is not part of any object, it cannot use instance variables. The *RectangleViewer* is handled in a similar way.

We can define the top level class as follows:

```
/**
 * A simple system to display a Rectangle's
 * properties.
 */
public class RectangleDisplay {

    /**
     * Run the program.
     */
    public static void main (String[] argv) {
        Rectangle theModel;
        RectangleViewer theUserInterface;
        theModel = new Rectangle(100,50);
        theUserInterface = new RectangleViewer();
        theUserInterface.displayRectangle(theModel);
    }
}
```

When the program is run, the method `main` is invoked. (How to run a program is described in detail in Appendix i.) The method allocates space for the two local variables, creates *Rectangle* and *RectangleViewer* instances storing references to these instances in the local variables, and gives the *RectangleViewer* the command `displayRectangle`. This is the last statement in the method `main`. When this statement completes, the program terminates.

There are a few items to note.

- Recall that a variable declaration can include an initializing expression. Thus, we could have written:

```
Rectangle theModel = new Rectangle(100,50);
RectangleViewer theUserInterface =
                              new RectangleViewer();
```

and eliminated the assignment statements.

- The variables themselves are not necessary. A constructor invocation returns a reference to a newly created object. Since we have a reference to the object, we can give it a command without storing the reference value in a variable. Thus we could have reduced the body of `main` to a single statement:

```
(new RectangleViewer()).displayRectangle(
        new Rectangle(100,50));
```

- The dimensions of the *Rectangle* that will be displayed are "hard coded" into the program.

If we want to display a different *Rectangle*, we must edit the program and recompile. This is clearly not an ideal situation. Improvement, however, will have to wait until we discuss input in a later chapter.

You might wonder why we went to the trouble of building a separate class to display a *Rectangle* rather than simply including the displayRectangle method in the *Rectangle* class itself. The basic reason is that modeling a rectangle and communicating with a user are two completely different kinds of responsibilities. The model should be designed to solve the problem independently of how the system communicates the solution to the user. The user interface is generally a rather complex subsystem which requires more frequent change than the problem model. It is fundamentally important that we design coherent classes that in some sense encompass a single concept. The importance of this point will become evident as we build more substantial and realistic systems. For the present, we must limit ourselves to simple, almost trivial, examples to illustrate the structure of a well-designed program. In fact, if all we wanted to do was compute the area and perimeter of a rectangle, there would be little point in using an object-oriented approach at all. A couple of lines of code in the main method would do the trick.

RectangleDisplay and *RectangleViewer* are shown in Listing 3.5.

Listing 3.5   *RectangleDisplay* and *RectangleViewer*

```
/**
 * A simple system to display a Rectangle's properties.
 */
public class RectangleDisplay {

    /**
     * Run the program.
     */
    public static void main (String[] argv) {
        Rectangle theModel;
        RectangleViewer theUserInterface;
        theModel = new Rectangle(100,50);
        theUserInterface = new RectangleViewer();
        theUserInterface.displayRectangle(theModel);
    }
}


/**
 * A trivial object to display a Rectangle.
 */
public class RectangleViewer {
```

continued

Listing 3.5   *RectangleDisplay* and *RectangleViewer* (cont'd)

```java
/**
 * Create a viewer.
 */
public RectangleViewer () {
}

/**
 * Write the properties of the specified Rectangle to
 * standard output.
 */
public void displayRectangle (Rectangle rectangle) {
    int outputValue;
    outputValue = rectangle.length();
    System.out.println("length: " + outputValue);
    outputValue = rectangle.width();
    System.out.println("width: " + outputValue);
    outputValue = rectangle.area();

    System.out.println("area: " + outputValue);
    outputValue = rectangle.perimeter();
    System.out.println("perimeter: " + outputValue);
}
}
```

DrJava: running RectangleDisplay

It is possible to run a program from DrJava. Open `RectangleDisplay.java`, located in folder `rectangle`, in ch3, in nhText.

In the *Interactions* pane, key

> `java rectangle.RectangleDisplay`

Output will appear in the *Interactions* pane.

1. Modify the `main` method to create a *Rectangle* with different dimensions.
2. Save and recompile. Run the program again and verify the correctness of the output.
3. Modify the `main` method as shown above, so that the local variables `theModel` and `theUserInterface` are not used. Save and recompile.
4. Open the file `RectangleViewer.java` in the same folder. Modify the method `displayRectangle` so that the local variable `outputValue` is not needed. Save and recompile.
5. Run the program and verify the correctness of the output.

3.5.2 The method *toString*

Even though we do not put user interface functionality in model classes, it is useful to include a query that returns a *String* representation of an object's state. In Java, this method is specified by convention as:

public String toString ()
      A *String* representation of the object.

The implementation should produce a concise, easy to read, informative description of the object and its state. The result should contain the values of all relevant object properties. For example, we might define the method in the class *Rectangle* as follows:

```
/**
 * A String representation of this object.
 */
public String toString () {
    return "Rectangle: length = " + length +
            " width = " + width;
}
```

where we assume `length` and `width` are instance variables.

The method `toString` is useful for testing and debugging since it gives a concise picture of the current state of an object. It is also invoked automatically when one operand of the concatenation operator is a reference value. For example, consider the expression

```
"rect: " + rect
```

where `rect` is a *Rectangle* variable. Since the left operand of the + operator is a *String*, the operator denotes concatenation. The right operand is a reference value: a reference to a *Rectangle*. The reference is "converted" to a *String* by invoking the object's `toString` method. Thus the above expression is equivalent to

```
"rect: " + rect.toString()
```

and the expression evaluates to something like

```
"rect: Rectangle: length = 100 width = 50"
```

3.6   Testing an implementation

Testing is a fundamental part of building a software system. The testing we consider here is called *unit testing*. We test a class we are implementing to make sure that it behaves as expected. This is part of the job of implementing the class. *Functional testing*, on the other hand, involves testing the entire system to ensure that it meets the customer's specifications. Functional testing is a different beast entirely, and is often the responsibility of a team different from the programming team that implements the system.

It is an unfortunate fact that programmers spend more time debugging than writing code. As a result, the best way to improve productivity is to reduce debugging time, and the best way to reduce debugging time is to adopt an aggressive testing regimen. In our opinion, an incremental test-driven implementation procedure is the most effective means of reducing the time required to track down and correct bugs.

There are several aspects to this approach. First, the implementation proceeds in relatively small increments. The process is to code a little, test a little. Each time you add a new bit of functionality, you test it immediately. Second, the implementation is "test-driven." That is, you write the test for a feature before implementing the feature. Writing the test gives a very concrete specification of how the feature is to behave. Once the test is written, you write code to satisfy the test. In fact, developing a test sometimes exposes inconsistencies or a lack of completeness in the specification.

Testing can be a very boring business. If we expect programmers to test continuously and rigorously, the testing process must be easy and routine. To that end, a number of testing frameworks have been developed to help automate the process. With these tools, testing becomes a natural part of the implementation process. We study testing in some detail in a later chapter. Here, we build a minimal system for creating and exercising an object. This will give us some idea of how the testing process works, and allow us to see a few new features of Java.

3.6.1 A class to test

Even though it is a very simple class that we already know how to implement, we use *TrafficSignal* as an example of how test-driven development proceeds. We'll start with a definition of the class in which methods and constructors have been "stubbed." Stubs are method and constructor bodies that don't actually do anything useful, but conform to the syntactic rules of Java. They are "place holders" that satisfy the compiler so that documentation can be produced and tests conducted. Of course, a stub will ultimately be replaced with an actual implementation.

In practice, we rarely start with a completely stubbed class. As we've mentioned before, in building a class design, specification, implementation, and testing are all incremental and concurrent activities.

Constructors and commands can be stubbed by simply leaving the body empty. Queries are stubbed with a single simple return statement. (If the query returns a reference value, it is generally stubbed with a return statement that returns null.) We omit comments in the text, to more clearly illustrate the implementation. The code you write, of course, should contain doc comments.

```java
public class TrafficSignal {

    public static final int GREEN = 0;
    public static final int YELLOW = 1;
    public static final int RED = 2;

    private int light;
```

```
public TrafficSignal () {
}

public int light () {
    return 0;
}

public void change () {
}

}
```

The class will compile successfully, but certainly won't behave as required. The query `light` always returns 0, and the command `change` does nothing at all.

3.6.2 The *TrafficSignalTest* class

We want to create a *TrafficSignal* instance and exercise it by querying it and giving it commands. To do this, we need another object to act as client to the *TrafficSignal*. We call this object a *TrafficSignalTest*. The *TrafficSignalTest* will be a user interface object, and report results to the user.

> **class** TrafficSignalTest
> A simple class to test the class *TrafficSignal*.

We'll put this class in the same package as the class *TrafficSignal*. As it does not need to be accessed from outside the package, we need not make the class public.

The only property of a *TrafficSignalTest* is the *TrafficSignal* to be tested. Its only function is to test the *TrafficSignal*. So we specify a single command for the class:

> **public void** runTest ()
> Test a *TrafficSignal*.

How does the *TrafficSignalTest* get a *TrafficSignal* to test? As was the case with the *RectangleViewer* above, there are several possibilities:

- the *TrafficSignal* could be provided as an argument, either to the *TrafficSignalTest* constructor or to the method `runTest`;
- the *TrafficSignal* could be created by the *TrafficSignalTest*, either in its constructor or in the method `runTest`.

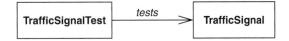

Figure 3.13 *TrafficSignalTest* **is client to** *TrafficSignal*.

With no good reason at present to choose one over the other, we create the *TrafficSignal* in the *TrafficSignalTest* constructor, and store a reference to the newly created *TrafficSignal* in an instance variable. We use an instance variable because we want the stored value to be available after the constructor completes.

Stubbing the method `runTest`, we can write a compilable definition of the class *TrafficSignalTest*:

```
/**
 * A tester for the class TrafficSignal.
 */
class TrafficSignalTest {

    private TrafficSignal signal; // the object to test

    /**
     * Create a TrafficSignalTest
     */
    public TrafficSignalTest () {
        signal = new TrafficSignal();
    }

    /**
     * Run the test.
     */
    public void runTest () {
    }

}
```

3.6.3 The initiating class

To run the program, we need a more public class containing the method `main` as explained above. The method `main` simply creates a *TrafficSignalTest* object, and commands the *TrafficSignalTest* to run the test:

```
/**
 * A simple test system for the class TrafficSignal.
 */
public class Test {

    /**
     * Run a TrafficSignal test.
     */
    public static void main (String[] argv) {
        TrafficSignalTest test;
```

```
            test = new TrafficSignalTest();
            test.runTest();
        }
    }
```

As before, we could eliminate the variable and assignment, and write `main` as a single statement:

```
public static void main (String[] argv) {
    (new TrafficSignalTest()).runTest();
}
```

3.6.4 Writing the tests

So now we have a system that compiles and runs, but doesn't do anything. We need to write some tests. Let's start by writing a test that checks the initial state of the *TrafficSignal*. We could write the test code directly in the method `runTest`. But as we added additional tests, the method would become excessively long and unmanageable. Rather than putting the test code directly in `runTest`, it is preferable to put each test in its own method and invoke these test methods from `runTest`. This will give a more manageable structure to our test class.

We name the method that tests the initial state, logically enough, `testInitial-State`. Now this method is *not* part of the specification of the *TrafficSignalTest* class. It is not available to clients of the class, and will be invoked only from inside the class itself. Its purpose it to help organize the implementation of *TrafficSignalTest*, and in fact it is part of the implementation. Therefore the method is declared to be *private* rather than *public*:

```
private void testInitialState () ...
```

We invoke this method from `runTest`. Since the method is defined in the same class as `runTest` and will be executed by the same object that is executing `runTest`, we can invoke the method without prefixing an object name, that is, we can write:

```
public void runTest () {
    testInitialState();
}
```

If we want, we can emphasize the fact that the object executing `runTest` will also execute `testInitialState` by writing:

```
public void runTest () {
    this.testInitialState();
}
```

Figure 3.14 illustrates execution of a test in an interaction diagram. The method `testInitialState` is executed by the same object executing `runTest`. Note that no instance of the class *Test* is created. The `main` method of this class is executed when the program is run.

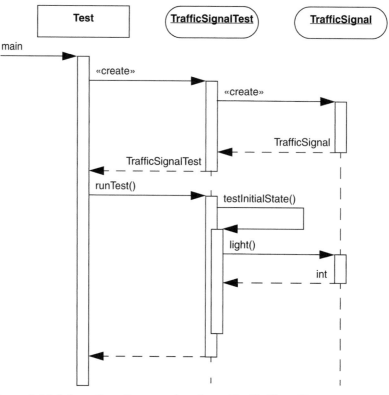

Figure 3.14 **Interaction diagram showing a *TrafficSignalTest*.**

What do we need to do to test the initial state? We need to get the light and make sure that it's green. To get the light, we can query the *TrafficSignal* object:

```
signal.light()
```

To know that the result is correct, we must somehow "see" the results: we want to produce output that we can examine. Using the method System.out.println, we can write testInitialState so that it displays the result obtained from the query:

```
private void testInitialState () {
    System.out.println("testInitialState:");
    System.out.println(
        "Initial light: " + signal.light());
}
```

Running the test

When we run the program, we see the following line displayed:

```
testInitialState:
Initial light: 0
```

The program gives the correct result—the initial light is green, which is represented by the integer value 0—but for the wrong reason. We have stubbed the method light as

```java
public int light () {
    return 0;
}
```

so it will always produce 0 no matter what! A failed test always means that the implementation is not correct, but a successful test does not guarantee a correct implementation. And a successful test of a function that we have not yet implemented should always cause us to look for an explanation.

Implementing the constructor and query

Next we implement the *TrafficSignal* constructor and method light:

```java
public TrafficSignal () {
    light = TrafficSignal.GREEN;
}

public int light () {
    return light;
}
```

and again run the test. This time we get the correct result because we have correctly implemented the constructor and query.

Testing the command

Now we build a test for the command change. In order to ensure that the *TrafficSignal* is working properly, we should give the command at least three times and see the light cycle from green back to green. As before, we put this test in its own method and invoke it from runTest:

```java
public void runTest () {
    testInitialState();
    testChange();
}
```

The method itself is straightforward:

```java
private void testChange () {
    System.out.println("testChange:");
    System.out.println(
        "Starting light: " + signal.light());
    signal.change();
    System.out.println(
        "After 1 change: " + signal.light());
```

```
signal.change();
System.out.println(
    "After 2 changes: " + signal.light());
signal.change();
System.out.println(
    "After 3 changes: " + signal.light());
}
```

Recompiling and running produces the following output:

```
testInitialState:
Initial light: 0
testChange:
Starting light: 0
After 1 change: 0
After 2 changes: 0
After 3 changes: 0
```

This is not surprising, since we've not yet implemented change. It's still stubbed as a do-nothing method. But we have verified that the test method works.

Finally, we implement change as above:

```
public void change () {
    light = (light + 1) % 3;
}
```

Recompiling and running one more time should produce a successful test, with the following output:

```
testInitialState:
Initial light: 0
testChange:
Starting light: 0
After 1 change: 1
After 2 changes: 2
After 3 changes: 0
```

We now have a nice, simple, test system for the class *TrafficSignal*. If later we need to modify or extend the class, we can easily add new tests to the system. Furthermore, our existing tests will help ensure that additions or modifications don't break the implementation.

The complete implementation of *TrafficSignalTest* and *Test* are given in Listing 3.6.

Listing 3.6   The classes *TrafficSignalTest* and *Test*

```
package trafficSimulation;

/**
 * A simple test system for the class TrafficSignal.
 */
public class Test {

   /**
    * Run a TrafficSignalTest.
    */
   public static void main (String[] argv) {
      TrafficSignalTest test;
      test = new TrafficSignalTest();
      test.runTest();
   }
}

/**
 * A tester for the class TrafficSignal.
 */
class TrafficSignalTest {

   private TrafficSignal signal;     // the object to test

   /**
    * Create a TrafficSignalTest
    */
   public TrafficSignalTest () {
      // create a signal to test:
      signal = new TrafficSignal();
   }

   /**
    * Run the test.
    */
   public void runTest () {
      testInitialState();
      testChange();
   }
```

continued

Listing 3.6   The classes *TrafficSignalTest* and *Test* (cont'd)

```java
/**
 * Test the TrafficSignal's initial state.
 */
private void testInitialState () {
    System.out.println("testInitialState:");
    System.out.println(
        "Initial light: " + signal.light());
}

/**
 * Test the method change.
 */
private void testChange () {
    Sustem.out.println("testChange:");
    System.out.println(
        "Starting light: " + signal.light());
    signal.change();
    System.out.println(
        "After 1 change: " + signal.light());
    signal.change();
    System.out.println(
        "After 2 changes: " + signal.light());
    signal.change();
    System.out.println(
        "After 3 changes: " + signal.light());
}
}
```

DrJava: writing a test for Counter

Open the files `Counter.java` and `CounterTest.java`, in folder `counters`, in ch3, in nhText. The file `Counter.java` contains a stubbed implementation of the familiar *Counter* class and `CounterTest.java`, a stubbed implementation of test class.

1. Write a *Test* class containing a `main` method, similar to that described above, and save it in the folder `counters`.

2. Compile and run the program in the *Interactions* pane.

   ```
   > java counters.Test
   ```

   Of course, there is no output yet.

3. Add a `testInitialState` method to *CounterTest*, and invoke the method in `runTest`. Save, recompile, and run the program.

4. Implement the *Counter* constructor and the method `currentCount` in *Counter*. Save, recompile, and run the test.

5. Add a method `testIncrement` to *CounterTest*, invoked in `runTest`. Save, recompile, and run.

6. Implement the *Counter* method `incrementCount`. Save, recompile, and run.

7. Add a method `testReset` to *CounterTest*, invoked in `runTest`. Save, compile, and run

8. Implement the *Counter* method `reset`. Save, compile, and run.

The steps in the above exercise probably seem somewhat excessive and extreme. The example is trivial and completely familiar to you by now. The point of the exercise is to get a feel for writing a test, implementing a feature, and then testing the feature. This process is essential when you develop more complex classes.

A couple of items should be addressed before we leave this exercise. First, is it necessary to test every method that we write? The answer is, of course, no. Methods such as `reset` and `currentCount` are completely straightforward, and many experienced programmers would not bother testing them. On the other hand, errors often occur in the least expected places. A little overly aggressive testing is preferable to a lot of tedious debugging.

Second, you may wonder why we go through the trouble of building a test system when we can easily test the class interactively with DrJava. Again, our examples at this point are necessarily very simple, and the payoff from the strategies we're introducing comes when we build larger, more realistic classes. In fact, the two forms of testing complement each other. Interactive testing is quick and immediate. On the other hand, coding a test with a test system has the following advantages.

- It helps us think through cases and precisely define the expected behavior of a feature before we write the feature. Writing the feature becomes easier: we simply have to build something that satisfies the tests.

- It gives us a permanent, repeatable test of a feature. As we add to and modify the class, we automatically repeat tests of previously implemented features. If a modification accidentally breaks some existing feature, the test will tell us.

- As we'll see later, test reporting can be automated. Manually verifying the correctness of a few simple tests is easy. But tests for a complex class can be substantial. We don't want to manually verify the correctness of voluminous test output. A test system can be designed to automatically verify the correctness of a test, and to produce output only in the event of a failed test.

3.7   Java in detail: *static* and *final* features

3.7.1   *Static* methods and the class *Math*

In Section 3.5, we specified a simple class modeling rectangles. Suppose we want to add a method to that class that computes the diagonal of a rectangle:

> **public double** diagonal ()
>> The diagonal of this *Rectangle*.

The diagonal can be computed from the length and width:

$$diagonal = \sqrt{length^2 + width^2}$$

Squaring a value is easy, but how do we get the square root? We could attempt to write code to compute the square root directly in the method diagonal, but we would find this rather difficult with the limited amount of Java that we currently know. Besides, square roots are used in many situations besides computing rectangle diagonals, and knowing how to compute a square root doesn't sound like it ought to be a responsibility of a *Rectangle*.

It would be useful if there was a server object that knew how to compute square roots, and other mathematical functions, such as the trigonometric functions, as well. Let's assume for the moment that there is a class *Math* that includes this kind of functionality:

> **public class** Math
>> The class *Math* contains methods for performing basic numeric operations such as square root and trigonometric functions.

> **public double** sqrt (**double** a)
>> The positive square root of the specified value.

>> ...

Now if length and width are **int** instance variables, we can write the method diagonal with the help of a *Math* object:

```
public double diagonal () {
    Math calculator = new Math();
    double a = (double)(length*length + width*width);
    return calculator.sqrt(a);
}
```

Note that the expression

```
length*length + width*width
```

produces an **int**. We cast the **int** to a **double** before assigning it to the **double** variable a.

If we think carefully about the *Math* object calculator, it appears to be a very unusual object. In the first place, it really doesn't "model" anything. It is just a collection of functions that are related only in that they are "mathematical." Its only role is to provide service via these functions. Second, the *Math* object has no state at all. Any instance is indistinguishable from any other. The method sqrt simply reports the square root of its argument to its client. It does not depend in any way on the object calculator. In fact, there seems little point in instantiating an object at all.

Java provides a mechanism for defining methods that are not dependent on the state of an object. A method can be defined as *static*, in which case it is associated with the *class* rather than with an *instance* of the class. Static methods are referred to in Java as "class methods," as opposed to "instance methods," which are associated with particular objects. In fact, there is a standard predefined[1] class *Math* that includes a square root function specified as:

> **public static double** sqrt **(double** a)
>   The positive square root of the specified value.

The function is invoked by prefixing the name of the class rather than the name of a class instance. The diagonal method can be written as:

```
public double diagonal () {
    double a = (double)(length*length + width*width);
    return Math.sqrt(a);
}
```

All of the methods in the standard class *Math* are static. Since there is no need to instantiate the class, the constructor for the class is declared private.

Since a static method is not associated with any instance, its implementation clearly cannot reference instance variables. For example, we could not declare the *Rectangle* method diagonal to be static because it must access instance variables length and width of some particular *Rectangle* instance.

Object-oriented design involves distributing system responsibilities to cooperating objects. Static methods, therefore, are on the periphery of object-oriented programming and should rarely appear in an object-oriented design. If you find that you are specifying more than a very few specialized methods as static, you are almost certainly creating a poor design.

3.7.2 *Final* features

Now that we have an idea of what static means, let's take another look at the definition of named constants. Recall that named constants are defined as *static final*, for example,

> **public static final int** GREEN = 0;

The specification *static* implies that the feature is associated with the class itself, rather than with an instance of the class. Hence the use of the class name when referring to the feature:

```
light = TrafficSignal.GREEN;
```

---

1. This class is defined in the package java.lang mentioned in Section 2.9.

The keyword **final** means that the value to which the identifier is bound cannot be changed. We can declare instance variables and even parameters *final*. For example, we could declare the instance variables of a *Rectangle* to be final:

```
public class Rectangle {
    ...
    private final int length;
    private final int width;
}
```

After these variables are assigned values in the constructor,

```
public Rectangle (int length, int width) {
    this.length = length;
    this.width = width;
}
```

their values cannot subsequently be modified. We could not, for example, have a *Rectangle* method:

```
✗        public void changeLength (int newLength) {
            this.length = newLength;  // No! length is final!
        }
```

A parameter is initialized with the argument provided by the client. If a parameter is defined to be final, such as,

```
public void incrementCount (final int amount) ...
```

it cannot be modified in the body of the method. For instance

```
✗        public void incrementCount (final int amount) {
            amount = amount*2;       // No! amount is final!
            int twice = amount*2;    // This is ok.
            ...
```

It is generally considered to be good practice to treat parameters as final even if they are not declared as such.

Note that the modifier **final** applied to a variable refers to the *value stored in the variable*, not to an object denoted by a reference value. Suppose the parameter pile in nim *Player* method takeTurn was defined to be **final**:

```
public void takeTurn (final Pile pile) ...
```

When the method is invoked, a method variable is allocated and initialized with a *reference-to-Pile* value provided as argument

The fact that the parameter is final means that the *value* stored in this variable cannot be changed. For instance, the method cannot contain the statement:

```
✗        pile = new Pile(10); // No! pile is final!
```

However, the method is not prevented from giving the *object* a command that might change the object's state. The method *can* contain the statement

```
pile.remove(1);      // OK! This doesn't change the
                     // reference value stored in pile.
```

3.7.3 Importing static features

The import statement introduced in Section 2.9, can also be used to import static features into a compilation unit. There are two formats for this purpose:

```
import static className.identifier ;
import static className.* ;
```

In the first case, the identifier must name a static feature defined in the specified class. For example,

```
import static Math.sqrt;
import static TrafficSignal.GREEN;
```

These statements allow the identifiers to be used without being prefixed with the class name. We can write

```
return sqrt(a);
```

and

```
light = GREEN;
```

rather than

```
return Math.sqrt(a);
```

and

```
light = TrafficSignal.GREEN;
```

The second format allows all static features defined in a a class to be used without being prefixed with the class name. For instance,

```
import static TrafficSignal.*;
```

allows the simple identifiers GREEN, RED, and YELLOW to be used in place of the qualified names TrafficSignal.GREEN, TrafficSignal.RED, and TrafficSignal.YELLOW.

3.8   Summary

We started this chapter with a brief overview of designing with objects. In designing an object, we ask what should the object know and what should the object do. That is, we enumerate the "knowing responsibilities" and the "doing responsibilities" of the object. These responsibilities are determined by the object's role in supporting the functionality of the system. System functionality is distributed to the comprising objects by assigning a set of responsibilities to each object. "Knowing responsibilities" translate to queries when the object is defined. "Doing responsibilities" translate into queries or commands. Itemizing an object's responsibilities determines the object's features and its relationship to other objects that comprise the system.

We developed several examples in which one object acts as client to another. In our examples, the client object was provided with a reference to a server as a method argument. The client was then able to use the server by invoking its methods.

A command invocation is a form of statement. The format for invoking a command is

```
object.command (arguments);
```

The processor executes the method body associated with the command, which generally results in the object changing state.

A query invocation is a form of expression, since it computes and returns value. The format is similar to a command invocation:

```
object.query (arguments)
```

A constructor invocation creates a new object, and returns a reference to the newly created object. The format is

```
new class (arguments)
```

When a method with formal parameters is invoked, a method variable is allocated for each formal parameter and initialized with the argument provided by the client. A local variable is another kind of method variable. Local variables are created when a method is invoked and used to hold intermediate results needed during the computation. Method variables are substantially different from instance variables. Instance variables contain data that is part of the object's state. They are created when the object is created, and should always contain a meaningful value. Method variables are created when a method is invoked, and contain values that are used only for a specific computation.

We next developed a simple but complete system containing a model object and a user interface object. To complete the program, we introduced a class with a single method named `main`. This is the method that is executed when the program is run. Its only function is to create the initial objects and get the system started. In our example, it creates a model object and user interface object, and then "starts" the user interface, passing it the model as argument. We restrict ourselves to this style of using a "special" class that contains only the method `main`, and using `main` only to initialize and start the object-oriented system.

We concluded the chapter with a brief introduction to unit testing. To reduce time spent debugging and improve programmer efficiency, we adopt a test-driven implementation strategy. The basic idea is to develop a test for each feature or bit of functionality before implementing the feature or adding the functionality. We saw how to construct a class to be used to test another existing class. An instance of the testing class invokes commands and queries of the object under test, and displays information about its state. By comparing actual results with expected results we can determine if the object under test behaves correctly.

SELF-STUDY EXERCISES

3.1   Assume that mrBill is an *Explorer*, and steelGuy is a *Denizen*. Write a command invocation that instructs mrBill to poke steelGuy.

3.2   Assume that thePile is a *Pile*, and count an **int** variable. Write a statement that queries the *Pile* for the number of sticks remaining, and stores the number in the variable count.

3.3   Write a *Counter* method that will set the *Counter* to any specified value. (The class *Counter* is defined in the previous chapter.)

3.4   Given that myCounter is a *Counter*, write a command invocation that sets myCounter to 3. Assume the method specified in the previous question.

3.5   The following statement appears in the *Explorer* constructor, to initialize the *Explorer*'s instance variable strength to 10:

        int strength = 10;

What's wrong with the statement?

3.6   Explain the basic difference in how instance variables, parameters, and local variables are used.

Which type of variable can be accessed directly by a client?

3.7   Fill in the blanks in the following statements.

   a.   A parameter gets its initial value from the _____; a local variable is initialized by _____.

   b.   A test to determine if the system meets the customer's specification is called a(n) _____. A test to determine if a class is implemented correctly is called a(n) _____.

   c.   The method that gets executed when a program is run is named _____.

3.8   Given that day, month, and year are **int** variables, write a statement that will display their values, labeled appropriately.

3.9   Modify the *TrafficSignalTest* method runTest so that it creates the *TrafficSignal* to test, stores a reference to it in a local variable, and passes the reference as an argument to the testInitialState and testChange methods. Assume these methods are specified as

        private void testInitialState (TrafficSignal signal)
        private void testChange (TrafficSignal signal)

3.10   What does it mean to say that an implementation is "test driven"?

EXERCISES

3.1   Design and implement *Explorer* commands that will change an *Explorer*'s strength and tolerance.

3.2   Suppose the class *Student* has an instance variable

```
private int grade;
```

containing the *Student*'s test grade. Write a *Student* method

```
public int adjustedGrade (int highGrade)
```

that works as follows. The argument is the highest grade scored on the test. The maximum adjustment is the difference between the highest grade and 100. For example, if the highest grade is 90, the maximum adjustment is 10. The *Student*'s adjustment is determined by the ratio of the *Student*'s grade to the highest grade. For example, if the *Student*'s grade is 45 (50% of the highest grade), the *Student*'s adjustment is 5 (50% of the maximum adjustment). The *Student*'s adjusted grade is 50 (45+5).

Use local variables to store intermediate results.

3.3   Design and implement a class modeling a retail item, as suggested in Section 3.4. Include a method `toString`.

3.4   Design and implement a simple class modeling a *Room* in the maze game. A *Room* should have a *String* description that is given when the *Room* is created.

3.5   Two *Rooms* in a maze can be connected by a passageway. Of course, we will define a class to model passageways. Write specifications for queries that will determine which *Rooms* the passageway connects.

3.6   Suppose an instance of the class *Room* of the maze game must keep track of whether or not the *Explorer* is in the *Room*. Add a **boolean** instance variable to store this data, and a query **public boolean** `occupied()` to report whether or not the *Explorer* is in the *Room*.

Note that a **boolean** variable can be assigned a value by using a **boolean** literal:

```
occupied = true;
occupier = false;
```

Initialize the variable in the constructor, and implement two methods

```
public void enter ()
```
        The *Explorer* has entered this *Room*.

```
public void exit ()
```
        The Explorer has exited this Room.

that set the variable.

3.7   Modify the *Explorer* method `move` so that the *Rooms* involved are informed of the *Explorer*'s coming and going.

Illustrate the interaction between an object commanding the *Explorer* to move, the *Explorer*, and the *Room* objects using an interaction diagram.

3.8 Exercises 2.4 and 2.14 ask you to implement a class modeling a three-way lamp: a lamp with off, low, medium, and high settings. Design and implement a class that will test the three-way lamp, implement the test system and run the test.

3.9 Design and implement a class that will test the modulus counter of Exercise 2.2 and Exercise 2.13. Since the constructor for a modulus counter has a parameter, we will want to create several different modulus counters with different constructor arguments. We'll do this by having the `runTest` method create the counters, and pass them to the test methods. The private test methods will take a modulus counter as argument. For instance,

```
private void testStepCount (ModCounter counter)
```

The `runTest` method will create several counters—perhaps using 0, 1, and 3 as constructor arguments—and invoke the test methods for each counter.

Implement the test system and run the test.

3.10 Implement and test a class modeling circles. The constructor should specify the radius of the circle. The class has queries for radius, diameter, area, and circumference. Use the named constant PI defined in the `java.lang` class *Math* for the value of π.

3.11 Using a web browser, access the Java API documentation for the predefined class *Math*. (If you don't have the documentation locally, it can be accessed through the document *http://java.sun.com/apis.html.*) Scan the class definition. What package contains this class?

Are all the methods in this class static?

SELF-STUDY EXERCISE SOLUTIONS

3.1 `mrBill.poke(steelGuy);`

3.2 `count = thePile.sticks();`

3.3
```
/**
 * Set this Counter to the specified value.
 */
public void set (int value) {
    tally = value;
}
```

3.4 `myCounter.set(3);`

3.5 The statement is a local variable declaration: it creates and initializes a local variable, and has no effect on the instance variable.

3.6   An instance variable stores some aspect of an object's state: the value of some property of the object; a parameter is used to pass information from a client to the server when the client invokes a server method or constructor; a local variable is used to store a temporary result during execution of a method or constructor.

None can be accessed directly by a client. (An argument provided by the client is used to initialize a parameter; but the client cannot directly access the variable.)

3.7   *a.*   client; server (or method, or object executing the method)

b.   functional test; unit test

c.   main

3.8
```
System.out.println("day: " + day + ", month: " + month
    + ", year: " + year);
```

3.9
```
public void runTest () {
    TrafficSignal signal = new TrafficSignal();
    testInitialState(signal);
    testChange(signal);
}
```

3.10   The test for a feature is written before the feature is implemented. Then the feature is implemented to satisfy the test.

CHAPTER 4   **Conditions**

In the previous chapters, we saw how to implement methods using method invocations and simple assignment and return statements. In this chapter, we introduce *conditions* and *conditional statements*. By using conditional statements, a method can behave in different ways depending on state of the object. As we'll see, this is essential for building objects that are at all interesting.

We also introduce the notions of *precondition*, *postcondition*, and *class invariant*. Together, these play a fundamental role in system design and verification of program correctness. Preconditions and postconditions form an essential part of a method's specification.

Along the way, we look in detail at *boolean expressions*: expressions that produce a boolean value when evaluated. Boolean expressions are used to express preconditions and postconditions, and are an integral part of conditional statements.

Objectives

After studying this chapter you should understand the following:

- the notions of preconditions, postconditions, and invariants;
- the purpose of a conditional statement;
- the function of boolean expressions;
- the purpose of a compound statement.

Also, you should be able to:

- write and evaluate boolean expressions;
- write conditional statements of various forms;
- implement methods that use conditional statements;
- implement a class tester which automatically verifies test results.

4.1   Conditional statements

We implemented several classes in the previous chapters. Now we'll extend the specifications a bit, and see some new algorithmic constructs to support the extended specification.

Postconditions and invariants

The class *Counter*, as developed in Chapter 2, is shown in Listing 4.1. The method cur-rentCount is specified as

```
/**
 * The number of items counted.
 */
public int currentCount () { ...
```

The specification stipulates that a client invoking the method is delivered a value of type **int**. We remarked previously that we could be more precise in specifying the result of the query: the integer result is non-negative. That is, for every *Counter* object, the query currentCount will always return a value greater than or equal to zero. We now include this in the doc comment for the method:

```
/**
 * The number of items counted.
 *
 * @ensure  this.currentCount() >= 0
 */
public int currentCount () { ...
```

The word "@ensure" is a *javadoc tag*. Tags are recognized by *javadoc* and used to format the documentation generated. The notation is not part of the programming language Java. Remember that comments are ignored by the compiler, and can contain anything at all.

The comment tells the client that the implementor guarantees that the method will deliver a result that is greater than or equal to 0. (">=" means "greater than or equal to"; it's the way we write "≥" in Java.) Such a commitment is called a *postcondition*. It is a condition that the implementor promises will be satisfied when the method completes execution. We sometimes use the word "result" in a comment to refer to the value returned by a query. For instance, we could have written the postcondition as

```
 * @ensure   result >= 0
```

Even though the postcondition is included in a comment, it is an important part of the method specification. The correctness of a client will generally depend on the postcondition being satisfied.

We can write anything in a comment, and it will be ignored by the compiler. Since the return type of the method is defined as **int**,

```
public int currentCount () ...
```

Listing 4.1   **The class *Counter***

```java
/**
 * A simple integer counter.
 */
public class Counter {

    private int count;       // current count

    /**
     * Create a new Counter, with the count initialized
     * to 0.
     */
    public Counter () {
        count = 0;
    }

    /**
     * The number of items counted.
     */
    public int currentCount () {
        return count;
    }

    /**
     * Increment the count by 1.
     */
    public void incrementCount () {
        count = count + 1;
    }

    /**
     * Reset the count to 0.
     */
    public void reset () {
        count = 0;
    }

}
```

the compiler will make sure that the value returned is an **int**. But neither the compiler nor the run-time system will make sure the result is not negative. In a sense, documentation is little more than advertising. The implementor must make sure that the method satisfies its specification.

The query currentCount returns the value stored in the private instance variable count. We need to make sure that this instance variable will never contain a negative value. We document this as well:

```
private int count;      // current count
                        // invariant: count >= 0
```

The assertion that count will always be non-negative is called a *class invariant*. An *invariant* is a condition that will always hold true. A *class invariant* is an invariant concerning instance properties that will always be true of all instances of the class.

But still, all we've done is advertise. To make sure that the invariant holds, we need to examine every place in the program where the variable is given a value and verify that it can never be given a negative value.

There are three places where count is set: in the constructor, where it is given an initial value of 0; in the method reset, where it is set to 0; and in the method incrementCount, where it is incremented by 1. Clearly a variable that can be set only to 0 and incremented will never contain a negative value. Thus we can conclude that the implementation conforms to the specification, that is, the implementation is correct.

---

postcondition: a condition the implementor guarantees will hold when a method or constructor completes execution.

invariant: a condition that always holds true.

class invariant: an invariant regarding properties of class instances; that is, a condition that will always be true for all instances of a class.

Suppose we add a command to decrement the count, which we specify as follows:

```
public void decrementCount ()
        Decrement the count by 1.
```

Now we have a design decision to make. What should happen if the method decrementCount is invoked when the count is 0? If we decide that the count can have a negative value, we must remove the postcondition from the specification of currentCount. We no longer guarantee that count will return a value greater than or equal to 0. On the other hand, if we decide that the count should never be negative, we must specify what happens in the case where decrementCount is invoked with the count 0. Lets adopt the latter approach and specify the method as:

```
public void decrementCount ()
        Decrement positive count by 1; zero count remains zero.
```

The assignment statement

```
count = count - 1;
```

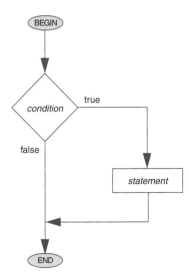

Figure 4.1 **An *if-then* statement.**

will decrement the count. But we need to make sure that this statement is done only when
count is greater than 0. We want to *guard* the assignment statement with the condition
"count > 0." To do this, we need a new kind of statement called a *conditional* statement. A conditional statement permits us to specify the conditions under which an action
is to be performed. That is, it lets us specify that a certain action is to be performed only if
appropriate conditions are met. We look at two variants, called *if-then* and *if-then-else*.

4.1.1 The *if-then* statement

An *if-then* statement has the form

```
if (condition)
    statement
```

Note that this is a *composite* statement. It includes another statement as a component. This
component statement can be any kind of statement at all, even another if-then statement.

The meaning is straightforward. The condition is evaluated, and if it is *true* the
included statement is performed. If the condition is *false*, the included statement is not
performed. The condition "guards" the included statement. This is illustrated in
Figure 4.1.

We can use an if-then to guard the assignment in the method decrementCount:

```
/**
 * Decrement positive count by 1;
 * zero count remains zero
 */
```

```
public void decrementCount () {
    if (count > 0)
        count = count - 1;
}
```

Now the assignment is done only if `count` is positive. If `count` is 0, the assignment is not done and the value of `count` remains 0.

(Notice our convention for indenting. The statement that makes up the "body" of the if-then is indented a uniform amount from the keyword **if**.)

A number of questions remain to be answered. In particular, we need to take a more complete and careful look at conditions. But first, we introduce another variant of the conditional statement, the *if-then-else*.

DrJava: using if-then

Open `Counter.java`, located in `counters`, in `ch4`, in `nhText`. (If you already have a class named `Counter` open, you should close it, using the *Close* option from the *File* menu.)

1. Add the method `decrementCount` as described above. Be sure to include appropriate documentation. Save and compile.

2. In the *Interactions* pane, create a *Counter* and test it, verifying that the `decrementCount` method works properly.

3. Add a parameter `maxValue` to the *Counter* constructor. This is the maximum value a *Counter* can record.

4. Modify the method `incrementCount` so that it will increment the count only if the count is less than the maximum value provided in the constructor. When the counter reaches the maximum value, further invocations of `incrementCount` leave it unchanged.

   Be sure to properly document the constructor and the method `incrementCount`. Note that you ***should not*** refer to private instance variables in doc comments. For example, if you store the maximum value of the count in a variable named `maxCount`, you cannot refer to this variable in a doc comment. Instance variables are part of the implementation and not part of the specification visible to a user of the class.

5. Save, compile, and test. Be sure to test `decrementCount` after max count has been reached.

4.1.2 The *if-then-else* statement

Take a look at the implementation of the *Explorer* method `takeThat` from the previous chapter:

```
public void takeThat (int hitStrength) {
    tolerance = tolerance - hitStrength;
}
```

If the argument `hitStrength` is greater than `tolerance`, `tolerance` becomes negative. Let's suppose we want to consider an *Explorer* with a tolerance of 0 to be defeated, and restrict the tolerance of an *Explorer* to be a non-negative integer. As before, we document this as a postcondition for the query and as an invariant of the instance variable:

```
private int tolerance;    // current tolerance
                          // invariant: tolerance >= 0

/**
 * Damage (hit points) required to defeat
 * this Explorer.
 *
 * @ensure   tolerance >= 0
 */
public int tolerance () {
    return tolerance;
}
```

The variable `tolerance` is assigned a value in the constructor, where it is given its initial value, and in the method `takeThat` where it is reduced. We need to ensure that the value assigned in each case is not negative.

First consider the `takeThat` method. As we said above, the variable `tolerance` will be assigned a negative value if the argument provided by the client, `hitStrength`, is greater than the current value of `tolerance`. To prevent this, we can guard the assignment as we did above:

```
public void takeThat (int hitStrength) {
    if (hitStrength <= tolerance)
        tolerance = tolerance - hitStrength;
}
```

("`<=`" means "less than or equal." It's the way we write "≤" in Java.)

Now the assignment is done only if `hitStrength` is less than or equal to the current value of `tolerance`. If `hitStrength` is 10 and `tolerance` is 15, then tolerance will be reduced to 5. But if `hitStrength` is 10 and `tolerance` is 5, nothing will be done, and `tolerance` will remain 5. This is clearly not correct. If `hitStrength` is greater than `tolerance`, we want `tolerance` to be reduced to 0, its minimum value. We can try to accomplish this by writing two guarded statements:

```
public void takeThat (int hitStrength) {

    if (hitStrength <= tolerance)
        tolerance = tolerance - hitStrength;
```

```
        if (hitStrength > tolerance)
            tolerance = 0;
}
```

Let's be clear about what's happening here. We have written two if-then statements that will be done one after the other in the order written. In the first, we decide whether or not to do the assignment

```
        tolerance = tolerance - hitStrength;
```

Then, as a separate and independent decision, we decide whether or not to do the assignment `tolerance = 0;`. This is illustrated in Figure 4.2.

We mean these two alternatives to be exclusive, that is, we intend to do one or the other of the assignments, but not both. Is it possible for both conditions to be true? The answer is yes, because they are evaluated at different times. Suppose `tolerance` is 75, and the method is called with an argument of 50. The first condition is true, and the assign-

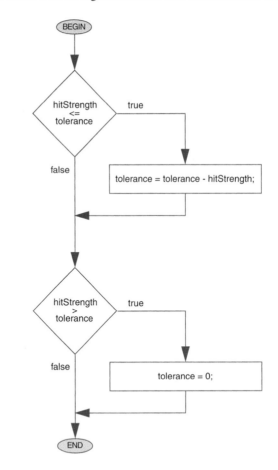

Figure 4.2 Two consecutive *if-then* statements.

ment sets tolerance to 25. Now the second if-then is done, and since `tolerance` has been changed to 25, this condition is also true: `tolerance` is set to 0. Clearly this is not what we want to happen.

We could correct the problem by reversing the order of the if-then statements:

```
if (hitStrength > tolerance)
    tolerance = 0;

if (hitStrength <= tolerance)
    tolerance = tolerance - hitStrength;
}
```

A better approach is to use an *if-then-else* statement. The form is

```
if (condition)
    statement₁
else
    statement₂
```

This is also a composite statement, having two component statements. As with the if-then, the included statements can be any kind of statements at all.

If the condition is true, *statement₁* is executed; if the condition is false, *statement₂* is done. That is, we choose to do either *statement₁* or *statement₂*, but not both, depending on the condition. This is shown in Figure 4.3.

We can now implement the method using an if-then-else:

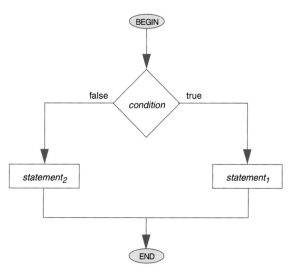

Figure 4.3 **An *if-then-else* statement.**

```
public void takeThat (int hitStrength) {
    if (hitStrength <= tolerance)
        tolerance = tolerance - hitStrength;
    else
        tolerance = 0;
}
```

If the argument (hitStrength) provided by the client is 20, for instance, and the value of tolerance is 100, then hitStrength <= tolerance is true, and first assignment is done: tolerance is assigned 80. On the other hand, if hitStrength is 20 and tolerance is 10, then hitStrength <= tolerance is false, and the "else" part is done: tolerance is assigned 0.

Finally, we must examine the constructor. Recall that an initial value is given to the instance variable tolerance in the constructor:

```
public Explorer (String name, Room location,
                 int strength, int tolerance) {
    ...
    this.tolerance = tolerance;
    ...
}
```

Suppose the constructor is called with a negative value for the parameter tolerance. What should we do in this case? A reasonable approach seems to be to give the *Explorer* the lowest possible tolerance value, namely 0. This will do for now. We write the following in the constructor:

```
public Explorer (String name, Room location,
                 int strength, int tolerance) {
    ...
    if (tolerance >= 0)
        this.tolerance = tolerance;
    else
        this.tolerance = 0;
    ...
}
```

These changes guarantee that the instance variable tolerance will never have a negative value, and thus the value returned by the query tolerance will be greater than or equal to 0.

DrJava: continuing the Counter

Open Counter.java, in counters, in ch4, in nhText. You should have modified this class by adding the method decrementCount and by adding a maximum count, as explained on page 180.

We want to add functionality to the *Counter* that allows the client to determine if the maximum count has been exceeded.

1. Add a **boolean** valued method named maximumExceeded. This method will return true if the command incrementCount has been invoked after the maximum value was reached. For now, you can leave it a stub. Save and compile.

2. Add a **boolean** instance variable to remember whether or not the maximum count has been exceeded. Make sure that it is properly initialized in the constructor. Modify maximumExceeded to return the value of this variable. Save, compile, and test.

3. Modify incrementCount so that the count is incremented if it is less than the maximum, and maximum exceeded is set to true otherwise. Modify reset so that it sets maximum exceeded to false. Save, recompile, and test.

DrJava: using the Debugger

DrJava includes a "debugger" that allows you to stop a computation at any point, and to watch the values of variables. We'll use the debugger to step through execution of the flawed implementation of the takeThat method, given on page 181.

Open Explorer.java, located in mazeGame, in ch4, in nhText. This file contains an "abbreviated" version of the *Explorer* class introduced in the previous chapter.

1. Turn on *Debug Mode*, by selecting it from the *Debugger* pull-down menu. (A debugger window will appear.)

2. In the edit window, click on the first line of the takeThat method. (The line that reads "if (hitStrength <= tolerance).")

3. Set a "breakpoint" on this line, by choosing *Toggle Breakpoint on Current Line* from the *Debugger* menu. The line will be highlighted in red. Computation will pause whenever this line is reached.

4. In the *Interactions* pane, create an *Explorer*. Note that the constructor needs only two integer arguments, representing strength and tolerance.

    ```
    > import mazeGame.*;
    > Explorer myHero = new Explorer(10,100);
    ```

5. Invoke the *Explorer*'s takeThat method:

    ```
    > myHero.takeThat(10);
    ```

    Execution of the method pauses when the breakpoint is reached. The line about to be executed is highlighted.

6. Click the *Watches* tab in the debug window. In the field labeled *Name*, key tolerance (and press *Return* or *Enter*). Note that the current value (100) of the variable is displayed.

7. Click *Step Into*, on the right side of the debug window. The current line is executed and the highlighting moves to the next line, that is, to the first assignment statement.

8. Click *Step Into* again. The assignment statement is executed, and the value of `tolerance` changes to 90.

9. Click *Step Into* one more time, and notice that the second assignment statement is skipped. Click *Resume*, and execution of the method completes.

10. Invoke the *Explorer*'s `takeThat` method again, this time with an argument value of 50:

    ```
    > myHero.takeThat(50);
    ```

    Again, step through the method by repeatedly clicking *Step Into*. Notice that this time, both conditions are true and both assignment statements are executed, leaving `tolerance` with the incorrect value of 0.

4.1.3 Compound statements

Before turning to the question of what conditions look like in general, let's see how we can combine a group of statements into one.

The if-then and if-then-else constructs allow only a single statement to be given as an option. The if-then has the form

```
if (condition)
    statement
```

and the if-then-else has the form

```
if (condition)
    statement₁
else
    statement₂
```

In each case, a single statement is to be done if the condition is true, and in the if-then-else, a single statement is to be done if the condition is false.

This seems a bit restrictive. Suppose the alternatives we want to choose from consist of several statements. For instance, suppose we wanted to set both `strength` and `tolerance` to 0 in the event that `takeThat` was called with an argument greater than `tolerance`. We could not simply write

```
if (hitStrength <= tolerance)
    tolerance = tolerance - hitStrength;
else
    tolerance = 0;
✗    strength = 0;
```

Despite the misleading indention, the "else" part of the conditional consists only of the single assignment

```
tolerance = 0;
```

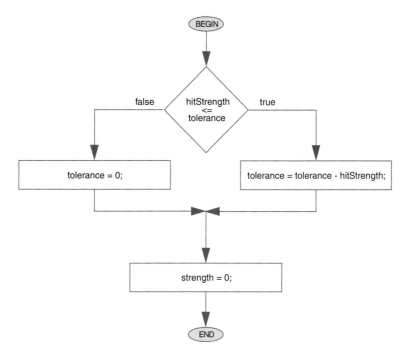

Figure 4.4 **The *else* part consists of a single statement.**

The assignment to `strength` *follows* the conditional. It is an entirely different statement and will be done no matter what the value of the conditional. This is illustrated in Figure 4.4.

If we put a sequence of statements between a pair of braces:

$$\{ \ statement_1 \ \ statement_2 \ \dots \ statement_N \ \}$$

the resulting construct is called a *block* or *compound statement*. The statements are simply done one after the other, in the order in which they are written. A compound statement is syntactically considered to be a *single statement*. The single statements specified as part of an if-then or if-then-else construct can be compound statements, as illustrated below. Note the convention for placement of the braces.

```
if (condition) {                    if (condition) {
    statement₁                          statement1₁

    ...                                 ...

    statementₙ                          statement1ₙ
}                                   } else {
                                        statement2₁

                                        ...

                                        statement2ₘ
                                    }
```

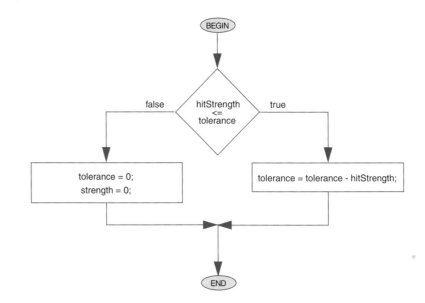

Figure 4.5 **The *else* part is a compound statement.**

We can now combine the two assignment statements from the preceding example into a single compound statement:

```
if (hitStrength <= tolerance)
    tolerance = tolerance - hitStrength;
else {
    tolerance = 0;
    strength = 0;
}
```

This is shown in Figure 4.5. We'll see many examples of these structures in subsequent chapters.

4.2   Boolean expressions

A condition, as described above, is either *true* or *false*. You may recall that the primitive type **boolean** introduced in Section 1.2.1 has two values, *true* and *false*. So when a condition is evaluated, a value of type **boolean** is the result. A condition is a *boolean expression*. Boolean expressions are fundamentally similar to the arithmetic expressions seen in Section 2.4. Arithmetic expressions produce arithmetic values when evaluated: values of type **int**, **double**, *etc*. Boolean expressions produce **boolean** values when evaluated.

Just as we have **int** literals to denote particular values of type **int**, and **int** variables that contain values of type **int**, we also have **boolean** literals and variables. We have been introduced to the **boolean** literals **true** and **false** in Section 1.9.2. A **boolean** variable can be defined just like any other type of variable. For instance, given the declarations

```
private boolean tooBig;
private int size;
```

the identifier `tooBig` denotes a portion of memory that holds a **boolean** value just as the identifier `size` denotes a portion of memory that holds an **int**. An assignment statement can be used to store a **boolean** value in a **boolean** variable. For example, note the similarities in the following pairs of statements:

```
tooBig = true;
size = 10;
```

and

```
tooBig = size > 10;
size = size + 1;
```

If `size` is 10, `size > 10` is a **boolean** expression yielding false when evaluated, just as `size + 1` is an **int** expression yielding 11 when evaluated.

The boolean expressions we have seen so far, involving operators such as < and <=, are called *relational expressions*. We'll introduce additional boolean expressions as we need them. A comprehensive presentation can be found in Section 4.5.

4.3   Handling multiple cases

One way of thinking about a conditional statement is that it divides the problem into *cases* that can be considered independently. The if-then-else in the method `takeThat`, for instance, separates the problem into the case where

```
hitStrength <= tolerance
```

and the case where

```
hitStrength > tolerance
```

takeThat:	
case: hitStrength <= tolerance tolerance = tolerance - hitStrength	case: hitStrength > tolerance tolerance = 0

In many problems, there are more than two cases, or the cases need to be further divided into subcases. These situations can be handled by nesting conditional statements.

That is, the component statements of an if-then or if-then-else can themselves be conditional statements.

Suppose we are implementing the class *Date*, suggested in Section 1.2.2. Instances of the class represent calendar dates, and have properties *year*, *month*, and *day*. We would like to implement a query that will tell whether or not the date occurs in a leap year. That is, we want to implement the method:

> **public boolean** isLeapYear ()
> This *Date* occurs in a leap year.

Note that this is a **boolean** method: when invoked, it will return either true or false. We commonly name a boolean method with an adjectival predicate describing the "true" case: isLeapYear, isOpen, isGreen, *etc.* When we document the method, we also describe the "true" case. For instance, if myBirthday is a *Date*, then the invocation

> myBirthday.isLeapYear()

will return true if "this *Date* (*i.e.*, myBirthday) occurs in a leap year."

We assume the Gregorian calendar rule, a year is a leap year if it is divisible by 4, unless it is also divisible by 100, in which case it is a leap year if and only if it is divisible by 400. For example, 1900 is not a leap year even though it is divisible by 4, but 2000 is a leap year.

Suppose the instance variable year contains the *year* attribute of a *Date*:

> **private int** year;   // the year

Now if we consider the rule given above, it should occur to us to divide the problem into the case where the year is divisible by 4, and the case where it is not:

isLeapYear:	
case: year divisible by 4 ???	case: year not divisible by 4 not a leap year

The "year divisible by 4" case needs to be further divided into subcases depending on whether or not the year is divisible by 100:

isLeapYear:		
case: year divisible by 4		case: year not divisible by 4 not a leap year
case: year divisible by 100 ???	case: year not divisible by 100 a leap year	

We could further subdivide the "year divisible by 100" case, but at this point, we'd rather just write the method.

How do we say "year divisible by 4" in Java? We use the remainder operator % (page 84) to compute the remainder of year divided by 4,

> year % 4

and see if that value is 0. The equality operator == is used to determine if two values are equal. (Remember that a single equal sign, =, denotes *assignment* and *not equality*.) So the following condition will be *true* exactly when the value of year is divisible by 4:

```
year % 4 == 0
```

Similar expressions can be used to determine if year is divisible by 100 or 400.

We use a local **boolean** variable aLeapYear to store the value we want to return. Look carefully at the statement

```
aLeapYear = (year % 400 == 0);
```

This is an assignment statement, storing a **boolean** value into the variable aLeapYear. The expression on the left of the assignment operator is a **boolean** expression that evaluates to true or false depending on whether or not year is divisible by 400.[1]

In the implementation below, note how the subcases are handled by nested conditionals. That is, one of the statements that comprise the outer if-then-else is itself an if-then-else. This is fine. An if-then-else is a kind of statement. The syntactic structure of this method is shown in Figure 4.6:

```
/**
 * This Date occurs in a leap year.
 */
public boolean isLeapYear () {
    boolean aLeapYear;
    if (year % 4 == 0)
        if (year % 100 == 0)
            // if divisible by 100,
            // must also be divisible by 400
            aLeapYear = (year % 400 == 0);
        else // divisible by 4, not by 100
            aLeapYear = true;
    else // not divisible by 4
        aLeapYear = false;
    return aLeapYear;
}
```

The TrafficSignal

Let's look again at the *TrafficSignal* class that we implemented in Chapter 2. Recall that we used values 0, 1, and 2 to represent the green, yellow, and red lights. Our implementation of the method change depended on this representation:

```
public void change () {
    light = (light + 1) % 3;
}
```

---

1. The parentheses are not required in the assignment. They are included to improve readability.

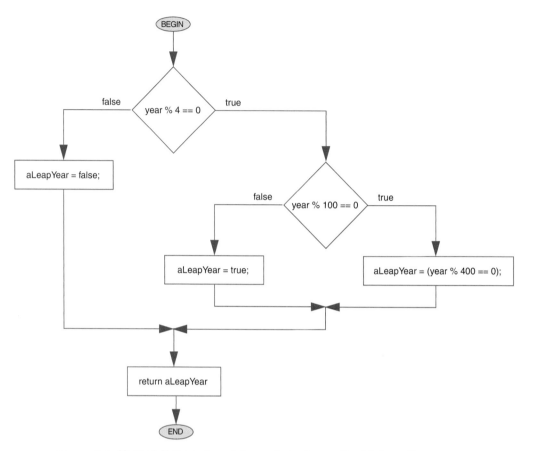

Figure 4.6 **Nested *if-then-else* statements in the method *isLeapYear*.**

Now we'll write a version that is independent of the particular values chosen to encode the lights.

Sometimes a problem naturally splits into more than two equivalent cases. There are clearly three cases here, depending on the current state of the signal:

change:		
case: light is GREEN change to YELLOW	case: light is YELLOW change to RED	case: light is RED change to GREEN

One way to handle multiple cases is to "cascade" if-then-else statements, that is, write a sequence of nested if-then-else statements in which a single case is handled in the true branch, and the false branch consists of another if-then-else:

```
if (case1)
    handleCase1
else if (case2)
    handleCase2
...
else if (penultimateCase)
    handlePenultimateCase
else
    handleLastCase
```

Even though we think of them as alternatives at the same level, the structure is actually a collection of nested conditionals. Using this structure, we write:

```java
public void change () {
    if (light == GREEN)
        light = YELLOW;
    else if (light == YELLOW)
        light = RED;
    else // light == RED
        light = GREEN;
}
```

Suppose we decide to add a left-turn arrow to the signal, and have the signal cycle from left-turn arrow to green to yellow to red. A *TrafficSignal* object now has four different states. We add a named constant representing the left arrow,

```java
public static final int LEFT_ARROW = ...;
```

and add this case to the method:

```java
public void change () {
    if (light == GREEN)
        light = YELLOW;
    else if (light == YELLOW)
        light = RED;
    else if (light == RED)
        light = LEFT_ARROW;
    else  // light == LEFT_ARROW
        light = GREEN;
}
```

(Of course, we must change the specification of the query `light`, adding `Traffic-Signal.LEFT_ARROW` as one of the possible values returned.) The implementation is illustrated in Figure 4.7:

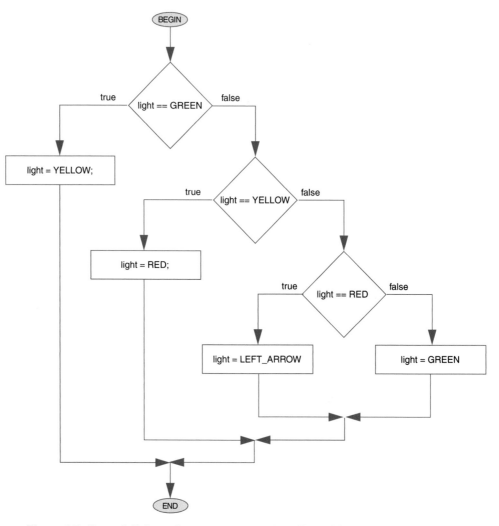

Figure 4.7 **Nested *if-then-else* statements to handle multiple cases.**

DrJava: checking the Date

Open `Date.java`, located in `date`, in `ch4`, in `nhText`. This contains the definition of a simple *Date* class, that includes the `isLeapYear` method defined above.

1. In the *Interactions* pane, create several *Date* objects and test the `isLeapYear` method.

    ```
    > import date.*;
    > Date noLeap1 = new Date(10,29,1943);
    > Date noLeap2 = new Date(1,1,1900);
    ```

```
> Date Leap1 = new Date(16,6,1904);
> Date Leap2 = new Date(2,2,2000);
```

2. Using the debugger as explained above, step through execution of the `isLeapYear` method and make sure you understand the flow of control as the method is executed.

3. If you are up to it, define a **boolean**-valued method `isLegalDate`. This method should return true if the *Date* is a legal date after 1752, and false otherwise. For instance, the method will return false for a date like February 29, 1943 (since 1943 was not a leap year) and for April 31, 2002 (since April has only 30 days). (This method will likely be long and unwieldy.)

4.3.1 Dangling *else*

Before moving to another example, we should mention one additional point about conditional statements. There is an ambiguity as to whether the structure

```
if (condition1)
    if (condition2)
        statement1
else
    statement2
```

is an if-then nested in an if-then-else, or an if-then-else nested in an if-then. That is, which "if" does the "else" go with? Which of the following two possible structures is implied?

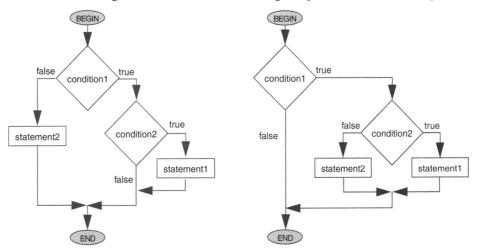

The answer is that an *else* clause is associated with the closest possible *if*. Thus, the figure on the right is correct. If you want an if-then nested in an if-then-else, that is, the figure on the left, you must make the if-then a compound statement by wrapping braces around it:

```
if (condition1) {
    if (condition2)
        statement1
} else
    statement2
```

4.4   Example: a combination lock

For a bit more practice, we develop another example involving conditions. In this example, we model a simple lock with an integer combination. The combination is set into the lock when it is created. To open a closed lock, the client must provide the correct combination.

A lock must know its combination and whether it is locked or unlocked. It must be able to lock and to unlock when provided with the proper combination. Thus the responsibilities of a lock can be summarized as follows.

Combination Lock responsibilities:

know:
>   the combination
>   whether open or closed (*i.e.*, unlocked or locked)

do:
>   close (lock)
>   open (unlock), when given the proper combination

While the lock must know its combination, this will certainly not be a feature available to clients. (If a client can query a lock for its combination, it's not a very secure lock! Here is an example of a property that does not have a corresponding query.) A lock will have only one query, to determine whether it is open or closed. It will have two commands, one to close the lock and one to open it.

Class: *CombinationLock*

queries:

>   *isOpen*   whether or not the lock is open

commands:

>   *close*   lock the lock
>   *open*   unlock the lock (*combination*)

We can write the class specification as follows.

public class CombinationLock
>   A lock with an integer combination.

public CombinationLock (**int** combination)
>   Create a lock with the specified combination.

public boolean isOpen ()
>   This *CombinationLock* is unlocked.

```
public void close ()
        Lock this CombinationLock.

public void open (int combinationToTry)
        Unlock this CombinationLock if the correct combination is
        provided.
```

The query returns a **boolean**: it returns true if the lock is open, false if the lock is closed.

What data should the object contain? The lock is responsible for knowing its combination and whether it is open or closed. We'll use instance variables to store these pieces of information:

```
private int combination;  // lock's combination
private boolean isOpen;   // the lock is unlocked
```

isOpen is a **boolean** variable, containing the value true if the lock is open, false if it is not. As before, we use the same identifier to name both the variable and query. This causes no problems, since the compiler can determine which we are referring to from the context. Note that there is data stored in the object that is not available to the client. A client can't query a lock for its combination. A client can determine only whether the lock is open or closed.

Though this is a simple object with an obvious implementation, let's build a test system before we go further. It's easy to stub an implementation and test system for the class, similar to the one we wrote for *TrafficSignal* in the last chapter. This is shown in Listing 4.2. We assume that all three classes are in the same package. We omit comments in the listing to emphasize the implementation.

We should first write a test for the initial state of a *CombinationLock*. But the constructor specification leaves some questions. Is any integer a legal combination? For instance, can a combination be negative? And does a newly minted lock start life open or closed?

Let's assume that a lock should initially be open, and that only combinations in the range 0 through 999 are legal. We need to include these in the constructor specification. That the lock is initially open is an attribute of the newly created lock. It is something we guarantee about the state of the newly constructed lock. We can express this as a constructor postcondition:

```
/**
 * Create a lock with the specified combination.
 *
 * @ensure     this.isOpen()
 */
public CombinationLock (int combination) ...
```

The requirement that the argument be in a specific range, however, is a requirement on the *client* when invoking the constructor. That is, we want to say the it is legal for a client to invoke this constructor only with an argument in the range 0 through 999. We do this with a *require* tag in the comment:

Listing 4.2   Stubbed implementation of *CombinationLock*

```java
public class CombinationLock {

    private int combination;
    private boolean isOpen;

    public CombinationLock (int combination) {
    }

    public boolean isOpen () {
        return true;
    }

    public void close () {
    }

    public void open (int combinationToTry) {
    }
}


class CombinationLockTest {

    private CombinationLock lock;

    public CombinationLockTest () {
    }

    public void runTest () {
    }
}


public class TestCombinationLock {

    public static void main (String[] argv) {
        (new CombinationLockTest()).runTest();
    }
}
```

```
/**
 * Create a lock with the specified combination.
 *
 * @require    0 <= combination && combination <= 999
 * @ensure     this.isOpen()
 */
public CombinationLock (int combination) ...
```

The operator `&&` is read "and." For the condition to be true, both sides of the `&&` operator must be true. That is, both `0 <= combination` and `combination <= 999` must be true. If either is false, then the entire condition is false. (The `&&` operator is fully explained in Section 4.5.)

The requirement we have added is called a *precondition*. It is a requirement placed on the *client*. The client must make sure that the condition is satisfied when the method is invoked. (Note that a precondition is a requirement on an *object invoking a method or constructor*. It has nothing to do with a user entering data from the console, for instance.) We have more to say about preconditions and postconditions in the next chapter.

---

precondition: a condition the client of a method or constructor must make sure
holds when the method or constructor is invoked.

Now we can proceed writing the test. When we tested the *TrafficSignal* in the last chapter, we created a single instance of the class to test. This was adequate, since one *TrafficSignal* instance behaves like any other. But *CombinationLocks* are created with different combinations. We probably want to test several different locks. In particular, it is a good idea to test locks with the largest and smallest legal combinations. Rather than constructing a single lock to test in the *CombinationLockTest* constructor, we write a method that creates and tests a lock with a given combination:

```
private void testLock (int combination)
        Test a lock with the specified combination.
```

and invoke this method in `runTest` for each lock that we want to test.

We'll test three different locks: one with the smallest possible combination, one with the largest possible, and one other. The method `runTest` invokes `testLock` for each of these locks, and looks like this:

```
public void runTest () {
    testLock(0);
    testLock(123);
    testLock(999);
}
```

Make sure that you understand what is happening here. The method `runTest` will invoke `testLock` three times in succession, passing a different argument value each time. The first time `testLock` is executed, its parameter `combination` will be initialized to 0; the second time, its parameter will be initialized to 123; the third time to 999.

Should we test a lock with an illegal combination? How would we expect an illegal lock to behave? Asking about creating an illegal lock is like asking about dividing by zero. It's not something that can be meaningfully done. So we'll ignore the case in which the argument is not legal. (It's ok if you're not completely convinced this is a good idea. Attribute it to laziness on our part for the present.)

The first thing the testLock method should do is create a lock and run the initial state test:

```
private void testLock (int combination) {
    lock = new CombinationLock(combination);
    testInitialState();
}
```

For instance, the first call to testLock shown above will result in a lock with combination 0 being created.

The initial state test should make sure that the lock is open:

```
private void testInitialState() {
    System.out.println(
        "Initial state: " + lock.isOpen());
}
```

We can't directly access the combination to see if it's correct, so we'll postpone testing the combination until we write a test for the open command.

But wait a minute. When we run the test, we get output that we have to examine manually to make sure that it is correct. This is annoying and error prone. And while it's not such a big deal with the little tests we're writing, we can easily imagine being inundated with output when we test complicated objects. We know what the result of the test should be when we write the test. So why not let the *CombinationLockTest* tell us if the test succeeded? And in fact, we really want to be bothered only if the test fails.

Let's write another little helper method

```
private void verify (boolean test, String message) {
    if (!test)
        System.out.println(
            "Verification failed: " + message);
}
```

This method takes two arguments, a **boolean** and a *String*. The exclamation mark ! is the "not" operator: !test evaluates to true if test is false, and evaluates to false if test is true. So if the **boolean** argument is false, the message is output; if the **boolean** argument is true, the method does nothing at all. Now we can write:

```
private void testInitialState() {
    verify(lock.isOpen(), "initial state");
}
```

When we run the test, we get output only if the test fails. The output will give us a hint as to which test failed.

You might complain that this is more work than just verifying the output manually. But methods like `verify` are generally useful when testing any class, and we have to write the code only once. If we depend on manual verification, we have to check the output every time we run the test. This is a very error prone activity. We often see what we expect to see, and overlook erroneous output. Ultimately we'd like to have a testing framework that provides methods like `verify` and allows us to easily build and run tests.

Implementing the *CombinationLock* constructor and the query `isOpen` is easy. The constructor gives initial values to the instance variables, and the query returns the value stored in the instance variable `isOpen`:

```
public CombinationLock (int combination) {
    this.combination = combination;
    this.isOpen = true;
}

public boolean isOpen () {
    return isOpen;
}
```

Recall that use of the keyword **this** is necessary in the assignment

```
this.combination = combination;
```

The left-hand side refers to the instance variable, and the right-hand side to the parameter. The keyword **this** is not necessary in the assignment

```
this.isOpen = true;
```

We write it just to give some symmetry to the two statements.

One question that comes to mind is what should we do if the argument to the constructor is not legal? For simplicity, we'll assume the argument is legal for now. Dealing with illegal values will be taken up in the next chapter

Next, let's write a test for the method `close`. Clearly, we want to close the lock and then verify that it is not open. There are two possibilities, and we should test both: close an open lock, and close a lock that is already closed. We can cover both, assuming the lock is

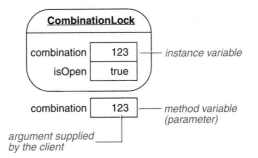

Figure 4.8 **CombinationLock being created.**

initially open, by giving the `close` command twice. We write a method to test `close`, and invoke it from `testLock`:

```
private void testClose() {
    lock.close();
    verify(!lock.isOpen(), "close open lock");
    lock.close();
    verify(!lock.isOpen(), "close closed lock");
}

private void testLock (int combination) {
    lock = new CombinationLock(combination);
    testInitialState();
    testClose();
}
```

The command `close` is also easy to implement:

```
public void close () {
    isOpen = false;
}
```

Finally, we write a test for the method `open`. Here, we have four cases to test:

- closed lock, correct combination: lock opens;
- open lock, correct combination: lock remains open;
- closed lock, incorrect combination: lock remains closed.
- open lock, incorrect combination: lock remains open;

The test depends on the combination, so we pass the correct combination as an argument:

```
private void testOpen (int combination) ...
```

It's easy enough to test the cases with the correct combination. But how do we get an incorrect combination? One way is to add some arbitrary small value to the combination, and then do "`% 1000`" to make sure that the result is in the proper range.

```
private void testOpen (int combination) {
    int badCombination = (combination + 1) % 1000;

    // test with correct combination:
    lock.close();
    lock.open(combination); // open closed lock
    verify(lock.isOpen(), "open closed lock");
    lock.open(combination); // open opened lock
    verify(lock.isOpen(), "open opened lock");

    // test with incorrect combination:
    lock.open(badCombination); // try opened lock
```

```
        verify(lock.isOpen(), "bad comb, opened lock");
        lock.close();
        lock.open(badCombination); // try closed lock
        verify(!lock.isOpen(), "bad comb, closed lock");
    }
```

We add an invocation of this method to testLock:

```
    private void testLock (int combination) {
        lock = new CombinationLock(combination);
        testInitialState();
        testClose();
        testOpen(combination);
    }
```

Note that the argument value passed to testLock is subsequently passed to testOpen.
To implement the method open, we might be inclined to write something like this:

```
    public void open (int combinationToTry) {
        isOpen = this.combination == combinationToTry;
    }
```

The expression on the right of the assignment is a **boolean** expression:

```
        this.combination == combinationToTry
```

It will be true if the value of the instance variable (**this**.combination) is equal to the
argument provided by the client (combinationToTry), and false otherwise. The variable on the left, isOpen, is a **boolean** variable. Thus the format of the assignment is
correct. The value true will be stored in isOpen if the combination provided by the client
is correct, and the value false will be stored if it is not.

But this implementation is not correct. When we run the test, we will see that one of
the testOpen cases fails. The test will produce the following output:

```
        Verification failed: bad comb, opened lock
        Verification failed: bad comb, opened lock
        Verification failed: bad comb, opened lock
```

We get three lines of output because runTest invokes the method testLock three
times. Each time testLock is invoked, it calls testOpen, which produces a line of
output.

Giving the command open to an unlocked lock should have no effect: the lock
should remain open. But consider the case illustrated in Figure 4.9, where the client provides an incorrect combination to an already open lock.
The expression

```
        this.combination == combinationToTry
```

compares 123 to 124 and evaluates to false. This value is then assigned to the instance
variable isOpen, effectively closing the lock. Attempting to open an already opened lock
with a bad combination should not close the lock.

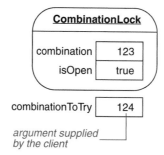

Figure 4.9 **CombinationLock** with method *open* being executed.

The correct implementation of the method uses a conditional statement that opens the lock if the combination is correct, and does nothing if the combination is not correct:

```
public void open (int combinationToTry) {
    if (this.combination == combinationToTry)
        isOpen = true;
}
```

The complete implementations of the lock and test system, again without comments, are given in Listing 4.3. (Note that the instance variable lock of *CombinationLockTest* is set to **null** in the constructor. There is no lock to test until the method testLock is invoked.)

Listing 4.3   The class *CombinationLock* and test system

```
public class CombinationLock {

    private int combination;
    private boolean isOpen;

    public CombinationLock (int combination) {
        this.combination = combination;
        this.isOpen = true;
    }

    public boolean isOpen () {
        return isOpen;
    }

    public void close () {
        isOpen = false;
    }
```

continued

Listing 4.3   The class *CombinationLock* and test system (cont'd)

```
    public void open (int combinationToTry) {
        if (this.combination == combinationToTry)
            isOpen = true;
    }
} // end of class CombinationLock


class CombinationLockTest {

    private CombinationLock lock;

    public CombinationLockTest () {
        this.lock = null;
    }

    public void runTest () {
        testLock(000);
        testLock(123);
        testLock(999);
    }

    private void testLock (int combination) {
        lock = new CombinationLock(combination);
        testInitialState();
        testClose();
        testOpen(combination);
    }

    private void testInitialState() {
        verify(lock.isOpen(), "initial state");
    }

    private void testClose() {
        lock.close();
        verify(!lock.isOpen(), "close opened lock");
        lock.close();
        verify(!lock.isOpen(), "close closed lock");
    }
```

continued

Listing 4.3   The class *CombinationLock* and test system (cont'd)

```java
    private void testOpen(int combination) {
        int badCombination = (combination + 1) % 1000;
        lock.close();
        lock.open(combination);
        verify(lock.isOpen(), "open closed lock");
        lock.open(combination);
        verify(lock.isOpen(), "open opened lock");
        lock.open(badCombination);
        verify(lock.isOpen(), "bad comb, opened lock");

        lock.close();
        lock.open(badCombination);
        verify(!lock.isOpen(), "bad comb, closed lock");
    }

    private void verify (boolean test, String message) {
        if (!test)
            System.out.println(
                "Verification failed: " + message);
    }
} // end of class CombinationLockTest


public class TestCombinationLockClass {

    public static void main (String[] argv) {
        (new CombinationLockTest()).runTest();
    }
}
```

DrJava: testing and modifying locks

Open the file `CombinationLock.java`, in `locks`, in `ch4`, in `nhText`. This file contains the definition of the class *CombinationLock* as described above. The files `CombinationLockTest.java` and `TestCombinationLock.java` contain the test system.

1. Run the test in the *Interactions* pane:

    ```
    > java locks.TestCombinationLock
    ```

    Since the test is successful, you will get no output.

2. Modify the definition of `close` in *CombinationLock* so that it reads

    ```
    isOpen = !isOpen;
    ```

    Save and compile. Is this also a correct implementation of the method?

3. Run the test again and observe the results. Is this what you expected?

4. Modify the *CombinationLock* constructor so that it takes an additional *String* argument, a password.

5. Add a method for changing the combination. The method requires two arguments: a new combination and the password. The combination is changed only if the password matches the password given in the constructor. Use `equals` to compare passwords, rather than `==`. Save and compile.

6. Open `CombinationLockTest.java`. Design and implement "change password test" method, and add its invocation to `testLock`. (Note: you will also need to modify the constructor invocation in `testLock`.) Save, compile, and run.

4.4.1 A digit-by-digit lock

As a final example, let's refine our model a bit and construct a lock in which the combination is entered one digit at a time. As before, we'll assume the lock has a three-digit combination. To open the lock, the client provides digits one at a time. If the client enters the three digits of the combination in order, the lock opens.

There are actually quite a few possible sequences of operations that can happen here, and we need a bit of analysis to make sure we understand the problem. To begin with, it doesn't matter how many digits the client provides, as long as the combination is given. For instance, if the combination is 123, we might observe the following:

Digit Entered	Lock Status
4	closed
1	closed
2	closed
4	closed
3	closed
1	closed
2	closed
3	open

Once the lock is open, entering additional digits doesn't close it:

Digit Entered	Lock Status
1	closed
2	closed
3	open
4	open
7	open

What happens if the client gives the command close when the combination has been partly entered? Does it matter if the lock is open or closed at the time?

Client Command	Lock Status
enter 1	closed
enter 2	closed
close	closed
enter 3	?

Client Command	Lock Status
enter 1	open
enter 2	open
close	closed
enter 3	?

We will specify that the command close resets the lock, so that the entire combination must be entered after close. In particular, the lock will not open after the digit 3 is entered in either of the above two cases.

And a final note. If the combination is partly entered correctly, and an incorrect digit is entered, we may or may not have to start over, depending on the combination. For instance, if the combination is 123 and the digits 1-2-2 are entered, we need three digits to open the lock:

Digit Entered	Lock Status	
1	closed	(need 2-3 to open)
2	closed	(need 3 to open)
2	closed	(need 1-2-3 to open)

On the other hand, if the combination is 223 and the digits 2-2-2 are entered, a 3 will still open the lock:

Digit Entered	Lock Status	
2	closed	(need 2-3 to open)
2	closed	(need 3 to open)
2	closed	(still need 3 to open)

Even after entering the third 2, the last two digits entered are still the first two digits of the combination.

We should have a fairly good idea of how the object works now and be able to write the specification. As before, the combination is set when the lock is created, and the only query is to determine whether the lock is open or closed. There will be a command to close the lock, but rather than an open command as we had above, there will be a command to enter a single digit. That is, we expect the lock to be able to accept the combination one digit at a time. A client must invoke the command at least three consecutive times to open the lock.

public class CombinationLock
    A lock with a three digit combination.

public CombinationLock (**int** combination)
>Create a lock with a given three digit combination;
>combination values < 100 are assumed to have leading zeros.
>
>**require:**
>>0 <= combination && combination <= 999
>
>**ensure:**
>>this.isOpen()

public boolean isOpen ()
>This lock is unlocked.

public void close ()
>Lock and reset this lock; partially entered combination is lost.

public void enter (**int** digit)
>Enter a digit of the combination; lock unlocks if the three digits of
>the combination are entered in order.
>
>**require:**
>>0 <= digit && digit <= 9

Before we proceed with the implementation, let's carefully specify the lock's responsibilities. What does the object need to know? As before, it needs to know the combination and whether it is open or closed. But it also needs to remember how much of the combination has been successfully entered. That is, if the combination is 456, and the digit 4 is entered, the lock must remember that the first combination digit has been entered and that it should open if the second and third are entered next. If the digit 5 is then entered, it must remember that the first two digits of the combination have been successfully entered, and it should open if the third is entered next. There are any number of ways to accomplish this. Probably the most straightforward is for the lock to remember the three digits last entered. If these match the combination, the lock opens. We summarize:

Combination Lock responsibilities:

know:
>the three-digit combination
>whether open or closed, that is, unlocked or locked
>the last three digits entered

do:
>close (lock)
>open (unlock), when given the proper combination
>accept a digit

We are now ready to develop the implementation. We keep the information as to whether the lock is open or not in a **boolean** variable as before. But rather than keeping the combination as a single integer, we keep the three digits separately. Thus a lock instance will have the following instance variables.

```
private boolean isOpen;    // the lock is unlocked
```

```
private int digit1;        // 1st combination digit
private int digit2;        // 2nd combination digit
private int digit3;        // 3rd combination digit
// invariant:
// digit1 >= 0 && digit1 <= 9 &&
// digit2 >= 0 && digit2 <= 9 &&
// digit3 >= 0 && digit3 <= 9
```

We also store the last three digits entered as separate integers. The value −1 will serve to indicate that a particular digit has not been entered, since this value cannot be a legally entered digit.

```
// last, secondToLast, thirdToLast are the last three
// digits entered, with last the most recent.
// a value of -1 indicates the digit has not been
// entered.
private int last;
private int secondToLast;
private int thirdToLast;
// invariant:
// -1 <= last && last <= 9 &&
// -1 <= secondToLast && secondToLast <= 9 &&
// -1 <= thirdToLast && thirdToLast <= 9
```

If the combination is 223, and the digits 2-2 have been entered to a closed lock, the object will look as shown in Figure 4.10.

We'll leave the test system as an exercise for the reader, and just implement the class. We start with the constructor. The client provides a three-digit integer as combination. The first question is how do we separate this integer value into its constituent digits? That is, if the client provides the integer 123 as argument, how do we get the 1, 2, and 3 to store into the instance variables digit1, digit2, and digit3? If we look at the operations

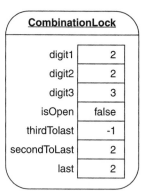

Figure 4.10 **Almost open *CombinationLock.***

available for integer values described in Section 2.4, integer quotient (/) and remainder (%) look promising. The integer quotient of 123 divided by 10 is 12; the remainder is 3.

$$123 \ / \ 10 \quad \Rightarrow \quad 12 \qquad\qquad 123 \ \% \ 10 \quad \Rightarrow \quad 3$$

These are exactly the operations we need to separate the number into its component digits:

```
public CombinationLock (int combination) {
    digit3 = combination % 10;
    combination = combination / 10;
    digit2 = combination % 10;
    digit1 = combination / 10;
    isOpen = true;
    last = -1;
    secondToLast = -1;
    thirdToLast = -1
}
```

If the argument is 123, then

the first assignment assigns 3 to digit3;
the second assignment assigns 12 to combination;
the third assignment assigns 2 to digit2;
the fourth assignment assigns 1 to digit1.

(Note: we might want to save the original combination value as well, for testing purposes.)
The query isOpen is the same as before.

```
public boolean isOpen () {
    return isOpen;
}
```

The command close has a little more work to do, since it also resets the lock.

```
public void close () {
    open = false;
    last = -1;
    secondToLast = -1;
    thirdToLast = -1;
}
```

Finally, we must implement the command enter. This method must set the instance variables last, secondToLast, thirdToLast, and isOpen. The digit being entered becomes the most recent digit entered (last); the previous last digit becomes the second to last, and so on. Finally, if the three digits match the combination, the lock opens. Note that the first three assignment statements cannot be written in a different order.

```
public void enter (int digit) {
    thirdToLast = secondToLast;
    secondToLast = last;
    last = digit;
```

```
        if (thirdToLast == digit1 && secondToLast == digit2
            && last == digit3)
          isOpen = true;
    }
```

The complete class definition is given in Listing 4.4.

4.5   Java in detail: Boolean expressions

We've already seen several examples of the most common kind of boolean expressions, *relational expressions*. A relational expression is composed of two arithmetic expressions joined with a *relational* or *equality* operator. These operators are:

$<$ less than
$<=$ less than or equal
$>$ greater than
$>=$ greater than or equal
$==$ equal
$!=$ not equal

For instance, if i1, i2, and i3 are **int** variables with values 10, –20, and 30, respectively, then

$$i1 < 12 \Rightarrow \textbf{true} \qquad\qquad i1 < 10 \Rightarrow \textbf{false}$$
$$i1 <= 10 \Rightarrow \textbf{true} \qquad\qquad i2 > 0 \Rightarrow \textbf{false}$$
$$i3 == i1 \Rightarrow \textbf{false} \qquad 2*i1 == i2+40 \Rightarrow \textbf{true}$$
$$i1 != 2 \Rightarrow \textbf{true} \qquad i2*(-1) != i1+i1 \Rightarrow \textbf{false}$$

Remember that "equals" is denoted with the operator $==$. A single equal sign, of course, denotes assignment.

A few further observations. Suppose we wanted to express the condition that the value of i1 was between 0 and 20. We might be tempted to write something like this:

✗   `0 < i1 < 20`

The problem is that the relational operators are *binary* and *left associative*. The above line is equivalent to

`(0 < i1) < 20`

which would "evaluate" as

$$(0 < i1) < 20 \Rightarrow \textbf{true} < 20 \Rightarrow ???$$

This is not legal. The left operand is a **boolean** value, and the right operand is an **int**. It is not meaningful to compare a **boolean** value with an **int**: "**true** < 20" is not syntactically correct. The expression $0 < i1 < 20$ does *not* say that i1 is between 0 and 20. To do this, we use the && operator as explained in Section 4.5.2.

Listing 4.4   **The digit by digit *CombinationLock***

===

```
/**
 * A lock with a three digit combination.
 */
public class CombinationLock {

    // Private Components:

    private boolean isOpen;       // the lock is unlocked
    private int digit1;           // 1st combination digit
    private int digit2;           // 2nd combination digit
    private int digit3;           // 3rd combination digit
    // invariant:
    // digit1 >= 0 && digit1 <= 9 &&
    // digit2 >= 0 && digit2 <= 9 &&
    // digit3 >= 0 && digit3 <= 9

    // thirdToLast, secondToLast, last are the last three
    // digits entered, with last the most recent.
    // a value of -1 indicates the digit has not been
    // entered.
    private int thirdToLast;      // the third to last digit
                                  // entered
    private int secondToLast;     // the second to last digit
                                  // entered
    private int last;             // the most recent digit
                                  // entered
    // invariant:
    // thirdToLast >= -1 && thirdToLast <= 9 &&
    // secondToLast >= -1 && secondToLast <= 9 &&
    // last >= -1 && last <= 9

    // Constructors:

    /**
     * Create a lock with the given three digit
     * combination; combination values < 100 are assumed
     * to have leading zeros.
     *
     * @require     0 <= combination && combination <= 999
     * @ensure      this.isOpen()
     */
```

continued

Listing 4.4   **The digit by digit *CombinationLock (cont'd)***

===

```java
public CombinationLock (int combination) {
   digit3 = combination % 10;
   combination = combination / 10;
   digit2 = combination % 10;
   combination = combination / 10;
   digit1 = combination % 10;
   isOpen = true;
   last = -1;
   secondToLast = -1;
   thirdToLast = -1;
}

// Queries:

/**
 * This lock is unlocked.
 */
public boolean isOpen () {
   return isOpen;
}

// Commands:

/**
 * Lock and reset this lock; partially entered
 * combination is lost.
 */
public void close () {
   isOpen = false;
   last = -1;
   secondToLast = -1;
   thirdToLast = -1;
}

/**
 * Enter a digit of the combination; lock unlocks if
 * the three digits of the combination are entered in
 * order.
 *
 * @require    0 <= digit && digit <= 9
 */
```

continued

Listing 4.4   The digit by digit *CombinationLock (cont'd)*

```
public void enter (int digit) {
    thirdToLast = secondToLast;
    secondToLast = last;
    last = digit;
    if (thirdToLast == digit1 && secondToLast == digit2
        && last == digit3)
        isOpen = true;
}


}
```

Second, if one of the operands is an **int** and the other is a **double**, the **int** is converted to a **double** before the comparison is made. (This is similar to how arithmetic operators are handled.)

$$i1 < 2.5 \Rightarrow 10 < 2.5 \Rightarrow 10.0 < 2.5 \Rightarrow \textbf{false}$$

Finally, since floating point values are approximations for real numbers (Section 1.2.1), we must be vary careful comparing floating point numbers for equality or inequality. Values that are mathematically equal may not have identical floating point representations. The following expression, for example, evaluates to *false*:

$$(1.0/6.0+1.0/6.0+1.0/6.0+1.0/6.0+1.0/6.0+1.0/6.0) == 1.0$$
$$\Rightarrow \textbf{false} \ (!)$$

In fact we rarely use the operators == and != with floating point values.

4.5.1 Reference equality and object equality

The equality operators == and != can be used to compare values of any type, including reference values. Two reference values can be legally compared only if they are of the same type. For instance, given the following declarations

```
Counter counter1;
Counter counter2;
Explorer myHero;
```

the expression

```
counter1 == counter2
```

compares the values stored in the two variables for equality. However, the expression

✗   `counter1 == myHero`

is not legal, since `counter1` contains a *reference-to-Counter* and `myHero` contains a *reference-to-Explorer*.

Two reference values are equal when they refer to the *same object*. Sometimes, though, we want to consider two *different* objects as equal. Constructing two *Strings*, for example, is likely to produce two different objects, even if the characters that comprise the *Strings* are identical. For instance, if `string1`, `string2`, and `string3` are *String* variables, and we write

```
string1 = "c";
string2 = "ab" + string1;
string3 = "a" + "bc";
```

then `string2` and `string3` will reference two distinct objects. The expression

```
string2 == string3
```

asks if `string1` and `string2` reference *the same object*, and in this case returns false.

To compare strings for equality, we should use the *String* method `equals`, which returns a **boolean** result. The method invocation

```
string2.equals(string3)
```

returns true if `string2` and `string3` are composed of the same sequence of characters.

(Note: every occurrence of a *String* literal does not result in a new *String* instance being created. For example, if we wrote

```
String hello = "aloha";
String goodbye = "aloha";
```

or even

```
String hello = "al" + "oha";
String goodbye = "alo" + "ha";
```

the compiler would be clever enough to create a single *String* instance containing "aloha" and store references to this instance in the variables `hello` and `goodbye`.)

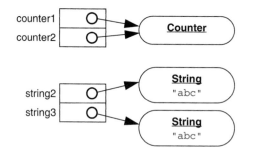

*Figure 4.11 **counter1** == **counter2**, but **string2** != **string3**.*

4.5.2 Boolean operators

There are two binary operators and a unary operator for building composite boolean expressions. The unary operator is written ! and read "not." The binary operators are && and ||, and usually read "and then" and "or else" respectively.[1]

```
! booleanExpression
booleanExpression && booleanExpression
booleanExpression || booleanExpression
```

The "not" operator evaluates to *true* if its operand is *false*, and *vice versa*. If, as above, i1 is an **int** variable with value 10,

```
!(i1 > 9)  ⇒ !(true)  ⇒ false
!(i1 < 9)  ⇒ !(false) ⇒ true
```

Since ! has high precedence (the same as unary + and –), the parentheses are needed in the above expressions. Without them, the expression would not parse correctly.

✗   `! i1 > 9 ⇒ (!i1) > 9`

which is not legal.

Liberal use of the "not" operator can make a program difficult to read. For instance

```
i1 >= 9
```

is clearer than

```
!(i1 < 9)
```

A good general rule is to avoid the "not" operator whenever possible.

The "and then" operator evaluates to *true* only if both its operands are *true*; "or else" evaluates to *true* if either (or both) of its operands are *true*. This is usually expressed by a "truth table" as shown in Figure 4.12.

Some examples, again assuming that i1 contains the value 10:

```
(i1 > 10) || (i1 == 10)   ⇒ false || true    ⇒ true
(i1 > 10) || (i1 < 0)     ⇒ false || false   ⇒ false
```

b1	b2	b1 && b2	b1 || b2
true	true	true	true
true	false	false	true
false	true	false	true
false	false	false	false

Figure 4.12 **Truth table for the operators && and ||.**

1. These operators are sometimes simply called "and" and "or."

$$(i1 > 0) \ \&\& \ (i1 < 5) \qquad \Rightarrow \textbf{true} \ \&\& \ \textbf{false} \qquad \Rightarrow \textbf{false}$$
$$(i1 > 0) \ \&\& \ (i1 < 20) \qquad \Rightarrow \textbf{true} \ \&\& \ \textbf{true} \qquad \Rightarrow \textbf{true}$$

As the precedence of the operators && and || is lower than the relational and equality operators, the parentheses are not essential in the above examples. However parentheses usually enhance the readability of boolean expressions, and we often include them even though they are not absolutely needed. (Operator precedence is summarized in Figure 4.13.)

Using the "and then" operator, we can now express the condition that the value of i1 is between 0 and 20:

```
(0 < i1) && (i1 < 20)
```

The first operand is false if i1 is 0 or less, and the second is false if i1 is 20 or greater. Either situation makes the entire expression false. Put another way, $0 < i1 < 20$ (mathematically) if and only if i1 makes both $0 < i1$ and $i1 < 20$ true. In general, the mathematical relation $a < b < c$ translates to the Java expression $a < b$ && $b < c$.

You can construct rather baroque expressions with boolean operators. Consider the following, which attempts to determine if the value of the **int** variable year is a leap year:

```
(year % 100 != 0 && year % 4 == 0) ||
(year % 100 == 0 && year % 400 == 0)
```

Such expressions quickly become unreadable. You can accomplish the same result with a more tractable series of steps, as we saw on page 191. Even a relatively simple boolean expression can be misread if sufficient care is not taken. For instance, the expression

```
(i1 != 0) || (i1 != 1)
```

is always true no matter what the value of i1.

"and-then" and "or-else" are lazy

The operators && and || are somewhat unique in that they evaluate their left operand first, and evaluate the right operand only if necessary. For instance, if i1 is 10, the following expressions are evaluated as shown:

$$(i1 < 10) \ \&\& \ (i1 > 0) \qquad \Rightarrow \textbf{false} \ \&\& \ (i1 > 0) \Rightarrow \textbf{false}$$
$$(i1 < 11) \ || \ (i1 > 100) \Rightarrow \textbf{true} \ || \ (i1 > 100) \Rightarrow \textbf{true}$$

The right operands, (i1 > 0) in the first case and (i1 > 100) in the second, are not evaluated.

There might seem little point to this, but consider an example like

```
(x == 0) || (y/x < 10)
```

where x and y are **int** variables. If the left operand is true, that is, if x is 0, evaluating the right operand will result in an attempt to divide by 0 and a run-time error. The rules for *high*

unary + unary − !
`*` `/` `%`
`+` `-`
`<` `<=` `>` `>=`
`==` `!=`
`&&`
`||`

low

Figure 4.13 **Precedence of common operators.**

evaluating the `||` operator ensure that `(y/x < 10)` will not be evaluated if `x` is 0. The entire expression will evaluate to true without the division being attempted.

DeMorgan's laws

As we mentioned above, the use of "not" operator can make an expression particularly difficult to read. For instance, the expression

```
!(i1 > 5 && i1 < 8)
```

is *true* when `i1` is less than or equal to 5, or when `i1` is greater than or equal to 8. Two equivalences, known as DeMorgan's laws, can simplify such expressions. If `b1` and `b2` are arbitrary boolean expressions, then

```
!(b1 && b2) ≡ !b1 || !b2
!(b1 || b2) ≡ !b1 && !b2
```

Thus the above expression can be rewritten as

```
!(i1 > 5) || !(i1 < 8)
```

or simply as

```
i1 <= 5 || i1 >= 8
```

DrJava: evaluating boolean expressions

In the *Interactions* pane, create several **`int`** variables and initialize them:

```
> int i1 = 1;
> int i2 = 2;
> int i3 = 3;
> int z = 0;
```

Evaluate the following expressions. In each case, determine what the result should be before keying the expression.

```
> i3 <= i2+2          > i3 <= i1+2          > i1 != 2
> !(i1 = 2)           > !(i1 == 2)
> i1 == 2 || i1 == 1
> !(i1 == 1 && i1 == 2)
> i1 == 2 || i1 != i3
> z != 0 && 100/z < 50
> 100/z < 50 && z != 0
```

✳ 4.6   Java in detail: logical operators and conditional expressions

Logical operators

In addition to the boolean operators "not" (!), "and then" (&&), and "or else" (| |), Java provides binary boolean operators "and" (&), "or" (|), and "exclusive or" (^). The operators & and | are similar to && and | |, except that both operands are always evaluated. For ^, the result is true if the operand values are different; otherwise the result is false. These operators are very rarely used.

- be1 & be2 evaluates to true if and only both be1 and be2 evaluate to true.
- be1 | be2 evaluates to true if and only if either be1 or be2 or both evaluate to true.
- be1 ^ be2 evaluates to true if and only if either be1 or be2, but not both, evaluates to true.

Conditional expression

A conditional expression consists of a **boolean** expression and two component expressions. It has the format

```
booleanExpression ? expression1 : expression2
```

The **boolean** expression is first evaluated. If true, the value of *expression1* is the value of the conditional expression. If false, the value of *expression2* is the value of the conditional expression. For instance, if a and b are **int** variables, the expression

```
a > b ? a : b
```

produces the maximum of a and b. The assignment statement

```
max = a > b ? a : b;
```

has the same effect as the conditional statement

```
if (a > b)
    max = a;
else
    max = b;
```

✳ 4.7   Java in detail: the *switch* statement

In addition to if-then and if-then-else statements, Java provides another mechanism to handle conditional computations: the *switch* statement. A switch is a rather baroque structure, originally derived from a 1960's assembly language technique called a "branch table." Like a cascade of if-then-else statements, a switch offers a number of possible alternative actions. However, the actions are not independent. What the switch offers is a sequence of actions that can be started at various points.

A switch statement consists of an integer or character valued expression and a *switch block*:

switch (*expression*) *switchBlock*

Like a compound statement, a switch block is a sequence of statements enclosed in braces. But the statements in a switch block can be prefixed with one or more *labels*. A label has one of the following forms:

case *constantExpression* :
default :

A *constant expression* is an expression that can be evaluated by the compiler: essentially, an expression involving only literals and named constants. It must denote an integer or character. The label **default** can appear at most once in a switch block, and if it appears, it must be the last label in the block.

Given the named constant definitions

```
public static final int CLUB = 1;
public static final int DIAMOND = 2;
public static final int HEART = 3;
public static final int SPADE = 4;
```

and assuming that suit is an **int** variable, consider the following statement:

```
switch (suit) {
case DIAMOND:
case HEART:
    redCardCount = redCardCount + 1;
case SPADE:
    spadeCount = spadeCount + 1;
case CLUB:
    blackCardCount = blackCardCount + 1;
default:
    cardCount = cardCount + 1;
}
```

The first assignment is prefixed with two labels (**case** DIAMOND:, **case** HEART:), while each other statement is prefixed with a single label.

To execute the switch statement, the processor evaluates the expression and then continues with the statement following the label that matches the value of the expression. If no label matches the value of the expression, the processor continues at the default label. If there is no default label, execution of the switch statement is complete.

In the example above, the processor evaluates the expression `suit`. If the value of `suit` is 2 or 3, execution continues with the first assignment (`redCardCount = redCardCount + 1;`). If the value of `suit` is 4, execution continues with the second assignment. If the value is 1, execution continues with the third assignment. Finally, if the value of `suit` is something besides 1, 2, 3, or 4, execution continues with the last assignment. This is illustrated in Figure 4.14.

Note that execution of the switch is *not terminated* by reaching another label. Execution is complete only if no label matches the value of the expression and there is no default label, or the end of the switch block is encountered. In the example above, if `suit` is 1 (CLUB), then both the variables `blackCardCount` and `cardCount` are incremented.

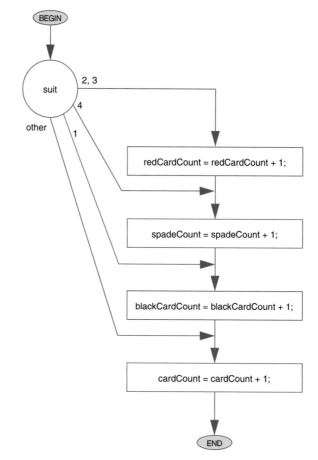

Figure 4.14 **A *switch* statement.**

However, if `suit` is 2 (`DAIMOND`), then the variables `redCardCount`, `spadeCount`, `blackCardCount`, and `cardCount` are all incremented! This is probably not what the programmer had in mind.[1]

To force termination of a switch statement at an arbitrary point, a *break* statement is used. A break statement consists of the keyword **break** followed by a semicolon:

```
break;
```

If we assume the obvious intention, the switch statement of the previous example can be corrected by inserting a break statement after the first assignment, and moving the last assignment outside the switch statement:

```
switch (suit) {
case DIAMOND:
case HEART:
    redCardCount = redCardCount + 1;
    break;
case SPADE:
    spadeCount = spadeCount + 1;
case CLUB:
    blackCardCount = blackCardCount + 1;
}
cardCount = cardCount + 1;
```

The resulting structure is illustrated in Figure 4.15.

As a more realistic example, we rewrite the method `change` from page 193 using a switch statement rather than cascading if-then-else's.

```
public void change () {
switch (light) {
case GREEN:
    light = YELLOW;
    break;
case YELLOW:
    light = RED;
    break;
case RED:
    light = LEFT_ARROW;
    break;
case LEFT_ARROW:
    light = GREEN;
    break;
}
```

Note that the cases can be written in any order. The final break statement is not required, since it occurs at the end of the switch statement. Including it, however, reduces

---

1. Actually, I'm the programmer and this "misreading" example is what I had in mind.

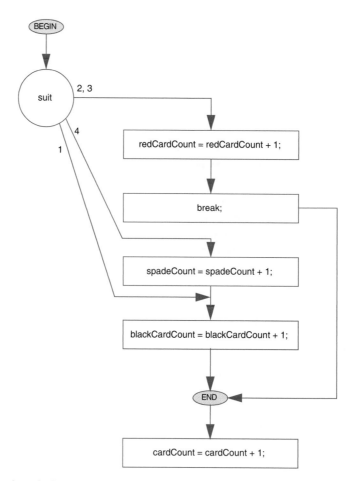

Figure 4.15 **A *switch* statement, modified.**

the chance of error if the statement is subsequently modified. We suggest that any switch statement you write have this property. That is, we recommend not writing switch statements in which execution of one case "falls through" to the following case.

Again, remember that the type of the expression and case labels in a switch statement must be **int**, **byte**, **short**, or **char**. Floating point or **boolean** expressions are not allowed.

4.8   Summary

In this chapter, we've introduced boolean expressions and conditional statements. Conditional statements allow us to specify alternative computations and the circumstances under which each is to be performed. The particular action to be done is determined by the processor at execution time, depending on the current data values.

The two forms of conditional statement we've seen are if-then and if-then-else.

- With an if-then, we specify an action that is to be performed only if a given condition is true, that is, a guarded action:

```
if (condition)
    statement
```

- With an if-then-else, we specify two possible actions, one of which will be done:

```
if (condition)
    statement₁
else
    statement₂
```

Since the syntax of the Java language permits only a single statement as a conditional alternative, we need a way to package a number of statements into one. This is the compound statement. By putting braces around a sequence of statements, we form a single compound statement:

```
{ statement₁ statement₂ … statementₙ }
```

The condition of a conditional statement is syntactically a boolean expression: an expression that evaluates to a **boolean** value, true or false. We saw several kinds of operators useful for constructing boolean expressions, including relational operators <, <=, >, and >=, equality operators == and !=, and boolean operators &&, ||, and !.

We also introduced preconditions, postconditions, and invariants. These are not formally part of the Java language but are important in the specification and correctness verification of our designs. Since they are not part of the language *per se*, we include them in comments.

The client of a method is responsible for making sure that all preconditions of the method are satisfied before invoking the method. The method will work correctly only if preconditions are satisfied. Preconditions are documented in a require clause of the method specification.

The implementor of a method is responsible for making sure that all postconditions of the method are satisfied when the method completes. Postconditions are documented in an "ensure clause" of the method specification.

Invariants are conditions that always hold. In particular, class invariants are conditions that are always true of all instances of a class. A class instance is a consistent and coherent model of whatever entity the class represents if the class invariants hold.

SELF-STUDY EXERCISES

4.1   For each of the following statements, indicate whether it applies to a precondition or a postcondition.

   a.   Is the responsibility of the client.

   b.   The algorithm implementing the method must make sure that it gets satisfied.

   c.   Must be true when the method is invoked.

   d.   Guaranteed true when the method completes.

   e.   Is expressed with a "require" clause in the documentation.

   f.   Is expressed with an "ensure" clause in the documentation.

4.2   A class invariant is a claim about an object's state. Explain.

4.3   Given that x, y, and z are **int** variables containing the values 4, 6, and 8, respectively, evaluate each of the following boolean expressions.

   (a) x < 4   *(b)* x <= 4   *(c)* x > 4 || y == 6
   (d) x > 4 && y == 6   *(e)* !(x > 4)
   (f) x != 4 || x != 5   *(g)* x + 2 != y
   (h) x == 8 || y == 8 || z == 8
   (i) (y < z && y < x) || y >= x
   (j) x != 4 && z/(x-4) == 1
   (k) z/(x-4) == 1 && x != 4

4.4   Given that i and j are **int** variables, simplify each of the following.

   (a) !(i < 10 && j > 0)   *(b)* !(i < 10 || j > 0)
   (c) !(i < 10 && j == 0)   *(d)* !(i <= 10 && i > 0)
   (e) !((i <= 10 && i > 0) || j > 0)
   (f) !(i != 0 || j != 0)

4.5   For which values of the **int** variable i is the expression

$$(i != 1 || i != 0)$$

   true? Compute the negation of this expression, and check against the negation of your original answer.

4.6   Given that x, y, and z are **int** variables, write a boolean expression that will be true:

   a.   if x is greater than y.

   b.   if x is greater than both y and z.

   c.   if x is greater than either y or z.

   d.   if x equal to the product of y and z.

   e.   if x ends in 0, that is, if x is divisible by 10.

f. if x is even.

g. if x is between y and z, inclusive, where y is known to be less than z.

4.7 On page 215, the observation is made that the operators == and ! = are rarely used to compare floating point values. How might you compare floating point values for equality?

4.8 Suppose that x and max are **int** variables, and done a **boolean** variable.

a. Write a statement that will increment x by 1 only if done is false.

b. Write a statement that will increment x by 1 only if x is less than max.

4.9 Given that x, y, and z are **int** variables, write statements to accomplish the following.

a. Assign to z the larger of x and y.

b. Assign to x the absolute value of x.

c. Assign to z the largest of x, y, and z.

4.10 Suppose that value, max, and min are **int** variables. The following code fragment should set value to min if it is smaller than min, and to max if it is larger than max. It is not correctly written. Add braces to make the code correct.

```
if (value >= min)
    if (value > max)
        value = max;
else
    value = min;
```

4.11 Assume that x is an **int** variable. For each of the following code fragments, state which initial values of x will result in x being incremented by 4.

a.
```
if (x == 1)
    x = x + 1;
else if (x == 2)
    x = x + 2;
else if (x == 3)
    x = x + 3;
else
    x = x + 4;
```

b.
```
if (x == 1)
    x = x +1;
if (x == 2)
    x = x + 2;
if (x == 4)
    x = x + 4;
```

4.12 If a and b are **int** variables, what's wrong with the following statement?

```
if (a = b)
    a = a + 1;
```

```
    else
        b = b + 1;
```

4.13 Given the definitions

```
String day = "jour";
String hello = "bonjour";
String goodDay = "bon" + day;
String greetings = goodDay;
```

evaluate each of the following.

a. `hello == goodDay`

b. `goodDay == greetings`

c. `hello == greetings`

d. `goodDay.equals(hello)`

e. `goodDay.equals("hello")`

✶ 4.14 Consider the following statement, where i and j are **int** variables:

```
switch (i) {
case 0:
case 1:
    j = 1;
    break;
case 2:
    j = 2;
case 3:
    j = 3;
default:
    j = 4;
}
```

What will the value of j be after the statement is executed if i is:

(a) 0?   *(b)* 2?   *(c)* 4?   *(d)* −1?

✶ 4.15 Given that i and j are **int** variables, what's the difference in the following two expressions?

```
i != 0 && j/i > 10
i != 0 & j/i > 10
```

✶ 4.16 Write a condition expression that evaluates to the absolute value of the **int** variable x.

EXERCISES

4.1 Rephrase each of the following in the form of if-then or if-then-else statements. Use ordinary English to express the conditions and actions.

      a. Don't do the homework and you're grounded!

      b. Pass the exam or drop the course.

      c. If you have the money, go to the movies; otherwise, clean your room.

      d. I have to work overtime in the warehouse unless Peter is there.

      e. I go to school on Tuesday and Thursday, work on Monday, Wednesday, and Friday, and hang out on weekends.

4.2   Given that `score` is a *Student* instance variable of type **int** containing a student's test score, write a *Student* method `passed` that returns true if the student's score is 70 or above, and returns false otherwise. Do you need a conditional statement to write this method?

4.3   If `score` is an **int** variable containing a student's test score, and `grade` is a **char** variable, write a statement that will assign the letter 'A' to `grade` if `score` is 93 or above, 'B' to `grade` if `score` is between 85 and 92, 'C' if `score` is between 77 and 84, 'D' if `score` is between 70 and 76, and 'F' if `score` is below 70.

4.4   Suppose that the class *Location* models a location on the display screen. The methods

        public int x()
        public int y()

return the distance of the location (in pixels) right from the upper left corner, and down from the upper left corner respectively:

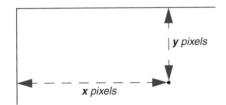

The class *Rectangle* models a rectangle on the screen. It has properties

        private Location location;
        private int height;
        private int width;

where `location` is the location of the upper left corner of the *Rectangle*, `height` is the vertical dimension, and `width` is the horizontal dimension (in pixels).

Write a *Rectangle* method

        public boolean contains (Location point)

that tells whether or not the specified *Location* is inside (or on the perimeter of) the *Rectangle*.

4.5   Consider the class *Student* sketched in Section 1.1. Assume that fees are assessed as follows:

0 – 3 credit hours:	$500
4 – 6 credit hours:	$750
7 – 9 credit hours:	$1000
10 or more credit hours:	$1250

A *Student* object has an instance variable,

```
private int creditHours;    // credit hours enrolled in
```

Write a *Student* method `fees` that returns the fee amount as an **int**.

4.6   Suppose a class *Employee* contains the following instance variables:

```
private int hours;       // hours worked in the week
private double rate;     // hourly pay rate (dollars)
```

Write a definition of a method `pay` that returns the *Employee*'s pay for the week, where the *Employee* is paid the hourly rate for the first 40 hours worked, and paid time and a half for overtime.

4.7   Review the nim *Player* class, discussed in Section 3.2. Implement the *Player* method `takeTurn`, where the *Player*'s strategy is as follows: if one stick can be left in the pile by removing 1, 2, or 3 sticks, do so. Otherwise, remove a single stick from the pile.

The method should first query the pile to determine the number of sticks remaining. After determining how many sticks to remove, the method should invoke the *Pile* method `remove`. The method will look something like this:

```
public void takeTurn (Pile pile) {
    int left;        // number in the pile
    int take;        // number to take
    left = pile.sticks();
    // determine number to take
    ...
    pile.remove(take);
    this.sticksTaken = take;
}
```

Test the implementation.

4.8   Implement and test the balls and strikes counter described in Exercise 2.1. Use the "test-driven" implementation strategy: first build a test system and stubbed implementation of the class.

4.9   Implement and test a dollars and cents counter. The counter should provide the following functionality:

```
public int dollars ()
```
> The dollar count.

> **ensure:**
>> `this.dollars() >= 0`

```
public int cents ()
```
The cents count.

ensure:
```
0 <= this.cents() && this.cents() <= 99
```

```
public void add (int dollars, int cents)
```
Add the specified dollars and cents to this *Counter*.

```
public void reset ()
```
Reset this *Counter* to 0.

ensure:
```
this.dollars() == 0 && this.cents() == 0
```

Suppose the following method were added to the counter:

```
public void subtract (int dollars, int cents)
```
Subtract the specified dollars and cents from this *Counter*.

What problems would this present in the design?

4.10   Write, compile, and run a simple program with the following `main`:

```
public static void main (String[] argv) {
    boolean a = false;
    boolean b = false;
    if (a = b)
        System.out.println("Equal!");
    else
        System.out.println("Not equal!");
}
```

Be sure that the "condition" has only one equal sign: a = b. Explain the results.

4.11   A three digit *CombinationLock* is created with the following constructor invocation

```
new CombinationLock(023)
```

The lock refuses to open when given the combination 0-2-3, but opens with the combination 0-1-9. Explain. (Hint: read about literals in Section 1.9.2 or Section 1.9.3.)

4.12   The digit-by-digit combination lock of Section 4.4.1 remembers the last three digits entered. In fact, it needs only to remember the last two. Modify the implementation eliminating the variable `thirdToLast`.

4.13   Design and implement a class *PairedCounter* as follows. A *PairedCounter* is similar to the modulus counter of Exercise 2.2 and Exercise 2.13. However, it can have a *partner*, set with the command

```
public void setPartner (PairedCounter partner)
```
Set the partner of this *PairedCounter* as specified.

If a *PairedCounter* has a non-null partner, then whenever it executes an increment count command that resets it to 0, it also resets its partner.

4.14   Implement the balls and strikes counter of Exercise 4.8 using two *PairedCounters*, as constructed in Exercise 4.13.

4.15   Modify the test system of Section 4.4 to test the digit-by-digit lock. Code and test the digit-by-digit lock.

4.16   Rewrite the class modeling a three-digit combination lock. Rather than having the lock explicitly remember the last three digits entered, make the lock remember if the last digit entered was the first digit of the combination, and if the last two digits entered were the first two digits of the combination. That is, replace the instance variables thirdToLast, secondToLast, and last with these:

```
private boolean haveFirst;
    // the last digit entered was digit1
private boolean haveSecond;
    // the last two digits entered were digit1 and digit2
```

Implement and test.

SELF-STUDY EXERCISE SOLUTIONS

4.1   *a.*   precondition

b.   postcondition

c.   precondition

d.   postcondition

e.   precondition

f.   postcondition

4.2   A class invariant is a condition involving an object's properties that is always true. That is, it is a condition that is satisfied by any legal state of the object.

4.3   *(a) false*   *(b) true*   *(c) true*   *(d) false*   *(e) true*   *(f) true*
        (g) false   *(h) true*   *(i) true*   *(j) false*   *(k)* divide by zero error

4.4   *(a)* i >= 10 || j <= 0   *(b)* i >= 10 && j <= 0
        (c) i >= 10 || j != 0   *(d)* i > 10 || i <= 0
        (e) (i > 10 || i <= 0) && j <= 0   *(f)* i == 0 && j == 0

4.5   True for all values of i. Negation is i == 1 && i == 0.

4.6   *a.*   x > y   *b.*   x > y && x > z   *c.*   x > y || x > z
        d.   x == y*z   *e.*   x % 10 == 0   *f.*   x % 2 == 0
        g.   y <= x && x <= z

4.7 Rather than testing that the values are equal, test that they are "sufficiently close." For example, if x, y, and delta are **double** variables, the expression

```
y-delta <= x && x <= y+delta
```

will be *true* if x differs from y by no more than delta.

4.8   *a.*   **if** (!done)
       x = x+1;

     b.   **if** (x < max)
       x = x+1;

4.9 There are several ways to accomplish each of these tasks. We show one possibility for each.

     a.   **if** (x > y)
       z = x;
     else
       z = y;

     b.   **if** (x < 0)
       x = -x;

     c.   **if** (x > z)
       z = x;   // z is now larger of x and original value of z
     if (y > z)
       z = y;

4.10   **if** (value >= min) {
     if (value > max)
       value = max;
  } **else**
     value = min;

4.11   *a.*   Any value other than 1, 2, or 3.

     b.   Only 4.

4.12 The "condition" a = b is an assignment, not a comparison for equality.

4.13 *(a) false*   *(b) true*   *(c) false*   *(d) true*   *(e) false*

4.14 *(a)* 1   *(b)* 4   *(c)* 4   *(d)* 4

4.15 The first expression will evaluate to false if i is 0; the second will result in a divide by zero error.

4.16 One possibility: x > 0 ? x : -x

CHAPTER 5

Programming by contract

We've now seen boolean expressions and conditional statements in some detail. Conditional statements allow us to define a number of alternative courses of action. The specific action taken depends on the run-time value of the condition. The same conditional statement might result in different actions being performed at different times in the computation, since the condition can be true at some times, false at others.

We've also introduced the notions of precondition, postcondition, and invariant. These are all conditions, assertions that can be true or false. Preconditions, postconditions, and invariants are not formally part of the Java language. They are not constructs recognized by the compiler or understood by the interpreter. However, they play an important role in the design, specification, and verification of systems. We include them in comments, and they directly influence the implementations we develop.

Since they are not part of Java *per se*, the language syntax does not restrict how we express preconditions, postconditions, and invariants. We have considerable flexibility in specifying these conditions, and can be quite informal if we want. On the other hand, we do not have the compiler and interpreter making sure that what we write is not utter nonsense. We use the Java syntax for boolean expressions wherever practical.

In this chapter, we further develop the ideas of precondition and postcondition, and introduce a programming style called *programming by contract*. The point of programming by contract is to clearly delineate in a method's specification the respective responsibilities of client and server. Preconditions and postconditions play a key role in defining these responsibilities.

Objectives

After studying this chapter you should understand the following:

- programming by contract, defensive programming, and the difference between the two;
- consequences of a client's lack of adherence to a contract;
- purpose and use of the assert statement.

Also, you should be able to:

- express the responsibilities of client and server as a contract;
- use assert statements to verify a client's preconditions;
- use contracts to reason about a program's behavior.

5.1   Programming by contract

Let's return to an issue raised in the previous chapter: the range of possible values that might be returned from an *Explorer*'s `tolerance` query. We have decided that this value has a lower bound of 0, and documented this fact in the specification of the method:

```
/**
 * Damage (hit points) required to defeat
 * this Explorer.
 *
 * @ensure      tolerance >= 0
 */
public int tolerance () ...
```

In order to guarantee this, we modified the constructor and the `takeThat` method so that they never assign a negative value to the instance variable `tolerance`, regardless of the arguments provided by the client. We need to look at these two cases a little more carefully.

In the case of `takeThat`, we protect against the client providing a hit strength that's greater than the current tolerance of the *Explorer*:

```
public void takeThat (int hitStrength) {
    if (hitStrength <= tolerance)
        tolerance = tolerance - hitStrength;
    else
        tolerance = 0;
}
```

This does not at all seem unreasonable. We shouldn't expect a client to worry about the tolerance of the *Explorer* when striking a blow. We didn't take the tolerance of the opponent into account, for instance, when we implemented the *Explorer*'s method `poke`:

```
public void poke (Denizen opponent) {
    opponent.takeThat(strength);
}
```

There may, in fact, be no method for obtaining the tolerance of a *Denizen*.

In summary, we do not consider it an error for a client to call `takeThat` with an argument greater than `tolerance`. It is simply a possibility that the implementation of `takeThat` must account for.

On the other hand, a call to the constructor with a negative initial value for `toler-`
`ance` seems quite different. This is something that should not happen. It is an error and
the fault of the client who makes the call. We document our expectation that the client will
provide a non-negative value when invoking the constructor as follows:

```
/**
 * Create a new Explorer with the specified name,
 * initial location, strength, and tolerance.
 *
 * @require    strength >= 0
 *             tolerance >= 0
 */
public Explorer (String name, Room location,
                      int strength, int tolerance) ...
```

We introduced this notation in the previous chapter. Recall that conditions labeled
"require" are called *preconditions*. They are requirements placed on the *client*. We are stating that *client must make sure* that the arguments provided for `strength` and `toler-`
`ance` are non-negative. *Postconditions*, labeled "ensure," are requirements on the
implementor of the method. Preconditions and postconditions are part of a programming
style called *programming by contract*. The basic idea is that use of an object feature (query
or command) or constructor is considered to involve a "contract" between the client and
server. For an invocation of a feature or constructor to be correct, the client must make
sure that the preconditions are satisfied at the time of the call. If the preconditions are satisfied, then the server guarantees that the postconditions will be satisfied when the method
completes (*i.e.*, upon "return"). If the preconditions are not satisfied, that is, if the client
does not meet his end of the contract, then the server *promises nothing at all*.

---

programming by contract: a programming style in which the invocation of
a method is viewed as a contract between client and server, with each having explicitly stated responsibilities.

Understand that this is not an issue of a user entering bad data. The user interface is
responsible for interacting with a user and making sure that bad data doesn't get into the
system. What we're concerned with here is one object, a client, invoking a method of
another object. If a client invokes a method without the preconditions being satisfied, it is
due to a programming error in the client.

The point of this approach is to delineate, clearly and explicitly, responsibilities
between the client and the server, and ultimately between the user of a method and the
implementor of the method. We want to make sure that any possible error that can arise at
run time is detected. But we'd like to do as little explicit error checking as possible. Specifically, we'd like to test for every possible error condition only once. One reason is fairly
obvious: program efficiency. However, there is a much more important reason for this
approach. The most consequential impediment to writing correct, maintainable code is
complexity. Adding error checking can make a simple straightforward algorithm unduly

convoluted. An approach in which each routine validates all of its arguments—sometimes called *defensive programming*—can result in an excessively high degree of "code pollution." The trick is to make a program reliable but not so convoluted as to be unmaintainable. Clearly there are many design trade-offs here, and we'll talk more about error handling in Chapter 15. We use preconditions and postconditions to prescribe explicitly who—client or server—is responsible for what.

We can completely specify the behavior of the constructor by adding postconditions, like this:

```
/**
 * Create a new Explorer with the specified name,
 * initial location, strength, and tolerance.
 *
 * @require    strength >= 0
 *             tolerance >= 0
 * @ensure     this.name().equals(name)
 *             this.location() == location
 *             this.strength() == strength
 *             this.tolerance() == tolerance
 */
public Explorer (String name, Room location,
                 int strength, int tolerance) ...
```

The postconditions precisely and concisely describe the relationship between the parameters of the constructor and the properties of the newly created object. The notation means that if the newly created object is queried with the method name, for example, it will return the string provided as the first argument of the constructor. That is, in the condition

```
this.name().equals(name)
```

`this.name()` refers to the value that the newly created object (`this`) will return when the method name is invoked. The identifier name on the right refers to the first parameter of the constructor.

Granted, the ensure clause is a bit redundant here. It essentially repeats what is said in the descriptive sentence beginning "Create…," and could be omitted without a substantial loss in clarity or precision.

We have now completely specified the behavior of the constructor for the client. But remember the format we use for writing precondition and postconditions is a convention intended to convey information to the human reader: it is not part of the programming language. The client must make sure that the preconditions are satisfied *before* the method is invoked, in which case the implementor guarantees that the postconditions will be satisfied *upon completion* of the method.

Implied preconditions and postconditions

There are two situations in which preconditions and/or postconditions are generally assumed and not made explicit. First, in the constructor above, the first two arguments reference a *String* and a *Room*, respectively. Recall from Section 1.5 that there is a special null value, denoted by the literal **null**, that doesn't reference any object.

We assume that an argument value cannot be null unless the specification explicitly allows it. We also assume that the value returned by a query cannot be null unless the specification explicitly allows this possibility.

Therefore the constructor precondition above is equivalent to

```
*  @require    name != null
*              location != null
*              strength >= 0
*              tolerance >= 0
```

However, we rarely write these non-null requirements in the specification.

Second, the type of a numeric property implies some expected "range of reasonable use." For example, the query `currentCount` of a *Counter* is specified as

public int currentCount ()
    The number of items counted.

    ensure:
        this.currentCount() >= 0

The return type (**int**) determines an upper bound on the returned value, namely, 2,147,483,647. Thus the counter can only be legitimately incremented if its value is less than this limit:

public void incrementCount ()
    Increment the count by 1.

    require:
        this.currentCount() < 2147483647

The underlying assumption, however, is that instances of this class will only be used in situations where the count will not exceed the range of the type **int**. Thus we will rarely write a precondition like the one shown above.

5.1.1 Verifying preconditions: the *assert* statement

So we have placed preconditions, `strength >= 0` and `tolerance >= 0`, on the constructor. If the client invokes the constructor with non-negative `strength` and `tolerance` arguments, we are committed to produce a new, well-formed *Explorer* object. If the client invokes the method with either argument negative, *we promise nothing at all*. This is important to realize. If the client does not adhere to its end of the contract, the implementation is not committed to any particular action.

In fact, if the client does not adhere to the contract, the program is erroneous and the behavior of an erroneous program is, by definition, unpredictable.

But of course *something* must happen. What we do depends to some degree on how much we trust our client. It may be that we are absolutely convinced that the constructor will never be called with a negative second argument—perhaps we're writing the client code ourselves—in which case we need do nothing. But systems change, and initial values are often computed in complex (and error-prone) ways. We can easily imagine, for instance, employing a nontrivial function that determines a random initial value for `tolerance` or `strength`.

The real problem with not verifying the values of the constructor arguments is that we can end up violating a class invariant. Suppose we simply leave the constructor as we originally wrote it:

```
public Explorer (String name, Room location,
                      int strength, int tolerance) {
    this.name = name;
    this.location = location;
    this.strength = strength;
    this.tolerance = tolerance;
}
```

If the client violates the precondition, there is no specific requirement on the constructor *with regard to the contract*. However, we have an *internal implementation requirement* in the form of the invariant condition on the component `tolerance`:

```
private int tolerance;      // current tolerance
                            // invariant:
                            // tolerance >= 0
```

Executing the constructor with the precondition violated will result in an *Explorer* object being created that does not satisfy the invariant. For this reason, rather than for the requirements of the contract, the original implementation is not particularly satisfactory.

We can, of course, return to the implementation suggested in the previous chapter, in which the argument value provided for `tolerance` is explicitly checked by the constructor:

```
public Explorer (String name, Room location,
                      int strength, int tolerance) {
    ...
    if (tolerance >= 0)
        this.tolerance = tolerance;
    else
        this.tolerance = 0;
}
```

But this is not entirely satisfactory either, since it treats an error condition (violation of the precondition) as a normal, expected, occurrence, and introduces the explicit checking we're trying to avoid.

What would we like to happen if the client violates the precondition? Perhaps the most we could hope for is that the interpreter or run-time system would recognize that the precondition was violated and generate an informative run-time error. Ideally, we'd like this to happen without having to write anything but the precondition. (Remember a major point of this approach is to avoid cluttering our code with excessive error checks.) That is, we'd like the interpreter to automatically check that preconditions are satisfied whenever a method is invoked. If the preconditions are met, the method executes normally. If not, the computation is interrupted and the user informed of the error condition. Error reporting of this kind is particularly useful while we're developing, testing, and debugging a system.

Java's *assert statement*[1] can be used in verifying preconditions. The statement has two formats. The simpler form is

assert *booleanExpression* ;

The boolean expression is evaluated, and if it is true, the statement has no effect. If it is false, the statement raises an error condition—an *exception*. This will stop execution of the program and display some information about the cause of the exception. We can use *assert* statements to verify preconditions in the constructor as follows:

```
public Explorer (String name, Room location,
                        int strength, int tolerance) {
    assert strength >= 0;
    assert tolerance >= 0;

    this.name = name;
    this.location = location;
    this.strength = strength;
    this.tolerance = tolerance;
}
```

If a client invokes the constructor with a negative tolerance argument, the program will terminate and we'll get a message that looks something like this:

```
Exception in thread "main" java.lang.AssertionError
    at mazeGame.Explorer.<init>(Explorer.java:16)
    at mazeGame.ExplorerTest.runTest(TestExplorer.java:16)
    at mazeGame.TestExplorer.main(TestExplorer.java:7)
```

(Exactly what the message looks like depends on the system we're running and where the error occurred.)

The second form of the *assert* statement is

assert *booleanExpression* : *expression* ;

As before, the boolean expression is evaluated, and if it is true, the statement has no effect. If it is false, the second expression is evaluated and the result incorporated into the exception message. For instance, we might write

---

1. The *assert statement* is available in Java version 1.4 and later.

```
assert tolerance >= 0 :
    "precondition: tolerance (" + tolerance + ") >= 0";
```

Here the expression produces a *String* that includes the argument value of `tolerance`. (Remember, + is concatenation in this expression.) If a client invokes the constructor with a negative tolerance argument, the message will look something like this:

```
Exception in thread "main" java.lang.AssertionError:
precondition: tolerance (-10) >= 0
    at mazeGame.Explorer.<init>(Explorer.java:16)
    at mazeGame.ExplorerTest.runTest(TestExplorer.java:16)
    at mazeGame.TestExplorer.main(TestExplorer.java:7)
```

We tend to use assert statements sparingly in our examples. This is not to indicate a style to be copied, but to reduce distractions in the examples.

Assertions are disabled by default

There is a difficulty with *assert* statements that leads some programmers to avoid them for precondition testing. When the program is run, the interpreter, unless told to do otherwise, simply ignores them. Assertions are explicitly enabled with command line switches as explained in Appendix i.

Because of the possibility that a program might be run without precondition testing, some programmers prefer to test preconditions explicitly with *if* statements. But as we have said, an *if* statement implies an ordinary, expected case that must be handled by the program. A precondition failure, on the other hand, is an error and occurs only in an incorrect program.

DrJava: the assert statement

Open the file `CombinationLock.java`, located in `locks`, in ch5, in nhText. This file contains a definition of the class *CombinationLock*, as presented in the previous chapter.

Note that the package name is `ch5.locks`. We'll incorporate the chapter number in a package name from now on, so that classes with the same name don't become confused.

1. Select *Preferences...* from the *Edit* pull-down menu. A *Preferences* window will appear.

2. Choose the category *Miscellaneous* from the *Preferences* window. Click on the check box *Allow Assert Keyword...*, making sure that this option is activated. Press *Apply* and *OK*.

3. In the *Interactions* pane, create a *CombinationLock* with an invalid combination

    ```
    > import ch5.locks.*;
    > CombinationLock myLock = new CombinationLock(1000);
    ```

    and note the result.

4. Modify the assert statement, adding an expression:

```
assert 0 <= combination && combination <= 999 :
       "bad combination: " + combination;
```

Note the condition is separated from the following expression by a colon.

Save and recompile.

5. In the *Interactions* pane, again create a *CombinationLock* with an invalid combination and note the result.

5.2   Further examples

Named constants in preconditions and postconditions

First, let's look at the *TrafficSignal* query `light`. Recall that in the class *TrafficSignal*, we defined three named constants, GREEN, YELLOW, and RED, to represent the different lights. The method `light` was specified in Section 2.5 as

public int light ()
> The current light that is on. Returns `TrafficSignal.GREEN`,
> `TrafficSignal.YELLOW`, or `TrafficSignal.RED`.

We can express this a little more clearly with a postcondition:

public int light ()
> The current light that is on.

> **ensure:**
> ```
> this.light() == TrafficSignal.GREEN ||
> this.light() == TrafficSignal.YELLOW ||
> this.light() == TrafficSignal.RED
> ```

Named constants should be used in preconditions and postconditions rather than literals whenever possible. Furthermore, though we occasionally resort to informal English when writing preconditions and postconditions, standard Java syntax is preferable. There is no chance for ambiguities creeping into our statements if we stick to the formal language notation.

Specifying a command

Next, let's take another look at the *Explorer* method `takeThat`, which we have specified as:

public void takeThat (**int** hitStrength)
> Receive a poke of the specified number of hit points.

We've decided that we won't require hitStrength be bounded by our *Explorer*'s current tolerance. But we might want to put a lower limit of 0 on the value of this argument. (Unless we decide that some pokes can *increase* our *Explorer*'s tolerance: pokes with a magic wand?)

> **public void** takeThat (**int** hitStrength)
>   Receive a poke of the specified number of hit points.
>
> **require:**
>   hitStrength >= 0

It is important to realize that if we don't put this precondition on hitStrength, the method *must be prepared to accept a negative argument.* Furthermore, the documentation must explain exactly what a negative argument means.

We might consider making the precondition hitStrength > 0. After all, what's the point of a 0-point hit? But unlike a negative point hit, a 0-point hit has a reasonable meaning. It's a poke that does no damage. We can understand it without additional explanation. In general, our methods will be simpler and easier to use if we don't arbitrarily exclude reasonable argument values, even if we don't expect some of these values to occur ordinarily.

What kind of postcondition can we write to describe to the client the effect of the method? We want to indicate that the *Explorer*'s tolerance will decrease: that the value returned by the query tolerance() after execution of takeThat will be less than the value returned by this query before execution of takeThat. To do this, we must be able to refer to the state of the *Explorer* when the method is invoked as well as to the state of the *Explorer* when the method completes. (It is common for a command postcondition to describe the state of the object after the command is executed in terms of the object's state when the command is invoked.)

When writing a postcondition, we use "this" to refer to the state of the object at the time the method completes, and "old" to refer to the state of the object *at the time the method is invoked.* The notation "old" is not a Java construct; it is a convention used in a comment specifying a precondition.

We might start by writing something like this:

> **ensure:**
>   this.tolerance() ==
>   old.tolerance() - hitStrength

As noted, this.tolerance() refers to the tolerance property of the object when the method completes, and old.tolerance() refers to the tolerance property when the method begins. The condition says that the value returned by tolerance after the method is complete will be the tolerance value when the method was called minus the argument value.

But this postcondition is not correct: if hitStrength is greater than tolerance, tolerance will end up 0, and not old.tolerance() - hitStrength. We can correct the problem by writing:

ensure:
```
      this.tolerance() ==
         max (old.tolerance() - hitStrength, 0)
```

This says that after the method competes, tolerance will be the larger of 0, and the starting tolerance minus the argument.

The postcondition is now correct but almost certainly too strong, since it promises the client exactly how the method is implemented. Suppose we decide later in the development that the *Explorer* should be able to do something to lessen the effect of a poke; put on a parka, for instance. Not only would the postcondition need to be changed, but since a client's correctness depends on our promises, any client that invoked the method would need to be reexamined as well. We don't want a client to depend on irrelevant implementation details.

The following would probably be an adequate postcondition:

ensure:
```
      this.tolerance() <= old.tolerance()
```

It simply promises that the *Explorer*'s tolerance, after executing the method, will be no greater than it was when the method was called.

The definition of `takeThat` can be written as follows:

```
/**
 * Receive a poke of the specified number of
 * hit points.
 * @require     hitStrength >= 0
 * @ensure      this.tolerance() <= old.tolerance()
 */
public void takeThat (int hitStrength)
    if (hitStrength <= tolerance)
       tolerance = tolerance - hitStrength;
    else
       tolerance = 0;
}
```

Note that if the method is invoked with a negative `hitStrength`, `tolerance` is increased and the postconditions not satisfied. But if the client violates the preconditions, the sever is under no obligation to comply with the postconditions.

Assigning responsibilities

As a final example, let's look at the nim game class *Pile* from Section 3.2. Remember that a *Pile* instance modeled a pile of sticks from which players in turn removed 1, 2, or 3 sticks. The command `remove` is used to remove sticks:

```
public void remove (int number)
```
         Reduce the number of sticks by the specified amount.

There are at least three "what if" questions that come to mind when we read this specification:

- what if `number` is negative? Is this legal? If so, what does this mean?
- what if `number` is greater than the number of sticks remaining the pile?
- what if `number` is not 1, 2, or 3?

Each of these questions must be answered to complete the specification of the method. In each case, we can write a precondition that excludes the case, and put the responsibility on the client. Or we can handle the case in the method.

For instance, we can write a precondition requiring `number` to be non-negative. Then it's the client's responsibility to make sure that the argument is not negative, and it's a programming error if the method is ever invoked with a negative argument. Or we can decide that the method will accept a negative argument, in which case we must document clearly what this means. But we must choose one or the other. If we don't exclude negative arguments, a client can legitimately invoke the method with a negative argument and expect something reasonable to happen.

What should we do in each case? First, it does not seem meaningful for a client to remove a negative number of sticks. (Maybe there should be a method for adding sticks to the pile, but this shouldn't happen in a method named `remove`.) A negative argument would certainly be due to a program bug, and is not something we want to handle quietly. We'll exclude this possibility with a precondition:

require:
```
number >= 0
```

(We might also wonder whether an argument of 0 should be allowed. But "remove 0 sticks" has a clear meaning, so we'll accept a 0 argument.)

It's not so obvious how to handle the second case, where `number` is greater than the number of sticks remaining in the pile. We could say that if a client attempts to remove more sticks than remain in the pile, all the sticks are removed. But attempting to remove more sticks than there are in the pile also seems likely to be a client error. So we'll exclude this case too, though handling it in the method could also be justified:

require:
```
number >= 0
number <= this.sticks()
```

Finally, what if `number` is not 1, 2, or 3? The number of sticks than can legally be removed by a player is determined by the rules of the game. Knowing the rules of the game really doesn't seem like it should be the *Pile*'s responsibility. So we won't restrict the argument further.

Adding a postcondition, the complete specification reads as follows:

public void remove (**int** number)
Reduce the number of sticks by the specified amount.
require:
```
number >= 0
number <= this.sticks()
```

ensure:

```
this.sticks() == old.sticks() - number
```

Note that in the precondition, the expression `this.sticks()` refers to the number of sticks in the pile *when the method is invoked*. In the postcondition, the expression `this.sticks()` refers to the number of sticks *when the method completes*.

DrJava: preconditions and postconditions

Open the file `Toy.java`, located in folder `exercise`, in ch5, in nhText. The class does not model anything, but simply serves the exercise.

1. In the *Interactions* pane create an instance of the class:

    ```
    > import ch5.exercise.*;
    > Toy t = new Toy();
    ```

2. Since each of the functions `twice` and `increment` take integer arguments and return integer values, they can be composed. That is we can write the expressions:

    ```
    > t.next(t.twice(0))
    > t.twice(t.next(0))
    ```

3. Try the expressions above. Find other values for which the composition is legal and evaluate them.

4. Now try other input values for which the composition is not quite legal, such as:

    ```
    > t.twice(t.next(5))
    > t.next(t.twice(3))
    ```

    As you can see, the expressions are evaluated, but `twice`'s and `next`'s contracts are broken in the process.

5. To avoid illegal compositions, add an assert statement to method `twice`.

    ```
    assert 0 <= number && number <= 10;
    ```

    Before compiling, you must make sure that the preference *Allow Assert Keyword* has been activated. (See page 242.) Save and compile.

6. In the *Interactions* pane, create a *Toy* instance as above, and key

    ```
    t.twice(t.next(5))
    ```

    Read the error message produced.

7. Add the appropriate assert statement to `next`. Save compile, and evaluate `t.next(t.twice(3))`.

5.3   Preconditions and postconditions: a summary

Preconditions

Preconditions must be satisfied by the client when invoking the method. Occasionally, preconditions constrain the order in which methods can be invoked or require that an object be in a certain state before a given method can be invoked. For instance, it might be necessary that a door be unlocked before it can be opened, or that an automobile be started before it can be moved. Most often, however, preconditions constrain values that the client can provide as arguments when invoking the method. This is the case in the Explorer constructor and takeThat command considered above. The precondition for takeThat, for example, requires that the client provide a non-negative argument.

Remember that if an argument is not constrained by a precondition, the method must be prepared to accept *any value of the specified type*.

Query postconditions

When an object responds to a query, it does not change state. It simply provides a value to the client. Thus query postconditions inevitably say something about the value returned. We sometimes use the term "result" to refer to the value returned by the query. For instance, we might specify the *Counter* method currentCount in either of the following ways:

> **public int** currentCount ()
>> Current count; the number of items counted.
>
>> **ensure:**
>>> this.currentCount() >= 0

> **public int** currentCount ()
>> Current count; the number of items counted.
>
>> **ensure:**
>>> result >= 0

Command postconditions

Commands result in a change of state. Thus command postconditions typically describe the new state of the object, its state after execution of the command. The new state is often compared to the previous state, the state of the object when the command was invoked. For this reason, it is convenient to have a notational convention for referring to the state of the object when the command is invoked. We use "old" for this purpose, as illustrated above with the *Explorer* method takeThat.

Constructor postconditions

Not surprisingly, constructor postconditions typically describe the initial state of the newly created object. This is the case with the *Explorer* constructor given above.

Preconditions and postconditions are part of the specification

It is important to remember that preconditions and postconditions for public methods are part of an object's specification. As such, they should *never* mention private implementation components. The following specification of the *Counter* method `reset`, for instance, is incorrect. The *Counter* instance variable `count` is part of the implementation: it is not part of the object's specification, and is meaningless to the client.

> **public void** reset ()
> Reset the count to 0.
>
> **ensure:**

✗
> count == 0 *This is not correct! count is private.*

The method `currentCount`, however, is part of the public specification of the class. The following is the proper way to express the postcondition:

> **public void** reset ()
> Reset the count to 0.
>
> **ensure:**
> this.currentCount() == 0

✷ 5.4   Enumeration classes

In defining the classes *TrafficSignal* and *PlayingCard* in Chapter 2, we used named constants to define what are essentially "types" with only a few values. For instance, there are three possible values for a *TrafficSignal* light: green, yellow, and red. To represent these values, we used integers named `TrafficSignal.GREEN`, `TraficSignal.YEL-LOW`, and `TraficSignal.RED`. Similarly, there are four possible values for a *Playing-Card* suit, and thirteen values for a *PlayingCard* rank. In each case, we used integers to represent these values.

The problem with this approach is that there is no way for the compiler to ensure that a client uses appropriate integers for these values. There is nothing to prevent a client from writing, for example,

> **new** PlayingCard(27,-4)

Of course, we can check at run-time with an assert statement:

```
public PlayingCard (int suit, int rank) {
    assert suit == SPADE || suit == HEART ||
        suit == DIAMOND || suit == CLUB;
    ...
```

But compile time checking, when we can achieve it, is much more effective than run-time checking.

An alternative approach is to use an *enumeration*. An enumeration is a class having a small number of fixed, named, instances. We can define an enumeration classes in the class *PlayingCard* as follows.

```
public class PlayingCard {

    public enum Suit {clubs, diamonds, hearts, spades}
    public enum Rank {two, three, four, five, six,
        seven, eight, nine, ten, jack, queen, king, ace}
    ...
```

The format of the definition includes the keyword **enum**, followed by the name of the class, followed by a list of class instances.

These definitions define classes *PlayingCard.Suit* and *PlayingCard.Rank*. *Playing-Card.Suit* comprises four objects, named clubs, diamonds, hearts, and spades. *PlayingCard.Rank* comprises thirteen objects named two, three, *etc*. These objects are essentially "named constants." PlayingCard.Suit.clubs, for example, is a named constant in much the same way as PlayingCard.CLUB in our original definition of *PlayingCard*. However, PlayingCard.Suit.clubs denotes a *PlayingCard.Suit* object, while PlayingCard.CLUB denotes an **int**.

We can now define the *PlayingCard* constructor and queries in terms of the classes *Suit* and *Rank*, as shown in Listing 5.1. A client is required to provide *PlayingCard.Suit* and *PlayingCard.Rank* arguments when invoking the constructor:

```
new PlayingCard(
    PlayingCard.Suit.clubs, PlayingCard.Rank.ace);
```

Furthermore, since the enumeration classes and instance identifiers are static, they can be imported into a compilation unit with a static import statement. (See Section 3.7.3.) If the client compilation unit includes

```
import static PlayingCard.*;
```

the constructor can be invoked as

```
new PlayingCard(Suit.clubs, Rank.ace);
```

If the client compilation unit includes

```
import static PlayingCard.Suit.*;
import static PlayingCard.Rank.*;
```

the constructor can be invoked as

```
new PlayingCard(clubs, ace);
```

There is one other advantage to using enumerations. In an enumeration class, the method toString is defined to return the name of the object as a *String*. For instance,

```
PlayingCard.Suit.clubs.toString() ⇒ "clubs"
```

Listing 5.1   **The class *PlayingCard***

```
public class PlayingCard {

    public enum Suit {clubs, diamonds, hearts, spades}
    public enum Rank {two, three, four, five, six, seven,
        eight, nine, ten, jack, queen, king, ace}

    private Suit suit;
    private Rank rank;

    public PlayingCard (Suit suit, Rank rank) {
        this.suit = suit;
        this.rank = rank;
    }

    public Suit suit () {
        return suit;
    }

    public Rank rank () {
        return rank;
    }

    public String toString () {
        return rank + " of " + suit;
    }
}
```

This can be helpful in testing and debugging. With our original *PlayingCard* class, `card.suit()` returns an **int**. The statement

```
System.out.println("suit: " + card.suit());
```

produces something like

```
suit: 1
```

Using enumerations, this statement writes a more readable

```
suit: clubs
```

5.5   Summary

In this chapter, we introduced a programming style called programming by contract. The basic idea is to make explicit the respective responsibilities of client and server in a method invocation. To this end, the invocation of a server method by a client is viewed as involving a contract between the client and the server. The server promises to perform the action specified by the method and to ensure that the method's postconditions are satisfied, but only if the client meets the preconditions. Preconditions are the client's responsibility; postconditions are the server's. If the client fails to meet the preconditions, the contract is void: the server is not obligated to behave in any specific way.

Using this approach, it is a programming error for a client to invoke a method without satisfying the method's preconditions. We talk more about errors in Chapter 15. Conversely, if the client satisfies the preconditions, the server must accomplish the action as specified.

Preconditions can be verified using Java's assert statement. If the boolean expression in the assert statement is true, the statement has no effect. If it is false, an error exception occurs and the program terminates.

Preconditions most often constrain the values a client can provide as argument. Postconditions for a query generally say something about the value returned. Postconditions for a command generally describe the state of the object after the command is completed in terms of the state before the command was begun.

SELF-STUDY EXERCISES

5.1   What is "programming by contract"? For what language constructs are contracts defined? How is the contract between client and server specified?

5.2   How does programming by contract help manage complexity and improve efficiency in a software system?

5.3   Compare how the system deals with bad data entered by the user and illegal arguments passed to a method.

5.4   Indicate whether each of the following statements is true or false.

    a.   In programming by contract, the server is always required to meet specified postconditions.

    b.   In programming by contract, the server should verify client-provided arguments and correct them if possible.

    c.   Java's run-time system checks the validity of preconditions and postconditions.

5.5   Consider the class *JetCalibrator* partially given below. What this class models is not important.

```
1.    public class JetCalibrator {
2.
3.       /**
4.        * @ensure       -5 <= this.jetSetting() &&
5.        *                this.jetSetting() <= 5
6.        */
```

```
7.        public int jetSetting () ...
8.
9.        /**
10.        * @require    -3 <= offSet && offSet <= +3
11.        */
12.       public void adjust (int offSet) ...
13.
14.        /**
15.        * @ensure      this.jetSetting () >= 0
16.        */
17.       public void normalize () ...
18.
19.       private int jet;    // invariant:
20.                           // -5 <= jet && jet <= +5
21.    }
```

Which of the following statements are true?

a. Ensuring that the condition of line 10 holds is the responsibility of the client.

b. In a correct program, the method `adjust` will never be invoked with an argument of 4.

c. The implementation of the method `adjust` must check the value of `offSet` in case the user enters a value that is out of range.

d. The condition of line 15 implies that the server will never execute the method `normalize` when the property `jetSetting` is negative.

e. The condition of line 20 implies that the value of the instance variable `jet` will never be 6.

5.6   Let c, i, and j be variables defined as follows:

```
JetCalibrator c = new JetCalibrator (...);
int i;
int j;
```

where *JetCalibrator* is the class sketched in Exercise 5.5. Which of the lettered statements are true after the following sequence is executed?

```
i = c.jetSetting ();
c.normalize ();
j = c.jetSetting ();
```

a. i and j are guaranteed to have the same value.

b. i can be –5.

c. j can be –5.

5.7   Given the variables of Exercise 5.6, suppose the following statements are executed:

```
i = 4;
c.adjust(i);
j = c.jetSetting();
```

Which one of the following are true?

a. j will be 4.

b. It is not possible to tell what will happen.

c. The program is guaranteed to crash.

5.8   Write an assert statement to verify the precondition of the method `takeThat`, shown on page 245.

5.9   The following are specifications for constructors and methods in a *Counter* class. Critique their completeness.

(a)   **public** Counter (**int** a, **int** b)
               Create a new *Counter*.

(b)   **public void** increment ()
               Increment this *Counter*.

(c)   **public void** reset ()
               Reset this *Counter* to the starting value.

               ensure:
                   this.count() == Counter.STARTING_VALUE

5.10   The class *CombinationLock* defined in Section 4.4 includes a method `close`, specified as

               public void close ()
                   Lock this *CombinationLock*.

and an instance variable isOpen, defined as

               private boolean isOpen;   // the lock is unlocked

Here are three implementations of the method `close`:

(a)
```
public void close () {
    isOpen = false;
}
```

(b)
```
public void close () {
    assert isOpen;
    isOpen = false;
}
```

(c)
```
public void close () {
    isOpen = !isOpen;
}
```

What preconditions. if any, should be added to the method to make each of these implementations correct?

EXERCISES

5.1 Add preconditions and/or postconditions as appropriate to the balls and strikes counter class of Exercise 4.8.

5.2 Add appropriate assert statements to the *Pile* method `remove`, as specified on page 246. Write and run a test in which the precondition is violated and note the error message produced.

5.3 Add preconditions and postconditions to the *Rectangle* class specified in Listing 3.4. Add assert statements to the implementation. Modify the `RectangleDisplay` program so that it attempts to create an illegal *Rectangle*. Run the program and observe the error message generates.

5.4 Add preconditions and postconditions to the class *PlayingCard*, specified in Listing 2.5.

5.5 Add appropriate assert statements to the digit-by-digit lock of Listing 4.4.

5.6 Write assert statements that explicitly versify that the name and location arguments of the *Explorer* constructor are not null.

5.7 Suppose that for the *Employee* method `pay` of Exercise 4.6, `hours` and `rate` are parameters rather than instance variables. That is, suppose the method is specified as

```
public double pay (int hours, double rate)
```

Write a complete specification, including reasonable preconditions and postconditions, for this method.

5.8 Assume that the method `dayOfWeek` takes a day of the year and year as arguments, and returns the day of the week. That is, `dayOfWeek` is specified

```
public int dayOfWeek (int day, int year)
```

and `dayOfWeek(51,1999)` will tell us that the 51st day of 1999 was a Saturday.

Assume that the class *Date* has named constants defined for each day of the week:

```
public static final int MONDAY = ...
    ...
```

Write a complete specification, including reasonable preconditions and postconditions, for this method.

5.9 Write, compile, and run a simple program with the following `main`. Explain the results.

```
public static void main (String[] argv) {
    int i = 2147483647;
    i = i + 1;
    System.out.println("i = " + i);
}
```

5.10 Suppose we want to build a maze game in which *Denizens*, when poking an *Explorer*, sometimes magically increase the *Explorer's* tolerance. We represent a magic tolerance-giving hit by furnishing a negative argument to the `takeThat` method. Furthermore, we allow an *Explorer* to have deficit tolerance, also represented by a negative value. An *Explorer* with deficit tolerance can be revived only by a tolerance-giving poke. Can we reuse the class *Explorer* as it exists in this new game? Explain your answer.

5.11   Can an assert statement be used to verify query postconditions? Why do you think preconditions are verified far more often than postconditions?

Can an assert statement generally be used to verify command postconditions? Why or why not?

SELF-STUDY EXERCISE SOLUTIONS

5.1   Programming by contract is a programming style in which the invocation of a method is viewed as a contract between client and server, with each having explicitly stated responsibilities. Contracts are defined for methods and constructors. Contracts are specified by the doc comment preceding the method or constructor. In particular, preconditions (require) detail responsibilities of the client, postconditions (ensure) detail responsibilities of the server.

5.2   By localizing responsibilities, the number of methods that must contain code to verify the validity of data is minimized. The result is reduced complexity and improved efficiency.

5.3   It is the responsibility of the user interface subsystem to interact with the user and prevent bad data from being entered. Sometimes this is easy, for instance, if the user enters a name when a data is expected. Sometimes this is impossible, for instance, if the user keys "7" rather than "8" when entering the price for a can of beans. A client invoking a server a method with an illegal argument, however, is the result of a program bug. We can only hope that the program will terminate with an error message.

5.4   All three statements are false.

5.5   *(a) true*   *(b) true*   *(c) false*   *(d) false*   *(e) true*

5.6   *(a) false*   *(b) true*   *(c) false*

5.7   *(b)* is true.

5.8   **assert** hitStrength >= 0;

5.9   *(a)* The specification adds nothing. What are the parameters? What is the initial value of the *Counter*?

(b) Increment by how much? One would guess one, but it would be better to be explicit. No preconditions imply that the method can be invoked at any time.

(c) Specifications are satisfactory. No preconditions imply that the method can be invoked at any time.

5.10   *(a)* No preconditions are needed.

(b) and *(c)* both need **this**.isOpen() as a precondition. *(b)* will fail if this precondition is not satisfied, and *(c)* will leave open a lock that is already closed. (This is probably not a reasonable precondition. There is no obvious reason for requiring that the client to make sure that the lock is open before attempting to close it.)

CHAPTER 6   **Testing**

The development of a class involves design, specification, implementation, and testing. The process is iterative and incremental: any of these activities can disclose flaws requiring previous steps to be repeated. We have learned how to specify and implement a simple class, and we've seen several examples of simple test systems. We now address the issue of testing more carefully. Testing is fundamental. It validates the implementation of the class, and ultimately the design and implementation of the entire system. But testing can be a difficult topic to become comfortable with. While many guidelines have been developed, there are no hard and fast rules that tell us we have devised an adequate series of tests. Nevertheless, it is important to go about testing in a coherent, well-organized way. Every test we conduct should have a clear purpose.

In this chapter, we briefly discuss testing in general, including *functional testing* and *unit testing*. Functional testing involves testing an entire system to make sure that it conforms to the customer's requirements. Unit testing is testing individual system components to verify that they perform correctly. Every class that we implement should be adequately tested before it is incorporated into a system. We concentrate on unit testing for most of the chapter. We introduce the idea of a test plan, a comprehensive blueprint for ensuring that a method satisfies its specification. Finally, we present an example illustrating the development and implementation of a test plan.

Objectives

After studying this chapter you should understand the following:

- functional testing and unit testing, their similarities and differences;
- implementation driven testing *vs.* test driven implementation;
- the role of a test plan.

Also, you should be able to:

- implement a test plan with a test class.

6.1   Functional testing and unit testing

Testing is an activity with the goal of determining whether or not an implementation functions as intended, and of determining if the implementation is correct. Since it is impossible to exhaustively test any but the simplest system, testing can show that a system contains errors but can't guarantee that a system is completely correct. Thus the purpose of testing is to uncover errors in the implementation: a successful test is one that reveals some previously undiscovered error.

Testing consists of two phases. First, test activities are determined and test data selected. Then the test is conducted and test results compared with expected results. Though a system cannot be tested with all possible data, testing needs to be in some sense comprehensive. Test activities and data must be judiciously chosen to thoroughly exercise the system. It is this process of determining test activities and selecting test data that we refer to as *test design*.

Functional testing

As we saw in Chapter 3, there are two broad categories of testing: *functional testing* and *unit testing*. The goal of functional testing is to determine that the system as a whole meets the customer's specifications. This kind of testing is sometimes referred to as *black box testing*. The test designer ignores the internal structure of the implementation in developing the tests. The expected external behavior of the system drives the selection of test activities and data. The system is treated as a "black box" whose behavior can be observed, but whose internal structure is unknown.

Test design generally begins with an analysis of

- the functional specifications of the system, and
- the ways in which the system will be used (referred to as "use cases").

"Use cases" are artifacts created in the analysis of a system and used to guide its design and implementation. The test is decomposed into several test cases, each addressing a specific use or a specific functionality. A test case is defined by

- a statement of case objectives;
- the data set for the case;
- the expected results.

The result of the design effort is a *test plan*. A test plan is a document that describes the test cases giving the purpose of each case, the data values to be used, and the expected results. The test plan directs the running of the tests.

Functional testing is a complex and extensively studied subject. Many strategies and methodologies have been proposed, and many different approaches are used in practice. Developing an adequate test plan for a large system is clearly an involved, many leveled business, well beyond the scope of this text. Here our attention will be limited to testing the implementation of individual system components.

> **functional testing:** testing to determine that the system as a whole meets the customer's specifications. The system is treated as a "black box" whose behavior can be observed, but whose internal structure is unknown.

Unit testing

Developing and conducting functional tests is often the responsibility of a team different from the programming team that implements the system. Unit testing, on the other hand, is part of the job of implementing the system. Unit testing consists of incrementally testing classes as they are implemented in order to ensure that they function properly. Unit testing and implementation are complementary activities, done concurrently.

As with functional testing, successful unit testing requires development of an adequate test plan. At this level, though, the test plan is generally not a separate document. Instead the test plan is expressed in the testing code itself.

When we do unit testing, we sometimes do *implementation driven testing* and sometimes *test driven implementation*. "Implementation driven" simply means that tests for a module are developed based upon its implementation. Developing and refining test cases based on the implementation is sometimes referred to as *white box testing*. (Perhaps "transparent box testing" would be a better name.) In white box testing, knowledge of the implementation is used to select and refine test cases. For example, if we are testing code that contains an if-then-else statement, it would be judicious to ensure that both the true and false branches of the if-then-else are exercised in the tests.

With test driven implementation, the tests for a feature are written before implementing the feature. Tests are based on specifications only. That is, we generate test cases based on method specifications, including preconditions and postconditions. There are a number of significant advantages to test driven implementation, not the least of which is that the tests provide a very concrete goal for the implementation: we must write an implementation that satisfies the tests. Since we are testing the behavior of an individual method without benefit of the method implementation, this form of test design is sometimes referred to as *gray box testing*.

> **unit testing:** incremental testing of classes as they are implemented in order to ensure that they function properly. Testing can be "white box testing" where the tests are developed based on the unit's implementation, or "gray box testing" where tests are developed based solely on a method's specification.

6.2   Developing a test plan

When we implement a feature we are inclined to be satisfied with a bit of *ad hoc* testing. But indiscriminate, haphazard testing is likely to leave critical and problematic cases untested. And there is no doubt that skimping on testing is false efficiency. We will pay the price later with tedious, time-consuming debugging. It is essential that we carefully analyze the specification of the feature we are building, and develop a plan that thoroughly tests the feature. Additionally, we do not want to waste effort with pointless testing. Every test we perform should be chosen with a clear purpose, and should contribute to our confidence in the correctness of the feature. Thus the plan should in some sense identify the minimal testing required to adequately test the feature. While a plan need not be formal or elaborate, careful specification-directed testing is critical to programmer productivity.

What should we consider when developing a test plan? First, we should analyze the feature to identify cases that should be tested. For example, when we tested the *CombinationLock* command `open` in Section 4.4, we noted that the state of the *CombinationLock* could be opened or closed, and the combination given could be correct or incorrect. Thus we identified four cases to test:

- open a closed lock with the correct combination;
- open an already opened lock with the correct combination;
- attempt to open a closed lock with the incorrect combination;
- attempt to open an already opened lock with the incorrect combination.

As we've seen, it is easy to build an implementation that fails to handle one of the cases correctly. An incorrect implementation could easily pass a test that did not include all four cases.

The set of possible states the object under test can assume is an important aspect of case analysis. Occasionally, an object has so few states that it is possible to test them all. The *TrafficSignal* of Section 2.5 for instance, has only three distinct states. Our test checked the behavior of a *TrafficSignal* in each of its possible states. More often an object has a large number of possible states. A *CombinationLock*, for example, has 2000 possible states: there are 1000 possible combination values, and two possible "is open" values. Furthermore, the *CombinationLock* `open` method has a `combinationToTry` argument, which can have any one of 1000 legitimate values. Thus 2,000,000 method invocations would be required to completely test the *CombinationLock* `open` command. Attempting this would be a monumental waste of time, as we can adequately test the method with far fewer invocations.

To help ensure that the tests are representative without being excessive, the set of possible data is partitioned into *equivalency groups*. Values are considered to be in the same group if they are not likely to test differently. That is, the assumption is that if the system behaves correctly for one instance of an equivalency group, it will behave correctly for all instances of that group. Test cases are chosen from each equivalency group. Particular attention is paid to cases that lie on group boundaries, that is, cases in one group that are as close as possible to being in another. In developing tests for the *CombinationLock* in Chapter 4, since all combinations are treated similarly, there is only one equivalence group. Hence we chose to test one "representative" combination (123), and two boundary cases: the smallest allowed combination (0), and the largest allowed (999). As subtle implementation errors only appear in limiting cases, it is particularly important to test the boundaries.

Finally, it is sometimes important to consider sequences of actions. For example, suppose we are testing a simple counter as introduced in Section 2.2. We want to test both the `reset` and `incrementCount` methods. Rather than simply thinking about each method in isolation, we might consider testing `incrementCount` followed by `incrementCount`; `incrementCount` followed by `reset`; `reset` followed by `incrementCount`; `reset` followed by `reset`. This might seem overkill here, since the state of a *Counter* is so very simple. But here are many situations in which the interaction between methods is not so straightforward and well worth testing.

Testing illegal data

Should the test plan include cases in which the data is invalid? Whether it should or not depends on the source of the "bad data" and the expected behavior of the program. For example, suppose we are developing a functional test for a system and are concerned with the possibility of a user entering bad data. Perhaps the user must enter a date in a specific format, and it is possible that the user will not enter the date correctly. It is the responsibility of the user interface to interact with the user, and the behavior of the user interface should be clearly specified in this kind of situation. Perhaps an explanatory message will be displayed to the user and the user will be asked to reenter the date. The expected behavior of the system is stipulated, and the system should be tested to verify that the actual behavior is as expected.

The case of a method being invoked with an invalid precondition is another matter entirely. This will never happen in a correct program. It can only happen as the result of a bug in the program itself. To test a method by invoking it with an invalid precondition is to test the behavior of the method in an erroneous program. But the behavior of an erroneous program is unspecified and unpredictable. So it generally does not make sense to include test cases in which a precondition does not hold.

Occasionally, we expect a particular behavior if certain preconditions are violated. There is nothing wrong with testing for this if we are so inclined. However, we should be cautious about describing such behavior in a method's specification. Including a description of a method's behavior when preconditions are not satisfied can encourage programmers to ignore preconditions and depend on the advertised behavior.

6.3   An example

Developing the test plan

As an example, let's develop a plan for testing a digit by digit combination lock, similar to the one specified in Section 4.4.1.

Recall that such a lock has three features, a query and two commands:

public boolean isOpen ()
>This lock is unlocked.

public void close ()
>Lock and reset this lock; partially entered combination is lost.

public void enter (**int** digit)
>Enter a digit of the combination; lock unlocks if the digits of the combination are entered in order.
>
>**require:**
>>digit >= 0 && digit <= 9

A client repeatedly invokes the enter method to enter digits one at a time. If the client enters the digits of the combination in the correct order, the lock is opened. Since the number of cases to consider in a three digit lock is substantial, we'll simplify the example by testing a lock with a two digit combination.

The state of a lock includes not only the combination and whether the lock is open or closed, but also the most recent digit entered by the client. That is, the object knows if the first digit of the combination has just been entered. In considering cases to test, we should consider all three facets of the state. Specifically, we want to test

- cases in which the lock is open, and cases in which the lock is closed;
- cases in which the first digit of the combination has been entered, and cases in which it has not;
- cases with various combinations.

For convenience, we'll refer to a closed lock in which the first digit has been entered as "almost open," and a closed lock that requires both digits as "reset."

What combinations should we test? We might consider the following equivalency groups: combinations specified with a single digit integer (the first digit is implicitly 0); combinations in which the two digits are different, such as 12; combinations in which the two digits are the same, such as 77. It is also a good idea to test the boundaries: that is, the largest (99) and smallest (00) combinations. We'll assume that the case where both digits are the same is adequately covered with the 00 and 99 combinations, but we'll explicitly include a case in which the combination is given by a single digit integer. To be precise, we'll test locks with the combinations 0 (*i.e.*, 00), 1 (*i.e.*, 01), 12, and 99.

With four combination values, two values for "is open," and two value for "first digit has been entered," we already have 16 interesting states to test. The number of cases to consider in a thorough set of tests can quite easily get out of hand! Not all tests, though, need to be performed on all states. For example, if a test is independent on the combination, there is little to be gained from repeating it with locks having different combinations.

Next let's consider the tests we want to perform. Basically we would like to test the initial state, test that the lock opens properly, and test that the lock closes properly. We consider each in turn.

1.   *Test initial state:*

We have no direct way of checking that the combination has been stored correctly. The only aspect of the initial state we can check is that the lock is open. We must trust other tests to implicitly verify the combination has been correctly stored.

- Test the lock is initially open.

2. *Test opening the lock:*

Cases to consider are states in which the lock is already opened, and states in which the lock is closed.

2.a. The lock is already opened.

About all that we need to test in this case is that entering an incorrect combination will not cause an open lock to close.

- Test that entering digits will not close an opened lock.

2.b. The lock is closed.

Clearly the most complicated test. We want to make sure that the correct combination opens the lock and that an incorrect combination doesn't. There are two subcases: states in which the first digit of the combination has not been entered (the lock is "reset"), and states in which it has ("almost open").

2.b.i. The lock is reset.

- Test that entering the correct combination opens the lock.
- Test that entering an incorrect combination doesn't open the lock.

Are there any special cases worth considering here? Perhaps giving the combination digits in the incorrect order, giving an incorrect first digit and the correct second. Giving the correct first digit and incorrect second will be covered in the next case.

2.b.ii. The lock is almost open.

We need not test that entering a correct second digit will open the lock, since this case is implicitly covered when testing that the correct combination opens the lock. We need only consider situations in which the correct first digit is followed by an incorrect second digit.

One situation worth checking is the case in which the first digit of the combination is entered twice. We should make sure that subsequently entering the second digit will still open the lock, as illustrated in the diagram below. Assuming the combination is 12, the left circle represents a state in which the first combination digit has not been entered (reset), the middle circle represents a state in which the first digit has been entered (almost open), the right circle represents a state in which the lock is open.

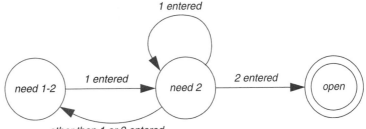

- Test that an almost open lock remains almost open if the digit entered is not the correct second digit, but is the correct first digit.

- Test that an almost open lock is reset if the digit entered is neither the first nor second digit of the combination.

  Note that these subcases do not exist if both digits of the combination are identical.

3. *Test closing the lock:*

    These tests are rather straightforward. We must make sure that closing a lock also resets the lock.

- Test that an open lock is closed and reset after executing `close`.

- Test that a reset lock remains reset after executing `close`.

- Test that an almost open lock is reset after executing `close`.

Implementing the test plan

We have identified the locks we want to test and the tests we want to perform. Let's write the test system. We'll try to handle a minimal number of cases that adequately test the implementation. For instance, we won't apply tests that are independent of the combination to all the locks. We could, of course, add tests if we feel it necessary.

Some programmers prefer including test methods in the class to be tested, essentially building a "self-testing" class. An advantage of this approach is that test routines can access private instance variables of the object being tested. We prefer a separate test class. Adding test methods to a class complicates the class in a way unrelated to its primary function. Furthermore, separating the testing function gives us a bit more flexibility in designing tests, and is the approach we'll use when employing testing frameworks.

The basic structure of the test system is similar to the one we built in Section 4.4. The test object will be an instance of the class *CombinationLockTest*. This class defines a single public method `runTest`. The system `main` method creates a *CombinationLockTest* instance and invokes its `runTest` method:

```
public class TestCombinationLockClass {
    public static void main (String[] argv) {
        (new CombinationLockTest()).runTest();
    }
}
```

As before, the class *CombinationLockTest* will include a helper method `verify`:

```
private void verify (boolean test, String message) {
    if (!test)
        System.out.println(
            "Verification failed: " + message);
}
```

Since we have decided to test four locks, we could structure our test class around a `testLock` method that tests an individual lock, much like we did in Section 4.4. Rather than passing the combination as argument to this method, it would be better to pass the individual digits of the combination:

```
/**
 * Create and test a lock with the specified
 * two digit combination.
 */
private void testLock (int digit1st, int digit2nd)
```

The combination can easily be computed from the digits:

```
int combination = 10*digit1st + digit2nd;
```

If we passed the combination as a single integer, then the test object would have to separate the combination into digits, performing the same computation that the *CombinationLock* constructor performs. That is, the tester would do the same computation whose correctness it should be testing. This is generally not a good idea.

As we proceeded to write the tests, we would notice that locks in which the combination consists of the same digit repeated (such as 99) must be treated somewhat differently from locks in which the combination digits are different. This is not at all an uncommon situation. Objects often behave differently depending on how they are created. So rather than structure the tester with a `testLock` method, we'll take a somewhat different approach. The collection of objects on which a test is to be performed is sometimes called a *test fixture*. We'll consider the four locks that we want to test to be a test fixture, and define instance variables to reference them:

```
private CombinationLock lock00;   // lock with comb. 00
private CombinationLock lock01;   // lock with comb. 01
private CombinationLock lock12;   // lock with comb. 12
private CombinationLock lock99;   // lock with comb. 99
```

Next, we write an auxiliary method to create a test fixture. We'll create a new test fixture for each test, to make sure that the tests are independent of each other.

```
private void setUp () {
    lock00 = new CombinationLock(0);
    lock01 = new CombinationLock(1);
    lock12 = new CombinationLock(12);
    lock99 = new CombinationLock(99);
}
```

It will also be handy to have an auxiliary method to close the locks:

```
private void closeLocks () {
    lock00.close();
    lock01.close();
    lock12.close();
    lock99.close();
}
```

Now we can write the test methods. We begin each method by creating a test fixture. The initial state test will only test that the lock is open. Since this is independent of the combination, we don't need to check each lock in the test fixture. Testing one lock should suffice.

```
private void testInitialState () {
    setUp();
    verify(lock12.isOpen(),"Initially open: lock 12");
}
```

We'll write five tests to verify that the lock opens properly, corresponding to the cases that we described above.

```
private void testOpenLock ()
```
>   Test that entering an incorrect combination does not close an open lock.

```
private void testCorrectCombination ()
```
>   Test that entering the correct combination opens a lock.

```
private void testIncorrectCombination ()
```
>   Test that entering an incorrect combination doesn't open a lock.

```
private void testFirstDigitTwice ()
```
>   Test that entering the first combination digit twice leaves the lock almost open (unless two combination digits are the same).

```
private void testCorrectFirstDigit ()
```
>   Test that entering the first combination digit followed by an incorrect digit different from the first leaves the lock reset.

Coding the tests is straightforward, if a bit tedious.

```
private void testOpenLock () {
    setUp();
    lock12.enter(3);  lock12.enter(4);
    verify(lock12.isOpen(),"Open lock: lock 12");
}


private void testCorrectCombination () {
    setUp();  closeLocks();

    verify(!lock00.isOpen(),"Lock closed: lock 00");
    lock00.enter(0);  lock00.enter(0);
    verify(lock00.isOpen(),"Correct comb: lock 00");

    verify(!lock01.isOpen(),"Lock closed: lock 01");
    lock01.enter(0);  lock01.enter(1);
    verify(lock01.isOpen(),"Correct comb: lock 01");

    verify(!lock12.isOpen(),"Lock closed: lock 12");
```

```
        lock12.enter(1); lock12.enter(2);
        verify(lock12.isOpen(),"Correct comb: lock 12");

        verify(!lock99.isOpen(),"Lock closed: lock 99");
        lock99.enter(9); lock99.enter(9);
        verify(lock99.isOpen(),"Correct comb: lock 99");
    }

    private void testIncorrectCombination () {
        setUp(); closeLocks();

        lock00.enter(1); lock00.enter(0);
        verify(!lock00.isOpen(),"Incorrect comb: lock 00");

        lock01.enter(1); lock01.enter(1);
        verify(!lock01.isOpen(),"Incorrect comb: lock 01");

        lock12.enter(2); lock12.enter(1);
        verify(!lock12.isOpen(),"Incorrect comb: lock 12");

        lock99.enter(0); lock99.enter(9);
        verify(!lock99.isOpen(),"Incorrect comb: lock 99");
    }

    private void testFirstDigitTwice () {
        setUp(); closeLocks();

        lock01.enter(0); lock01.enter(0);
        verify(!lock01.isOpen(),"1st, 1st: lock 01");
        lock01.enter(1);
        verify(lock01.isOpen(),"1st, 1st, 2nd: lock 01");

        lock12.enter(1); lock12.enter(1);
        verify(!lock12.isOpen(),"1st, 1st: lock 12");
        lock12.enter(2);
        verify(lock12.isOpen(),"1st, 1st, 2nd: lock 12");
    }

    private void testCorrectFirstDigit () {
        setUp(); closeLocks();

        lock01.enter(0); lock01.enter(2); lock01.enter(1);
        verify(!lock01.isOpen(),"1st, X, 2nd: lock 01");

        lock12.enter(1); lock12.enter(0); lock12.enter(2);
```

```
        verify(!lock12.isOpen(),"1st, X, 2nd: lock 12");
    }
```

To test that a lock closes properly, we write three tests corresponding to the case we identified above. We've already implicitly tested closing an open lock in the testCorrectCombination method. Again, we don't feel obligated to test each lock in the test fixture.

```
    private void testCloseOpenedLock () {
        setUp();
        lock12.enter(1);
        lock12.close();
        verify(!lock12.isOpen(),"close opened: lock 12");
        // Verify the lock is reset:
        lock12.enter(2);
        verify(!lock12.isOpen(),"reset opened: lock 12");
    }

    private void testCloseResetLock () {
        setUp(); closeLocks();
        lock12.close();
        verify(!lock12.isOpen(),"close reset: lock 12");
    }

    private void testCloseAlmostOpenLock () {
        setUp(); closeLocks();

        lock00.enter(0);
        lock00.close();
        lock00.enter(0);
        verify(!lock00.isOpen(),
            "reset almost open: lock 00");

        lock12.enter(1);
        lock12.close();
        lock12.enter(2);
        verify(!lock12.isOpen(),
            "reset almost open: lock 12");

        lock01.enter(0);
        lock01.close();
        lock01.enter(1);
        verify(!lock01.isOpen(),
            "reset almost open: lock 12");
    }
```

Implementation driven testing and test driven implementation

In the example, we have developed the test system independent of the model implementation. If the *CombinationLock* had already been implemented, we could use the implementation to direct development of the test plan (white box testing). We could, for example, verify that our assumptions that certain operations are independent of the combination are accurate.

On the other hand, if the class has not been implemented, we would develop the test plan and implement the class at the same time: test driven implementation. We might begin by stubbing the *CombinationLock* class. Then we would follow the implementation strategy we've seen before:

- implement a test;
- run the test, and observe it fail;
- implement the features required by the test;
- run the test again and verify the correctness of the implementation.

In either situation, the model must first be analyzed, and test cases identified.

DrJava: testing with JUnit

JUnit is a useful framework for building Java unit tests. In this exercise, we will see how to access JUnit through DrJava, and how a simple JUnit test is constructed.

Open the file `CombinationLockTest.java`, located in `locks`, in `ch6`, in `nhText`. This contains a skeletal JUnit test for the *CombinationLock* class described above. Note that

- the file imports `junit.framework.TestCase`, and
- the test class extends `TestCase`.

The significance of the extends clause will be explained in a later chapter. For now, it is simply some syntax that must be included in the definition of a test class.

Each test method must be specified as

```
public void testSomething ()
```

In particular, a test method has no parameters, and its name begins with the word "test." There are two test methods written here, `testInitialState` and `testOpenLock`. These perform exactly the same tests as the methods with the same names in the above section.

There is a method specified as

```
protected void setUp ()
```

This method creates the test fixture, exactly as the method `setUp` in the previous section. Note that the method is specified as protected, and not public or private. Again, the significance of this will be explained in a later chapter.

When the test is run, each test method will be executed. The method `setUp` is automatically invoked before each test method. It does not need to be invoked explicitly in the test method. Thus each test method is executed against a newly created test fixture. The test methods are guaranteed to be independent of each other.

Note that this is exactly what we did with the test in the previous section. But the method `runTest` of the previous section is not required, and the test methods do not explicitly invoke `setUp`.

To verify the results of an action, the test methods invoke `assertTrue`. This method takes two arguments, a *String* and a **boolean**. It is essentially the same as the method `verify` from the previous section. If the **boolean** is false, an error is reported. The error report includes the *String* given as the first argument.

The file `CombinationLock.java` contains an implementation of the two-digit lock. The method close is not completed, and the implementation contains a deliberate error.

1. Make sure that *CombinationLockTest* is open in the edit window.

2. Press the *Test* button on the tool bar. This runs the test specified by *CombinationLockTest*. The tests will fail because of the error in *CombinationLock*.

3. Open `CombinationLock.java`, correct the error, save and compile.

4. Open *CombinationLockTest* again. (Simply click on the name in the "opened files pane" to the left of the edit window. Run the test. This time, the tests should be successful.

5. Add the method `closeLocks` as defined above to *CombinationLockTest*. Save and recompile.

6. Add methods `testCloseOpenedLock` and `testCloseResetLock`, as specified in the previous section, to *CombinationLockTest*. Remember, these methods must be specified public and should not explicitly invoke `setUp`. Also, don't forget to replace calls of `verify` with calls of `assertTrue`, with the arguments in the correct order. Save and recompile.

7. Run test. The newly added tests should fail, since the method `close` in *CombinationLock* is not yet implemented.

8. Implement `close`. Save and recompile *CombinationLock*, and run the test again. The test should succeed.

9. Add the remaining tests, as defined in the previous section, to *CombinationLockTest*. After adding each test, save, compile, and test.

6.4   Summary

In this chapter, we considered the problem of testing. We noted that testing can demonstrate that a system contains errors, but can never completely guarantee a system's correctness.

Functional testing tests the system to verify that it meets the customer's specifications. Functional tests are designed from the functional specifications of the system. They are generally "black box tests," in that they test the external behavior of the system while treating the implementation structure as unknown. Unit tests verify that a systems components work properly. Unit tests are the responsibility of the programmers developing the components and are part of the job of implementing the system. Functional testing, on the other hand, is often the responsibility of a separate team.

All testing requires the development of a test plan. A test plan describes the tests to be conducted: the purpose of the test, the data to be used in the test, the expected results. For unit testing, the test plan is formalized in the test code itself. For functional testing, the test plan is an independent document that directs the testing.

Developing a test plan involves identifying a number of cases to be tested. In a functional test, these "use cases" describe ways in which the system will be used. In a unit test, cases are often determined by the possible states of the object under test. The behavior of the object is tested in any number of representative or critical states.

SELF-STUDY EXERCISES

6.1   What is the basic difference between functional testing and unit testing? Which is the responsibility of the implementor?

6.2   True or false: a test plan is only important in functional testing.

6.3   True or false: when testing a method, it is important to always include test data that will make preconditions false.

6.4   A system requires a user to enter his or her current age. A method readAge is included in the user interface, and is responsible for getting his or her age from the user. A method computePremium is included in the model. It requires the user's age as an argument, and has a precondition on this argument requiring it to be in the range 0 to 120, inclusive. Should these methods be tested with an age value of 969? Explain.

6.5   What is the difference between implementation driven testing and test driven implementation?

6.6   In testing locks with three digit combinations, would it be reasonable to test both a lock with the combination 123 and a lock with the combination 234? Why or why not?

6.7   What is a test fixture?

6.8   Consider the command remove from the nim game class *Pile*, specified as:

```
public void remove (int number)
        Reduce the number of sticks by the specified amount.

    require:
        number >= 0
        number <= this.sticks()

    ensure:
        this.sticks() == old.sticks() - number
```

(See Section 5.2.) Which of the following would be reasonable tests for this method?

       a.   Test with an argument of 0.

       b.   Test with an argument greater than 3.

       c.   Test with a *Pile* containing no sticks.

       d.   Test with an argument greater than the number of sticks in the *Pile*.

6.9   The nim game class *Pile* has only one attribute: the number of sticks it contains, and one command, `remove`. (See Section 3.2.) In developing a test for this class, how many different *Pile* instances would you include in a test fixture?

6.10   The nim game class *Player* has a method `takeTurn`, specified as follows:

        public void `takeTurn (Pile pile)`
              Remove 1, 2, or 3 sticks from the specified *Pile*.

(See Section 3.2.) In developing a test for this method, how many different *Pile* instances would you consider using as arguments?

EXERCISES

6.1   Using the test system developed in this chapter, find the errors in the following implementation of *CombinationLock*.

```
public class CombinationLock {

    public CombinationLock (int combination) {
        this.digit1st = combination/10;
        this.digit2nd = combination%10;
    }

    public boolean isOpen () {
        return isOpen;
    }

    public void enter (int digit) {
        if (needSecond)
            isOpen = (digit == digit2nd);
        else
            needSecond = (digit == digit1st);
    }

    public void close () {
        isOpen = !isOpen;
    }

    private int digit1st;          // 1st digit of the
```

```
                                        // combination
        private int digit2nd;           // 2nd digit of the
                                        // combination
        private boolean isOpen;         // lock is open
        private boolean needSecond;     // 2nd combination
                                        // digit will open the
                                        // lock (i.e., 1st has
                                        // been entered.)


    }
```

6.2   Develop a test plan for the method isLeapYear of Section 4.3.

6.3   Given that score is a *Student* instance variable of type **int** containing a student's test score, and letterGrade is a method returning a **char** as follows: the **char** 'A' is returned if score is 93 or above, 'B' if score is between 85 and 92, 'C' if score is between 77 and 84, 'D' if score is between 70 and 76, and 'F' if score is below 70. Develop a test plan for the method letterGrade.

6.4   Develop a test plan for the method fees of Exercise 4.5.

6.5   Develop a test plan for the method pay of Exercise 4.6.

6.6   Reexamine the test plan you implemented for testing the modulus counter of Exercise 3.9. Revise and reimplement the test plan if necessary.

6.7   Develop a test plan for testing the class *Pile* (Section 3.2).

6.8   Reexamine the test plan you implemented for testing the class *Player* of Exercise 4.7. Revise and reimplement the test plan if necessary.

6.9   Reexamine the test plan you implemented for testing the three digit lock of Exercise 4.15. Revise and reimplement the test plan if necessary.

6.10 Implement and test the class *Explorer*, specified in Section 3.3. Use a test driven implementation strategy. You will need minimal definitions of the classes *Room* and *Denizen*.

SELF-STUDY EXERCISE SOLUTIONS

6.1   Functional testing tests the system to ensure that it conforms to the customer's specifications. Unit testing tests a system component to ensure that it is correct. Unit testing is the responsibility of the implementor.

6.2   False, a test plan is essential for all testing.

6.3   False.

6.4   The readAge method should be tested in the case that the user attempts to enter "invalid data," since it should have some clearly defined behavior in this case. The computePremium method need not be tested with invalid data. In a correct program, it will never be called with an argument value of 969.

6.5   Implementation driven testing tests an existing implementation. The structure of the implementation is taken into account when the tests are designed. With test driven implementation, the test for a feature is written first, and based on the specification of the feature. Then the feature is implemented.

6.6   No. These combinations are in the same equivalency group. If one of the locks passes the test, the other will certainly pass as well. Testing both locks does not increase the level of confidence in the correctness of the implementation.

6.7   A set of objects that will participate in a test.

6.8   *a.*   Yes, a valid argument and boundary value.

        b.   Yes. Even though this is not allowed by the game, it is not prohibited by the method.

        c.   Yes. Again, this is not prohibited by the method. Of course, the only valid argument in this case is 0.

        d.   No. This case is prohibited by the precondition. What would the expected result be?

6.9   At least one "representative" *Pile* containing a reasonable number of sticks, and a *Pile* with no sticks. Perhaps also a *Pile* that could be emptied in one legal move.

6.10   Good choices would be a *Pile* with more than three sticks, and a *Pile* with three or fewer sticks. Note that there is no explicit precondition here requiring the *Pile* have at least one stick. However, since the command must remove at least one stick, an empty *Pile* is implicitly excluded. It would be preferable to make this condition explicit.

CHAPTER 7

Building a text-based user interface: iteration and composition

In Section 1.6, we saw that a system can be divided into basic subsystems, including model, external interface, and data management. In Section 3.5, we built a simple user interface for a *Rectangle*, called a *RectangleViewer*. The *RectangleViewer* did nothing more than display a Rectangle's attributes. Now we want to construct a more useful user interface, one that will accept user input as well as produce output. The user interfaces we design in this chapter are text based, that is, input is in the form of text keyed by the user, and output is in the form of text displayed in the window in which the program is run. We've still a way to go before we can create the kind of event-driven graphical interfaces we'd like our systems to have. Before we tackle that topic, we need to understand more about the structure of Java applications. But text-based interfaces can be useful in many circumstances, in particular when testing and developing a system.

Input and output functions are provided in Java through a collection of standard library classes. These facilities are quite powerful and flexible, and as a result, somewhat complex. Since we want to see how to construct a user interface without getting bogged down in the byzantine structure of Java's standard i/o classes, we use our own simple i/o classes in this chapter.

We also introduce a new algorithmic structure in this chapter called *iteration*. The language's iterative, or looping, constructs allow us to specify an action that is to be repeated until some condition is satisfied. We use iteration in a rather simple way here, to allow a user to make a sequence of menu choices for instance.

Objectives

After studying this chapter you should understand the following:

* independence of servers from clients;

- likeliness of the user interface to change;
- i/o streams;
- structure of a simple text-based user interface;
- purpose and structure of a while loop;
- how existing classes can be composed to define a new class.

  Also, you should be able to:

- use input/output objects to read and write data;
- build a simple text-based user interface;
- use and trace a basic while statement;
- define classes whose implementations contain other classes as components.

7.1   Relating the user interface and the model

Recall that the user interface and model are two fundamental subsystems of an application. Before we design a user interface, we should get a clear idea of how the user interface and model are related. The model consists of the objects that solve the problem at hand. The function of the user interface is to interact with the user, getting input from the user, thereby allowing the user to control the model, and giving output to the user, reporting on the status of the model. Issues such as how the user provides input, what negotiation is necessary to ensure that the user provides acceptable input, what the output looks like, are the responsibility of the user interface. It is the user interface that communicates with and gathers appropriate input data from the user, and formats and displays results to the user. By identifying this as a separate subsystem, we gain flexibility in design. All the details of user interaction are isolated ("encapsulated") in the user interface. These details can easily be changed without affecting the fundamental function of the system.

A server is independent of its clients

The interface and model interact in a client-server relation. Should the interface function primarily as client with the model as server, or *vice versa*? Notice that in a client-server relationship, the server is *independent* of the client, while the client is *dependent* on the server: the client must know about the server, but the server need not know about the client. Client code explicitly references server features, and if the server's specification is changed, the client must be modified appropriately. We say server changes "propagate" to the client. The server, on the other hand, does not directly reference the client. Changes in the client will not effect the server. The server can be implemented before the client has been specified.

A system is easier to maintain if changes can be "localized" and not propagate to more stable system elements. Thus a key to good system design is to structure the system so that stable components are independent of those likely to require modification. If a sta-

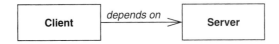

Figure 7.1 **A client depends on its server.**

ble component interacts with one that is likely to change, it is preferable to have the former function as server, with the later as client. (If a client must interact with a server that is likely to be changed, the dependency of the client on the server should, of course, be minimized.)

The user interface is more likely to change than the model

Now the responsibility of the model is to "solve the problem," while the user interface provides a mechanism for viewing and controlling the solution process. From this point of view, the user interface is inherently dependent on the model. Furthermore, the user interface is typically one of the least stable parts of the system, and often among the last to be finalized in system design. Consider the university registration system we've mentioned several times previously. The basic function of the system—to allow students to register for classes—is not likely to change. Model classes, modeling students, courses, and so on, require very little modification over time. However, the user interface, defining how we interact with the system, can change dramatically. Input, for instance, was once done with punched cards. Now we expect to provide input with a touch-tone phone or internet browser.

Since we want the model to be as independent of the user interface as possible, we would like to structure the system so that the user interface acts as client, with the model as server. The user interface queries the model to get state information to report to the user, and gives the model commands as directed by the user.

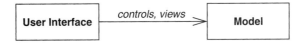

Figure 7.2 **The user interface is client to the model.**

There are two distinct functions of the user interface that we'll ultimately distinguish. First, the user interface must display information about the model state to the user. This is an output function: the user interface provides the user with a *view* of the model. Second, the user interface must provide a means by which the user can *control* the model. This is an input function. There are instances in which the model must direct the user interface to gather data from the user. In these cases, the model is client to the user interface. We must carefully design this dependency to be as minimal as possible.

Ultimately, we want to build graphical user interfaces that interactively respond to user actions. This kind of system is called *event-driven*, since it is designed to respond to "events" that are the result of user actions: moving the mouse, clicking on a menu item, keying a line of text, *etc.* At the moment, we don't have all the tools we need to build a proper event-driven system. But we'll try to keep as close as possible to the event-driven model in our text-based interface.

7.2   Stream-based i/o

An application may have access to several data *streams*. A data stream is essentially no more than a sequence of bytes. If the bytes denote characters, in the ASCII character set for instance, we refer to the stream as a *character stream*. If the stream is a source of data for an application, it is an *input stream*. If it is a destination (or sink), it is an *output stream*. An application *reads* data, removing it from an input stream, and *writes* data, appending it to an output stream.

Figure 7.3   **Input and output streams.**

The actual source of the data in an input stream might be a user's keyboard, a file, another program, a network connection, an external device, *etc.* Likewise, the destination of an output stream could be a terminal window, a file, another program, a network connection, and so on.

Three standard streams, generally available to every program, are *standard input*, *standard output*, and *standard error*. The first, obviously enough, is an input stream; the other two are output streams. (Error messages are written to standard error, never to standard output.) The default source and destination for these streams are keyboard for input, and the display window in which the program is being run for output. The source and destination can be redirected by the operating system when an application is run.

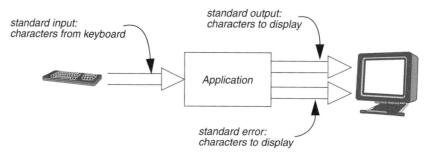

Figure 7.4   **Standard input and output streams.**

7.2.1   Writing standard output and reading standard input

Output

We've been introduced to the predefined object `System.out`. This object provides methods for writing to standard output, including the familiar

> **public void** println (String s)
> > Write the specified *String* to standard output and then terminate the line.

This command writes the *String* to standard output followed by a "line terminator." Subsequent output will begin on the next line. Exactly what constitutes a line terminator is operating system dependent. On a Unix system, for instance, it is a newline character, `'\n'`. On some other systems it is a return character `'\r'` followed by a newline character.

The command `print` writes a *String* without the line terminator:

> **public void** print (String s)
> > Write the specified *String* to standard output.

The command `println` without an argument writes a line terminator:

> **public void** println ()
> > Terminate the current line by writing the line terminator to standard output.

So the command

    System.out.println(s);

is equivalent to the pair of commands

    System.out.print(s);
    System.out.println();

Also note that the pair of commands

    System.out.print("Anarchists ");
    System.out.println("Unite!");

has the same effect as the single command

    System.out.println("Anarchists Unite!");

In both cases, a single line of output is produced.

The runtime system or operating system might sometimes buffer characters until a line terminator is written. For instance, if the command

    System.out.print("Anarchists ");

is executed, the eleven characters in the string `"Anarchists "` might be stored in a memory buffer rather than being immediately written to the user's window. Then when the command

    System.out.println("Unite!");

is executed, the entire line is displayed.

Sometimes we want to make sure that characters are written and not buffered. `System.out` provides a command `flush` to guarantee this:

> **public void** flush ()
>> Flush the stream: write any buffered output to standard output and then flush that stream.

Executing

```
System.out.print("Anarchists ");
System.out.flush();
```

will ensure that the characters in the string `"Anarchists "` are written to the screen (without line termination).

Input

Java's standard mechanisms for handling input are very flexible, and as a result, rather complex and likely to overwhelm beginning programmers. There are no standard easy-to-use input objects comparable to `System.out`. However, the class *Scanner* defined in the standard package `java.util` will serve out present needs. We postpone an examination of the standard input classes until Chapter 16.

Although a *Scanner* can be tailored in a number of ways, the basic default configuration is adequate for our purposes and we will not consider more complex options here.

A *Scanner* reads characters from an input character stream, specified when the *Scanner* is created:

> **public** Scanner (*InputSource* source)
>> Create a *Scanner* to read from the specified `source`.

The input source from which a *Scanner* reads can be one of several possible kinds of obejects. Here, we limit ourselves to reading from standard input, modeled by the predefined object `System.in`, and assume characters are keyed from the keyboard. To create a *Scanner* reading from standard input, we write something like:

```
Scanner input = new Scanner(System.in);
```

A *Scanner* sees its input as a sequence of *tokens* separated by *white space*. White space is made up of characters such as spaces, tabs, line terminators, and so on. A token is a sequence of "nonwhite" characters. For instance, if the user keys

> ••••12•-34••5ab•c?↵

where "•" represents a space and "↵" represents the line termination character(s) at the end of the line, the *Scanner* will see four tokens: 12, -34, 5ab, and c?.

The basic *Scanner* method `next` reads the next token from the input stream:

> **public** String next ()
>> Find and return the next token in the input stream.

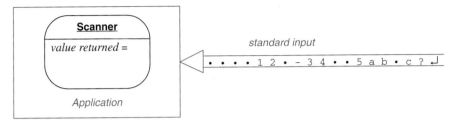

before executing next()

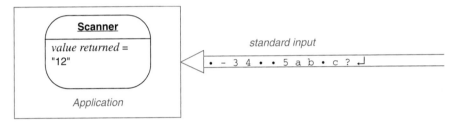

after executing next()

Figure 7.5 A *Scanner* executing *next()*.

If the user keys the line shown above, executing `next` causes the *Scanner* to read up through the character 2. The characters following 2 and the line terminator(s) remain in the input stream, as illustrated in Figure 7.5. The method returns the *String* `"12"`.

Given the input line above, the statements

```
String one = input.next();
String two = input.next();
String three = input.next();
String four = input.next();
```

will assign `"12"` to one, `"-34"` to two, `"5ab"` to three, and `"c?"` to four.

Note that the method `next` is neither a proper command nor a proper query. It is not a proper command since it returns a value. It is not a proper query since it changes the state of the *Scanner*: successive invocations of `next` return different results.[1]

If there are no tokens in the input stream, that is, if the input stream is empty or contains only white space, the method simply waits until the user keys a line containing non-

---

1. What's wrong with methods that both return a value and change state? They are inherently more complex than proper commands and queries. The use of such methods makes it harder to reason about a program's behavior and verify a program's correctness. For instance, if `f` is an integer-returning method that might change state, we cannot deduce something as simple as `f()-f() == 0`.

blank characters. For instance if `next` were invoked a fifth time with the above input, the method would wait until the user entered another (nonblank) line of input.

If there are no tokens remaining in the input stream and the input stream is "closed" or "terminated," the method will fail and raise an error condition called an *exception*. We deal with failure in a later chapter. For now, we'll be content with the default behavior, which is to terminate the program with an appropriate error message. (How one "closes" standard input from the keyboard is system dependent, but generally involves keying a character like CONTROL-D or CONTROL-Z on a line by itself.)

The method `next` returns the next token in the input stream as a *String*. There are also methods that read tokens having the form of integer, double or boolean constants, and return the corresponding **int**, **double**, or **boolean** values.[1]

> **public int** `nextInt ()`
> Return the **int** value denoted by the next token in the input stream.

> **public double** `nextDouble ()`
> Return the **double** value denoted by the next token in the input stream.

> **public boolean** `nextBoolean ()`
> Return the **boolean** value denoted by the next token in the input stream.

The method `nextInt` requires that the next token have the format of an optionally signed integer literal. Given the input line shown above, the statements

```
int one = input.nextInt();
int two = input.nextInt();
```

will assign the **int** values 12 and -34 to the variables `one` and `two` respectively. Invoking `nextInt` a third time will cause the method to fail and raise an exception, since the next token, `5ab`, does not have the form of an optionally signed integer literal. The methods `nextDouble` and `nextBoolean` have similar requirements.

In order to verify preconditions for the various `next` methods, *Scanner* includes queries for determining the existence and format of the next token:

> **public boolean** `hasNext ()`
> This *Scanner* has another token to scan. May block waiting for input. Does not advance past any input.

> **public boolean** `hasNextInt ()`
> The next token in this *Scanner*'s input can be interpreted as an **int**. Does not advance past any input.

> **public boolean** `hasNextDouble ()`
> The next token in this *Scanner*'s input can be interpreted as a **double**. Does not advance past any input.

---

1. There are similar methods `nextByte`, `nextShort`, `nextLong`, and `nextFloat`, and `has-NextByte`, `hasNextShort`, `hasNextLong`, and `hasNextFloat`.

public boolean hasNextBoolean ()
> The next token in this *Scanner*'s input can be interpreted as a **boolean**.
> Does not advance past any input.

We can use these queries to state preconditions for the next methods:

public String next ()
> Find and return the next token in the input stream.
>
> **require:**
> > this.hasNext()

public int nextInt ()
> Return the **int** value denoted by the next token in the input stream.
>
> **require:**
> > this.hasNextInt()

public double nextDouble ()
> Return the **double** value denoted by the next token in the input stream.
>
> **require:**
> > this.hasNextDouble()

public boolean nextBoolean ()
> Return the **boolean** value denoted by the next token in the input
> stream.
>
> **require:**
> > this.hasNextBoolean()

Finally, the nextLine reads the rest of the input line:

public String nextLine ()
> Advance past the current line and return any input that was skipped,
> excluding line terminator(s).

DrJava: exercising a Scanner

1. In the *Interactions* pane, create a *Scanner* that reads from standard input.

   ```
   > import java.util.*;
   > Scanner input = new Scanner(System.in);
   ```

2. Command the *Scanner* to read a token.

   ```
   > input.next()
   ```

   A box will be displayed in which to enter input.

3. Click in the box and enter the following line of text. End by pressing *Enter* or *Return*.

   •••123••123abc••-345⏎

   As above, "•" represents a space and "⏎" represents the line termination.

The *String* returned will be displayed:

```
"123"
```

4. Query to determine if the next token can be interpreted as an **int**.

```
> input.hasNextInt()
false
```

5. Get the next two tokens on the line.

```
> input.next()
"123abc"
> input.nextInt()
-345
```

6. Note that a query to determine if there is another token in the input stream

```
> input.hasNext()
```

will again display the box and wait for input. Enter the following text in the box:

```
Just•some•text⏎
```

7. Now read the "rest of the line" with nextLine:

```
> input.nextLine()
```

Is the result what you expected? Can you explain the result? Remember that has-Next does not "consume" any input, and nextLine returns the remaining characters on the line excluding any line termination characters.

8. Exercise the *Scanner* until you are sure that you understand its behavior.

7.3   An example: building an interface for *Rectangle*

In Section 3.5, we built a very simple interface *RectangleViewer* for the class *Rectangle*. You may recall that the dimensions of the *Rectangle* were "hard coded" into the application, and the interface simply displayed the properties of the *Rectangle* to the user. Now let's build a more useful interface that lets the user specify the dimensions of the *Rectangle* and ask for the property to be displayed.

We name the interface class *RectangleTUI*, for "text-based user interface." It has a simple parameterless constructor and only one public method:

> **class** RectangleTUI
>   A simple text-based interface for *Rectangles*.
>
> **public** RectangleTUI ()
>   Create a new RectangleTUI instance.
>
> **public void** start ()
>   Run the interface.

The application simply creates an interface and executes its start method:

```
public class RectangleExample {

    public static void main (String[] argv) {
        (new RectangleTUI()).start();
    }
}
```

What properties should the interface *RectangleTUI* have? It needs a *Rectangle* to interact with, and a *Scanner* to get input from the user:

```
private Rectangle rectangle;      // the model
private Scanner in;               // standard input
```

These instance variables should be initialized in the constructor:

```
public RectangleTUI () {
    this.rectangle = null;
    this.in = new Scanner(System.in);
}
```

Since the first thing we will do is create a *Rectangle* with user-provided dimensions, we initialize the variable `rectangle` to null. Alternatively, we could start with some default-sized *Rectangle*.

Next let's write a method that creates a *Rectangle*, getting the dimensions of the *Rectangle* from the user. This method will be invoked from the `start` method.

```
private void createRectangle ()
```
Create a new *Rectangle* with user-provided dimensions.

Recall that the *Rectangle* constructor requires length and width:

```
public Rectangle (int length, int width)
```
Create a new *Rectangle* with specified length and width.

> **require:**
> ```
> length >= 0 && width >= 0
> ```

The `createRectangle` method must get these values from the user.

We want to prompt the user for each value and then read the number keyed by the user. Since we'll do this "prompt-read" operation several times, it will be handy to write a little helper method so that we don't have to repeat the same sequence of statements over and over.

```
private int readIntWithPrompt (String prompt) {
    System.out.print(prompt); System.out.flush();
    int input = in.nextInt();
    in.nextLine();
    return input;
}
```

The method writes out the prompt given as argument and reads the integer keyed by the user in response to the prompt. flush is called to make sure that the prompt is not buffered by the operating system. The invocation of nextLine clears anything else on the line. The method nextLine returns a *String* consisting of the skipped input, but we don't do anything with the returned value. Effectively, we use the method as a simple command. The **int** value read by nextInt is returned.

There are wo things to notice about this method. First, it is not very robust, since the user can crash the system by keying something other than an integer to the prompt. We'll fix this problem in a bit. Second, like nextInt, this method is neither a proper command nor a proper query. However, this is a private helper method, and not part of the specification of a class. It's use is local to the implementation of the *RectangleTUI*. In these circumstances, we occasionally excuse the use of such methods.

Now we can make a first attempt at writing the method createRectangle:

```
private void createRectangle () {
    int length;
    int width;
    length = readIntWithPrompt(
        "Rectangle length (a non-negative integer): ");
    width = readIntWithPrompt(
        "Rectangle width (a non-negative integer): ");
    this.rectangle = new Rectangle(length,width);
}
```

When the program is run, we expect a dialogue like the following, where the user's input is indicated by italics:

```
Rectangle length (a non-negative integer): 10
Rectangle width (a non-negative integer): 5
```

But we have one small issue to deal with. The *Rectangle* constructor requires its arguments to be non-negative. If the user keys in something other than an integer, the program will crash. But what if the user keys a negative value? Whether this is likely or not, it is the client's responsibility to make sure that the constructor arguments satisfy the preconditions. Since it is possible for the user to key in negative values, the createRectangle method must check the arguments before invoking the constructor.

What should we do if the user keys in a token that is not an integer or keys in a negative value? There are two obvious choices: use some default value, or ask the user again for input. If we assume that bad input is likely a keying error on the user's part, the second choice seems preferable. So we want to get a value from the user, check to make sure it's valid, and if not, ask the user for the value again. Clearly an obtuse user can continue to key invalid input. We need a way to repeatedly ask for a value until the user keys in one we will accept. To do this, we use a new kind of statement which we introduce next.

7.3.1 Repeating actions: the *while* statement

The process of repeating an action a number of times is called *iteration*. There are several statements in Java that can be used for iteration. The simplest is the *while* statement, or *while-loop*. The while statement is a structured statement. Like the if-then, it has a condition and another statement as components. The syntax is:

> **while** (*condition*)
> *statement*

As with the if-then, the condition is a **boolean** expression. The component statement is called the *body* of the while. The body can be any kind of statement, and is often a compound statement.

When the while statement is executed, the condition is evaluated first. If the condition is true, then the component statement is performed, and the entire process is repeated. Thus the body is repeatedly executed until the condition evaluates to false, at which point the while statement is complete. This is illustrated in Figure 7.6. Because of its structure, the statement is often called a "*while-loop.*"

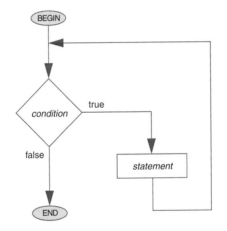

Figure 7.6 **A *while* statement.**

The statement that comprises the loop body might not be executed at all, might be executed once, or might be executed more than once. Executing the body should have the potential of changing the value of the condition.

You should compare the structure of the while statement shown in Figure 7.6 with the if-then pictured in Figure 4.1. Although there is some superficial similarity, these statements exhibit quite distinct behavior, and are used for completely different purposes.

We consider only very simple iteration in this chapter.

---

iteration: a process in which an operation is performed several times.

DrJava: exercising a while statement

Open the file `Examples.java`, located in `ch7`, in `nhText`. This file does not contain the definition of a proper class. It simply contains a few methods that will allow us to watch an iteration being executed.

Look at the method `charCount`. It counts the number of occurrences of a character in a *String*. You may recall from Chapter 1 the *String* method `length` returns the number of characters in the *String*, and `charAt(i)` returns the character at position `i` in the *String*. (The first character in the *String* is at position 0.) This method compares each character in the *String* to the character argument, and counts any matches.

1. Set debug mode, and put a breakpoint on the while statement in method `char-Count`. (See page 185 if you do not remember how to use the debugger.)

2. Invoke the method `charCount` in the *Interactions* pane:

    ```
    > import ch7.*;
    > Examples.charCount('z',"azbz")
    ```

    (The method is static, and so an *Examples* instance is not needed. See page 166 for information about static methods.)

3. Click the *Watches* tab, and enter `count`, `index`, `c`, `current`, and `s` in the *Name* column.

4. In the *Interactions* pane, key

    ```
    ... > s.length()
    4
    ... > s.charAt(0)
    'a'
    ... > s.charAt(1)
    'z'
    ```

5. Press *Step Into* a number of times, noting the flow of control in the method and the change in values of the variables. Note in particular that the while statement starts with the evaluation of the conditional, and every time the body of the loop is completed, the flow comes back to the top of the loop to again evaluate the loop's condition.

6. When this method completes, exercise the other methods in a similar fashion.

7.3.2 Completing the *createRectangle* method

The actions that we want to repeat are the actions that get input from the user. Let's start by verifying that integers we get are nonnegative, and so are legal arguments for the *Rectangle* constructor. We repeatedly ask the user for values until we are satisfied with the result:

```
while ( condition )
    length = readIntWithPrompt(
        "Rectangle length (a non-negative integer): ");
```

```
while ( condition )
    width = readIntWithPrompt(
        "Rectangle width (a non-negative integer): ");
```

In each case, the condition that continues the iteration is that the value provided by the user is negative. When we get a non-negative value from the user, we terminate the iteration:

```
while (length < 0)
    length = readIntWithPrompt(
        "Rectangle length (a non-negative integer): ");

while (width < 0)
    width = readIntWithPrompt(
        "Rectangle width (a non-negative integer): ");
```

Now we have only one issue remaining: in the first while statement, we reference the variable length (in the condition) before it is given a value. The same happens with the variable width in the second while statement. This is not legal. We must give these variables some initial value before referencing them. What value should they be initialized to? We want the while conditions to be true initially: otherwise, the body of the loop won't be executed at all. We can initialize length and width to any values that will make the conditions true:

```
private void createRectangle () {
    // initialize to insure at least one execution of
    // the loops:
    int length = -1;
    int width = -1;
    while (length < 0)
        length = readIntWithPrompt(
          "Rectangle length (a non-negative integer): ");
    while (width < 0)
        width = readIntWithPrompt(
          "Rectangle width (a non-negative integer): ");
    // assert: length >=0 && width >= 0
    this.rectangle = new Rectangle(length,width);
}
```

We are now guaranteed that length and width will both be greater than or equal to 0 when the constructor is invoked. If the user enters a negative value, we'll see a dialogue something like this:

```
Rectangle length (a non-negative integer): -10
Rectangle length (a non-negative integer): -10
Rectangle length (a non-negative integer): 10
Rectangle width (a non-negative integer): -5
Rectangle width (a non-negative integer): 5
```

Now let's look at the `readIntWithPrompt` method. We want to make sure that the user keys in a legal integer in response to the prompt, and continue to prompt until we're satisfied. The method `hasNextInt` will tell whether or not the user has keyed in a valid integer, but we don't want to invoke this method until after the prompt is given. The method can be written as follows:

```
private int readIntWithPrompt (String prompt) {
    System.out.print(prompt); System.out.flush();
    while (!in.hasNextInt()) {
        in.nextLine();
        System.out.print(prompt); System.out.flush();
    }
    int input = in.nextInt();
    in.nextLine();
    return input;
}
```

Note that the body of the while statement is a compound statement, since there is a sequence of three commands that will be repeated. Also notice that the formatting of the statement is similar to that of the if-then.

We give the prompt first, outside the loop. If the user keys in something other than a legal integer, we clear any remaining characters from the line, and prompt again. When the loop terminates, we can be sure that the next token to be read has the proper format. (We could, of course, include the check for a nonnegative value in this method. But since that would make the code a bit more complex, we leave the tests separate for now.)

7.3.3 Finishing the user interface

Now that we've written a method to create a *Rectangle*, let's write the method `start`. After the *Rectangle* is created, the user must be able to query the *Rectangle* for its properties. We want to display a menu enumerating the possible actions, and read the user's choice. We expect a dialogue something like this:

```
Enter the number denoting the action to perform:
Display length..............1
Display width...............2
Display area................3
Display perimeter...........4
Create new rectangle........5
Exit........................0
Enter choice: 2

Width is 5
```

After an action has been completed, the menu should be displayed again. That is, we want the following sequence of actions to be repeated:

1. display menu;
2. get user's choice;
3. perform requested action.

As always, it will simplify things to define auxiliary methods to carry out these steps. The local methods are specified as follows.

> **private void** displayMenu ()
> > Display the menu to the user.

> **private void** executeChoice (**int** choice)
> > Perform the indicated action, and display results to the user.

We can use the method readIntWithPrompt to get the user's choice.

First, we name the choices with identifiers:

```
private static final int LENGTH = 1;
private static final int WIDTH = 2;
private static final int AREA = 3;
private static final int PERIMETER = 4;
private static final int NEW = 5;
private static final int EXIT = 0;
```

Next we sketch the method start:

```
public void start () {
    createRectangle();
    int choice;
    while ( ? ) {
        displayMenu();
        choice = readIntWithPrompt("Enter choice: ");
        executeChoice(choice);
    }
}
```

What should the while condition be? The iteration should continue until the user selects the 'Exit' option. The loop terminates when choice is EXIT:

```
while (choice != EXIT) { ...
```

Again we must initialize a variable, choice, before it is referenced. Any value other than EXIT will do, but we'll define a value to mean that the user has not yet made a choice,

```
private static final int NO_CHOICE = -1;
```

and initialize choice to that value:

```
public void start () {
    createRectangle();
    int choice = NO_CHOICE;
    while (choice!= EXIT) {
```

```
                    displayMenu();
                    choice = readIntWithPrompt("Enter choice: ");
                    executeChoice(choice);
                }
        }
```

All we have left to do is implement the methods `displayMenu` and `executeChoice`. These are rather straightforward.

```
            private void displayMenu () {
                System.out.println();
                System.out.println(
                    "Enter the number denoting the action " +
                    "to perform:");
                System.out.println(
                    "Display length.............." + LENGTH);
                System.out.println(
                    "Display width..............." + WIDTH);
                System.out.println(
                    "Display area................" + AREA);
                System.out.println(
                    "Display perimeter..........." + PERIMETER);
                System.out.println(
                    "Create new rectangle........" + NEW);
                System.out.println(
                    "Exit......................." + EXIT);
            }

            private void executeChoice (int choice) {
                System.out.println();
                if (choice == LENGTH)
                    System.out.println(
                        "Length is " + rectangle.length());
                else if (choice == WIDTH)
                    System.out.println(
                        "Width is " + rectangle.width());
                else if (choice == AREA)
                    System.out.println(
                        "Area is " + rectangle.area());
                else if (choice == PERIMETER)
                    System.out.println(
                        "Perimeter is " + rectangle.perimeter());
                else if (choice == NEW)
                    createRectangle();
                else if (choice == EXIT)
                    System.out.println("Goodbye.");
```

```
      else
          System.out.println(choice + " is not valid.");
  }
```

Note that we invoke `createRectangle` if the user chooses the "Create new rectangle" option. If the user enters a choice other than those displayed on the menu, `executeChoice` attempts to educate the user. The entire interface, without comments, is shown in Listing 7.1.

DrJava: running the application

Open the files `RectangleExample.java` and `RectangleTUI.java`, located in `figures`, in `ch7`, in `nhText`.

You can run the application by keying

```
> java ch7.figures.RectangleExample
```

in the *Interactions* pane. You might want to expand the *Interactions* pane a bit (by grabbing the top bar) so that you can see the full menu when it is written.

Now let's use the debugger to watch the execution a bit more closely.

1. Open `RectangleTUI.java` in the editor pane, set *Debug Mode*, and toggle a breakpoint on the line containing the while. (See page 185 if you do not remember how to use the debugger.)

2. In the *Watches* pane, enter `choice` as the name of the variable to watch.

3. To use the debugger, we'll explicitly run the `main` method of *RectangleExample*. In the *Interactions* pane, enter

```
> import ch7.figures.*;
> RectangleExample.main(null);
```

4. Enter data as before. Execution will pause when the while statement is reached.

5. Step through execution of the loop several times by successively pressing the *Step Over* button. When you are required to enter data, you may need to click in the *Console* pane, on the line containing the prompt.

To see the difference between *Step Over* and *Step Into*, notice what happens when you reach the `displayMenu();` line. When you press *Step Over*, the method `displayMenu` is executed, and execution pauses at the next line, the line beginning `choice = ....` On the next iteration, when `displayMenu();` is reached, press *Step Into*. Notice that execution breaks at the first statement of the method `displayMenu`. You can now step through execution of that method, statement by statement. Pressing *Step Out* finishes execution of `displayMenu`.

Listing 7.1 *Rectangle* **text-based user interface.**

```java
package figures;

import java.util.*;

public class RectangleExample {

    public static void main (String[] argv) {
        (new RectangleTUI()).start();
    }
}


class RectangleTUI {

    private static final int NO_CHOICE = -1;
    private static final int LENGTH = 1;
    private static final int WIDTH = 2;
    private static final int AREA = 3;
    private static final int PERIMETER = 4;
    private static final int NEW = 5;
    private static final int EXIT = 0;

    private Rectangle rectangle;
    private Scanner in;

    public RectangleTUI () {
        this.rectangle = null;
        this.in = new Scanner(System.in);
    }

    public void start () {
        createRectangle();
        int choice = NO_CHOICE;
        while (choice != EXIT) {
            displayMenu();
            choice = readIntWithPrompt("Enter choice: ");
            executeChoice(choice);
        }
    }
```

continued

Listing 7.1   *Rectangle* text-based user interface. (cont'd)

```
private void createRectangle () {
    int length = -1;
    int width = -1;
    while (length < 0)
        length = readIntWithPrompt(
        "Rectangle length (a non-negative integer): ");
    while (width < 0)
        width = readIntWithPrompt(
        "Rectangle width (a non-negative integer): ");
    this.rectangle = new Rectangle(length,width);
}

private void displayMenu () {
    System.out.println();
    System.out.println(
        "Enter the number denoting the action " +
        "to perform:");
    System.out.println(
        "Display length.............." + LENGTH);
    System.out.println(
        "Display width.............." + WIDTH);
    System.out.println(
        "Display area................" + AREA);
    System.out.println(
        "Display perimeter.........." + PERIMETER);
    System.out.println(
        "Create new rectangle........" + NEW);
    System.out.println(
        "Exit......................." + EXIT);
}

private void executeChoice (int choice) {
    System.out.println();
    if (choice == LENGTH)
        System.out.println(
            "Length is " + rectangle.length());
    else if (choice == WIDTH)
        System.out.println(
            "Width is " + rectangle.width());
```

continued

Listing 7.1   ***Rectangle* text-based user interface. (cont'd)**

```
        else if (choice == AREA)
            System.out.println(
                "Area is " + rectangle.area());
        else if (choice == PERIMETER)
            System.out.println(
                "Perimeter is " + rectangle.perimeter());
        else if (choice == NEW)
            createRectangle();
        else if (choice == EXIT)
            System.out.println("Goodbye.");
        else
            System.out.println(choice + " is not valid.");
    }

    private int readIntWithPrompt (String prompt) {
        System.out.print(prompt); System.out.flush();
        while (!in.hasNextInt()) {
            in.nextLine();
            System.out.print(prompt); System.out.flush();
        }
        int input = in.nextInt();
        in.nextLine();
        return input;
    }
}
```

7.4   A second example: using composition

The simple combination lock built in Section 4.4 can be specified as follows:

> **public class** CombinationLock
>> A lock with an integer combination.
>
> **public** CombinationLock (**int** combination)
>> Create a lock with the specified combination.
>>
>> **require:**
>>> 0 <= combination && combination <= 999
>>
>> **ensure:**
>>> this.isOpen()

public boolean isOpen ()
> This *CombinationLock* is unlocked.

public void open (**int** combinationToTry)
> Unlock this *CombinationLock* if the correct combination is provided. If this *CombinationLock* is already open, it remains open regardless of whether or not the correct combination is provided.
>
> **require:**
> > ```
> > 0 <= combinationToTry &&
> > combinationToTry <= 999
> > ```

public void close ()
> Lock this *CombinationLock*.
>
> **ensure:**
> > ```
> > !this.isOpen()
> > ```

(The astute reader will complain that literals rather than named constants appear in the preconditions.)

Suppose that we have a class *Oracle*. An *Oracle* is an object that dispenses fortunes. Its specification is given below.

public class Oracle
> A dispenser of fortunes. An *Oracle* will give a fortune only if it is awake. The normal sequence of actions is: wake the *Oracle*; get a fortune; put the *Oracle* back to sleep.

public Oracle ()
> Create new *Oracle*. This *Oracle* is initially asleep.
>
> **ensure:**
> > ```
> > !this.isAwake()
> > ```

public boolean isAwake ()
> This *Oracle* is awake.

public String fortune ()
> The prophecy currently seen by this *Oracle*.
>
> **require:**
> > ```
> > this.isAwake()
> > ```

public void awaken ()
> Wake this *Oracle*. The *Oracle* will divine a fortune when it wakes.

public void sleep ()
> Put this *Oracle* to sleep.

We want to build an application that lets a user access a "locked oracle." That is, the user can get a fortune from the oracle only by providing the correct key. To do this, we use the existing classes *CombinationLock* and *Oracle*, and create two new classes, one modeling a locked oracle, and the other defining the user interface.

First let's specify the class *LockedOracle*. A key is specified when a *LockedOracle* is constructed. The key is required to generate a fortune.

public class LockedOracle
> A keyed dispenser of fortunes. A *LockedOracle* will give a fortune only if the correct key is provided. A *LockedOracle* must be told to conjure a fortune before the fortune can be retrieved.

public static final String NO_FORTUNE
> *String* indicating no fortune has been conjured.

public LockedOracle (**int** key)
> Create new *LockedOracle* with the specified key.
>
> **require:**
> > 0 <= key && key <= 999

public String fortune ()
> The prophecy currently seen by this *LockedOracle*. If a fortune has not been conjured, the *String* NO_FORTUNE is returned.

public void conjureFortune (**int** keyToTry)
> Prophesy. This *LockedOracle* will make a prophecy only if the correct key is presented.
>
> **require:**
> > 0 <= keyToTry && keyToTry <= 999

Having specified the *LockedOracle*, we could proceed to define the user interface. But we'll implement this model class first.

7.4.1 Constructing a class by composition

We have all the functionality that we need in the existing classes *CombinationLock* and *Oracle*, specified above. Clearly we want to build a *LockedOracle* by putting together a *CombinationLock* and an *Oracle*. This process of defining a new class by putting together existing classes is called *object composition*. Composition is the most important and most fundamental way of building new classes from existing classes.

When we design with composition, we determine a collection of other *collaborator* objects that support an object's responsibilities. The object is equipped with collaborators, or *components*, by means of instance variables that reference the components. Some aspects of the composite object's responsibilities can be delegated to its components. Complicated functions can be broken down into subactions to be accomplished by appropriate components.

The relation between a composite or *composed* object and one of its components is sometimes called the *has-a* relation, or the *includes* relation. It is illustrated in static diagrams with a small diamond, as shown in Figure 7.7. A component class is also referred to as a *core* class.

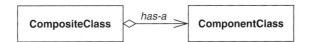

Figure 7.7 A class can be constructed from an existing class by composition.

Though there are exceptions, composites are typified by several properties. First, it is generally the case that the composite and its components have the same lifetime. That is, the components are created when the composite is, and are "meaningful" only in their role of comprising the composite. Often the components are created in the constructor of the composite object.

Additionally, clients of the composite are typically not given access to the components. A client cannot query the composite object and obtain a reference to one of the components. A request for service goes directly to the composite. This object may parcel out portions of the job to its components, as illustrated in Figure 7.8. But the client never deals directly with the components. Note the interaction here between composite and components is client-server, with the composite the client and the component the server.

> **composition:** the process of defining a new class by putting together existing classes. An instance of the new class, the composite, references instances of the existing classes, its components.

Implementing LockedOracle

Now it should be clear that we want the *LockedOracle* class to be a composite, with *CombinationLock* and *Oracle* components. We'll define appropriate instance variables, which we'll initialize in the constructor.

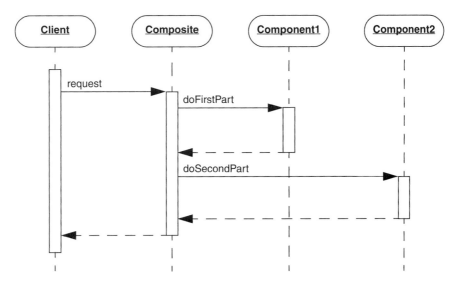

Figure 7.8 A composite delegates parts of a task to its components.

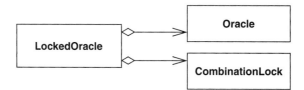

Figure 7.9 A *LockedOracle* has an *Oracle* and a *CombinationLock.*

Looking ahead just a bit, we can see that the command `conjureFortune` changes the state of the *LockedOracle*. This aspect of the state can be queried by the method `fortune`. To support this behavior, we'll also need a component variable to reference the "current prophecy." Thus we define three instance variables,

```
private CombinationLock lock;
private Oracle oracle;
private String fortune;
```

which are initialized in the constructor:

```
public LockedOracle (int key) {
    lock = new CombinationLock(key);
    lock.close();
    oracle = new Oracle();
    fortune = NO_FORTUNE;
}
```

We also need to define the named constant `NO_FORTUNE`:

```
public static final String NO_FORTUNE =
                "Sorry, no fortune for you.";
```

The query `fortune` simply returns the value of the instance variable:

```
public String fortune () {
    return this.fortune;
}
```

The command `conjureFortune` first attempts to open the lock, and wakes the oracle only if it succeeds:

```
public void conjureFortune (int keyToTry) {
    lock.open(keyToTry);
    if (lock.isOpen()) {
        oracle.awaken();
        fortune = oracle.fortune();
        oracle.sleep();
        lock.close();
    } else
        fortune = NO_FORTUNE;
}
```

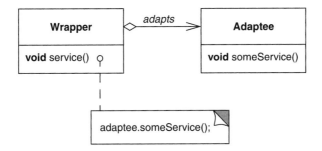

Figure 7.10 **A wrapper adapts an existing class to required specifications.**

Wrapping: the adapter pattern

One further point to note before we move on to the user interface: in the problem at hand, the class *Oracle* has the basic functionality that we require—producing fortunes—but the wrong specification. This is a fairly common problem: an existing class has the needed functionality, but the wrong interface. A general approach to the problem is to *wrap* the existing class in a class with the proper specification, that is, define a new class with the desired specification having the existing class as a component. The new class simply forwards requests for service to the component class. We call the new class a *wrapper* or *adapter*, and the resulting structure is sometimes called the *adapter pattern*. This is illustrated in Figure 7.10. The figure implies that the implementation of the *Wrapper* method `service` involves invoking the *Adaptee* method `someService`. In our example, the adapter *LockedOracle* refines and extends the specification of the existing *Oracle* class, adding the functionality of a lock.

7.4.2 Implementing the user interface

Now that we've completed the model, we can build the user interface. We call the interface class *LockedOracleTUI*. The *LockedOracle* that the interface interacts with will be provided as a constructor argument. The class has one public method.

    class `LockedOracleTUI`
        A simple text-based interface for a *LockedOracle*.

    public `LockedOracleTUI (LockedOracle oracle)`
        Create a new interface for the specified *LockedOracle*.

    public void `start ()`
        Run the interface.

The application creates an oracle and an interface, and executes the interface's `start` method:

```
public class OracleExample {
    public static void main (String[] argv) {
```

```
LockedOracle oracle = new LockedOracle(123);
LockedOracleTUI ui =
    new LockedOracleTUI(oracle);
ui.start();
    }
}
```

Note that the key is hard-coded into the application. This is similar to what we did with the *Rectangle* example in Section 3.5. Of course, this is not the most desirable approach, since the application must be modified and recompiled to change the key. We adopt it only in the interest of simplifying the example.

Instance variables and constructor are much as before:

```
private LockedOracle oracle;
private Scanner in;

public LockedOracleTUI (LockedOracle oracle) {
    this.oracle = oracle;
    this.in = new Scanner(System.in);
}
```

In interacting with the user, we want to ask if the user wants to speak to the oracle, and then get a key from the user. The interaction should look something like this, with the user's input in italics:

```
Fortune? (Key yes or no): yes
Enter key (0-999): 123
To iterate is human, to recurse, divine.

Fortune? (Key yes or no): yes
Enter key (0-999): 124
Sorry, no fortune for you.

Fortune? (Key yes or no): no
Good-bye.
```

As always, it will be handy to write auxiliary methods. One method will get the user's yes or no response, and return it as a boolean. The other method will get a legal key from the user. Again, we grit our teeth and write mongrel commands that return a value.

> **private boolean** readYes (String prompt)
> Read a yes or no response from the user. Return *true* if user keys "yes."

> **private int** readKey (String prompt)
> Read and return a legal key.
>
> **ensure:**
>   0 <= this.readKey() && this.readKey() <= 999

Using these methods, we can write the method start.

```
public void start () {
    String fortune;
    boolean goOn = true;
    while (goOn) {
        goOn = readYes("Fortune? (Key yes or no): ");
        if (goOn) {
            int key = readKey("Enter key (0-999): ");
            oracle.conjureFortune(key);
            fortune = oracle.fortune();
            System.out.println(fortune);
            System.out.println();
        }
    }
    System.out.println("Good-bye.");
}
```

This method is a little more complex than most of the methods we've seen so far, but it should not be difficult to understand.

Now we have only the auxiliary methods to write. The method readYes will be similar to what we've done before. We'll use the method next to get the user's input:

```
private boolean readYes (String prompt) {
    String input = "";
    while (?) {
        System.out.print(prompt); System.out.flush();
        input = in.next();
        in.nextLine();
    }
    return ?;
}
```

There is only one issue left: what shall we consider acceptable input? We have instructed the user to key "yes or no." Will we accept "Y"? "Yes"? "YES"? Let's decide to require that the word "yes" or "no" be spelled out, but not insist on lowercase. That is, we'll accept "Yes" or "YES" but not "Y." Now varying the case gives eight possibilities for "yes" and four for "no." Do we want to compare the input to twelve values? Conveniently, the class *String* contains a method toLowerCase, specified as:

public String toLowerCase ()
> A new *String* object that contains the characters of this *String* converted to lowercase.

So we can convert the user's input to lowercase before checking it.

```
private boolean readYes (String prompt) {
    String input = "";
    while (!(input.equals("yes") ||
            input.equals("no"))) {
```

```
        System.out.print(prompt); System.out.flush();
        input = in.next();
        input = input.toLowerCase();
        in.nextLine();
    }
    return input.equals("yes");
}
```

Note the use of `equals` for comparing *Strings*. This was explained in Section 4.5.1.

The `readKey` method is a little more complex. We need to prompt the user, make sure the token in an integer, read the integer, make sure the integer is valid. The following will do. The variable `haveGoodKey` is set to true when the user enters an acceptable key. As long as the variable is false, the iteration continues.

```
private int readKey (String prompt) {
    int key = -1;
    boolean haveGoodKey = false;
    while (!haveGoodKey) {
        System.out.print(prompt); System.out.flush();
        if (in.hasNextInt()) {
            key = in.nextInt();
            haveGoodKey = (0 <= key && key <= 999);
        }
        in.nextLine();
    }
    return key;
}
```

✳ 7.5   Java in detail: the *do* statement

Though the while statement is the most commonly used statement for iteration, and is the simplest and easiest to verify, Java provides two other looping constructs: the *do statement* and the *for statement*. We look at the do statement here, and consider the for statement in a later chapter.

The do statement is similar to the while, except that the condition follows the body of the loop. The syntax for the do statement is

```
do
    statement
while ( condition ) ;
```

Note the required semicolon terminating the statement. The semantics is illustrated in Figure 7.11. As with the while statement, the body of the loop consists of a single statement, which is often a compound statement.

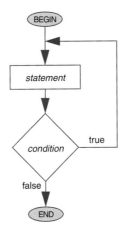

Figure 7.11 **A *do* statement.**

The essential difference between a while statement and a do statement is that the body of the loop is always executed at least once in a do statement. With a while statement, the body of the loop might not be executed at all (if the condition is initially false). Any variables referenced in the condition of a while statement must be initialized before the while statement is executed. In a do statement, these variables are often initialized in the first iteration of the loop body. *RectangleTUI* methods `createRectangle` and `start` are written below using do statements rather than while statements. Notice the use and formatting of the compound statement as the loop body.

```java
private void createRectangle () {
    int length;
    int width;
    do {
        length = readIntWithPrompt(
        "Rectangle length (a non-negative integer): ");
    } while (length < 0);
    do {
        width = readIntWithPrompt(
        "Rectangle width (a non-negative integer): ");
    } while (width < 0);
    this.rectangle = new Rectangle(length,width);
}

public void start () {
    int choice;
    createRectangle();
    do {
        displayMenu();
        choice = readIntWithPrompt("Enter choice: ");
        executeChoice(choice);
    } while (choice != EXIT);
}
```

DrJava: exercising a do statement

Open the file `RectangleTUIDo.java`, located in `figures`, in `ch7`, in `nhText`. This file contains an implementation of the textual user interface that uses a do statement rather than a while statement in the `start` method.

1. Set *Debug Mode*, and toggle a breakpoint on the line containing the `displayMenu();` in the method `start`. (See page 185 if you do not remember how to use the debugger.)

2. Run the `main` method of *RectangleExampleDo*. In the *Interactions* pane, enter

   ```
   > import ch7.figures.*;
   > RectangleExampleDo.main(null);
   ```

3. Enter data as before. Execution will pause when the `displayMenu();` statement is reached.

4. In the *Watches* pane, enter `choice` as the name of the variable to watch.

5. Note that execution of the loop has begun before the condition has been tested. Step through execution of the loop several times by successively pressing the *Step Over* button.

7.6   Summary

In this chapter, we learned to build a simple text-based user interface. We reviewed the relationship between client and server, and observed that while a client is dependent on its server, a server is independent of its client. In designing a system, it is preferable to make stable components independent of those likely to require change. Since the user interface is generally considerably less stable than the model, we favor designs in which the user interface acts as client to the model. In cases where the model must collaborate with the user interface, we need to minimize the interface for this collaboration.

We next introduced i/o streams. A stream is a sequence of bytes, sometimes viewed as characters, to which an application can append data (an output stream) or from which an application can read data (an input stream). Java has an extensive library of classes to deal with streams. However to simplify matters in this introduction, we use only basic functionality from the predefined object `System.out` for output, and the *Scanner* class from `java.util` for input.

We concluded by presenting two simple applications with their text-based user interfaces. In the process of building the user interfaces, we introduced the while statement or while-loop: a Java construct that specifies a sequence of actions to be repeated until a condition fails to hold.

In the design of the *LockedOracle* class, we saw how to compose existing classes to construct a new class. The relation between a composite class and its component classes is called the *has-a* relation. The *LockedOracle* class wraps *Oracle*, adapting its specification to that required by the system: the adapter pattern.

SELF-STUDY EXERCISES

7.1   What are the fundamental subsystems of a system developed using objects?

7.2   What are the fundamental responsibilities of a user interface? Why should the user interface be identified as a separate subsystem?

7.3   What is a text-based user interface?

7.4   What are data streams? What standard streams are provided for an application, and what
are their purposes?

7.5   What's the difference between the following two method invocations?

```
System.out.println("Hark!");
System.out.print("Hark!");
```

7.6   Taking a wild guess, what do you think the following does?

```
System.err.println("Oh, fudge.");
```

7.7   Suppose an input stream contains the following:

••⌐•Joe:2•23⌐••⌐•••32.4ft/sec••⌐end⌐

input is a *Scanner* instance reading from the stream. The following commands are done
in order. For each method invocation, indicate what the input stream will contain after the
method is executed, and what will be returned.

a.   input.next() ⇒ ?
b.   input.hasNextInt() ⇒ ?
c.   input.nextInt() ⇒ ?
d.   input.hasNext() ⇒ ?
e.   input.hasNextInt() ⇒ ?
f.   input.nextLine() ⇒ ?
g.   input.nextLine() ⇒ ?
h.   input.next() ⇒ ?
i.   input.next() ⇒ ?

7.8   Suppose an input stream contains only the following:

••⌐•⌐

and is "terminated" after these characters. input is a *Scanner* instance reading from the
stream. Which of the following commands will fail?

a.   input.nextInt();
b.   input.next();
c.   input.nextLine();

7.9   Suppose an input stream contains the following two lines:

10•ft.⌐12•ft.⌐

input is a *Scanner* instance reading from the stream. Write statements that will assign the number on the first line (10) to the **int** variable width, and the number on the second line (12) to the **int** variable length.

7.10   What's the difference between "iteration" and "looping"?

7.11   For each of the following, how many times will the phrase "Please wait" be written?

a.
```
int i = 1;
while (i < 3) {
    System.out.println("Please wait");
    i = i + 1;
}
```

b.
```
int i = 1;
while (i < 0) {
    System.out.println("Please wait");
    i = i + 1;
}
```

c.
```
int i = 1;
while (i > 0)
    System.out.println("Please wait");
    i = i + 1;
```

7.12   Given the i is an **int** variable, indicate the number of times the body of each of the following loops will be performed:

a. `i = 1;` `while (i <= 10)` `{ ... i = i+1;}`
b. `i = 0;` `while (i <= 10)` `{ ... i = i+1;}`
c. `i = 0;` `while (i < 10)`   `{ ... i = i+1;}`
d. `i = 0;` `while (i <= 10)` `{ ... i = i+2;}`
e. `i = 10;` `while (i > 0)`   `{ ... i = i-1;}`
f. `i = 10;` `while (i > 1)`   `{ ... i = i-1;}`
g. `i = 10;` `while (i > 0)`   `{ ... i = i-2;}`
h. `i = 10;` `while (i != 0)`   `{ ... i = i-1;}`
i. `i = 9;` `while (i != 0)`   `{ ... i = i-2;}`
j. `i = 0;` `while (i != 10)` `{ ... i = i+3;}`

7.13   Assume that a and b are **int** variables with initial values 18 and 48 respectively. Trace the following program fragments and indicate what will be written.

a.
```
while (a != b) {
    if (a > b)
        a = a - b;
    else
        b = b - a;
System.out.println("result is: " + a);
```

b.
```
int q = 0;
int r = a;
while (r > b) {
    q = q + 1;
    r = r - b;
}
System.out.println("q = " + q " and r = " + r);
```

Try different values for a and b. What happens if a is 1 and b is 0?

7.14 Consider the following, where i and sum are **int** variables:

```
i = 1;
sum = 0;
while (i != 10) {
    sum = sum + i;
    i = i + 1;
}
```

a. What is the final value of i? of sum?

b. What does this loop compute?

7.15 Consider the following, where i and sum are **int** variables:

```
i = 1;
sum = 0;
while (i != 10) {
    sum = sum + i;
    i = i + 2;
}
```

a. What is the final value of i? of sum?

b. What does this loop compute?

7.16 Write a method that computes the sum of the integers from 1 to *n*, for any positive integer *n*.

7.17 Write a method that computes the sum of the odd numbers from 1 to *n*, for any positive integer *n*.

7.18 Explain the following diagram:

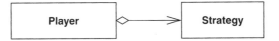

7.19 What are the collaborators of a *LockedOracle*?

✳ 7.20 What are the two essential differences between while and do statements?

EXERCISES

7.1   Using a web browser, access the Java API documentation for the class *System*. (If you don't have the documentation locally, it can be accessed through the document *http://java.sun.com/apis.html.*) Find the definition of the constant out. Of what class is it?

Go to the specifications for this class (for instance, by clicking on the class name link). Read the specifications for the methods print (String s) and println(). How many methods does this class have named println? How are the methods distinguished?

What is the difference between the methods write(int b) and print(int i)?

As an experiment, run a simple program with the following main:

```
public static void main (String[] argv) {
    System.out.write(65);
    System.out.println();
    System.out.print(65);
    System.out.println();
}
```

Explain the results.

7.2   Review the results of Exercise 5.9. Mathematically, the following loop should not terminate. Given the results of Exercise 5.9, how many times will the body of the following loop actually be executed?

```
int i = 1;
while (i > 0)
    i = i + 1;
```

7.3   Revise the *Rectangle* interface so that the menu, in addition to the other choices, offers a choice to display all properties. If this choice is selected, length, width, area, and perimeter are displayed.

7.4   Revise the *Rectangle* interface so that the first menu offers two choices: create a rectangle or exit from the program. After the user has created a rectangle, a new menu offers choices for displaying *Rectangle* properties or exiting. The exit option from this second menu results in the first menu again being displayed.

7.5   Implement a text-based user interface for the class modeling circles, implemented in Exercise 3.10.

7.6   Implement a text-based user interface for the class *Counter* (Listing 2.1). The interface should offer the user the options of incrementing the *Counter*, resetting the *Counter*, or exiting. If the user chooses to increment or reset the *Counter*, the value of the *Counter* should be immediately displayed.

7.7   Implement a text-based user interface for the balls and strikes counter of Exercise 4.8.

7.8 Implement the class *Oracle* specified on page 299. An *Oracle* should have only two fortunes, and alternate between them.

7.9 Revise the *LockedOracle* interface so that it offers a menu with two choices: get fortune or exit. The fortune choice results in the user being asked for the key. The exit choice terminates the program.

7.10 Define a simple class *Money* to model a dollars and cents amount. Instances should be immutable. The constructor takes two arguments,

public Money (**int** dollars, **int** cents)

and the class has two queries, one for dollars and one for cents.

Using the dollars and cents counter of Exercise 4.9 as a component, implement and test a class modeling a no-interest checking account. A checking account should have an account number and maintain a balance in dollars and cents. The query for balance returns a *Money* instance. It should have commands for making a withdrawal and for making a deposit. A withdrawal that exceeds the balance is not permitted.

7.11 Implement a text-based user interface for the checking account of Exercise 7.10. The interface should provide options for creating an account, querying for the balance, making a withdrawal, and making a deposit. If the user chooses the withdrawal or deposit options, the interface requests the amount and displays the resulting balance.

SELF-STUDY EXERCISE SOLUTIONS

7.1 Model, external interface, data management.

7.2 The basic functions of the user interface are to get input from the user, thereby allowing the user to control the model, and to give output to the user, reporting on the status of the model. Issues such as how the user provides input, what negotiations are necessary to ensure that the user provides acceptable input, and what the output looks like, are the responsibility of the user interface.

The user interface should be a separate subsystem so that it can be changed without affecting the rest of the system. The model can be reused with other user interfaces without having to retrofit it.

7.3 A text-based interface is one in which input is in the form of text keyed by the user, and output is in the form of text displayed in the window in which the program is run.

7.4 A data stream is a sequence of bytes to which an application can append data (an output stream) or from which an application can read data (an input stream). Standard streams are system input (for input), system output (for output), and system error (for reporting errors).

7.5 System.out.println("Hark!") writes five characters to standard output followed by line termination characters(s). System.out.print("Hark!") doesn't terminate the line.

7.6   Writes a line of output (containing "Oh, fudge.") to standard error.

7.7   *a.*   `input.next()` ⇒ `"Joe:2"`
          input stream: •23↵••↵•••32.4ft/sec••↵end↵

       b.   `input.hasNextInt()` ⇒ `true`
          input stream: •23↵••↵•••32.4ft/sec••↵end↵

       c.   `input.nextInt()` ⇒ 23
          input stream: ↵••↵•••32.4ft/sec••↵end↵

       d.   `input.hasNext()` ⇒ `true`
          input stream: ↵••↵•••32.4ft/sec••↵end↵

       e.   `input.hasNextInt()` ⇒ `false`
          input stream: ↵••↵•••32.4ft/sec••↵end↵

       f.   `input.nextLine()` ⇒ `""`
          input stream: ••↵•••32.4ft/sec••↵end↵

       g.   `input.nextLine()` ⇒ `"••"`
          input stream: •••32.4ft/sec••↵end↵

       h.   `input.next()` ⇒ `"32.4ft/sec"`
          input stream: ••↵end↵

       i.   `input.next()` ⇒ `"end"`
          input stream: ↵

7.8   Invocations `input.nextInt()` and `input.next()` will fail.

7.9   `width = input.nextInt();`
      `input.nextLine();` or `input.next();`
      `length = input.nextInt();`

7.10   As we have used the terms, they are essentially equivalent. To be more careful, "iteration" is a problem solving technique in which the solution is obtained in a series of similar "steps," each step building on the partial solution provided by the previous step. "Looping" is a programming language mechanism for carrying out an iterative solution.

7.11   *a.*   Twice.

       b.   The phrase will not be printed at all: the condition is initially false.

       c.   The loop will continue forever (or at least until someone manually kills the program). The value of i is not changed in the body of the loop.

7.12   *a.*   10   *b.*   11   *c.*   10   *d.*   6   *e.*   10   *f.*   9
        g.   5   *h.*   10   *i.*   non terminating   *j.*   non terminating

7.13   *a.*   `result is: 6`

       b.   `q = 2 and r = 12`

      If a is 1 and b is 0, neither loop terminates.

7.14   *a.*   Final value of i is 10; final value of sum is 45.

      b.   Computes sum of the integers from 1 through 9.

7.15   This loop appears to be intended to compute a sum of odd integers. But it does not terminate, as i never equals 10.

7.16
```
public int sum (int n) {
    i = 1;
    sum = 0;
    while (i != n) {
        sum = sum + i;
        i = i + 1;
    }
    return sum;
}
```

7.17
```
public int sum (int n) {
    i = 1;
    sum = 0;
    while (i <= n) {
        sum = sum + i;
        i = i + 2;
    }
    return sum;
}
```

7.18   A *Player has-a Strategy.* Every instance of the class *Player* will have as a component an instance of the class *Strategy.*

7.19   *Oracle* and *CombinationLock.*

7.20   The body of a do is always executed at least once, while the body of a while might not be executed at all. Any variables referenced in a while condition must be initialized prior to executing the while statement. Variables referenced in the condition of a do are often initialized in the first iteration of the loop body.

CHAPTER 8　Putting a system together

We've seen how to specify, implement, and test objects, and in the last chapter, how to put together a model with a simple text-based user interface. Now we are ready to consider the design of a modest but complete system. Our purpose is to get an idea of what's involved in system design, and to see how a collection of objects work together to solve a problem. We start with an overview of the design and implementation process, outlining the steps involved in producing a complete system. Then, as a case study, we build a system that plays the game simple nim, introduced in Chapter 3. Our example is limited in scope for several reasons: we want a system we can comprehend in its entirety, and haven't yet acquired all the tools we need for a completely satisfactory design. Consequently, we settle for a rather small system of limited functionality.

Objectives

After studying this chapter, you should understand the following:

- phases of the software life cycle;
- iterative and compositional nature of the software life cycle;
- functional specification of a system;
- identifying classes, their responsibilities, and relationships among the classes, as fundamental system activities.

Also, you should be able to:

- differentiate between system design and algorithm design;
- identify potential classes, their responsibilities, and relationships, for a simple problem;
- draw a static diagram of the design of a simple system;
- implement a simple system.

8.1   Software life cycle

System development begins with *problem analysis*, a thorough examination of the problem to be solved. Problem analysis results in a document that carefully and precisely describes *what* the system is intended to do. This description is primarily concerned with the system's *functionality*, and is usually called a *system specification* or *functional specification*. The specification is essentially the contract between the customer—the person who will use the system—and the developer. It explicitly describes, for the customer, the product to be delivered, and tells the developer what must be produced.

The initial system specification is rarely complete and is often ambiguous and inconsistent. Furthermore, the circumstances in which the system will be used, and hence the customer's requirements, are not static. Even in situations such as military procurement, where specifications are voluminous and detailed, the resulting system is rarely exactly as initially envisioned. (An extreme example: the Internet was originally conceived by cold war era planners to be a military data network with the critical property of no single point of failure.) Accordingly, system specifications must be modified and amended as the design and implementation proceed. It is this difficulty in "hitting a moving target" that the object-oriented design methodology attempts to address. Some software development strategies, such as Extreme Programming (XP), require an "on-site customer" available to the development team throughout the design and implementation process.

Once the system is specified, the *design* phase begins. Design involves *defining* a collection of objects (actually classes) and their interactions that will satisfy the specifications. Note that *system design* involves *object specification*.

Following design, *system implementation* can be started. The actual (software) modules that will make up the system are built, using programming languages and other software development tools. This is the coding, or programming, part of system development. It's what we've been dealing with, at a fundamental level, in the first few chapters.

As modules are implemented, they must be *tested* to ensure that they conform to specifications, that is, that they behave as expected. This requires the creation of *test plans* to direct the testing process. As we have seen, module implementation can be *test-driven*, with tests written before a module is implemented.

The final step in the implementation process is the integration of the modules to produce a complete system. This step also requires testing, called integration or functional testing. The design of a functional test is much more demanding than the design of a unit test. System specification is distributed over many modules that interact in complicated and often subtle ways. The test design involves not only black box testing based on system specification and use cases, but also white box testing, checking for unexpected interactions between system components.

The entire process is *iterative* and *incremental*. The design effort often uncovers inadequacies in the specifications which must be addressed before the design can be completed. Testing typically uncovers design and implementation flaws which must be corrected. Test plans must be continually updated as the process proceeds. System integration and integration testing must be performed incrementally. It is a fatal strategy to leave

---

The software life cycle involves

- analysis;
- specification;
- design;
- implementation;
- testing;
- maintenance.

The process is

- iterative;
- incremental;
- compositional.

Figure 8.1 **The software life cycle.**

system integration as one final step. As time passes, additional functionality is required, and must be integrated into the system design and implementation.

The process is also *compositional*. That is, the system itself, the objects, and the algorithms implementing each object's features are all composed of simpler pieces, which are themselves composed of pieces, *etc.* The iterative process of design-implement-test occurs at all compositional levels. Consequently the development of a system is not cleanly divided into separate specification-design-implement-test phases: these activities are carried out concurrently in different parts of the system.

Of course, the process is not complete when the system is put into production. As we have mentioned several times, a system's specifications are not fixed, but constantly evolve. The problem a system is designed to solve inevitably changes over time. *System maintenance* involves modifying a system to meet changing requirements, as well as correcting problems not detected before the system is put into production.

8.2   Design of a system

As a case study, we design a system to play the game of "simple nim," introduced in Section 3.2. In this game, there are two players and a pile of sticks. Each player, in turn, removes one, two, or three sticks from the pile. The player who removes the last stick loses.

Our initial implementation will play a number of games and simply show the results to the user. That is, the games will be played "computer vs. computer." The user determines whether to play another game and how many sticks to start with. Later we'll consider modifications that allow the user to participate in the play and allow different strategies to be employed by the players.

There is a fairly easy to determine perfect strategy for the game: one of the players can always win no matter what the other player does, as long as the number of sticks in the pile is known. Which player has the perfect strategy depends on the number of sticks in the pile. This fact is not particularly relevant to our system design.

8.2.1 Functional specification

Basic functionality

Since we've already determined what we want the system to do, no real problem analysis is required. We can state the functionality required of the system as follows.

Basic function of the system: Play a number of games of "simple nim," reporting the results to the user.

System functionality:

1. Allow the user to specify the number of sticks the pile contains at the start of the game.

2. For each player in turn, determine what play to make (number of sticks to remove) and make the play.

3. Display the state of the game after each play, that is, the number of sticks taken, the number of sticks left, and when the game is over, who won.

4. Allow the user to determine whether or not to play another game.

User interface

The functional specification also describes the system as it appears to the user. We prescribe a simple text-based user interface.

1. When the program is run, the user is offered the following menu:

```
Enter the number denoting the action to perform:
Run game..............1
Exit.................2
Enter choice:
```

2. Entering 2 terminates the program.

3. Entering 1 produces the following prompt:

```
Enter number of sticks (a positive integer):
```

4. A play by play description of the game is displayed, similar to the following:

```
Player Player1 takes 1 stick(s), leaving 4.
Player Player2 takes 3 stick(s), leaving 1.
Player Player1 takes 1 stick(s), leaving 0.
Player Player2 wins.
```

5. The original menu is again displayed.

8.2.2 Preliminary design

Before we begin a extensive design, we should mention that there are many possible approaches and rarely one best solution for any nontrivial problem. But not all designs are equal. Proposed solutions can be evaluated against specific measurement norms, and different approaches can be compared with regard to various criteria. The task of the designer is to explore the solution space—the set of possible solutions for a problem—and evaluate alternatives.

We need more experience before we can attempt this kind of detailed evaluation of alternatives. Our goal, at the moment, is to see a collection of objects working together in a complete system. Therefore, we aim for simplicity in the design, without introducing new linguistic constructs. A careful and thorough analysis of the solution presented, though, would likely identify better alternatives.

Identifying objects

Design involves defining a collection of objects that will work together to satisfy the specifications. This is a nontrivial iterative process. While a number of techniques have been suggested for identifying objects in a system, there is no substitute for experience. The broader your experience, the greater variety of solution patterns you have at hand for attacking a particular problem.

Of course, we really specify *classes* in the design. The objects are created dynamically when the system is run. We can properly describe the first step in design as identifying a potential collection of classes. There are several different kinds of classes that come together in any system design. Some are derived directly from the external system being modeled: a student registration system, for instance, almost certainly needs a class modeling students. These classes are often "there for the picking" and are the kind of classes we have been considering in the preceding chapters.

But classes that directly model aspects of the external system are not sufficient. Other classes are *architectural* and form the underlying structure of the solution. These structural classes are not directly involved in addressing functional requirements of the system, but are used to define relationships between system components. Although such classes often occur in common patterns, identifying appropriate architectural classes for a system is one of the most difficult aspects of design, requiring considerable experience.

Finally, some classes support the algorithms that implement system functionality. These *implementation classes* are generally well understood, as they are derived from algorithmic data structures that have been studied and used for many years. We encounter these classes in later chapters, when we see how to implement some common library classes.

An initial collection of potential classes can be developed by carefully examining the functionality required of system. Then as responsibilities are allocated to these classes and relationships between them identified, other potential model classes, architectural classes, and organizational approaches will suggest themselves. Since this is our first attempt at system design, we present an adequate collection of classes with little more than intuitive justification.

In the problem at hand, we need a user interface and model. No data management component is required. We'll use a text-based user interface similar to those of the last chapter. What objects comprise the model? The game is described in terms of two players and a pile of sticks. It seems clear that we want objects modeling the two *players*. The sticks are really not very interesting in themselves. So rather than modeling the individual sticks, we'll define an object to represent the *pile* of sticks. (If our game was poker, however, we'd want objects representing the individual cards, and if we were playing chess we'd want objects representing the individual pieces. Deciding what not to model is as critical to a design as deciding what to model.)

As we proceed with the design, we encounter functions that don't seem to be natural responsibilities of any of these objects. For instance, someone must decide whose turn it is, when the game is over, and who wins. We might attempt to assign these responsibilities to the player or pile objects, but the development would become very awkward. It is useful to introduce a structural object responsible for managing the game. Game rules that are independent of the individual players can be encapsulated in this object, which we'll call the *game*.

System design involves defining a collection of objects that interact to solve the problem.

Classes can be
    model classes, that model some aspect of the problem;
    architectural classes, that form the underlying structure of the solution; or
    implementation classes, that support the implementing algorithms.

Determining responsibilities

Now that we've identified some objects, we can begin to assign responsibilities. We have a user interface and four model objects: two players, the pile, and the game. Let's concentrate on the model for the moment. We must determine the responsibilities of each object, that is, what each object must know and what each object must do. The functionality required of the system determines what should and shouldn't be included. We must take care not to get too concerned with simulating reality rather than modeling system requirements.

The design process produces class definitions and not individual objects. The two player objects behave identically and so are instances of the same class. Consequently we have three model classes to consider: *Pile*, *Player*, and *Game*.

We've already seen versions *Player* and *Pile* in Section 3.2. The *Pile* is a rather simple class that does no more than manage the sticks. The *Pile* need only know how many sticks remain, and be able to remove sticks.

A *Player*'s primary responsibility is to make a play, that is, determine how many sticks to remove and remove them from the pile. We give the *Player* a name so that we can identify an individual *Player* to the user. (Note that the only real purpose in naming a

Player is for the benefit of the user interface.) We also make the *Player* responsible for knowing how many sticks it took on its last turn.

(There are many situations in which we have little *a priori* reason for choosing one alternative over another. For instance, we could also argue that knowing how many sticks were taken should be the responsibility of the *Game* or the *Pile*. We choose not to give the responsibility to the *Pile* because we view the *Pile* as a simple, minimal, class that knows nothing of the play of the game. We choose not to give the responsibility to the *Game* because this would strengthen the *Player* to *Game* relationship. Suppose that after making a move, the *Player* provides this information to the *Game* by invoking a *Game* method. The *Player* is then a client of the *Game*. We'll see that minimizing relationships between classes is one of the keys to developing a successful design. Since the *Game* already knows the *Player*, the *Game* can query the *Player* for the information if necessary.)

The *Game* must know the *Players* and the *Pile*. It must know who is to play next and who played last. It must know when the game is over and who the winner is. And since we are thinking of the *Game* as a repository of game rules, we assign the *Game* the responsibility for knowing how many sticks can be taken on a turn. (Again, we might argue that this knowledge should reside with the *Player* or even the *Pile*. Putting this information in the *Pile* seems inappropriate, since the *Pile* knows nothing of the game rules. In Section 3.2, we imply that the *Player* has this information. However, the *Game* seems a more appropriate choice given its basic function of "running the game." Also, it will allow a slightly more flexible *Player*. We can imagine a *Player* playing in games with slightly different rules; it is not as reasonable to consider a *Game* in which the players are playing by different rules. Therefore we try to put information regarding "rules" in the *Game* rather than in the *Player*.)

What should the *Game* do? Note that the *Game* state includes who played last, who plays next, whether the game is over, *etc.* There should be a *Game* command that changes this state information. So we assign the responsibility of conducting a play to the *Game*. By a "play," we mean one of the *Players* taking a turn and removing sticks from the *Pile*.

As we identify a specific object's responsibilities, we also try to identify *collaborators*: other objects whose services the specific object requires in order to carry out its responsibilities. The *Pile* is a complete server: it requires no other objects to satisfy its responsibilities. The *Player*, on the other hand, needs the *Pile* in order to make a play. The *Player* must determine from the *Pile* how many sticks are left, and then command the *Pile* to remove a specified number of sticks.

We summarize this information in Figure 8.2. For each class, we give a general description of the class, and then enumerate specific responsibilities and collaborators, other classes a given class needs to accomplish its responsibilities.

The user interface will be a text-based interface similar to those we built in the previous chapter. It must allow the user to determine whether to terminate the program or to play another game. In the latter case, it must allow the user to specify the number of sticks to be used in the game. The user interface must report each move and the winner to the user. The user interface must interact with the *Game* to have a game played, and must interact with the *Game* and the *Players* to get relevant information to display to the user.

Note that for each play, the user interface reports the number of sticks remaining in the *Pile*. Is the *Pile* a collaborator of the user interface? That is, should the user interface

Class: *Pile*
a pile of sticks for playing simple nim

Responsibilities: **Collaborators:**

do:
remove sticks
know:
the number of sticks remaining
in the *Pile*

Class: *Player*
a player of the simple nim game

Responsibilities: **Collaborators:**

do:
make a play by removing sticks   *Pile*
from the *Pile*
know:
Player's name
the number of sticks removed
on this *Player*'s most
recent turn

Class: *Game*
a manager of a simple nim game

Responsibilities: **Collaborators:**

do:
conduct a play of the game,   *Players, Pile*
instructing the appropriate
Player to take a turn
know:
the *Players*
the *Pile*
number of sticks that can be
taken on a turn
which *Player* plays next
which *Player* played last
when the game is over   *Pile*
which *Player* won when game
is over

Figure 8.2 Model class responsibilities.

gets this information directly from the *Pile*? If so, then the *Game* must provide a method like

public Pile pile ()
The *Pile* for this *Game*.

But the *Pile* is a subsidiary of the game, and the *Game* should have control over who does what with the *Pile*. This method makes the *Pile* available to any arbitrary client who might alter its state independently of the *Game*. So rather than getting the *Pile* from the *Game*, we'll have the user interface get the number of sticks remaining from the *Game*. We summarize the user interface responsibilities in Figure 8.3.

Our class specifications are not yet complete. We have not completely resolved the interaction of the user interface and the model objects, nor have we addressed object creation responsibilities. Nevertheless, we should have an idea of how the model objects will work together to satisfy the system requirement.

8.2.3 Relations between objects

Now that we have identified responsibilities and collaborators, we can sketch the relationships that exist between these objects. Considering the *Game* first, we can describe the relation between the *Game* and the *Players*, and between the *Game* and the *Pile*, as composition. The *Game* has two *Players* and it has a *Pile*. This is illustrated in Figure 8.4. The small "2" means that the relation between *Game* and *Player* is a "one-to-two" relation: the *Game* has exactly two *Players*.

Note that we have not pictured the relation between *Game* and *Player* as the diamond-ended "includes" relation. In a sense, the relation between *Game* and *Pile* is stronger than the relation between *Game* and *Player*. The *Game* owns and is responsible for the *Pile*. The

Class:	NimTUI	
	text-based user interface for the simple nim system	
Responsibilities:		**Collaborators:**
do:		
	allow the user to indicate whether or not another game is to be played	
	allow user to specify the number of sticks to be used in a game	
	have a game played	*Game*
	display each play of a game, when the game is over, and which player has won	*Game, Players*

Figure 8.3 **User interface responsibilities.**

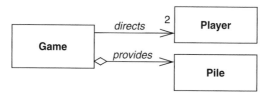

Figure 8.4 A *Game* is a composite object.

Pile has no meaning independently of the game. We expect the *Game* and *Pile* to have identical lifetimes, and in fact, we will give the *Game* creation responsibility for the *Pile*. The *Players*, on the other hand, exist independently of any particular game. They are not subsidiary to the *Game* in the sense that the *Pile* is. For this reason, we do not picture the relation between *Game* and *Player* as the "includes" relation. But we'll not be rigid in our notation, since we intend our diagrams to serve only as informal aids, and not definitive elements of the design.

The relation of an object to a component is typically an instance of the client-server: the object *uses* its components to fulfill its responsibilities. This is the case here. The *Game* will be a client of the *Pile* and of the *Players*. The *Game uses* these objects by giving them commands and queries. For instance, the *Game* instructs each *Player* in turn to make a play.

The *Player* objects will *use* the *Pile* by removing sticks from it. This is a simple instance of client-server.

Figure 8.5 *Player* is client to *Pile*.

To see the interaction of the *Game*, the *Players*, and the *Pile*, consider the scenario shown in Figure 8.6.

Here we illustrate the situation in which the game is not over (there are sticks remaining in the pile), and *player1* is next to play. To determine if the game is over, the *Game* queries the *Pile* to ascertain the number of sticks remaining. As there are sticks remaining, the *Game* instructs one of the *Players*—*player1* in this case—to take a turn. The *Player* queries the *Pile* to determine how many sticks remain, and then removes some number of sticks from the *Pile*. When the *Game* is given the command *play* again, the *Game* will instruct *player2* to take a turn.

We must still consider creation responsibilities. Since we have decided that the *Pile* is a part of the *Game*, it is appropriate to make the *Game* responsible for creating the *Pile*. The *Players* and the *Game*, however, exist independently. We do not want to make either responsible for creating the other. We consider the *Players* and the *Game* top-level model objects, and worry about their creation later.

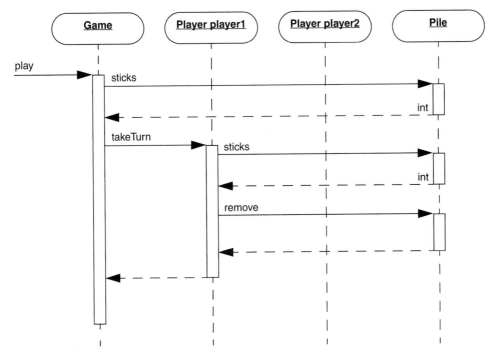

Figure 8.6 **Case: game not over, *player1*'s turn.**

8.2.4 Class specification

We could, and probably should, go back and refine our statement of responsibilities and collaboration. But since our system is fairly simple and we've got a good idea the about the relationships we need to model, we begin specifying the classes.

We include the class definitions in a package nim. Note that there is no need, at least initially, to make most of the classes public.

Pile specifications

We start with the specification of the *Pile*, since this object is purely a server and doesn't need to know about other objects. We've specified this class once, in Listing 3.1, and refined the specification in Section 5.2, pages 245 through 247. These specifications are adequate, and we simply repeat them here with minor refinements.

> **class** Pile
> > A pile of sticks for playing simple nim.
>
> > **public** Pile (**int** sticks)
> > > Create a new *Pile*, with the specified number of sticks.
> >
> > > **require:**
> > > > sticks >= 0

```
public int sticks ()
```
> The number of sticks remaining in this *Pile*.
>
> **ensure:**
> ```
> this.sticks() >= 0
> ```

```
public void remove (int number)
```
> Reduce the number of sticks by the specified amount.
>
> **require:**
> ```
> number >= 0
> number <= this.sticks()
> ```
>
> **ensure:**
> ```
> this.sticks() == old.sticks() - number
> ```

We do not define the class to be **public**. Hence, instances of this class will be accessible only from within the package nim. Since this is the case, the keyword **public** in each of the method headings is extraneous. We could have written

```
int sticks ()
```

for instance. A method not declared **public** is only available to clients defined in the same package. But since the class itself is not **public**, a *Pile* instance can only be accessed inside the package anyway. If access to an object is restricted, access to its methods is also inherently restricted. Nevertheless, we will continue to mark methods **public** to emphasize that they are part of the object's specification.

Player specification

Next we specify the *Player* class. We built this class before as well, in Section 3.2. The main responsibility of a *Player* is to make a play, that is, to remove sticks from the *Pile*. We give each *Player* a name, so that the user can easily distinguish the *Players*.

We require that a *Player* be given a name when created, and provide queries for the *Player*'s knowing responsibilities:

```
class Player
```
> A player in the game simple nim.

```
public Player (String name)
```
> Create a new *Player* with the specified name.
>
> **ensure:**
> ```
> this.name().equals(name)
> ```

```
public String name ()
```
> This *Player*'s name.

```
public int sticksTaken ()
```
> Number of sticks removed on this *Player*'s most recent turn.
> Returns 0 if this *Player* has not yet taken a turn.
>
> **ensure:**
> ```
> this.sticksTaken() >= 0
> ```

Now we must specify the command that instructs the *Player* to make a play. As in Section 3.2, we name this method `takeTurn`. In order to make a play, the *Player* must have access to the *Pile* and must know the maximum number of sticks that can be removed on a turn. As the *Pile* and the maximum number of sticks are both known by the *Game*, the *Player* must get this information from the *Game*.

Let's consider the *Pile* first. There are several ways that the *Player* can get a reference to a *Pile*:

1.   the *Pile* is provided as an argument to the *Player* constructor;

2.   the *Player* directly queries the *Game*;

3.   the *Player* provides a method, something like

> **public void** `setPile` `(Pile pile)`
> Specify the *Pile* this *Player* is to use.

for the *Game* to invoke and inform the *Player* of the *Pile*;

4.   the *Game* provides the *Pile* as an argument to the `takeTurn` method.

The first alternative is not very satisfactory, since the *Player* gets the reference to the *Pile* from the *Game*, and the *Game* does not have creation responsibility for the *Player*. The *Player* may well be created before the *Game*.

The second alternative implies that the *Player* must know (*i.e.*, have a reference to) the *Game*: the *Player* will be a client of the *Game*. We will need to decide how the *Player* gets a reference to the *Game*. Furthermore, since the *Game* is already a client of the *Player*, this would create a "cyclic dependency": the *Game* knows the *Player*, who knows the *Game*. This kind of structure is very rigid and can make maintenance and modification difficult. (For instance, neither class could be tested independently of the other.) It should be avoided if possible.

In the last two alternatives, the *Game* provides the *Pile* as a method argument. The third alternative requires additional *Player* functionality, in the form of the `setPile` method. Furthermore, a sequential dependency is introduced: the `setPile` method must be invoked before the `takeTurn` method can be invoked. Thus the fourth alternative seems the most attractive.

We might also note that a general rule of design states that the later a "binding" (such as the association of the *Player* with the *Pile*) takes place, the more flexible the resulting system. In this case, we have postponed the binding to the latest possible moment. The *Game* doesn't provide the *Player* with a *Pile* until the *Player* is asked to take a turn.

The situation with the maximum number of sticks that can be removed on a turn is similar. We will have the *Game* provide this information to the *Player* as an argument to the `takeTurn` method, which is specified as follows.

> **public void** `takeTurn` `(Pile pile,` **int** `maxOnATurn)`
> Take a turn: remove sticks from the specified *Pile*. `maxOnATurn` is the maximum number of sticks a *Player* can remove on a turn. A *Player* will remove at least one stick.
>
> **require:**
> `pile.sticks() > 0 && maxOnATurn > 0`

ensure:
```
1 <= this.sticksTaken() &&
this.sticksTaken() <= maxOnATurn &&
pile.sticks() ==
    old.pile.sticks() - this.sticksTaken()
```

Two final items to note. We require that the *Pile* passed as argument not be empty. This responsibility falls on the *Game* when it invokes the method. If we do not require this, the *Player* must be prepared to deal with an empty *Pile*, even though this situation should not occur in a well-regulated game. Also, the postcondition explicitly relates the `sticksTaken` feature to the `takeTurn` operation.

Game specification

The *Game* is responsible for managing the game and knowing relevant game state information. We require that the *Game* be provided with the *Players* when it is constructed:

public Game (Player player1, Player player2,
    int sticks)
> Create a nim *Game*, with the specified *Players* and the specified number of sticks. The first *Player* specified (`player1`) plays first in the game.
>
> **require:**
> ```
> sticks > 0
> ```

The user interface will get state information about the game from the *Game*, including (as we mentioned on page 323) the number of sticks remaining. State information the user interface will need includes:

- the number of sticks remaining;
- which *Player* took the previous turn;
- which *Player*'s turn is next;
- whether or not the game is over;
- if the game is over, who won.

(Note that "who took the previous turn" and "whose turn is next" are not redundant bits of information. At the start of the game, there is no "previous turn.") We specify a query for each of these pieces of information.

public int sticksLeft ()
> The number of sticks remaining in the pile.
>
> **ensure:**
> ```
> this.sticksLeft() >= 0
> ```

public Player nextPlayer ()
> The *Player* whose turn is next.

public Player previousPlayer ()
> The *Player* who last played; returns *null* if no play has been made yet.

public boolean gameOver ()
> The game is over.

public Player winner ()
> The winning *Player*: the one who did not make the last play in the game. Returns *null* if the game is not over.
>
> **ensure:**
>> if this.gameOver()
>>> this.winner() != this.previousPlayer()

Finally, we need a command to instruct the *Game* to conduct a play.

public void play ()
> Conduct a play of the game, allowing the appropriate *Player* to take a turn. Has no effect if the game is over.

We could place !this.gameOver() as a precondition for this method. Since we choose not to do so, we must address the case where the method is invoked after the game has ended.

User interface specification

The user interface is a client of the *Game* and the *Players*. Since several games might be played, we give the user interface creation responsibility for the *Game*. Since we might want to let the user name the *Players*, we give the user interface creation responsibility for the *Players* as well. (We admit these decision are somewhat *ad hoc*.)

class NimTUI
> A simple text-based user interface for the simple nim system.

public NimTUI ()
> Create a new user interface.

public void start ()
> Start the interface.

The initiating class will look like this:

```
public class NimGame {
    public static void main (String[] argv) {
        (new NimTUI()).start();
    }
}
```

We have now determined all creation responsibilities, which are summarized in Figure 8.7.

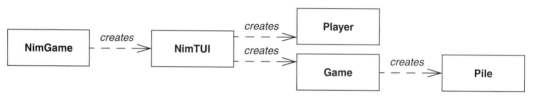

Figure 8.7 **Creation responsibilities in the nim game.**

User interface—model interaction

We implement the system in the next section. But before moving on, there is one additional issue we should address. The user interface determines whether or not the user wants to run a game. But the *Game* has only a method for conducting a single play of the game:

> **public void** play ()
>> Conduct a play of the game, allowing the appropriate *Player* to take a turn. Has no effect if the game is over.

To play an entire game, this method must be repeatedly invoked. That is, there must be a loop that looks something like this:

> **while** (!game.gameOver())
>   game.play();

Where should this loop reside? That is, who has the responsibility of repeating plays until the game ends? The obvious choices are the *Game* or the user interface.

A good argument can be made that this responsibility belongs to the *Game*, or at least to the model. First, the *Game* is the repository of game rules and is responsible for "managing" the game. Clearly the fact that turns are taken repeatedly until the game ends is part of the rules, and causing this to happen is part of game management. Second, an important design goal is to make the user interface as "dumb" as possible, that is, knowledge of how the model works should be encapsulated in the model, and not seep out into the user interface.

However, if we looked ahead a little bit, we would see that such loops often reside *in the user*. In an event-driven system, the system is essentially idle until the user performs some action: clicks a mouse button, enters text, *etc*. The system responds to this user generated event, and then returns to its idle state, awaiting the next event. If we imagine that one of the players is the user, the repetition occurs because the user repeatedly makes moves. In order to capture a bit of this spirit, we will give the responsibility for continuing play until the game ends to the user interface.

8.3   Implementing the system

Given the specification, the implementation of the system is mostly straightforward. While we prefer test driven implementation, we'll show test details only for the class *Player*.

Additionally, we omit comments from the listings to more clearly illustrate the implementation, and do not aggressively include `assert` statements to check preconditions.[1]

We assume that all of the classes are in the package nim. Each class definition will be in a file beginning with the statement

```
package nim;
```

8.3.1 The top level

As shown in Figure 8.7, the `main` method creates the *NimTUI*. This is the "top level" object in our design. The *NimTUI* method `start` is invoked to run the system.

```
/**
 * The game of simple nim. User observes game
 * played by means of a simple text based interface.
 */
public class NimGame {
    public static void main (String[] argv) {
        (new NimTUI()).start();
    }
}
```

8.3.2 The class *Pile*

Since *Pile* is the only completely independent class in the system, it makes sense to implement it first. The implementation is quite simple. We give it without further comment in Listing 8.1.

8.3.3 The class *Player*

Next we can implement *Player*. We'll illustrate a test-driven implementation, assuming we've built a test driver similar to the ones of Sections 4.4 and 6.3.

We start with a stubbed implementation as shown in Listing 8.2. The test fixture will certainly require a *Player*. The test class will have a *Player* instance variable, and a `setUp` method to create the test fixture:

```
private Player player;

private void setUp () {
    player = new Player("Player");
}
```

---

1. Yes, the noise you hear is your instructor grinding his or her teeth.

Listing 8.1   The class *Pile*

```
class Pile {

    private int sticks;

    public Pile (int sticks) {
        this.sticks = sticks;
    }

    public int sticks () {
        return sticks;
    }

    public void remove (int number) {
        assert number <= sticks :
            "precondition: number <= this.sticks()";
        sticks = sticks - number;
    }

    public String toString () {
        return "Pile: " + sticks + " sticks.";
    }
}
```

First, we should test the initial state of the *Player*. The specifications tell us that the initial value returned by sticksTaken should be 0.

```
private void testInitialState () {
    setUp();
    verify(player.name().equals("Player"),
        "name set initially");
    verify(player.sticksTaken() == 0,
        "sticksTaken initially 0");
}
```

If we run the test, it will not simply fail, but will in fact crash with a *NullPointerException*. In the first invocation of verify, we attempt to evaluate the expression

```
player.name().equals("Player")
```

To evaluate the expression, the *Player*'s method name is invoked, returning a *String*. The *String*'s method equals is then invoked. But the stubbed *Player* method name returns the value *null*. This is a reference value that does not reference any object. Thus there is no object to query with equals. The result is a *NullPointerException* failure.

Listing 8.2   **Stubbed implementation of the class** *Player*

```java
class Player {

    public Player (String name) {
    }

    public String name () {
        return null;
    }

    public int sticksTaken () {
        return 0;
    }

    public void takeTurn (Pile pile, int maxOnATurn) {
    }
}
```

This particular kind of failure is not uncommon. By default, Java initializes reference typed instance variables to null. Thus, an attempt to use such a variable that has not been explicitly initialized will result in a *NullPointerException* failure.

To satisfy the initial state test, we must implement the queries name and sticks-Taken as well as the constructor. This is straight forward:

```java
    private String name;
    private int sticksTaken;

    public Player (String name) {
        this.name = name;
        this.sticksTaken = 0;
    }

    public String name () {
        return name;
    }

    public int sticksTaken () {
        return sticksTaken;
    }
```

(Note a small anomaly here: our implementation will pass the test even if we forget to implement sticksTaken, since the stubbed implementation just happens to give the proper value.)

Next we test the method `takeTurn`. This method requires two arguments, a *Pile* and maxOnATurn, the maximum number of sticks that can be removed on a turn. Preconditions guarantee that the *Pile* is not empty, and that maxOnATurn is positive. What cases should we consider? The following seem reasonable:

- maxOnATurn is smaller than the number of sticks in the *Pile*;
- maxOnATurn is equal to the number of sticks in the *Pile*;
- maxOnATurn is larger than the number of sticks in the *Pile*.

We should also test the boundaries of *Pile* size and maxOnATurn. Given these considerations, we'll test the following cases:

Pile size	maxOnATurn
5	3
3	3
2	3
1	3
5	1
1	1

There are any number of ways of organizing the tests. We'll include four *Piles* in the test fixture:

```
private Player player;
private Pile pile5;          // Pile with 5 sticks
private Pile pile3;          // Pile with 3 sticks
private Pile pile2;          // Pile with 2 sticks
private Pile pile1;          // Pile with 1 stick

private void setUp () {
    player = new Player("Player");
    pile5 = new Pile(5);
    pile3 = new Pile(3);
    pile2 = new Pile(2);
    pile1 = new Pile(1);
}
```

and write a separate test method for each value of maxOnATurn:

```
/**
 * Test the takeTurn method with maxOnATurn 1.
 */
private void testTakeTurnMax1 () {
    player.takeTurn(pile5,1);
    verify(pile5.sticks() == 4,
        "takeTurn size 5, max 1");
    verify(player.sticksTaken() == 1,
        "sticksTaken size 5, max 1");
```

```
    player.takeTurn(pile1,1);
    verify(pile1.sticks() == 0,
        "takeTurn size 1, max 1");
    verify(player.sticksTaken() == 1,
        "sticksTaken size 1, max 1");
}
```

When we consider the case in which maxOnATurn is 3, verification is a little more complex. For instance, if the *Pile* size is 3 or larger, the *Player* can take 1, 2, or 3 sticks. Since we have not yet implemented takeTurn, we don't know exactly what the resulting *Pile* size will be. However, the postconditions translate nicely into verification conditions.

```
/**
 * Test the takeTurn method with maxOnATurn 3.
 */
private void testTakeTurnMax3 () {
    player.takeTurn(pile5,3);
    verify(1 <= player.sticksTaken() &&
        player.sticksTaken() <= 3,
        "sticksTaken size 5, max 3");
    verify(pile5.sticks() == 5 - player.sticksTaken(),
        "takeTurn size 5, max 3");

    player.takeTurn(pile3,3);
    verify(1 <= player.sticksTaken() &&
        player.sticksTaken() <= 3,
        "sticksTaken size 3, max 3");
    verify(pile3.sticks() == 3 - player.sticksTaken(),
        "takeTurn size 3, max 3");

    player.takeTurn(pile2,3);
    verify(1 <= player.sticksTaken() &&
        player.sticksTaken() <= 2,
        "sticksTaken size 2, max 3");
    verify(pile2.sticks() == 2 - player.sticksTaken(),
        "takeTurn size 2, max 3");

    player.takeTurn(pile1,3);
    verify(player.sticksTaken() == 1,
            "sticksTaken size 1, max 3");
    verify(pile1.sticks()== 0,
        "takeTurn size 1, max 3");
}
```

The difference between "grey box" testing and "white box" testing is clear from this test. If we had the implementation of takeTurn, we would know exactly what the resulting size of the *Pile* should be in each case. As we have written the test, it will serve no matter how simply or cleverly we implement `takeTurn`.

Looking at the specifications of `takeTurn` and the tests, we can see that the simplest implementation of the method is the one we wrote in Chapter 3: always remove one stick from the *Pile*.

```
public void takeTurn (Pile pile, int maxOnATurn) {
    pile.remove(1);
    sticksTaken = 1;
}
```

This is legal because the preconditions of `takeTurn`,

```
pile.sticks() > 0
maxOnATurn > 0
```

guarantee that the *Pile* will have at least one stick, and that we are allowed to remove one stick. The invocation of `remove` is legal, since the preconditions of `remove`,

```
number >= 0
number <= this.sticks()
```

where `number` is the argument, are satisfied.

Of course, this is not a particularly interesting game strategy. But it satisfies the specifications, and we'll leave it for now. You are invited to develop more interesting strategies in the exercises.

DrJava: developing Player with JUnit

Review the use of JUnit, pages 271 through 272. Open files `Player.java` and `PlayerTest.java`, located in folder `nim`, in `ch8`, in `nhText`. `Player.java` contains a stubbed implementation of the class *Player*, and `PlayerTest.java` a skeletal JUnit test.

Following the pattern described in the section above, implement and test the class *Player*, using JUnit to conduct the tests.

8.3.4 The class *Game*

The *Game* is also easy to build from the specifications. An implementation, again without comments, is shown in Listing 8.3. We write an auxiliary method `otherPlayer` that returns the opponent of the *Player* passed as argument.

Listing 8.3   **The class *Game***

```java
class Game {

   private static final int MAX_ON_A_TURN = 3;
   private Player player1;
   private Player player2;
   private Player nextPlayer;
   private Player previousPlayer;
   private Pile pile;

   public Game (Player player1, Player player2,
                    int sticks) {
      assert sticks > 0 :
         "precondition: initial sticks > 0";
      this.player1 = player1;
      this.player2 = player2;
      this.nextPlayer = player1;
      this.previousPlayer = null;
      this.pile = new Pile(sticks);
   }

   public int sticksLeft () {
      return pile.sticks();
   }

   public Player nextPlayer () {
      return nextPlayer;
   }

   public Player previousPlayer () {
      return previousPlayer;
   }

   public boolean gameOver () {
      return pile.sticks() == 0;
   }

   public Player winner () {
      if (gameOver())
         return otherPlayer(previousPlayer);
      else
         return null;
   }
```

continued

Listing 8.3   **The class *Game* (cont'd)**

```
public void play () {
    if (!gameOver()) {
        nextPlayer.takeTurn(pile,MAX_ON_A_TURN);
        previousPlayer = nextPlayer;
        nextPlayer = otherPlayer(nextPlayer);
    }
}

public String toString () {
    return "Game with players: " + player1 + ", and "
            + player2;
}

private Player otherPlayer (Player player) {
    if (player == player1)
        return player2;
    else
        return player1;
}
}
```

8.3.5 The class *NimTUI*

Only the user interface remains to be implemented. It is shown in Listing 8.4. The structure is similar to those developed in Chapter 7. As always, we have included a number of auxiliary methods to simplify the code. The only thing a bit unusual here is the loop in playGame method. As we mentioned on page 332, this iteration seems to more appropriately belong in the model. But here it remains for the time being.

One thing a bit annoying is that when the game is played, all the moves appear on the screen almost instantly. Because things happen so fast, we don't get a sense of the moves being made sequentially over time. To solve this problem, we can slow things down a bit. Our local library class *nhUtilities.utilites.Control*[1] contains a method sleep specified as follows:

public static void sleep (**int** seconds)
Sleep for the specified number of seconds.

Invoking this method causes the program to simply pause for a bit. We can slow down the display of moves by invoking this method in the run loop. For instance, if we write

---

1. To use a library, the *classpath* must contain the directory in which the library resides. See Appendix i for details on classpath.

```
private void playGame (int numberOfSticks) {
    game = new Game (player1, player2, numberOfSticks);
    while (!game.gameOver()) {
        game.play();
        reportPlay(game.previousPlayer());
        nhUtilities.utilities.Control.sleep(1);
    }
    reportWinner (game.winner());
}
```

the move will be written about every second.

Listing 8.4   The class *NimTUI*

```
import java.util.*;

    // Main menu options:
    private static final int NO_CHOICE = 0;
    private static final int PLAY_GAME = 1;
    private static final int EXIT = 2;

    private Player player1;      // the Players
    private Player player2;
    private Game game;
    private Scanner in;

/**
 * A simple text-based user interface for the game of
 * simple nim, played computer vs. computer.
 */
class NimTUI {

    /**
     * Create a new user interface.
     */
    public NimTUI () {
        this.player1 = new Player("Player1");
        this.player2 = new Player("Player2");
        this.game = null;
        this.in = new Scanner(System.in);
    }

    /**
     * Start the interface.
     */
```

continued

Listing 8.4   **The class *NimTUI* (cont'd)**

```java
public void start () {
   int choice = NO_CHOICE;
   while (choice != EXIT) {
      displayMainMenu();
      choice = readIntWithPrompt("Enter choice: ");
      executeChoice(choice);
   }
}

/**
 * Play a game with the specified number of sticks.
 */
private void playGame (int numberOfSticks) {
   game = new Game (player1, player2, numberOfSticks);
   while (!game.gameOver()) {
      game.play();
      reportPlay(game.previousPlayer());
   }
   reportWinner(game.winner());
}

/**
 * Display the main menu.
 */
private void displayMainMenu () {
   System.out.println();
   System.out.println(
      "Enter the number denoting the action " +
      "to perform: ");
   System.out.println(
       "Run game.............." + PLAY_GAME);
   System.out.println(
       "Exit.................." + EXIT);
}

/**
 * Execute choice from main menu.
 */
private void executeChoice (int choice) {
   System.out.println();
   if (choice == PLAY_GAME) {
      int numberOfSticks = readNumberOfSticks();
      playGame(numberOfSticks);
```

continued

Listing 8.4   The class *NimTUI* (cont'd)

```java
        } else if (choice == EXIT)
            System.out.println("Good-bye.");
        else
            System.out.println(choice + "is not valid.");
    }

    /**
     * Read and return the number of sticks to play with.
     *
     * @ensure  this.readNumberOfSticks() > 0
     */
    private int readNumberOfSticks () {
        int number = -1;
        while (number <= 0) {
            number = readIntWithPrompt(
                    "Enter number of sticks " +
                    "(a positive integer): ");
        }
        return number;
    }

    /**
     * Report that the specified Player won.
     */
    private void reportWinner (Player player) {
        System.out.println();
        System.out.println("Player " + player.name() +
                " wins.");
        System.out.println();
    }

    /**
     * Read and return an int in response to the specified
     * prompt.
     */
    private int readIntWithPrompt (String prompt) {
        System.out.print(prompt); System.out.flush();
        while (!in.hasNextInt()) {
            in.nextLine();
            System.out.print(prompt); System.out.flush();
        }
```

continued

Listing 8.4   **The class *NimTUI* (cont'd)**

```
        int input = in.nextInt();
        in.nextLine();
        return input;
    }

    /**
     * Report the play of the specified Player.
     */
    private void reportPlay (Player player) {
        System.out.println("Player " + player.name() +
                " takes " + player.sticksTaken() +
                " stick(s), leaving " + game.sticksLeft()
                + ".");
    }
}
```

DrJava: running the application

Before running the application, we must add the directory containing the nhUtilites library to the classpath.

- Close all the files in DrJava (*Close All* option from the *File* pull-down menu.)
- Choose *Preferences…* from the *Edit* menu. A *Preferences* window will appear.
- Choose *Resource Locations* in the *Category* pane.
- Press the *Add* button under the *Extra Classpath* pane. A file section window will appear.
- In the *Select* window, select the folder that *contains* the folder nhUtilities. This folder should now appear in the *Extra Classpath* pane.
- Click *Apply* and *OK* in the *Preferences* window.

The folder containing nhUtilities has been added to your classpath. (For details on classpath, see Appendix i.)

Folder nim, located in ch8, in nhText, contains an implementation of the nim game. (Of course, you've completed the implementation of *Player* in the previous exercise. Note that these classes are labeled public to simplify interaction with the *Interactions* pane.)

1. Open one of the nim game files. (The only purpose is to add the directory containing nim to the classpath.)

2. In the *Interactions* pane, create a Pile.

```
    > import ch8.nim.*;
    > Pile myPile = new Pile(7);
```

```
> myPile
Pile: 7 sticks.
> myPile.remove(2);
> myPile
Pile: 5 sticks.
```

3. Create two *Players*.

```
> Player p1 = new Player("Spike");
> Player p2 = new Player("Biff");
> p1.sticksTaken()
0
> p1.takeTurn(myPile,3);
> p1.sticksTaken()
1
> myPile.sticks()
4
```

4. Create a *Game*. Note that the *Game* creates its own *Pile*.

```
> Game game = new Game(p1,p2,7);
> game.sticksLeft()
7
> game.nextPlayer().name()
"Spike"
> game.play();
> game.nextPlayer().name()
"Biff"
> game.previousPlayer().name()
"Spike"
> game.previousPlayer().sticksTaken()
1
> game.sticksLeft()
6
> game.play();
> game.nextPlayer().name()
"Spike"
> game.previousPlayer().name()
"Biff"
> game.sticksLeft()
5
```

5. A *NimTUI* creates *Players* and *Games*. Create a *NimTUI* and start it.

```
> NumTUI ui = new NimTUI();
> ui.start();
```

8.4   Summary

In this chapter, we have seen how to put together a complete, simple system. We began by considering the life cycle of a system: problem analysis, specification, design, implementation, testing, and maintenance. We noted that these were not a series of sequential steps, but rather a process that is iterative, incremental, and compositional.

As a case study, we carried out the design and implementation of a system to play the simple nim game. System design involved identifying classes, assigning responsibilities to the classes, determining fundamental relationships between classes, and writing detailed class specifications.

Finally, we implemented the system and noticed that the implementation was quite straightforward given the system specification. Implementing the *Player* class gave us an opportunity to see another example of test-driven design. The user interface we built was a simple, text-based interface, similar to what we've seen before.

SELF-STUDY EXERCISES

8.1   What is the "functional specification" of a system? What role does the functional specification serve with respect to customer and developer?

8.2   Comment on the following observation: "It is important to have a functional specification finalized before development begins so that the developers know beforehand exactly what the completed system will look like."

8.3   What steps does the "software life cycle" involve?

8.4   Which step involves algorithm design?

8.5   Give two reasons why it is helpful to have an "on-site" customer available to the design team throughout design and implementation.

8.6   Why is the software development process described as "compositional"?

8.7   System maintenance involves what activities?

8.8   Draw a static diagram showing all the classes of the nim game and their relationships.

8.9   How would the specification of *Pile* change if the `remove` precondition `number <= this.sticks()` were omitted?

8.10   Rewrite the *Pile* method `remove` assuming `number <= this.sticks()` is not a precondition.

8.11   What cases should be considered in testing the class *Pile*?

8.12   Suppose the `assert` command were removed from the *Game* constructor, and the user interface allowed the user to specify that a game was to be played with 0 sticks. What would happen when the user chose this option?

Would it matter if the condition `player == player1` in the *Game* method `otherPlayer` were replaced with `player.equals(player1)`?

8.13 Modify the implementation of the class *Player* so that rather than taking one stick on a turn, the *Player* takes as many as possible.

8.14 Modify the implementation of the class *Player* so that if it is possible on the *Player*'s turn to leave one stick remaining in the *Pile*, the *Player* does so.

EXERCISES

8.1 Consider systems to play the following games:

   a. tic-tac-toe;

   b. monopoly;

   c. chess;

   d. poker;

   e. a rogue-like, maze-crawling game;

   f. an adventure-like, cave exploration game.

For each, develop a list of some potential model classes, specify responsibilities for some fundamental model classes, and create a set of diagrams that illustrate important relationships between some of these model classes.

8.2 Do the same steps specified in the previous exercise for any of the following systems:

   a. a system to manage inventory in a video store;

   b. a system to schedule classrooms on a campus;

   c. a system to manage windows on a computer desktop;

   d. a system to produce and edit architectural plans for houses.

8.3 Modify the implementation of *NimTUI* so that the user gets to name the *Players*.

8.4 There is an easy to determine perfect strategy for the simple nim game. That is, if the number of sticks is known, one of the players has a winning strategy. Consider the situation from the point of view of the player whose turn it is. One stick left is clearly a losing situation. But 2, 3, or 4 sticks left are winning situations, since by making an appropriate choice, the player can leave the other player with the last stick. If there are 5 sticks left, it is a losing situation since no matter what the player does, the other player is left with a winning situation, that is, the other player is left with 2, 3, or 4 sticks. Continuing in this manner, we see that if there are 6, 7, or 8 sticks left, the player can leave the other player with 5 – that is, leave the other player in a losing situation. So 6, 7, or 8 are winning situations. Summarizing:

number of sticks:	1	2	3	4	5	6	7	8	9	10	11	12	13	...
win/lose:	L	W	W	W	L	W	W	W	L	W	W	W	L	...

Modify the implementation of the class *Player* so that the *Player* uses a "perfect" strategy.

(Hint: you will find the remainder operator, %, handy in writing this method.)

8.5   It might be more interesting if the user got to determine the plays in the nim game rather than simply observing the play. Modify *Player* to include a command `setNumber-ToTake` that tells the *Player* how many sticks to take on its next turn.

8.6   Given the modification of *Player* in the previous exercise, modify the user interface so that the user provides the number of sticks each *Player* is to take on each turn.

8.7   Modify the *Game* and user interface so that the play loop is in the *Game* rather than the user interface. That is, the *Game* method `play` plays an entire game rather than a single turn.

You will notice that the *Game* must now notify the user interface after each individual play. Have it do so by invoking a user interface method `notify`. You will also notice that the interface must be made known to the *Game*. Have it do so by invoking a *Game* method `register`.

8.8   Consider the *TrafficSignal* of Section 2.5. (A test for this class was implemented in Chapter 3.) Construct a class *Intersection* that has two *TrafficSignals*: an east-west signal and a north-south signal. When one signal is green or yellow, the other must be red. The class should have a command `change`, and queries for the light color of each of its signals.

Note that in terms of the *Intersection*'s response to a `change` command, there are three cases:

- if the north-south *TrafficSignal* is green, the *Intersection* must give only the north-south *TrafficSignal* a `change` command;

- if the east-west *TrafficSignal* is green, the *Intersection* must give only the east-west *TrafficSignal* a `change` command;

- otherwise, the *Intersection* gives both *TrafficSignals* a `change` command.

The user interface should allow the user to give the *Intersection* a `change` command, and should write out the colors of the two signal lights.

8.9   Design and implement a simple "maze crawl" game described in the following.

The maze is composed of a number of rooms. Each room has a description. Each room has four exits, labeled north, south, east, and west. The exits are connected to other rooms. That is, if you leave a room through an exit, you end up in another room (or possibly back in the same room). The maze is not cartesian. That is, if you leave room A by the south exit and end up in room B, moving north from room B will not necessarily put you back in room A. (But some exit from B should put you back in A.)

An explorer, controlled by the user, moves from room to room through the maze.

The user interface should permit the user to specify the direction in which the explorer moves, and then write out a description of the room entered.

You may "hard code" the maze in your program. Three or four rooms should be adequate.

8.10   Consider the class *Intersection* described in Exercise 8.8. The state of an *Intersection* instance determines which signals will be instructed to change when the *Intersection* is instructed to change. Suppose an *Intersection* starts with the north-south signal green and the east-west signal red. The *Intersection* responds to the first `change` command by instructing the north-south signal to change. The *Intersection* has also changed state: it responds to the next `change` command by instructing both signals to change.

If we represent the state of the *Intersection* with the signal(s) it will instruct to change, we can picture the state transitions of the *Intersection* as follows,

$$NS \Rightarrow NS, EW \Rightarrow EW \Rightarrow NS, EW \Rightarrow NS \Rightarrow NS, EW \Rightarrow \ldots$$

where "NS" means north-south and "EW" means east-west. That is, the *Intersection* will respond to the first `change` command by instructing the north-south signal to change; it will respond to the next `change` command by instructing both the north-south and the east-west signals to change; it will respond to the next `change` command by instructing the east-west signal to change; and so on.

Now suppose we capture this state information in an object. That is, suppose we define a class *IntersectionState*, with the following features:

> **public** IntersectionState (TrafficSignal signal1,
>   TrafficSignal signal2)
> > Create an *IntersectionState* that changes the specified *TrafficSignals*.

> **public void** execute ()
> > Change this *IntersectionState*'s *TrafficSignals*.

> **public** IntersectionState next ()
> > The next state after this one.

> **public void** setNext (IntersectionState next)
> > Set the next state.
>
> > **ensure:**
> > > this.next() == next

We give the class *Intersection* a third, dummy *TrafficSignal* since some states only change only one *TrafficSignal*, but the *IntersectionState* constructor requires two:

> **private** TrafficSignal northSouth;
> **private** TrafficSignal eastWest;
> **private** TrafficSignal dummy;

In the *Intersection* constructor, we create four *IntersectionStates*, and link them together in a circular fashion:

```
IntersectionState state1 =
        new IntersectionState(northSouth, dummy);
IntersectionState state2 =
        new IntersectionState(northSouth, eastWest);
IntersectionState state3 =
        new IntersectionState(eastWest, dummy);
IntersectionState state4 =
        new IntersectionState(northSouth, eastWest);
```

```
state1.setNext(state2);
state2.setNext(state3);
state3.setNext(state4);
state4.setNext(state1);
```

Finally, we give the class *Intersection* an instance variable that references the current state:

private IntersectionState current;

Now if we have done things correctly, the implementation requires no *if* statements at all. The *Intersection* command change becomes:

```
public void change () {
    current.execute();
    current = current.next();
}
```

Complete this implementation of *Intersection*.

SELF-STUDY EXERCISE SOLUTIONS

8.1   The functional specification is a document that defines system requirements. It defines *what* the system must be able to do, but not *how* the system will accomplish its goals. The functional specification is essentially the contract between customer and developer. It defines what the developer agrees to produce, and what product the customer will accept.

8.2   While it is important to have the scope of a project agreed upon beforehand, customers and developers must realize that requirements and specifications will change during development. Changes in the contract must be negotiated between the customer and developer.

8.3   Analysis, specification, design, implementation, testing, maintenance.

8.4   Implementation.

8.5   Two reasons (among many): initial functional specifications are often incomplete and inconsistent, and decisions regarding functional behavior need to be made during design and implementation; customer's needs and desires change as the design evolves.

8.6   The system itself, the objects, and the algorithms implementing each object's features are all composed of simpler pieces, which are themselves composed of pieces.

8.7   System maintenance involves modifying a system to meet changing requirements, as well as correcting problems detected after the system is put into production.

8.8   Something like the following:

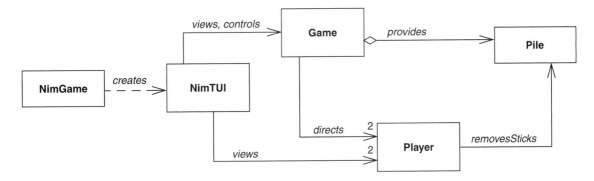

8.9   The specifications would need to say what happens if number > this.sticks(), and the postcondition modified. Perhaps:

> **public void** remove (**int** number)
>> Reduce the number of sticks by the specified amount. If number is greater than the number of sticks in this *Pile*, all the sticks are removed.
>
>> **require:**
>>> number >= 0
>
>> **ensure:**
>>> this.sticks() == old.sticks() - number ||
>>> this.sticks == 0

8.10 **public void** remove (**int** number) {
```
    if (number > sticks)
        sticks = 0;
    else
        sticks = sticks - number;
}
```

8.11 Probably a *Pile* with one stick (boundary case) and a *Pile* with more than one stick, and removing fewer sticks than are in the *Pile*, and removing all sticks that are in the *Pile* (boundary case).

8.12 The loop in *NimTUI*'s playGame method would immediately terminate (since game.gameOver() would return *true*), game.winner() would return player1 (since previousPlayer is **null** and so not equal to player1), and player1 would be reported as the winner.

In the second case, the program would fail with a *NullPointerException*. The method otherPlayer would be invoked with a **null** argument (previousPlayer), and attempting to invoke the method equals would cause the failure.

8.13 **public void** takeTurn (Pile pile, **int** maxOnATurn) {
```
    int size = pile.sticks();
    int number;
```

```
      if (size > maxOnATurn)
         number = maxOnATurn;
      else
         number = size;
      pile.remove(number);
      sticksTaken = number;
   }
```

8.14
```
   public void takeTurn (Pile pile, int maxOnATurn) {
      int size = pile.sticks();
      int number;
      if (size <= maxOnATurn+1)
         number = size-1;
      else
         number = 1;
      pile.remove(number);
      sticksTaken = number;
   }
```

CHAPTER 9   Interfaces

In the last chapter, we saw how to put together a complete system that involved a number of interacting objects. But it turns out that some of the relationships we established were too strong. For example, when we made *Game* client to the class *Player*, we tied the *Game* to a particular implementation of the *Player*'s strategy. We offered a trivial strategy implementation in the text and suggested several possible alternatives in the exercises. Nevertheless, when we implement the class *Player* we must chose some particular algorithm to implement the play strategy. And *Game* is welded to this implementation.

In this chapter, we see how to use abstraction to fix this problem. In particular, we see how to use the Java *interface* construct to abstract the functionality required by a client of a server. We also introduce the important idea of *subtyping*, by which a reference value can be in more than one type. Along the way, we also encounter some significant structural patterns, including one that allows a server to communicate fundamental state information to a client.

Objectives

After studying this chapter you should understand the following:

- the role of abstraction in the specification of a server;
- the use of interfaces to specify servers independent of implementation details;
- the notion of subtype, and fundamental property of a subtype;
- contractual requirements in the implementation of an interface;
- multiple inheritance of interfaces;
- the notion and use of the strategy pattern.

Also, you should be able to:

- specify and implement an interface;
- use an interface to capture commonality among similar classes.

9.1   Modeling alternative implementations

In the previous chapter, we designed and implemented an elementary system that played the game simple nim. Let's take a more careful look at the class *Player*. The basic function of a *Player* is to take a turn, as expressed in the method `takeTurn`:

public void takeTurn (Pile pile, **int** maxOnATurn)

> Take a turn: remove sticks from the specified *Pile*. maxOnATurn is the maximum number of sticks a *Player* can remove on a turn. A *Player* will remove at least one stick.
>
> **require:**
> ```
> pile.sticks() > 0
> maxOnATurn > 0
> ```
>
> **ensure:**
> ```
> 1 <= this.sticksTaken() &&
> this.sticksTaken() <= maxOnATurn &&
> pile.sticks() ==
>       old.pile.sticks() - this.sticksTaken()
> ```

The specifications tell us that when this method is invoked, the *Player* will remove at least one, and no more than `maxOnATurn`, sticks. The specifications do not tell us how the *Player* will determine how many sticks to remove. There are any number of strategies a *Player* might use and satisfy the specifications. In the last chapter, we implemented a rather timid player who always removed one stick:

```
public void takeTurn (Pile pile, int maxOnATurn) {
    pile.remove(1);
    sticksTaken = 1;
}
```

In the exercises, we suggested other possibilities: a greedy player, for instance, who always takes the maximum possible, or a clever player who uses a "perfect strategy."

Of course when we implement the method we must choose some particular strategy. But the rest of the program is *independent of the strategy* we choose: the rest of the program depends only on the specification of the method.

Suppose we define several player classes implementing different strategies: perhaps *TimidPlayer*, *GreedyPlayer*, *CleverPlayer*. We would like to choose what kinds of players to use when we construct the system. That is, we would like to be able to write initiating code like this:

```
public NimTUI () {
    this.player1 = new TimidPlayer("Player1");
    this.player2 = new CleverPlayer("Player2");
    this.game = null;
    this.in = new Scanner(System.in);
}
```

We might even let the user choose what kind of players will play the game.

The problem is that all of the code is written in terms of the class *Player*. The *Game* constructor, for example, requires two *Players* as arguments, not a *TimidPlayer* and a *CleverPlayer*. The *Game* method `winner` returns a *Player* as result, not a *TimidPlayer* or *CleverPlayer*. If we have three different player classes, we will need to replicate *NimTUI* and *Game* code nine times to handle all the possible combinations. Methods like `winner` can no longer simply return a *Player*, and pose a particular problem. Adding more player variants makes matters even worse.

This is not a very satisfactory situation. From the point of view of the *NimTUI* or the *Game*, the players are identical: the specification for all three player classes is the same, and the client classes *depend only on the specification*. The difference is in how the `takeTurn` method is implemented. But in all cases, the implementation satisfies the specifications. This is an example of *abstraction*, as discussed in Section 0.1.1. (It would not be a bad idea to reread pages 5 and 6 at this point.) *Player* abstracts *TimidPlayer*, *Greedyplayer*, and *CleverPlayer*. What is common to these classes is that they all have the same specification: they all offer the same contract to a client. In particular, they all know how to `takeTurn` when requested to do so. The client, the *Game* in this case, does not care what particular kind of player it is dealing with.

Abstraction is common in ordinary life. If we rent a car we assume a certain specification: we assume that the driver's seat is the left front (at least, in most of the world), that there will be a wheel for steering and that turning the wheel in one direction will cause the car to turn in that direction, that the right-most pedal is the accelerator, and so on. We might be pleased if the car has a navigational system or an alarm that sounds if we follow too closely behind another vehicle, but we would not be unduly distressed if we did not find these features. On the other hand, we would be rudely surprised if the left-most pedal caused the car to accelerate or if no turn signal control was close to hand. We understand a basic abstraction of any car we might drive, and expect this specification to be satisfied no matter how the car is built. It is this fact that allows us to easily move from one car to another. The abstraction is essentially the contract between the client (the driver) and the implementor (the car builder).

As we have seen so far, when we define a class we define an abstraction *along with its implementation*. This creates a relationship between client and server that is too strong. The server's definition includes not only its specification—what the server does—but also its implementation – how it does it. Consider the relationship between *Game* and *Player*. The *Game* is tied to a particular *Player* implementation, even though *Player* strategy is not relevant to the *Game*.

There are several mechanisms for defining server abstractions that are independent of any implementation. These mechanisms allow us to

- write client code based only on the specification of the server, and
- write server implementations that are independent of the client, and that can even be added after the system is in production.

The most fundamental Java mechanism for expressing abstraction is the *interface* facility, which we consider next.

> An abstraction should be independent of its implementations; the implementations must respect the abstraction's contract.

9.2   Interfaces

A Java *interface* looks much like a class with the implementation omitted. An interface can contain only method specifications, called *abstract methods*, and named constant definitions. There are no constructors, no method bodies, and no instance variables. There is, in fact, no trace of an implementation. You do not "instantiate" an interface. As we shall see, an interface defines an abstract view of a group of classes. It is used to specify the minimal functionality that a client requires of a server.

Let's look at the classes *Player*, *Game*, and *NimTUI* from the previous chapter. Both the *Game* and the *NimTUI* are player clients. *Game* invokes the *Player* method `takeTurn`, and provides *Player* references to the *NimTUI* through methods `previousPlayer`, `nextPlayer`, and `winner`. The *NimTUI* queries the *Player* for `name` and `sticksTaken`. The *Player* functionality required by these clients is defined by the specification of the methods `takeTurn`, `name`, and `sticksTaken`. Thus, if we want to use an interface to specify the functionality these clients require of a *Player*, the interface must contain specifications of these three methods. (The astute reader will note that the *Game* and the *NimTUI* have different views of a *Player*. To the *Game*, a *Player* is an object that responds to the `takeTurn` command; to the *NimTUI*, it is an object that can be queried for `name` and `sticksTaken`.)

9.2.1   Interface definition

Syntactically, an interface definition looks very much like a class definition. The keyword **class** is replaced with the keyword **interface** and method bodies are replaced with semicolons. For example, we can define an interface modeling a player as follows:

```
/**
 * A player in the game simple nim.
 */
interface Player {

    /**
     * This Player's name.
     */
    public String name ();

    /**
     * Number of sticks removed on this Player's most
```

```
 * recent turn. Returns 0 if this Player has not yet
 * taken a turn.
 *
 * @ensure      this.sticksTaken() >= 0
 */
public int sticksTaken ();

/**
 * Take a turn: remove sticks from the specified
 * Pile. maxOnATurn is the maximum number of sticks
 * a Player can remove on a turn. A Player will
 * remove at least one stick.
 *
 * @require     pile.sticks() > 0
 *              maxOnATurn > 0
 * @ensure      1 <= this.sticksTaken() &&
 *              this.sticksTaken() <= maxOnATurn &&
 *              pile.sticks() == old.pile.sticks() -
 *                  this.sticksTaken()
 */
public void takeTurn (Pile pile, int maxOnATurn);

}
```

Like a class, an interface is a member of a package. Also like a class, an interface can be public or "package private." Since the above interface definition does not begin with the keyword **public**, it is package private, that is, available only within the package in which it is defined. (We should also note that a package cannot contain both a class and an interface with the same name. The package nim, for example, could not contain both a class and an interface named Player.)

Method specifications in which the method body is replaced by a semicolon are called *abstract methods*. The keyword **abstract** can be used in these definitions. Thus, we could have written

```
public abstract String name ();
```

All method specifications included in an interface are public and abstract. Hence, the language does not require these keywords when specifying a method in an interface. We could, for example, write the specification of the method name in any of the following equivalent ways:

```
public abstract String name ();
public String name ();
abstract String name ();
String name ();
```

9.2.2 Interface implementation

An interface specifies functionality required by a client. It is not a source of objects: we cannot instantiate an interface. An object, however, can *satisfy* an interface. That is, an object can supply the functionality required by the interface. An object satisfies an interface if it is an instance of a class that *implements* the interface. A class implements an interface by

- naming the interface in an *implements clause* in the class heading, and
- including definitions for all the methods specified in the interface.

For example, suppose we want to define a class *TimidPlayer* that implements the interface *Player* defined above. The class definition will look like this:

```
class TimidPlayer implements Player {
    ...
    // definitions of class members as before
    ...
}
```

The class must contain definitions of methods `name`, `sticksTaken`, and `takeTurn` as specified in the interface *Player*. The class will also contain definitions of constructors, instance variables, *etc*. The class can contain other public methods besides those specified in the interface. But the definitions of methods specified in the interface must match these specifications exactly. (If method headings in the class definition don't match the headings in the interface, the result will be a compilation error stating that the class "should be declared abstract." This indicates that the class is missing the implementation of some method specified in the interface.)

In static diagrams, we denote an interface by placing the word "interface" in guillemets, and represent the "implements" relation with a triangle-headed arrow as shown in Figure 9.1.

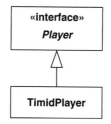

Figure 9.1 *TimidPlayer* **implements the interface** *Player*.

Abstraction

The triangle-headed arrow, in fact, represents the *abstraction relation*. Recall from Section 0.1.1 that "to abstract" means to eliminate details or distinctions. To categorize both a '68 Datsun 510 and a Maybach 57 as "cars" is an abstraction: it ignores several differences. To

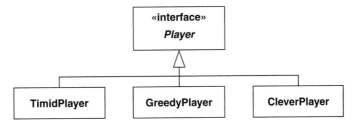

Figure 9.2 *Player* abstracts *TimidPlayer*, *GreedyPlayer*, and *CleverPlayer*.

call them "sedans" is less abstract; to call them "vehicles" is more abstract. In the example we are considering, *Player* is an abstraction of *TimidPlayer*. Considered as a *Player*, the implementation details of *TimidPlayer* are ignored.

We can also build implementations of the classes *GreedyPlayer* and *CleverPlayer* that implement the interface *Player*. We need only make sure that these classes implement the methods specified in *Player*, and name the class *Player* in an implements clause. Note that *Player* is an abstraction of all three classes. When viewed as *Players*, these classes are equivalent since they all satisfy the same specification. A *CleverPlayer* and a *TimidPlayer* are equivalent as *Players* in the same sense that a Datsun and a Maybach are equivalent as cars: they satisfy the requirements of the definition.

There is a considerable amount of terminology used to describe abstraction. The abstraction relation is sometimes called *generalization*: thus we say "the interface *Player* generalizes or abstracts the class *TimidPlayer*." The relation of the less abstract entity to the more abstract is sometimes called "*is-a*." Thus, *TimidPlayer is-a Player*.

> **interface:** a language construct that specifies functionality without any hint at implementation. An interface contains method specifications but no method implementations.

DrJava: implementing an interface

Open the file `Pair.java`, located in folder `exercise`, in `ch9`, in `nhText`. This file contains a simple interface definition. Open `StringPair.java` in the same directory. This file defines a class that implements the interface.

1. Compile `StringPair.java`. Notice the error message. The error message says essentially that "a class definition that does not override all abstract methods must be an abstract class." We'll see what an abstract class is in the next chapter. But recognize this error message as telling you that you have not implemented all the methods specified in the interface.

2. Implement the method `setFirst` in the obvious way:

   ```
   public void setFirst (Object obj) {
       this.first = (String)obj;
   }
   ```

Save and compile. There is still a method that has not been implemented.

3. Implement the method setSecond with a *String* argument:

    ```
    public void setSecond (String string) {
        this.second = string;
    }
    ```

    Save and compile. Note that the compilation still does not succeed. The method set-Second defined in *StringPair* does not match the specification in *Pair*.

4. Modify the definition of setSecond, but leave the name of the parameter string:

    ```
    public void setSecond (Object string) {
        this.second = string;
    }
    ```

    Save and compile. Note that the compile succeeds. The names of the parameters need not be the same in the interface and implementing class. Only the number and type must match.

9.2.3 Subtyping

So we now understand what an interface is and how to specify that a class implements an interface. How do we make use of this?

Recall the discussion of values and types in Chapter 1. A *type* is a set of *values* that can be used in the same way: anything we can do with one value of a type we can do with another value of the same type. Associated with each object is a *reference value* that identifies the object. A reference value is typed according to the class of the object it references. For example, suppose we execute the following two declarations:

```
TimidPlayer firstPlayer = new TimidPlayer("Wakko");
TimidPlayer secondPlayer = new TimidPlayer("Yakko");
```

Two objects are instantiated, and references to these objects are stored in variables firstPlayer and secondplayer:

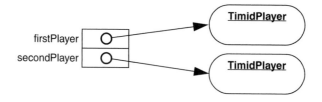

The type of these reference values is *reference-to-TimidPlayer*. Any operation we can perform on the value stored in firstPlayer (querying for name, for example), we can perform on the value stored in secondPlayer.

An interface also defines a type. A value is included in the type if it *references an instance of a class that implements the interface*. Suppose we have the structure depicted in Figure 9.2. Any value of type *reference-to-TimidPlayer*, *reference-to-GreedyPlayer*, or *reference-to-CleverPlayer* is also of type *reference-to-Player*. In other words, the type *reference-to-Player*, defined by the interface, is essentially the union of the types *reference-to-TimidPlayer*, *reference-to-GreedyPlayer*, and *reference-to-CleverPlayer*.

The type *reference-to-TimidPlayer* is said to be a *subtype* of the type *reference-to-Player*. (Notice that considered as sets of values, *reference-to-TimidPlayer* is a subset of *reference-to-Player*.) *Reference-to-Player* is a *supertype* of *reference-to-TimidPlayer*.[1]

Type conformance

A type defined by an interface can be used like any other reference type. It can be the type of an instance variable or parameter, and can be the return type of a query. So we can define the class *Game* exactly as in Listing 8.3, even if *Player* is an interface and not a class. Instance variables can be defined to be of type *Player*,

```
private Player player1;
private player player2;
```

constructors and methods can have *Player* parameters,

```
public Game (Player player1, Player player2,
    int sticks)
```

and queries can return values of type *Player*:

```
public Player nextPlayer () ...
```

Subtyping captures the essence of abstraction. If a client expects to be given a server of type *Player*, then a value of any *Player* subtype can be provided and the client is satisfied. The subtype object is guaranteed to provide all the functionality required by the client. It is a fundamental property of subtypes that

if type A is a subtype of type B, then an A value can be provided wherever a B value is required.

In particular,

if type A is a subtype of type B, then an A expression can be written in any context requiring a B value.

Thus, the *Game* constructor can be invoked with arguments that reference *TimidPlayers*, *GreedyPlayers*, etc.

When we discuss types, we must sometimes distinguish between the *static* or *syntactic* type of an expression and the *dynamic* type of the value of the expression. For example, the *Game* method nextPlayer is specified as

```
public Player nextPlayer ()
```
        The *Player* whose turn is next.

---

1. Having beaten the point into submission, we'll simplify terminology and refer to reference types by the class or interface name. Thus "type *Player*" rather than "type *reference-to-Player*."

Thus, if game is a *Game*, the type of the expression

```
game.nextPlayer()
```

is *Player*. The type of this expression can be determined by the compiler from the program text. It is not dependent on what actually happens when the program is run. We refer to this as the *static* type of the expression.

When the expression is evaluated during program execution, the value returned will reference some particular object: perhaps a *TimidPlayer*. Thus, the *dynamic* type of the value returned by the expression is *TimidPlayer*. The dynamic type cannot in general be determined by the compiler. In fact, the above expression will likely be evaluated many times during execution of the program, sometimes returning a reference to one kind of player, sometimes returning a reference to another kind. All we can determine from the program text is that the dynamic type will be a subtype of *Player*.

Suppose we have a variable, parameter, and return type of type *Player*:

```
private Player nextPlayer;
private void reportPlay (Player player) ...
public Player winner () ...
```

Then the following contexts all require expressions of type *Player*:

```
nextPlayer = Player expression required;
```

```
reportPlay(Player expression required);
```

```
public Player winner () {
    ...
    return Player expression required;
}
```

By the fundamental property stated above, an expression of type *TimidPlayer*, for instance, can be written in any of these contexts. If

```
TimidPlayer timid = new TimidPlayer("Wakko");
```

then the assignment

```
nextPlayer = timid;
```

is legal. This certainly makes sense, since *TimidPlayer* is a subtype of *Player*: every value of type *TimidPlayer* is also a value of type *Player*.

Similarly, given the variable declarations

```
TimidPlayer firstPlayer = new TimidPlayer("Wakko");
TimidPlayer secondPlayer = new TimidPlayer("Yakko");
CleverPlayer thirdPlayer = new CleverPlayer("Guy");
GreedyPlayer fourthPlayer = new GreedyPlayer("Sis");
```

the following are all legal constructor invocations:

```
new Game(firstPlayer, secondplayer)
new Game(firstPlayer, thirdPlayer)
```

```
new Game(thirdPlayer, fourthPlayer)
new Game(thirdPlayer, new TimidPlayer("Dot"))
```

The *Game* does not distinguish *Player* subtypes: it views the arguments through the interface *Player*.

Now the *Game* method nextPlayer returns a *Player*:

> **public** Player nextPlayer ()
> > The *Player* whose turn is next.

The value returned will reference either a *TimidPlayer*, a *GreedyPlayer*, or a *CleverPlayer* (assuming these are the only subtypes of *Player*). But all we can assume about the value returned is that the object it references will satisfy the interface *Player*. If game is a *Game* instance, we cannot write the following:

✗   TimidPlayer next = game.nextPlayer();

The assignment operator, =, requires a *TimidPlayer* reference on the right, to store into the *TimidPlayer* variable next. But game.nextPlayer() is of type *Player*, and *Player* is not a subtype of *TimidPlayer*.

These type conformance rules are *syntactic* and *static*, and are checked by the compiler at compile time. They depend on the static type of the expression written in the program, not the actual class of the object referenced at run-time. Consider the following:

```
Game game = new Game(
                new TimidPlayer("Yakko"),
                new TimidPlayer("Dot"));
```
✗   TimidPlayer next = game.nextPlayer();

The assignment to next is not allowed, even though we *know* the value returned will reference a *TimidPlayer*. Syntactically, game.nextPlayer() is an expression of type *Player*, and not of type *TimidPlayer*.

A few simple examples should help clarify this point. Suppose we have the following variable declarations:

```
Player p1;
Player p2;
TimidPlayer tp = new TimidPlayer("Wakko");
CleverPlayer cp = new CleverPlayer("Guy");
```

The following assignments are all legal, since in each case the right operand of the assignment is required to be of type *Player*:

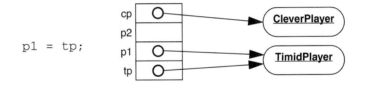

p1 = tp;

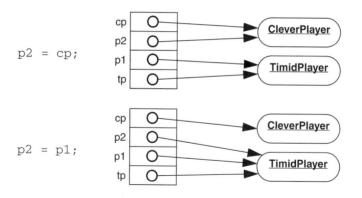

The following are not legal:

✗	`tp = p1;`	`// p1 is not of type TimidPlayer`
✗	`cp = p2;`	`// p2 is not of type CleverPlayer`
✗	`cp = tp;`	`// tp is not of type CleverPlayer`

Note that in the first assignment statement, it does not matter whether p1 actually references a *TimidPlayer* when the statement is executed. The (static) type of the variable p1 is *Player*; *Player* is not a subtype of *TimidPlayer*; so p1 cannot be used in a context requiring a *TimidPlayer*.

> **subtype:** a type whose constituent values are also members of another (super) type. If A is a subtype of B, then an expression of type A can be written in any context requiring a value of type B.

DrJava: subtyping and type conformance

Open the files `Player.java`, `TimidPlayer.java`, `CleverPlayer.java`, and `Exercise.java` located in folder nimExercise, in ch9, in nhText. These are minimal, "dummy" definitions, just for the purpose of this exercise.

Note that the interface *Player* specifies only a single method, `myClass`. The classes *TimidPlayer* and *CleverPlayer* each implement the method in their own way. Also, *TimidPlayer* defines an additional method, `isTimid`, and *CleverPlayer* defines an additional method, `isClever`.

1. In the *Interactions* pane, create a *TimidPlayer*, a *CleverPlayer*, and a *Player* variable.

```
> import ch9.nimExercise.*;
> TimidPlayer timmie = new TimidPlayer();
> CleverPlayer lassie = new CleverPlayer();
> Player player;
```

`timmie` and `lassie` behave as expected,

```
> timmie.myClass()
"TimidPlayer"
> timmie.isTimid()
true
> lassie.myClass()
"CleverPlayer"
> lassie.isClever()
true
> lassie.isTimid()
Error: No 'isTimid' method in 'ch9.nim.CleverPlayer'
```

while `player` has not yet been initialized:

```
> player
Error: Variable 'player' uninitialized
```

2. A reference to a *TimidPlayer* can be assigned to `player`, since *TimidPlayer* is a subtype of *Player*:

    ```
    > player = timmie;
    > player.myClass()
    "TimidPlayer"
    ```

    But we cannot access *TimidPlayer* features through `player`. The view of the object via `player` shows only the functionality of a *Player*:

    ```
    > player.isTimid()
    Error: No 'isTimid' method in 'ch9.nim.Player'
    ```

3. A reference to a *CleverPlayer* can also be assigned to `player`:

    ```
    > player = lassie;
    > player == lassie
    true
    > player.myClass()
    "CleverPlayer"
    ```

4. But the following is not allowed,

    ```
    > lassie = player;
    Error: Bad types in assignment
    ```

    since the static type of `player` is *Player*, the assignment to `lassie` requires an expression of type *CleverPlayer*, and *Player* is not a subtype of *CleverPlayer*.

5. Now look at the definition of *Exercise*. Note that the constructor requires two *Players*. Since *TimidPlayer* and *CleverPlayer* are subtypes of *Player*, we can create an *Exercise* as follows:

    ```
    > Exercise e = new Exercise(timmie, lassie);
    ```

6. The expression `e.getPlayer(1)` returns a *TimidPlayer* instance:

```
> e.getPlayer(1).myClass()
"TimidPlayer"
> e.getPlayer(1) == timmie
true
```

but has a static type of *Player*:

```
> player = e.getPlayer(1);
> timmie = e.getPlayer(1);
Error: Bad types in assignment
```

9.2.4 Putting it together

So what does the updated system look like? The classes *Pile* and *Game* remain exactly as in the previous chapter. *Game* constructors, methods, and instance variables are written in terms of the type *Player*. It does not matter that *Player* is now an interface and not a class.

The class *NimTUI* is the same as in the previous chapter, except that the constructor invocations must instantiate classes, not the *Player* interface. *NimTUI* will still have instance variables of type *Player*:

```
private Player player1;
private Player player2;
```

But the initialization code will create specific kinds of players. For instance,

```
public NimTUI () {
    this.player1 = new TimidPlayer("Player1");
    this.player2 = new GreedyPlayer("Player2");
    this.game = null;
    this.in = new Scanner(System.in);
}
```

If we do things this way, we must edit the code and recompile to change the kinds of players that are playing the game. A much more attractive approach is to permit the user to choose the kinds of players. This modification is suggested in the exercises.

Finally, *Player* is an interface as defined on page 356, with *TimidPlayer*, *Greedy-Player*, and *CleverPlayer* implementing classes. The basic relationships between *NimTUI*, *Game*, and *Player* are shown in Figure 9.3.

DrJava: programming with interfaces

Close all open files. Open the file NimTUI.java, located in nim, in ch9, in nhText. Notice that the variables player1 and player2 are of type *Player*, and that a *Timid-Player* and *GreedyPlayer* are created in the constructor. (The directory does not contain source files for *GreedyPlayer* and *CleverPlayer*.)

1. In the *Interactions* pane, run the application.

```
> java ch9.nim.NimGame
```

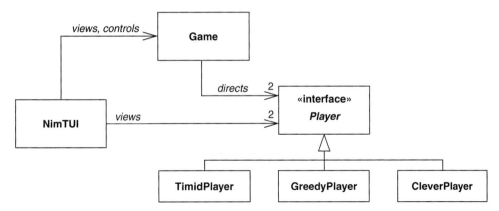

Figure 9.3 **Fundamental relationships between nim game components.**

2. Modify the *NimTUI* constructor so that a *CleverPlayer* rather than a *GreedyPlayer* is created. Save and compile.

3. Run the application again. Notice that the application is independent of the choice of players made in the interface.

9.3   Clients and interfaces

An interface defines the functionality a client requires of a server. Classes that implement an interface can be quite diverse. Let's revisit the maze game, first introduced in Section 3.3. Suppose that the maze can contain various kinds of items: potions, rings, swords, and so on, each modeled by an appropriate class. Suppose further that among the maze inhabitants are gnomes whose only function is to move items around. Then from the point of view of a gnome, rings and swords are equivalent: they are items that can be moved. Thus we might have an interface defined as

```
interface Movable {

    /**
     * Move this item to the specified Room.
     */
    public void moveTo (Room newLocation);

}
```

and implemented by classes such as *Ring*, *Potion*, *etc.*:

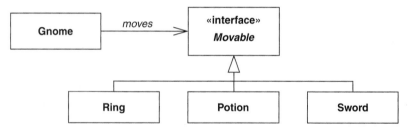

Note that in other respects, these classes are quite different. But to the *Gnome* client, they are equivalent.

Implementing classes and contracts

Now as we have seen, the interaction between client and server is defined in terms of a contract specified in part by method preconditions and postconditions. An implementing class is obligated to respect the contract offered by the server interface. An implementing class can weaken the preconditions and strengthen the postconditions of a method specified by the interface, but not *vice versa*.

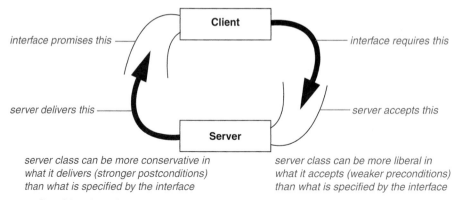

Consider the *Player* method `takeTurn`. Preconditions require the *Pile* supplied as argument to be non empty:

```
/**
 *  ...
 * @require     pile.sticks() > 0
 *  ...
 */
public void takeTurn (Pile pile, int maxOnATurn);
```

It would be permissible for an implementing class to weaken this precondition, allowing an empty *Pile*:

```
/**
 *  ...
 * @require     pile.sticks() >= 0
 *  ...
 */
public void takeTurn (Pile pile, int maxOnATurn) ...
```

This cannot possibly affect a client of *Player*. The client will make sure that the stronger condition is met, even if it is dealing with a more liberal server. However, the implementing class must guarantee that if the *Pile* is not empty, at least one stick will be removed. This is the contract offered by *Player* to its clients.

On the other hand, it is not legitimate for an implementing class to strengthen a precondition, say by requiring that maxOnATurn be no greater than the number of sticks in the *Pile*:

```
     /**
      *  ...
      * @require     pile.sticks() > 0
✗     *               maxOnATurn <= pile.sticks()
      *  ...
      */
     public void takeTurn (Pile pile, int maxOnATurn) ...
```

This requirement is not part of the *Player* contract, and we cannot expect a client to conform to it.

To see how the rule applies to postconditions, note that the takeTurn postcondition promises that a *Player* will take at least one stick:

```
/**
 *  ...
 * @ensure      1 <= this.sticksTaken() &&
 *              this.sticksTaken() <= maxOnATurn
 *  ...
 */
public void takeTurn (Pile pile, int maxOnATurn);
```

An implementing class (*TimidPlayer* for instance) might strengthen this postcondition by guaranteeing to take exactly one stick:

```
/**
 *  ...
 * @ensure      this.sticksTaken() == 1
 *  ...
 */
public void takeTurn (Pile pile, int maxOnATurn) ...
```

Again, this cannot cause problems for the client: the client is satisfied as long as the *Player* takes one or more.

But an implementing class is not permitted to weaken the postcondition. For instance, an implementing class could not allow the possibility of not taking any sticks:

✗
```
/**
 *  ...
 *  @ensure     0 <= this.sticksTaken() &&
 *              this.sticksTaken() <= maxOnATurn
 *  ...
 */
public void takeTurn (Pile pile, int maxOnATurn) ...
```

Player promises that at least one stick will be removed. A client may not be prepared to deal with the possibility that a *Player* does not take any sticks.

9.4   Multiple inheritance and interface extension

Let's carry the maze game example, revisited at the start of the previous section, a little further. Suppose that an *Explorer* wields a weapon. There are various kinds of weapons that share a common set of features. Thus we might define an interface *Weapon*:

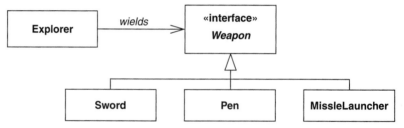

Note now that the class *Sword* implements both *Weapon* and *Movable*:

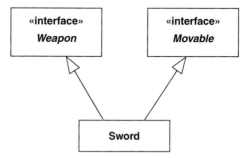

This is sometimes termed *multiple inheritance*. The class *Sword* must name both interfaces in the implements clause:

```
class Sword implements Weapon, Movable { ...
```

and must provide implementations for methods specified in *Weapon* as well as for those specified in *Movable*.

Interface extension

Suppose we decide that all *Weapons* should be *Movable*. That is, *Movable* is an abstraction of *Weapon*:

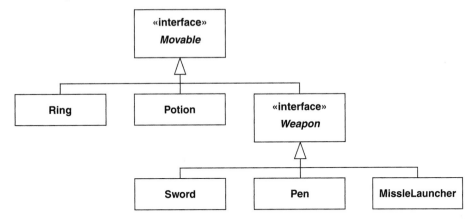

In this case, the interface *Weapon extends* the interface *Movable*. (We can't say "*Weapon* implements *Movable*," since *Weapon*, being an interface, doesn't implement anything.) We must include an *extends* clause in the definition of *Weapon*:

```
interface Weapon extends Movable { ...
```

The definition of the interface *Weapon* doesn't need to contain specifications of methods already specified in *Movable*: *Weapon* won't contain a specification of `moveTo`, for instance. We say that *Weapon inherits* the abstract methods specified in *Movable*.

A class that implements *Weapon* will also implement *Movable*. For example, the class *Sword* is now simply specified as

```
class Sword implements Weapon { ...
```

Since a *Weapon* is a *Movable*, *Sword* implements both interfaces, and must provide implementations for methods specified in both *Weapon* and *Movable*.

Just as a class can implement more than one interface, an interface can extend more than one interface. For instance, given that *DataInput* and *DataOutput* are interfaces, we could define an interface *DataIO* as follows:

```
interface DataIO extends DataInput, DataOutput { }
```

This interface inherits specifications from both *DataInput* and *DataOutput*. A class that implements *DataIO* must implement the methods specified both by *DataInput* and by *DataOutput*. Note that as we have written it, the interface *DataIO* does not specify any additional methods. (Though, of course, it could.) Interface hierarchies are not particularly common and tend to be very shallow.

Finally, we should note that the subtype and supertype relations are *transitive*: if *A* is a subtype of *B,* and *B* is a subtype *C*, then *A* is a subtype of *C* (and *C* is a supertype of *A*). In the illustration on page 371, *Pen* is a subtype of *Weapon* and *Weapon* is a subtype of *Movable*. Thus *Pen* is also a subtype of *Movable*.

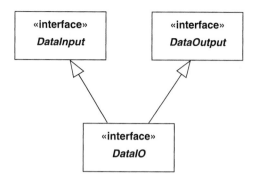

Figure 9.4 **An interface can extend more than one parent.**

9.5   Modifying the system: user vs. computer

At this point, let's see what's involved in allowing the user to play the nim game. That is, we want the same simple nim game and text-based user interface, but we want the user to play against "the computer" rather than just watching the game.

The initial menu will be similar to the previous one:

```
Enter the number denoting the action to perform:
Play game.............1
Exit.................2
Enter choice:
```

If the user chooses to play a game, the user will be prompted for the number of sticks and whether or not the user plays first:

```
Enter number of sticks (a positive integer):
User plays first? (Key yes or no):
```

On the user's turn, the user will be prompted for the number of sticks to take. A game will look like this, with the user's input shown in italics:

```
Enter the number denoting the action to perform:
Play game.............1
Exit.................2
Enter choice: 1

Enter number of sticks (a positive integer): 5
User plays first? (Key yes or no): yes

Enter number to take (a positive integer, at most 3): 3
User takes 3 stick(s), leaving 2.
Computer takes 1 stick(s), leaving 1.
```

```
Enter number to take (a positive integer, at most 1): 1
User takes 1 stick(s), leaving 0.

Computer wins.
```

9.5.1 Player classes

The most obvious change is in *Player* functionality. We now need two different kinds of players. One player decides its own move, exactly as before; the other gets its move from an external source, the user. To model these two kinds of players, we define two classes, *IndependentPlayer* and *InteractivePlayer*. Both classes implement the interface *Player*, as defined on page 356. *IndependentPlayer* is specified exactly as the class *Player* was in Chapter 8. The *InteractivePlayer*, on the other hand, gets its move from some client.

We include a method `setNumberToTake` to tell the *InteractivePlayer* how many sticks to take on its next turn. The user interface will invoke this method after the number is obtained from the user.

class InteractivePlayer **implements** Player
> A player in the game simple nim that gets moves from a client.

public InteractivePlayer (String name)
> Create a new *InteractivePlayer* with the specified name.

> **ensure:**
> > this.name().equals(name)

public String name ()
> This *InteractivePlayer*'s name.

public int sticksTaken ()
> Number of sticks removed on this *InteractivePlayer*'s most recent turn. Returns 0 if this *InteractivePlayer* has not yet taken a turn.

> **ensure:**
> > this.sticksTaken() >= 0

public void setNumberToTake (**int** number)
> Set the number of sticks this *InteractivePlayer* should take on its next turn.

> **require:**
> > number > 0

public void takeTurn (Pile pile, **int** maxOnATurn)
> Take a turn: remove sticks from the specified *Pile*. maxOnATurn is the maximum number of sticks a *Player* can remove on a turn.

> If this.setNumberToTake(number) is invoked before this *InteractivePlayer* removes sticks, and if the argument number provided in the most recent invocation is not greater than

maxOnATurn nor greater than `pile.sticks()`, then number sticks will be removed. Otherwise, one stick will be removed.

require:
```
pile.sticks() > 0
maxOnATurn > 0
```

ensure:
```
1 <= this.sticksTaken() &&
this.sticksTaken() <= maxOnATurn &&
pile.sticks() ==
    old.pile.sticks() - this.sticksTaken()
```

9.5.2 The user interface

The user interface must also be modified somewhat. It will now create an *InteractivePlayer* and a *IndependentPlayer* when instantiated:

```
private InteractivePlayer user;
private IndependentPlayer computer;

public NimTUI () {
    this.user = new InteractivePlayer("user");
    this.computer =
        new IndependentPlayer("computer");
    this.game = null;
    this.in = new Scanner(System.in);
}
```

(As suggested before, we might want to let the user name the players.)

In addition to determining the number of sticks, the user also gets to say who plays first:

```
private void executeChoice (int choice) {
    System.out.println();
    if (choice == PLAY_GAME) {
        int numberOfSticks = readNumberOfSticks();
        boolean userPlaysFirst = readYes(
            "User plays first? (Key yes or no): ");
        playGame(numberOfSticks,userPlaysFirst);
    } else if (choice == EXIT)
        System.out.println("Good-bye.");
}
```

The method `readYes` is shown on page 304.

We've added a parameter to `playGame` indicating whether or not the user wants to play first. Recall that when the *Game* is constructed, the *Player* passed as first argument plays first.

```
private void playGame (int numberOfSticks,
        boolean userPlaysFirst) {
    if (userPlaysFirst)
        game = new Game (user, computer,
            numberOfSticks);
    else
        game = new Game (computer, user,
            numberOfSticks);
    while (!game.gameOver()) {
        game.play();
        reportPlay(game.previousPlayer());
    }
    reportWinner(game.winner());
}
```

Note that the *Game* constructor requires two *Player* arguments. Since both *InteractivePlayer* and *IndependentPlayer* are *Player* subtypes, both invocations of the *Game* constructor in the above method are correct.

9.5.3 User interface – model interaction

Now we come to a fundamental issue: how does the user interface know when to get a play from the user? There are two possible approaches:

- the user interface checks to see whose turn it is before invoking the *Game* method `play`;
- the *InteractivePlayer* tells the user interface when it needs a move.

The first alternative certainly seems the simplest way to address the problem at hand. We need only add a conditional to the play loop,

```
while (!game.gameOver()) {
    if (game.nextPlayer().equals(user)) {
        int numberToTake = readNumberToTake();
        user.setNumberToTake(numberToTake);
    }
    game.play();
    reportPlay(game.previousPlayer());
}
```

where `readNumberToTake` is similar to `readNumberOfSticks`, and gets the number to take from the user.

The difficulty is that the user interface is becoming more closely involved in the play of the game, which is properly the function of the model. We want a "dumb" user interface, as isolated from the model as possible. We've already stepped onto the slippery slope by putting the play loop in the user interface. If we choose the first alternative, we continue to add knowledge about the mechanism of the game itself to the user interface. The more knowledge a component has, the more potential changes that component must be able to accommodate. The role of the user interface is to manage input and output: its knowledge about how the model works should be minimized. By choosing this alternative, we essentially make the user interface the model driver.

The problem with the second alternative is that it requires that the model be client to the user interface. But as we've seen, we don't want the model dependent on the user interface. The user interface is properly client to the model.

However, it is not uncommon that a client needs to know that a server has reached some particular state. That's the situation we have here: the user interface (client) needs to know that the model (server) has reached a state in which it needs input from the user. We'll see a general solution to the problem, called the *observer pattern*, later. For now, let's see how a *InteractivePlayer* can let the user interface know it is ready to make a move.

If the *InteractivePlayer* is to tell the user interface it needs a move, the *InteractivePlayer* must know the user interface. But we want this relationship to be as weak, as minimal as possible. Since we want to be able to change the user interface without modifying *InteractivePlayer*, we don't want the *InteractivePlayer* to know the specific kind of user interface it is dealing with. All the *InteractivePlayer* is concerned with is that there is someone who wants to be notified when it is about to make a move. What that someone does about it is not important to the *InteractivePlayer*. Thus we define an interface

> **interface** InteractiveController
>> Models an object that needs to be informed when a *InteractivePlayer* is about to make a play.

> **public void** update (InteractivePlayer player)
>> The specified *InteractivePlayer* is making a play.

Before removing sticks from the pile, the *InteractivePlayer* notifies an *Interactive-Controller* by invoking its update method.

```
public void takeTurn (Pile pile, int maxOnATurn) {
    controller.update(this);
    ...
}
```

```
private InteractiveController controller;
```

The method invocation uses the key word **this**. **this** is a reference to the object executing the method. Thus the *InteractivePlayer* sends a reference to itself as argument to the *InteractiveController*.

The interaction between *InteractivePlayer* and *InteractiveController* is illustrated in Figure 9.5. The *Game* instructs the *InteractivePlayer* to take a turn. The *InteractivePlayer* notifies the *InteractiveController* by invoking the *InteractiveController*'s update

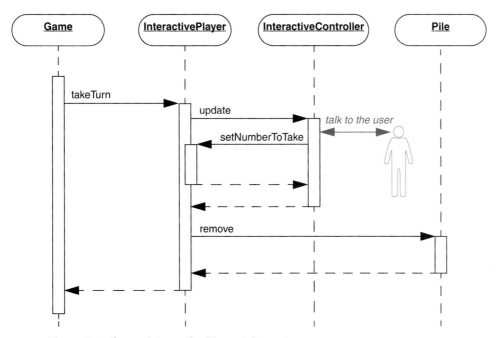

Figure 9.5 Case: *InteractivePlayer* takes a turn.

method. The *InteractiveController* finds out from the user how many sticks to take, and tells the *InteractivePlayer* by invoking the *InteractivePlayer*'s `setNumberToTake` method. The *InteractivePlayer* completes its turn removing sticks from the *Pile*.

There is one last issue to address before we can complete the definition of *Interactive-Player*. How does the *InteractivePlayer* know the *InteractiveController*? That is, how does the *InteractivePlayer* get a reference to a *InteractiveController*? Someone must provide it. So we add one more method to *InteractivePlayer*:

> **public void** register (InteractiveController control)
> > Set the *InteractiveController* this *InteractivePlayer* is to report to. This *InteractivePlayer* will notify `control` (by invoking its `update` method) before taking its turn.

We give a complete implementation of *InteractivePlayer*, without comments, in Listing 9.1. Note that the *InteractivePlayer* informs the *InteractiveController* before making a play, but in fact is not dependent on whether or not a *InteractiveController* has registered.

The class TUIController

Finally, we must update the user interface to support the *InteractiveController* functionality. We could modify *NimTUI* to implement that interface. But code implementing a dialogue with an external user can become involved. Furthermore, we can easily imagine a

---

Listing 9.1   **The class *InteractivePlayer***

```
class InteractivePlayer implements Player {

    private String name;
    private int numberToTake;
    private int sticksTaken;
    private InteractiveController controller;

    public InteractivePlayer (String name) {
        this.name = name;
        this.numberToTake = 0;
        this.sticksTaken = 0;
        this.controller = null;
    }

    public String name () {
        return name;
    }

    public int sticksTaken () {
        return sticksTaken;
    }

    public void takeTurn (Pile pile, int maxOnATurn) {
        if (controller != null)
            controller.update(this);   // numberToTake set here
        int pileSize = pile.sticks();
        int number = 1;
        if (numberToTake > 0 && numberToTake <= maxOnATurn
                && numberToTake <= pileSize)
            number = numberToTake;
        pile.remove(number);
        sticksTaken = number;
    }

    public void setNumberToTake (int number) {
        this.numberToTake = number;
    }

    public void register (InteractiveController control) {
        this.controller = control;
    }
}
```

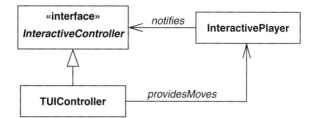

Figure 9.6 *InteractiveController* isolates *InteractivePlayer* from the user interface.

situation in which we have more than one *InteractivePlayer*. So rather than building this functionality into the existing *NimTUI*, we define a separate class that implements *InteractiveController*. This class is responsible for getting moves from the user and giving them to a *InteractivePlayer*. We call this class *TUIController*. (See Figure 9.6.)

When talking to the user, the *TUIController* writes a prompt something like:

```
Enter number to take (a positive integer, at most 3):
```

Thus, the *TUIController* must know the maximum number of sticks that can be removed on the user's turn. This information comes from the *Game*. So we add the following method to the *Game*:

```
/**
 * The maximum number of sticks that can be removed on
 * the next turn. Returns 0 if the game is over.
 */
public int maxOnThisTurn () {
   if (pile.sticks() < MAX_ON_A_TURN)
      return pile.sticks();
   else
      return MAX_ON_A_TURN;
}
```

When it is constructed, the *TUIController* is provided with a *InteractivePlayer* to control and a *Game*. The *TUIController* does not need to store a reference to the *InteractivePlayer* in an instance variable since the *InteractivePlayer* is passed as an argument to the update method. We show the implementation, again without comments, in Listing 9.2.

The *TUIController* can be created by the *NimTUI* when the *Game* is created:

```
private void playGame (int numberOfSticks,
   boolean userPlaysFirst) {
   if (userPlaysFirst)
      game = new Game (user, computer,
         numberOfSticks);
   else
      game = new Game (computer, user,
         numberOfSticks);
```

Listing 9.2   **The class *TUIController***

```java
class TUIController implements InteractiveController {

    private Game game;
    private Scanner in;

    public TUIController (InteractivePlayer player,
        Game game, Scanner in) {
        this.game = game;
        this.in = in;
        player.register(this);
    }

    public void update (InteractivePlayer player) {
        int numberToTake = readNumberToTake();
        player.setNumberToTake(numberToTake);
    }

    private int readNumberToTake () {
        int number = 0;
        int max = game.maxOnThisTurn();
        while (!(0 < number && number <= max)) {
            System.out.print("Enter number to take " +
                "(a positive integer, at most " + max +
                "): ");
            System.out.flush();
            if (in.hasNextInt())
                number = in.nextInt();
            in.nextLine();
        }
        return number;
    }
}
```

```java
        new TUIController(user,game,in);
        while (!game.gameOver()) {
            game.play();
            reportPlay(game.previousPlayer());
        }
        reportWinner(game.winner());
```

Note that the *NimTUI* does not need to store a reference to the *TUIController*. Once the *TUIController* is created, it functions independently of the *NimTUI*. The *Interactive-Player*, of course, maintains a reference to the *TUIController*.

DrJava: running an interactive game

Close all the open files. Open the file `TUICOntroller.java`, located in `interactiveNim`, in `ch9`, in `nhText`. This file contains the definition of an interactive user interface, similar to that built above.

1. Run the application in the *Interactions* pane.

    > `java ch9.interactiveNim.NimGame`

2. Play several games, and be sure you understand what is happening. You might want to put a breakpoint on the first statement of *InteractivePlayer*'s `takeTurn` method, and step through the method observing how the controller's `update` method is invoked. When this method is invoked, the controller gets input from the user and invokes the *InteractivePlayer*'s `setNumberToTake` method before returning.

3. Note that the instance variable `computer` in *NimTUI* is declared to be of type *Player*, and is initialized with a *TimidPlayer*. Change the initialization to *CleverPlayer*, save, recompile, and run the application again.

✳ 9.6   Reclaiming lost ground: the strategy pattern

If we look at the various player classes from Section 9.1, we will notice a considerable amount of duplicate code. In fact, the only difference in the classes *TimidPlayer*, *Greedy-Player*, and *CleverPlayer* is the body of the `takeTurn` method. Everything else is identical.

Duplicate code is one of the prime causes of maintenance headaches, and should be avoided whenever possible. Can we reduce the amount of duplicate code in the player classes? There are (at least) two approaches we might take. We consider one here, and look at a somewhat more general approach in a later chapter.

In Chapter 7, we introduced the concept of composition, specifically the includes or "has-a" relation:

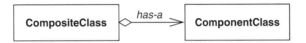

Recall that the idea is that the composite object can delegate some of its responsibilities to its component. A request for service is directed by a client to the composite object, and forwarded by the composite object to the component.

Applying this idea to the *Player*, suppose we make *Player* a class (so that it can implement all the common functionality), but give a *Player* a component that determines what move to make:

A *Player* will have an instance variable referencing a *PlayStrategy*,

```
private PlayStrategy strategy;
```

and the `takeTurn` method delegates the responsibility for determining how many sticks to take to the *PlayStrategy*:

```
public void takeTurn (Pile pile, int maxOnATurn) {
    int number =
        strategy.numberToTake(pile, maxOnATurn);
    pile.remove(number);
    sticksTaken = number;
}
```

Now clearly we don't want *Player* tied to a particular strategy. That would put us right back where we started. So *PlayStrategy* should be an interface that can be implemented in various ways, as illustrated in Figure 9.7. This kind of structure is sometimes referred to as the *strategy pattern*. The interface is defined in Listing 9.3.

We can implement *TimidStrategy*, for instance, as follows, with comments omitted:

```
class TimidStrategy implements PlayStrategy {

    public void numberToTake (Pile pile,
        int maxOnATurn) {
        return 1;
    }
}
```

The easiest way to equip a *Player* with a *PlayStrategy* is to provide one as a constructor argument:

```
public Player (String name, PlayStrategy strategy)
```
Create a *Player* with the specified name and strategy.

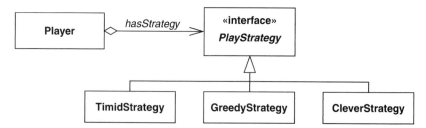

Figure 9.7 **A *Player* has-a *PlayStrategy*.**

Listing 9.3   **The Interface *PlayStrategy.***

```
/**
 * A player strategy in the game simple nim.
 */
interface PlayStrategy {

    /**
     * The number of sticks to be removed from the specified
     * Pile. maxOnATurn is the maximum number of sticks
     * a Player can remove on a turn. At least one stick
     * will be removed.
     *
     * @require     pile.sticks() > 0
     *              maxOnATurn > 0
     * @ensure      this.numberToTake() >= 1 &&
     *              this.numberToTake() <= maxOnATurn &&
     *              this.numberToTake() <= pile.sticks()
     */
    public int numberToTake (Pile pile, int maxOnATurn);

}
```

But an important result of using the strategy pattern is that a *Player*'s strategy can be changed *dynamically*. With the approach of Section 9.2, a *Player*'s strategy is fixed when the *Player* is created. That is, we create either a *TimidPlayer*, *GreedyPlayer*, or *CleverPlayer*. But here, we can include a method that allows a *Player*'s strategy to be changed after the *Player* is instantiated:

> **public void** setStrategy (PlayStrategy strategy)
> Set this *Player*'s strategy to the one specified.

This ability to dynamically change an object's behavior is one of the principal reasons for using the strategy pattern.

We show an implementation of this version of *Player*, again without comments, in Listing 9.4.

Note that we cannot directly adapt *InteractivePlayer* to this approach. The problem is that *InteractivePlayer* not only implements takeTurn differently, but also has additional functionality in the form of the setNumberToTake and register methods. We could define these methods in the class *Player*, and have *TimidStrategy*, *GreedyStrategy*, and *CleverStrategy* ignore input from a controller. But this is not attractive. We will see a better solution in a later chapter.

Listing 9.4   **The class *Player* with *PlayStrategy*.**

```java
class Player {

    private String name;
    private int sticksTaken;
    private PlayStrategy strategy;

    public Player (String name, PlayStrategy strategy) {
        this.name = name;
        this.strategy = strategy;
        this.sticksTaken = 0;
    }

    public String name () {
        return this.name;
    }

    public int sticksTaken () {
        return this.sticksTaken();
    }

    public void setStrategy (PlayStrategy strategy) {
        this.strategy = strategy;
    }

    public void takeTurn (Pile pile, int maxOnATurn) {
        int number = strategy.numberToTake(pile, maxOnATurn);
        pile.remove(number);
        this.sticksTaken = number;
    }
}
```

9.7   Java in detail: casting and *instanceof*

In Section 9.2.3, we saw that type conformance was a static issue, that is, the legality of a construct depends on the static type of the constituent expressions as determined by the compiler rather than the run-time type of the values produced by evaluating the expressions. For instance, given variable definitions

```java
Player player;
InteractivePlayer user;
```

the assignment statement

✗   `user = player;`

is not legal, regardless of whether or not `player` references an *InteractivePlayer* when the statement is executed. Even if we write

```
Player player;
InteractivePlayer user =
    new InteractivePlayer("Louis");
player = user;
```
✗   `user = player;`

the last assignment is not legal. Syntactically, the type of the expression `player` is *Player*, and *Player* is not a subtype of *InteractivePlayer*. Thus `player` cannot be used in a context requiring an *InteractivePlayer*, even if we know `player` will reference an *InteractivePlayer* at run time.

In cases where we are certain of the dynamic type of a value, we can *cast* the expression to this type. The format of a cast expression is

`(type) expression`

(We limit our attention here to cases in which the type is a reference type, and the expression evaluates to a reference value. Casting numeric values was discussed in Section 2.7.)

For instance if we write

`(InteractivePlayer)player`

we are saying that we are certain that `player` references an *InteractivePlayer*, and we want to treat the object referenced by `player` as an *InteractivePlayer*. If `player` does not reference an *InteractivePlayer* when the expression is evaluated, the cast will fail with a *ClassCastException* and the program will terminate.

Since the static type of the expression

`(InteractivePlayer)player`

is *InteractivePlayer*, we can legally write the assignment

`user = (InteractivePlayer)player;`

where `user` and `player` are as above.

Feature selection, ".", has higher precedence than casting. If `game` is a *Game*, we can write

`(InteractivePlayer)game.winner()`

to cast the result of the expression `game.winner()` to *InteractivePlayer*. But we cannot write

✗   `(InteractivePlayer)player.setNumberToTake(1);`

This parses as

✗   `(InteractivePlayer)(player.setNumberToTake(1));`

which will not compile since *Player* does not define a `setNumberToTake` method. Explicit parentheses must be used to cause the cast to happen first:

        ((InteractivePlayer)player).setNumberToTake(1);

A cast to a supertype is always safe. For example, given the structure shown on page 371,

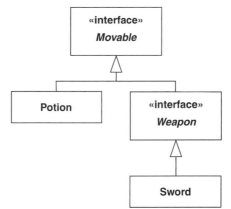

and the declarations

        Sword sword;
        Weapon weapon;

the cast `(Weapon)sword` is always safe. (Though it might not be clear at this point why we'd want to do this.) A cast to a subtype, `(Sword)weapon` for instance, will fail during execution if `weapon` does not reference a *Sword* instance. A cast that cannot possibly succeed, `(Potion)sword` for example, will result in a compile time error.

The boolean operator **instanceof** is used to determined the type of value an expression produces at run-time. This operator requires a reference-valued expression as left operand and a reference type as right operand:

        expression **instanceof** *type*

It returns *true* if the expression evaluates to a value of the specified type. For example, the expression

        player **instanceof** InteractivePlayer

returns *true* if the variable `player` references an *InteractivePlayer* when the expression is evaluated.

Suppose `game` is a variable of type *Game*, and we want to tell the next player how many sticks to take if it is an *InteractivePlayer*. We can write

        Player next = game.nextPlayer();
        if (next **instanceof** InteractivePlayer) {
            int number = readNumberToTake();
            ((InteractivePlayer)next).setNumberToTake(number);
        }

We can safely cast next to *InteractivePlayer* inside the if statement. If next did not refer to an *InteractivePlayer*, the **instanceof** operator would have returned *false*.

Use instanceof judiciously

While it is sometimes appropriate to use **instanceof** (and we sometimes have no choice), this operator often indicates problems in the structural design of a system. Consider a standard case in which a client accesses some service as shown in Figure 9.8.

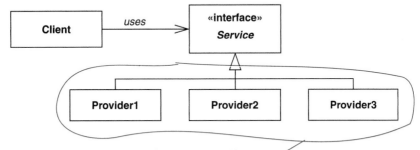

Client is independent of the collection of alternative providers

Figure 9.8 Interface isolates client from concrete service providers.

The purpose of the interface is to encapsulate the functionality required by the client. At run-time, the client will deal with some specific provider object. But as long as the provider satisfies the interface, the client does not care what specific kind of provider it's dealing with. The client is independent of the collection of concrete classes that can provide the service. We can add additional classes that satisfy the interface, or even remove classes, and it will not matter to the client.

If the client uses the operator **instanceof** to determine the particular kind of provider it is dealing with and behaves accordingly, a relationship is established between the client and the set of concrete providers. The client now depends on the possible classes of the object providing the service. But this is exactly the dependency that the interface is intended to remove. There is clearly something wrong with the abstractions being used. When you are inclined to use **instanceof**, make sure that you are not subverting a basic design abstraction.

DrJava: casting and instanceof

Again open the files Player.java, TimidPlayer.java, CleverPlayer.java, and Exercise.java located in folder nim, in ch9, in nhText.

1. In the *Interactions* pane, create a *TimidPlayer*, a *CleverPlayer*, and a *Player* variable.

```
> import ch9.nim.*;
> TimidPlayer timmie = new TimidPlayer();
```

```
> CleverPlayer lassie = new CleverPlayer();
> Player player;
```

and assign a *TimidPlayer* reference to `player`

```
> player = timmie;
```

2. Note that we can determine the run-time class of the object with the operator
`instanceof`:

```
> player instanceof TimidPlayer
true
> player instanceof CleverPlayer
false
```

3. The expression `(TimidPlayer)player` has static type *TimidPlayer*. Note that

```
> timmie = (TimidPlayer)player;
```

succeeds.

4. Modify the method `getPlayer` so that it casts its return value to *TimidPlayer*:

```
public TimidPlayer getPlayer (int which) {
    if (which == 1)
        return (TimidPlayer)player1;
    else
        return (TimidPlayer)player2;
}
```

Save and compile. Note that the compilation is successful. The expressions `(Timid-Player)player1` and `(TimidPlayer)player2` are both of type *TimidPlayer*, so the compiler is content.

5. In the *Interactions* pane, create an *Exercise* as above:

```
> import ch9.nim.*;
> TimidPlayer timmie = new TimidPlayer();
> CleverPlayer lassie = new CleverPlayer();
> Exercise e = new Exercise(timmie, lassie);
```

6. Note that when `getPlayer` is invoked, the cast of `player1` to *TimidPlayer* succeeds

```
> e.getPlayer(1)
ch9.nim.TimidPlayer@60991f
```

while an attempted cast of `player2` to a *TimidPlayer* fails:

```
> e.getPlayer(2)
java.lang.ClassCastException:
  at ch9.nim.Exercise.getPlayer(Exercise.java:17)
  ...
```

9.8   Summary

In this chapter, we introduced the fundamental notions of interface and subtyping. An interface definition is syntactically similar to a class definition, but with no hint of an implementation. An interface is not instantiated to produce objects. Rather, an interface captures the functional requirements a client has of a server.

An interface can be implemented by any number of concrete classes. To implement an interface, a class must name the interface in an implements clause, and implement all the methods specified in the interface. If a class C implements an interface I, the reference type defined by the class C is a subtype of the type defined by the interface I. This means that an expression of type C can be written in any context requiring an I. Essentially, if a client requires the services defined by the interface I, an instance of class C can provide those services.

Java's type conformance rules are syntactic and static: they are verified by the compiler from the program text. Thus if e is an expression of type A, and A is a supertype of B, we cannot write e in a context requiring a B value even if we are certain that evaluating e will deliver a B value at run-time. In this case, we must cast e to the appropriate type: $(B) e$. If we are not certain that e will deliver a B value, we can guard the cast by using the operator **instanceof**:

```
if (e instanceof B) {
    ... (B) e ...
}
```

We noted, however, that use of **instanceof** often involves undermining the basic abstraction defined by the supertype. This operator should be used with care.

In developing our examples, we encountered two structural patterns used to solve commonly occurring problems. First is a situation in which a client needs to know when a server reaches some state. The client informs the server of its interest by invoking a server method (*register*). When the server reaches the relevant state, it informs the client by invoking a client method (*update*). To keep the server as independent as possible from the client, the server knows the client through a minimal interface. This structure is sometimes called the observer pattern. An example is the *InteractivePlayer* and *InteractiveController* of Section 9.5.3:

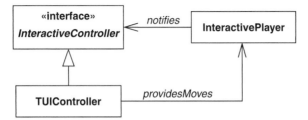

Second is a situation in which some behavior of an object is encapsulated in a component. The component is defined by an interface, and the object's behavior can be changed dynamically by replacing the component. This is referred to as the strategy pattern, and was illustrated in the player-with-strategy example of Section 9.6:

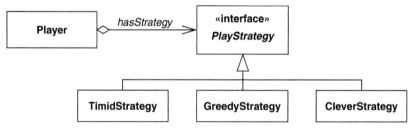

SELF-STUDY EXERCISES

9.1 In what sense does the interface *Player* capture the commonality between classes *Timid-Player*, *CleverPlayer*, and *GreedyPlayer*?

9.2 Suppose that the interface *Comparable* is defined as follows:[1]

```
interface Comparable {

    /**
     * This Comparable is greater than the specified
     * Comparable other.
     * @require    this.isComparableTo(other)
     */
    public boolean greaterThan (Comparable other);

    /**
     * This Comparable can be compared to the specified
     * Comparable other.
     */
    public boolean isComparableTo (Comparable other);
}
```

In what ways must the class *PlayingCard* (as specified in Section 2.6 for instance) be modified so that it implements this interface?

The type *PlayingCard* is a _____ of *Comparable*, and the type *Comparable* is a _____ of *PlayingCard*.

9.3 *a.* What is the difference between the following definitions of the interface *Comparable*?

```
interface Comparable { ... }
public interface Comparable { ... }
```

---

1. The standard interface *Comparable* defined in `java.lang` is somewhat different from the one we use in this exercise.

b.   What is the difference between the following definitions of the method
greaterThan in the interface *Comparable*?

> **boolean** greaterThan(Comparable other);
>
> **public abstract boolean** greaterThan(Comparable other);

9.4   To implement the interface *Comparable*, the class *Date* contains the following:

> **class** Date **implements** Comparable {
>
>   ...
>
>   **public boolean** greaterThan (Date other) ...
>   **public boolean** isComparableTo (Comparable other) ...
> }

Is this adequate?

9.5   Suppose that both *Date* and *PlayingCard* implement the interface *Comparable*. If *d* is a
Date, and *p* a *PlayingCard*, in what sense are they the same type? Is the assignment

> card = date;

legal, where card and date are variables of type *PlayingCard* and *Date* respectively?

Is the method invocation

> card.greaterThan(date)

legal?

9.6   Assume the structure shown on page 386. Given the definitions

> Movable movable;
> Weapon weapon;
> Sword sword;
> Potion potion;

and that the class *Sword* contains the method

> **public void** sharpen ()

the class *Potion* contains the method

> **public** Potion mix (Potion other)

and the interface *Weapon* contains the method

> **public void** break ()

which of the following are legal?

a.   movable = sword;
b.   sword = weapon;
c.   weapon = (Sword)potion;
d.   weapon.sharpen()
e.   ((Sword)movable).sharpen()

     f.   `potion.mix(movable)`

     g. `potion.mix((Potion)movable)`

     h. `sword.break()`

9.7   The interface *Cloneable* is defined as

             public interface `Cloneable {}`

    In what ways must the class *PlayingCard* be modified so that it implements this interface?

9.8   The following method is specified in an interface

```
public int swatchCount (Color color)
```
        The number of swatches of the specified *Color.*

       require:
```
color.equals(Color.PURPLE) ||
color.equals(Color.GREEN) ||
color.equals(Color.GOLD)
```

       ensure:
```
this.swacthcCount(color) > 0
```

    Which of the following specifications can be included in a class that implements the interface?

    (a)
```
/**
 * The number of swatches of the specified Color.
 * @require    color.equals(Color.PURPLE) ||
 *             color.equals(Color.GOLD)
 * @ensure     this.swacthcCount(color) > 0
 */
public int swatchCount (Color color) { ... }
```

    (b)
```
/**
 * The number of swatches of the specified Color.
 * @require    !color.equals(Color.WHITE)
 * @ensure     this.swacthcCount(color) > 0
 */
public int swatchCount (Color color) { ... }
```

    (c)
```
/**
 * The number of swatches of the specified Color.
 * @require    color.equals(Color.PURPLE) ||
 *             color.equals(Color.GREEN) ||
 *             color.equals(Color.GOLD)
 * @ensure     this.swacthcCount(color) >= 0
 */
public int swatchCount (Color color) { ... }
```

(d)
```
        /**
         * The number of swatches of the specified Color.
         * @require    color.equals(Color.PURPLE) ||
         *             color.equals(Color.GREEN) ||
         *             color.equals(Color.GOLD)
         * @ensure     this.swacthcCount(color) > 1
         */
        public int swatchCount (Color color) { ... }
```

9.9   Given that `game` is a *Game*, add parentheses to the expression

        `(InteractivePlayer)game.nextPlayer()`

to illustrate the order in which the operations of feature selection (`.`) and casting are carried out. Are the parentheses necessary?

Add parenthesis to the statement

        `(InteractivePlayer)game.nextPlayer().setNumberToTake(1);`

to make the statement legal. Why are the parentheses needed here?

9.10   Assume that a *Rectangle* has a query

        `public int area ()`

with the obvious meaning. Implement the *Comparable* method `greaterThan`, as specified in Exercise 9.2, for the class *Rectangle*, where *Rectangles* are compared by area. (Assume that a *Rectangle* can only be compared with another *Rectangle*.)

✳ 9.11   Suppose the class *Employee* has a method `pay` that computes the *Employee*'s pay for a pay period:

        `public int pay ()`
                This *Employee*'s pay for the current pay period, in dollars.

If the *Employee* is promoted or changes departments, the algorithm used to compute pay must be changed. Explain how composition and abstraction can be used to solve this problem.

EXERCISES

9.1   In Listing 3.3, we specified a simple maze game class, *Explorer*. An *Explorer* is client to a *Denizen*. Define *Denizen* as an interface, capturing only the functionality required by an *Explorer*. Could *Explorer* also implement this interface?

9.2   In Exercises 2.15 and 3.10, we implemented classes modeling rectangles and circles. Define an interface *ClosedFigure* that captures the commonality of these classes.

9.3 Assume that a *Date* has queries

```
public int day ()
public int month ()
public int year ()
```

with the obvious meanings. Implement the *Comparable* method `greaterThan`, as specified in self-study Exercise 9.2, for the class *Date*. (A *Date* is comparable only to another *Date*.)

9.4 Consider the following interface definition, modeling a binary integer operation (such as addition) with identity.

```
public interface OperatorWithIdentity {

    /**
     * Perform this operation with the specified
     * operands.
     */
    public int operate (int left, int right);

    /**
     * The identity for this operator. For any int i,
     *     this.operate(this.identity(),i) ==
     *     this.operate(i,this.identity()) == i
     */
    public int identity ();

}
```

Define a class *Addition* that models the integer operation of addition, and implements the interface.

Define a class *Multiplication* that models the integer operation of multiplication, and implements the interface.

9.5 Experimentally determine whether or not an interface can specify a static method.

9.6 Modify the nim game so that before a game, the user is asked to choose the type of each player. (Options are timid player, greedy player, clever player, or interactive player.) A *TUIController* should be created for each *InteractivePlayer*.

9.7 A chess board is made up of 64 squares, 8 rows and 8 columns. Rows are numbered 1 to 8, bottom to top; columns are numbered 1 to 8, left to right.

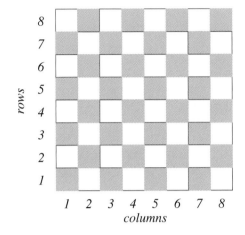

Define an interface *Piece* modeling chess pieces. The interface should include two methods, a boolean query `canMoveTo` and a command `moveTo`. Both take row and column as arguments. The first tells whether or not the piece can move to the specified row and column, and the second moves the piece to the specified row and column if possible.

A bishop moves diagonally, while a rook moves vertically and horizontally. Thus the bishop and rook shown below can move into any square covered by the arrows.

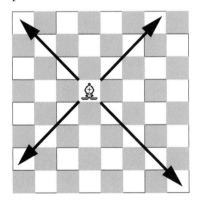 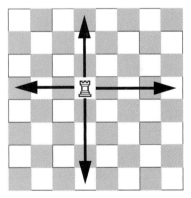

Define classes *Rook* and *Bishop* that implement the interface *Piece* and model the appropriate pieces. (In implementing the methods, ignore the possibility that other pieces might be on the board.)

9.8 The class *Employee* models employees of a particular company. An *Employee* has methods

> **public int** hours ()
>> The number of hours this *Employee* has worked in the current pay period.

public double pay ()
    This *Employee*'s pay for the current period in dollars.

Different kinds of employees are paid in different ways, and the way an employee is paid can be changed at any time. Thus an *Employee* has a component of type *PayCalculator*, and the *Employee* method pay simply forwards responsibility for computing pay to the *PayCalculator*:

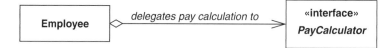

Define the class *Employee* and the interface *PayCalculator*. Define two classes implementing *PayCalculator*, one that pays the employee at some fixed hourly rate and one that pays the employee time and a half for overtime.

9.9   The class *Room* models a room in the maze game. A *Room* is initially undiscovered. When the *Explorer* enters the *Room*, it becomes known. A *Room* can be occupied (the *Explorer* is in the *Room*) or unoccupied.

    Design a class *Room* that models these aspects. (You can ignore any other *Room* properties in this exercise.)

    Define an interface *RoomViewer* that models an object that wants to be informed when a *Room* changes its state. (This interface should look like the interface *InteractiveController* of Section 9.5.3.)

    Define a class *TUIViewer* that implements the interface. When the *Room* changes state, the *TUIViewer* should query the *Room* to determine its current state, and write an appropriate message to System.out.

9.10   Modify the *Intersection* of Exercise 8.10 so that *IntersectionState* is an interface. The interface is implemented by two classes: one modeling a state in which two signals are changed, and one modeling a state in which one signal is changed. There should now be no need for the "dummy" *TrafficSignal*.

9.11   Modify the system described in Section 9.5 so that both the "user player" and the "computer player" get moves from "controllers." That is, both players are built using the observer pattern. Specifically, modify the system as follows.

    a.   Both user and computer are declared to be of type *InteractivePlayer*. (*InteractivePlayer* and *InteractiveController* are no longer good, meaningful names. Feel free to change them.)

    b.   A class *TimidController* is defined to implement *InteractiveController*. Rather than getting moves from the user, a *TimidController* always tells the player to take one stick.

    c.   The "computer" is given a *TimidController* as its controller.

Expand the system with other kinds of algorithmic controllers, such as *GreedyController* and *CleverController*. Modify the user interface so that the user can specify what kind of opponent he or she wants to play against.

✳   9.12   Modify the system described in Section 9.5 so that both the "user player" and the "computer player" get moves from "strategies." That is, both players are built using the strategy pattern, as described in Section 9.6. The "user player" has a strategy that gets moves from the user, much like the *TUIController* of Section 9.5.

9.13   A *DigitCounter* is a simple single digit, zero to nine, counter with the following features:

public int digit ()
> The current digit of this *DigitCounter*.

ensure:
> `0 <= this.digit() && this.digit() <= 9`

public void step ()
> Increment this *DigitCounter*.

public void reset ()
> Reset this *DigitCounter* to 0.

ensure:
> `this.digit() == 0`

Each *DigitCounter* has a *neighbor* representing the next higher order digit in a number:

Thus a multi-digit counter is modeled by stringing together *DigitCounters*:

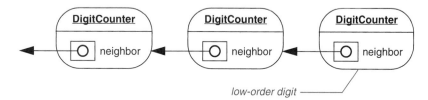

If a *DigitCounter*'s digit is less than 9, it simply increments its digit in response to the command `step`. However, if its digit is 9, it sets its digit to 0 and gives its neighbor a `step` command (thereby modeling the "carry" operation).

When a *DigitCounter* is given the command `reset`, it sets its digit to 0 and gives its neighbor a `reset` command.

A *DigitCounter* will also have methods `count` and `toString`:

public int count ()
> The count maintained by this *DigitCounter* and its high-order neighbors.

public String toString ()
> String representation of the count maintained by this *DigitCounter* and its high-order neighbors.

A *DigitCounter* implements count by getting the count from its neighbor, multiplying it by 10, and adding its digit. Similarly, it implements toString by getting its neighbor's *String* representation and tacking on its digit.

The question is how to handle the high-order *DigitCounter*. To do this, we define an interface *AbstractDigit*, and make a *DigitCounter*'s neighbor an *AbstractDigit*. Two classes

implement *AbstractDigit*: *DigitCounter* and *NullDigit*. *NullDigit* simply does nothing if given a step or reset command.

We make the high-order *DigitCounter*'s neighbor a *NullDigit*:

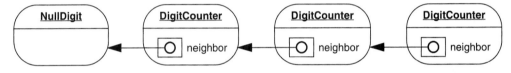

Notice that the *DigitCounter* does not care what kind of neighbor it has. Its implementation should never check to see what the type of its neighbor is.

Implement a class *ThreeDigitCounter* that counts from 0 to 999, and is constructed from three *DigitCounters* (and a *NullDigit*).

9.14   Notice in the previous exercise that the query digit is not particularly useful, and that there is a strong similarity between the features of a *DigitCounter* and a *ThreeDigit-Counter*. Develop a more general implementation that eliminates the need for the class *ThreeDigitCounter*.

SELF-STUDY EXERCISE SOLUTIONS

9.1   These classes have the same specification that is captured in the interface *Player*.

9.2   The class heading must include an implements clause

```
class PlayingCard implements Comparable { ...
```

and the class must include implementations of the methods greaterThan and isComparableTo:

```
public boolean greaterThan (Object other) { ... }
public boolean isComparableTo (Object other) { ... }
```

The type *PlayingCard* is a *subtype* of *Comparable*, and the type *Comparable* is a *super-type* of *PlayingCard*.

9.3   *a.*   In the first case, the interface is visible only in the package in which it is defined. In the second case, it is visible throughout the program.

       b.   There is no difference.

9.4   No, the definition of `greaterThan` in *Date* does not match the specification in *Comparable*. The parameter must be of type *Comparable*.

9.5   They are both of type *Comparable*, since *Comparable* is a supertype of both *PlayingCard* and *Date*.

     The assignment is not legal, because the right-hand side of the assignment operator requires a *PlayingCard*.

     The method invocation is syntactically legal, because `greaterThan` requires a *Comparable* argument. However, the invocation is not correct unless `card.isComparableTo(date)`.

9.6   *a.*   Legal.
       b.   Not legal.
       c.   Not legal.
       d.   Not legal.
       e.   Legal.
       f.   Not legal.
       g.   Legal.
       h.   Legal.

9.7   It need only include an implements clause. Since no methods are specified in the interface, no specific methods need to be implemented to satisfy the interface.

9.8   *(a)* Not correct; the precondition is strengthened.

     (b) Ok; the precondition is weakened.

     (c) Not correct; the postcondition is weakened.

     (d) Ok; the postcondition is strengthened.

9.9   `(InteractivePlayer)(game.nextPlayer())`

     The parentheses are not necessary, since feature selection (`.`) has higher precedence than casting.

     `((InteractivePlayer)game.nextPlayer()).setNumberToTake(1);`

     Without the parenthesis, the statement would require invoking the `setNumberToTake` method for game.nextPlayer() before doing the cast. But game.nextPlayer() is of type *Player*, and a *Player* does not have such a method.

9.10
```
public boolean greaterThan (Comparable other) {
    assert other instanceof Rectangle;
    Rectangle otherRec = (Rectangle)other;
    return this.area() > otherRec.area();
}
```

✳ 9.11 As shown on the next page, the *Employee* can be given a component, say *PayStrategy*, that is delegated the responsibility of computing the *Employee*'s pay. This component will be defined by an interface that has different implementations. The actual *PayStrategy* object referenced by the *Employee* can be changed dynamically, at run-time, as needed.

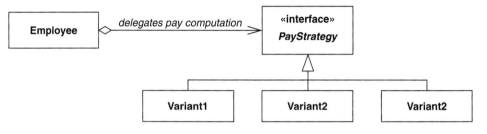

CHAPTER 10   **Inheritance**

In the last chapter, we introduced interfaces as a mechanism for expressing abstraction. An interface expresses the functionality required by a client, and decouples the client from any particular server implementation. Now we'll see that an abstraction can also be defined by a class. That is, a class can generalize or abstract a number of other classes, called *subclasses*, in somewhat the same way that an interface generalizes its implementing classes. The subclasses are said to *extend* the generalizing class.

When one interface extends another, the extending interface inherits the (abstract) method specifications of the other. A class includes an implementation as well as a specification. When a class extends another class, the extending class inherits the implementation as well.

An important aspect of inheritance is that a subclass can redefine the implementation of an inherited method. Thus instances of different subclasses can perform the same function in different ways. This behavior is referred to as polymorphism or dynamic binding. We spend the majority of this chapter investigating this relation between two classes, and its implications.

In the latter part of the chapter, we look at Java's rules for feature accessibility and scoping. That is, we look at the rules that determine from where in a program a particular method or variable can be accessed. To this point, all of our methods and instance variables have been either public or private. Now we introduce two additional feature categories, protected and package private, and see that, unfortunately, the reality is not as simple as we might like.

Objectives

After studying this chapter you should understand the following:

- generalizing classes by means of another class;
- extension, inheritance, and the subtyping relation defined by subclasses;
- method overloading, method overriding, and method polymorphism;
- class extension and class composition, and their differences;
- accessibility of public, private, protected, and package private features;
- Java's scoping rules.

Also, you should be able to:

• define a class extending an existing class;

• implement a class using an existing class via extension or composition.

10.1   Abstraction and classes

In the previous chapter, we saw that abstraction could be realized with an interface. An interface *generalizes* a class or less abstract interface:

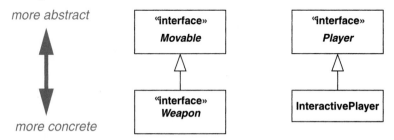

The more concrete interface *extends* the more abstract interface; the more concrete class *implements* the more abstract interface. In the diagram above, *Weapon* extends *Movable*, *InteractivePlayer* implements *Player*.

We can also define the abstraction relation between classes. That is, we can specify that one class generalizes or abstracts another class. Figure 10.1 illustrates an abstraction hierarchy of classes.

When dealing with classes, we say that the more concrete class *extends* the more abstract. Referring to the figure, we say the class *Circle extends ClosedFigure*, a *Circle is-a ClosedFigure*, *Circle* is a *subclass* of *ClosedFigure*, or *Circle* is a *descendent* of *Closed-Figure*. We also say *ClosedFigure generalizes Circle*, *ClosedFigure* is an *abstraction* of *Circle*, *ClosedFigure* is a *superclass* of *Circle*, or *ClosedFigure* is an *ancestor* of *Circle*.

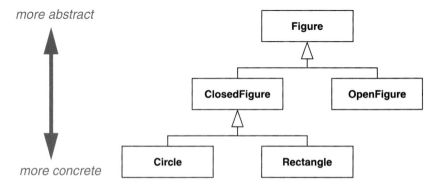

Figure 10.1 **A class hierarchy.**

The terminology is transitive, so that we can also say that *Circle extends Figure*, *etc*. (If we intend to limit the relation to child-parent, we say "directly extends", "is an immediate subclass of," "is an immediate superclass of," "is parent of," or "is child of.")

Class extension defines a subtype

As with interfaces, class extension creates a subtype relation between the types defined by the two classes. Thus, considering the classes shown in Figure 10.1, the type (*reference-to*) *Circle* is a subtype of the types *ClosedFigure* and *Figure*. An expression of type *Circle* can be written in any context requiring a *ClosedFigure* or *Figure*.

Expressions can be cast up or down the class hierarchy. Given variable declarations

```
Figure top;
Circle soleil;
```

the following are legal (though not necessarily safe) expressions

```
(ClosedFigure)top
(Circle)top
(ClosedFigure)soleil
```

while this is not:

✗   `(Rectangle)soleil`

(Since *Circle* is a subtype of *ClosedFigure*, a cast up the hierarchy like `(ClosedFigure)soleil` is almost never done. However, see Self-study Exercise 10.6, part *(e)*.)

10.1.1 Class inheritance is single inheritance

There is one significant difference between extending or implementing an interface, and extending a class. As we saw in the last chapter, a class can implement, and an interface can extend, any number of interfaces:

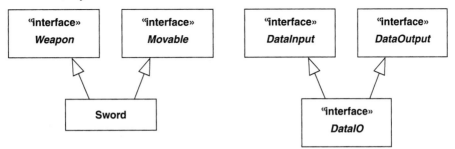

A class can have any number of "interface parents." On the other hand, every class (with one exception) extends *exactly one other class*. That is, every class has exactly one parent in the class hierarchy. This property is referred to as *single inheritance*. The lone exception is the class *Object*, defined in the standard library package `java.lang`, (We first encountered this package in Section 2.9, as home of the class *String*.) This class is at the top (or the *root*) of the hierarchy, and has no parent. Thus every class is a subclass of *Object*.

A parent class is specified with an *extends clause* in the class heading:

public class Circle **extends** ClosedFigure { ...

Object is the default parent. If a class does not explicitly specify a parent class in an extends clause, the class by default extends *Object*.

If a class also implements an interface, the implements clause follows the extends clause. For example, to define the structure shown in Figure 10.2, we would write

class Poison **extends** Potion **implements** Weapon { ... }

class Potion **implements** Movable { ... }

Note that *Poison* is a subtype of *Moveable* and *Object* as well as of *Weapon* and *Potion*. It is the possibility of this kind of structure that makes a cast from *Potion* to *Weapon* legal. If potion is a variable of type *Potion,* it is possible that potion will contain a (*reference-to*) *Poison* value at run-time. Thus the expression (Weapon)potion is syntactically legal. It is accepted by the compiler, and checked at run-time.

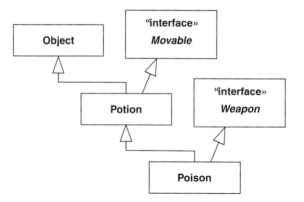

Figure 10.2 **Poison** extends **Potion**, implements **Weapon**.

10.2 Extension and inheritance

An interface defines a set of features that are guaranteed to be provided by an implementing class. Since the interface contains no implementation, the implementing class is required to implement the features.

The situation is somewhat different with a class. As with an interface, the generalizing class defines a set of features that are guaranteed to be provided by an extending class. For example, if *Circle* extends *ClosedFigure*, then a *Circle* will provide all the functionality of a *ClosedFigure*. But *ClosedFigure* is a class, and already has implementations for its features. The class *Circle inherits* the public features of *ClosedFigure* along with their implementations. The class *Circle* does not need to independently implement these inherited features.

Let's take a more careful look at this mechanism, called *class extension*. Suppose as above, the class *ClosedFigure* has subclasses *Rectangle* and *Circle*:

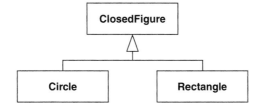

Instances of class *Circle* (and instances of class *Rectangle*) inherit all the functionality of class *ClosedFigure*: if a *ClosedFigure* can be queried for its location and area, then so can a *Circle*. A *Circle*, of course, might have features not shared by other *ClosedFigures*. We might be able to query a *Circle* for its radius, for instance. Furthermore, different subclasses might implement common features in different ways. *Circle* and *Rectangle*, for example, will implement area differently.

Suppose a *ClosedFigure* has features to get and change its location. (We don't particularly care what a *Location* is, except that it represents the location of a figure. Perhaps it includes coordinates in a Euclidean plane.)

```
public class ClosedFigure {

    private Location location;
    ...
    public Location location () {
        return this.location;
    }

    public void moveTo (Location newLocation) {
        this.location = newLocation;
    }
    ...
}
```

We make the class *Circle* a subclass of *ClosedFigure* by using an extends clause in the class definition:

```
public class Circle extends ClosedFigure {
    ...
    public int radius () {
        ...
    }
    ...
}
```

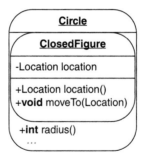

Figure 10.3 **Class *Circle* extends class *ClosedFigure*.**

Since *Circle* extends *ClosedFigure*, a *Circle* instance will automatically inherit all of the features of a *ClosedFigure*. We can imagine that the *Circle* has a *ClosedFigure* "embedded" in it, as illustrated in Figure 10.3. (Recall that a "plus sign" preceding the feature emphasizes that the feature is public, while a "minus sign" emphasizes that it is private.)

If we have a *Circle* instance, we can query the instance for its location as well as for its radius. Assume the constructor for a *Circle* provides some default *Location* and requires that a radius be specified. If we create a *Circle* `circle`

```
Circle circle = new Circle(10);
```

we can query `circle` as follows:

```
Location loc = circle.location();
int distance = circle.radius();
```

Technically speaking, a subclass does not "inherit" private features of its superclass.[1] Thus even though a *Circle* has a *ClosedFigure* with instance variable `location` "embedded" in it, the variable `location` is *private* to *ClosedFigure*. It can't be directly accessed as a *Circle* feature, even in the class *Circle*. That is, we can't write a statement like

✗   `this.location = null;`

in the class *Circle*, though we can write

✓   `this.moveTo(null);`

We'll examine this situation more carefully later in the chapter, when we study feature accessibility.

> **inheritance:** a mechanism by which an extending class or interface automatically possesses all of the nonprivate features of its parent class or interface.

---

1. This is according to Java's definition of the term "inherit." Informally, we would like to say that private features are inherited by the subclass, but not directly accessible from the subclass.

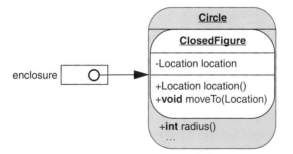

Figure 10.4 **The view from *enclosure* shows only a *ClosedFigure*.**

Subtyping and inheritance

As we mentioned above, the type *Circle* is a subtype of *ClosedFigure*. The rules for type conformance are the same, regardless of whether the type is defined by a class or an interface. Thus a *Circle* expression can be written wherever a *ClosedFigure* value is needed:

```
        Circle ring = new Circle(10);
        ClosedFigure enclosure;
 ✓      enclosure = ring;      // This is ok since Circle is a
                               // subtype of ClosedFigure.
```

And as we have seen in the last chapter, type conformance rules are static. Thus we are not permitted to write

```
 ✗      int distance = enclosure.radius();
                // A ClosedFigure is not necessarily a Circle
```

even if we are sure that `enclosure` will in fact reference a *Circle* when the statement is executed. A *ClosedFigure* does not have a `radius` method. (See Figure 10.4.)

We can, of course, cast from the more abstract type to the more concrete:

```
        if (enclosure instanceof Circle)
            int distance = ((Circle)enclosure).radius();
```

DrJava: inheritance and private features

Open files `Base.java` and `SubBase.java`, which are located in directory `inheritanceExercise`, in ch10, in nhText. These files contain dummy class definitions used to illustrate features by a subclass.

Note that class *SubBase* extends class *Base*, and that *Base* contains three public methods, one private method, and a private instance variable. Method `publicMethod1` returns the value of the private instance variable `state`, `publicMethod3` changes the value of this variable, and `publicMethod2` invokes `privateMethod`. The *SubBase* method `report` invokes the public methods it has inherited.

1. In the *Interactions* pane, create a *SubBase* instance.

```
        > import ch10.inheritanceExercise.*;
```

```
> SubBase sub = new SubBase();
```

2.   Invoke the *SubBase* method `report`,

```
> sub.report();
```

Note that the *SubBase* clearly has an embedded state obtained from the superclass *Base*.

3.   Remove the comments from the *SubBase* statements that access the private method and instance variable. Save and compile. The compilation fails, since the private features can't be accessed in the subclass. In Java terms, they are "not inherited."

DrJava: class extension and subtyping

Open `Top.java`, `Middle.java`, and `Bottom.java` located in folder subtypingExercise, in ch10, in nhText. These files contain dummy class definitions to illustrate subtyping. Note that the class *Bottom* extends *Middle*, which extends *Top*. Thus *Bottom* is a subtype of both *Middle* and *Top*, while *Middle* is a subtype of *Top*.

1.   In the *Interactions* pane, define variables and create instances of *Top*, *Middle*, and *Bottom*.

```
> import ch10.subtypingExercise.*;
> Top top;
> Middle mid = new Middle();
> Bottom bot = new Bottom();
```

2.   Since *Middle* and *Bottom* are subtypes of *Top*, the following are legal

```
> top = mid;
> top = bot;
```

But even though `top` happens to be referencing a *Bottom* instance,

```
> top instanceof Bottom
true
top instanceof Middle
true
```

these assignments are not legal:

```
> mid = top;
Error: Bad types in assignment
> bot = top;
Error: Bad types in assignment
```

3.   Now assign a reference to the *Middle* object to `top`:

```
> top = mid;
```

The view we have of the object through the variable `top` is of an object with the functionality of a *Top*:

```
> top == mid
true
> mid.middleCommand();
middleCommand done.
> top.middleCommand();
Error: No 'middleCommand' method in
    'ch10.subtypingExercise.Top'
> ((Middle)top).middleCommand();
middleCommand done.
```

10.3   Constructors and subclasses

Constructors are not inherited: each class must define its own constructors. A constructor is responsible for initializing instance variables defined in a superclass as well as those expressly defined in the class itself. Hence the first thing a constructor does is invoke a constructor of its parent class. (A constructor can also invoke another constructor of the same class. In any case, the parent class constructor is ultimately invoked.)

For example, *Circle* is a subclass of *ClosedFigure* and we have suggested that the constructor for a *Circle* require a radius as argument:

```
public class Circle extends ClosedFigure {

    public Circle (int radius) {
        ...
```

But *ClosedFigure* has an instance variable `location`, and this variable must be properly initialized when a *Circle* instance is created. To do this, the *Circle* constructor invokes the *ClosedFigure* constructor with the keyword **super**. The format is

```
super(arguments);
```

For instance we can write

```
public class Circle extends ClosedFigure {

    private int radius:

    public Circle (int radius) {
        super();
        this.radius = radius;
    }
    ...
}
```

Of course, for this to be legal the superclass *ClosedFigure* must *have* a constructor requiring no arguments, and this constructor must properly initialize *ClosedFigure* instance variables.

The keyword **this** is used in a constructor to invoke another constructor of the same class. Suppose we want to equip the class *Circle* with a second constructor that creates an instance with a default radius of 1. The second constructor can invoke the first as follows:

```
public class Circle extends ClosedFigure {

    private int radius;

    public Circle (int radius) {
        super();
        this.radius = radius;
    }

    public Circle () {
        this(1);       // invoke above constructor
    }                  // with argument 1.
        ...
}
```

Next let's extend *Circle* with a class *ColoredCircle*:

```
public class ColoredCircle extends Circle { ...
```

A constructor for *ColoredCircle* invokes a *Circle* constructor to initialize *Circle* features. For example

```
public class ColoredCircle extends Circle {

    private Color color;

    public ColoredCircle (int radius, Color color) {
        super(radius);
        this.color = color;
    }
        ...
}
```

If we write a constructor that neither calls a superclass constructor explicitly nor calls another constructor of the same class, it implicitly begins with

```
super();
```

That is, the constructor begins with an invocation of the superclass constructor requiring no arguments, which the superclass must have. For instance, the *ColoredCircle* constructor

```
public ColoredCircle (Color color) {
    this.color = color;
}
```

is equivalent to

```
public ColoredCircle (Color color) {
    super();
    this.color = color;
}
```

Notice that invocation of a class's constructor results in invocation of a constructor for each of the class's ancestors. For instance, an invocation of a *ColoredCircle* constructor

```
new ColoredCircle(c)
```

will call a *Circle* constructor, which will call a *ClosedFigure* constructor, which will call an *Object* constructor.

If a class doesn't contain a constructor definition, a default constructor requiring no arguments is automatically provided. This default constructor is equivalent to

```
public Class () {
    super();
}
```

Finally, note that the key words **this** and **super** as constructor invocations can appear only as the first statement of another constructor.

DrJava: constructor invocation

Open Top.java, Middle.java, and Bottom.java located in folder constructorExercise, in ch10, in nhText. These files contain dummy class definitions to illustrate the order in which constructors are executed.

1. In the *Interactions* pane, create a *Bottom* instance using the constructor with parameter.

   ```
   > import ch10.constructorExercise.*;
   > Bottom b1 = new Bottom(1);
   The Bottom class, constructor with parameter
   ```

2. Next create a *Bottom* using the constructor with no parameters. Note that this constructor first invokes the other.

   ```
   > Bottom b2 = new Bottom();
   The Bottom class, constructor with parameter
   The Bottom class, constructor without parameter
   ```

3. Next, modify the class *Bottom* so that it extends *Middle*.

   ```
   public class Bottom extends Middle { ...
   ```

   Save and recompile.

4. Again, create a *Bottom* instance using the constructor with parameter. Note that the *Middle* constructor is the first thing executed. (Actually, the *Middle* constructor first invokes a constructor for *Object*. But that constructor produces no output.)

```
> import ch10.constructorExercise.*;
> Bottom b1 = new Bottom(1);
The Middle class
The Bottom class, constructor with parameter
```

5. Finally, modify *Middle* so that it extends *Top*.

```
public class Middle extends Top { ...
```

Save and recompile.

6. Once more create a *Bottom*, and note the constructor invocations.

```
> import ch10.constructorExercise.*;
> Bottom b1 = new Bottom(1);
The Top class
The Middle class
The Bottom class, constructor with parameter
```

10.4   Overloading, overriding, and polymorphism

Next we want to look at an important inheritance-related feature of the language called *method overriding*. The language also provides a feature called *method overloading*. These two features are quite different semantically and serve entirely different purposes. But they look similar, are often confused, and sometimes interact in rather nonobvious ways. Although we are primarily interested in overriding, we begin our discussion with overloading.

10.4.1 Method overloading

Overloading is a simple idea: a class can contain distinct methods with the same name as long as invocations of these methods can be distinguished by the compiler. In particular, they must differ in number and/or type of parameters. For instance, a class could contain three methods specified as:

```
public int report (int x)
public int report (Object obj)
public void report (int x, int y)
```

These are completely separate, independent methods. They simply all happen to be named report. Which method is invoked is determined, obviously enough, by the number and types of arguments. For example, the call report(2,3) would invoke the third of the three methods, while the call report(2) would invoke the first.

A class cannot contain two methods with the same name and the same number and type of parameters, even if the methods have different return types. For example, a class could not contain two methods specified as

✗   **public void** report **(int** x)
✗   **public** Object report **(int** i)

even though one is a query returning an *Object*, and the other is a command.

Overload resolution is static

A key point to remember is that overload resolution is *static*. That is, the method to be executed is determined by the compiler based on the static types of the argument expressions as they are written in the program. It does not depend on the actual run-time argument values.

Suppose a class *Reporter* has two methods named report, defined as:

❶
```
public void report (Object obj) {
    System.out.println("The argument is an object.");
}
```

❷
```
public void report (Circle circle) {
    System.out.println("The argument is a circle.");
}
```

Let the variables circle, figure, and object be defined and initialized as follows, where as before, we assume that *Circle* is a subclass of *Figure*:

```
Circle circle = new Circle(1);
Figure figure = circle;
Object object = figure;
```

Note that the three variables all contain the same value, a reference to a *Circle* instance.

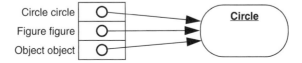

Now suppose that reporter is an instance of class *Reporter*. Consider the following three statements:

```
reporter.report(circle);
reporter.report(object);
reporter.report(figure);
```

The first statement will invoke method ❷, and result in "The argument is a circle" being written. The second will invoke method ❶. The expression object has (static) type *Object*, and so reporter.report(object) refers to the method with an *Object* parameter. This determination is made by the compiler from the program text. It does not matter that at run-time, when the statement is executed, the variable object will in fact reference a *Circle*. The third statement will also invoke method ❶. The expression figure is of type *Figure*; *Figure* is a subtype of *Object* but not of *Circle*. (And so a *Figure* expression can be written in a context requiring an *Object*.) Again, it does not matter that the variable `figure` will reference a *Circle* at run-time.

Overloading and inheritance

The rules for overload resolution are the same regardless of whether a class inherits or explicitly defines the overloaded methods. For example, suppose that the class *Reporter* mentioned above inherits one of the `report` methods:

```
class Parent {
    ...
    public void report (Object obj) {
        System.out.println(
            "The argument is an object.");
    }
}

class Reporter extends Parent {
    ...
    public void report (Circle circle) {
        System.out.println("The argument is a circle.");
    }
}
```

Class *Reporter* still has two different methods named `report`, and the statement

```
reporter.report(object);
```

results in "The argument is an object" being written. This is not different from the previous situation.

Using overloading

As we have seen in the above examples, injudicious overloading can be misleading. A good rule is never overload a method by changing the type of a parameter to a subtype or supertype. (This is the case with the `report` method above.) Some designers suggest an even more conservative approach: never overload two methods with the same number of parameters.

Methods are reasonably overloaded if they have the same function but offer alternative ways of providing arguments. Suppose we want a method that moves a figure to a particular point in a window. We might allow the client to provide the location by giving *x, y* Cartesian coordinates,

```
public void moveTo (int x, int y)
```
> Move this *Figure* to the specified point, where x is distance from the left of the window (in pixels) and y is distance from the top of the window (pixels).

or by explicitly specifying the point:

> **public void** moveTo (Point newLocation)
> Move this *Figure* to the specified *Point*.

(Here we assume that *Point* is a class modeling a point in a window.)

The library class *java.io.PrintStream*, for example, contains ten different methods named println. (System.out is a *PrintStream*.) Included are:

> **public void** println (String s)
> Print a *String* and then terminate the line. If the argument is null then the *String* "null" is printed. Otherwise, the *String*'s characters are converted into bytes according to the platform's default character encoding.

> **public void** println (**int** x)
> Print an integer and then terminate the line. The *String* produced by String.valueOf(int) is translated into bytes according to the platform's default character encoding.

Methods are also overloaded to provide default parameter values. For instance, we might offer two methods for coloring a circle, one in which the color is explicitly given and one in which a default value is used:

> **public void** fill (Color color)
> Fill this *Circle* with the specified *Color*.

> **public void** fill ()
> Fill this *Circle* with the foreground *Color*.

The class *String*, for example, contains two methods for extracting a substring: one in which the client specifies the end of the substring, and one in which a default is used:

> **public** String substring (**int** beginIndex)
> Returns a new *String* that is a substring of this *String*. The substring begins with the character at the specified index and extends to the end of this string.

> **public** String substring (**int** beginIndex, **int** endIndex)
> Returns a new *String* that is a substring of this *String*. The substring begins at the specified beginIndex and extends to the character at index endIndex - 1. Thus the length of the substring is endIndex-beginIndex.

(The first character in a *String* is at index 0. So

> "smiles".substring(1,5)

returns "mile" for example.)

> **overloading:** (*method overloading*) providing a class with several distinct methods having the same name.

DrJava: method overloading

Open the files `Parent.java` and `Child.java` located in folder `overloadingEx-`
`ercise`, in `ch10`, in `nhText`. These are minimal, "dummy" definitions, just for the purpose of this exercise.

Note that method `report` is overloaded in *Child*: *Child* has two methods named
`report`, one inherited from *Parent* and one defined in *Child*.

1. In the *Interactions* pane, create several objects as follows.

```
> import ch10.overloadingExercise.*;
> Object obj = new Object();
> Parent p = new Parent();
> Child c = new Child();
> Parent pc = c;
```

2. Note which methods are invoked in the following. Remember that overload resolution
   depends on the static type of the expressions. In particular, it is not relevant that pc
   happens to reference a *Child*. The static type of pc is *Parent*.

```
> c.report(c);
Child, Child parameter
> c.report(obj);
Parent, Object parameter
> c.report("abc");                    (A String is an Object.)
Parent, Object parameter
> c.report(p);                        (A Parent is an Object.)
Parent, Object parameter
> c.report(pc);                       (Static type of pc is Parent.)
Parent, Object parameter
> c.report((Child)pc);                (Static type of (Child)pc is Child.)
Child, Child parameter
```

3. Also note that, since the static type of pc is *Parent*, and *Parent* has only one method
   named `report`, there is no need for overload resolution in the following even though
   pc happens to reference a *Child*.

```
> p.report(c);
Parent, Object parameter
> pc.report(c);
Parent, Object parameter
```

10.4.2 Method overriding

We have seen that a subclass inherits all the (public) features of its parent class. For
instance, every Java class comes equipped with a method `equals`, effectively defined as

```
public boolean equals (Object obj) {
    return this == obj;
}
```

The reason every class has this method is that the method is defined for the class *Object*, and as we observed in Section 10.1.1, every class is a subclass of *Object*.

A class can redefine the implementation of a method that it inherits. Such a redefinition is called *overriding*. The redefinition must have the same number and type of parameters as the original (inherited) definition. The return type of the redefinition must be the same as, or a subtype of, the original return type.[1]

For example, we might redefine equals in the class *Circle* so that two *Circles* with the same radius are considered equal, regardless of their locations:

```
public class Circle extends ClosedFigure {
    ...
    public boolean equals (Object c) {
        if (c instanceof Circle)
            return this.radius() == ((Circle)c).radius();
        else
            return false;
    }
    ...
}
```

Note the use of the operator **instanceof**, and the cast of the *Object* c to *Circle*. We could not simply write c.radius(), because c is an *Object*, and *Objects* do not have a radius feature.

We can also redefine equals for the class *Rectangle*, so that two *Rectangles* with the same length and width are equal. The classes *ClosedFigure*, *Circle*, and *Rectangle* now each have a different implementation of the equals method. (*ClosedFigure* inherits the method from *Object*. See Figure 10.5.)

Now consider the following:

```
      Scanner in = new Scanner(System.in);
      ClosedFigure figure1;
      ClosedFigure figure2;
      int n;
❶     n = in.nextInt();
      if (n == 0) {
          figure1 = new Circle();
          figure2 = new Circle();
      } else {
          figure1 = new Rectangle();
          figure2 = new Rectangle();
      }
❷     boolean b = figure1.equals(figure2);
```

1. Priot to Java version 5.0, the return type of the redefinition was required to be the same as the original return type.

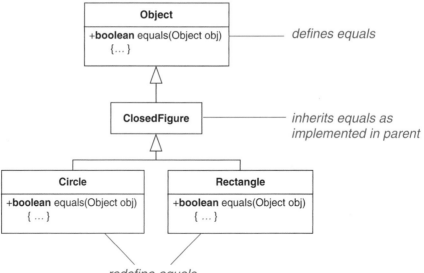

Figure 10.5 Overriding the method *equals* in classes *Circle* and *Rectangle*.

figure1 and figure2 are *ClosedFigure* variables. When ❷ is reached, they will both reference *Circles* or will both reference *Rectangles*, depending on the value assigned n at ❶. Which equals method is executed at ❷ depends on the object figure1 references when the statement is reached. If figure1 references a *Circle*, the equals defined in *Circle* will be invoked; if figure1 references a *Rectangle*, the equals defined in *Rectangle* will be invoked. This behavior is referred to as *dynamic binding, dispatching*, or *polymorphism* (since figure1 can "take the form of" a *Circle* or a *Rectangle*). Note that even though figure1 is a *ClosedFigure* variable, the *ClosedFigure* version of equals will not be used.[1]

You should note that this is no different from the situation in the previous chapter. There an interface *Player* is implemented by several classes, *TimidPlayer, CleverPlayer*, and so on. The interface defines the method takeTurn:

public void takeTurn (Pile pile, **int** maxOnATurn);

This abstract method is inherited and overridden in each implementing class. Each class provides its own implementation of the method, exactly as *Circle* and *Rectangle* provide their own implementations of equals above. When a statement such as

nextPlayer.takeTurn(pile, MAX_ON_A_TURN);

is executed, the actual takeTurn method that is performed depends on the object nextPlayer references.

---

1. Overriding equals is fraught with pitfalls. We take a careful look at the problem in Section 12.8.

Unlike overload resolution, override resolution is *dynamic*. The particular implementation of a method that is to be performed is determined at run-time, and depends on the object actually executing the method.

Accessing an overridden implementation

A class that overrides a method can call its parent's overridden implementation with the key word **super**. For instance, assume the class *ClosedFigure* defines methods `moveTo` and `location` as specified previously:

> **public void** moveTo (Location newLocation)
> Move this *ClosedFigure* to the specified *Location*.

> **public** Location location ()
> The location of this *ClosedFigure*.

Suppose we want to equip a *ClosedFigure* subclass, say *Circle*, with a method that reverses the most recent move:

> **public void** moveBack ()
> Move this *Circle* back to where it was before the most recent move.

(For simplicity, we can only "undo" the most recent move.)

We must override the inherited `moveTo` method, and remember the location we are moving from. We might write the following:

```
public class Circle extends ClosedFigure {
    ...
    private Location previousLocation
    ...
    public void moveTo (Location newLocation) {
        this.previousLocation = this.location();
        super.moveTo(newLocation);
    }
    ...
}
```

The method first saves its current *Location* in the instance variable `previousLocation`, and then invokes the `moveTo` method as implemented in the class *ClosedFigure*.

---

overriding: providing an alternative implementation of an inherited method.

polymorphism: dynamic behavior by which the algorithm performed when a method is invoked is determined at run-time by the class of the object executing the method.

Overriding and overloading

As we have seen, overloading and overriding are different aspects of the language. Over-loading involves several distinct methods with the same name in a single class. Which method to be invoked is determined by the compiler, and depends on the (static) type of the argument expressions. Overriding involves a single method with different implementa-tions in different classes. Which implementation is performed depends on the object exe-cuting the method at run-time.

Nevertheless, overloading and overriding are easily confused. Suppose a programmer attempts to override `equals` by writing the following:

```
public class Circle {
   ...
   public boolean equals (Circle c) {
      return this.radius() == c.radius();
   }
   ...
}
```

This definition *overloads* the `equals` method inherited from *Object*, but does not override it. The reason is that the parameter of the method defined in *Circle* has a different type from that of the inherited method. The class *Circle* now has *two* methods named `equals`, one inherited from *Object* and specified as

```
public boolean equals (Object obj)
```

and the other explicitly defined in the class, and specified as

```
public boolean equals (Circle c)
```

If we have

```
Circle circle1 = new Circle(1);
Circle circle2 = new Circle(1);
Object object2 = circle2;
```

then

```
circle1.equals(circle2)
```

returns true, while

```
circle1.equals(object2)
```

returns false. The reason is that two different methods are being invoked. The first expres-sion invokes the method defined in *Circle* while the second expression invokes the inher-ited method. The overloaded name `equals` is resolved by the compiler depending on the (static) type of the argument: *Circle* in the first case, *Object* in the second. (Recall that the default implementation of `equals` inherited from *Object* returns true if and only if the object and its argument are in fact the same object.)

Casting changes the static type of the expression, and hence the method to be invoked. Thus

```
circle1.equals((Object)circle2)
```

returns false, and

```
circle1.equals((Circle)object2)
```

returns true.

What does the expression

```
object2.equals(circle1)
```

evaluate to? `object2` is an *Object*, and *Object* has only one method named `equals`: the method specified as

public boolean equals (Object obj)

There is no overload resolution to be done. Furthermore, even though `object2` references a *Circle* at run-time, *Circle* does *not override* this method. So the result of the expression will be false.

In the above examples, there was no overriding at all. The identifier `equals` was simply overloaded in the class *Circle*. Next, let's look at a case involving both overloading and overriding. Suppose the class *Parent* defines a method `report`,

```
class Parent {
    ...
```
❶
```
    public void report (Object obj) {
        System.out.println("Parent.report(Object)");
    }
}
```

which is overridden and overloaded in a subclass:

```
class Child extends Parent {
    ...
```
❷
```
    public void report (Object obj) {
        System.out.println("Child.report(Object)");
    }

    public void report (Circle obj) {
        System.out.println("Child.report(Circle)");
    }
}
```

Given

```
Child child = new Child();
Parent parent = child;
Circle circle = new Circle(1);
```

what does the command

```
parent.report(circle);
```

produce? The expression `parent` is of type *Parent*, and the class *Parent* has only one method named `report`: there is no overload resolution to worry about. *Parent*'s `report` (labeled ❶) requires an *Object* as argument, and `circle` fits the bill (since *Circle* is a subtype of *Object*).

Now this method ❶ is *overridden* in the class *Child* (labeled ❷), and `parent` actually references a *Child* when the command is executed. Thus the overriding implementation ❷ is executed, and the message "Child.report(Object)" is written.

DrJava: method overriding

Open the files `Parent.java` and `Child.java` located in folder `overridingEx-ercise`, in `ch10`, in `nhText`. These are identical to those of the previous exercise, except that *Child* overrides the method `report` inherited from *Parent*.

1. In the *Interactions* pane, create several objects as before.

    ```
    > import ch10.overridingExercise.*;
    > Object obj = new Object();
    > Parent p = new Parent();
    > Child c = new Child();
    > Parent pc = c;
    ```

2. Note which methods are invoked in the following. Remember that *Child* has two methods named `report`, while *Parent* has one.

    ```
    > c.report(obj);
    Child, Object parameter
    > c.report(c);
    Child, Child parameter
    > p.report(obj);
    Parent, Object parameter
    > p.report(c);
    Parent, Object parameter
    ```

3. As before, which *Child* method is invoked depends on the static type of the argument.

    ```
    > c.report(pc);
    Child, Object parameter
    ```

4. The method `report` with *Object* parameter is defined in *Parent*, overridden in *Child*. Since `pc` references a *Child*, we have the following:

    ```
    > pc.report(obj);
    Child, Object parameter
    ```

5. Now `pc` is of static type *Parent*, and *Parent* has only one method named `report`. Thus there is no overload resolution to be done in the invocation `pc.report(arg)`. The static type of `arg` is not relevant. Hence, the invocation

    ```
    > pc.report(c);
    ```

will invoke the method `report` with *Object* argument defined in *Parent*. But pc happens to reference a Child, and Child overrides the implementation of this method. Thus,

```
> pc.report(c);
Child, Object parameter
```

10.4.3 Overriding and contracts

We have seen in Section 9.3 that a class implementing an interface is obligated to respect the contract offered by the interface. The reason is that the type defined by the class is a subtype of the type defined by the interface. But the type defined by a class is also a subtype of the type defined by its parent superclass. That is, a subclass instance can turn up where a superclass instance is expected. For example, a method

public void invert (ClosedFigure f)

with a *ClosedFigure* parameter can be invoked with a *Circle* as argument, assuming that *Circle* is a subclass of *ClosedFigure*. Hence a subclass is obligated to respect the contract offered by its parent superclass.

Let us restate the rules regarding precondition and postconditions introduced in Section 9.3.

- When overriding a method, preconditions can be weakened but cannot be strengthened.
- When overriding a method, postconditions can be strengthened but cannot be weakened.

Assume the class *ClosedFigure* contains a method `fill` specified as follows:

public void fill (Color c)
Paint this *ClosedFigure* with the specified *Color*.

ensure:
this.backgroundColor().equals(c)

The server promises to paint the figure with and set the background color to the specified *Color*.

Suppose the class *MonochromeFigure* extends *ClosedFigure*:

public class MonochromeFigure **extends** ClosedFigure ...

A *MonochromeFigure* can now be supplied wherever a *ClosedFigure* is required. In particular, a client invoking the *ClosedFigure* method `fill` may actually be dealing with a *MonochromeFigure*. Thus, while the subclass *MonochromeFigure* can override the method `fill`, it is still bound to the contract *as specified in ClosedFigure*.

Suppose further that *MonochromeFigure* overrides `fill` as follows:

```
/**
 * Paint this MonochromeFigure black or white.
 * @require    c.equals(Color.white) ||
 *             c.equals(Color.black)
 */
```

```
public void fill (Color c) {
    assert c.equals(Color.white) ||
                c.equals(Color.black);
    ...
```

The precondition has been strengthened, and the method no longer respects the inherited contract. A *ClosedFigure* client that innocently tries to fill a *ClosedFigure* with gray, for instance, will unexpectedly fail if the *ClosedFigure* happens to be *MonochromeFigure*.

A complementary problem results from weakening postconditions. Suppose the *MonochromeFigure* method `fill` treated any color other than white as if it were black. It might be specified as follows.

public void fill (Color c)
> Paint this *MonochromeFigure* white or black.

ensure:
> if c.equals(Color.white)
> > this.backgroundColor().equals(c)
>
> else
> > this.backgroundColor().equals(Color.black)

Instead of guaranteeing that the background color will be the one specified, the method guarantees it will be the one specified only if the argument is white or black. The postcondition is weakened. Again, this can cause problems for the *ClosedFigure* client that expects the postconditions specified in *ClosedFigure* to be met.

DrJava: contracts and inheritance

Close all open files. Open the file `Client.java`, located in `contractExercise`, in `ch10`, in `nhText`. Note that a *Client* is provided a *Server* when the *Client* is created. The *Client* method report invokes the *Server* method `divisibleBy3` with an argument, because of the precondition, guaranteed to be between 0 and 100, inclusive.

1. Click *Javadoc*, select the folder `docs` in `contractExercise`.

2. Choose the class *Server* in the Javadoc Viewer, and look at the detail specification of the method `divisibleBy3`. The method promises to tell whether or not an argument is divisible by 3 if the argument is in the range 0 to 100, inclusive.

3. In the *Interactions* pane, create a *Client* and exercise it a bit.

    ```
    > import ch10.contractExercise.*;
    > Client c = new Client(new Server());
    > c.report(15);
    15 is a good value.
    ```

4. Now create a Client with a ServerSubClass server, and exercise it.

    ```
    > c = new Client(new ServerSubClass());
    > c.report(15);
    15 is a not good value.
    ```

What's wrong here? A *ServerSubClass* is a *Server*, and is bound by *Server* contracts.

10.5   Java in detail: feature accessibility

To this point, all the features defined for a class—methods, instance variables, named constants—have been labeled either public or private. Public features are part of the class specification and are visible to clients of the class. Private features are part of the implementation and are not available to clients. Java provides two other accessibility categories for class features: *protected* features and *package private* or *restricted* features. Protected features are intended to be inherited by and accessible in a subclass. Package private features are accessible in the class's package. We will now take a closer look at the issue of "feature accessibility." We touch only the most significant points, and make no claim of completeness.

Accessibility is a static issue

The first thing to note is that the issue of feature access has to do with the structure of the *program text* and not with the run-time state of the system. Specifically, the question to be answered is, "From where in the program text can this feature be accessed?" and not, "Which objects can access this feature?"

   To see what this means, observe that a feature labeled *private* is accessible from within the class in which it is defined. Consider the following example:

```java
public class Circle {

    private int r;

    public Circle (int radius) {
        this.r = radius;
    }
    public boolean equals (Object obj) {
        if (obj instanceof Circle)
❶          return r == ((Circle)obj).r;
        else
            return false;
    }

    public int radius() {
        return r;
    }
}
```

At ❶, the *private* instance variable r of the argument obj is being accessed. (We use the name r rather than radius to clearly distinguish the private instance variable from the public query.) If we write

```java
Circle c1 = new Circle(10);
Circle c2 = new Circle(12);
```

c1 and c2 are two distinct instances of the class *Circle*, each with its own private instance variable r. If we query c1 with

```
c1.equals(c2)
```

c1 will execute the *Circle* method `equals`, and legally access the private variable r of c2 at line ❶. The reason is that the private *Circle* feature r, of *any Circle*, can be referenced from anywhere in the text of the class *Circle*.

Suppose we again consider extending *Circle* with a class *ColoredCircle*:

```
public class ColoredCircle extends Circle {

    private Color c;

    public ColoredCircle (int radius, Color color) {
        super(radius);
        c = color;
    }

    public boolean equals (Object obj) {
        if (obj instanceof ColoredCircle)
            return r == ((Circle)obj).r &&
                c == ((ColoredCircle)obj).c;
        else
            return false;
    }

    public Color color () {
        return c;
    }

}
```

❶✗ (at the `return r == ((Circle)obj).r &&` line)

Now even though a *ColoredCircle* instance executing the `equals` method and the method argument `obj` are both *Circles*, and *Circles* have instance variables named r, *neither* of the references to r at ❶ is legal: r is private to *Circle* and can be accessed only from inside that class. Since *ColoredCircle* does not *inherit* the private component r from

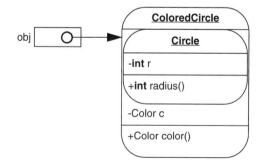

Figure 10.6 A *ColoredCircle* is-a *Circle*.

Circle, the instance variable cannot be directly accessed from *ColoredCircle*. Even if we cast an object to a *Circle*, its r instance variable can be accessed only from within the definition of the class *Circle*, where the private instance variable r is defined.

The method can be written legally as follows:

```
public boolean equals (Object obj) {
    if (obj instanceof ColoredCircle)
        return this.radius() == ((Circle)obj).radius()
            && c == ((ColoredCircle)obj).c;
    else
        return false;
}
```

The method radius is public, inherited by *ColoredCircle*, and available in the class *ColoredCircle*. (There are, however, more subtle problems with this overriding of equals, as we shall see in Section 12.8. Self-study Exercise 10.7 and Exercise 10.2 provide hints.)

Of course, just because a construct is possible does not mean that it is proper. We prefer to view private features as part of the implementation of an object that should not be directly accessed by a client, even if the client happens to be an instance of the same class.

Feature accessibility is limited by class accessibility

We saw early on (in Section 2.8) that a class might or might not be labeled public. A class that is not labeled public is package private and can be accessed only from within its own package. Rather obviously, if the class is not visible outside its package, neither are any of its features. That is, access to features of a nonpublic class, even if the features are labeled public, is limited to the package containing the class definition. Package private classes are used as a structural mechanism to further hide details from clients. A package private class usually serves as a supporting class for some public class.

Though we haven't seen any examples yet, it is also possible for a class to be defined inside of another class. Such a class is called an *inner class*. The accessibility of an inner class is determined by the same rules as the accessibility of other class features. In most cases, inner classes are declared private, and their use limited to the class in which they are defined.

10.5.1 Protected features

A *protected* feature, either a method or instance variable, is labeled **protected**, rather than **public** or **private**. A subclass inherits protected features, and these features are accessible in the subclass. Consider the class *Circle* defined in the previous section. If the instance variable r is declared protected rather than private,

```
public class Circle {

    protected int r;

        ...
}
```

it is accessible in a subclass. The references to r in the following are legal.

```
public class ColoredCircle extends Circle {

    private Color c;

    ...

    public boolean equals (Object obj) {
        if (obj instanceof ColoredCircle) {
            ColoredCircle other = (ColoredCircle)obj;
            return r == other.r &&
                c == other.c;
        } else
            return false;
    }

    ...

}
```

✓

Unfortunately, declaring a feature protected extends its visibility considerably. A feature declared protected is accessible from anywhere in the package containing the class in which the feature is defined. Thus the protected variable r defined in *Circle* can be invoked from anywhere in the package containing *Circle*. As we'll see in the next chapter, we should consider a protected feature to be part of the contract a class offers to its subclasses, and not a feature to be accessed by other clients.

There are several points to note about protected features. First, a protected feature is inherited, so every subclass of the defining class has the feature. Suppose that a protected feature, let us say an instance variable f, is defined in class *p1.Parent*:

```
package p1;

public class Parent {

    protected int f;

    ...

}
```

Suppose further that *Child* is a subclass of *Parent*, and *Grandchild* a subclass of *Child*, as shown at the top of the followign page. Then instances of class *Child* and *Grandchild* inherit (and can access) the feature f. For example, the method

```
public void clearChildF (Child c) {
    c.f = 0;
}
```

which accesses the feature f of a *Child*, can appear in the class *Child*, and the method

```
public void clearGrandchildF (Grandchild g) {
    g.f = 0;
}
```

which accesses the feature f of a *Grandchild*, can appear in the class *Grandchild*.

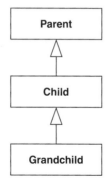

Second, the feature is accessible from anywhere in the package p1. For instance, the methods `clearChildF` and `clearGrandchildF` can appear anywhere (*i.e.*, in any class) in the package p1. In particular, they can appear in the class *Parent*. It does not matter which packages contain *Child* and *Grandchild*.

Finally, a protected feature of a class is accessible in any superclasses "through which" the feature was inherited. Since *Grandchild* inherits the feature f "through *Child*," the method `clearGrandchildF` can also appear in the class *Child*, again regardless of the packages that contain *Child* and *Grandchild*. However, `clearChildF` cannot appear in *Grandchild*, unless *Grandchild* happens to be in package p1.

The behavior of protected features is sometimes rather obscure. Assume again that the variable r is declared protected in *Circle*. In the class *ColoredCircle*, the following is legal:

```
public boolean equals (Object obj) {
    if (obj instanceof ColoredCircle)
        return r == ((ColoredCircle)obj).r ...
```
✓

The type of the expression `(ColoredCircle)obj)` is *ColoredCircle*, and we can reference a *ColoredCircle*'s inherited instance variable r in the class *ColoredCircle*. However, the following is not legal, assuming that *Circle* and *ColoredCircle* are defined in different packages:

```
public boolean equals (Object obj) {
    if (obj instanceof ColoredCircle)
        return r == ((Circle)obj).r ...
```
✗

The type of the expression `((Circle)obj)` is *Circle*, and we cannot access a *Circle*'s instance variable r from the class *ColoredCircle*.

We emphasize that to limit class coupling and localize the effects of change, access to protected features should only occur in descendents of the defining class. Furthermore, the strength of a design is improved if we keep instance variables private, and control access through commands and queries, which can be public or protected as appropriate.

10.5.2 Package private features

Sometimes a situation arises in which we want to permit a closely related class that is not a subclass to have access to a feature. For example, consider the classes *Explorer* and *Room* from the maze game. Suppose that the *Explorer* must know which room it is in, and the *Room* must know its contents:

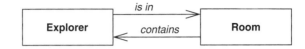

Explorer has a command `move`, and in the process of executing this command an *Explorer* might leave one *Room* and enter another. If the system is to remain consistent, the command `move` must inform a *Room* that the *Explorer* is entering or leaving. To this end, we equip a *Room* with methods for adding and removing an *Explorer*:

void add (Explorer e)
> The specified *Explorer* has entered this *Room*, and should be added to this *Room*'s contents. Should only be invoked by an *Explorer* when it enters this *Room*.

void remove (Explorer e)
> The specified *Explorer* has left this *Room*, and should be removed from this *Room*'s contents. Should only be invoked by an *Explorer* when it leaves this *Room*.

How should we label these methods? We can't declare them *private*, because they must be invoked from the class *Explorer*. We don't want to make them *public*, because they should only be invoked by an *Explorer* when he leaves or enters the *Room*. If they are invoked from anywhere else, we could easily end up with inconsistencies in the system.

A possibility is to make them *package private* or *restricted*. If a feature is not declared public, protected, or private, it is by default *package private*. A package private feature is accessible anywhere in the package containing the class in which the feature is defined.[1] Essentially, a package private feature looks like a public feature inside the package, and like a private feature outside the package. Therefore if the *Room* features `add` and `remove` are package private, and if *Room* and *Explorer* are in the same package, then an *Explorer* can invoke the features.

Note that as we have described them, the classes *Explorer* and *Room* are very closely related (*tightly coupled*). Not only does each depend on the other, but each depends on the implementation of the other. Like private features, package private features are part of a class's implementation and not part of the specification that the class presents to its clients. Note also that the specifications `add` and `remove` refer to implementation specifics of *Explorer*. This tight mutual dependence is not a happy situation, as it complicates maintenance, modification, and class reuse. When we see such structures, we should carefully examine the design to see if another approach would produce more independent classes.

---

1. It is also inherited by subclasses that are in that package.

The package private option allows only very coarse control over access to a feature. A class can be in only one package, and a package private feature can be accessed from anywhere in the package. Declaring a feature, particularly an instance variable, protected or package private weakens encapsulation and compromises the integrity of the class. Such features introduce possible points of interaction with every current and future member of the package. This can lead to increased system complexity particularly during system maintenance. Maintenance programmers often have very subtle problems to solve, little time to solve them, and no clear understanding of the overall system architecture. Thus they are likely to exploit the kind of encapsulation weaknesses created by protected and package private features. The result is a system in which modules are related in obscure and complex ways: a system whose maintainability is significantly diminished.

The misuse of feature accessibility, as specified by the system architecture, leads to what is termed *architectural drift* or *architectural erosion*. The system becomes *brittle*, frustrating further maintenance efforts. If a feature is neither public nor private, it is incumbent upon a maintenance programmer to determine why this is so, and to make sure that any new use of the feature does not compromise the system structure.

10.5.3 Inner classes

We mentioned above that a class can be a member of another class. In fact, there are several situations in which the definition of one class is contained in another. A class whose definition is contained in the body of another class is a *nested class*. A class that is not nested is a *top level class*.

A nested class can be defined

- directly in a containing class, like any other class feature, or
- in the body of a method or constructor.

In the first case, the class is a *member class*. Like other class features, member classes can be public, private, protected, or package private. A member class can also be static, in which case it is associated with the containing class rather than with an instance of the containing class.

A class defined in the body of a method or constructor is a *local class* if it has a name, and an *anonymous class* if it does not. Like a local variable, a local class is visible only inside the method in which it is defined. We won't use local classes in the remainder of this text. We encounter anonymous classes in Chapter 14.

If a nested class is not a static member class, then it is an *inner class*. We limit our attention to inner member classes for the remainder of this section.

The definition of an inner member class is nested inside its containing class. In the definition

```
public class Outer { ...
    private class Inner {
        ...
    } // end of class Inner
    ...
} // end of class Outer
```

the class *Inner* is a member of the top level class *Outer*. Since *Inner* is private, it is accessible only from inside the definition of *Outer*.

Feature access is determined only by the top level class. For instance, a private member of an outer class can be accessed in an inner class, and a private member of an inner class can be accessed from anywhere in its containing outer class. Consider the following:

```
public class Outer {
    private int size;

    ...

    private class Inner {
        private Inner next;

        ...

    } // end of class Inner

    ...

} // end of class Outer
```

The private *Outer* variable `size` is visible in class *Inner*. Class *Inner* can contain a method like this:

```
    private void evaporate () {
✓       size = size - 1;

        ...

    }
```

Similarly, the private variable `next` of a *Inner* can be accessed from anywhere in class *Outer*. *Outer* can contain this method:

```
    private Inner advanceFrom (Inner n, int i) {
        while (i > 0) {
✓           n = n.next;
            i = i-1;
        }
        return n;
    }
```

Note that a nonstatic member class is a member of *some instance* of the containing class. Figure 10.7 illustrates an instance of the class *Outer*, with `size` (an instance vari-

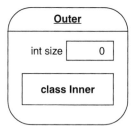

Figure 10.7 An inner class is a member of an instance.

able) and *Inner* (a class) members. Do not confuse this membership relationship between a class and an instance with object composition or extension. Each inner class instance is associated with an instance of the containing class.

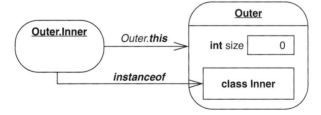

The containing class instance can be referenced from the inner class by prefixing the keyword **this** with the name of the containing class. From inside the class *Inner* defined above, the expression `Outer`.**this** refers to the *Outer* instance of which the *Inner* class is a member. For example, the first line of the method `evaporate` could be written

```
Outer.this.size = Outer.this.size - 1;
```

This syntax is necessary if the inner class and containing class have members with the same name. If the class *Inner* also contains the definition of an instance variable `size`, the assignment

```
this.size = Outer.this.size;
```

stores the value of the *Outer*'s instance variable into the *Inner*'s instance variable.

If an inner class is not private, it is accessible from outside the containing top level class. The name of the type defined by the inner class is formed by prefixing the outer class name to the inner class name. For example, suppose *Inner* is a public inner class contained in class *Outer*:

```
public class Outer {
    ...
    public class Inner {
        ...
    } // end of class Inner
    ...
} // end of class Outer
```

The type defined by the inner class is *Outer.Inner*:

```
Outer bag = new Outer();
Outer.Inner node = bag.new Inner();
```

In particular, note the syntax for creating the instance `node`.

DrJava: accessibility

Open files `Parent.java`, `Child.java`, `ChildPackage1.java`, `Grand-Child.java`, and `ParentPack.java`. These are located in folders `package1`, package2, and package3, in accessibilityExercise, in ch10, in nhText. These contain dummy class definitions, intended only for this exercise.

Note that *Parent*, *Child*, and *GrandChild* are in different packages. *ParentPack* and *ChildPackage1* are in the same package as *Parent*. *Child* extends *Parent*, and *GrandChild* extends *Child*. *ChildPackage1* also extends *Parent*.

Assignment statements that have been commented out are erroneous according to Java's accessibility rules.

- Note that the package private feature res behaves like a public feature inside the package, and like a private feature outside the package. In particular, it is inherited by *ChildPackage1*, but not by *Child*.

- Note that the protected feature pro is inherited by *Child* and *GrandChild*. The feature can be seen in a *GrandChild* from class *Child*, since *GrandChild* inherits the feature "through" *Child*. The feature cannot be seen in a *Parent* from class *Child*.

1. Can the feature pro be seen in a *Child* from the class *GrandChild*? That is, can the assignment

   ```
   child.pro = 3;
   ```

   appear in the class *GrandChild*, where child is a *Child*? Add a method containing such an assignment to *GrandChild* and compile.

2. Remove the comments from several of the commented assignment statements (one at a time) and recompile. Note that the compilation fails.

10.6   Java in detail: scoping rules

At this point, we digress a bit to take a look at Java's scoping rules. As with the accessibility rules discussed in the previous section, scoping rules are static, having to do with the program text and not with the run-time state of the system. In fact, the rules regarding feature access that we looked at in the last section are part of the language scoping rules. Again, we touch only the most significant points and do not attempt a complete presentation.

An identifier may occur many times in a program in many different contexts. An identifier can be introduced as the name of a variable in a variable definition or parameter specification, or as the name of a method in a method definition. Such an occurrence is referred to as a *defining* or *naming occurrence* of the identifier. For instance, the following are defining occurrences of the identifiers takeThat, hitStrength, count, and temp.

```
public void takeThat (int hitStrength)
private int count;
int temp;
```

A defining occurrence establishes the identifier as the name of some entity. (Of course, identifiers are also used to name packages, classes, and so on. Here we're concerned only with identifiers that name variables and methods.)

Other occurrences, such as occurrences of an identifier in an expression, are called *applied occurrences*. An applied occurrence is simply the use of an identifier to refer to the thing it names. For example, both occurrences of the identifier `count` in the assignment

```
count = count + 1;
```

are applied occurrences. They refer to a particular **int** variable created by a definition such as the one shown above.

An applied occurrence is sometimes prefixed with an object reference. For example, in the assignment statement

```
this.room = monster.location();
```

the applied occurrences of `room` and `location` are prefixed with object references **this** and `monster`. (An identifier can also be prefixed with a package or class name, but we ignore those cases here.)

Scoping rules, sometimes referred to as *static scoping rules*, are language rules that associate applied identifier occurrences with defining occurrences. For example, if a class is defined as

```
      public class Counter {
❶         private int count;

          ...

          public void increment () {
❷            count = count + 1;
          }
      }
```

scoping rules specify that the applied occurrences of `count` at ❷ are associated with the defining occurrence at ❶. We say the applied occurrence "refers to" or "references" the defining occurrence. Thus we say the applied occurrences of `count` at ❷ "refer to" the instance variable defined at ❶.

Now certainly the run-time semantics of the program are intimately connected with the static program syntax. If line ❷ above is performed during program execution, the variable incremented will be an instance variable of a *Counter*, created because of the definition at line ❶. But during execution of the program, there might be no *Counter* object created, or there might be thousands of *Counters*. Thus at any point, there might be many variables named `count` or none at all. The scoping rules refer to the text, and not directly to entities created dynamically during program execution.

The *scope* of a definition is the section of program text in which applied occurrences of an identifier refer to the identifier introduced by the definition. In the above example, the scope of the variable definition at ❶ is the text of the class *Counter*. Applied occurrences of the identifier `count` in this segment of the program text refer to the definition at ❶. (Technically it is a *definition* that has scope, though we informally refer to the "scope of an identifier.")

We've already looked at scoping issues regarding instance variables and methods. Here we consider method variables, that is, local variables and parameters.

The scope of a local variable definition is from the definition to the end of the compound statement (or method body) containing the definition. A parameter is treated like a local variable defined just inside the method body. Thus the scope of parameter definition is the method body. For instance, in the method

```
public boolean smallerThan (Rectangle r) {
    double myArea;
    double yourArea;
    myArea = pi*radius*radius;
    yourArea = r.length() * r.width();
    return myArea < yourArea;
}
```

the scope of the parameter r is the body of the method smallerThan; the scopes of the local variable myArea and yourArea extend from the variable definitions to the end of the method smallerThan. Applied occurrences of these identifiers in the body of the method refer to method variables created when the method is invoked. Furthermore, these definitions have no effect outside of the method. One cannot write a reference to the variable myArea, for instance, except inside the body of smallerThan.

Note that the scope of a local variable begins with its definition. It cannot be referenced prior to its definition:

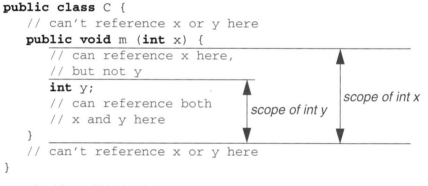

```
public class C {
    // can't reference x or y here
    public void m (int x) {
        // can reference x here,
        // but not y
        int y;
        // can reference both
        // x and y here
    }
    // can't reference x or y here
}
```

scope of int y

scope of int x

For example, this would be legal

```
✓   public boolean smallerThan (Rectangle r) {
        double area1 = 100.0;
        double area2 = area1; // in the scope of area1
```

but this would not

```
✗   public boolean smallerThan (Rectangle r) {
        double area1 = area2; // not in the scope of area2
        double area2 = 100.0;
```

A local variable definition can appear almost anywhere in a method body. The scope extends to the end of the compound statement containing the definition:

```
public void m (int x) {
    if (x > 0) {
        int i = 1;
        ...
    }
    ...
}
```

scope of int i

Though a method can contain definitions of several distinct variables with the same name, the scopes of these definitions cannot overlap. For instance, the following method contains legitimate definitions for two variables named sum, one a **double** and one an **int**:

```
public double m (int x) {
    double result;
    if (x > 1) {
        int sum = x;
        result = sum/2;
    } else {
        double sum = x;
        result = sum/2;
    }
    return result;
}
```

✓

scope of int sum

scope of double sum

But the following is not legal, since the scopes of the **int** sum and the **double** sum overlap:

```
public double m (int x) {
    double result;
    double sum = x;
    if (x > 1) {
        int sum = x;
        result = sum/2;
    } else {
        result = sum/2;
    }
    return result;
}
```

✗

scope of int sum

scope of double sum

Finally, we note that a method variable can "hide" an instance variable with the same name, but a method variable cannot be prefixed with an object reference. At line ❷ of the following,

```
public class Circle {
    ...
```

❶   `private int radius;`
          `...`
          `public void setRadius (int radius) {`
❷   `this.radius = radius;`
          `}`
              `...`
      `}`

the identifier `radius` on the right of the assignment denotes a method variable (the parameter), while **`this`**`.radius` denotes an instance variable defined at ❶.

10.7   Summary

In this chapter, we examined abstraction as defined by a hierarchy of classes. We noted that every class (except *Object*) extends exactly one parent superclass, and that the type defined by a (sub)class is a subtype of the type defined by its superclass. Thus, considering types, the extends relation between a class and its parent superclass is much the same as the implements relation between a class and an interface.

Unlike an interface, a class contains an implementation, including instance variables, constructors, and method bodies. When a class extends another class, it inherits the implementation of its parent. The extending class can, of course, add to or modify the inherited implementation. Though a class does not inherit its parent's constructors, the first thing a constructor does when a class is instantiated is invoke a constructor of the class's parent. Effectively, when a class is instantiated, a constructor from each ancestor is executed, beginning with *Object* and ending with a constructor of the instantiated class. Thus the implementation components contributed by each of the class's ancestors are initialized in the appropriate order.

A class inherits an implementation from its parent, but can modify that implementation. In particular, a class can override an inherited method, providing an implementation different from that defined by its parent. A subclass, however, is committed to the contract its parent offers clients. This implies that when a method is overridden, its preconditions can be weakened but not strengthened, and its postconditions can be strengthened but not weakened.

Overriding should not be confused with overloading. Overloading means supplying a class with several distinct methods having the same name. The methods are distinguished by their parameter lists. Overloading is resolved by the compiler according to the static types of the argument expressions that appear in a method invocation. Overriding, on the other hand, means giving an inherited method a different implementation than it has in the parent superclass. The implementation executed depends on the class of the object that actually performs the method at run-time.

Finally, we examined Java's accessibility and scoping rules. Class features, that is, instance variables and methods, can be declared to be public, private, protected, or package private. Public features constitute the specification of the class, and define the view offered to the class's clients. Private, protected, and package private features should be considered part of the implementation. Private features are accessible only in the class definition. Good practice keeps all instance variables private. Protected features are inherited by subclasses, and are part of the contract a class offers its subclasses. Unfortunately, a protected feature is also accessible anywhere in the package containing the class defining the feature. Thus declaring a feature protected significantly opens its accessibility. A package private feature is accessible in the package containing the class defining the feature. If a feature must be available to a few "closely related" classes, a possible approach is to declare the feature package private and put the closely related classes in the same package.

The scoping rules for method variables are rather simple. A method variable is accessible from its definition to the end of the compound statement (or method body) in which it is defined. A parameter is accessible anywhere in the method body. A method can define several method variables with the same name as long as their scopes do not overlap.

SELF-STUDY EXERCISES

10.1   Class *A* generalizes class *B*. How else can this relationship be described?

10.2   Indicate whether each of the following statements is true or false:

a.   If class *A* extends class *B*, class *A* is a subclass of class *B*, and class *B* is a superclass of class *A*.

b.   If class *A* extends class *B* and class *B* extends class *C*, then class *A* is a subclass of class *C*.

c.   An instance of a superclass can be treated as if it were an instance of any of its subclasses.

d.   Polymorphism implies that the method actually invoked at run-time is dependent on the run-time class of the method's arguments.

e.   Public features of a public class are accessible from any class in any package.

f.   Access to package private features of a class is limited to classes in the same package only if the class is not public.

10.3   Consider the following three classes:

```java
public class Grandparent {
    public Grandparent () {
        System.out.println("Grandparent");
    }
}

public class Parent extends Grandparent {
    public Parent () {
        System.out.println("Parent");
    }
}
```

```
public class Child extends Parent {
    public Child () {
        System.out.println("Child");
    }
}
```

What is the parent class of *Grandparent*?

Is *Child* a subclass of *Grandparent*?

What will be displayed when a new instance of *Child* is created?

10.4 Given the class definitions of *Grandparent*, *Parent*, and *Child* from the previous question, is the type *Child* a subtype of the type *Grandparent*?

Why is the definition

```
Grandparent grandpa = new Child();
```

legal?

Given the above definition of grandpa, and the definitions

```
Grandparent grandma = new Grandparent();
Child child = new Child();
```

Which of the following assignments are legal?

a. `grandma = child;`

b. `child = grandpa;`

c. `child = (Child)grandpa;`

d. `if (grandpa instanceof Child)`
`    child = grandpa;`

10.5 Given the definitions above of *Grandparent*, *Parent*, *Child*, grandpa, grandma, and child. The method hasKids is specified as

```
public boolean hasKids (Parent p)
```

Which of the following are legal?

a. `hasKids(grandma)`

b. `hasKids(grandpa)`

c. `hasKids(child)`

d. `hasKids((Parent)grandma)`

e. `hasKids((Parent)grandpa)`

10.6 Consider the two classes defined below:

```
public Parent {
    public int report (Object obj) {
        return 1;
    }
}
```

```
    public int report (Parent p) {
        return 2;
    }
}

public Child extends Parent {
    public int report (Parent p) {
        return 3;
    }
    public int report (Child c) {
        return 4;
    }
}
```

How many methods named `report` does the class *Child* have?

What methods in *Parent* are overridden in *Child*?

Given the definitions:

```
Object obj = new Parent();
Parent parent1 = new Parent();
Parent parent2 = new Child();
Child child = new Child();
```

what do the following method invocations return?

(a) `parent1.report(obj)`   *(b)* `parent2.report(parent1)`
(c) `parent2.report(obj)`   *(d)* `parent2.report(child)`
(e) `((Parent)child).report(child)`

10.7   Suppose that `equals` is overridden in both *Circle* and *ColoredCircle* as suggested in Section 10.5:

```
public class Circle {
    private int radius;
        ...
    public boolean equals (Object obj) {
        if (obj instanceof Circle)
            return this.radius == ((Circle)obj).radius;
        else
            return false;
    }
}
public class ColoredCircle extends Circle {
    private Color color;
        ...
    public boolean equals (Object obj) {
        if (obj instanceof ColoredCircle)
```

```
                    return super.equals(obj) &&
                        this.color.equals(
                            ((ColoredCircle)obj).color);
                else
                    return false;
            }
        }
```

That is, two *Circles* are equal if their radii are equal, and two *ColoredCircles* are equal if they are equal as *Circles* and have the same color.

Given the definitions

```
        Circle c1 = new Circle(3);
        Circle c2 = new ColoredCircle(3,Color.BLUE);
```

what does the expression

```
        c1.equals(c2)
```

evaluate to?

What does the expression

```
        c2.equals(c1)
```

evaluate to?

Does this bother you?

10.8   Given the definitions of the classes *Circle* and *ColoredCircle* suggested in Section 10.3, can the following method legally appear in the class *Circle*? Can it appear in the class *ColoredCircle*? Why or why not?

```
            public ColoredCircle copyWithColor (Color c) {
                ColoredCircle cc = new ColoredCircle(c);
                ((Circle)cc).radius = this.radius;
                return cc;
            }
```

10.9   Each of the classes *A*, *B*, and *C* is defined in a different package:

```
            package Apackage;
            public class A {
                protected int x;
                ...
            }

            package Bpackage;
            public class B extends Apackage.A {
                ...
            }
```

```
package Cpackage;
public class C extends Bpackage.B {
    ...
}
```

Can the method definition

```
public void setX (Bpackage.B aB) {
    aB.x = 1;
}
```

appear in the class *A*? in the class *B*? in the class *C*?
in some other Apackage class? in some other Bpackage class?

Can the method definition

```
public void setX (Cpackage.C aC) {
    aC.x = 1;
}
```

appear in the class *A*? in the class *B*? in the class *C*?
in some other Apackage class? in some other Cpackage class?

EXERCISES

10.1 Using a web browser, access the Java API documentation for the predefined class *java.io.PrintStream*. How many overloaded methods do you find? Can you find two overloaded methods that differ only in that the parameter of one is a subtype of the parameter of the other? Are these overloadings likely to be confusing?

Access the Java API documentation for the predefined class *java.lang.String*. How many overloaded methods do you find? Do any of the overloaded methods have the same number of parameters? Are these overloadings likely to be confusing? Does *String* override equals?

10.2 Using a web browser, access the Java API documentation for method equals in the predefined class *java.lang.Object*, and carefully read the specification. Look at the overriding definitions of equals for the classes *Circle* and *ColoredCircle* in Self-study Exercise 10.7, and the questions posed in that exercise. Are the requirements given for the method equals in *Object* satisfied by these overridings?

Suppose the method was overridden only in *Circle*: say *Circle* defines equals as **final**. Are the requirements now satisfied by this overriding?

Suppose *ColoredCircle* defines equals as follows:

```
public boolean equals (Object obj) {
    if (obj instanceof ColoredCircle)
        return super.equals(obj) &&
```

```
                        this.color.equals(
                            ((ColoredCircle)obj).color);
            else if (obj instanceof Circle)
                return super.equals(obj);
            else
                return false;
        }
```

What do the expressions c1.equals(c2) and c2.equals(c1) evaluate to, where c1 and c2 are as in Self-study Exercise 10.7?

Using the *ColoredCircle* definition of equals shown above, give examples of three *Circles* c1, c2, and c3 such that c1.equals(c2) and c2.equals(c3) are *true*, but c1.equals(c3) is *false*. (Hint: two of the *Circles* should be *ColoredCircles*.)

10.3   The class *java.lang.Class* models the run-time class of an object. *Object* defines a method

public final Class getClass ()
     The run-time class of this *Object*.

and *Class* defines a method

public String getName ()
     The name of the entity (class, interface, array class, primitive type, or void) represented by this *Class* object, as a *String*.

Implement a simple program that will defines classes *Parent* and *Child*, where *Child* is a subclass of *Parent*, creates two instance

```
Parent p1 = new Parent();
Parent p2 = new Child();
```

and then invokes getClass on each:

```
System.out.println(p1.getClass().getName());
System.out.println(p2.getClass().getName());
```

10.4   Suppose that each *Room* in a maze game is connected to two other *Rooms*. Connections are "one-way." That is, if *Room A* is connected to *Room B*, *Room B* is not necessarily connected to *Room A*. A *Room* may be connected to itself.

A *Room* has a query to determine if it is connected to another specified *Room*:

public boolean connectedTo (Room r)
     This *Room* is connected to the specified *Room*.

The *Explorer* in the maze game has a query to determine its location, and a command to change location. However, it can only move between *Rooms* that are connected by a passage:

public Room location ()
     This *Explorer*'s current location.

> **public void** moveTo (Room newLocation)
>> Move to the specified *Room* if it is connected to this *Explorer*'s current location. Otherwise, this *Explorer* remains in the current location.

Some rooms in the maze are enchanted, and there is a special kind of explorer, a wizard, who can move into an enchanted room even if it is not connected to the wizard's current room. Enchanted rooms and wizards are modeled by subclasses of *Room* and *Explorer*.

Implement and test a simple version of the program. You may "hard code" the maze in your program. Three or four rooms should be adequate. (Assume that a *Room*'s state doesn't change when an *Explorer* enters.)

10.5   In Exercise 9.8, a class *Employee* was described that modeled employees of a company who were paid in different ways. Composition was used to solve the problem: each *Employee* was equipped with a *PayCalculator* that was responsible for computing the pay of the *Employee*.

Redo the exercise using extension rather than composition. Define a class *Employee*, that implements methods such as

> **public** String name ()
>> This *Employee*'s name.

> **public int** hours ()
>> The number of hours this *Employee* has worked in the current pay period.

and stubs the method pay:

```
/**
 * This Employee's pay for the current period
 * in dollars.
 */
public int pay () {
    return 0;
}
```

Implement two subclasses, *FullTimeEmployee* and *PartTimeEmployee*, that compute pay in different ways. A *FullTimeEmployee* gets time and a half for overtime, and a *PartTimeEmployee* doesn't.

Which approach, composition or extension, seems the most flexible? In each case, what is involved in changing an employee from full time to part time?

10.6   The class *IntVector* models finite, immutable, integer sequences. An *IntVector* can be empty, or it can be constructed from an integer and another *IntVector*, by prefixing the integer to the front of the *IntVector*. For instance, by prefixing the integer 3 to the empty *IntVector*, (), we get the one-element *IntVector*, (3). By prefixing 4 to this *IntVector*, we get the two-element *IntVector*, (4, 3). By prefixing 5 to this two-element *IntVector*, we get the three-element *IntVector*, (5, 4, 3), and so on.

The first element of a non-empty *IntVector* is its *head*, and the rest is its *tail*. Thus the head of (5, 4, 3) is 5, and the tail is (4, 3). Note that the head and the tail are the two pieces used to construct the *IntVector*. In particular, the head of (3) is 3, and the tail is the empty *IntVector*, ().

The class is specified as follows.

> **public class** IntVector
> > A finite, possibly empty, sequence of integers.
>
> > **public** IntVector ()
> > > Create a new empty *IntVector*.
> > >
> > > **ensure:**
> > > > this.isEmpty()
> >
> > **public boolean** isEmpty ()
> > > This *IntVector* is empty.
> >
> > **public** IntVector prefix (**int** i)
> > > A new *IntVector*, constructed by prefixing the specified int to this *IntVector*.
> > >
> > > **ensure:**
> > > > !(this.prefix(i)).isEmpty()
> >
> > **public** int head ()
> > > The first element of this *IntVector*.
> > >
> > > **require:**
> > > > !this.isEmpty()
> >
> > **public** IntVector tail ()
> > > An *IntVector* equal to this *IntVector* with the first element removed.
> > >
> > > **require:**
> > > > !this.isEmpty()
> >
> > **public boolean** equals (Object obj)
> > > The argument is an *IntVector*, and represents the same sequence of integers as this *IntVector*.
> >
> > **public** String toString ()
> > > A *String* representation of this *IntVector*.

There are two kinds of *IntVector*: empty and nonempty. Invoking the *IntVector* constructor will produce a new empty *IntVector*.

We model nonempty *IntVectors* by subclassing *IntVector*:

> **class** ConstructedVector **extends** IntVector ...

The *ConstructedVector* constructor will produce a new, nonempty *IntVector*:

```
public ConstructedVector (int head, IntVector tail)
```
Create a new nonempty *IntVector* with the specified first element and specified tail.

ensure:
```
!this.isEmpty()
this.head()==head && this.tail().equals(tail)
```

An *IntVector* instance that is not a *ConstructedVector* represents an empty vector. For instance, `isEmpty` simply returns true in *IntVector* and false in *ConstructedVector*. So `isEmpty` effectively tells the run-time class of the object. Also note that if `iv` is an *IntVector*, then

```
iv.prefix(2).head() == 2, and
iv.prefix(2).tail().equals(iv)
```

Implement and test *IntVector* and its subclass *ConstructedVector*. Do not use any loops in your implementation. Use if statements and the `instanceof` operator only in the `equals` method.

Implement `toString` in the following way.

- In *IntVector*, it returns the *String* `"()"`.
- In *ConstructedVector*, it returns the *String*
  `"( " + this.head() + this.tail().continueString()`,
  where `continueString` is a protected method that

-- returns the *String* `")"` in *IntVector*, and

-- returns the *String*
  `", " + this.head() + this.tail().continueString()`
  in *ConstructedVector*.

Can the method `continueString` be private rather than protected? Can it be package private?

Write a method that, given an *IntVector*, will produce the sum of the integers.

10.7   In addition to instance variables and methods, a class can have another class as a member.

Reorganize the classes of Exercise 10.6 so that *ConstructedVector* is a private inner class of *IntVector*. The definition of *IntVector* will look like this:

```
public class IntVector {
    ...
    private static class ConstructedVector
        extends IntVector {
        ...
    }
}
```

Now *ConstructedVector* can be accessed only from inside the definition of *IntVector*. As with any class member, declaring the class static means that there will be only one class member *ConstructedVector* for the class *IntVector*, rather than a class for each *IntVector* instance.

Can the method `continueString` now be declared as private? That is, if `continueString` is private, does the implementation in *ConstructedVector* override the implementation in *IntVector*

SELF-STUDY EXERCISE SOLUTIONS

10.1   *A* is a superclass of *B*; *A* is an abstraction of *B*; *A* is an ancestor of *B*; *B* extends *A*; *B* is a subclass of *A*; *B* is a descendent of *A*.

10.2   *a.*   True.

      b.   True

      c.   False.

      d.   False.

      e.   True.

      f.   False.

10.3   *Object* is the parent of *Grandparent*. *Child* is a subclass of *Grandparent*, since the "subclass" relation is transitive.

Three lines will be displayed, in this order:

```
Grandparent
Parent
Child
```

10.4   *Child* is a subtype of *Grandparent*, and therefor the assignment of a *reference-to-Child* value to a *Grandparent* variable is legal.

      a.   Legal, since *Child* is a subtype of *Grandparent*.

      b.   Not legal, since *Child* is not a subtype of *Grandparent*. The fact that `grandpa` happens to reference a *Child* when the statement is executed (at run-time) is not relevant.

      c.   Legal, since the expression `(Child)grandpa` is of *type* Child. The run-time system will verify that `grandpa`, in fact, references a *Child* when the statement is executed.

      d.   The statement is not legal, for the same reason as *(b)*.

10.5   *a.*   Not legal, since *Grandparent* is not a subclass of *Parent*.

      b.   Not legal, since a *Grandparent* is not a *Parent*. It does not matter that `grandpa` references a *Child*; its static type is *Grandparent*.

      c.   Legal, since *Child* is a subclass of *Parent*.

    d. Will be accepted by the compiler, since the type of the expression `(Parent)grandma` is *Parent*. But the case will fail at run-time, since `grandma` references a *Child*, not a *Parent*.

    e. Legal. The cast will succeed, since `grandpa` references a *Child*, which is a *Parent*.

10.6   *Child* has three methods named `report`, having *Object*, *Parent*, and *Child* parameters.

The method `report(Parent)` is overridden in *Child*.

(a) returns 1. The static type of `obj` is *Object*; that `obj` happens to reference a *Parent* when the expression is evaluated is not relevant.

(b) returns 3. `report(Parent)` is overridden in *Child*, and `parent2` references a *Child* when the expression is evaluated at run-time.

(c) returns 1. `report(Object)` is not overridden in *Child*, and as with *(a)*, it is not relevant that `obj` happens to reference a *Parent*.

(d) returns 3. This is a tricky case. The static type of `parent2` is *Parent*. So the compile time overload resolution is between `report(Object)` and `report(Parent)`, as specified in *Parent*. The argument `child` is of type *Child*, which is a subtype of both *Parent* and Object. But *Child* is closer to *Parent*, so the overload resolution is to the method `report(Parent)`. Ar run-time, `parent2` actually references a *Child*, which overrides the implementation of `report(Parent)`.

(e) returns 3. This is also a tricky case. The static type of `(Parent)child` is *Parent*, so the analysis of this case is exactly as the previous case, *(d)*.

10.7   The first expression evaluates to *true* and the second to *false*. This should bother you because the relation *equals* is symmetric, that is, *c1 equals c2* should imply that *c2* equals *c1*.

10.8   The method can appear in the class *Circle* but not in the class *ColoredCircle*. The *Circle* instance variable `radius` is declared private, and so can only be accessed in the class *Circle*.

10.9   The method `setX(Bpackage.B)` can appear in class *A* or *B*, or in any `Apackage` class.

The method `setX(Cpackage.C)` can appear in class *A*, *B*, or *C*, or in any `Apackage` class.

CHAPTER 11　Modeling with abstraction

In the previous chapter, we examined class extension and inheritance, the language mechanisms for implementing abstraction. We saw how to exploit extension and polymorphism to define different implementations of a feature, where the run-time type of the server object determines which implementation will be executed.

In this chapter, we consider the use of abstraction in class design a little more carefully, and compare it with composition. We start by introducing abstract classes, classes that contain abstract methods and cannot be instantiated. Abstract classes are used as a basis for building other, concrete classes by extension. We compare the roles of interfaces, abstract classes, and concrete classes in a system design. An important observation is that a class has two kinds of "customers": client classes, that use the features of the class, and subclasses, that extend the class. In general, these different kinds of customers need different things from a class, and the class offers different contracts to clients and subclasses.

Finally, we compare the two fundamental mechanisms for constructing classes: extension and composition. We note that these two approaches are not as obviously distinct as they first seem. There are many situations in which either can be applied to a particular design problem. In general, we should favor composition over inheritance. Composition usually produces designs that are more flexible and easier to change; designs in which the effect of change can be localized and controlled.

Objectives

After studying this chapter you should understand the following:

- the roles played by interfaces, abstract classes, and concrete classes;
- the use of protected features for the benefit of subclasses;
- the two kinds of clients a class can have, and the additional documentation required by subclass clients regarding the implementation of superclass features;
- class extension and class composition, and their proper use.

Also, you should be able to:

- use abstract classes to specify class generalization;
- use interfaces, abstract classes, and concrete classes to model a system.

11.1   Abstract classes

Let's revisit a problem we noticed in Chapter 9. Recall that we have an interface *Player* implemented by several classes:

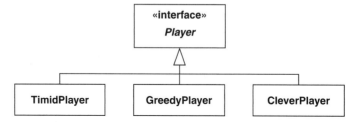

The difficulty is that the classes are identical except for the implementation of the method `takeTurn`. The classes contain a considerable amount of duplicate code, and, as we have often noted, duplicate code should be avoided whenever possible.

Suppose we put a class between the interface and player variants to contain the duplicate code. We'll call it *AbstractPlayer*:

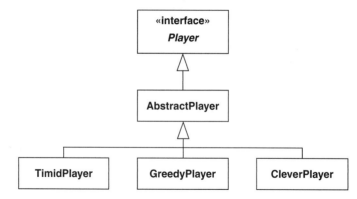

Now *AbstractPlayer* can contain implementations of methods common to all the player variants, such as `name` and `sticksTaken`, and the player subclasses can simply inherit these methods.

There are a couple of issues to address with this approach. First, what do we do with the method `takeTurn` in *AbstractPlayer*? We could give it a stubbed implementation, but that does not seem entirely satisfactory. Second, we have introduced *AbstractPlayer* as a basis on which to build other classes, and not as a source of objects. We do not expect clients to instantiate *AbstractPlayer*.

The Java *abstract class* feature addresses these issues. An abstract class is a class that

- can contain abstract methods, and therefore
- cannot be instantiated.

Otherwise, it is like any other class. It defines a type. It occupies a position in the class hierarchy. It can be the parent of other classes, abstract or not, and has a unique parent which may or may not be abstract. It can define nonabstract methods and instance variables. It has one or more constructors. (If an abstract class cannot be instantiated, why does it have constructors? An abstract class will have descendent subclasses that are not abstract and can be instantiated. As we saw in Section 10.3, instantiating a class results in constructors for all of its ancestors being invoked.)

A class is declared abstract by use of the keyword **abstract**,

> **abstract class** AbstractPlayer **implements** Player { ...

and denoted in diagrams by a slanted font:

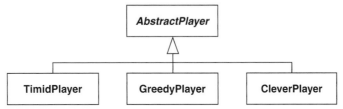

To emphasize the distinction, we sometimes refer to a class that is not abstract as *concrete*.

An abstract class can inherit abstract methods (from an interface for example) without implementing them. Thus there is no need to specify the method takeTurn in the class *AbstractPlayer*: the abstract method is inherited from *Player*. However, in contrast to what is permitted in an interface, an abstract method must be labeled **abstract** in an abstract class. For example, if the method takeTurn were specified in *AbstractPlayer* rather than being inherited from *Player*, its definition would look like this:

> **public abstract void** takeTurn (
>   Pile pile, **int** maxOnATurn);

The keyword **abstract** is required here.

> **abstract class:** a class that cannot be instantiated, but is used as a basis on which to build other classes by extension.

✳ 11.1.1 Interfaces, abstract classes, and concrete classes

We now have three closely related but distinct structures: interfaces, abstract classes, and concrete classes. It is important to realize that each has its purpose.

An interface is used to specify the functionality required by a client. In the nim game, the interface *Player* defines the functionality required by the *Game* and the user interface. An interface establishes the client's view of things, and isolates the client from the many possible server implementations. A client should be programmed to access a server specified by an interface. During program execution, some concrete object will fill the role defined by the interface. Thus the class *Game* is programmed using *Player*, and during execution, the *Game* is provided with concrete instances of *TimidPlayer*, *GreedyPlayer*, *etc.*

The purpose of a class is to provide an implementation. A class, even an abstract class, defines instance variables and includes method and constructor implementations.

An abstract class provides a basis on which to build concrete server implementations. It actualizes the generalization relationship, factoring out common implementation details from the subclasses. In the nim game, a complete *Player* implementation can be built from *AbstractPlayer* by implementing a move strategy. Abstract classes serve to structure the system design rather than provide run-time objects that actually participate in problem solution.

A concrete class completes the implementation of the server specified by an interface. Concrete classes furnish run-time objects, and are not generally suited to serve as a basis for extension. In the nim game, the actual *Player* objects are instances of concrete classes such as *TimidPlayer*, *GreedyPlayer*, etc.

Classes related by inheritance are "tightly coupled" semantically. Subclasses share the structure of their parent class, and often share a common implementation of common functionality. Class inheritance produces a family of closely related classes. Though they are difficult to justify *a priori*, we suggest the following guidelines in the use of abstract classes.

- An abstract class should "factor out" common implementation details of its concrete subclasses. These common implementation details may be in the form of method implementations or data components.

- Abstraction provides opportunities to exploit polymorphism. Common functionality specified in the parent abstract class can be given different implementations appropriate to each concrete subclass. However, an abstract class should be used to model a generalized object, not simply to capture common functionality or exploit polymorphism. The class abstracts a set of classes that are related in what they model.

- The decision to use generalization should be made with care. A class can extend only one class, and a subclass is closely dependent on its parent. The features defined in an abstract class must not be susceptible to change, as any change in an abstract class will propagate to its descendents and their clients. In other words, an abstract class must be stable.

An interface, on the other hand, defines only a specification. Neither the structure nor implementation-level behavior of an object satisfying the interface is prescribed. Two classes that implement the same interface are related only in that they support the functionality defined by the interface. A hierarchical family of closely tied classes is not created, as is the case with class inheritance.

Advantages of interfaces include the following.

- Interfaces are by definition abstract; they do not fix any aspect of an implementation.

- A class can implement more than one interface.

- Interfaces allow a more generalized use of polymorphism, in that instances of relatively unrelated classes can be treated as identical for some specific purpose.

An example

Suppose we want to specify that a figure appearing in a diagram has a *Location* and *Dimension*. Though we don't particularly care about the details, a *Location* might be given in terms of the Cartesian coordinates of the upper left corner of the figure, and a *Dimen-*

sion might include length and width. Omitting comments, we define the following interface:

```
public interface Depictable {
    public Location location ();
    public Dimension dimension ();
}
```

and define classes that implement the interface, such as:

```
public abstract class GeometricalFigure
    implements Depictable {
    ...
}


public class Rectangle extends GeometricalFigure {
    ...
    public Location location () { ... }
    public Dimension dimension () { ... }
    ...
}
```

Now clients of the interface *Depictable* contain methods that manipulate *Depictables*. For instance, a class might contain a method that determines whether an arbitrary point is contained within a diagram figure modeled as a *Depictable*:

```
public boolean isIn (Location point,
    Depictable figure) {
    Location l = figure.location();
    Dimension d = figure.dimension();
    ...
}
```

If we later decide to expand the kinds of things that can appear in a diagram, for example by creating a class *WordBalloon* that extends an existing class *ArtClip*,

```
public abstract class ArtClip { ... }


public class WordBalloon extends ArtClip
    implements Depictable { ... }
```

we can pass instances of the newly created class to the `isIn` method without modifying either the method or its clients.

On the other hand, if *Depictable* were an abstract class, we'd either have to somehow merge the *ArtClip* and *Depictable* hierarchies so that *WordBalloons* could be passed to methods like `isIn`, or overload these methods to accept *WordBalloon* arguments as well as *Depictable* arguments. Such methods would be mostly rewritten code, accommodating a different type of argument. By specifying the parameter of a method like `isIn` as an

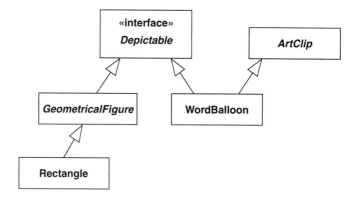

Figure 11.1 **An interface allows relatively unrelated classes to be treated identically.**

interface, any class in any family can be tailored to provide suitable arguments for the method.

The primary intent of an interface is to separate an object's implementation from its specification. There are substantial benefits to be gained from manipulating objects solely in terms of the specifications defined in an interface. Clients remain independent of the specific types of the objects they interact with, and independent of the classes that implement these objects. New classes can be created that implement an interface, or existing implementations modified, without affecting clients that depend solely on the interface. This greatly reduces the interdependencies between subsystems, and produces more flexible and manageable code. The benefits are so consequential that the adage "program to an interface, not to an implementation" is often stated as a fundamental principle of object-oriented design. This means that developers should not write code that interacts with an object *per se*. Rather, client code should be able to interact with any object that satisfies an interface.

11.2   Specifying a class for extension

There are two distinct ways in which one class can utilize another. A class can be a client to another class and use the other class as a server, exactly as we have seen all along. But a class can also extend another class, using the other class as a basis for its implementation.

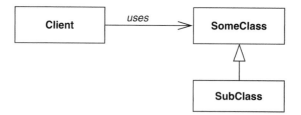

Figure 11.2 **A class can utilize another class by acting as client or by extending.**

It should not be surprising that clients and subclasses have essentially different views of the original class. To see this, let's return to the *AbstractPlayer* example. The principal purpose of *AbstractPlayer* is to capture implementations common to the different kinds of players, and so reduce duplicate code. We might start by writing *AbstractPlayer* as follows, as usual omitting comments:

```
abstract class AbstractPlayer implements Player {

    private String name;
    private int sticksTaken;

    public AbstractPlayer (String name) {
        this.name = name;
        this.sticksTaken = 0;
    }

    public String name () {
            return this.name;
    }

    public int sticksTaken () {
        return this.sticksTaken;
    }

    public String toString () {
        return "Player: " + name + ", took: " +
                sticksTaken;
    }

}
```

AbstractPlayer inherits the abstract method `takeTurn` from *Player* and does not override it with an implementation. It provides implementations for the other methods.

Now when we implement *TimidPlayer*, we need only build a constructor and an implementation for `takeTurn`:

```
class TimidPlayer extends AbstractPlayer {

    public TimidPlayer (String name) {
        super(name);
    }

    public void takeTurn (Pile pile, int maxOnATurn) {
        pile.remove(1);
❶       this.sticksTaken = 1;
    }

}
```

But when we try to compile *TimidPlayer*, the compiler informs us that it "cannot resolve" the symbol `sticksTaken` at line ❶. The private instance variable `sticksTaken`, defined in *AbstractPlayer*, is not inherited and not accessible from *TimidPlayer*.

We might try adding a definition of `sticksTaken` to *TimidPlayer*:

```
class TimidPlayer extends AbstractPlayer {
    private int sticksTaken;
        ...
}
```

Although this will satisfy the compiler, it will not produce the correct results. We now have two instance variables named `sticksTaken`, one accessed from *AbstractPlayer* and one from *TimidPlayer*:

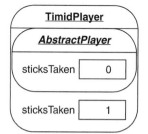

The assignment statement in *TimidPlayer* assigns 1 to one of these variables, and the method `sticksTaken` defined in *AbstractPlayer* returns the value of the other.

We could override the method `sticksTaken` in *TimidPlayer*, but we would need to do this in every player variant, reintroducing the duplicate code we are trying to avoid. The problem is that a subclass has a different, stronger relation to its parent class than a client does. In our case, the subclass needs to be able to tell its parent "store this *sticksTaken* value." The subclass needs a different "contract" with its parent than a client needs.

Protected features

A solution, as we have seen in the previous chapter, is to define the variable `sticksTaken` protected in *AbstractPlayer*:

```
abstract class AbstractPlayer implements Player {
    private String name;
    protected int sticksTaken;
        ...
}
```

The variable is now accessible in *TimidPlayer*, and the *TimidPlayer* implementation originally given above is correct. In particular, at line ❶, the value 1 is assigned to the variable declared in *AbstractPlayer* as desired.

A better approach is to allow controlled access to the instance variable through a *protected method*. We can leave the instance variable `sticksTaken` private in *AbstractPlayer*, and include a method

```
    protected void setSticksTaken (int number) {
        this.sticksTaken = number;
    }
```

TimidPlayer will then invoke this method:

```
    public void takeTurn (Pile pile, int maxOnATurn) {
        pile.remove(1);
        setSticksTaken(1);
    }
```

Accessing component data by queries and commands limits class coupling, and localizes the effects of change.

Unfortunately, a feature declared protected is accessible from anywhere in the package containing the class in which the feature is defined. Thus the protected method `set-SticksTaken` defined in *AbstractPlayer* can be invoked from anywhere in the package containing *AbstractPlayer*.

In the case at hand, *AbstractPlayer* is itself package private and not public. Thus access to the class itself, and hence to all of its features, is limited to its package. Since declaring a feature protected exposes it to the entire package (at least), there is no effective difference in this case between declaring a feature protected and declaring it public. In either case, the feature is accessible throughout the package.

Nevertheless, we should treat the protected label as indicating that a feature is intended to be inherited by and accessible in a subclass, but is not part of the class specification. Clients defined in another package cannot access a protected feature; clients defined in the same package should also refrain from accessing it. Protected contracts are only offered to subclasses.

11.2.1 Planning for extension

A class serves two different kinds of "customers," clients and subclasses, having significantly different needs. A Java class definition does not cleanly distinguish between the contract a class offers its clients and the one it offers its subclasses. (In fact, a Java class definition does not cleanly distinguish specification from implementation.) Nevertheless, it is incumbent upon us when we design a class to consider the possibility of extending the class and the requirements a subclass will have.

A subclass depends on the implementation of its parent. As we have seen in *Abstract-Player*, a subclass often requires access to the underlying implementation structure of its parent, which can be provided by means of protected features. Furthermore, the correctness of a subclass can depend on the algorithms used to implement parent methods, as illustrated in the following example.

Suppose we have a class modeling a three-digit combination lock, similar to those of Chapter 4. Assume the class has methods that allow the combination to be entered either digit by digit, or as a single integer:

```
    public class ThreeDigitLock
```
A combination lock with a three digit combination.

```
public void enterDigit (int digit)
```
Enter a digit of the combination; lock unlocks if the three digits of the combination are entered in order.

require:
```
0 <= digit && digit <= 9
```

```
public void enterCombination (int combination)
```
Enter the three digit combination specified; lock unlocks if the three digits of the combination are entered in order.

require:
```
0 <= combination && combination <= 999
```

Let's say we want to build a version of the lock that keeps track of the total number of digits entered. We'll call this an *InstrumentedLock*. An obvious approach is to extend *ThreeDigitLock*, overriding enterDigit and enterCombination:

```
public class InstrumentedLock extends ThreeDigitLock {

    private int digitCount;
    ...
    public void enterDigit (int digit) {
        digitCount = digitCount + 1;
        super.enterDigit(digit);
    }

    public void enterCombination (int combination) {
        digitCount = digitCount + 3;
        super.enterCombination(combination);
    }
    ...
}
```

But there is a problem if *ThreeDigitLock*'s enterCombination method is implementing by invoking enterDigit three times:

```
public class ThreeDigitLock {
    ...
    public void enterCombination (int combination) {
        int remainder = combination;
        int position = 100;
        while (position > 0) {
            enterDigit(remainder / position);
            remainder = remainder % position;
            position = position / 10;
        }
    }
    ...
}
```

❶

What happens when *InstrumentedLock*'s enterCombination method is invoked? First the digitCount is incremented by three, then *ThreeDigitLock*'s enterCombination implementation is executed. This algorithm invokes enterDigit three times, at ❶. But enterDigit is overridden in *InstrumentedLock*, and digitCount is incremented three more times. The result is that digitCount is incremented by 6 rather than by 3.

Given the implementation of enterCombination in *ThreeDigitLock*, enterCombination in *InstrumentedLock* should not increment digitCount. The design of the subclass *InstrumentedLock* depends on the algorithm used to implement enterCombination in *ThreeDigitLock*. *ThreeDigitLock* must therefore document the method's implementation, something like this:

> **public void** enterCombination (**int** combination)
>> Enter the three digit combination specified; lock unlocks if the three digits of the combination are entered in order.
>>
>> This implementation invokes enterDigit three times, once for each digit in the specified combination.
>>
>> **require:**
>>> 0 <= combination && combination <= 999

This added documentation is not part of the method's specification: it is of no interest to a client, and a client should not make use of it. It is part of the contract that the method offers to a subclass. *ThreeDigitLock* is committed to this implementation just as it is committed to its specification. If the implementation is changed so that enterDigit is not invoked, *InstrumentedLock* will be broken.

The general rule is:

- if a class is to be extended, any use *in the class* of the class's overridable (*i.e.*, not private) methods must be documented.

That is exactly the case we have above. The class *ThreeDigitLock* invokes its public method enterDigit. This "self-use" of an overridable method must be documented.

There is one more related issue:

- if a class is to be extended, its constructors should not invoke any of the class's overridable methods.

The problem is that a method in a subclass can get invoked before the subclass constructor has a chance to initialize the state of the object. A simple, though somewhat contrived, example should illustrate the point. Consider the following classes, which provide methods by which an object can identify its run-time class:

```
public class Parent {

    private String parentClass;

    public Parent () {
        parentClass = "Parent";
    }
}
```

```
    public String myClass () {
        return parentClass;
    }
}


public class Child extends Parent {

    private String childClass;

    public Child () {
        super();
        childClass = "Child";
    }

    public String myClass () {
        return childClass;
    }
}
```

Child extends *Parent* and overrides the method `myClass`. If we define

```
Parent parent1 = new Parent();
parent parent2 = new Child();
```

then `parent1.myClass()` returns `"Parent"`, while `parent2.myClass()` returns `"Child"`. In *Child*, `myClass` references the instance variable `childClass`, initialized in the *Child* constructor. The *Child* constructor, as always, begins by invoking the constructor of its parent.

Now suppose the *Parent* constructor invokes the method `myClass`:

```
    public Parent () {
        parentClass = "Parent";
❶      System.out.println(myClass());
    }
```

When a *Child* is created, its constructor invokes the *Parent* constructor before doing anything else. The *Parent* constructor invokes the method `myClass` at ❶. But `myClass` is overridden, and so the *Child* implementation of `myClass` is executed. This returns the value of the variable `childClass` which has not yet been initialized. Thus the invocation of `myClass` at ❶ returns null, violating an implicit postcondition.

The essential point of all this is that a subclass is very tightly related to its parent, and care must be taken in designing and documenting a class that is intended to be extended. Determining the contract to be offered subclasses is not always easy. In particular, the structural details that a subclass will need access to are not always obvious.

We can prevent extension by declaring a class *final*. For instance, if we specified

          public final class ThreeDigitLock { ...

then the extension by *InstrumentedLock* would not be allowed. We can also prevent overriding of a particular method by declaring the method *final*. For example,

          public final void enterCombination (**int** combination) ...

prevents overriding of the method enterCombination a subclass.

    A good practical rule is to consider only abstract classes and interfaces to be suitable for extension, and to treat concrete classes solely as a source of fully implemented runtime objects.

DrJava: planning for extension

Open the file Point.java, locates in extensionExercise, in ch11, in nhText. This file defines a class *Point*, modeling a point with (x, y) coordinates. (This class is intended only for the exercise. It is not a serious attempt to model a point in a plane.)

    Open the file RelativePoint.java. The class *RelativePoint* extends *Point*. When a *RelativePoint* is created, x and y offsets are given. Setting the point is always relative to these offsets.

1.   In the *Interactions* pane, create a *RelativePoint*.

       > import ch11.extensionExercise.*;
       > RelativePoint p = new RelativePoint(10,10);

2.   Setting the coordinates of p is relative to the offset.

       > p.setX(5);
       > p.setY(5);
       > p.x()
       15
       > p.y()
       15

3.   Now set the coordinates of p using setPoint.

       > p.setPoint(10,10);
       > p.x()
       30
       > p.y()
       30

What went wrong? setPoint, as implemented in *RelativePoint*, invokes super.setPoint (setPoint as implemented in *Point*) with arguments (20, 20). *Point*'s setPoint method invokes setX with argument 20. But setX is overridden in *RelativePoint*, and p is a *RelativePoint*. So the implementation of setX in *RelativePoint* is executed with an argument of 20. This invokes the super.setX (setX as implemented in *Point*) with an argument of 30!

Since `setPoint` is implemented in *Point* in terms of `setX` and `setY`, `setPoint` should not be overridden in *RelativePoint*. Note that *RelativePoint* depends on the implementation of *Point*.

4.   Modify *RelativePoint* by removing the overriding implementation of `setPoint`. Save, compile, test.

5.   Modify the implementation of *Point* so that `setPoint` directly assigns new values to `x` and `y` rather than invoking `setX` and `setY`. Save, compile, test. Notice that changing the implementation of *Point* has broken *RelativePoint*.

Now open files `Cylinder.java` and `RectangularCylinder.java`, located in folder `extensionExercise`, in `ch11`, in `nhText`. The abstract class *Cylinder* models a cylinder, and *RectangularCylinder* models a cylinder with a rectangular base. Note that *Cylinder* computes the volume of the cylinder in the constructor and stores the value in the instance variable `volume`.

1.   In the *Interactions* pane, create a *RectangularCylinder*.

```
> import ch11.extensionExercise.*;
> RectangularCylinder c =
    new RectangularCylinder(10,5,3);
```

2.   Query the *RectangularCylinder* for its volume.

```
> c.volume()
0
```

What went wrong here? The *RectangularCylinder* constructor invokes the *Cylinder* constructor, which invokes the method `baseArea`. This method is overridden in *RectangularCylinder*, and so the implementation in *RectangularCylinder* is executed. But this implementation uses instance variables `length` and `width`. These instance variables have not yet been initialized. (We have not yet reached the two assignment statements in the *RectangularCylinder* constructor.) The default values of these variables is 0. Hence, `baseArea` returns 0.

11.3   Composition revisited

In Section 7.4.1, we introduced the process of *composition* for creating new classes from existing ones. There are several different situations in which composition is used. Most commonly, composition is used when a component is an intrinsic part of an object. If we consider an instance of the class *Book*, for example, components like *preface*, *index*, *etc.* are intrinsic parts of the object. An index does not exist except as part of a *Book*.

Another use of composition is in the definition of a class formed as an aggregation of components, where the components exist independently of the aggregation. For instance, a class modeling a *Course* at a university might include a list of enrolled *Students* and an *Instructor*. These objects come together in the *Course*, but they exist independently of any particular *Course*. They are not created when the *Course* is created, and do not cease to

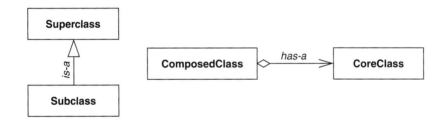

Figure 11.3 **A class can be constructed by extension or composition.**

exist when the *Course* object is deallocated. In general, they are "known" by objects other than the *Course*.

A third use of composition is to "wrap" an existing class in order to alter its interface. We saw this idea in Section 7.4.1, where we wrapped an *Oracle* with a *LockedOracle*. In each of these cases, the resulting composed class delegates certain responsibilities to its components.

11.3.1 Extension and composition

As illustrated in Figure 11.3, extension and composition are two fundamental ways of building a new class from existing classes. Extension implements the *is-a* relation, and composition implements the *has-a* relation. We use extension to build a subclass from an existing superclass. When we use composition, we construct a class (a *composed* class) from one or more component or *core* classes. Both are sometimes referred to as instances of "code reuse" since we're reusing the code from the superclass in creating the subclass, and reusing the code from a core class in building the composed class.

Though *is-a* and *has-a* are fundamentally different relations, we are often faced with situations in which either could be employed in the development of new classes. For example, consider the nim *Player* and its implementations discussed in Chapter 9 and in Section 11.1. It seems perfectly straightforward to say that a *CleverPlayer is-a Player*, and to model the relation with inheritance. *CleverPlayer* inherits all the features of *Player*, and overrides the move method.

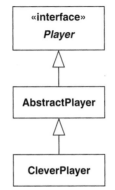

But as we saw in Section 9.6, we can also view a player as *having* a move strategy. Different players have different strategies, and so make their moves in different ways. A player might even change strategies during its lifetime. In this case, the move strategy that differentiates player behavior is a *Player* component.

The purpose of a *PlayStrategy* is to determine the move to be made on the *Player*'s turn, that is, to determine the number of sticks to be removed. Different *PlayStrategy* instances determine which move to make in different ways. Thus we define *PlayStrategy* as an interface, which specific concrete strategies implement:

```
interface PlayStrategy {

    int numberToTake (Pile pile, int maxOnATurn);

}
```

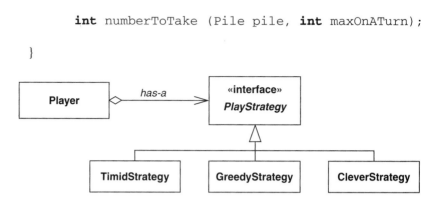

An instance of a *PlayStrategy* subclass is sometimes called a *function object*. Its only purpose is to provide the functionality implemented by the numberToTake method.

WARNING!! Saying that the purpose of an object is to *do* something is often the sign of a faulty design. Specifically, it's often a case of a function masquerading as an object, when the function should properly be one of the responsibilities of some other more coherent object. The structure discussed here, though, is commonly used and considered acceptable practice. The basic responsibility for making a move rests with the *Player*. The *Player* delegates the responsibility of determining the move to its *PlayStrategy* component.

The *Player*'s strategy is set in the constructor, and can be changed with the method setStrategy. The *Player* method takeTurn queries the *PlayStrategy* to determine the number of sticks to take.

```
class Player {

    private String name;
    private PlayStrategy strategy;
    private int sticksTaken;

    public Player (String name,
        PlayStrategy strategy) {
        this.name = name;
```

```
            this.strategy = strategy;
            this.sticksTaken = 0;
        }
        ...
        public void setStrategy (PlayStrategy strategy) {
            this.strategy = strategy;
        }

        public void takeTurn (Pile pile, int maxOnATurn) {
            int number =
                strategy.numberToTake(pile, maxOnATurn);
            pile.remove(number);
            this.sticksTaken = number;
        }
    }
```

It might seem that we are still really using abstraction here to achieve different *Player* behaviors, and to some extent that is true. The interface *PlayStrategy* abstracts the various concrete strategies. But the implementation hierarchy is very shallow, and completely separate from any class hierarchy that *Player* might be a part of. One *Player* behaves differently from another because it *has* a different strategy, not because it *is* an instance of a different class.

11.3.2 Extension, composition, and reuse

There are no absolute guidelines for determining whether we should employ extension or composition in building a specific class. Different situations call for different approaches, and there is no substitute for experience. Nevertheless, it is useful to compare the advantages and disadvantages of each, so that we can begin to understand which technique is appropriate in various circumstances. In making this comparison, we should distinguish the classes being reused and the classes resulting from reuse.

	reused class:	*resulting class:*
extension:	superclass	subclass
composition:	core class	composed class

Two advantages often mentioned regarding extension are code reuse and polymorphism. Since a subclass inherits the features of its superclass, extension provides a substantial degree of code reuse. Furthermore, polymorphism is a powerful tool for extending an application. If a client uses an instance of a particular class, the client, without modification, can be applied to a subclass instance. Extension allows us to extend the functionality of class without affecting the clients of the original class.

On the other hand, a superclass and subclass are strongly coupled. A change to a superclass specification (reused class) affects its subclasses and their clients as well as its own clients. The change propagates outward to clients, and downward to subclasses and

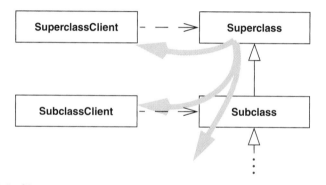

Figure 11.4 **Changes to a superclass specification propagate to clients and subclasses.**

their clients. And as we have seen in Section 11.2.1, encapsulation is broken in that changes to the superclass implementation also propagate to subclasses. A major source of headaches is that classes are not always designed and documented for extension. Further, a subclass by definition is committed to maintain the specifications inherited from its super-class. No changes can be made to a subclass specification that affect the specification of a superclass.

Composition also offers opportunities for code reuse, in that core classes can be used in the construction of different composed classes. A principal advantage of composition is that it is possible to change an object's behavior dynamically, at run time. For example, the behavior of a nim *Player*-with-*PlayStrategy* is determined by the *Player's PlayStrategy* component. This component can be set and changed dynamically during execution of the program. With inheritance, on the other hand, the *Player's* behavior depends on the partic-ular *Player* subclass that is instantiated, and is fixed when the *Player* is created.

Composition also supports stronger encapsulation than does inheritance. Changes to the core class (reused class) need not result in changes to the specification of the com-posed class. Thus core class changes do not affect clients of the composed class. Further-more, it is generally easy to change the specification of the composed class without modifying the core class. With inheritance, changes in a superclass propagate to sub-classes and their clients, and it is difficult to change the specification of a subclass without breaking the specification of its superclass. Finally, a composed class depends only on the specification of a core class, not its implementation. Implementation changes in the core class do not propagate to the composed class.

Let's look again at the *InstrumentedLock* of Section 11.2.1. We noted that this class depended on the implementation of the superclass *ThreeDigitLock*. Specifically, changes

Figure 11.5 **Changes to a core class need not affect clients of the composed class.**

in the implementation of *ThreeDigitLock*'s enterCombination method required changes to *InstrumentedLock*'s enterCombination method. Suppose we implement *InstrumentedLock* by wrapping *ThreeDigitLock* rather than extending it:

```
public class InstrumentedLock {

    private int digitCount;
    private ThreeDigitLock lock;

    public InstrumentedLock (int combination) {
        lock = new ThreeDigitLock(combination);
        ...
    }
    ...
    public void enterDigit (int digit) {
        digitCount = digitCount + 1;
        lock.enterDigit(digit);
    }

    public void enterCombination (int combination) {
        digitCount = digitCount + 3;
        lock.enterCombination(combination);
    }
    ...
}
```

Now *InstrumentedLock* is independent of the implementation of *ThreeDigitLock*. Changing the implementation of *ThreeDigitLock*'s enterCombination method will not affect *InstrumentedLock*. However, we have lost subtyping. *InstrumentedLock* is no longer a subtype of *ThreeDigitLock*. If a client expects a *ThreeDigitLock*, we cannot deliver an *InstrumentedLock*. The proper solution to this problem is for both *ThreeDigit-Lock* and *InstrumentedLock* to implement the same interface, as illustrated in Figure 11.6. The client can then be programmed in terms of this interface.

In summary, modifying the reused class with extension is likely to affect more of the system than modifying the reused class with composition. Modifying the resulting class

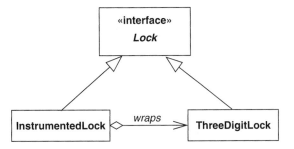

Figure 11.6 InstrumentedLock wraps ThreeDigitLock; both implement Lock.

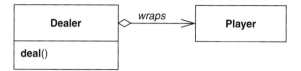

Figure 11.7 **Composition can add functionality to an object.**

with composition will not affect the reused class. On the other hand, modifying the resulting class with extension may not be feasible if the modification changes the specification of inherited features. The resulting class can be modified only if changes are limited to adding new data or methods to the superclass. We conclude that reuse through composition produces more flexible code. However, we must not ignore the advantages of polymorphism. On the surface, we lose polymorphism with composition. But we can gain it back by composing with interfaces and defining core classes that implement them.

11.3.3 Extension, composition, and modifying functionality

Extension is sometimes used to model *roles* that class instances can perform, and sometimes to provide alternate implementations of the same functionality. The former can result in awkward constructions in which detailed knowledge of an object's possible roles is spread throughout the application. The latter can lead to a combinatorial explosion in the class hierarchy as the system evolves through cycles of maintenance. Suppose we are modeling a card game in which a player takes on the role of dealer. It seems natural to model dealer functionality by extending *Player*, that is, by defining class *Dealer* that extends *Player*. But difficulties arise when we want a given *Player* to change roles. One approach to handling this situation is to make *Player* a component of *Dealer*, as shown in Figure 11.7. That is, to *wrap* the additional functionality around the *Player*. This can be done dynamically, during run time, by setting the *Player* component of the *Dealer* instance. The extended functionality of dealing does not characterize a *Player*. Rather it is required for a role that a *Player* may fill. The fact that a *Player* might change roles is a very strong hint that composition is the appropriate mechanism.

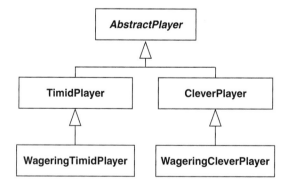

Figure 11.8 **Using inheritance for implementation can lead to *class explosion*.**

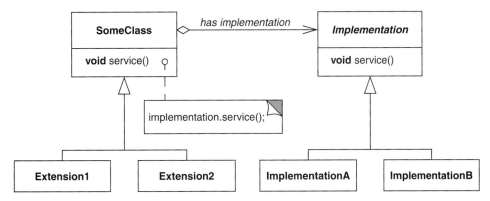

Figure 11.9 The *bridge pattern* separates implementation and application hierarchies.

If we use extension to provide alternate implementations of some functionality, problems may arise if we later want to extend the base class to add new features. For example, we saw how we can use inheritance to provide nim *Players* with different move strategies, by extending the class *AbstractPlayer* and overriding the `takeTurn` method. If we later decide that we want to create *Players* with some additional functionality, *Players* who can wager for instance, we can't simply extend *AbstractPlayer*: we already have a family of classes that differ in how `takeTurn` is implemented. We must extend each of the different *AbstractPlayer* subclasses, as shown in Figure 11.8. The problem here is that we are trying to make *AbstractPlayer* part of two distinct hierarchies: an "implementation" hierarchy that captures `takeTurn` implementation differences, and an "application" hierarchy that extends the functionality of *Player*.

One general solution to this situation is to separate the hierarchies and use composition. The resulting structure, illustrated in Figure 11.9, is called the *bridge pattern*. The class forwards all implementation dependent functions to its *Implementation*. The *Implementation* can be an abstract class or interface, and is the root of a shallow implementation hierarchy. This is essentially what we did by giving the *Player* a *PlayStrategy*. Different implementations of *Player* behavior are taken care of by different implementations of *PlayStrategy*.

In summary, we suggest favoring composition over extension. Extension should not be used simply for code reuse or to take advantage of polymorphism. We must keep in

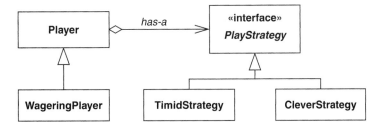

Figure 11.10 Composition can be used for alternate implementations.

mind the life cycle of the system: it's harder to maintain extension-based code than composition-based code. Extension should be limited to cases where there is a legitimate, permanent *is-a* relation between classes, and where the specification of the superclass is stable. Interfaces can be employed to maintain separation between specification and implementation, and to provide reuse and polymorphism across class hierarchies. Composition can be used to add functionality or to provide alternate implementations of some specific functionality.

✳ 11.4 Extension and state

The "kind" of thing an object models and the "state" of an object are closely related. For instance, in a university registration system we might have several categories of students: junior division students, undergraduates, graduate students, *etc.* (Perhaps students are classified as "junior division" until they complete some specified number of credit hours.) One obvious approach is to differentiate among the various kinds of student by making the classification part of the state of a *Student* object:

```java
public class Student {
    ...
    // Student classifications:
    public static final int JUNIOR_DIVISION = 0;
    public static final int UNDERGRADUATE = 1;
    public static final int GRADUATE = 2;
    private int classification;
    ...
    public int classification () { ... }
    ...
    public void setClassification (int class) { ... }
    ...
}
```

Some of the functionality of a *Student* is state dependent. That is, how the *Student* object behaves in response to a command or query depends on the *Student*'s state. In particular, it sometimes depends on the *Student*'s classification. Code that depends on a student's classification does a case analysis using conditional statements. For instance, a method to register someStudent might look like this:

```java
int classification = someStudent.classification();
if (classification == Student.JUNIOR_DIVISION) {
    handle JUNIOR_DIVISION case
} else if (classification == Student.UNDERGRADUATE) {
    handle UNDERGRADUATE case
} else if (classification == Student.GRADUATE)
    ...
```

The problem is that the method containing this code is dependent on the set of possible student classifications. Furthermore, we are likely to find identically structured conditional statements scattered throughout the implementation. Adding a new classification requires modifications in a number of places, complicating maintenance. Long conditionals handling many cases are hard to understand and difficult to modify or extend. Such structures are generally undesirable in an object-oriented system.

An obvious alternative is to model different classifications by subclassing *Student*, rather than including classification as part of a *Student*'s state. Classification-dependent behavior is handled by providing different implementations to common methods in each subclass. Adding a new classification is handled by defining a new subclass. Clients depend on polymorphism to supply the appropriate behavior. The conditional case analysis disappears. The selection is handled by the polymorphism dispatching mechanism at run-time.

The approach using inheritance introduces more classes, and is less compact than a state-based approach. However, experience has shown that the distribution of behavior over different classes is particularly beneficial if there are many alternatives, a situation that would otherwise necessitate long conditionals.

11.4.1 State as an object

There is one difficulty with subclassing, though,. The class of an object is fixed when the object is created. It cannot be changed dynamically during program execution. For example, suppose *JuniorDivisionStudent* and *Undergraduate* are subclasses of *Student*. An instance of *JuniorDivisionStudent* is created to represent an individual student when he or she is first admitted to the university. At some point, the student is admitted to a college and becomes an undergraduate. However, there is no way to convert the *JuniorDivisionStudent* object to an *Undergraduate* object. The best that can be done is to create a new *Undergraduate* object to represent the student and copy information from the old *JuniorDivisionStudent* object. The problem is that other objects reference the old object. (A *Course*, for instance, might have a list of *Students* enrolled.) Making sure that all references to the old object are updated to the new one is difficult, error-prone, and complicates the system structure considerably.

A closer look shows that the use of inheritance to handle the *Student*'s classification-based behavior is inappropriate. An approach similar to that seen above with the "strategy" interface can be used to avoid this difficulty. Rather than employing extension directly, we use composition. That is, we define an interface (or abstract class) that isolates state-dependent behavior, and equip an object with a state-defining component that implements the interface. Different behaviors are achieved by providing different subclasses for this component, each with its own implementation. State-dependent requests are simply forwarded to the state component. For instance, the *Student* class can be structured as follows:

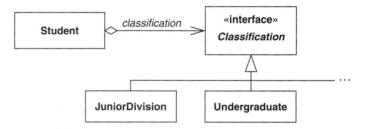

Classification-dependent behavior is specified in the interface or abstract class *Classification*. *Student* forwards responsibility for functions like registration to the *Classification*:

```
public class Student {
    ...
    private Classification classification;
    ...
    public void register () {
        classification.register();
    }
    ...
}
```

An additional advantage to this approach is that state transitions—the changes from one state to another—become explicit, and can be delegated to the state subclasses. Such an approach can produce an extremely flexible and easily modifiable design.

11.5   Summary

In this chapter, we considered in some detail how to use abstraction and composition in the structure of a system design. We began by looking at abstract classes. An abstract class is different from an ordinary concrete class in two respects: it can contain abstract methods, and it cannot be instantiated. Though an abstract class bears some similarity to an interface, an abstract class contains an implementation component and is included in the class hierarchy. An abstract class is used as a foundation on which to build completely implemented concrete classes. An interface, on the other hand, contains no implementation at all and is used to specify what a client requires of a collaborating server.

We noted that a class has two distinct kinds of "customers": clients, that use the class through its specification, and subclasses that extend the class. These different kinds of customers have very different needs, and the contract that a class offers its subclasses is generally not the same as the contract it offers its clients. The dependency of a subclass on its parent superclass is quite strong, and at the implementation level. You must carefully consider this relation when defining a class that is intended to be extended. A good rule is to view only abstract classes and interfaces as suitable for extension.

Next we compared the two primary means of constructing new classes from existing ones, composition and extension. We noted that we could achieve alternate implementations of a specified functionality either by extending the class, or by providing the class with a "strategy" component. Functionality can be added to a class with extension or by wrapping. We observed that composition led to fewer maintenance problems than extension. In general, composition produces a more flexible and maintainable structure than extension. Extension should be limited to cases where there is a legitimate, permanent *is-a* relation between classes, and where the specification of the superclass is stable.

We concluded by noting that the state of an object could be modeled with extension. In cases where an object can dynamically change state, combining composition and inheritance—by providing an object with a state component that is subclassed to define specific state-dependent behavior—produces a flexible maintainable system.

SELF-STUDY EXERCISES

11.1 Indicate whether each of the following statements is true or false:

    a. If a method is qualified as abstract, the class that contains it must also be qualified as abstract.

    b. An abstract class cannot extend a concrete class.

    c. A class can directly extend more than one abstract class.

    d. An abstract class has exactly one parent class.

    e. An abstract class can implement an interface.

11.2 How is an abstract class different from a concrete class? Why does an abstract class have at least one constructor?

11.3 Consider the class:

```
public class Greeter {

    private String greetings;

    public Greeter () {
        String greetings = "Hello!";
    }
    public void displayGreetings () {
        System.out.println(greetings);
    }
}
```

What will be displayed by the statement

```
(new Greeter()).displayGreeting()
```

and why?

11.4   Consider the class:

```java
public class Greeter {

    private String greetings;

    public Greeter () {
        greetings = "Hello!";
    }

    public void displayGreetings () {
        System.out.println(greetings);
        String greetings = "Salut!");
        System.out.println(greetings);
    }
}
```

What will be displayed by the statement

```java
(new Greeter()).displayGreeting()
```

and why?

11.5   The following method is shown on page 461:

```java
public void enterCombination (int combination) {
    int remainder = combination;
    int position = 100;
    while (position > 0) {
        enterDigit(remainder / position);
        remainder = remainder % position;
        position = position / 10;
    }
}
```

Trace the method when invoked with an argument of 123, showing the value of the variables `remainder` and `position`, and the expression `remainder/position`, each time the while condition `position > 0` is evaluated.

11.6   Suppose in classes *Parent* and *Child* on page 461, the instance variables were both named `myClass`, rather than `parentClass` and `childClass`.

   a.   What will be written when a *Child* is created, if the *Parent* constructor is

```java
public Parent () {
    myClass = "Parent";
    System.out.println(myClass());
}
```

   b.   What will be written when a *Child* is created, if the *Parent* constructor is

```
public Parent () {
    myClass = "Parent";
    System.out.println(myClass);
}
```

Now suppose that the instance variable myClass is declared protected in *Parent*, and *Child* declares no instance variable:

```
public class Parent {
    protected String myClass;
    ...
}

public class Child extends Parent {

    public Child () {
        super();
        myClass = "Child";
    }
    ...
}
```

c. What will be written when a *Child* is created, if the *Parent* constructor is

```
public Parent () {
    myClass = "Parent";
    System.out.println(myClass());
}
```

11.7 Does a subclass depend on the specification of its superclass?

Does a subclass depend on the implementation of its superclass?

Does a client of a subclass depend on the specification of the superclass?

11.8 Does a composed class depend on the specification of a core class?

Does a composed class depend on the implementation of a core class?

Does the client of a composed class depend on the specification of a core class?

11.9 How can composition be used to provide alternate implementations of some particular functionality?

11.10 How can composition be used to add functionality to a class?

EXERCISES

11.1 Using a web browser, access the Java API documentation for the package java.util. Find an example in this package of an interface implemented by an abstract class that is extended by at least two concrete subclasses.

11.2   Using a web browser, access the Java API documentation for method `removeRange` in the predefined class *java.util.AbstractList*. (Exactly what this method does is not particularly important.) What part of the documentation is intended for a client, and what part for a subclass?

11.3   An application requires two kinds of counters: a standard step-counter that starts at 0 and can be incremented and decremented by 1, and a "cell-division" counter that starts at 1, is doubled by the increment operation, and decremented by 1. Model these counters with an abstract class and two concrete classes.

11.4   Model the two counters of the previous exercise using composition. Define a class *Counter* that delegates responsibility for incrementing to an *Incrementor*. Make *Incrementor* an interface, and make the interface and implementing classes private nested members of *Counter*. Make the constructor for *Counter* private (!) and define two static methods

```
public static Counter createStandardCounter ()
public static Counter createCellDivisionCounter ()
```

that produce the two flavors of *Counter*.

The nested classes should be static (so they can be created by the static `create` methods), and their constructors should have a *Counter* as argument, for example,

```
private static class AddOneIncrementor
    implements Incrementor {
    ...
    private AddOneIncrementor (Counter counter) ...
```

11.5   Exercise 9.7 introduced classes modeling pieces in a chess game. Define an abstract class *AbstractPiece* that defines methods

public boolean isWhite ()
>   This piece is white.

public String name ()
>   The name of this piece, as a *String*.

public Square location ()
>   The location of this piece. Returns *null* if this piece is no longer in play.

public boolean canMoveTo (Square location)
>   This piece can legally move to the specified *Square*.

public void moveTo (Square newLocation)
>   Move this piece to the specified *Square* if it can legally do so. Otherwise, this piece does not change location.

public void remove ()
>   Remove this piece from play.

Implement as much as possible in the abstract class. In particular, implement `moveTo` in terms of `canMoveTo`.

Implement classes *Rook* and *Bishop*, modeling these chess pieces, as subclasses of *AbstractPiece*.

11.6 In Section 9.5, we introduced the class *InteractivePlayer*, modeling a nim player that gets its moves from the user. Define a set of interfaces, abstract classes, and concrete classes to model nim players. There are two kinds of players: interactive players, who get moves from the user, and independent players, who algorithmically determine their own moves. Further, there are three kinds of independent players: timid players, greedy players, and clever players.

11.7 We want to add to the players of the previous question the ability of remembering how many games the player won and lost. Consider how this might be done by using extension and by using composition, wrapping the additional functionality around the player.

11.8 Define a class *Elevator* that models a simple elevator. An elevator starts at the bottom floor, moves upward one floor at a time until it reaches the top floor, and then moves downward one floor at time until it reaches the bottom floor. The only aspects of the elevator we are interested in is the floor it is on, and the direction of movement. The the specification of the class will look like this:

> **public class** Elevator
>> A simple elevator.
>
> **public** Elevator (**int** floors)
>> Create an *Elevator* traversing the specified number of floors.
>
> **public int** floor ()
>> The floor this *Elevator* is on. The bottom floor is numbered 1.
>
> **public boolean** goingUp ()
>> This *Elevator* is going up.
>
> **public void** move ()
>> Move to the next floor.

Implement the *Elevator* using the "state as object" strategy. Define a private inner class *State*. An *Elevator* has a *State* component. A *State* knows the floor, the direction of movement, and the next state. Thus,

> **private class** State
>> A state of the *Elevator*.
>
> **private** State (**int** floor, **boolean** goingUp)
>> Create a *State* for the specified floor and direction.
>
> **public int** floor ()
>> The floor of this *State*.
>
> **public boolean** goingUp ()
>> This is a "going up" *State*.
>
> **public** State next ()
>> The *State* after the *Elevator* moves.

public void setNext (State next)
Set the *State* after this *State*.

When an *Elevator* is created, one *State* is created for the bottom floor (going up), one for the top floor (going down), and two for each of the intermediate floor (going up and going down). For instance, if there are three floors, four states are created: floor 1 going up, floor 2 going up, floor 2 going down, floor 3 going down.

The *States* are linked together in a circular fashion:

Your implementation should contain no if statements. The only structured statements required should be loops in the constructor to create the *States*.

SELF-STUDY EXERCISE SOLUTIONS

11.1 *a.* True.
  b. False.
  c. False.
  d. True.
  e. True.

11.2 An abstract class can have abstract methods while a concrete class cannot. An abstract class cannot be instantiated while a concrete class can. An abstract class is used as a basis for extension while a concrete class is used as a source of objects.

11.3 The statement will display

```
null
```

The reason is that the constructor declares an automatic variable greetings, whose scope is the body of the constructor. The instance variable greetings is never initialized.

11.4 The statement will display

```
Hello!
Salut!
```

The scope of the variable greetings defined in the method displayGreetings is from the declaration to the end of the method body. The first occurrence of the identifier `greetings` in the method body refers to the instance variable; the last occurrence refers to the automatic variable.

11.5
remainder	position	remainder/position
123	100	1
23	10	2
3	1	3
0	0	*not a number*

11.6 *a.* Same as before: null. The names of the instance variables do not matter. There are still two distinct variables.

   b. "Parent" will be written. Code in the class *Parent* references the instance variable defined in the class *Parent*.

   c. 'Parent" will be written. There is only one variable involved. That variable is initialized in the *Parent* constructor, and then assigned in the *Child* constructor. The out happens after the variable has been assigned `"Parent"` and before it is assigned `"Child"`.

11.7 The answer to all three questions is "yes."

11.8 The answer to the first is "yes," but the answer to the last two is "no."

11.9 By defining a component that is responsible for the function, and forwarding the responsibility to the component. The component can then be extended (or implemented) to provide different implementations.

11.10 By wrapping the class. The wrapper implements the new functionality and forwards other requests to the component.

CHAPTER 12   Lists

In many applications, we must deal with a collection of objects: a deck of cards, a group of employees, a set of transactions. A *container* is an object whose purpose is to hold a collection of other objects. Containers of some kind are almost always provided as a built-in feature of a programming language, and a variety of containers are generally available as library classes. Programmers can also define their own container classes.

In this chapter, we consider a fundamental container called a *list*. Although several kinds of lists are provided in the standard Java libraries, we introduce a particularly straightforward and simple version here. For the present we concentrate on understanding the specification of list features, and how to use them. We'll see various implementation possibilities in later chapters.

Container classes are typed according to the kind of objects they can contain. For instance, a list of playing cards is a different kind of object from a list of students. However, these two objects are very similar in that they have (essentially) the same set of features with the same implementations: we can add items, remove items, check to see if an item is on the list, *etc*. To handle this situation, we introduce the notion of a *generic* class or interface. Using a generic structure, we can write the specification and implementation for a list once, and "instantiate" the generic structure to produce different list classes for particular types of objects.

When using a container, we find that we are frequently required to perform some operation on each element in the container. This is essentially an iterative process, and we see here how to perform such an iterative process with a list, employing the while statement introduced in Chapter 7.

Common list operations involve searching the list to see if it contains a particular item. Thus we must consider exactly what is meant by the "equality" of two objects. As we will see, defining equality in a completely satisfactory fashion is not entirely trivial.

We conclude by examining a straightforward, default implementation of a list. We follow the pattern, introduced in the previous chapter, of defining an interface to specify the functionality and an abstract class to provide a base implementation.

Objectives

After studying this chapter, you should understand the following:

- the notion of container and its features;

- the specification of a list as a container;
- iteration as the control mechanism to process list entries;
- the notion of equality, and the pitfalls in overriding the method `equals`.

Also, you should be able to:

- use the class *DefaultList<Element>* to create and manipulate list instances;
- implement iterative algorithms that manipulate lists.

12.1   Containers

Situations often arise in which we must deal with a *collection* of objects: a *Student*'s schedule is a set of *Courses*, a *Course* contains a group of enrolled *Students*, a *PokerHand* contains a number of *Cards*, a *Receipt* is a list of *Items*, *etc*. To manage such collections, objects called *containers* are used. A *container* is simply an object whose purpose is to contain a collection of other objects.

Basic container operations include:

- adding an item to the container;
- removing an item from the container;
- determining whether or not a particular item is in the container;
- performing some specific operation on each item in the container.

Performing some action with each item in a container is sometimes called a *for each* operation: "*for each* item in the container, …"

Suppose we use a container to manage the collection of *Students* enrolled in a *Course*. We want to enroll (add) *Students* to the *Course*, drop (remove) *Students* from the *Course*, and determine if a particular *Student* is enrolled in the *Course*. We also want to perform "for each" operations such as computing the final grade for each enrolled *Student*.

> **container:** an object whose purpose is to contain other objects.

Containers are homogeneous

A fundamental property of a container is that it is *homogeneous*: all the items in the container are of the same type. If all the items are of the same type, we know exactly which operations they can perform. This is important when a "for each" operation is done. If we are to compute the final grade for each item in a container, for example, we must be sure that all the items are *Students* so that the operation "compute the final grade" makes sense.

Requiring that all the items in a container are of the same type is not unduly restrictive. Using abstraction, we can be as liberal or as conservative as necessary regarding what kind of items we admit into a container. We can even construct a container in which items need only be of type *Object*. (Though it hard to imagine many applications in which a particular container can actually contain any kind of object at all.)

Container characterizations

A mathematical set is a simple, familiar container. Sets have two properties that are sometimes used to characterize containers. First, a set cannot contain "duplicates." It can contain only one instance of any particular value. Adding items to a set that are already members does not change the set:

$$\{1, 2, 3\} \cup \{2, 3\} = \{1, 2, 3\}$$

Second, a set has no "structure." An item is either in the set or it is not. There is no other relationship imposed on the set members

$$\{1, 2, 3\} = \{2, 1, 3\} = \{3, 1, 2\}$$

Other forms of containers permit multiple occurrences of an item and impose a structural relationship on the container elements. For example, the same number might appear more than once on a list of test scores, or the same patient might appear several times in a physician's weekly appointment schedule. A queue of students waiting to pay fees relates the students sequentially: one is first, and one is last; for each student in the queue (except the last), there is a unique "next" student, and for each student in the queue (except the first) there is a unique "previous" student. The relationship is the result of membership in the queue. In this chapter, we consider containers called *lists* in which duplicates are permitted and that impose a simple sequential relation on their members.

12.2   Lists

A *list* is a container that holds a finite sequence of reference values, all of the same type. (We will say "list of objects" rather than a "list of references," but we should remember that the list's components are references to the "contained" objects.) Several important properties are implied by this definition.

- A list is *finite*. In particular, a list might contain just one element or it might contain no elements at all. If a list does not contain any elements, it is said to be *empty*.

- A list is a *sequence*. That is, assuming there are several elements on the list, there is a first element, a second element, and so forth.

- A list is *homogeneous*. All the elements of a list are of the same type.

Furthermore, as we mentioned above, a list can contain multiple instances of an item: the same reference value might occur several times on the list. What we mean is that it is *possible* to add an item to a list more than once. There is nothing in the list mechanism to prevent it. But in many specific cases it will not make sense for an item to appear more than once on a list. For example, a student should not appear more than once on a list of students enrolled in a course.

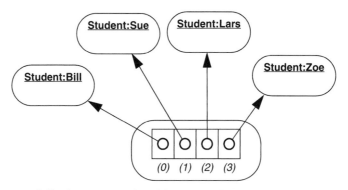

Figure 12.1 **A list is a composite object containing references to other objects.**

Since a list is a sequence, we can reference elements by their relative position on the list. For historical reasons, list elements are indexed by their offset from the beginning of the list rather than by their ordinal position. The first element on the list is at index 0, the second element is at index 1, and so on. Figure 12.1 shows a list of four *Students*, indexed 0 through 3. Note that indexes range from 0 to one less than the number of elements on the list.

> **list:** a container in which the items are organized in a sequence.

12.2.1 Structuring lists

Suppose we model a list of *Students* such as shown in the figure with a class *StudentList*. What functionality do we expect an instance of this class to support? As we mentioned in the first section, we want to add and remove items and determine whether or not a particular item is on the list:

> **public void** add (Student student)
> > Add the specified *Student* to the end of this list.
>
> **public void** remove (Student student)
> > Remove the first occurrence of the specified *Student* from this list. Has no effect if the *Student* is not on this list.
>
> **public boolean** contains (Student student)
> > This list contains the specified *Student*.

Note that in the specification of remove, we must indicate which occurrence of the item will be removed (since an item can appear on a list more than once), and what happens in the event that the item is not on the list.

We have also said that we often want to perform "some operation on each item in the container." For example, we might want to compute the final grade of each *Student* on the list. An index is a handy way of accessing an item on the list:

```
public int size ()
```
      Number of elements in this list.

```
public Student get (int index)
```
      The *Student* with the specified index.

      require:
```
0 <= index && index < this.size()
```

```
public void set (int index, Student student)
```
      Replace the element at the specified position with the specified *Student*.

      require:
```
0 <= index && index < this.size()
```

A client can create a new, empty *StudentList*

```
StudentList roll = new StudentList();
```

and populate the list with statements such as

```
roll.add(new Student("Bill",...));
```

The client can query its size with

```
roll.size()
```

and access a particular *Student* on the list with an expression like

```
roll.get(index)
```

where index is an **int** variable containing a nonnegative value less than `roll.size()`. For instance, if `finalGrade` is a *Student* method, we can write

```
if (roll.get(0).finalGrade() >= 70) ...
```

to determine if the first *Student* on the list has a passing grade.

    Now suppose we need to create a class to model a list of *PlayingCards*. We define a class with basically the same features as *StudentList*. Methods like size will have the same specifications, while other methods are modified to reflect that list elements are now instances of *PlayingCard*:

```
public void add (PlayingCard card)
```
      Add the specified *PlayingCard* to the end of this list.

```
public void remove (PlayingCard card)
```
      Remove the first occurrence of the specified *PlayingCard* from this list. Has no effect if the *PlayingCard* is not on this list.

```
public boolean contains (PlayingCard card)
```
      This list contains the specified *PlayingCard*.

```
public PlayingCard get (int index)
```
      The *PlayingCard* with the specified index.

```
public void set (int index, PlayingCard card)
```
Replace the element at the specified position with the specified *PlayingCard*.

require:
```
0 <= index && index < this.size()
```

We model each different kind of list with a distinct class based on the entries of the list. For instance,

```
public class StudentList
```
A list of *Students.*

```
public class PlayingCardList
```
A list of *PlayingCards.*

We can then safely write code like:

```
StudentList roll = new StudentList();
roll.add(new Student("Bill",...));
if (roll.get(0).finalGrade() >= 70) ...
```

and

```
PlayingCardList hand = new PlayingCardList();
hand.add(new PlayingCard(PlayingCard.SPADE,2));
if (hand.get(0).suit() == PlayingCard.SPADE) ...
```

We expect the following to produce compiler errors:

✗   `roll.add(new PlayingCard(PlayingCard.SPADE,2));`
     (Cannot add a *PlayingCard* to a *StudentList.*)

✗   `hand.get(0).finalGrade()...`
     (`hand.get(0)` is a *PlayingCard*, which does not have a `finalGrade` method.)

There are difficulties with this simple approach, however. If we implement the class *StudentList*, and subsequently implement *PlayingCardList*, the implementations will be virtually identical. To implement *PlayingCardList*, all we would do is copy *StudentList* and replace all references to the class *Student* with references to *PlayingCard*. (In fact, that's exactly what we did when we wrote the specifications for *PlayingCardList* above.)

This violates a basic software engineering guideline:

Do not repeat yourself!

Disregarding this rule adversely effects software evolution.[1] Since changes in one instance of the repeated code generally must be replicated in all instances, we end up maintaining an ill-defined set of classes—classes that are related only in that they contain common code.

---

1. Martin Fowler and Kent Beck refer to duplicated code as "number one in the stink parade."

Furthermore, we want to write methods that do things like count the number of items on a list, reverse the items on the list, merge two lists into one, build a new list with the first *n* elements of a list, *etc*. For example, the following method swaps two elements on a *StudentList*:

```
/**
 * Swap element at index i with element at index j.
 * @require    0 <= i && i < list.size()
 *             0 <= j && j < list.size()
 */
public void swap (StudentList list, int i, int j){
    Student temp = list.get(i);
    list.set(i,list.get(j));
    list.set(j,temp);
}
```

If we want a method to swap two elements on a *PlayingCardList*, we have more opportunity to repeat ourselves. The algorithms are identical:

```
/**
 * Swap element at index i with element at index j.
 * @require    0 <= i && i < list.size()
 *             0 <= j && j < list.size()
 */
public void swap (PlayingCardList list, int i, int j){
    PlayingCard temp = list.get(i);
    list.set(i,list.get(j));
    list.set(j,temp);
}
```

Such methods depend only on the list structure, and are independent of the kind of items the list can contain. Nevertheless, we are required to reimplement the methods for each type of list.

Using abstraction to capture "list-ness"

An obvious approach is to attempt to use abstraction to capture the commonality of list classes like *StudentList* and *PlayingCardList*. What is common is that they both model list structures, with features as specified above. They differ only in the type of elements that can be on the list.

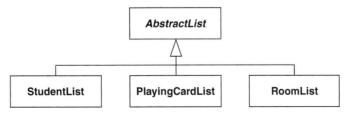

But this approach presents some problems. The first question is how will methods like add and get be specified in *AbstractList*? (Remember, we want to implement these methods in *AbstractList*, so that the various concrete list classes can simply inherit the implementations.) The only possible choice is to specify the list elements as *Objects*:

> **public void** add (Object object)
> Add the specified *Object* to this list.

> **public** Object get (**int** index)
> The *Object* on this list with the specified index.

When we extend *AbstractList* to produce a *StudentList*, we want to make sure that get returns a *Student*. Since *Student* is a subclass of *Object*, we can override get in *StudentList* with[1]

```
public Student get (int i) {
    return (Student) super.get(i);
}
```

Methods like add that take an *Object* argument cause more of a problem. We can't override add with

```
public void add (Student student) {
    super.add(student);
}
```

This will only *overload* add. Thus add must remain specified with an *Object* parameter in *StudentList*, and we can no longer count on the compiler to verify that only *Students* will be added to a *StudentList*. The best we can do is override add and explicitly check the type of the argument at run-time:

```
public void add (Object student) {
    assert student instanceof Student;
    super.add(student);
}
```

But there is a more serious problem. The specification of add in *AbstractList* is

> **public void** add (Object object)
> Add the specified *Object* to this list.

---

1. Restricting the return type to a subtype when overriding a method is allowed only in Java version 5.0 and later. In earlier versions of Java, the return type of an overriding implementation must be the same as the overridden implementation. Thus, in versions prior to 5.0, get would be specified in *StudentList* as

    ```
    public Object get (int index)
    ```

    requiring an item from a *StudentList* to be cast before it can be used as a *Student*:

    ```
    ((Student)roll.get(0)).finalGrade()
    ```

    The compile time type check is replaced with a run-time check, defeating much of the purpose of defining *StudentList* as a separate class.

while the specification in *StudentList* is

> **public void** add (Object student)
>> Add the specified *Object* to this list.
>
> **require:**
>> student instanceof Student

The precondition has been strengthened in *StudentList*, violating the fundamental rule introduced in Section 9.3 and repeated in Section 10.4.3.

The crux of the problem is that *StudentList* should *not* be a subtype of *AbstractList*. It's not the case that a *StudentList is-a AbstractList*, and can be used in any context requiring an *AbstractList*. Consider the following simple method:

```
public void addAnObject (AbstractList list) {
    list.add(new Object());
}
```

An invocation of this method requires an *AbstractList* as argument. If *StudentList* is a subtype of *AbstractList*, the method can be invoked with a *StudentList* argument. But this is clearly wrong. Only *Students* should be added to a *StudentList*.

We have used extension for code reuse: we want to implement the list methods once, and inherit these implementations in the concrete, homogeneous list classes. But with extension we also get subtyping, which in this case we do not want. Nevertheless, this was the only reasonable approach prior to Java version 5.0, and was incorporated into the original Java libraries. Java version 5.0 introduced a *generics* facility which solves the problem cleanly. We consider this next.

12.2.2 Using generics to capture "list-ness"

We have seen that the specifications of *StudentList* and *PlayingCardList* are virtually identical. Likewise, if we were to look at the implementations of classes *StudentList* and *PlayingCardList*, we would see that they are identical as well. The only difference in both specification and implementation is that occurrences of the identifier Student in *StudentList* are replaced with the identifier PlayingCard in *PlayingCardList*. Thus we could share specification and implementation if we could write a class definition in which the list element type were a "parameter," with an appropriate "argument," such as Student or PlayingCard, to be supplied when a list object is created.

The *generics* facility, introduced in Java version 5.0, allows us to do exactly this. We can write class, interface, or method definitions that have *type* parameters. In particular, we can declare a *List* class in which the *element type* is a parameter, using the syntax

> **public class** List<Element> { ...

We use the definition to create a specific kind of list by supplying the element type as argument:

> List<Student> roll = **new** List<Student>();
> List<PlayingCard> hand = **new** List<PlayingCard>();

The specification and implementation of *List<Element>* uses the type parameter `Element` as the type of the list elements:

```
public class List<Element> { ...
    ...
    public void add (Element element) { ... }
    ...
    public Element get (int index) { ... }
    ...
}
```

(The identifier "`Element`" is simply a formal parameter; any identifier will do.)

Using a generic class to create a specific class by supplying an argument, for example `List<Student>`, is referred to as *generic instantiation*. This should not be confused with *class instantiation*, the creation of an object with the operator **new**. To avoid some confusion, we refer to the use of a generic class to create a specific class as *application* rather than instantiation.

Methods can also be generic. For example, the `swap` method mentioned above can be written

```
public <Element> void swap (List<Element> list,
    int i, int j) {
    Element temp = list.get(i);
    list.set(i,list.get(j));
    list.set(j,temp);
}
```

No special syntax is required to invoke a generic method. To invoke `swap`, we write

```
swap(roll,0,1);
swap(hand,0,hand.size()-1);
```

where, as above, `roll` and `hand` are instances of *List<Student>* and *List<PlayingCard>* respectively.

Generics and subtyping

That a type *A* is a subtype of a type *B* does not imply that *List<A>* is a subtype of *List<B>*. For instance, suppose *Weapon* is a subtype of *Movable*, as in Chapter 9. If

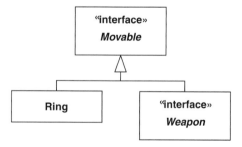

List<Weapon> were a subtype of *List<Movable>* then according to the fundamental rule of subtypes, a *List<Weapon>* could be provided in any context requiring a *List<Movable>*. For instance, the method

```
public void putRingInPack (Ring ring,
    List<Movable> pack) {
    pack.add(ring);
}
```

could be invoked with a *List<Weapon>* as argument. But this is not correct. A *Ring* is not a *Weapon*, and cannot be added to a *List<Weapon>*.

Specifically, *List<Movable>* has a method specified as

```
public void add (Moveable element)
```

while *List<Weapon>* has a method

```
public void add (Weapon element)
```

The precondition for the second method is stronger than the precondition for the first. The add defined in *List<Weapon>* requires its argument to be a *Weapon*, while the add defined in *List<Movable>* requires only that its argument be a *Movable*. If *List<Weapon>* were a subtype of *List<Movable>*, this would not be correct: subtypes shouldn't strengthen preconditions.

Note that this is the same argument that we made against using abstraction to capture "list-ness" above.

Code reuse

Being able to reuse code offers substantial advantages. In addition to having to write and test less code, we avoid code duplication with its countless maintenance headaches.

We have seen how Java supports code reuse through class composition and inheritance. Generic structures provide additional opportunities for reuse. Employing these tools has an immediate payoff in improving programmer productivity. But the cost of generic programming is in the need to test generic code for all expected applications. And reused code should be carefully tested when it is to be employed in some new, not previously anticipated, situation.

12.3   List specification

We use generic interfaces and classes to define lists. Following the pattern outlined in the previous chapter, we'll define an interface (rather than a class) *List<Element>* that captures the basic functionality a list should have, and an abstract class *AbstractList<Element>* implementing this interface. The abstract class will serve as a basis on which to develop various list implementations. We'll also define a concrete class *DefaultList<Element>* that implements the interface. These are all defined in the package nhUtilities.containers.

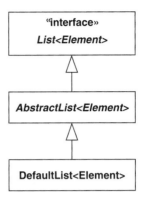

Let's look at some of the features we expect a list to have. One property we're interested in is how many elements are on the list. We provide a query:

public int size ()
>   Number of elements in this *List*.

>   **ensure:**
>   this.size() >= 0

The case in which the list contains no elements is of particular importance. Though it's redundant—saying the list is empty is the same as saying its size is 0—we provide a separate query for this case.

public boolean isEmpty ()
>   This *List* contains no elements.
>   this.isEmpty() == (this.size() == 0)

Observe that an *empty* list is not the same as a *null* value. An empty list *is* an object. If we declare a *List<Student>* variable,

        List<Student> roll;

the variable will initially contain the null value. However, after the assignment,

        roll = **new** DefaultList<Student>();

roll will contain a reference to a newly created empty list, as illustrated in Figure 12.2.

If the list is not empty, we want to be able to access the individual elements of the list. As we've seen, we can reference elements by their relative position or index.

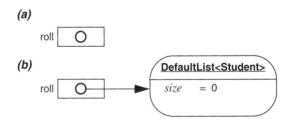

Figure 12.2   Variable roll contains null (a) and references the empty list (b).

> **public** Element get (**int** index)
>   The *Element* with the specified index.
>
>   **require:**
>   0 <= index && index < this.size()

Note carefully how this method works. If roll is an object of class *List<Student>*, then

        roll.get(3)

gives us (a reference to) the fourth element on the list, that is, the element with index 3. Specifically, it gives us a a reference to a *Student* instance. For this query to be legal, we require there be at least four elements on the list.

If the list is empty (this.size == 0), we cannot invoke get. The precondition cannot be satisfied, no matter what value the argument has: index cannot possibly be greater than or equal to 0 *and* less than 0.

What commands should we provide for modifying the list? It seems clear that we'll want to add and remove elements. We provide two methods for adding an element:

> **public void** add (Element element)
>   Append the specified *Element* to the end of this *List*. Equivalent to
>   this.add(this.size(),element).
>
>   **require:**
>   element != null
>
>   **ensure:**
>   this.size() == old.size() + 1
>   this.get(this.size()-1).equals(element)

> **public void** add (**int** index, Element element)
>   Insert the specified *Element* at the specified index.
>
>   **require:**
>   element != null
>   0 <= index && index <= this.size()
>
>   **ensure:**
>   this.size() == old.size() + 1
>   this.get(index).equals(element)
>   for all j: index <= j && j < old.size() implies
>   old.get(j).equals(this.get(j+1))

The preconditions emphasize that the value null cannot appear on a list. Read the postconditions carefully. Note that the first version of add appends an element to the end of the list. If a list has five elements, and we append an element, the new element becomes the sixth. The rest of the list remains unchanged. The postcondition

        this.size() == old.size() + 1

means that the list is one element longer after appending than it was before.

The second variant adds the item at the specified index, and "pushing in front of" existing items. The postcondition says that the element that used to be at `index` is now at `index+1`, the element that used to be at `index+1` is now at `index+2`, *etc.* If a list has five elements and the command

```
add(2,item);
```

is performed, `item` is inserted at index 2 (it becomes the third element), the old third element becomes the new fourth, the old fourth element becomes the new fifth, the old fifth becomes the new sixth. In this case, the postcondition says "for all *j* between 2 and 4, the element with old index *j* has index *j+1* after the add is done." Note that invoking `add` with `index == this.size()` appends the item to the end of the list.

We include a method for removing a specified element, and a method for removing an element at a specified position:

public void remove (Element element)
> Remove the first occurrence of the specified *Element* from this *List*. Has no effect if the *Element* is not contained in this *List*.

public void remove (**int** index)
> Remove the element with the specified index.
>
> **require:**
> ```
>     0 <= index && index < this.size()
> ```
> **ensure:**
> ```
>     this.size() == old.size() - 1
>     for all j: index <= j && j < this.size() implies
>         this.get(j).equals(old.get(j+1))
> ```

The second `remove` method allows us to remove an arbitrary element from the list. The postconditions indicate that the list shrinks by one when we delete an element, and the elements after the one deleted move up one position toward the beginning of the list. If a list has six elements and the command

```
remove(2);
```

is performed, the third element (index 2) is deleted, the old fourth element becomes the new third, the old fifth becomes the new fourth, and the old sixth becomes the new fifth. In this case, the second postcondition says "for all *j* between 2 and 4, the element with new index *j* is the element that was previously at index *j+1*."

The method `set` allows us to replace an arbitrary element of the list with another element:

public void set (**int** index, Element element)
> Replace the element at the specified position with the specified *Element*.
>
> **require:**
> ```
>     0 <= index && index < this.size()
>     element != null
> ```
> **ensure:**
> ```
>     this.get(index).equals(element)
> ```

There are also two methods for determining whether or not an element is on a list. The method `indexOf` gives an index of the element.

public boolean contains (Element element)
    This *List* contains the specified *Element*.
```
this.contains(element) ==
    (this.indexOf(element) >= 0)
```

public int indexOf (Element element)
    The index of the first occurrence of the specified element, or −1 if this *List* does not contain the specified element.

    ensure:
```
if this.indexOf(element) >= 0
    this.get(this.indexOf(element)).equals
        (element)
        for all j: 0 <= j && j < this.indexOf(element)
            implies !this.get(j).equals(element)
if this.indexOf(element) == -1
    for all indexes j,
        !this.get(j).equals(element)
```

Recall that a list might contain several occurrences of the same element. The method `indexOf` returns the index of the first occurrence, that is, the smallest index of the element.

Finally, the method `copy` provides a copy of the list. This is a distinct container object that contains the same values as the original. Note that the postcondition guarantees that a list and its copy are not the same object, but have the same size and contain the same values.

The complete specification of the interface is given in Listing 12.1. We'll give a simple implementation of the interface in Section 12.9. Now we want to understand how to write client code using lists. We instantiate *DefaultList<Element>* when we need a list, and access its features by means of the interface.

Listing 12.1 **Specification for *List<Element>***

---

nhUtilities.containers
Interface List<Element>

    public interface List<Element>
        A finite list of *Elements*.

Queries

---

continued

Listing 12.1   **Specification for *List<Element>* (cont'd)**

---

public int size ()
> Number of elements in this *List*.

> **ensure:**
>> this.size() >= 0

public boolean isEmpty ()
> This *List* contains no elements.
>> this.isEmpty() == (this.size() == 0)

public Element get (**int** index)
> The *Element* with the specified index.

> **require:**
>> 0 <= index && index < this.size()

public boolean contains (Element element)
> This *List* contains the specified *Element*.
>> this.contains(element) ==
>>> (this.indexOf(element) >= 0)

public int indexOf (Element element)
> The index of the first occurrence of the specified element, or −1 if this *List* does not contain the specified element.

> **ensure:**
>> if this.indexOf(element) >= 0
>>> this.get(this.indexOf(element)).equals
>>>> (element)
>>> for all indexes j: j < this.indexOf(element) implies
>>>> !this.get(j).equals(element)
>> if this.indexOf(element) == -1
>>> for all indexes j,
>>>> !this.get(j).equals(element)

Commands

---

public void add (Element element)
> Append the specified *Element* to the end of this *List*. Equivalent to this.add(this.size(),element).

> **require:**
>> element != null

> **ensure:**
>> this.size() == old.size() + 1
>> this.get(this.size()-1).equals(element)

continued

Listing 12.1 **Specification for *List<Element>* (cont'd)**

=====

```
public void add (int index, Element element)
```
Insert the specified *Element* at the specified index.

require:
```
element != null
0 <= index && index <= this.size()
```

ensure:
```
this.size() == old.size() + 1
this.get(index).equals(element)
for all j: index <= j && j < old.size() implies
    old.get(j).equals(this.get(j+1))
```

ensure:
```
this.get(index).equals(element)
```

```
public void remove (Element element)
```
Remove the first occurrence of the specified *Element* from this *List*. Has no effect if the *Element* is not contained in this *List*.

```
public void remove (int index)
```
Remove the element with the specified index.

require:
```
0 <= index && index < this.size()
```

ensure:
```
this.size() == old.size() - 1
for all j: index <= j && j < this.size() implies
    this.get(j).equals(old.get(j+1))
```

```
public void set (int index, Element element)
```
Replace the element at the specified position with the specified *Element*.

require:
```
element != null
0 <= index && index < this.size()
```

```
public List<Element> copy ()
```
A copy of this *List*.

ensure:
```
this.copy() != this
this.copy().size() == this.size()
for all indexes  j,
    this.get(j).equals(this.copy().get(j))
```

=====

DrJava: exercising Lists

An instance of the class *Integer*, defined in `java.lang`, wraps an **int** value so that it can be treated as an object. (See Section 1.7.) An *Integer* is immutable. The **int** value is specified in the constructor, and can be accessed with the *Integer* method `intValue`:

> **public int** `intValue ()`
> The value of this *Integer* as an **int**.

1. In the *Interactions* pane, create an *Integer* list:

```
> import nhUtilities.containers.*;
> DefaultList<Integer> list =
    new DefaultList<Integer>();
```

2. Verify that the list is initially empty, and add several items to the list.

```
> list.isEmpty()
true
> list.add(new Integer(1));
> list.add(new Integer(3));
> list.add(new Integer(0));
> list.add(new Integer(1));
> list.size()
4
> list.toString()
"[ 1, 3, 0, 1]"
```

3. Query the list for several items.

```
> list.get(0)
1
> list.get(1)
3
> list.get(list.size()-1)
1
```

4. Remove the item at index 0, and verify the correctness of the operation.

```
> list.remove(0);
> list.size()
3
> list.toString()
"[ 3, 0, 1]"
```

5. Try to access the item with index 3 and note the results.

6. Create a *DefaultList<String>* and exercise it.

12.4 Iteration

We mentioned in Section 12.1 that a common requirement is to perform some operation with each element of a container. This is a form of *iteration*. Iteration was introduced in Section 7.3.1, and defined as a process in which an operation is to be performed several times. In the situation at hand, "several times" translates into "once for each element in the container."

Section 7.3.1 also introduced the while statement to control an iteration. Recall that a while statement is a structured statement with another statement, the body, as a component:

```
while ( condition )
    statement
```

The body determines the action that is to be repeated, and is often a compound statement (see Section 4.1.3). Before each execution of the body, the condition is evaluated. When the condition is false, the iteration is complete. This is illustrated in Figure 12.3.

The statement that comprises the loop body might not be executed at all, might be executed once, or might be executed more than once. As was pointed out in Section 7.3.1, executing the body should have the potential of changing the value of the condition. For a while statement to be correct, we must make sure that if the condition is initially true, executing the body a sufficient number of times will cause it to become false.

It is possible that the condition of a while statement will remain true no matter how many times the body is executed, and the while statement will never terminate. Such a situation is called an "infinite loop." Infinite loops are usually the result of programmer error, though there are rare situations where we intend to program an infinite loop.

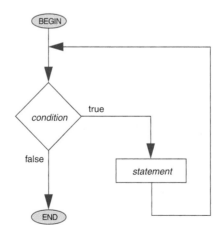

Figure 12.3 **A *while* statement.**

12.4.1 *while* loops and lists

The general format of a while statement used to iterate over the elements of a container is:

```
while ( more elements to process )
    process the next element
```

The elements in a list can be accessed by index. If we want to process each element in the list, an obvious approach is to start with the first element (index 0), then proceed to the second (index 1), and so on, until we're done. We use its index to access each element of the list. If `list` is the list, the approach can be outlined as follows:

```
int i;         // index of the next element to process
i = 0;
while ( more list elements to process ) {
    process list.get(i);
    i = i + 1;
}
```

The first two lines are referred to as "loop initialization." Loop initialization declares and initializes any local variables required by the iteration.

Note the relationship between the index variable `i` and the set of elements processed. For each iteration, the value of `i` identifies the next element to be processed. As we iterate, all of the elements with index less than `i` have been processed:

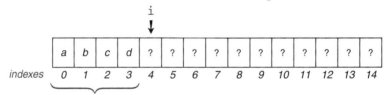

These elements have been processed

In particular, when we start the while loop, `i` is 0 and no elements have been processed. All elements have been processed when `i` is `list.size()`.

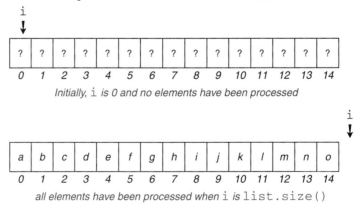

Initially, `i` is 0 and no elements have been processed

all elements have been processed when `i` is `list.size()`

To process every element, i should take on each value in the range 0 through list.size()-1. We are done when i reaches list.size():

```
int i;
i = 0;
while (i < list.size()) {
    process list.get(i);
    i = i + 1;
}
```

If the list is empty, list.size() is 0 and the condition i < list.size() is initially false. The loop terminates without executing the body at all. If the list is not empty, the condition is true. The element with index 0 is processed, and i is incremented to 1. The while condition is again evaluated. If the list contains only one element, this condition is now false and the loop terminates having processed the one element. Otherwise, the element with index 1 is processed, i is incremented to 2, and the process continues.

Note that we are guaranteed that the preconditions for get are satisfied. get requires that its argument is greater than or equal to 0, and less than list.size(). Since i is initialized to 0 and incremented in the loop, we are sure that it is at least 0. The while condition guarantees that i is less than list.size() when get is invoked.

When we write a while loop, we must make sure that the iteration terminates by making certain that the while condition will eventually become false. Incrementing i by 1 each time we execute the loop body ensures that the loop will terminate as long *as the length of the list does not increase*. Thus the operation "*process* list.get(i)" must not increase the length of the list.

In the code sketched above, the query list.size() is executed for each iteration of the loop. If the length of the list does not change, we can query the list once for its length, and save the value in a local variable:

```
int i;
int length;
length = list.size();
i = 0;
while (i < length) {
    process list.get(i);
    i = i + 1;
}
```

12.5 Examples

12.5.1 Summing items on a list

As a first example, suppose that we have a list of the students enrolled in a course, a *List<Student>*, and we would like to compute the average (mean) of their final exam grades. Assume that the class *Student* defines the query:

public int finalExam ()
This *Student*'s grade on the final exam.

We write a method that, given the list of students, returns the average final exam grade:

public double finalAverage (List<Student> students)
The average (mean) of the final exam grades of the specified *Students*.
require:
students.size() > 0

To compute the mean, we must sum up all the exam grades and then divide by the number of students. We use a while loop to iterate through the list, adding up the grades. A local variable sum, initialized to 0, will contain the sum of the grades:

```
int sum;
sum = 0;
```

The operation we want to perform on each list element is to get the final exam grade and add it to sum:

```
sum = sum + students.get(i).finalGade();
```

Using the template for iterating through a list given above, we write

```
int i;      // index of students
int length; // number of Students on the list
int sum;    // sum of grades up to, but not including,
            // the i-th Student

sum = 0;
length = students.size();
i = 0;
while (i < length) {
    sum = sum + students.get(i).finalExam();
    i = i+1;
}
```

(To simplify documentation, we refer to the element with index *i* as "the *i*-th.")

To make sure we understand what's happening, let's trace how the variables change as the method is executed. Assume the list students has four elements, as illustrated in Figure 12.4.

After executing the first three assignments, the variables length, sum, and i will have the following values:

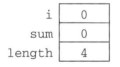

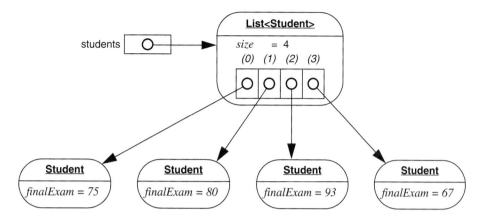

Figure 12.4 **The *List<Student>*.**

Since the condition is true, the body of the while is performed. The first assignment in the body queries students for its first element, queries this *Student* for its final exam grade, and adds it to sum. The second statement increments i. After performing the body of the iteration once, the variables will be

i	1
sum	75
length	4

The condition is still true, so the body is performed a second time. students is queried for its second element (since i is 1), and this *Student's* final exam grade is added to sum. The variable i is again incremented. After two iterations, we have

i	2
sum	155
length	4

After a third iteration of the *while*, the variables look like this:

i	3
sum	248
length	4

Once again the condition is true, so the body is done a fourth time:

i	4
sum	315
length	4

Now the condition is false, and the iteration is complete. The body of the while statement was performed four times, once for each element of the list.

We still have to compute the average by dividing sum by length. We have one minor problem here: we want a **double**, but sum and length are both **ints**. If we divide sum by length, we get the **int** quotient, which isn't exactly what we want. We need to convert the values of sum and length to **double**, so that we get the **double** quotient. We saw in Section 2.7 that we can convert an **int** to a **double** with a cast operation. We write

```
return (double)sum / (double)length;
```

(We actually only need to convert one of the values, since if one operand of the operator is **double**, the other will automatically be converted to **double**.)

The complete method is shown in Listing 12.2. Why do you think we require the list to be nonempty?

12.5.2 Summing selected elements of a list

Let's modify the above problem a bit. Assume that some students did not take the test, and are represented in the data by test grades of "−1." These grades should not be included when computing the average.

We have two modifications to make to the method. First, we don't want to add the "−1" grades into the sum. Second, we can't compute the average by simply dividing the

Listing 12.2   **The method** *average*

```
/**
 * The average (mean) of the final exam grades of the
 * specified Students.
 *     @require    students.size() > 0
 */
public double average (List<Student> students) {
   int i;        // index of students
   int length;   // number of Students on the list
   int sum;      // sum of grades up to, but not
                 // including, the i-th Student

   sum = 0;
   length = students.size();
   i = 0;
   while (i < length) {
      sum = sum + students.get(i).finalExam();
      i = i+1;
   }
   return (double)sum / (double)length;
}
```

sum by the number of elements of the list, since this number includes the "–1" grades. We must count the valid test grades on the list to get the divisor. The modified method is given in Listing 12.3.

Note the precondition: we require that there be at least one legitimate test grade on the list. Why is this important?

12.5.3 Finding the minimum

The above examples have used local variables in the while condition and in the body of the loop. These variables must be initialized before they are referenced, and must be updated in the body of the loop in such a way as to guarantee that the while condition will ultimately become false.

Listing 12.3 **The method *average*, revised**

```
/**
 * The average (mean) of the final exam grades of the
 * specified Students. Negative grades are not included.
 *     @require    students.size() > 0
 *                     for some index i,
 *                         students.get(i).finalExam() >= 0
 */
public double average (List<Student> students) {
    int i;         // index of students
    int length;  // number of Students on the list
    int sum;      // sum of non-negative grades up to, but not
                   // including, the i-th Student
    int count;   // number of non-negative grades up
                   // to, but not including, the i-th
    sum = 0;
    count = 0;
    length = students.size();
    i = 0;
    while (i < length) {
        if (students.get(i).finalExam() >= 0) {
            sum = sum + students.get(i).finalExam();
            count = count+1;
        }
        i = i+1;
    }
    return (double)sum / (double)count;
}
```

Loop variable initialization is critical to the correct execution and termination of a loop. In many cases initialization is straightforward. But there are other cases where careful thought must be given. As a example, let's find the lowest final exam grade for a group of *Students*. Again, we assume that the list provided as argument is not empty.

> **public int** minFinalExam (List<Student> students)
>> The lowest final exam grades of the specified *Students*.
>
>> **require:**
>>> students.size() > 0

Essentially, all we have to do is look at the final exam grade of each *Student* on the list, and remember the lowest we see. We need two local variables, one to index the list, and one to remember the lowest grade seen. We can define them as follows:

```
int i;      // index of the next Student to look at
int low;    // lowest final exam grade of the Students
            // looked at so far; that is, lowest of
            // Students with indexes less than i.
```

low *is the minimum of these*

The iterative step is clear: look at the final exam grade of the next *Student*, and remember it if it is the smallest so far:

```
while (i < students.size()) {
    if (students.get(i).finalExam() < low)
        low = students.get(i).finalExam();
    i = i+1;
}
```

The only question remaining is how to initialize i and low. It seems reasonable to initialize i to 0, since the first *Student* we need to look at has index 0. But what should low be initialized to? According to the specification, it should be the "lowest final exam grade of the *Students* looked at so far." But what is this when we haven't yet looked at any? We could set low to an initial value that is higher than any anticipated grade. But this is dangerous, since the *Student* method finalExam doesn't specify any upper bound for the value returned. The best approach is to initialize low to the grade of the first *Student* (with index 0) on the list. (We are guaranteed that the list is not empty.) Then, as low is the "lowest of *Students* with indexes less than 1," we initialize i to 1. Note that the initial state is consistent with the picture above:

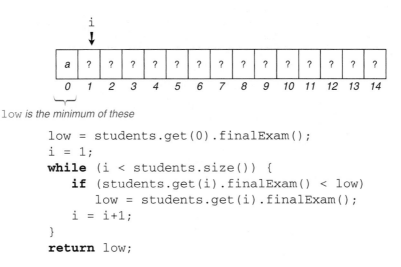

low *is the minimum of these*

```
low = students.get(0).finalExam();
i = 1;
while (i < students.size()) {
    if (students.get(i).finalExam() < low)
        low = students.get(i).finalExam();
    i = i+1;
}
return low;
```

It is worth pointing out how the specification of variable behavior drives the details of the algorithm. For example, suppose we had defined low to be the lowest exam grade up through and including the i-th *Student*:

```
int low;      // lowest final exam grade of the Students
              // with indexes through i.
```

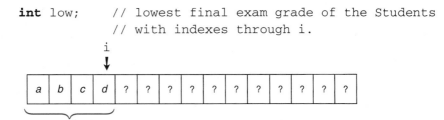

low *is the minimum of these*

With this picture, the initialization of i, the while condition, and the order of statements in the loop body all change:

```
low = students.get(0).finalExam();
i = 0;
while (i < students.size()-1) {
    i = i+1;
    if (students.get(i).finalExam() < low)
        low = students.get(i).finalExam();
}
return low;
```

12.5.4 Determining if an object is on a *List*: searching the *List*

For the next example, we will implement the method indexOf using the other *List* methods. Recall that indexOf returns the index of the first occurrence of an item on a list, or −1 if the item is not on the list.

```
public int indexOf (Element element)
```
The index of the first occurrence of the specified element, or −1 if this *List* does not contain the specified element.

The method must examine each item on the list and see if it is equal to the argument `element`. The operation performed with an item compares it to the argument

```
this.get(i).equals(element)
```

(Since the method is defined in the class we are implementing, we use **this** to refer to the list.)

In the previous examples, the iteration looked at every item on the list. But here we want to find the *first* occurrence of the argument on the list. We should stop the iteration as soon as we find what we're looking for. We can write a first approximation as follows:

```
int i = 0;  // index of the next element to examine
while (!this.get(i).equals(element)) ...
```

What to do if the `i`-th element is not what we're looking for? Simply move on to the next one:

```
int i = 0;  // index of the next element to examine
while (!this.get(i).equals(element))
   i = i +1;
```

Note that "process the `i`-th element" happens in the while condition. The body of the loop is a single simple assignment to move to the next element.

When the loop exits, `i` indexes the element we're searching for. That is, `this.get(i).equals(element)` is true when the loop terminates.

```
int i = 0;  // index of the next element to examine
while (!this.get(i).equals(element))
   i = i +1;
return i;
```

This would be a satisfactory implementation if we were certain that the argument was on the list. But what if it's not? In this case, we iterate through the entire list without finding the argument, and must return −1. Thus there are *two different conditions* that can terminate the iteration: all the elements on the list are examined without finding the one we're looking for, or the one we're looking for is found. We should make these two conditions explicit when we write the while condition.

```
int i = 0;  // index of the next element to examine
while (i < this.size() &&
       !this.get(i).equals(element))
   i = i +1;
```

A few points should be noted. First, recall that the operator `&&` is lazy. That is, the right operand is evaluated *only if* the left operand is true:

```
!this.get(i).equals(element)
```

will be evaluated only if

```
i < this.size()
```

is true. The laziness is critical here. The method get has a precondition that requires 0 <= i && i < this.size(). If i < this.size() is false, we *must not invoke* get(i). If we do, we violate the precondition with unpredictable results. Thus the order in which the relational expressions are written is important in this case.

Second, i is the index of the next element in the list to look at. The following statement is always true during execution of the method:

No list element with index less than i is equal to the argument element.

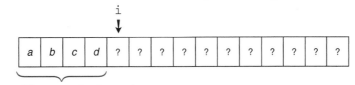

None of these equals element

The statement is true initially, since i is 0 and there are no list elements with index less than i. (We say the statement is "vacuously true.") And it remains true as the loop executes because i doesn't get incremented unless the element with index i isn't what we're looking for. Such a statement that is true no matter how many times the body of the loop has been executed is called a *loop invariant*. This statement describes the essence of the iteration: the iteration pushes i along making sure that the invariant remains true.

Finally, either i < this.size() or !this.get(i).equals(element) must be false when the loop terminates. (If they were both true, the while condition would be true and the loop would not have terminated.) That is, either

```
i == this.size(), or
this.get(i).equals(element)
```

If i == this.size(), the invariant implies that the element is not on the list. (If it were, it would have an index less than this.size()). On the other hand, if this.get(i).equals(element), the invariant implies that this is the smallest value of i for which this is true. We can determine what value to return by seeing which of these conditions holds when the loop terminates:

```
public int indexOf (Element element) {

    int i = 0;  // index of the next element to examine
    while (i < this.size() &&
            !this.get(i).equals(element))
        i = i+1;

    if (i < this.size())
        return i;
    else
        return -1;
}
```

12.5.5 Removing duplicates

As a final example, we write a method that removes duplicates from a list. Let's suppose we want to implement a class modeling a set of integers:

public class IntegerSet
      A finite set of *Integers*.

We were introduced to the class *Integer*, defined in java.lang, in Section 1.7. An *Integer* instance wraps an **int** value so that it can be treated as an object. An *Integer* is immutable. The **int** value is specified in the constructor, and can be accessed with the *Integer* method intValue:

public int intValue ()
      The value of this *Integer* as an **int**.

A set, of course, cannot contain duplicate entries.

One approach to implementing a set is to use a component list to contain the set elements:

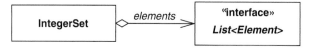

public class IntegerSet {
     private List<Integer> elements;
        ...
}

Now further assume that we want to be able to populate a newly created set from a list. That is, we define a constructor like this:

public IntegerSet (List<Integer> elements)
      Create a new *IntegerSet* containing the elements of the specified *List*.

The obvious implementation is to copy the argument list:

public IntegerSet (List<Element> elements) {
     this.elements = elements.copy();
        ...
}

(Why copy and not just assign? We don't want the *IntegerSet* instance variable referring to the *same object* as the argument provided by the client. If it did, then any subsequent changes to the argument object would effect the state of the set and *vice versa*.)

But a list can contain duplicate values and a set cannot. So we implement a private auxiliary method to remove duplicates,

private void removeDuplicates ()
      Remove duplicates from the component *List*.

which we invoke in the constructor:

```
public IntegerSet (List<Element> elements) {
    this.elements = elements.copy();
    removeDuplicates();
}
```

The basic design of the method `removeDuplicates` is to iterate through the list and make sure that any repetitions of the item being considered are removed. The fundamental invariant for the loop is

No element with index less than i *appears more than once on the list.*

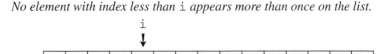

No duplicates of these on the list

As i moves through the list, any duplicates of elements "behind" i have been removed. We can sketch the method as

```
private void removeDuplicates () {
    int i = 0;
    while (i < elements.size()) {
        // remove duplicates of the item with index i
        i = i + 1;
    }
}
```

Note that executing the body of the loop might well remove elements and change the size of the list. Therefore we must recompute the size (by invoking `elements.size()`) for each iteration. Since the list can only get smaller, we have no problem with loop termination.

We write another auxiliary method to accomplish the "remove duplicates of the item with index i" step, and invoke it in the `removeDuplicates` method:

```
private void removeDuplicates () {
    int i = 0;
    while (i < elements.size()) {
        removeDuplicatesOfItemAt(i);
        i = i + 1;
    }
}
```

The thing to notice is that there can be no duplicate of item i with an index less than i. This is because duplicates of elements with indexes less than i have already been removed from the list. So the iteration to find duplicates of item i need only look at elements following item i.

```
private void removeDuplicatesOfItemAt (int i) {
    int j;                // index of element to check
    Integer item;         // remove duplicates of this
    item = elements.get(i);
    j = i+1;
    while (j < elements.size()) {
        if (item.equals(elements.get(j)))
            elements.remove(j);
        else
            j = j+1;
    }
}
```

The invariant for the loop is

The item with index i *does not appear in the list with an index greater than* i *and less than* j.

None of these equals list.get(i)

Again, since the list changes size as we delete elements, we must recompute its length for each iteration. Also notice that the index j is not incremented when an element is deleted. The deletion automatically causes the next element in the list to move up to the j-th position, so that the *current* value of j indexes the *next* element to be compared.

If we replace the invocation of removeDuplicatesOfItemAt with its body in the method removeDuplicates, the resulting structure shows one while loop inside the body of another:

```
i = 0;
while (i < elements.size()) {
    Integer item = elements.get(i);
    int j = i+1;
    while (j < elements.size())
        if (item.equals(elements.get(j)))
            elements.remove(j);
        else
            j = j+1;
    i = i+1;
}
```

The loops are said to be *nested*. Although this saves writing a method, the code is harder to read, understand, and test. Separating the inner loop in a well-defined method markedly improves the situation. We can, for instance, write and test the method implementing the inner loop before writing and testing the method implementing the outer loop.

DrJava: tracing nested loops

Open the file `IntegerSet.java`, located in `sets`, in `ch12`, in `nhText`. This file contains a minimal implementation of the class *IntegerSet*, as sketched above.

1. Activate debug mode, and set a breakpoint on the if statement in the method `removeDuplicates`. (See page 185 for how to use the debugger.) Click the *Watches* tab, and enter `i` and `j` in the *Name* column as variables to watch.

2. In the *Interactions* pane, create an IntegerSet

   ```
   > import ch12.sets.*;
   > import nhUtilities.containers.*;
   > List<Integer> list = new DefaultList<Integer>();
   > list.add(new Integer(1));
   > list.add(new Integer(2));
   > list.add(new Integer(3));
   > list.add(new Integer(4));
   > list.add(new Integer(5));
   > IntegerSet set = new IntegerSet(list);
   ```

3. Step through execution of `removeDuplicates`, by successively pressing *Step Into*, and observe how the variables `i` and `j` behave.

12.6 Loop structure: a summary

As we have seen in the examples, loops generally have four fundamental parts: initialization, continuation condition, body, and conclusion:

```
initialization
while (condition) {
    body
}
conclusion
```

Initialization statements initialize variables used in the condition and in the body of the loop. This is a critical part of setting up the loop. If loop variables are to be initialized properly, their meaning and behavior must be clearly understood. It is good practice to document the behavior of each loop variable carefully.

The *condition* determines whether or not the body of the loop is to be executed. It is sometimes said to "guard" the loop body. We can be certain that the condition is satisfied when the loop body is reached. When the condition becomes false, the iteration terminates.

The loop *body* defines one step in the solution process: executing the loop body brings us one step closer to satisfying the goal of the loop. We must also ensure that executing the loop body brings us one step closer to satisfying the exit condition. That is, we must make sure that the loop condition will ultimately become false, and the loop will terminate.

The *concluding statements* are not always necessary. When we reach the concluding statements, we know that the loop variables will contain values that make the condition false. The concluding statements use the values produced by the loop.

The examples we have seen in this chapter are all instances of counting loops. With a counting loop, we know how many times the body of the loop must be performed. For instance, in the method `average`, the body of the loop must be done once for each student on the list: it is done `students.size()` times. We simply keep a counter or index that is incremented on each iteration. The loop terminates when the counter indicates that the body has been performed the appropriate number of times. Many loops, such as the loop in the *NimTUI* of Chapter 8, are not simple counting loops.

12.7   Java in detail: the *for* statement

The patterns we've seen when iterating over a list are extremely common. So common, in fact, that the language has a special construct, the *for* statement, that can be used in exactly these cases. There are two variants of the for statement. One wraps initialization, condition, and update in the statement header. The other implements the "for each" operation mentioned on page 484. We consider the first variant here, and the "for each" in the next section.

The first for statement variant has the format:

```
for (initializationStatement; condition;
        updateStatement)
    bodyStatement
```

The *initializationStatement* and the *updateStatement* are assignment statements stripped of their trailing semicolons. Execution of the for statement is equivalent to the following, as illustrated in Figure 12.5:

```
initializationStatement;
while (condition) {
    bodyStatement
    updateStatement;
}
```

An iteration processing each element of a list similar to the while loop on page 503 can be written as follows.

```
int i;
for (i = 0; i < list.size(); i = i+1)
    process list.get(i);
```

Note the placement of the semicolons inside the parentheses.

For example, the iteration in the method `average` (Listing 12.3) could be written with a for statement as shown below.

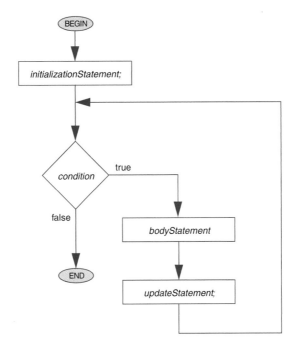

Figure 12.5 **A *for* statement.**

```java
for (i = 0; i < length; i = i+1) {
    if (students.get(i).finalExam() >= 0) {
        sum = sum + students.get(i).finalExam();
        count = count+1;
    }
}
```

We continue to use while statements in our examples, since the order in which things happen is a bit easier to see in this kind of loop.

A local variable can be declared in the initialization statement. However, the scope of such a variable is limited to the loop. For instance, we could write

```java
for (int i = 0; i < list.size(); i = i+1) ...
```

But we could not reference i outside of the loop:

```java
for (int i = 0; !list.get(i).equals(item); i = i+1) {
    ...
}
```
✗   `return i;   // can't reference i here!`

Finally, though not commonly done, the initialization and update can actually consist of several, comma separated statements. For example, the following

```java
for (int i=0, j=list.size()-1; i < j; i=i+1, j=j-1) ...
```

declares two local variables, i and j, initialized respectively to 0 and list.size()-1. Each is updated after the loop body is executed.

A "for each" statement

We have seen a number of examples where, in order to perform some operation on each element in a list., we access each list element by index. The basic structure of this kind of iteration is

```java
int index = 0;
while (index < list.size()) {
    process list.get(index);
    index = index+1;
}
```

or using the for statement introduced above,

```java
int index;
for (index = 0; index < list.size(); index = index+1)
    process list.get(index);
```

Java provides a variant of the for statement in which each element of a container is accessed without explicitly using an index. As mentioned above, this statement effectively implements the "for each" operation of page 484.

The format of the "for each" variant is

```java
for (type identifier : container)
    bodyStatement
```

Type is the type of elements in the container. For example, if roll is a *List<Student>*, we can write

```java
for (Student s : roll) ...
```

The statement comprising the body of the loop is repeated for each element of the container. The identifier names a variable that references a different container element on each iteration, as illustrated in Figure 12.6. The scope of the identifier is the loop body.

For example, using this variant of the for statement, the method average (Listing 12.3) can be written as follows.

```java
public double average (List<Student> students) {
    int sum = 0;
    int count = 0;
    for (Student s : students) {
        if (s.finalExam() >= 0) {
            sum = sum + s.finalExam();
            count = count + 1;
        }
    }
    return (double)sum / (double)count;
}
```

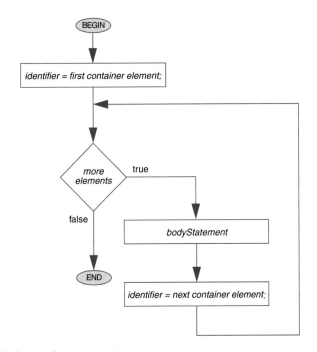

Figure 12.6 **A *for each* statement.**

A few items should be noted.

- The "for each" construct should generally be avoided in iterations where the container is modified by adding or removing elements.

- To be used in a "for each" statement, a container must implement the interface *java.lang.Iterable* or be an array. Arrays are introduced in the next chapter. Every container type, such as *List*, should implement or extend the interface.

We will continue to use indexes explicitly rather than the "for each" statement. Indexes make it much easier to write loop invariants.

12.8   What does "equal" mean?

The implementations of `indexOf` and `removeDuplicates` in Section 12.5 used `equals` when searching the list. We should take a closer look at the notion of equality in Java, consider the circumstances under which `equals` should be overridden, and the implications of overriding `equals`.

We encountered the equality operator, `==`, in Chapter 4. This operator compares two *values* for equality. Two reference values are equal when they reference the same object. So if `s1` and `s2` are *Student* variables,

```
Student s1 = ...
Student s2 = ...
```

`s1 == s2` is true only if `s1` and `s2` refer to exactly the same object.

In Section 10.4.2, we learned that every class inherits the method `equals` from *Object*. In *Object*, the method is defined as

```
public boolean equals (Object obj) {
    return this == obj;
}
```

Therefore if the method is not overridden, writing `s1.equals(s2)` is the same as writing `s1 == s2`. The result is true if and only if `s1` and `s2` reference the same object.

Of course, a class can override the definition of `equals`. For example, the class *String* overrides `equals` so that two *Strings* are equal if they represent the same sequence of characters, even if they are not the same object. Given

```
String s1 = new String("abc");
String s2 = new String("abc");
```

`s1 == s2` returns *false*, while `s1.equals(s2)` returns *true*. The variables `s1` and `s2` contain different reference values, denoting different objects. But as *Strings*, these objects are considered equal.

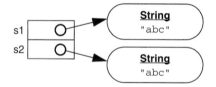

12.8.1 Overriding equals

Under what circumstances should `equals` be overridden in a class, and what are the implications? Our first consideration should be whether an instance of the class *uniquely represents* an entity in the problem domain. That is, whether there is "something" in the problem that is modeled by a single class instance. For example, if we're building a university registration system, we expect each student at the university to be represented by a single instance of the class *Student*. If several *Student* objects are created for the same actual student, there is likely a problem in the system.

On the other hand, suppose we have a class *Date*,[1] modeling days of the calendar with integer-valued properties *year*, *month*, and *day*, denoting the year:

public class Date
A calendar date.

---

1. The class outlined here represents dates somewhat differently than the standard class `java.util.Date`.

public Date (**int** day, **int** month, **int** year)
> Create a new *Date*, representing the specified day, month, and year.

public int year ()
> The year.

public int month ()
> Month of the year.

public int day ()
> Day of the month.

We expect that there might be several instances of the class all representing the same actual date. Class instances do not *uniquely* represent dates.

A general rule is that equals should not be overridden in classes whose instances are uniquely representative of problem entities. We should only consider overriding equals in classes where multiple instances might denote the same entity. We would not override equals in the class *Student*, but might in the class *Date*.

Another important observation is that mutable objects, objects whose state can change, are almost always uniquely representative. Suppose two different instances of a mutable class represent the same problem entity. For example, suppose two different *Student* objects represent the same student. If the objects are mutable, it is possible to change one without changing the other, resulting in an inconsistent picture of the student. We must make sure that whenever one object is modified, the other is modified as well. This is generally a nontrivial problem, and greatly complicates the design. With immutable objects whose state cannot change, maintaining consistency is not an issue.

Thus a second general guideline is that overriding equals should only be considered in classes whose instances are immutable. Think carefully if your are tempted to override equals in a class whose instances can change state. Use only immutable attributes when redefining equals in such a class.

✳ 12.8.2 Problems when overriding equals

Unfortunately, overriding equals is not as straightforward as it first seems. The problems are real but somewhat subtle. Let's consider an example from the previous chapter, where the class *Circle* extends *ClosedFigure* and overrides equals:

```
public class Circle extends ClosedFigure {

    public Circle (int radius) { ... }
    ...
    /**
     * Two Circles are equal if and only if they have
     * the same radius.
     */
    public boolean equals (Object obj) {
        if (obj instanceof Circle)
```

```
            return this.radius() ==
                ((Circle)obj).radius();
        else
            return false;
    }
    ...
}
```

Assuming that `equals` is not overridden in *ClosedFigure*, there are no problems. But now suppose we extend *Circle* with *ColoredCircle*, and again override `equals`:

```
public class ColoredCircle extends Circle {

    public ColoredCircle (int radius, Color c) { ... }
    ...
    /**
     * Two ColoredCircles are equal if and only if they
     * have the same radius and Color.
     */
    public boolean equals (Object obj) {
        if (obj instanceof ColoredCircle)
            return super.equals(obj) &&
                this.color().equals(
                    ((ColoredCircle)obj).color());
        else
            return false;
    }
    ...
}
```

We have introduced several problems. First, notice that we have broken subtyping by weakening the postcondition of *Circle*'s `equals`. The contract offered by *Circle* essentially says

if c is a *Circle*,
```
    this.equals(c) == (this.radius() == c.radius()).
```

ColoredCircle, however, promises only that

if c is a *ColoredCircle*,
```
    if this.equals(c), then this.radius() == c.radius().
```

A *Circle* client can see unequal *Circles* with the same radius: if two *Circles* happen to be *ColoredCircles* of different colors, they test as unequal even if the client is viewing them as *Circles* and not *ColoredCircles*. The following method

```
public void report (Circle c1, Circle c2) {
    if (c1.radius() == c2.radius())
        System.out.println("Circles are equal.");
```

```
    if (!c1.equals(c2))
        System.out.println("Circles are not equal.");
}
```

will report that its arguments are both equal and not equal if invoked as

```
report(new ColoredCircle(1,Color.BLUE),
           new ColoredCircle(1,Color.RED));
```

There is another problem as well. The specification for equals in the class *Object* promises that the method satisfies the following three conditions:

- it is *reflexive*: that is, for any reference value x, x.equals(x) is true;
- it is *symmetric*: that is, for any reference values x and y, if x.equals(y) is true, then so is y.equals(x).
- it is *transitive*: that is, for any reference values x, y, and z, if x.equals(y) and y.equals(z) are both true, then so is x.equals(z).

Now suppose c1 references a *Circle*, and c2 a *ColoredCircle* with the same radius:

```
Circle c1 = new Circle(1);
Circle c2 = new ColoredCircle(1,Color.BLUE);
```

c1.equals(c2) is true, but c2.equals(c1) is false. That is, the symmetric property is violated. The expression c1.equals(c2) executes the method equals as defined in the class *Circle*. This method compares only radii. The expression c2.equals(c1) executes the method equals as defined in the class *ColoredCircle*. This method requires that the argument be a *ColoredCircle*, and that both the radii and colors match.

How serious is this problem? Recall the implementation of indexOf from the previous section:

```
public int indexOf (Element element) {
    int i = 0;
    while (i < this.size() &&
               !this.get(i).equals(element))
        i = i+1;
    if (i < this.size())
        return i;
    else
        return -1;
}
```

Suppose list is a *List<Circle>* containing c1 as its first element (index 0). If we invoke

```
list.indexOf(c2)
```

the method returns 0, since **this**.get(i).equals(element) returns true when i is 0.

However, if the loop condition were written

```
while (i < this.size() &&
           !element.equals(this.get(i)))
```

the method would return −1, since element.equals(this.get(i)) returns false when i is 0. This is not a happy situation. The behavior of the method should not depend on an arbitrary choice in writing the condition.

Fixing the problems with equals

A first attempt to rectify the problems might be to have *ColoredCircle* equals use its parent's version when appropriate:

```
public boolean equals (Object obj) {
    if (obj instanceof ColoredCircle)
        return super.equals(obj) &&
            this.color().equals(
                ((ColoredCircle)obj).color());
    else if (obj instanceof Circle)
        return super.equals(obj);
    else
        return false;
}
```

Now if the argument is a *Circle*, but not a *ColoredCircle*, the two objects will be compared as *Circles*. Thus if

```
Circle c1 = new Circle(1);
Circle c2 = new ColoredCircle(1, Color.BLUE);
```

both c1.equals(c2) and c2.equals(c1) return true.

This does not quite fix the subtyping problem however. The method report, shown above, if invoked

```
report(new ColoredCircle(1, Color.BLUE)),
            new ColoredCircle(1, Color.RED));
```

will still report that the arguments are both equal and not equal.

Furthermore, we have now violated the transitivity property. Suppose

```
Circle c1 = new ColoredCircle(1, Color.BLUE);
Circle c2 = new Circle(1);
Circle c3 = new ColoredCircle(1, Color.RED);
```

Then c1.equals(c2) and c2.equals(c3) are both true, but c1.equals(c3) is false.

Another approach is to use the getClass method defined in *Object* and inherited by all classes. This method returns an instance of the class *java.lang.Class*, which describes the run-time class of the object. For example, given

```
Circle c1 = new Circle(1);
Circle c2 = new ColoredCircle(1, Color.BLUE);
```

even though both c1 **instanceof** Circle and c2 **instanceof** Circle are true, c1.getClass() is not equal to c2.getClass(). c1.getClass() returns an object modeling the class *Circle*, while c2.getClass() returns an object modeling *ColoredCircle*.

Using this method, we can write a version of equals that won't return true unless the run-time classes of the objects are the same. For *Circle*, equals is defined as

```java
public boolean equals (Object obj) {
    if (this.getClass().equals(obj.getClass())
        return this.radius().equals(
                ((Circle)obj).radius());
    else
        return false;
}
```

and for *ColoredCircle*, it is defined as

```java
public boolean equals (Object obj) {
    if (this.getClass().equals(obj.getClass())
        return
            this.radius().equals(
                    ((Circle)obj).radius()) &&
            this.color().equals(
                ((ColoredCircle)obj).color());
    else
        return false;
}
```

Now given the definitions of c1 and c2 above, both c1.equals(c2) and c2.equals(c1) return false.

This approach ensures that the symmetric and transitive properties are satisfied. But subtyping is still broken. The report method still reports that *Circles* with the same radius are not equal if the arguments happen to be *ColoredCircles* with different colors.

Unfortunately, given that equals is embedded in the class *Object*, there is no easy, completely satisfactory solution. The problem can sometimes be avoided by wrapping rather than extending. For instance, if *ColoredCircle* wraps rather than extends *Circle*,

```java
public class ColoredCircle {
    private Circle circlePart;
    ...
    public ColoredCircle (int radius, Color c) {
        this.circlePart = new Circle(radius);
        ...
    }
    ...
}
```

there is no subtyping to break. We can then regain some lost ground by having both classes implement a common interface:

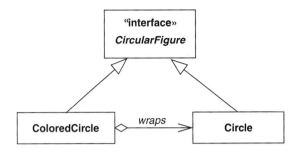

One overriding is safe: consider making it final

Note that problems can arise only when `equals` is overridden in a class after it has already been overridden in a superclass. Thus another guideline says that `equals` should be overridden at most once in any inheritance sequence. This leads some programmers to use the **final** attribute when overriding `equals`. (Recall that a method declared to be **final** cannot be subsequently overridden.)

DrJava: overriding equals

Open files `FauxString.java`, `CaseFreeString.java`, and `Test.java`, located in folder `equals`, in `ch12`, in `nhText`. *FauxString* mimics the class *String*. *CaseFreeString* extends *FauxString*. (We define *FauxString* because the class *java.lang.String* is final, and so cannot be extended.)

Like *String*, *FauxString* overrides `equals` so that two strings made up of the same sequence of characters are equal. *CaseFreeString* extends *FauxString*, and redefines `equals` so that two strings with the same sequence of characters, ignoring case, are equal.

1. In the *Interactions* pane, create several *FauxStrings* and *CaseFreeStrings*.

    ```
    > import ch12.equals.*;
    > FauxString f1 = new FauxString("abc");
    > FauxString f2 = new FauxString("abc");
    > CaseFreeString c1 = new CaseFreeString("abc");
    > CaseFreeString c2 = new CaseFreeString("ABC");
    ```

2. Note the behavior of `equals` in each class.

    ```
    > f1.equals(f2)
    true
    > c1.equals(c2)
    true
    ```

3. Invoke the method `Test.report`, which takes two *FauxStrings* as arguments.

```
> Test.report(f1,f2);
The FauxStrings are equal.
The Strings are equal.
> Test.report(c1,c2);
The FauxStrings are equal.
The Strings are not equal.
> Test.report(c1,f1);
The FauxStrings are not equal.
The Strings are equal.
```

4. Note that the symmetric property of `equals` does not hold.

```
> f1.equals(c1)
true
> c1.equals(f1)
false
```

5. Modify the definition of `equals` in *CaseFreeString* so that it uses the implementation in *FauxString* if its argument is a *FauxString*:

```
public boolean equals (Object s) {
    if (s instanceof CaseFreeString)
        return this.toString().equalsIgnoreCase(
            s.toString());
    else if (s instanceof FauxString)
        return super.equals(s);
    else
        return false;
}
```

Save and compile.

6. Notice that the symmetry property holds,

```
> import ch12.equals.*;
> FauxString f1 = new FauxString("abc");
> CaseFreeString c1 = new CaseFreeString("abc");
> CaseFreeString c2 = new CaseFreeString("ABC");
> f1.equals(c1)
true
> c1.equals(f1)
true
> f1.equals(c2)
false
> c2.equals(f1)
false
```

but transitivity doesn't:

```
> f1.equals(c1)
true
```

```
> c1.equals(c2)
true
> f1.equlas(c2)
false
```

12.9   Implementing the interface *List*

As we shall see in subsequent chapters, there are many different ways of implementing a list structure. In this section, we sketch a simple default implementation that will often suffice.

12.9.1 The class *AbstractList*

In Section 12.3, we observed that we could use an abstract class as a basis for constructing list implementations. The abstract class defines a number of list methods in terms of a few basic methods. A concrete class, then, need only implement these basic methods.

For example, in Section 12.5.4, we implemented the method indexOf using methods size and get. This implementation can be included in the class *AbstractList<Element>*. As we've seen in Section 11.2, the documentation of the method must reference this "self use" of an overridable method. Omitting the *ensure* clause, the method is documented as follows:

public int indexOf (Element element)

> The index of the first occurrence of the specified element, or −1 if this *List* does not contain the specified element.

> This implementation iterates over the list using get until the specified element is found or the end of the list is reached.

The second part of the documentation is part of the contract offered a subclass.

So what methods can we write in terms of others? The following are obvious possibilities:

```
public boolean isEmpty () {
   return this.size() == 0;
}

public boolean contains (Element element) {
   return this.indexOf(element) != -1;
}

public void add (Element element) {
   this.add(this.size(),element);
}
```

```java
public void set (int i, Element element) {
    this.remove(i);
    this.add(i, element);
}

public void remove (Element element) {
    int i = this.indexOf(element);
    if (i != -1)
        this.remove(i);
}
```

We can also provide an implementation of toString:

```java
public String toString () {
    String s = "[";
    int n = this.size();
    if (n > 0) {
        s = s + this.get(0).toString();
        int index = 1;
        while (index < n) {
            s = s + ", " + this.get(index).toString();
            index = index+1;
        }
    }
    s = s + "]";
    return s;
}
```

This leaves only five methods undefined:

```java
public int size();
public void get (int index);
public void add (int index, Element element);
public void remove (int index);
public List<Element> copy ();
```

As mentioned above, the interface *List<Element>* and the class *AbstractList<Element>* are defined in the package nhUtilities.containers.

12.9.2 The class *DefaultList*

Finally, let's build a simple concrete class extending the interface by wrapping a class from java.util that has the functionality we need.

If we extend *AbstractList<Element>*, we have only five basic methods to implement:

```java
public int size();
public void get (int index)
```

```
public void add (int index, Element element)
public void remove (int index)
public List<Element> copy ()
```

To improve efficiency, we'll also override set.

The class *java.util.Vector<Element>* provides the functionality required. A *Vector* is a list-like container in which elements are accessed by index, but with a rather unpleasantly bloated interface. As attitudes about the design of the standard libraries have shifted, this class has been "retrofitted" several times. Unfortunately, once a library class is published and in wide use, the only practical way of modifying a class is expansion.

In Section 7.4.1, we learned that one way to solve the problem of an existing class with the needed functionality, but the wrong interface, is to *adapt* or *wrap* the existing class. (See Figure 7.10 on page 303.) Thus the implementation of *DefaultList* will have a *Vector* component:

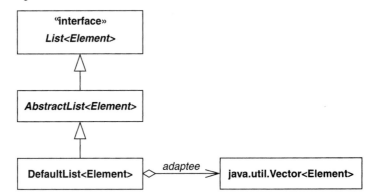

Vector<Element> defines these methods, among others:

```
public int size ()
public Element get (int index)
public void add (int index, Element element)
public void removeElementAt (int index)
public void setElementAt (Element element, int index)
```

A *DefaultList* delegates responsibility for adding, removing, *etc.*, to its component *Vector*. The definition of *DefaultList* is straightforward. We show it, without comments, in Listing 12.4.

DefaultList is a generic class. When we instantiate the class, we provide the actual element type as an "argument" to the constructor. Thus,

```
DefaultList<Student> roll =
    new DefaultList<Student>();
DefaultList<PlayingCard> hand =
    new DefaultList<PlayingCard>();
```

or even, since *DefaultList<Student>* is a subtype of *List<Student>*,

```
List<Student> roll = new DefaultList<Student>();
```

But not

✗   List<Object> roll = **new** DefaultList<Student>();

Even though *Student* is a subtype of *Object*, *List<Student>* is a not a subtype of *List<Object>*. The reason is as we explained on page 492. We cannot correctly provide a *List<Student>* in every context requiring a *List<Object>*.

Finally, note that we're begging the question of how to implement a list here: we're implementing a list by employing a class that (essentially) implements a list. The obvious next question is "Well, how does *java.util.Vector* work?" The answer to that question must wait until the next chapter.

Listing 12.4   The class *DefaultList<Element>*

```
package nhUtilities.containers;

public class DefaultList<Element>
        extends AbstractList<Element> {

   private java.util.Vector<Element> elements;

   public DefaultList () {
      this.elements = new java.util.vector<Element>();
   }

   public int size () {
      return this.elements.size();
   }

   public Element get (int index) {
      return this.elements.get(index);
   }

   public void add (int index, Element element) {
      this.elements.add(index,element);
   }

   public void remove (int index) {
      this.elements.removeElementAt(index);
   }

   public void set (int index, Element element) {
      this.elements.setElementAt(element,index);
   }
```

continued

Listing 12.4   **The class *DefaultList<Element>* (cont'd)**

```
public DefaultList<Element> copy () {
    DefaultList<Element> copy =
        new DefaultList<Element>();
    int i = 0;
    while (i < this.size()) {
        copy.add(this.get(i));
        i = i+1;
    }
    return copy;
}
}
```

✳ 12.10 Generic type checking is done at compile time

The idea of generics is not new. The programming language Ada, for instance, developed in the early '80's, had a fully developed generic facility. However, generics were added late to Java, and are included only in versions 5.0 and later.[1]

As substantive modification to the Java run-time system was not considered practical at this point, generic definitions and type checking were added as a compiler function. The result is that at run-time, all evidence of type parameters and arguments have been "erased" from the program.

For example, recall that the method getClass (page 524), defined in *Object* and inherited by all classes, returns an instance of the class *java.lang.Class* that models the run-time class of an object. If

```
List<Student> roll = new DefaultList<Student>();
List<Circle> loops = new DefaultList<Circle>();
Object obj = roll;
```

then

```
roll.getClass().equals(loops.getClass())
```

returns true, and both

```
roll.getClass().toString(), and
loops.getClass().toString()
```

return `"class nhUtilities.containers.DefaultList"`. The type verification expressions

---

1. Interestingly, "generic" was a reserved word original version of Java. Clearly, a generic facility was intended to be part of the language from its inception.

```
obj instanceof List<Student>
obj instanceof List<Circle>
```

both return true, though the compiler generates "unchecked cast" warnings. The compiler is clever enough to reject the expression

```
roll instanceof List<Circle>
```

with an "inconvertible types" error message.[1]

Further explanation of the implications of compile-time generics is beyond the scope of this text. But it is unfortunate that, rather than being provided with a simple and elegant generic semantics, we are left with a retrofitted kludge in which compiler details must be thought through in order to understand basic operational rules.

12.11 Summary

In this chapter, we examined the specification and application of a simple container called a list. A list is a finite sequence of objects, all of the same type. An individual element on the list can be accessed by an integer index, denoting how far the element is from the front of the list.

List classes are characterized by the kind of items they can contain. Thus one class models a list of *Students*, while another class models a list of *PlayingCards*. The specifications and implementations of these different list classes are almost identical. To avoid having to repeat the same code over and over for each different list class, Java provides a generic facility. This allows us to define interfaces, classes, and methods with "type parameters." Thus we define the interface *List<Element>* where *Element* is a type parameter. We "instantiate" the generic by providing an actual "type argument": *List<Student>* is a list of *Students*, *List<String>* a list of *Strings*, and so on.

It is often the case that we want to perform some operation on each element in a container. With a list, we can access the elements by index. So the standard pattern is to use a while loop and index to iterate through the list:

```
int i;
i = 0;
while (i < list.size()) {
    process list.get(i);
    i = i + 1;
}
```

Common operations involve searching a container to see if it holds a particular object. To do this, we must have an exact idea of what it means for two objects to be "equal." For mutable objects, "equal" generally means "identical." With immutable objects, though, it is sometimes the case that several distinct objects can represent the "same thing." For

---

1. Java's generic mechanism is still being developed. Details may have changed by the time you read this.

example, two different *Strings* might contain the same sequence of characters, or two different *Dates* might denote the same actual date. In these case, we might want to override the inherited method `equals` so that distinct objects that represent the "same thing" compare as equal. If we do this, we must be very careful. The method `equals` should satisfy the reflexive, symmetric, and transitive properties. It is difficult to satisfy these properties if `equals` is overridden more than once in a chain of subclasses.

List<Element> is defined as a generic interface that captures the functionality of a sequential container. Following the pattern we introduced in the last chapter, we define an abstract class *AbstractList<Element>* that implements most of the functionality and provides a basis for developing complete concrete implementations. Our default concrete implementation, *DefaultList<Element>*, wraps the standard library class, *java.util.Vector<Element>*.

SELF-STUDY EXERCISES

12.1   Class *Course* models a course offered at a university. A *Student* has an instance variable `schedule` referencing the list of courses the *Student* is enrolled in.

    a.   Write a declaration for this variable.

    b.   Write a statement that initializes the variable `schedule` to an empty list of *Courses*.

    c.   Write a *Course* method `enroll` that adds a *Student* to the *Course*.

    d.   Modify the method `enroll` so that the *Student* is added to the *Course* only if he or she is not already enrolled.

    e.   Write a *Course* method `drop` that removes a *Student* from the *Course*.

12.2   Given that `myHand` is a *List<PlayingCard>*, where *PlayingCard* is as defined in Chapter 2 (Listing 2.5).

Given

```
Card aceOfSpades = new PlayingCard(
    PlayingCard.SPADE, PlayingCard.ACE);
```

    a.   Write a statement that will add the ace of Spades as the first card in `myHand`.

    b.   Write a statement that will replace the first card in `myHand` with the ace of Spades.

    c.   Write a statement that will remove the last card from `myHand`.

    d.   Write an expression that will determine whether or not the first and last cards in `myHand` are of the same suit.

12.3   Explain why *List<String>* is not a subtype of *List<Object>*, even though *String* is a subtype of *Object*.

12.4   The **int** value wrapped by an *Integer* can be accessed with the *Integer* method `intValue`:

```
public int intValue ()
```
        The value of this *Integer* as an **int**.

Complete the following method, that returns the number of negative *Integers* on a list.

```
public int negativeCount (List<Integer> list) {
    int i;       // index of next item to consider
    int count;   // number of negative values found
    ...
}
```

12.5 State the (informal) invariant condition for the loop of the previous exercise.

12.6 Write a method `removeNegatives` that removes all negative *Integers* from a list of *Integers*.

12.7 Rewrite the method `minFinalExam` of Section 12.5.3 using a for statement.

12.8 Given that `list` is a *List<Integer>*, explain the difference between the following two statements:

```
List<Integer> temp = list;
List<Integer> temp = list.copy();
```

Explain the difference in the following two methods.

(a)
```
public int positiveCount (List<Integer> list) {
    List<Integer> temp = list;
    temp.removeNegatives();
    return temp.size();
}
```

(b)
```
public int positiveCount (List<Integer> list) {
    List<Integer> temp = list.copy();
    temp.removeNegatives();
    return temp.size();
}
```

12.9 How many times is the assignment statement

```
count = count + 1;
```

executed in the following? (That is, what is the final value of count?)

```
int count = 0;
int i = 0;
while (i < 3) {
    int j = 0;
    while (j < 3) {
        count = count + 1;
        j = j + 1;
    }
    i = i + 1;
}
```

12.10 How many times is the assignment statement

```
count = count + 1;
```

executed in each of the following?

(a)
```
int count = 0;
int i = 0;
while (i < 3) {
    int j = i;
    while (j < 3) {
        count = count + 1;
        j = j + 1;
    }
    i = i + 1;
}
```

(b)
```
int count = 0;
int i = 0;
int j = 0;
while (i < 3) {
    while (j < 3) {
        count = count + 1;
        j = j + 1;
    }
    i = i + 1;
}
```

12.11 Write an overriding implementation of `equals` for the class *Date*, sketched on page 520. Two *Dates* representing the same day should be considered equal.

EXERCISES

Note: be sure to import `nhUtilities.containers.*` into compilation units that use the *List* interface and *DefaultList* class.

12.1 Review the systems considered in the exercises of Chapter 8. Identify some class features that might be implemented with lists.

12.2 The **int** value wrapped by an *Integer* can be accessed with the *Integer* method `intValue`:

> **public int** intValue ()
> The value of this *Integer* as an **int**.

Write a method that will count the number of even values on a specified *List<Integer>*.

12.3 Suppose a class *Course* has an instance variable referencing the list of students who are enrolled in course:

```
private List<Student> enrollees;
```

How will this variable be initialized in the *Course* constructor?

Write a *Course* method for enrolling a specified *Student*:

```
public void enroll (Student student)
```

How can you handle the case in which the specified *Student* is already enrolled in the *Course*?

Write a *Course* method for dropping a specified *Student*.

12.4   Assume that the class *Student* defines the query

```
public int finalGrade ()
```

Write a *Course* method that takes a *List<Student>* as argument, and returns the number of enrolled students on the list who have failed, where a final grade of less than MINIMUM_PASS is considered failing.

Write a method that returns a list of the students who have failed. That is, implement

```
public List<Student> failingStudents ()
```

12.5   Given the class *PlayingCard* defined in Chapter 2 (Listing 2.5), write a method that determines whether or not all the elements of a specified *List<PlayingCard>* are of the same suit.

12.6   Given the class *PlayingCard* defined in Chapter 2 (Listing 2.5), write a method that determines whether or not a specified *List<PlayingCard>* contains a pair, that is, contains two cards of the same value.

12.7   Rewrite the "nested loop" version of removeDuplicates (Section 12.5.5) using for statements in place of the while loops. Note that the *updateStatement* in the for loop can be *empty*.

12.8   Redo Exercise 8.9, using a *List<Room>* to model the *Rooms* that make up a maze.

12.9   An unstructured container that does not permit duplicate occurrences of an item is called (surprise) a set. Complete the definition of the class *IntegerSet*, sketched in Section 12.5.5. An *IntegerSet* should support the operations size(), isEmpty(), add(Integer), remove(Integer), contains(Integer). Also include the query isSubSetOf:

```
public boolean isSubSetOf (IntegerSet other)
```
                   This *IntegerSet* is a subset of the specified *IntegerSet*.

Define a generic class based on your definition of *IntegerSet*.

One problem is that, since sets are not indexed, there is no obvious way to perform an operation on every element of a set. Can you suggest a possible approach to this problem?

12.10   Consider the following two implementations of indexOf:

(a)   ```
public int indexOf (Element element) {
     boolean found = false;
```
```

```
            int i = 0;
            while (i < this.size() && !found) {
                fount = this.get(i).equals(element);
                i = i+1;
            }
            if (i < this.size())
                return i;
            else
                return -1;
        }
```

(b)   ```
        public int indexOf (Element element) {
            int item = -1;
            int i = 0;
            while (i < this.size()) {
                if (this.get(i).equals(element))
                    item = i;
                i = i+1;
            }
            return item;
        }
```

Neither is correct. Look at the invariant given for indexOf on page 511. Find the problems in the above implementations by attempting to develop invariants for these loops.

12.11 Review the interface *OperatorWithIdentity* defined in Exercise 9.4. Define a function foldl as follows: foldl takes an *OperatorWithIdentity* and a *List<Integer>* as arguments:

```
        public int foldl (OperatorWithIdentity op,
            List<Integer> list)
```

If the list is empty, foldl return the identity of the operator.

If the list has only one element, foldl returns its value.

Otherwise, if the list is $[x_1, x_2, x_3, \ldots, x_{n-1}, x_n]$, foldl returns the value

$$(\ldots(x_1 \text{ op } x_2) \text{ op } x_3) \ldots \text{ op } x_{n-1}) \text{ op } x_n)$$

For instance, if list is $[\,1, 2, 3, 4\,]$,

```
        foldl (new Addition(), list) ⇒ (((1 + 2) + 3) + 4) ⇒ 10
        foldl (new Multiplication(), list) ⇒ (((1 × 2) × 3) × 4) ⇒ 24
```

Can you implement foldl with just a while statement, and no if statement?

12.12 Define a function foldr similar to foldl of the previous exercise, but that associates to the right. That is, if the list is $[x_1, x_2, x_3, \ldots, x_{n-1}, x_n]$, foldr returns the value

$$(x_1 \text{ op } (x_2 \text{ op } (x_3 \text{ op } \ldots (x_{n-1} \text{ op } x_n)\ldots)$$
```

12.13 Review the chess board of Exercise 9.7. Define a class *Square* that models a square of a chess board. A *Square* should have the following properties:

- row number;
- column number;
- whether or not it is occupied;
- if it is occupied, (a reference to) the occupying *Piece*.

We can model a row with a list of eight *Squares*. Given the declaration

```
List<Square> row1;
```

write code that will create a list of eight squares, referenced by `row1`. The first *Square* on the list, at index 0, should be row 1, column 1, the second *Square* row 1, column 2, and so on.

Now we can model a chess board with a list of rows. That is, a list whose elements are lists of *Squares*:

```
List<List<Square>> board;
```

`board.get(0)` is the first row, and `board.get(0).get(0)` is the first *Square* of the first row.

Define a class *ChessBoard* that models the board as described above. A *ChessBoard* should be initialized to have eight rows of eight *Squares* each. The *ChessBoard* should provide access to *Squares* by row and column. That is, it should define a method

```
public Square squareAt (int row, int column)
```

SELF-STUDY EXERCISE SOLUTIONS

12.1 *a.* `private List<Course> schedule;`

b. `schedule = new DefaultList<Course>();`

c.
```
public void enroll (Student student) {
    schedule.add(student);
}
```

d.
```
public void enroll (Student student) {
    if (!schedule.contains(student))
        schedule.add(student);
}
```

e.
```
public void drop (Student student) {
    schedule.remove(student);
}
```

12.2 *a.* `myHand.add(0,aceOfSpades);`

b. `myhand.set(0,aceOfSpades);`

c. `myHand.remove(myhand.size()-1);`

d. `myHand.get(0).suit()==myHand.get(myHand.size()-1).suit()`

12.3   A *List<String>* cannot be used in every context requiring a *List<Object>*. For instance, if
list is a variable of type *List<Object>*, then

```
list.add(new Integer(1));
```

is legal. But the statement would be incorrect if list references a *List<String>* at run
time. (Which it could do if *List<String>* were a subtype of *List<Object>*.) The add
method of *List<String>* requires its argument to be a *String*.

12.4
```
i = 0;
count = 0;
while (i < list.size()) {
    if (list.get(i).intValue() < 0)
        count = count + 1;
    i = i + 1;
}
return count;
```

12.5   count is the number of negative Integers on the list with index less than i.

12.6
```
public void removeNegatives (List<Integer> list) {
    i = 0;
    while (i < list.size()) {
        if (list.get(i).intValue() < 0)
            list.remove(i);
        i = i + 1;
    }
}
```

12.7
```
public int minFinalExam (List<Student> students) {
    low = students.get(0).finalExam();
    for (int i = 1; i < students.size(); i = i+1)
        if (students.get(i).finalExam() < low)
            low = students.get(i).finalExam();
    return low;
}
```

12.8   After the first assignment, variables temp and list contain the same value: they both
refer to the same object. In the second assignment, temp refers to a different object. This
object is a list containing the same elements as the list referenced by list. For instance,
after the first assignment things look like this,

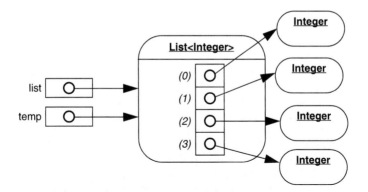

while after the second they look like this:

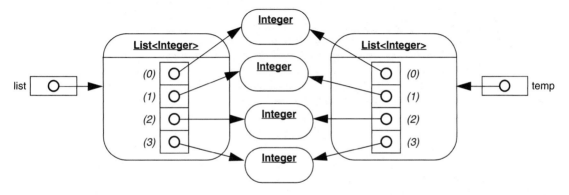

In method *a*, the list passed as argument is modified. In method *b*, it is not.

12.9   9.

12.10   *(a)* 6   *(b)* 3

12.11 **public boolean** equals (Object obj) {
         if (obj **instanceof** Date)
            return this.day() == ((Date)obj).day() &&
               this.month() == ((Date)obj).month() &&
               this.tear() == ((Date)obj).year();
         else
            return false;
      }

CHAPTER 13　Implementing lists: array implementations

In the previous chapter, we specified the generic class *List<Element>* and saw a simple implementation that wrapped the standard library class *java.util.Vector*. In this chapter, we build implementations on a primitive language-provided structure called an *array*. As we'll see, a *Vector* also uses an array to store its component elements.

In Chapter 20, we'll see a fundamentally different approach to building list structures called a linked implementation. These two implementation approaches, array-based and linked, are fundamental, and are used to build many kinds of structural relationships between problem components. As we proceed, we will also encounter several important relationships between classes used to effect various implementations. These relational patterns solve commonly occurring specific design problems, and can be applied to many different applications.

Objectives

After studying this chapter you should understand the following:

- the idea of an array and array index;
- list implementations using arrays and the Vector class;
- shallow and deep copies;
- the method `clone` and the interface *Cloneable*.

Also, you should be able to:

- define array variables, create arrays, and access array components;
- write algorithms having arrays as parameters;
- define classes whose components include array instances.

13.1   Arrays

An *array* is a contiguous sequence of variables all of the same type. The individual variables are identified by *index values* or *indexes*. In Java, index values are integers, beginning with 0.

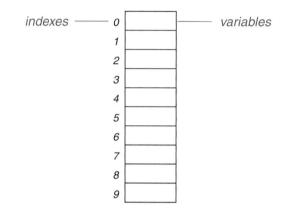

Figure 13.1   A 10-element array.

The variables that comprise an array are called the *components* or *elements* of the array, and can have a primitive type (**char**, **int**, **boolean**, **double**, *etc.*) or a reference type (*Student*, *Object*, *etc.*) The *length* of the array is the number of component variables that comprise the array. Note that just as with a *List*, if the length of an array is n, the component variables are indexed 0 through $n - 1$.

There are two important aspects of an array. First, the length of an array is fixed when the array is created. Second, since contiguous memory is allocated for the variables, accessing a particular variable in the array requires a constant amount of time independent of the array length. For example, suppose the variables comprising a particular array each occupy four bytes and the array is allocated memory starting at memory location 100:

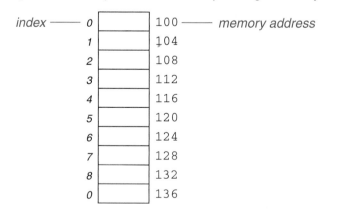

The address of the variable with index i is $100 + 4 \cdot i$. The address of the variable with index 6, for instance, is $100 + 4 \cdot 6 = 124$. In general, the address of an array element can be computed as (*starting address of the array*) + (*variable size*) · (*element index*). This computation requires a fixed amount of time, and is independent of either the index or the length of the array. (Many kinds of computer processors have specialized instruction formats designed for doing exactly this calculation very efficiently.)

Arrays in Java are encapsulated in objects, called surprisingly enough, *array objects* or simply *arrays*. In addition to the component array variables and features inherited from the class *Object*, array objects have a public final **int** component `length`.

The class of an array is determined by the type of the component variables: an array with **int** components is an "*array-of-***int**," and an array with *Student* components is an *array-of-Student*, and so on. The class is written as the component type followed by a pair of brackets. Thus, **int** [] denotes the class *array-of-***int**, and Student [] denotes the class *array-of-Student*. (Note these are brackets, not braces or parentheses.)

Arrays of primitive values are often used explicitly, particularly in complex numeric algorithms where run-time efficiency is critical. Arrays, however, are rather low-level structures. We will limit our use of arrays to the implementation of other higher-level structures.

> **array:** a structure composed of a contiguous sequence of variables, all of the same type.

Defining arrays

As with any class, variables can be defined to reference instances of an array class. For example, the definitions

```
int[] grades;
Student[] cs2125;
```

create two variables, one of type *array-of-***int** named `grades` and the other of type *array-of-Student* named `cs2125`.

(These definitions can also be written

```
int grades[];
Student cs2125[];
```

but we will not use this syntax.)

While we might refer to a variable like `grades` as an "**int**-array variable" or an "**int**-array," it is important to remember that the variable contains a *reference* to an *array object*. In particular, declaring the variable *does not* create an array. Declaring a variable never automatically creates an object. Arrays are no different from other objects in this regard.

The above definitions result in the creation of two *null*-valued variables:

grades   ○
cs2125   ○

As with any other object, we use a constructor to create an array object. The constructor requires a single integer argument, the length of the array. The argument, however, is written inside the brackets that are part of the array class name. For instance, the assignments

```
grades = new int[5];
cs2125 = new Student[5];
```

create two arrays of length 5, and assign references to these arrays to the specified variables:

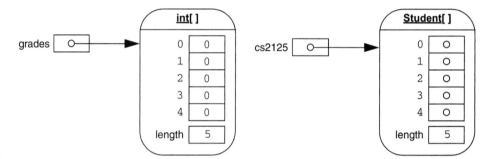

The component variables of the arrays are initialized with standard default values, for example, 0 for **int**, null for references. The length given in the constructor is simply an argument. It need not be a literal. (In fact, it generally *shouldn't* be a literal.) Any integer expression will do. For instance, the following are correct, assuming studentCount is an **int**:

```
cs2125 = new Student[studentCount];
grades = new int[4*cs2125.length];
```

Accessing array components

To access a component of an array, a reference to the array is followed by an index value in brackets. For example

```
grades[3]
```

is an **int** variable—the one with index 3 in the array referenced by the variable grades. This is an ordinary **int** variable, and can be used like any other **int** variable. We can write:

```
grades[3] = 100;
grades[4] = grades[3]/2;
```

and so on. Similarly, we can write:

```
cs2125[0] = new Student(…);
cs2125[0].payFees(100);
```

The expression in brackets that denotes the array element can be an arbitrary integer expression, as long as the value is not negative and is less than the length of the array. For instance, we can assign each component of the array grades the value 100 with the following iteration:

```
for (int i = 0; i < grades.length; i = i+1)
    grades[i] = 100;
```

The assignment

```
grades[i] = 100;
```

is performed a number of times, with i having a different value each time. The first time i has value 0 and the variable grades[0] is assigned 100. The second time, i is 1 and grades[1] is assigned. The variable i is successively assigned the index of each array component, and that component is then assigned 100.

An attempt to reference a nonexistent array element, that is, use of an index that is either negative or greater than or equal to the array length, results in a run-time error called an *ArrayIndexOutOfBoundsException*. This generally causes the program to terminate after producing an error message indicating the cause of the failure. For example, the following will store the value 100 in all components of the array grades, but will fail with an *ArrayIndexOutOfBoundsException* on the last iteration of the loop when i equals grades.length.

```
for (int i = 0; i <= grades.length; i = i+1)
    grades[i] = 100;
```

(To assign each component of the array the value 100, condition should be i < grades.length, as shown previously.)

✳ 13.2   Java in detail: arrays with array components and initializing arrays

Arrays with array components

The astute reader may wonder if we can create an array whose component variables are themselves array variables. The answer is yes. If we define a variable matrix as

```
int[][] matrix;
```

then matrix references an array whose component variables are of type int[]. That is, the component variables reference int arrays. The syntax for constructor invocation (and component access) is perhaps not quite as expected. For example,

```
matrix = new int[3][];
```

creates an array with 3 components, each of type **int** [ ]:

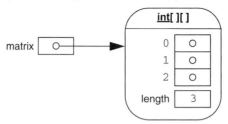

The statement

```
matrix = new int[3][4];
```

also creates three **int** arrays of 4 elements each:

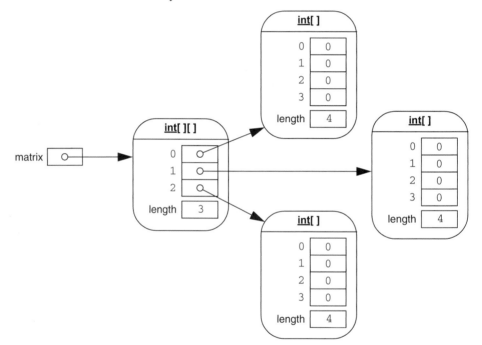

Array initializers

An array instance can be created with an *array initializer*. An array initializer is a comma separated sequence of expressions enclosed in braces. For instance,

```
int[] vec = {0,2,4,6};
```

creates a four-component **int** array, and initializes the component variables with the specified values: vec[0] contains 0, vec[1] contains 2, *etc.*

The initializer can contain arbitrary expressions of the appropriate type. The following, for example, initializes the array `vec` to the same four values as above:

```
int i = 1;
int[] vec = {0, 2*i, 2*i+2, 3*i};
```

An array initializer can appear only in an array declaration.

```
int[] vec;
✗   vec = {0,2,4,6};        // not a declaration
```

An array initializer can be an element of an array initializer. For example, the following:

```
int[][] matrix = {{0, 0, 0, 0}, {1, 2, 3}};
```

creates three arrays, where `matrix.length == 2`, `matrix[0].length == 4`, and `matrix[1].length == 3`.

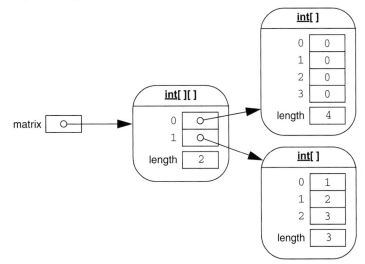

DrJava: exercising an array

Open the file `ArrayExercise.java`, located in `array`, in `ch13`, in `nhText`. This class contains two auxiliary methods for filling and displaying an integer array.

1. In the *Interactions* pane, create an array variable:

    ```
    > int[] v;
    ```

    Note that no array object has been created:

    ```
    > v
    Error: Variable 'v' uninitialized
    ```

2. Create an array object and assign a reference to it to v:

```
> v = new int[5];
> v.length
> v
```

3. Uses the method `show` to examine the contents of the array.

```
> import ch13.array.*;
> ArrayExercise.show(v);
```

4. Use the method `fill` to store different values into the array. Examine some elements.

```
> ArrayExercise.fill(v);
> v[0]
> v[1]
> ArrayExercise.show(v)
```

What happens if you examine the array element with index 5?

```
> v[5]
```

5. Create a new array variable initialized to v, and change its contents.

```
> int[] x = v;
> x.length
> x[2] = 100;
> v[2]
```

Make sure you understand what is happening here: x and v reference the same array object.

6. Now key the following:

```
> int[] fib = {0,1,1,2,3,5,8,13,21};
```

The expression in braces on the right is an "array initializer." Not only has a variable been created, but an array has been created and initialized.

```
> fib.length
> ArrayExercise.show(fib);
```

7. Key the following

```
> int[][] matrix = {{0,1},{2,3,4},{5,6}};
```

How many elements are in the array `matrix`? What is the type of the elements? Verify your answers:

```
> matrix.length
> matrix[0] instanceof int[]
> matrix[0].length
> ArrayExercise.show(matrix[0]);
```

13.3   An array-based list implementation

Now that we know what an array is, we can use arrays to implement lists. The idea is very straightforward: we allocate an array to hold (references to) the elements of the list. Array component 0 references the first element of the list element, component 1 references the second, and so on.

Note that the length of the list is bounded by the length of the array, and the array length is fixed when the array is created. To emphasize this fact, we'll call the class *BoundedList<Element>*, and require that a maximum list size be specified when an instance is created. Otherwise, it will have the same functionality as specified by the interface *List<Element>*.

public class BoundedList<Element>
    A list of *Elements* with a fixed maximum size.

    public BoundedList (**int** maxSize)
        Create a new *BoundedList* with a specified maximum size.

        require:
            maxSize >= 0

        ensure:
            this.isEmpty()

Should *BoundedList* extend *AbstractList* and implement *List*? There is one problem in doing this. The add methods specified in *List* make no mention of a maximum size:

public void add (Element element)
    Append the specified *Element* to the end of this *List*. Equivalent to
    this.add(this.size(),element).

public void add (**int** index, Element element)
    Insert the specified *Element* at the specified index.

    require:
        0 <= index && index <= this.size()

The add methods for *BoundedList*, on the other hand, requires that the list size be less than the maximum. The preconditions for *BoundedList* add will be stronger than the preconditions for *List* add. Thus *BoundedList* should not be a subtype of *List*.

We could modify the specifications of *List<Element>* to allow for both bounded and unbounded lists. For example, we might add the following queries to the interface *List*:

public boolean hasMaxSize ()
    This *List* has a maximum size.

public int maxSize ()
    The maximum size of this *List*. Returns –1 if this *List* has no maximum size.

Then we could specify add, for examples, as

```
public void add (Element element)
```
Append the specified *Element* to the end of this *List*. Equivalent to
`this.add(this.size(),element)`.

require:
```
    !this.hasMaxSize() ||
    this.size() < this.maxSize()
```

However, we choose not to do so at present. We'll simply implement *BoundedList* as an independent class.

The data components of a *BoundedList* include the array containing the list elements, and an **int** variable containing the list length. (Note that the *length* of the array is the *maximum length* of the list.)

Our immediate inclination is to write

```
private Element[] elements;
```

since we have a list of *Elements*. However, *Element* is a generic class parameter and, because of the way generics are implemented in Java, it is not legal to define an array using a type parameter to specify the type of the array elements.[1] (See Section 12.10.) The best we can do is to use an array of *Objects*:

```
private Object[] elements;     // elements of the list
private int size;              // size of the list
// elements[0] through elements[size-1] are valid;
// elements[size] through elements[elements.length-1]
// are not.
```

These variables are initialized by the constructor:

```
public BoundedList (int maxSize) {
    assert maxSize >= 0;
    elements = new Object[maxSize];
    size = 0;
}
```

A *BoundedList<Student>* is illustrated in Figure 13.2.

Other features can be implemented in a very straightforward fashion. We omit comments to simplify the presentation, though the add methods must now have preconditions requiring that the size of the list be less than the maximum size.

```
public int size () {
    return this.size;
}

public int maxSize () {
    return elements.length;
}
```

1. This may change in a future implementation. It may have been changed when you read this.

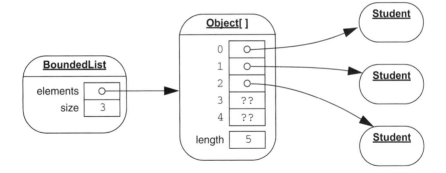

Figure 13.2 **A** *BoundedList.*

```
public Element get (int index) {
    assert 0 <= index && index < size;
    return (Element)elements[index];
}

public int indexOf (Element element) {
    int i = 0;
    while (i < size && !element.equals(elements[i]))
        i = i+1;
    if (i < size)
        return i;
    else
        return -1;
}

public void add (Element element) {
    assert size < elements.length;
    elements[size] = element;
    size = size+1;
}

public void add (int index, Element element) {
    assert 0 <= index && index <= size;
    assert size < elements.length;
    for (int i = size-1; i >= index; i = i-1)
        elements[i+1] = elements[i];
    elements[index] = element;
    size = size+1;
}
```

```
public void set (int index, Element element) {
    assert 0 <= index && index < size;
    elements[index] = element;
}

public void remove (int index) {
    assert 0 <= index && index < size;
    for (int i = index; i < size-1; i = i+1)
        elements[i] = elements[i+1];
    size = size-1;
}

public BoundedList<Element> copy () {
    BoundedList<Element> theCopy =
        new BoundedList<Element>(this.elements.length);
    theCopy.size = this.size;
    for (int i = 0; i < this.size; i = i+1)
        theCopy.elements[i] = this.elements[i];
    return theCopy;
}
```

Since the time required to access an array element is not dependent on either the element's index or the length of the array, the methods get(**int**), add(Element), and set(**int**,Element) are called *constant time* operations: the time required for their execution is constant, regardless of the size of the list or the length of the array.

On the other hand, the methods add(**int**,Element) and remove(**int**) must shuffle a portion of the array down or up. For instance, to insert a new element at position index in the list, the index-ed through last elements of the list must each be moved down one place in the array. If the list contains six elements, for example, and a new element is to be inserted at index position 2, then the last four elements in the array must be moved down to make room for the new element:

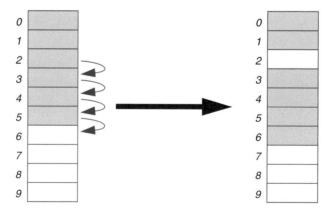

Elements must be moved starting with the last, or else some will be overwritten. If we wrote

```
for (int i = index; i < size; i = i+1)
    elements[i+1] = elements[i];
```

the result would be as shown in Figure 13.3, again assuming size is 6 and index is 2:

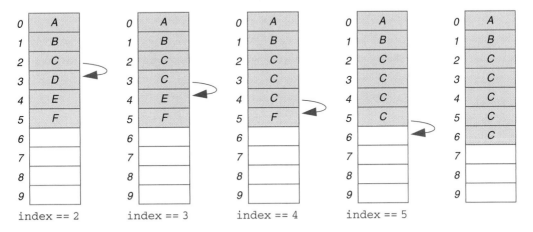

Figure 13.3 **Elements overwritten by an incorrect algorithm.**

On average, we expect to shuffle half the list elements when executing add(**int**, Element) or remove(**int**). If the list has n elements, we expect to execute about $n/2$ iterations of the loop. Thus the (average) time required to execute these methods is proportional to the size of the list. We say that these operations are *linear time* operations.

Also note that there is no need to set array components to null when elements are deleted with remove. Array components indexed from size through elements.length are considered invalid. It does not matter what values they contain.

The methods isEmpty, contains, remove(Element), and toString can be defined in terms of the above methods exactly as we did in Chapter 12.

13.3.1 Copies and clones

When a list is a component of an object, it is generally not desirable to allow clients to access the list. Suppose a class modeling a university course contains a list of enrolled students,

```
public class Course {
    private BoundedList<Student> students;
        ...
}
```

and a method providing clients the list:

```
public BoundedList<Student> roll () {
    return this.students;
}
```

The *variable* students is private and cannot be modified by a client, but the *list* can be manipulated in an arbitrary manner. For instance, if course is a *Course*, a client can contain the following:

```
course.roll().remove(0);
```

This is clearly not satisfactory. A much better solution is to provide a client with a copy of the list

```
public BoundedList<Student> roll () {
    return this.students.copy();
}
```

Now a client can't modify the *Course*'s list, but can still modify the list elements. For example,

```
course.roll().get(0).setAddress(newAddress);
```

will change the address of the first *Student* on the list. The reason is that when we copied the list, we did not also make copies of the list elements. The same *Student* objects are elements of both lists. This is acceptable. Since a *Student* object uniquely represents an actual student, we should not copy it. If there were several instances all representing the same student, maintaining consistency would be a nightmare.

The copy of the list produced by the method copy is referred to as a *shallow copy*. The list object is copied, but the elements on the list are not. The original list and the copy reference the same list elements. A shallow copy of the list of Figure 13.2 is illustrated in Figure 13.4.

When we implement a method to produce a copy of an object, we must decide how deep or how shallow the copy will be. The shallowest copy we can make copies instance variable *values* from the original object to the copy. A method to make a very shallow copy of a *BoundedList* would look like this:

```
public BoundedList<Element> veryShallowCopy () {
    BoundedList<Element> theCopy =
        new BoundedList<Element>(this.elements.length);
    theCopy.size = this.size;
    theCopy.elements = this.elements;
    return theCopy;
}
```

The copy produced by this method is shown in Figure 13.5. This is not a useful object, as the two lists share internal structure. Modifying one list will change the structure, leaving the other inconsistent. Adding or deleting an element, for instance, will change the size attribute of one list object but not the other.

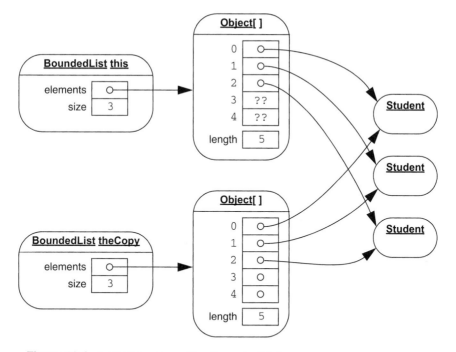

Figure 13.4 **A shallow copy of a *BoundedList*.**

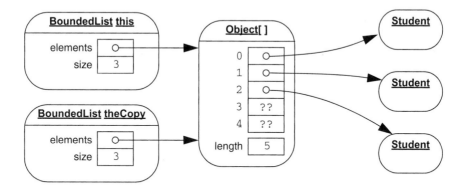

Figure 13.5 **A very shallow copy of a *BoundedList*.**

If we make copies of component objects, rather than simply copying values, the copy is *deep*. A method to make a deep copy of a *BoundedList* would look like this:

```
public BoundedList<Element> deeperCopy () {
    BoundedList<Element> theCopy =
        new BoundedList<Element>(this.elements.length);
    theCopy.size = this.size;
```

```
           for (int i = 0; i < this.size; i = i+1)
               theCopy.elements[i] =
                   ((Element)this.elements[i]).copy();
           return theCopy;
       }
```

Of course, for this to make sense we would have to insist that the class *Element* supports a method copy. The *Element* method copy could itself be either shallow or deep. A deep copy of the list of Figure 13.2 is illustrated in Figure 13.6

Java interface Cloneable

The class *Object* defines a method clone specified as

```
       protected Object clone ()
           throws CloneNotSupportedException
               Create a copy of this Object.
```

The clause "**throws** CloneNotSupportedException" means that the method may fail during execution, as we shall see below. (Note: failure and exceptions are treated in detail in Chapter 15.)

As defined in *Object*, clone produces a very shallow copy of the *Object*, that is, a copy in which instance variable values are simply copied as illustrated in Figure 13.5

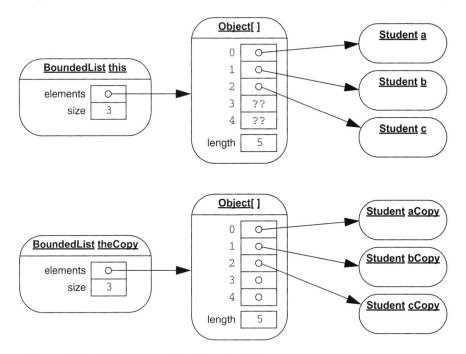

Figure 13.6 **A deep copy of a *BoundedList*.**

above. The method can be overridden if necessary to produce whatever kind of copy you want.

The intention is that the clone of an object is distinct from the object, equal to the object, and of the same run-time class of the object. That is, if `obj` is an object and `someType` a type, the following should all hold:

```
obj != obj.clone()
obj.equals(obj.clone())
obj instanceof someType if and only if
    obj.clone() instanceof someType
```

Since `clone` returns an *Object*, it is often necessary to cast the result:

```
Date date1 = new Date(...);
Date date2 = (Date)date1.clone();
```

The standard package `java.lang` defines an interface *Cloneable*, which specifies *no methods*:

```
public interface Cloneable { };
```

This interface should be implemented by any class that supports (or overrides) the method `clone`. The method `clone` as defined in the class *Object* first checks to see if the object executing the method is an instance of a class that implements *Cloneable*. If it does, a shallow copy of the object is produced. If it does not, the method fails with a *CloneNotSupportedException*. We say that a *CloneNotSupportedException* "has been thrown." As with an *ArrayIndexOutOfBoundsException* mentioned above, this failure generally causes the program to terminate with an appropriate error message.

For instance, suppose class *AClass* doesn't override the method `clone` it inherits from *Object*. If an *AClass* instance executes `clone`

```
AClass a = new AClass();
AClass b = a.clone();
```

the method `clone` first checks to see if the class of a, *AClass*, implements the interface *Cloneable*. If it doesn't, the invocation fails with a *CloneNotSupportedException*. Otherwise, a new instance of class *AClass* is created, and its instance variables are initialized with the values of the variables a. That is, `clone` works essentially as follows:

```
if (this instanceof Cloneable) {
    Object copy = new instance of this class;
    for each instance variable v of this
        copy.v = this.v;
    return copy;
else
    throw CloneNotSupportedException;
```

The statement "**throw** CloneNotSupportedException;" causes the method to fail.

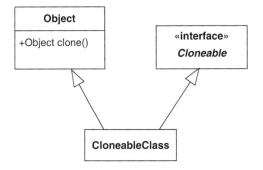

Figure 13.7 **Implementing a cloneable class in Java.**

Cloneable is a rather unusual interface. Implementing the interface does not require a class to implement any methods. Rather, it specifies that the class wants to "inherit" the method `clone` implemented in the class *Object*. Implementing the interface "turns on" the method inherited from *Object*. Ideally, the method `clone` would be defined and implemented in a class other than *Object*. Then a class that wanted this functionality would simply extend this class. But this is not practical in Java, since a class is limited to a single parent class.

(While this approach for providing "optional" functionality can be regarded as something of a general technique, its use leads to classes that are not particularly cohesive and structures that can become ungainly. We recommend not using it when defining your own classes.)

Should the class *BoundedList* implement *Cloneable*, and should we override the method `clone` rather than defining `copy`? We choose not to, because we don't want the copy of a *BoundedList* to be equal to the original list, as defined by the method `equals`. That is, we want

        `!list.equals(list.copy())`

The reason is simply to conform to the guideline that `equals` should not be overridden in a mutable class. (See Section 12.8.1.)

(We should note that the opposite design decision is made for the interface *List* defined in the package `java.util`. For this interface, two *Lists* are equal if they have the same size and if their corresponding elements are equal. We prefer to define another method, if necessary, to describe this equivalence. We'll have more to say about *java.util.List* in Section 21.4.)

DrJava: copies

Open the files `Composite.java` and `Component.java`, located in folder `copy`, in `ch13`, in `nhText`. Look at the definition of *Composite*, and note the difference in the two copy methods.

1.   Create a Composite, and two copies.

```
> import ch13.copy.*;
> Composite c1 = new Composite(3);
> Composite c2 = c1.shallowCopy();
> Composite c3 = c1.deepCopy();
```

2. Verify the nature of the copies.

```
> c1 == c2
> c1 == c3
> c1.getComponent() == c2.getComponent()
> c1.getComponent() == c3.getComponent()
> c1.getComponent().setValue(5);
> c2.getComponent().getValue()
> c3.getComponent().getValue()
```

3. Verify the kind of copy the inherited method clone creates. (Why is the cast necessary?)

```
> Composite c4 = (Composite)c1.clone();
> c1 == c4
> c1.getComponent() == c4.getComponent()
```

4. Remove the "implements Cloneable" clause from the class *Composite*, recompile, and save.

5. What happens now when you attempt to clone a *Composite*?

```
> import ch13.copy.*;
> Composite c1 = new Composite(3);
> Composite c2 = (Composite)c1.clone();
```

13.3.2 Advantages and limitations of an array implementation

The principal advantage of an array implementation is that elements of the list can be accessed efficiently, in constant time independent of the length of the list. As we mentioned above, the methods get(**int**), add(Element), and set(**int**,Element) all operate in constant time.

The limitations are also fairly obvious. The client must have a good idea of the ultimate size of a list when the list is created. Choosing a size that is too large will waste space; choosing a size too small will cause the program to fail.

Additionally, the operations remove(**int**) and add(**int**,Element) are linear. That is, the number of steps required increases in proportion to the size of the list. On average, half the list needs to be shifted up or down to add or remove an arbitrary element. (Note, though, that remove deletes the last element of the list in constant time, independent of the list length.) The method indexOf is also linear.

From these observations, it seems that an array-based implementation might not be a good choice for a very dynamic list—where elements are constantly being added and removed—but would be a good choice for a static list where the most common operation is accessing arbitrary elements by index.

13.4   Dynamic arrays

The interface *List<Element>*, as originally specified, sets no limit to the number of elements that can be added to an instance. There are no preconditions for the add methods preventing a client from adding an element to a full *List*. An instance of the class *BoundedList<Element>*, on the other hand, has a fixed maximum size, determined when the instance is created. We can distinguish between implementations with a maximum size, which we call *bounded*, and those with no upper bound, which we call *dynamic*.

A fairly obvious solution to the fixed size limitation is to create a larger array when necessary. That is, every time an item is added to the list, the method checks to see if there is room in the array. If not, a larger array is created, and the contents of the original one are copied into the new one. For example

```
private void makeRoom () {
    if (this.size == elements.length) {
        // need a bigger array, so
        // make one twice as big
        Object[] newArray =
            new Object[2*elements.length];
        // copy contents of old array to new
        for (int i = 0; i < elements.length; i = i+1)
            newArray[i] = elements[i];
        // replace old array with new
        elements = newArray;
    }
}

public void add (Element element) {
    makeRoom();
    elements[size] = element;
    size = size+1;
}
```

The disadvantage is that the add operation can now become expensive. But this array replacement operation shouldn't happen too often: in practice, we can't double a list that many times. Also as we have sketched the approach, we never replace a larger array with a smaller one, even if the list shrinks.

This is exactly the way that the class *java.util.Vector<Element>* works. (You should recall that we used this class to build *DefaultList<Element>* in Section 12.9.2.) An instance of the class *Vector* contains an *Object* array. If an element is added to the *Vector* and there is no more room in the array, the array is automatically replaced with a larger one.

The class includes three constructors:

```
public Vector ();
public Vector (int initialCapacity);
```

```
public Vector (int initialCapacity,
      int capacityIncrement);
```

The argument `initialCapacity` specifies the initial size of the array; `capacityIncrement` specifies how much larger to make the array when it needs to grow. For instance

```
new Vector<Integer>(100,20)
```

creates a *Vector<Integer>* instance containing a 100 element array. One hundred elements can be added to the *Vector*; but if a 101st element is added, the array is automatically replaced with one that is 120 elements in length.

A `capacityIncrement` of 0 means that the array should be doubled in size when it needs to grow larger. The default `initialCapacity` is 10; while default `capacityIncrement` is 0.

The class *Vector* has all of the functionality and most of the methods that we defined for lists. As we saw in Section 7.4.1, a class that provides required functionality but lacks the desired interface can be easily tailored to fit our needs by wrapping the class in a wrapper or adaptor class. That is, we define a new class that contains an instance of the original as a component. The new class has the desired specification, and simply delegates its responsibilities to the instance of the original class.

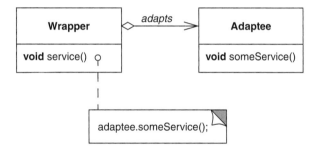

Figure 13.8 **A wrapper adapts an existing class to required specifications.**

The implementation of *DefaultList* has been given in Listing 12.4. We repeat it in Listing 13.1.

Note that the number of steps required to execute the methods is the same as with *BoundedList*. For instance, the method `remove` might appear to be constant at first glance. But the method calls `removeElement` from the class *Vector*, which is linear: it is essentially the same as *BoundedList* `remove`.

Listing 13.1   **The class *DefaultList\<Element>***

```
package nhUtilities.containers;

public class DefaultList<Element>
         extends AbstractList<Element> {

   private java.util.Vector<Element> elements;

   public DefaultList () {
      this.elements = new java.util.vector<Element>();
   }

   public int size () {
      return this.elements.size();
   }

   public Element get (int index) {
      return this.elements.get(index);
   }

   public void add (int index, Element element) {
      this.elements.add(index,element);
   }

   public void remove (int index) {
      this.elements.removeElementAt(index);
   }

   public void set (int index, Element element) {
      this.elements.setElementAt(element,index);
   }

   public DefaultList<Element> copy () {
      DefaultList<Element> copy =
         new DefaultList<Element>();
      int i = 0;
      while (i < this.size()) {
         copy.add(this.get(i));
         i = i+1;
      }
      return copy;
   }
}
```

13.5   Summary

In this chapter, we examined Java's array classes. An array is a primitive structure that consists of a contiguous sequence of variables, all of the same type. The component variables of an array can be of a primitive type or of a reference type. Since the components of an array are allocated in contiguous memory, access to an element requires only constant time, independent of the size of the array. An array constructor requires an integer argument specifying the size of the array. The size is fixed once the array is created.

We then used *Object* arrays to implement a variation of the interface *List<Element>*. The array is used to store the elements of the list. Since the maximum size of the list must be specified when the list is created, we named the class *BoundedList<Element>*. We noted that with an array-based implementation, methods such as `get(int)`, `set(int, Element)`, and `add(Element)` require constant time to execute, independent of the size of the list or length of the array. Methods `add(int, Element)` and `remove(int)`, however, are linear. The number of steps required, on average, increases in proportion to the size of the list.

We looked at several variations of what a `copy` method might be. A shallow copy copies instance variable values from the original object to the copy. If an object references another component object by means of an instance variable, both the object and its copy will reference the same component object. A deep copy, on the other hand, copies the component objects rather than just reference values. How shallow or deep a copy should be depends on the object being copied.

We considered the *Object* method `clone` and how a class "turns on" the cloning facility by implementing the interface *Cloneable*. The method `clone` should produce a different object that is equal to, and of the same class as, the cloned object.

Next, we considered a straightforward approach to solve the fixed size limitation of *BoundedList<Element>*. The idea is simply to create a new, larger array to hold list elements when the existing array is filled. The Java class *java.util.Vector<Element>* that we used to build *DefaultList<Element>* takes this approach. Elements are stored in an array. When an element is added to the *Vector* and there is no room in the array, a new, larger array is created. Elements are copied from the old array to the new.

SELF-STUDY EXERCISES

13.1   How many objects are created by each of the following:

   a.   `Object[] array;`

   b.   `array = new Object[100];`

13.2   Given that the method parameter `vector` is an **int** array,

            public void m (**int**[] vector) { ...

What is the index of the last element in the array?

Write statements that will assign 1 to the first and last elements of the array.

13.3   Write statements that will swap the first and last elements of vector, where vector is as in the previous exercise.

13.4   The following "clever" code is intended to swap the *i*-th and *j*-th elements of the **int** array vector without using a temporary variable.

```
vector[i] = vector[i] - vector[j];
vector[j] = vector[i] + vector[j];
vector[i] = vector[j] - vector[i];
```

Assume that vector is a five element array containing values 1 through 5:

```
[1,2,3,4,5]
```

Trace the statements with i equal to 2 and j equal to 3, and verify that the values are indeed swapped.

13.5   What happens with the statements of the previous exercise if both i and j are 1?

13.6   Write statements that will create 100 *Objects* and assign them as elements of array of Exercise 13.1.

13.7   Note that in the implementation of *BoundedList*, the contents of elements[size] through elements[length-1] are not relevant. Using this information, write a very simple implementation of a *BoundedList* method clear, that removes all elements from the *BoundedList*.

13.8   Look at the method veryShallowCopy on page 556. Suppose this method is used to make a copy of a list:

```
BoundedList<Integer> v = new BoundedList<Integer>(5);
v.add(new Integer(1));
v.add(new Integer(2));
v.add(new Integer(3));
BoundedList<Integer> copy = v.veryShallowCopy();
```

The copy is modified:

```
copy.remove(0);
```

What will copy.size() return? What will v.size() return? What will v.get(0) return? What will v.get(v.size()-1) return?

13.9   Assume that a *Date* is an immutable object with day, month, and year properties. What would you do to make *Date* a cloneable class?

13.10 Write a *BoundedList* method equivalent specified as follows:

public boolean equivalent (BoundedList<Element> other)
The specified *BoundedList* has the same size and capacity as this *BoundedList*, and the corresponding elements of the lists are equal.

EXERCISES

13.1   Write a method that takes an **int** [ ] as argument, and returns the number of negative values in the array.

13.2   Write a method that takes an **int** [ ] as argument, and reverses the values in the array. For instance, if the argument contains 5 elements [1, 3, 7, 9, 4] before the method is executed, then it should contain the values [4, 9, 7, 3, 1] after the method is executed. Do not create a new array.

13.3   Write a method that takes an **int** [ ] as argument, and shifts the values in the array up by one, moving the last value into the 0-*th* position. For instance, if the argument a and has ten elements, the value in a[0] is moved into a[1], the value in a[1] is moved into a[2], *etc*. The value in a[9] is moved into a[0]. Do not create a new array.

13.4   Write a method that takes two **int** [ ] arguments with the same length and computes the inner product assuming that the arrays represent vectors. The inner product of vectors *v1* and *v2* is given by the formula

$$\sum_{i=0}^{m-1} v1[i] \times v2[i]$$

where *m* is the length of the vectors.

13.5   Assume an **int** [ ] is used to store an arbitrarily large non-negative integer by storing each digit of the integer in an element of the array. The low-order digit is stored in the 0-*th* element of the array. For instance, if the integer 1234 were stored in an array a, a[0] would contain 4, a[1] would contain 3, a[2] would contain 2, and a[3] would contain 1.

Write a method that takes two **int** [ ] arguments storing non-negative integers as described above, and produces an **int** [ ] storing their sum.

13.6   Write a method that takes two **int**[] arguments storing non-negative integers as described in the previous exercise, and produces an **int**[] storing their product.

✳   13.7   The class *Matrix* models an integer matrix. Constructor arguments specify the number of rows and columns of the matrix:

        public Matrix (**int** rows, **int** columns)
                Create a matrix with the specified number of rows and columns.
            require:
                rows > 0 && columns > 0

A *Matrix* has an array component whose elements are the rows of the matrix. That is, a component

        private int[][] elements;

where elements[n] is the *n*-th row of the matrix. (Note that elements[n] is an **int**[].)

Implement the constructor, and methods for accessing and setting an arbitrary matrix element.

✳ 13.8 Let A be a matrix with n rows and p columns, and B a matrix with p rows and m columns. Denote the A element in row r column c by $a_{r,c}$, and denote the B elements in row r column c by $b_{r,c}$. Then the product $A \cdot B$ is the matrix with n rows and m columns, whose row r column c entry $p_{r,c}$ is defined as

$$p_{r,c} = \sum_{i=0}^{p-1} a_{r,i} \cdot b_{i,c}$$

Implement a *Matrix* method that takes a *Matrix* instance as argument, and returns the product of the *Matrix* and the argument.

✳ 13.9 Review the chess board of Exercises 12.13 and 9.7. Implement the class *ChessBoard*, where the board is built as an array rather than a list:

private Square[][] board;

13.10 Write an implementation of equals for *BoundedList* that returns true if the two *BoundedLists* have the same capacity, the same size, and their corresponding elements are equal. (Note: since all evidence of type parameters and arguments have been "erased" from the program at run-time, it is not possible to distinguish empty lists of different flavors. For instance, an empty *BoundedList<Integer>* will test equal to an empty *BoundedList<Boolean>* with the same capacity.)

13.11 Write a direct implementation of *DefaultList*, without using *Vector*.

13.12 The class *IntSet* models a set of small, nonnegative integers. A constructor argument specifies the maximum element of the set.

public IntSet (**int** maxElement)
> A subset of the integers 0, …, maxElement.

require:
> maxElement >= 0

An *IntSet* has a **boolean** array component that indicates which numbers are in the set. That is, a component

private boolean[] isIn;

where isIn[n] is *true* means that n is in the set.

Implement the constructor, methods for adding and removing elements, and a method for determining whether an arbitrary nonnegative integer is in the set.

13.13 Implement an *IntSet* method that takes an *IntSet* instance as argument, and returns the set union of the *IntSet* and the argument.

13.14 Implement an *IntSet* method that takes an *IntSet* instance as argument, and returns the set intersection of the *IntSet* and the argument.

13.15 Implement an *IntSet* method that takes an *IntSet* instance as argument, and returns the set difference of the *IntSet* and the argument.

SELF-STUDY EXERCISE SOLUTIONS

13.1 *a.* No objects are created, only a variable.

b. One object, the array object, is created.

13.2 ```
vector.length-1
vector[0] = 1;
vector[vector.length-1] = 1;
```

13.3 ```
int temp = vector[0];
vector[0] = vector[vector.length-1];
vector[vector.length-1] = temp;
```

13.4
After the first statement:	`vector[2] == -1`	`vector[3] == 4`
After the second statement:	`vector[2] == -1`	`vector[3] == 3`
After the third statement:	`vector[2] == 4`	`vector[3] == 3`

13.5 `vector[1]` get set to 0, regardless of its previous value.

13.6 ```
for (int i = 0; i < array.length; i = i+1)
    array[i] = new Object();
```

13.7 ```
public void clear () {
    this.size = 0;
}
```

13.8 `copy.size()` returns 2, while `v.size()` returns 3. `v.get(0)` returns an *Integer* with value 2, and `v.get(v.size()-1)` returns an *Integer* with value 3.

13.9 Have the class *Date* implement the interface *Cloneable*,

```
public class Date implements Cloneable ...
```

and override the method equals so that two *Dates* with the same day, month, and year properties compare as equal.

13.10 ```
public boolean equivalent (BoundedList<Element> other) {
    if (other.eleemtns.length == this.eleemtns.length &&
            other.size == this.size) {
        int i = 0;
        while (i < this.size &&
            this.elements[i].equals(other.elements[i]))
            i = i + 1;
        return i == this.size;
    } else
        return false;
}
```
```

CHAPTER 14

Sorting and searching

We introduced lists in Chapter 12 and saw how to use their basic features. In this chapter, we examine two fundamental list operations: arranging the elements in a specific order, called *sorting*, and determining whether or not a specified element is on a list, called *searching*. Sorting and searching are two of the most commonly performed operations on lists.

A list contains a finite sequence of elements, and we often want these elements arranged in some specific order. We might want to order a list of students alphabetically or by course grade. We might want to order a list of ball players by batting average or by number of home runs. A list in which the elements are maintained in some order is referred to as a *sorted list*. Many methods have been developed for sorting lists. We consider two algorithms in this chapter, called *selection sort* and *bubble sort*. These algorithms are easy to understand but not particularly efficient. In Chapter 19, we'll see a more sophisticated and efficient sorting algorithm known as *quick sort*.

Another common requirement is locating an item on a list. In Chapter 12, we wrote a rather straightforward method indexOf for finding a specified item on a list. The algorithm simply examines each element of the list until the searched for element is located. Here we see a more efficient search algorithm called *binary search*. Binary search requires the list to be sorted.

After developing the binary search, we take a careful look at how *loop invariants* are used to verify the correctness of the algorithm. Recall from the previous chapter that a loop invariant is a condition that remains true as we repeatedly execute the loop body. A key loop invariant captures the fundamental intent of the iteration. Loop invariants are indispensable aids in verifying the correctness of an iteration.

We should note that the primary goal of this chapter is to introduce some standard algorithms and algorithmic techniques. We are not particularly concerned here with class organization and object-oriented design.

Objectives

After studying this chapter you should understand the following:

- orderings and the ordering of list elements;
- the simple sorting algorithms selection sort and bubble sort;
- how to generalize sort methods.
- the binary search algorithm.
- the notion of a loop invariant, and its role in reasoning about methods.

Also, you should be able to:

- trace a selection sort and bubble sort with a specific list of values;
- sort a list by instantiating an ordering and using a predefined sort method;
- trace a binary search with a specific list of values;
- state and verify key loop invariants.

14.1   Ordering lists

If we want to order a list, there must be some ordering on the element class. For instance, the elements of a *List<Student>* are *Student* objects. If we want to order a *List<Student>*, we must have a way of comparing two *Student* objects to determine which should come first. That is, there must be an *ordering* on the class *Student*. While we don't want to be too formal about what we mean by an ordering, we assume the following.

- There is a **boolean** method inOrder defined for the class whose instances we want to order. This method defines the desired ordering.

For example, if we are considering the class *Student*, we need a method

public boolean inOrder (Student first, Student second)

Then if s1 and s2 are *Student* objects, the query

inOrder(s1,s2)

tells us whether or not s1 should precede s2 in the ordering. If inOrder(s1,s2) is true, s1 should come before s2. If inOrder(s1,s2) is false, then s1 need not come before s2. If we were ordering alphabetically by name, inOrder(s1,s2) would be true if s1's name preceded s2's name lexicographically. If we were ordering by decreasing grade, inOrder(s1,s2) would be true is s1's grade was greater than s2's.

We ignore for the moment the question of where this method is defined., and simply assume that it is available.

For notational convenience, we informally abbreviate inOrder(s1,s2) as

s1 < s2

and use

```
s1 >= s2
```

to mean !inOrder(s1,s2). We can read "s1 < s2" as "s1 comes before s2," but we'll often simply say "s1 is less than s2." Realize, though, that the ordering is generally something other than numerical "less than." As we mentioned above, inOrder(s1,s2) might mean s1's grade is higher than s2's grade. Of course, we can't write an expression like s1 < s2 in a program unless s1 and s2 are simple numeric values.

- An ordering is *antisymmetric*. That is, it cannot be the case that both s1 < s2 and s2 < s1. It cannot be the case that both s1 comes before s2, and s2 comes before s1. If inOrder(s1,s2) is true, then inOrder(s2,s1) must be false (This implies that an ordering is also *irreflexive*. That is, inOrder(s,s) is *false* for every s.

- An ordering is *transitive*. That is, if s1 < s2 and s2 < s3 for objects s1, s2, and s3, then s1 < s3. If both inOrder(s1,s2) and inOrder(s2,s3) are true, so is inOrder(s1,s3).

- It is possible that neither inOrder(s1,s2) nor inOrder(s2,s1) is true for objects s1 and s2. In this case, we say s1 and s2 are "equivalent with respect to the ordering." It does not matter which one comes first. For example, if we are ordering by decreasing course grade, inOrder(s1,s2) means s1 has a higher grade than s2. If two *Students* have the same grade, then neither inOrder(s1,s2) nor inOrder(s2,s1) is true. We would consider two students "equivalent" if they had the same grade. If we are ordering students alphabetically, students with identical names would be "equivalent." Notice that we do not insist that two equivalent objects be *equal*.

Given an ordering on the element class, to say that the list is *ordered* means that if s1 and s2 are both on the list, and s1 < s2, then s1 comes before s2 on the list: the index of s1 is less than the index of s2. We state this a little more precisely:

for all indexes i, j:
    inOrder(list.get(i),list.get(j)) implies i < j.

Let's make sure that we understand exactly what this says. list.get(i) and list.get(j) are two arbitrary list elements with indexes i and j respectively. If we are dealing with a *List<Student>*, they are objects of class *Student*. If list.get(i) < list.get(j) in the *Student* ordering, then list.get(i) must come before list.get(j) on the list, that is, i < j.

Equivalently, we could say that for all indexes i and j, if i < j then either list.get(i) < list.get(j) or they are equivalent. That is,

for all indexes i and j, i < j implies
    !inOrder(list.get(j),list.get(i)).

14.2   Two simple sorts

To order a list, we must rearrange the list elements putting them in the proper order. This process is called *sorting*. Sorting is a fundamental and thoroughly studied operation. Many different sorting algorithms have been developed, each with its advantages. We look at two rather straightforward approaches here. These are among the easiest sort algorithms to understand, but are not particularly efficient.

In presenting the algorithms, we illustrate with integers that are to be sorted in increasing order. This simplifies the explanation and allows the algorithms to be introduced without unnecessary distractions.

14.2.1 Selection sort

The first algorithm we look at is called *selection sort*. Intuitively, it works like this. Find the smallest element on the list, and put it in first; find the second smallest and put it second; and so on, until all elements have been placed in their proper position.

If we write this description down a little more carefully, it's easy to see the iteration.

1. Find the smallest of all the list elements.

7	6	4	2	3
(0)	(1)	(2)	(3)	(4)

Interchange it with the first (index 0) element.

2	6	4	7	3
(0)	(1)	(2)	(3)	(4)

2. Find the smallest of the list elements, from the second (index 1) to the end.

2	6	4	7	3
(0)	(1)	(2)	(3)	(4)

Interchange it with the second (index 1) element.

2	3	4	7	6
(0)	(1)	(2)	(3)	(4)

3. Find the smallest of the list elements, from the third to the end.

2	3	4	7	6
(0)	(1)	(2)	(3)	(4)

Interchange it with the third element.

2	3	4	7	6
(0)	(1)	(2)	(3)	(4)

4. Find the smallest of the list elements, from the fourth to the end.

2	3	4	7	6
(0)	(1)	(2)	(3)	(4)

Interchange it with the fourth element.

2	3	4	6	7

(0) (1) (2) (3) (4)

In the first step, we look at elements of the list starting with the index 0. In the second step, we look at elements starting with index 1, *etc*. When the second to last element has been positioned, we are done. The last element is automatically in the right place.

We summarize:

```
int first;      // index of first element to consider
                // on this step
int last;       // index of last element to consider
                // on this step
int small;      // index of smallest of
                // list.get(first)...list.get(last)

last = list.size() - 1;
first = 0;
while (first < last) {
    small = index of smallest of
        list.get(first) through list.get(last)
    interchange list.get(first) and list.get(small)
    first = first+1;
}
```

An informal invariant for this loop is

All the elements with index less than first *are in their proper position.*

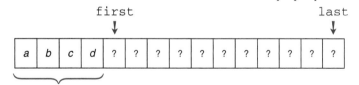

these elements are in their proper positions

As first moves through the list, all the elements "behind" first have been positioned.

To accomplish the step

```
small = index of smallest of
    list.get(first) through list.get(last)
```

we examine each element from (index) first through (index) last, and remember the smallest we see:

```
int next;    // index of next element to examine.
             // small is the index of the smallest of
             // list.get(first)...list.get(next-1).
```

```
        small = first;
        next = first+1;
        while (next <= last) {
            if (inOrder(list.get(next),list.get(small)))
                small = next;
            next = next+1;
        }
```

The invariant for the this loop is

The element with index small *is the smallest with an index greater than or equal to* first, *and less than* next.

small is the index of the smallest of these

The interchange step is also easily accomplished. Assuming list is a *List<Student>*, we write:

```
        Student temp = list.get(first);
        list.set(first, list.get(small));
        list.set(small, temp);
```

Note that we use a variable temp to keep a reference to the element at position first. If we simply wrote

```
        list.set(first, list.get(small));
        list.set(small, list.get(first));
```

we'd lose the reference to this element. For example, suppose first is 0 and small is 3 as illustrated below.

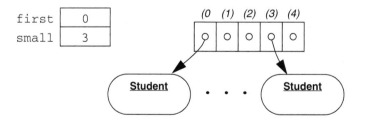

The statement

```
        list.set(first, list.get(small));
```

replaces the element with index first:

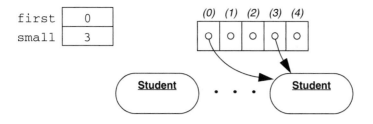

If we do not save a reference to the original first element in `temp`, we loose track of it.

Putting it all together, we make the "find smallest" and "interchange" steps separate methods. This makes the `sort` method a little easier to read. The complete algorithm is given in Listing 14.1. We assume in the code that we are sorting a *List<Student>*, and that the boolean method `inOrder`, defined for *Student* arguments, is available. We'll generalize later.

Listing 14.1 **Selection sort**

```
/**
 * Sort the specified List<Student> using selection sort.
 *     @ensure
 *         for all indexes i, j:
 *             inOrder(list.get(i),list.get(j)) implies i < j.
 */
public void sort (List<Student> list) {
    int first;      // index of first element to consider
                    // on this step
    int last;       // index of last element to consider
                    // on this step
    int small;      // index of smallest of
                    // list.get(first)...list.get(last)
    last = list.size() - 1;
    first = 0;
    while (first < last) {
        small = smallestOf(list, first, last);
        interchange(list, first, small);
        first = first+1;
    }
}
```

continued

Listing 14.1   Selection sort (cont'd)

```java
/**
 * Index of the smallest of
 * list.get(first) through list.get(last)
 *     @require   0 <= first && first <= last &&
 *         last < list.size()
 *     @ensure
 *         for all i: first <= i && i <= last implies
 *             !inOrder(list.get(i),list.get(result))
 */
private int smallestOf (List<Student> list,
    int first, int last) {
    int next;       // index of next element to examine.
    int small;      // index of the smallest of
                    // get(first)...get(next-1)
    small = first;
    next = first+1;
    while (next <= last) {
        if (inOrder(list.get(next), list.get(small)))
            small = next;
        next = next+1;
    }
    return small;
}


/**
 * Interchange list.get(i) and list.get(j)
 *     @require   0 <= i < list.size() && 0 <= j < list.size()
 *     @ensure
 *         list.old.get(i).equals(list.get(j))
 *         list.old.get(j).equals(list.get(i))
 */
private void interchange (List<Student> list,
    int i, int j) {
    Student temp = list.get(i);
    list.set(i, list.get(j));
    list.set(j, temp);
}
```

✳ 14.2.2 Analysis of selection sort

We've mentioned that the above algorithm is not particularly efficient. In this section, we try to get a general idea of how many steps are required to sort a list.

If we look carefully, we see that the algorithm consists of two **while** loops, one inside the other:

```
last = list.size() - 1;
first = 0;
while (first < last) {
    ...
    next = first+1;
    while (next <= last) {
        if ...
        next = next+1;
    }
    ...
    first = first+1;
}
```

The statements that get executed most often are the **if** and the assignment to next inside the inner loop. Can we determine how many times these statements get performed?

Let's assume there are n elements on the list. That is, list.size() equals n. The body of the outer loop is performed $n - 1$ times, with first successively taking on the values 0, 1, 2, ..., $n - 2$.

For each iteration of the outer loop, the inner loop body is done with next taking on the values first + 1, first + 2, ..., $n - 1$. That is, the body of the inner loop is done $n -$ first times. We summarize:

value of first	0	1	2	...	$n-3$	$n-2$
values of next	1, 2, ..., $n-1$	2, 3, ..., $n-1$	3, 4, ..., $n-1$	...	$n-2, n-1$	$n-1$
number of inner loop iterations	$n-1$	$n-2$	$n-3$	...	2	1

So to determine how many times the body of the inner loop is executed, we must sum:

$$(n-1)+(n-2)+...+2+1$$

This sum is well known, and evaluates to $(n^2 - n) / 2$. Thus the number of statements executed by the algorithm, and hence the time required for the algorithm to execute, increases roughly as the square of the length of the list. We say the algorithm is of "order n^2" or *quadratic*. This is fine for small lists, but might become a problem for lists with upwards of 1,000,000 elements.

n	$\dfrac{n^2 - n}{2}$
10	45
100	4,950
1,000	499,500
10,000	49,995,000
100,000	4,999,950,000
1,000,000	499,999,500,000

To get a bit of perspective, if a step takes one second to perform, it will take about 17,000 years to perform 499,999,500,000 steps. If a million steps can be done in a second, it still takes almost 6 days to perform 499,999,500,000 steps.

14.2.3 Bubble sort

In this section, we consider another simple sorting method called *bubble sort*. The method works as follows. Make a pass through the list comparing pairs of adjacent elements. If the pair is not properly ordered, interchange them. At the end of the pass, the last element will be in its proper place. Continue making passes through the list until all the elements are in place. We illustrate, again using a list of integers to be sorted in increasing order.

Pass 1

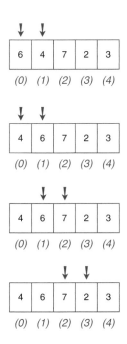

1. Compare first and second elements.

Since they are out of order (the second is less than the first), interchange them.

2. Compare second and third elements. Since they are in order, do nothing.

3. Compare third and fourth elements.

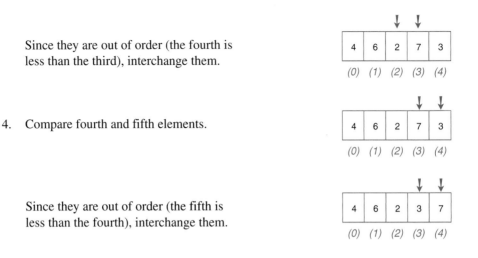

Since they are out of order (the fourth is less than the third), interchange them.

4. Compare fourth and fifth elements.

Since they are out of order (the fifth is less than the fourth), interchange them.

Notice that at the end of this pass, the last element is in place. (The algorithm is called the "bubble sort" because the largest element bubbles to the end of the list.)

The process is now repeated, "bubbling" the second largest element into place:

Pass 2

1. Compare first and second elements.

2. Compare second and third elements; interchange.

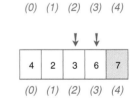

3. Compare third and fourth elements; interchange.

Two more passes are guaranteed to leave the list sorted.

Pass 3

1.   Compare first and second elements; interchange.

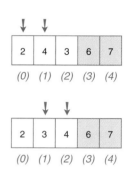

2.   Compare second and third elements; interchange.

Pass 4

1.   Compare first and second elements.

The algorithm is given in Listing 14.2. A little analysis will show that this algorithm takes essentially the same number of steps as the selection sort. That is, the inner loop body is performed $(n^2 - n) / 2$ times for a list of n elements.

We can improve the algorithm a bit with the following observation. If we make a pass through the list without interchanging any elements at all, then the list is ordered. If the list is ordered or nearly ordered to start with, we can complete the sort in fewer than $n - 1$ passes. For instance, if the list is ordered, we can determine this fact in one pass. If only one element is out of order, one pass sorts the list and a second pass tells us we are done. Thus if we expect to use the algorithm on "mostly ordered" lists, it pays to keep track of whether or not any elements have been interchanged. We modify the methods in a rather straightforward way to handle this. The modified algorithm is given in Listing 14.3.

Note that we have modified the method `makePassTo` so that it reports whether or not any items were swapped. It now behaves like both a command and a query. This is generally not a good idea. We like to keep commands and queries distinct, and in particular, a query should never change an object's state. But as this method just serves as a utility function for the sort and is not intended to define an object feature, we are not too concerned with this variance from standard practice.

Listing 14.2   **Bubble sort**

===

```
/**
 * Sort specified List<Student> using bubble sort.
 *     @ensure
 *        for all indexes i, j:
 *            inOrder(list.get(i),list.get(j)) implies i < j.
 */
public void sort (List<Student> list) {
    int last;        // index of last element to position
                     // on this pass

    last = list.size() - 1;
    while (last > 0) {
        makePassTo(list, last);
        last = last-1;
    }
}


/*
 * Make a pass through the list, bubbling an element to
 * position last.
 *     @require   0 < last && last < list.size()
 *     @ensure
 *        for all i: 0 <= i && i < last implies
 *            !inOrder(list.get(last),list.get(i))
 */
private void makePassTo (List<Student> list, int last) {
    int next;        // index of next pair to examine.
    next = 0;
    while (next < last) {
        if (inOrder(list.get(next+1),list.get(next)))
            interchange(list, next, next+1);
        next = next+1;
    }
}
```

===

Listing 14.3   **Bubble sort, modified**

```
/**
 * Sort specified List<Student> using bubble sort.
 */
public void sort (List<Student> list) {
    int last;      // index of last element to position
                   // on this pass
    boolean done;  // pass made with no interchanges

    last = list.size() - 1;
    done = false;
    while (!done && last > 0) {
        done = makePassTo(list, last);
        last = last-1;
    }
}

/*
 * Make a pass through list, bubbling an element to position
 * last, and report if anything needed to be changed.
 *     @require    0 < last < list.size()
 *     @ensure
 *         for all i: 0 <= i && i < last implies
 *             !inOrder(list.get(last),list.get(i))
 *         result == true iff
 *             for all i, j: 0 <= i <= last && 0 <= j <= last,
 *                 inOrder(list.get(i),list.get(j))
 *                 implies i < j.
 */
private boolean makePassTo (List<Student> list, int last) {
    int next;      // index of next pair to examine.
    boolean noItemsSwapped;
                        // no out of order items found
    next = 0;
    noItemsSwapped = true;
    while (next < last) {
        if (inOrder(list.get(next+1),list.get(next))) {
            interchange(list, next, next+1);
            noItemsSwapped = false;
        }
        next = next+1;
    }
    return noItemsSwapped;
}
```

14.2.4 Generalizing the sort methods

Before we take up searching, let's find a home for our sort methods. If we look back over the methods we have written, two things are clear.

- It does not matter what the method `inOrder` is, as long as it satisfies the requirements detailed in Section 14.1.

- It does not matter that we are sorting a *List<Student>*. We could replace *Student* with any object type, and the algorithms would be correct.

Clearly we do not want to write a separate sort method for each kind of list we might want to sort. We must make use of the fact that we have defined *List* to be a generic structure, that is, to have type *List<Element>*.

There are several ways in which we could proceed. We sketch two approaches.

Generic methods

We noted in the previous chapter that methods can be generic. We can define a method with type parameters, just as we can define a class or interface with type parameters. Syntactically, type parameters are enclosed in angles and appear before the return type in the method heading. For example, in the method definition

```
public <Element> void swap (List<Element> list,
    int i, int j) {
    Element temp = list.get(i);
    list.set(i,list.get(j));
    list.set(j,temp);
}
```

`Element` is a type parameter. When the method is invoked, the first argument will be a *List* of some type of element, and the local variable `temp` will be of that type.

No special syntax is required to invoke a generic method. When the method is invoked, the type to be used for the type parameter is inferred from the arguments. For example, if `roll` is a *List<Student>*,

```
List<Student> roll = ...
```

and the method `swap` is invoked as

```
swap(roll,0,1);
```

the association of the type *Student* with the type parameter `Element` is inferred from the type of the argument `roll`. The local variable `temp` created during the execution of the method will be of type *Student*.

Sorts as generic methods

One approach is to consider the sort methods as "utility algorithms," not really associated with a class, much like the mathematical function `sqrt`. We can make them static, and collect them in some utility class:

```
public class Sorts {

    public static void selectionSort ...

    public static void bubbleSort ...
        ...
}
```

This is not quite right. We want the methods to be generic, so we can use them to sort any kind of list:

```
public class Sorts {

    public static <Element> void selectionSort (
        List<Element> list) ...

    public static <Element> void bubbleSort (
        List<Element> list) ...
        ...
}
```

Now we've got to think about the method inOrder. We want to provide the sort method with the order to use when comparing list elements. We can furnish it as an argument if its an object. Thus we wrap up the method inOrder in an object so that we can pass it as an argument to the sort.

Specifically, we define an interface

```
/**
 * An ordering on the class Element.
 * The ordering is transitive, and antisymmetric
 */
public interface Order<Element> {

    /**
     * e1 precedes e2 in the ordering.
     * inOrder is antisymmetric:
     *    inOrder(x,y) implies !inOrder(y,x).
     * inOrder is transitive:
     *    inOrder(x,y) && inOrder(y,z) implies
     *    inOrder(x,z).
     */
    boolean inOrder (Element e1, Element e2);

}
```

A concrete order will implement this interface by defining the relation inOrder for some particular class. We are not particularly interested in the individual instances of the concrete order class. We need instances only so that we can pass the ordering as an argument to a sort method. The instances really have no distinguishing "properties" or semantic structure. They simply carry the method inOrder. An *Order* is another example of a *function object*. (See Section 11.3.1.) Its only purpose is to provide the inOrder method.

We define the sort methods to have both a list and an order as arguments. For example,

```
public static <Element> void selectionSort (
    List<Element> list, Order<Element> order)
```

The order also gets passed to auxiliary methods. The selection sort auxiliary method smallestOf will be defined as follows:

```
private static <Element> int smallestOf (
    List<Element> list, int first, int last,
    Order<Element> order) {
    int next;
    int small;
    small = first;
    next = first+1;
    while (next <= last) {
        if (order.inOrder(
            list.get(next),list.get(small)))
            small = next;
        next = next+1;
    }
    return small;
}
```

Let's look at an example. Suppose *Student* objects have a property:

```
public int finalGrade()
```

and we want to order a *List<Student>* by (decreasing) final grade. We can define a class:

```
/**
 * Order Students by decreasing finalGrade
 */
class GradeOrder implements Order<Student> {

    /**
     * s1.finalGrade() > s2.finalGrade()
     */
    public boolean inOrder (Student s1, Student s2) {
        return s1.finalGrade() > s2.finalGrade();
    }
}
```

Note that we don't explicitly define a constructor for the class. Since there are no data to initialize, the default constructor is adequate.

If `roll` is a *List<Student>*, the invocation

```
Sorts.selectionSort(roll, new GradeOrder());
```

will invoke the method with parameters `list` and `order` initialized as shown below. The list will be sorted according to the *Student* property `finalGrade`.

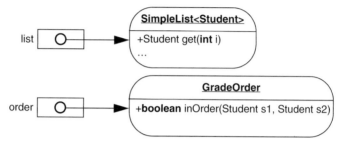

Anonymous classes

A class like *GradeOrder* really has no structural purpose in the design of a system. Its only function is to let us treat the ordering as an object so that we can pass it as a method argument. Java's *anonymous* class mechanism allows simultaneous class definition and instantiation.

In the above example, we needed an instance of a class implementing the interface *Order*. We first defined a class (*GradeOrder*) implementing the interface, and then instantiated the class to obtain the required object. With an anonymous class, we *define* the class and *instantiate* it in one expression. The syntax looks something like a combination of a constructor invocation and a class definition:

```
new InterfaceName () {
    // definitions
}
```

The class being defined has no name, and hence is called an *anonymous class*. An anonymous class is a nested class (see Section 10.5.3), contained in the method in which it is instantiated.

For example, we can create an object like the one used as a `sort` argument above by writing

```
new Order<Student>() {
    boolean inOrder(Student s1, Student s2) {
        return s1.finalGrade() > s2.finalGrade();
    }
}
```

Note that this expression both defines an anonymous class implementing the interface *Order<Student>, and* creates an instance of the class. The result of the expression is a reference to the newly created instance.

Now rather than explicitly defining a class *GradeOrder* and then instantiating it in the call to `selectionSort`, we can write the call like this:

```
Sorts.selectionSort(roll,
    new Order<Student>() {
        boolean inOrder(Student s1, Student s2) {
            return s1.finalGrade() > s2.finalGrade();
        }
    }
);
```

Though the syntax gets a bit cumbersome, it is cleaner than defining and naming a class just so that we can instantiate it once.

An anonymous class can be an extension of an existing abstract or concrete class as well as an implementation of an interface.

Sorts as generic objects

An alternate approach to finding a home for the sort method is to wrap up the sort method in an object just as we did the method `inOrder`. Then we can pass sorts around as arguments to other methods.

We can wrap the sort algorithm and the ordering in the same object. Omitting some of the comments, we define an interface *Sorter* as follows:

```
/**
 * A sorter for a List<Element>.
 */
public interface Sorter<Element> {

    /**
     * e1 precedes e2 in the sort ordering.
     */
    public boolean inOrder (Element e1, Element e2);

    /**
     * Sort the specified List<Element> according to
     * the order this.inOrder.
     */
    public void sort (List<Element> list);

}
```

Now we can provide specific sort algorithms in abstract classes, leaving the ordering abstract. For instance,

```
public abstract class SelectionSorter<Element>
    implements Sorter<Element> {

  /**
   * Sort the specified List<Element> using
   * selection sort.
   */
  public void sort (List<Element> list) {
     ...
  }
  ...
}
```

To create a concrete *Sorter*, we extend the abstract class and furnish the order:

```
class GradeSorter extends SelectionSorter<Student> {
   public boolean inOrder (Student s1, Student s2){
      return s1.finalGrade() > s2.finalGrade();
   }
}
```

Finally, we instantiate the class to get an object that can sort:

```
GradeSorter gradeSorter = new GradeSorter();
gradeSorter.sort(roll);
```

We can also use an anonymous class, avoiding the need for an explicit class and variable definition:

```
SelectionSorter<Student> gradeSorter =
    new SelectionSorter<Student>() {
       public boolean inOrder (Student s1, Student s2){
          return s1.finalGrade() > s2.finalGrade();
       }
    };
gradeSorter.sort(roll);
```

or even

```
(new SelectionSorter<Student>() {
   public boolean inOrder (Student s1, Student s2){
      return s1.finalGrade() > s2.finalGrade();
   }
}).sort(roll);
```

Note that here the anonymous class is defined as an extension of an abstract class, rather than as implementor of an interface.

![icon] *Dr.Java: sorting Lists*

Open the file `SortUtilities.java`, located in the directory `exercise`, in `ch14`, in `nhText`. This file contains the definitions of selection sort and (modified) bubble sort, as generic, static methods. These methods have one addition to the methods given above: they count and report the number of times the inner most loop body is done. This gives us a good measure of the run-time efficiency of the algorithms.

Open the file `Exercise.java` in the same directory. This file contains a handy method for generating lists of *Integers*, and the definition and instantiation of an anonymous *Order<Integer>* implementation.

1. Mimicking the definition `oddEven`, add two new order definitions to the class *Exercise*. One, referenced by the static variable `decreasing`, should implement the greater than relation on integers. The other, referenced by the static variable `increasing`, should implement the less than relation on integer. (It is easier to write these definition in the edit pane than in the *Interactions* pane.)

    Save and compile.

2. In the *Interactions* pane, create a *List<Integer>* of 10 increasing integers.

   ```
   > import ch14.exercise.*;
   > import nhUtilities.containers.*;
   > List<Integer> list = Exercise.generateList(10,1);
   > list
   [1, 2, 3, 4, 5, 6, 7, 8, 9, 10]
   ```

3. Using selection sort, sort the list in increasing order. (It is already in increasing order, so the list should not change.) Recall that if you want to continue a command on another line in the *Interactions* pane, you must press *Shift* while pressing *Enter* or *Return*.

   ```
   > SortUtilities.selectionSort(list,
       Exercise.increasing);
   > list
   ```

4. Using bubble sort, sort the list in increasing order.

   ```
   > SortUtilities.bubbleSort(list,Exercise.increasing);
   > list
   ```

   Note the different number of steps required by selection sort and bubble sort. Do you understand why?

5. Using bubble sort, sort the list in decreasing order and not the number of steps required.

   ```
   > SortUtilities.bubbleSort(list,Exercise.decreasing);
   > list
   ```

6. Look at the order referenced by the static variable `oddEven` in the class *Exercise*. Under what circumstances does an integer x come before an integer y in this order?

7. Create a random list of 20 integers, and sort it using selection sort and the `oddEven` order.

```
> list = Exercise.generateList(20,7);
> list
> SortUtilities.selectionSort(list,Exercise.oddEven);
> list
```

8. Generate the same list, and sort it with bubble sort.

```
> list = Exercise.generateList(20,7);
> list
> SortUtilities.bubbleSort(list,Exercise.oddEven);
> list
```

Are the sorted lists identical? Explain.

✳ 14.3 Ordered lists

While we occasionally sort a list for some singular purpose, it is more typical that we want to maintain the list in a specific order. Moreover, we tend to treat ordered and unordered lists in different ways. For instance, we may add an element to the end of an unordered list but want to put the element in the "right place" when adding to an ordered list. Because we tend to use them differently, we add *OrderedList* to our library as a distinct container:

> **public interface** OrderedList<Element>
>   A finite ordered list.

For the most part, an *OrderedList* will have the same features as a *List*, such as

> **public int** size ()
> **public boolean** isEmpty ()
> **public** Element get (**int** i)
> **public int** indexOf (Element element)
> **public void** remove (**int** i)

The method `add` inserts an element at the proper place rather than at the end of the list, and we don't include the method `set` since it may break the ordering.

> **public void** add (Element element)
>   Add the specified element to the proper place in this *OrderedList*.
>
>   **require:**
>   element != null
>
>   **ensure:**
>   this.size() == old.size()+1
>   for some index i,
>   this.get(i).equals(element)

We've seen how to isolate the notion of an order in an interface. We can use this idea to make the ordering a property of an *OrderedList*, and require that an *Order* be provided when an *OrderedList* is created. The constructor for an implementing class, say *DefaultOrderedList*, will look like this:

public DefaultOrderedList (Order<Element> order)
Create a new *DefaultOrderedList<Element>*, ordered by the specified *Order*.

ensure:
this.isEmpty()

We include a query for the order,

public Order<Element> ordering ()
The *Order* used to order this *OrderedList*.

and methods for populating an *OrderedList* from a *List*, and *vice versa:*

public void populateOrderedList (List<Element> list)
Populate this *OrderedList* from the specified *List*.

ensure:
this.size() == list.size()
for all indexes i,
this.get(i).equals(list.get(j)), for some j

public List<Element> toList ()
Create a new *List* containing the elements of this *OrderedList*.

ensure:
toList.size() == this.size()
for all indexes i,
toList.get(i).equals(this.get(i))

Methods like toList that create new instances are sometimes referred to as *factory methods.*[1]

Note that it is not appropriate to make *OrderedList<Element>* a subclass of *List<Element>*. A *List<Element>* has operations, such as set(**int**, Element) and add(**int**, Element), that an *OrderedList* does not. It may, however, be appropriate for both *List<Element>* and *OrderedList<Element>* to implement a common interface.

Qualified invariant

We can write a class invariant for an *OrderedList* that states that the items are, in fact, ordered:

---

1. We might like to specify a static factory method for creating an *OrderedList*, such as

public static <Element> OrderedList<Element> createOrderedList (
List<Element> list, Order<Element> order)

But Java does not permit static methods in an interface.

> **public interface** OrderedList<Element>
>   A finite ordered list.
>
>   class invariant:
>   for all indexes i, j:
>   ordering().inOrder(get(i),get(j)) implies
>   i < j.

But we must qualify the invariant. The items on the list exist and can be manipulated independently of the list. For instance, if we have a list of *Students* ordered alphabetically by name, the *Student* objects can be accessed directly by clients without using list methods. In particular, it's possible that a client might change the name of one of the *Students* on the list. Changing the name of a *Student* on a list ordered by name can, of course, invalidate the ordering, and the list has no control over this. Thus the list invariant must be qualified. It holds as long as no list item changes state in a way that effects the inOrder relation.

> **public interface** OrderedList<Element>
>   A finite ordered list.
>
>   class invariant:
>   for all indexes i, j:
>   ordering().inOrder(get(i),get(j)) implies
>   i < j.
>   Subject to no list item changing properties which determine the
>   relation ordering().inOrder.

Finally we include a command to make sure the list is properly ordered, and reorder it if necessary:

> **public void** validateOrder ()
>   Validate ordering, reordering if necessary.
>
>   **ensure:**
>   for all indexes i, j:
>   ordering().inOrder(get(i),get(j)) implies
>   i < j.

14.4 Binary search

One of the advantages of an ordered list is that it is easier to find an element in an ordered list than in an unordered one. Imagine, for instance, how much more difficult it would be to find a name in the telephone book or a word in the dictionary if they were not ordered alphabetically.

If we are looking up a word in the dictionary, we open the book more or less randomly and compare the first word on the page to the one we're looking for. If we're looking up the word "manciple" and we open the dictionary to a page that begins with "phlogiston," we immediately eliminate from consideration the pages following the one we're looking at. We know "manciple" comes before "phlogiston." We continue by looking at a page somewhat in the middle of those we have left, and again comparing what we see to what we're looking for.

If we formalize this process, we have a search algorithm called *binary search*.[1] The binary search algorithm looks for an item in an ordered list by first looking at the middle element of the list. Half the list can be eliminated, depending on how the middle element compares to the item searched for. That is, if the item searched for precedes the middle element, forget about the last half of the list. If the middle element precedes the item searched for, forget about the first half of the list. The process is then repeated with the remaining portion of the list.

Again, to simplify the presentation, we use integers ordered by increasing value. Suppose we want to search for the number 42 in the following 15-element list. The list is sorted in increasing numeric order: *x* precedes *y* if *x* is less than *y*. (The number happens not to be on the list, but we don't know that until we look.)

2	5	7	12	15	21	25	28	30	33	40	56	64	72	73
(0)	(1)	(2)	(3)	(4)	(5)	(6)	**(7)**	(8)	(9)	(10)	(11)	(12)	(13)	(14)

First, the middle element, the element at index 7, is compared to 42. Since 28 is less than 42, if 42 is on the list, it must be after 28. Thus the first half of the list need not be further examined:

2	5	7	12	15	21	25	28	30	33	40	56	64	72	73
(0)	(1)	(2)	(3)	(4)	(5)	(6)	(7)	(8)	(9)	(10)	**(11)**	(12)	(13)	(14)

The middle element of what's left is the element at position 11. This element, 56, is now compared to 42. Since 56 is greater than 42, the numbers after it in the list can be eliminated as possibilities.

2	5	7	12	15	21	25	28	30	33	40	56	64	72	73
(0)	(1)	(2)	(3)	(4)	(5)	(6)	(7)	(8)	**(9)**	(10)	(11)	(12)	(13)	(14)

Continuing, we next look at the element at index 9, the middle of what's left. This element, 33, is smaller than 42, so any remaining values below it are no longer considered.

2	5	7	12	15	21	25	28	30	33	40	56	64	72	73
(0)	(1)	(2)	(3)	(4)	(5)	(6)	(7)	(8)	(9)	**(10)**	(11)	(12)	(13)	(14)

---

1. Actually, formalizing a dictionary search is called an "interpolation search." If we were searching for the word "calash," for instance, we wouldn't start in the middle, but well toward the front of the book.

We're now down to one remaining element, at position 10. But this isn't what we're looking for, so we can conclude that 42 is not in the list.

Note that we have determined that 42 is not on the list by looking at only four elements. If the list were not sorted, we would need to look at all fifteen elements to determine that 42 was not on the list.

Let's develop a search method using this algorithm. We'll write a generic method that has the order as a parameter. There are, of course, other possibilities.

As a first step, we write an algorithm that tells us where an item should be if it is on the list. Its specification is as follows:

```
private <Element> int itemIndex (Element item,
    List<Element> list, Order<Element> order)
```
>   The proper place for the specified item on the specified list, found using
>   binary search.

>   **require:**
>   list is sorted according to order.

>   **ensure:**
>   0 <= result && result <= list.size()
>   for all indexes i: i < result implies
>   order.inOrder(list.get(i),item)
>   for all indexes i: i >= result implies
>   !order.inOrder(list.get(i),item)

Note clearly what this method gives us. It gives a list index such that all the elements prior to the index are smaller than the item searched for, and all of the items from the index to the end of the list are not:

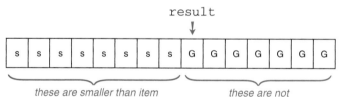

If the item is smaller than all the list elements, the method returns 0. It it is greater than all the list elements, the method returns list.size().

We can implement the method as follows:

```
private <Element> int itemIndex (Element item,
    List<Element> list, Order<Element> order) {

    int low;      // the lowest index being examined
    int high;     // the highest index begin examined

    /*
     * list.get(low)...list.get(high) is the segment
     * of the list still to be considered.
```

```
 *   for all indexes i: i < low implies
 *        order.inOrder(list.get(i),item)
 *   for all indexes i: i > high implies
 *        !order.inOrder(list.get(i),item)
 */

int mid;          // the middle item between low and
                  // high. mid == (low+high)/2

low = 0;
high = list.size() - 1;
while (low <= high) {
    mid = (low+high)/2;
    if (order.inOrder(list.get(mid),item))
        low = mid+1;
    else
        high = mid-1;
}
return low;
}
```

It is worth taking a careful look at this algorithm. The loop invariant, written in the method as a multiline comment, says that elements with indexes less than `low` are "smaller than" `item` with respect to the ordering, and elements with indexes greater than `high` are "greater than or equal to" `item`:

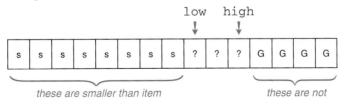

Let's first trace the algorithm with the list we used above. (Again, integers simplify the pictures.) Recall that we are searching for the value 42 in the following list:

2	5	7	12	15	21	25	28	30	33	40	56	64	72	73
(0)	(1)	(2)	(3)	(4)	(5)	(6)	(7)	(8)	(9)	(10)	(11)	(12)	(13)	(14)

When the method is invoked, `item` will be 42. `low` and `high` are initialized to 0 and 14, respectively.

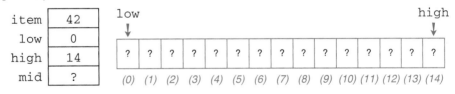

The first iteration of the loop body sets `mid` to 7, compares the element at index 7 with `item`, and adjusts `low`.

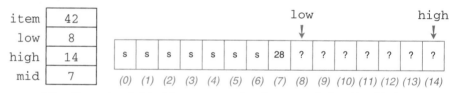

The second iteration sets `mid` to 11, compares the element at index 11 with `item`, and adjusts `high`.

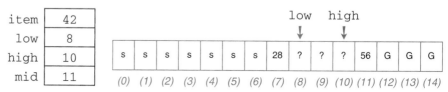

The third iteration compares the element at index 9 with `item` and adjusts `low`.

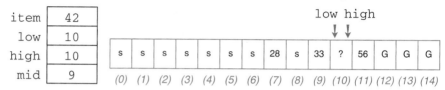

The final iteration examines the element at index 10 and adjusts `low` again.

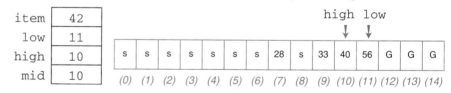

At this point `low > high`, the iteration terminates, and the value of `low` is returned. Note that the method postcondition is satisfied:

> for all indexes i: i < result implies
>   order.inOrder(list.get(i),item)
> for all indexes i: i >= result implies
>   !order.inOrder(list.get(i),item)

Let's do one more trace, this time with an item that is on the list. Suppose the method is invoked with the same list as above, and with `item` equal to 12. Again, `low` and `high` are initialized to 0 and 14, respectively.

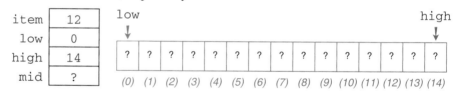

The first iteration of the loop body sets `mid` to 7, compares the element at index 7 with `item`, and adjusts `high`.

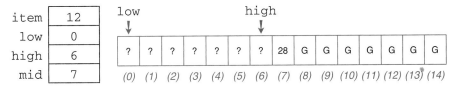

The second iteration sets `mid` to 3, compares the element at index 3 with `item` and, since `order.inOrder(list.get(mid),item)` is false, again adjusts `high`.

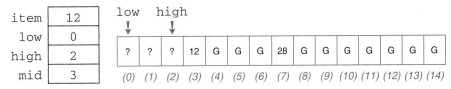

The third iteration compares the element at index 1 with `item` and adjusts `low`.

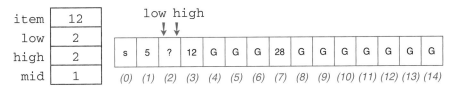

The final iteration examines the element at index 2 and adjusts `low` again.

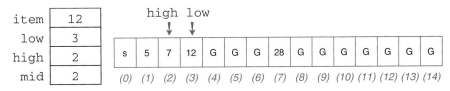

The value returned is 3, which is the index of the element 12 in the list.

In this example, we actually "found" the item we were searching for on the second iteration. So it might occur to us that we should include an explicit check for equality in the loop:

```
while (low <= high) {
    mid = (low+high)/2;
    if (list.get(mid).equals(item)) ...
```

A thorough analysis, however, would show that there is little to be gained from this additional test. The algorithm is made more complex and any "efficiency" achieved is more than offset by additional tests.

14.4.1 Completing the search

The method `itemIndex` gives us the index of the first list element that is not smaller than the item we're searching for. We'd like to write a search method using `itemIndex` as follows:

```
/**
 * The index of the specified item on the specified
 * list, located by binary search. Returns -1 if
 * the item is not on the list.
 *     @require
 *         item != null
 *         the order is total: that is,
 *         for any Elements x and y,
 *             x.equals(y) || order.inOrder(x,y) ||
 *             order.inOrder(y,x)
 *     @ensure
 *         if item equals no element of list then
 *             indexOf(item,list,order) == -1
 *         else
 *             item.equals(
 *                 list.get(indexOf(item,list,order))),
 *             and indexOf(item,list,order) is the
 *             smallest value for which this is true
 */
public <Element> int indexOf (Element item,
    List<Element> list, Order<Element> order) {
    int i = itemIndex(item, list, order);
    if (i < list.size() && list.get(i).equals(item))
        return i;
    else
        return -1;
}
```

This algorithm requires the ordering to be "complete" with respect to equality. That is, the order always specifies which of two unequal elements must come first. For instance, suppose `list` is a *List<Student>* ordered by social security number: `order.inOrder(s1,s2)` means s1's social security number is less than s2's. The method invocation `itemIndex(s,list,ssnOrder)` will give us the index of the first *Student* on the list whose social security number is greater than or equal to s's. Since no two *Students* have the same social security number, if s is on the list, it must be at the position returned by `itemIndex`. However, if the list is ordered by final grade, `itemIndex(s,list,gradeOrder)` will give us the index of the first *Student* on the list whose final grade is greater than or equal to s's. It is possible that s is on the list, but other *Students* with the same final grade come before s on the list. We cannot determine if s is on the list simply by looking at the element at `itemIndex(s,list,gradeOrder)`. We must search the list, starting at this position, until we either find s or we find a *Student* with a larger grade.

In finding a home for the binary search, we have choices similar to those for the sort methods. (Note that binary search would be an appropriate implementation of the `indexOf` method in an *OrderedList*.)

14.4.2 Sequential search and binary search

In Chapter 12, we wrote a search method that simply looked at each list element in order.

```
public int indexOf (Element element) {

    int i = 0;  // index of the next element to examine
    while (i < this.size() &&
            !this.get(i).equals(element))
        i = i+1;

    if (i < this.size())
        return i;
    else
        return -1;
}
```

This approach is called *sequential search* or *linear search*. How much better than linear search is binary search? If the list has *n* elements, and the element we are looking for is not on the list, the linear search algorithm requires *n* steps: we need to examine each of the *n* elements. If the element we are looking for is on the list, we expect to take about *n*/2 steps to find it.

Binary search, on the other hand, is guaranteed to work in $\log_2 n$ steps. If a list contains 1000 elements, binary search will locate an element in 10 steps ($2^{10} = 1024$). If a list contains 1,000,000 elements, binary search still requires only 20 steps ($2^{20} = 1024 \times 1024 \approx 1{,}000{,}000$).

The price we pay, of course, is that the list must first be sorted in order to use binary search.

Number of steps required by the algorithm with a list of length n grows in proportion to

- n^2 for *Selection sort*;
- n^2 for *Bubble sort*;
- n for *Linear search*;
- $\log_2 n$ for *Binary search*.

Figure 14.1 Relative efficiency (complexity) of search and sort algorithms.

DrJava: searching Lists

Open the file `SearchUtilities.java`, in directory `exercise`, in `ch14`, in `nhText`. This file contains the definitions of linear search and binary search, as generic, static methods. As with the sort methods, these methods count and report the number of steps required to complete the search.

1. In the *Interactions* pane, create a *List<Integer>* of 100 random integers.

   ```
   > import ch14.exercise.*;
   > import nhUtilities.containers.*;
   > List<Integer> list = Exercise.generateList(100,7);
   > list
   ```

2. Sort the list in increasing order.

   ```
   > SortUtilities.bubbleSort(list,Exercise.increasing)
   ```

3. Search the list for an element not on the list using linear search, and note the number of steps.

   ```
   > SearchUtilities.linearSearch(new Integer(17),list)
   ```

4. Search the list for the same element using binary search and note the number of steps.

   ```
   > SearchUtilities.binarySearch(new Integer(17),list,
       Exercise.increasing)
   ```

✳ 14.5   Verifying correctness: using a loop invariant

The iteration in the method `itemIndex` of the previous section is one of the first we've encountered that requires more than a casual analysis. In particular, we don't have an index stepping sequentially through the list elements as in most other cases we've seen. We'll use this as an example to illustrate how to verify the correctness of a loop, and to revisit a bit more carefully the important idea of a loop invariant.

We repeat the method with numbered lines for easy reference:

```
1.   private <Element> int itemIndex (Element item,
         List<Element> list, Order<Element> order) {
2.       low = 0;
3.       high = list.size() - 1;
4.       while (low <= high) {
5.           mid = (low+high)/2;
6.           if (order.inOrder(list.get(mid),item))
7.               low = mid+1;
8.           else
9.               high = mid-1;
10.      }
11.      return low;
12.  }
```

The purpose of the method is to find the index of the first list element (*i.e.*, the list element with lowest index) that is greater than or equal to a specified item. Specifically, the method postcondition states

> for all indexes i: i < result implies
>   order.inOrder(list.get(i),item)
> for all indexes i: i >= result implies
>   !order.inOrder(list.get(i),item)

Since the method returns the value of the variable low, we want low to satisfy this condition when the loop terminates

> for all indexes i: i < low implies
>   order.inOrder(list.get(i),item)
> for all indexes i: i >= low implies
>   !order.inOrder(list.get(i),item)

Verifying the correctness of the loop, and hence of the method, involves two steps. First we show that *if* the loop terminates, low will satisfy the above condition. This is termed *partial correctness*. That is, demonstrating partial correctness involves demonstrating that the loop is correct *assuming it terminates*. To complete the verification, we demonstrate that the loop will terminate in all cases.

---

partial correctness: the assertion that a loop is correct *if it terminates*.

total correctness: the assertion that a loop is both partially correct, and terminates.

To verify partial correctness, we first find a key *loop invariant*. As we've seen, a loop invariant is a condition that is true before and after each iteration of a loop, as illustrated in Figure 14.2. A key loop invariant captures the essential behavior of the loop. When the loop terminates, at the point labeled *(d)* in the figure, the invariant is true and the *while* condition is false. We want the combination of these two facts to guarantee that the loop has accomplished its purpose.

To show that a condition is a loop invariant, we argue inductively. First we verify that the condition is true when the loop test is reached for the first time, that is, the first time the point labeled *(a)* in Figure 14.2 is reached. (This is the induction base case.) Then assuming that the invariant holds before executing the loop body, we show that it will still hold after executing the loop body. That is, we assume the invariant is true at the point labeled *(b)* in Figure 14.2, and show it is still true when the point labeled *(c)* is reached. (This is the induction step.)

Preliminaries

Before we verify partial correctness, let's make sure that the reference list.get(mid) at line 6 is legal, that is, that the preconditions of get are satisfied. We must ensure that 0 <= mid && mid < list.size(). We know that low <= high at line 5, since this is the loop test and must be true to get into the loop. (We sometimes say the condition low

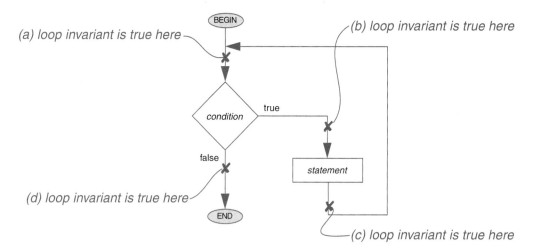

(a) loop invariant is true here

(b) loop invariant is true here

(d) loop invariant is true here

(c) loop invariant is true here

Figure 14.2 **A loop invariant.**

<= high *guards* the loop body.) This condition ensures that the value assigned to mid will be between low and high:

(1)   low <= mid <= high

Now *(1)* implies that low can only increase as the body of the loop is executed, and high can only decrease. Since low starts at 0 and high at list.size()-1, we can conclude that

        0 <= low <= mid <= high < list.size()

will hold whenever we reach line 6, and the reference list.get(mid) is correct.

The key invariant

The condition

(2)   for all indexes i: i < low implies
                order.inOrder(list.get(i),item)
            for all indexes i: i > high implies
                !order.inOrder(list.get(i),item)

is key to understanding the algorithm. This condition states that everything below low is smaller than item, and everything above high is greater than or equal to item:

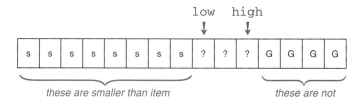

The operation of the loop is to maintain this relation while moving `low` and `high` closer together. When the loop exits, `low` equals `high+1`, and is the value we want:

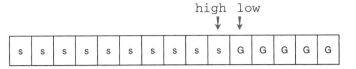

Let's informally verify that *(2)* is a loop invariant.

Note that the condition requires something of a set of list elements; specifically, those list elements with indexes less than `low` or greater than `high`. When we first reach the loop test, `low` is 0 and `high` is `list.size()-1`. There are no indexes less than `low` or greater than `high`. Thus the set of list elements of which something is required is empty, and the condition is vacuously true. (Loop invariants are often initially vacuously true.)

Now assume that condition *(2)* holds and we are about to execute the loop body: we have reached point *(b)* in Figure 14.2. We need to show that *(2)* is still true when we reach point *(c)*.

Given that condition holds before executing the if statement and that the list is sorted, it is rather easy to see that condition will remain true after executing the if statement, regardless of which alternative is performed.

Let's consider the case where `order.inOrder(list.get(mid),item)` is true, and the assignment

        low = mid+1;

at line 7 is executed. The facts that `order.inOrder(list.get(mid),item)` (the if condition) and the list is sorted guarantees that

        for all indexes i: i <= mid implies
            order.inOrder(list.get(i),item)

After the assignment, `low` equals `mid+1` and so

        for all indexes i: i < low implies
            order.inOrder(list.get(i),item)

The second part of *(2)*,

        for all indexes i: i > high implies
            !order.inOrder(list.get(i),item)

simply follows from the fact that *(2)* was true before the loop body was done. The value of `high` is not changed when the if condition is true.

The case in which the if condition is false can be argued in a similar manner.

Partial correctness

We have demonstrated that *(2)* is a loop invariant. In particular, it must also be true when the loop is exited: at point *(d)* in Figure 14.2. It is not difficult to determine that when the loop is exited, `low` equals `high+1`. (In fact, this is implied by the invariant.) If the list is empty, the loop body is not executed at all, and point *(d)* is reached with `low == 0` and `high == -1`. If the loop body is performed, we have seen that `low <= mid <= high` at line 6. The only ways the loop exit condition `low <= high` can become false is if either `mid == high` and `low` is set to `mid+1`, or if `low == mid` and `high` is set to `mid-1`. In either case, `low` equals `high+1` when the loop is exited.

Consequently, the following conditions are satisfied on loop exit

```
low == high+1
for all indexes i: i < low implies
    order.inOrder(list.get(i),item)
for all indexes i: i > high implies
    !order.inOrder(list.get(i),item)
```

which imply

```
for all indexes i: i < low implies
    order.inOrder(list.get(i),item)
for all indexes i: i >= low implies
    !order.inOrder(list.get(i),item)
```

This tells us that `low` is exactly the value we want to return. That is, `low` satisfies the method postcondition.

Loop termination

We have shown that the method is correct assuming the loop terminates. We must also verify that the loop will indeed terminate. This is also rather easy to see. When the loop body is executed, we have already noted that `mid` will be set to a value between `low` and `high`. That is, condition *(1)* will hold after line 5 is done. So the if statement will either increase `low` or decrease `high`, by at least one. Clearly this can only happen a finite number of times before `low` becomes larger than `high`, regardless of their initial values.

14.6   Summary

Sorting and searching are two fundamental list operations. In this chapter, we examined two simple sort algorithms, selection sort and bubble sort. Both of these algorithms make successive passes through the list, getting one element into position on each pass. They are order n^2 algorithms, which means that the time required for the algorithm to sort a list grows as the square of the length of the list. We also saw a simple modification to bubble sort that improved its performance on a list that was almost sorted.

After developing the algorithms, we considered how to generalize them so that they could be used for any type list and for any order. We proposed two possible homes for sort algorithms: as static generic methods, located in a utility class, and as abstract classes implementing a *Sorter* interface. With the later approach, we can dynamically create "sorter objects" to be passed to other methods. We also encountered Java's anonymous class construct. With this syntax, in a single expression we can create and instantiate a nameless class that implements an existing interface or extends an existing class.

After considering what an *OrderedList* container would look like, we developed a search method for sorted lists called binary search. This algorithm searches a list in much the same way we would search for a word in the dictionary or a number in the phone book. At each step of the algorithm, the middle of the remaining elements is compared to the element being searched for. This allows half the remaining elements to be eliminated from consideration. A major advantage of the binary search is that it needs to look at only $\log_2 n$ elements to find an item on a list of length n.

In evaluating the binary search algorithm, we saw that two steps were involved in verifying the correctness of the iteration. First, we demonstrated partial correctness: that the iteration is correct if it terminates. To do this, we found a key loop invariant that captured the essential behavior of the iteration. A loop invariant is a condition that remains true no matter how many times the loop body is performed. The key invariant insures that when the loop terminates it has satisfied its purpose. Verification of the key invariant provides a demonstration of partial correctness. Then to complete the verification, we showed that the iteration always terminates.

SELF-STUDY EXERCISES

14.1 Which of the following are legitimate orders, according to the requirements of Section 14.1?

  a. The relation "less than or equal" on the integers.
  b. The relation defined on the integers as "x comes before y if x is even and y is odd."
  c. The relation defined on the integers as "x comes before y if $x\%3 < y\%3$."
  d. The relation "is parent of" defined on the class *Person*.
  e. The relation "has beaten" defined on the class *FootballTeam*.
  f. The relation defined on the integers as "x comes before y if x is at least 10 greater than y."

14.2 Suppose that a *List<Student>* contains *Students A, B, C*, and *D*, in that order:

> *[A, B, C, D]*

  A and *C* have final grades of 80, *B* a final grade of 70, and *D* a final grade of 90. Trace a selection sort, with the order "higher final grade," and show the result.

14.3 Redo the previous problem, using bubble sort. What do you notice about the two results?

14.4 Suppose *A* and *B* are equivalent items, and that *A* initially precedes *B* on a list to be sorted. Is it possible that, after the sort, *B* will precede *A* if the sort algorithm is selection sort? If the sort algorithm is bubble sort?

14.5 In the illustration on page 575, the loop terminates when `first` equals `last`. Could we replace the condition in the while statement with `first != last`? (Hint: consider the empty list.)

14.6   Suppose the if condition in the bubble sort method `makePassTo` is changed to read

```
if (!inOrder(list.get(next),list.get(next+1))
```

Is the result of sorting a list always the same as with the original version? Is the sort still correct?

14.7   Assume sorts are defined as static generic methods in the class *Sorts*, as on page 587. Given that the class *Rectangle* has a method `area`, that returns an **int** and that `fig-ures` is a *List<Rectangle>*, write an invocation of selection sort that sorts the list by decreasing area. Use an anonymous class to define the order.

14.8   Redo the previous exercise, assuming that sorts are defined as generic objects, as on page 589.

14.9   Suppose all the items on a list are equivalent. For example, suppose the list is a *List<Stu-dent>* ordered by decreasing grade, and all the *Students* have a grade of 75. What will the binary search method `itemIndex` (page 596) return, if the item searched for is on the list?

What must be done to actually find the item on the list?

14.10   Would the binary search method `itemIndex` (page 596) still be correct if the while loop condition were changed to `low < high`?

14.11   Would the binary search method `itemIndex` (page 596) still be correct if the assignment to `high` in the loop is changed to `high = mid`?

EXERCISES

14.1   A *Student*'s name is kept as two *Strings*, accessed by queries `lastName` and `first-Name`. Using a web browser, access the Java API documentation for the class *String*. Using methods defined in *String*, write the definition of an *Order<Student>* that will order *Students* alphabetically.

14.2   Write a method that will sort a *List<PlayingCard>* by suit, and then by rank. For instance, all the spades should be together, and ordered by rank. Assume *PlayingCard* is defined as in Section 2.6.

14.3   Complete the binary search method `indexOf` (page 600) to accommodate lists contain-ing equivalent but unequal items.

14.4   A *merge* operation takes two sorted lists and combines them into a single sorted list. For instance

```
/**
 * Merge the specified Lists.
 * @require    list1 and list2 are ordered.
 * @ensure     merge(list1, list2) is ordered.
 */
```

```
public static <Element> List<Element> merge (
    List<Element> list1, List<Element> list2,
    Order<Element> order)
```

Implement the method, making sure that any iterations require no more than n_1+n_2 steps, where n_1 is the length of `list1` and n_2 is the length of `list2`.

14.5   An *insertion sort* can be described as follows.

   a.   Each element of the list is "positioned," starting with the second (index 1).

   b.   To position an element *e*, look at the elements preceding *e* on the list. For instance, if *e* is the tenth element, look at the ninth, then the eighth, then the seventh, *etc*. Elements greater than or equal to *e* are shifted one position up, leaving a "vacancy" after the first element encountered that is less than *e*. Put *e* into the vacancy.

   Implement insertion sort.

✲   14.6   Write an implementation *DefaultOrderedList<Element>* of *OrderedList<Element>* by wrapping a *DefaultList<Element>*.

✲   14.7   A key invariant for loop in the selection sort method `smallestOf` says that `small` is the index of the smallest element from `first` up to, but not including, `next`. A little more formally, it says

   for all indexes `i`: `first <= i && i < next` implies
   `list.get(i) >= list.get(small)`

or more properly,

   for all indexes `i`: `first <= i && i < next` implies
   `!inOrder(list.get(i),list.get(small))`

   Verify this invariant.

✲   14.8   A key invariant for the (outer) loop in selection sort says that the elements from 0 up to, but not including, `first` are in their proper position:

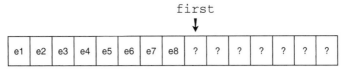

first

That is

   `list.get(0)` through `list.get(first-1)` are ordered, and
   `list.get(first)` through `list.get(last)` are all greater than
   or equal to `list.get(first-1)`.

   Verify this invariant.

✲   14.9   State and verify key loop invariants for the two bubble sort loops.

✲   14.10 State and verify key loop invariants for the methods written in Chapter 12.

14.11 A student attempting to write selection sort makes two mistakes. He starts the inner loop at
0, and reverses the test in the if statement. He ends up with the following method:

```
public void sort (List<Student> list) {
    int first = 0;
    int last = list.size() - 1;
    while (first <= last) {
        int next = 0;
        while (next <= last) {
            if (inOrder(list.get(first),list.get(next)))
                interchange(list,first,next);
            next = next+1;
        }
        first = first+1;
    }
}
```

Determine what this method does, and verify your hypothesis by finding key invariants for
the loops.

SELF-STUDY EXERCISE SOLUTIONS

14.1   *a.*   Does not satisfy the antisymmetric property, as we have defined this property. Antisymmetry says for any *x* and *y*, if "*x* comes before *y*" is true, then "*y* comes before *x*"
must be false. Let "comes before" be "less than or equal to," and let *x* and *y* both be 1.
Then since "1 less than or equal to 1" is true, antisymmetry requires that "1 less than
or equal to 1" is false. "Less than," of course, is an order.

b.   Satisfies the requirements of an order. The integers are partitioned into two sets of
equivalent values: all the evens are equivalent, and all the odds are equivalent. Notice
that the transitivity property is vacuously true. There are not three values *x*, *y*, and *z*
such that *x* comes before *y* and *y* comes before *z*. If *x* comes before *y*, *x* is even and *y*
is odd. No odd value comes before anything.

c.   This is an order. Here the integers are partitioned into five sets of equivalent values,
since *n*%3 can only be 0, 1, 2, –1, or –2 if *n* is an integer.

d.   This relation is not transitive: that *a* is parent of *b* and *b* is parent of *c* does not imply
that *a* is parent of *c*. The relation "is ancestor of" is an order, as long as we do not consider a person to be his or her own ancestor.

e.   This relation is neither inherently antisymmetric nor transitive. It's possible that two
teams play twice, and each beats the other. Also, that team *a* has beaten team *b*, and
team *b* has beaten team *c*, does not imply that team *a* has beaten team *c*.

f.   This is an order.

14.2   Selection sort produces *[D, C, A, B]*.

14.3   Bubble sort produces *[D, A, C, B]*. The sorts do not produce identical results, though both lists are correctly sorted. The difference is in the order of "equivalent" items *A* and *C*.

14.4   Yes, in the case of selection sort. (See Self-study Exercise 14.2 above.) No, in the case of bubble sort.

14.5   No. If the list is empty, `last` is initialized to –1 and `first` to 0. Since `first != last` is true, the body of the loop will be attempted causing the program to fail when it attempts to get an item from the empty list.

14.6   The sort is still correct, but the results are not always identical. For instance, the modified version of the bubble sort will sort the list of Self-study Exercise 14.2 as *[D, C, A, B]*.

14.7
```
Sorts.selectionSort(figures,
    new Order<Rectangle>() {
        public boolean inOrder(Rectangle r1, Rectangle r2) {
            return r1.area() > r2.area();
        }
    }
);
```

14.8
```
(new SelectionSorter<Rectangle> () {
    public boolean inOrder(Rectangle r1, Rectangle r2) {
        return r1.area() > r2.area();
    }
}).sort(figures);
```

14.9   It will return 0. The list must be searched sequentially.

14.10 No. If the loop exits with `low == high`, we do not know how the element with index `low` compares to `item`.

14.11 No. If `low == high`, the loop will not terminate because neither `high` nor `low` will be modified during execution of the loop body.

CHAPTER 15   **Failures and exceptions**

Though we would probably like to ignore the issue, we must admit that even the most carefully designed system may fail. In this chapter, we address the issue of failure: what it means for a system to fail, what are the possible causes of failure, and how a system failure can be handled.

We must first understand the mechanism provided by the language for detecting and dealing with failure. This is the *exception mechanism*. Exceptions are the means by which a method detects and reports failure, and are modeled by the class *Exception* and its subclasses.

Once we understand how the mechanism works, we must consider how to use it appropriately. We should understand the possible causes of failure, and what actions a method can take legitimately in the event of failure.

We conclude by noting that an application can define and generate its own exceptions, and by briefly considering what can be done about failures caused by logical errors in the program.

Objectives

After studying this chapter you should understand the following:

- the notion of program and method failure;
- the Java exception mechanism: throwing and catching an exception and exception propagation;
- how to deal with method failure.

  Also, you should be able to:

- catch exceptions in try-catch blocks;
- define and use exceptions based on problem constraints.

15.1   Failures

By *failure* we mean the inability of a system, at run-time, to accomplish its intended purpose. Since failure of a system ultimately is caused by failure of a method, we focus our discussion on method failure. We must consider what can cause a method to fail, and what we can do about it.

A method can fail for two fundamental reasons. It can fail because of

- a logical error in its implementation (a programming "bug"); or

- its inability to obtain some needed resource from the environment.

If a program contains an error, there is rarely anything that the program itself can do about it at run-time. The most we can hope for is a helpful error message that will assist in identifying and locating the problem.

The second situation includes a wide range of possibilities. A system may need resources from the hardware, the operating system, the file system, the network, a data base, and a user to achieve its purpose. For instance, it may need to acquire additional virtual memory, access to a particular file, or get input data in a particular format. In each case, the environment in which the system is running may be unable to provide the needed resource.

The occurrence of a detectable, abnormal situation that may lead to system failure is termed an *exception*. In many instances of program error, and in most instances of unavailable resources, exceptions are detected by the interpreter or run-time system. For example, if a program attempts to execute a query `s.name()` when `s` is *null*, the run-time system will detect the error. Similarly, if a program attempts to access a file that does not exist, the file system will report the problem to the run-time system. Clearly, we cannot expect the run-time system to detect every, or even most, logical errors. In some cases though, we can design the program so that the program itself will detect some logical errors.

Which exceptions we expect to occur and what we want to do about them depend on the circumstances in which the system is run. For instance, we may not expect program bugs in a mature, thoroughly tested system, but we are likely to encounter a number of logical errors during program development and be actively concerned with their detection. Similarly, the kinds of resource acquisition problems we anticipate depend on the specific environment in which the system is used. Thus we can rarely give a definitive answer as to how to handle a particular possible failure.

> **exception:** the occurrence of a detectable, abnormal situation which may lead to system failure.

15.2   The Java exception mechanism

The facilities provided by the language for detecting, reporting, and handling exceptions are collectively referred to as the *exception mechanism*. Before we examine it in detail, we must emphasize that the exception mechanism is not just another control structure. Its purpose is to deal with abnormal conditions, specifically with conditions that lead to failure. You should *never use the exception mechanism to handle normal, expected events*.

As we mentioned above, an exception can be detected by the run-time system or by the program itself. We consider run-time system detected exceptions first.

The Java run-time system or interpreter detects certain run-time errors, such as attempts to divide by zero or to use a *null* reference when an object is required. The run-time system notifies the program of the error by *throwing an exception*. An exception is said to be thrown from the point in the program at which the error occurred. (A program can also explicitly throw an exception, as we'll see shortly.)

A thrown exception involves a *transfer of control*: the processor stops executing the current sequence of statements, and begins executing statements at a different point in the program. The exception is said to be *caught* or *handled* at the point to which control is transferred.

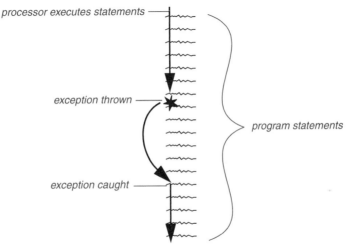

15.2.1 Exceptions as objects

An exception is modeled by an instance of the Java class *Throwable*. An object of this class carries information about the exception from the point at which the exception occurs to the point at which it is caught. The fundamental Java exception class hierarchy is shown in Figure 15.1.

The class *Error* and its subclasses represent conditions from which an ordinary program is not generally expected to recover. It includes linking and loading errors, and errors resulting from system resource limitations. We will not consider it further. Exceptions that an ordinary program might be interested in are instances of *Exception* and its subclasses.

A few of the standard exception classes defined by Java and detected by the run-time system are given below. They are all subclasses of *RuntimeException*.

- *ArithmeticException*: an exceptional arithmetic situation has arisen, such as an integer division with zero divisor.

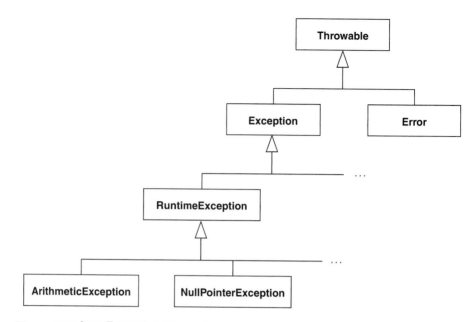

Figure 15.1 **Java Exception Hierarchy.**

- *ClassCastException*: an attempt has been made to cast a reference to an inappropriate type.
- *IllegalArgumentException*: a method was invoked with an invalid or inappropriate argument, or invoked on an inappropriate object.
- *NullPointerException*: an attempt was made to use a null reference in a case where an object reference was required.
- *SecurityException*: a security violation was detected.

15.2.2 Catching exceptions

Exceptions are caught or handled with a *try-catch* statement. The somewhat baroque syntax is as follows:

```
try {
    statements₁
} catch ( exception parameter₁ ) {
    statements₂
} catch ( exception parameter₂ ) {
    statements₃
} ...
```

The statement begins with the key word **try**, followed by a sequence of statements (possibly including local variable definitions) called the *try block*. The *try* block is followed by one or more *catch clauses*, which are also called *exception handlers*.

Each catch clause has a parameter of type *Exception* or one of its subclasses. For instance:

```
try {
    statements₁
} catch ( ArithmeticException e ) {
    statements₂
} catch ( NullPointerException e ) {
    statements₃
} catch ( Exception e ) {
    statements₄
}
```

As noted above, *ArithmeticException* and *NullPointerException* are subclasses of *Exception*. The run-time system throws an *ArithmeticException* if there is an attempt to divide by zero, and throws a *NullPointerException* if there is an attempt to use a null reference when a reference to an object is needed.

To execute the try-catch statement, the processor first performs the statements of the try block—labeled *statements₁* in the above example. If no exceptions occur, the try-catch is complete, and the catch clauses are ignored.

If an exception is thrown during execution of the *try* block, an attempt is made to match the exception to the catch clause parameters. The first catch clause whose parameter type is the same class as the exception or is a superclass of the exception, catches the exception. The mechanism for executing a catch clause is very much like the mechanism for invoking a method. A method variable is allocated for the parameter of the catch clause, and the variable is initialized with a reference to the thrown *Exception* instance. Then the body of the catch clause is performed.

In the above example, if an *ArithmeticException* (or a subclass of *Arithmetic-Exception*) is thrown during execution of *statements₁*, the exception is caught by the first catch clause, and *statements₂* are executed. A *NullPointerException* is caught by the second catch clause (*statements₃* executed). An *IllegalArgumentException* is caught by the third catch clause: *IllegalArgumentException* is neither a subclass of *ArithmeticException* nor of *NullPointerException*, but is a subclass of *Exception*. In each case, the parameter e references an object that models the exception.

Let's fill out the example a bit, to make sure we understand the mechanism. Suppose i and j are **int** variables, name a *String*, and s a *Student* variable. Consider the following:

```
1.   try {
2.       i = i/i;
3.       j = 0;
4.       name = s.name();
5.       j = 1;
6.   } catch (ArithmeticException e) {
7.       j = 3;
8.   } catch (NullPointerException e) {
9.       j = 4;
10.  } catch (Exception e) {
11.      if (e instanceof IllegalArgumentException)
12.          j = 6;
13.      else
14.          j = 5;
15.  }
16.  System.out.println("The value of j is " + j);
```

The try-catch statement starts at line 1 and ends at line 15. The method invocation System.out.println at line 16 follows the try-catch statement.

Note that the try-catch is set up to catch an *ArithmeticException* or a *NullPointer-Exception* explicitly. The catch clause at line 10 will catch any other exception.

In each catch clause, e is a formal parameter, a method variable, allocated and initialized when an exception is caught by the handler. It will contain a reference to the thrown *Exception* instance.

When the try-catch is executed, line 2 is first done. If i is 0, this statement causes an *ArithmeticException*, and control is transferred to the exception handler at line 6. Line 3 is never reached. The variable j is set to 3 at line 7, and the try-catch statement is finished. The remaining catch clauses are ignored. Line 16 writes out the number 3.

If i is not 0, line 2 completes successfully and line 3 and 4 are then done. If s happens to contain the null reference, attempting to query s.name() will generate a *NullPointerException*. Control is transferred to the exception handler at line 8. The variable j is set to 4, and the try-catch statement is finished. Line 16 writes out the number 4.

It is possible that execution of line 4 will result in an exception that is neither an *ArithmeticException* nor a *NullPointerException*. Such an exception will be caught by the handler at line 10. The formal parameter e will reference the object representing the exception. Line 11 checks to see if the exception is an instance of *IllegalArgumentException*. (Exactly what causes a *IllegalArgumentException* is not particularly relevant here; it is simply another subclass of *Exception*. Of course, the *IllegalArgumentException* could have been caught with a separate catch clause.) The variable j is set to 5 or 6 accordingly.

Otherwise, if the query s.name() completes successfully, j is set to 1 at line 5, and the try-catch statement is finished. The catch clauses are ignored. Line 16 writes out the number 1.

15.2.3 Propagated exceptions

What happens if a method does not catch an exception? That is, what happens if an exception is thrown by the execution of a statement that is not part of a try-catch, or if an exception is generated that does not match any of the catch clauses? In such a case, the exception is *propagated* to the calling method.

For instance, suppose an exception is thrown during execution of the *Student* method name, invoked from line 4 of the above example. If the method name does not handle the exception, the exception is propagated to the caller. In effect, the exception is thrown again at line 4. It will then be caught either by the handler at line 6, or by the handler at line 8, or by the handler at line 10, depending on the class of the exception.

An uncaught exception propagates up the *call chain* from each method to its caller. If no method in the call chain catches the exception, the program terminates with an error message. Suppose method nim.NimGame.main invokes nim.NimUI.start, which invokes nim.GameManager.play, which invokes nim.Player.makeMove, which attempts to divide by zero. If the *ArithmeticException* generated is not caught by makeMove, it will be propagated to play, and then to start, and then to main until a handler is found. (See Figure 15.2.) If none of the four methods catches the exception, the program terminates with an error message that might look something like this:

```
java.lang.ArithmeticException: / by zero
        at nim.Player.takeTurn(Player.java:36)
        at nim.Game.play(Game.java:114)
        at nim.NimTUI.start(NimTUI.java:29)
        at nim.NimGame.main(NimGame.java:11)
```

15.2.4 Checked and unchecked exceptions

The class *RuntimeException* and its subclasses are referred to as *unchecked exception classes*. Other exception classes are *checked exception classes*. The compiler verifies that checked exceptions are appropriately handled by analyzing which checked exceptions can result from execution of a method or constructor. If it is possible for a method to throw a checked exception to its caller, the method's specification must explicitly express this pos-

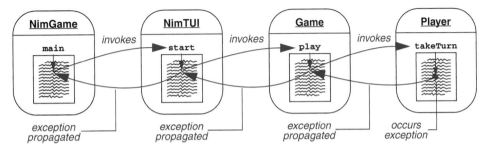

Figure 15.2 **Propagation of an exception up the call chain.**

sibility with a *throws* clause. That is, a *throws* clause must be included in a method specification if it is possible for a checked exception to be thrown in the method, and the method does not catch the exception. On the other hand, a method's specification need not document the possibility that an unchecked exception may be thrown and propagate to the caller.

For instance, the class *IOException* is not a subclass of *RuntimeException*, and so is a checked exception class. The method `readLine` defined in the class *java.io.Buffered-Reader* can throw the exception *IOException*. (It's not important what this method does, though you can probably make a good guess.) The method readLine is specified as:

```
public String readLine() throws IOException
```

An *IOException* that occurs in `readLine` is propagated to `readLine`'s caller. A method that invokes `readLine` and does not explicitly handle a resulting *IOException* propagates the exception to its caller. That is, it also throws an *IOException*. Such a method must also specify that it can throw an *IOException*. Consider the following, where `input` is a *java.io.BufferedReader*:

```
public void skip () throws IOException {
    String s;
    s = input.readLine();
}
```

As you can see, this method does not catch an *IOException* that might be generated by the call to `readLine`. The exception is simply propagated to `skip`'s caller. Thus the specification of the method `skip` must include the **throws** IOException clause.

If the method can throw several different checked exceptions, the classes are simply enumerated in the method specification. For example

```
public void skip () throws EOFException,
    FileNotFoundException {
    ...
}
```

Since *RuntimeExceptions* can occur almost everywhere, Java's designers thought it pointless to require documenting their possible occurrences.

DrJava: exceptions

Open the file `ExceptionGenerator.java`, located in `exercise`, in `ch15`, in `nhText`. This file defines an exercise class that generates some common exceptions.

1. In the *Interactions* pane, create an *ExceptionGenerator*.

```
> import ch15.exercise.*;
> ExceptionGenerator g = new ExceptionGenerator();
```

2. Invoke the method `tryIt` with arguments ranging from 0 through 6,

```
> g.tryIt(0)
```

```
> g.tryIt(1)
...
> g.tryIt(6)
```

and note the result in each case. Make sure that you understand the cause of each exception.

Notice that the assert statement generates an *Error* and not an *Exception*. The class *Error* and its subclasses represent conditions from which an ordinary program is not generally expected to recover. (Though it is hard to imagine an ordinary reprogram recovering from, say, a *NullPointerException*.)

Notice that exceeding the maximum value of an **int** does not generate an exception.

Now open files Catcher.java and Contractor.java located in the same directory. Note that *Contractor*'s doIt method invokes *ExceptionGenerator*'s tryIt after setting step to 1 and before setting step to 2.

Catcher's doIt method invokes *Contractor*'s doIt in a try statement, and then reports the value of *Contractor*'s step variable.

3. Note that *Contractor*'s doIt method has a throws clause in the heading, but *Catcher*'s does not. Why is this?

4. In the *Interactions* pane, create a *Catcher*.

```
> Catcher yogi = new Catcher();
```

5. Invoke Catcher's doIt with the following arguments and note the results.

```
> yogi.doIt(1)
> yogi.doIt(4)
> yogi.doIt(6)
> yogi.doIt(5)
```

Make sure that you understand the reasons for the output.

What happens when you invoke yogi.doIt(0)? Explain the result.

15.3   Dealing with failure: using exceptions

Now that we understand generally how Java's exception mechanism works, we need to consider how to use the mechanism to deal with failure. We will examine how a method can fail, and what we can do in each case.

A method fails if it is not able to accomplish its intended purpose. In Chapter 5, we introduced the notion of programming by contract. A method invocation is viewed as a "contract" between the client and the server, specified by method preconditions and postconditions. The client must make sure that the preconditions are satisfied when the method is called, in which case the server guarantees that the postconditions will hold when the method completes. The server promises to fulfill the contract only if the client satisfies the preconditions. The server has no obligation with regard to the contract if the client fails to meet the preconditions. As we have observed, the primary reasons for this approach are to simplify code and to make each component's responsibilities explicit.

Note that whether a method fails depends on what it promises to do. For instance, in Chapter 12 we specified a search method something like this:

public int indexOf (Element element)
> The index of the first occurrence of the specified element, or –1 if this *List* does not contain the specified element.

This method does not guarantee to return a legal list index. The possibility that the argument is not on the list is treated as normal. If the argument is not on the list, the method returns –1, and the client must be prepared to deal with this result.

Suppose the method were specified like this:

public int indexOf (Element element)
> The index of the first occurrence of the specified element on this *List*.

Now the method guarantees to find the item and return a legal index. If the item is not on the list, the method fails. This would not be a very good specification, since in general we have no way of knowing *a priori* whether or not the requested item is on the list.

Finally, we could make it the client's responsibility to ensure that the item searched for was on the list:

public int indexOf (Element element)
> The index of the first occurrence of the specified element on this *List*.
>
> **require:**
> > this.get(i).equals(element), for some i.

Here, the method *requires* that the item be on the list. It is a program error if the method is called with an argument not on the list, but not a failure of *this* method. Again, this is not a particularly good specification, since it puts an unreasonable burden on the client. The work involved in determining whether or not a particular item is on a list is almost surely equivalent to what is required to locate the item. Essentially, the client is asked to find the item on the list before calling this method to find the item on the list.

Specifically then, a method fails if it is unable to complete a contract even though its client has satisfied all preconditions. If a method detects that it will fail, it *must report failure* to its client. A method must *never* simply return to its caller, knowing that it has not satisfied the terms of the contract.

We can distinguish three cases in which a method may not be able to accomplish its purpose, even though its client has satisfied all preconditions.

- There is a logical error in the method. This is the most problematic case: we cannot in general expect an erroneous program to correctly recognize that it is erroneous.

- The method is not able to obtain necessary resources from its environment. We have mentioned a few examples above, such as an inaccessible file.

- The method invokes another method (a "subcontractor") which fails.

15.3.1 Dealing with exceptions

Let's consider the latter two cases first. We can assume that the method is notified of the failure by an exception. In order to get a resource, the method performs some action, such as invoking a system library method. If the resource is not available, this results in an exception. If the method calls a server and the server fails, the server should notify the method by throwing an exception. (Of course, it is possible that a server fails because of an undetected programming error, and returns without throwing an exception.)

In terms of the mechanism, we have seen that we can deal with an exception by catching the exception or by letting the exception propagate to the caller.

In terms of logical structure, there are two ways of dealing with a failure:

- clean up and report the failure to the caller (by throwing an exception); or
- try to correct the situation that caused the exception, and try again.

There are no other possibilities. A method *must not* return to its caller without either satisfying the contract or reporting failure.

Notice that there is no mention of writing "error messages." *"Reporting failure" means throwing an exception.* If necessary, the production of error messages can be allocated as a specific responsibility to some object. It is almost never the responsibility of the failing method.

An example should help explain the point. One of the constructors for the class *java.io.FileReader* requires a *String* argument denoting a file to be accessed. The constructor creates a *FileReader* instance that gets input from the named file. (Specifics of the class *FileReader* are not important to the example.)

```
public FileReader (String fileName)
    throws FileNotFoundException, SecurityException
```

This constructor throws a *FileNotFoundException* if the named file does not exist in the file system, and throws a *SecurityException* if the program does not have permission to read the file. (*SecurityException* is a subclass of *RuntimeException*, and so is an unchecked exception. Therefore it need not be explicitly mentioned in the method specification. We include it simply to clarify the example.) The constructor reports failure to its caller by throwing the appropriate exception.

Suppose we are writing a method that creates a *FileReader* by invoking this constructor. How do we handle failure of the constructor? Probably the most typical approach is to give up and report to our client that we have failed. Generally if our server fails, we have no choice but to fail also.

To report failure means to throw an exception. If we simply do not catch the exception thrown by the *FileReader* constructor, it will be propagated to our caller. Our method might look something like this:

```
public void getSomeData ()
    throws FileNotFoundException, SecurityException {
    FileReader in;
    in = new FileReader("DataFile");
    ...
}
```

If the *FileReader* constructor fails and throws, say, a *FileNotFoundException*, the exception is propagated to the caller of `getSomeData`, since `getSomeData` doesn't catch the exception. (Again, *SecurityException* does not need to be mentioned explicitly in the method specification, since it is an unchecked exception.)

We can also catch the exception, do some cleanup, and then throw either the same exception or a different one to our caller.

We use a *throw* statement to throw an exception explicitly. Its format is

```
throw exception;
```

For instance:

```
public void getSomeData ()
    throws FileNotFoundException, SecurityException {
    FileReader in;
    try {
        in = new FileReader("DataFile");
        ...
    } catch (FileNotFoundException e) {
        // cleanup
        ...
        throw e;
    } catch (SecurityException e) {
        // cleanup
        ...
        throw e;
    }
}
```

Here, the method `getSomeData` catches a *FileNotFoundException* or a *SecurityException*, does some cleanup, and throws the same exception to its caller.

Before we go on, we should briefly mention what we mean by "cleanup." A method cannot know how its caller will respond to the exception. The caller might be able to recover from the method's failure and continue. In that event, it is important that the method leave its object in a consistent state, that is, a state in which all class invariants are satisfied. Therefore upon discovering that it will fail, a method should make sure that the object is consistent before reporting failure to its caller.

Occasionally, it is possible to attempt recovery from a server failure. To concoct an example, suppose we expect the file `DataFile` to be occasionally locked by another program, and that we get a *SecurityException* if we attempt to access the locked file with the *FileReader* constructor. Suppose further that this is likely to be a transient situation: if we wait a few seconds, the lock will be removed. We can write our method so that, if we get a *SecurityException* when we try to create the *FileReader*, we wait a bit and then try one more time to access the file. For instance:

```
1.  public void getSomeData ()
2.      throws FileNotFoundException, SecurityException {
3.      FileReader in;
```

```
4.        boolean success = false;     // DataFile opened
5.                                     // successfully
6.        int tryNumber = 0;           // number of tries to
7.                                     // open DataFile
8.        int delay = 5;               // wait in seconds
9.                                     // between tries
10.       while (!success)
11.          try {
12.             tryNumber = tryNumber + 1;
13.             in = new FileReader("DataFile");
14.             success = true;
15.             ...
16.          } catch (SecurityException e) {
17.             if (tryNumber == 1)
18.                nhUtilities.utilities.Control.sleep(
19.                   delay);
20.             else
21.                throw e;
22.          }
23.    }
```

A few things to note in the above implementation:

- The *FileReader* constructor can generate two different exceptions: *FileNotFoundException* and *SecurityException*. The first is not caught, and is propagated to the caller. The second is caught by the catch clause at line 16.

- The actual body of the method is the try block of lines 12 through 15. The while loop is wrapped around the try statement to permit a "retry" in case the *FileReader* constructor fails. Note that the body of the while loop consists of a single try-catch statement.

- The variable success indicates whether or not we have successfully opened the file DataFile. If invocation of the *FileReader* constructor of line 13 is successful, success is set to **true** at line 14, and the rest of the method, indicated by line 15, is performed. Completing line 15 completes the try statement, which is the body of the loop. The while condition (!success) is again evaluated, and evaluates to false. This terminates the loop, and the method is complete.

- The variable tryNumber indicates how many times we have tried to open the file DataFile. If the *FileReader* constructor throws a *SecurityException* when we first reach line 14, the exception is caught at line 16. Since tryNumber is 1, the process waits about five seconds. (That's what the sleep invocation does. This method was introduced on page 340, in Chapter 8.) This completes the catch clause, which completes the try statement. Since success is still false, a second iteration of the while loop is begun. If the *FileReader* constructor succeeds this time, everything proceeds normally. If the constructor again throws a *SecurityException*, it is again caught at line 16. But this time tryNumber is 2. We give up and report failure to the caller by throwing at line 21 the same *SecurityException* we caught.

15.3.2 Application defined exceptions

It is sometimes useful to define our own exception classes. For instance, a client of the getSomeData method may only be interested in the fact that data was not obtained, and not in the specific reason we couldn't access the file. We could handle this by defining our own exception class, say *NoDataException*, and throwing this exception if we fail to get data for any reason.

We define our own exception classes by extending the class *Exception* or one of its subclasses. The java.lang class *Exception* has four constructors, specified as:

```
public Exception ()
public Exception (String message)
public Exception (String message, Throwable cause)
public Exception (Throwable cause)
```

The second and third constructors allow specification of a detail message that can be retrieved by the method getMessage. The third and fourth constructors allow bundling one exception inside another. The *Throwable* can be retrieved with the method get-Cause.

The definition of a program-defined exception is often as simple as the following:

```
public class NoDataException extends Exception {
    public NoDataException (String message,
        Throwable cause) {
        super(message,cause);
    }
}
```

We can now write a variation of getSomeData that throws a *NoDataException*. Note that we explicitly create a new instance of *NoDataException* to throw.

```
public void getSomeData () throws NoDataException {
    FileReader in;
    try {
        in = new FileReader("DataFile");
        ...
    } catch (FileNotFoundException e) {
        // cleanup
        ...
        throw new NoDataException(
            "DataFile does not exist",e);
    } catch (SecurityException e) {
        // cleanup
        ...
        throw new NoDataException(
            "DataFile cannot be accessed",e);
    }
}
```

Another reason for defining an exception class is to pass state information from the method detecting the exception to the method that will handle it. Such information can be essential in determining the course of a retry or useful in providing a more informative error message before the program is aborted. For example, if incorrectly formatted data is encountered while reading a file, we may want to report the location of the bad data. Such information can be packaged in an exception by the method discovering the error and passed along to the method responsible for reporting the error. It can be included in the *String* argument or as an explicit component of a program defined exception. For instance, an exception that reports which line in a file contains badly formatted data might be defined as follows:

```java
public class BadDataException extends Exception {

    private int lineNumber;

    public BadDataException (int lineNumber) {
        super();
        this.lineNumber = lineNumber;
    }

    /**
     * Line containing bad data
     */
    public int lineNumber () {
        return this.lineNumber;
    }
}
```

The method detecting the error creates an instance of *BadDataException* containing the number of the line with the bad data. The method handling the exception can query the *BadDataException* to determine line number.

Note that the purpose of an exception object is to carry information from the point where the error was detected to the point where the error is handled or reported. Thus exception objects are structured as immutable objects; their interface includes no state-changing commands.

15.3.3 Dealing with logical errors

As we mentioned above, detecting logical errors is an inherently difficult problem. A logical error often results in the run-time system throwing an exception, such as a *NullPointerException* or *ArithmeticException*. There is generally very little to do in this situation except fail. Sometimes a logical error causes a method to produce reasonable but incorrect results. In such cases, it may be virtually impossible to detect the error mechanically.

There are some instances, however, when we can get a good handle on the source of a logical error. Specifically, we can check preconditions, postconditions, and invariants. If a client invokes a method without preconditions being satisfied, it is an error.

We introduced the assert statement in Section 5.1.1 as a mechanism for verifying preconditions. Recall that there are two formats:

```
assert booleanExpression ;
assert booleanExpression : expression ;
```

In either case, the boolean expression is evaluated. If it is true, the statement has no effect. If it is false, a *java.lang.AssertError* is thrown. This is a subclass of *java.lang.Error* (see Figure 15.1), and is technically not an "exception."[1] In the second format of the assert, the expression is evaluated (it must yield a reference value) and the result is incorporated into the *AssertError*.

We can use assert statements to catch precondition violations without seriously complicating the structure of the method. For instance

```
/*
 * Interchange list.get(i) and list.get(j)
 *     @require   0 <= i, j < list.size()
 *     ...
 */
private <Element> void interchange (
   List<Element> list, int i, int j) {
   assert 0 <= i && i < list.size():
      "precondition: illegal i";
   assert 0 <= j && j < list.size():
      "precondition: illegal j";
   ...
```

If a client invokes the method without satisfying the preconditions, an exception is thrown reporting the nature and location of the error.

A method that does not satisfy its postconditions is also an error, and we can use asserts for checking postconditions. But postconditions tend to be a bit trickier to handle than preconditions, since they often involve comparing the object's state *after* method execution to the object's state *prior* to execution. Such a condition can only be verified if previous state information has been saved.

Finally, invariants tell us what conditions must hold at various points in the program. Again, we can use assert to verify that invariants are satisfied at critical points in the computation. As with postconditions, invariants are often too complex to verify with a simple condition. Nevertheless, we can sometimes identify conditions worth validating at key points in the program.

---

1. The distinction is that an error indicates serious problems that an application should not try to catch, while an exception indicates conditions that a application might want to catch.

Whether to include such checks depends to a large degree on where we are in the development process. We are much more concerned with logical errors early in the implementation, when the system is relatively unstable and has not been thoroughly tested and verified.

15.4   Summary

In this chapter, we addressed the issue of failure and examined the exception mechanism provided by Java to deal with failures. We saw that a method can fail for two fundamental reasons. It can fail because of:

- a logical error in its implementation (a programming "bug"); or
- its inability to obtain some needed resource from the environment.

An *exception mechanism* is provided by the language for detecting, reporting, and handling failure. An exception is a detectable, abnormal situation which may lead to system failure, and is modeled by an instance of the Java class *Exception*. An instance of this class carries information about the exception from the point at which the exception occurred (is thrown) to the point at which it is handled (is caught).

The language structure for handling exceptions is the *try-catch* statement. Exceptions thrown in the statements that comprise the *try* block can be handled in one of the *catch* clauses. An exception thrown in a method and not caught in the method is propagated to the method's caller.

A method fails if it cannot satisfy its contract even though the client has satisfied the method's preconditions. A method that fails must not simply return to its client. It must inform the client of the failure by throwing an exception.

When a client is notified of a server's failure (by the server's throwing an exception), there are only two possible courses of action the client can take. The client can

- attempt to correct the situation that caused the failure, and try again; or
- report failure to its caller, by throwing or propagating an exception.

Most often, the second alternative is the only one practical.

An application can define its own exception classes, by extending the class *Exception* of one of its subclasses. Program defined exceptions can be useful in providing more specific information about the cause of the failure.

Finally, logical errors, by their very nature, can be difficult to detect. Nevertheless, it can be useful, particularly during program development, to explicitly verify conditions, such as preconditions, that must hold in a correct program.

SELF-STUDY EXERCISES

15.1   What is a failure? What is an exception?

15.2   Consider the following method:

```
public int dummy () throws java.io.IOException {
    int value = 0;
    try {
        value = 1;
        contractor.doIt();
        value = 2;
    } catch (NullPointerException e) {
        value = value + 10;
    } catch (RuntimeException e) {
        value = value + 20;
    }
    return value;
}
```

What value does the method return if `contractor.doIt`:

a. throws a *NullPointerException*?
b. throws an *ArithmeticException*?
c. throws a *java.io.Exception*?
d. throws an *AssertionError*?
e. completes successfully?

15.3 What specifically does it mean for a method to fail? How does a method report failure to its client?

15.4 Consider the following method

```
/**
 * The number of lines in the specified file.
 * @ensure      this.lineCount() >= 0
 */
public int lineCount (File file) {
    file.open();
    int count = 0;
    while (!file.done()) {
        file.readLine();
        count = count + 1;
    }
    file.close();
    return count;
}
```

Which of the following are legitimate actions that can be taken by the method in the event that a `file` method throws an exception?

a. Ignore the exception, and let it propagate to the client.
b. Catch the exception, and return a value of –1 to the client.
c. Catch the exception, write out an error message, and terminate the program.

     d.   Catch the exception, write out an error message, and return a value of –1 to the client

     e.   Catch the exception, and throw another exception to the client.

15.5   In what way other than throwing or propagating an exception to its client might the above method deal with the failure of a `file` method?

EXERCISES

15.1   Suppose a search method is specified as:

```
public int indexOf (Element item) throws ItemNotFound
        The index of the first occurrence of the specified item on this
        List<Element>; throws ItemNotFound exception if this List<Element>
        does not contain the specified item.
```

and client code is written like this:

```
public enroll (Student student, List<Student> roll) {
    try {
        int i = roll.indexOf(student);
        // student is already enrolled
    } catch (ItemNotFound e) {
        roll.add(student);
    }
}
```

Comment on the reasonableness of the method specification and the method use.

15.2   Consider the following method for posting a withdrawal from an account.

```
public void withdraw (int amount) {
    this.balance = this.balance - amount;
    notifyObservers();
    log.logWithdrawal(this.accountNumber, amount);
}
```

A withdrawal is not complete unless it is successfully logged. But the method `logWithdrawal` might return a *LogFailureException* if the entry cannot be logged.

Modify the method so that it catches the exception and resets the balance to its original value before throwing an *UnsuccessfulWithdrawalException* to its client. Assume that `notifyObservers` must be done after updating the balance and before logging the withdrawal.

15.3   Modify the above method so that if `logWithdrawal` fails, it gives `log` the command `backupAndPurge`, and then tries to log the withdrawal again. If the second attempt fails, the method gives up and reports failure to its client. Ignore the possibility that `backupAndPurge` might fail.

15.4   In Chapter 7, we wrote a method to read an integer value after giving the user a prompt:

```
private int readIntWithPrompt (String prompt) {
    System.out.print(prompt); System.out.flush();
    while (!in.hasNextInt()) {
        in.nextLine();
        System.out.print(prompt); System.out.flush();
    }
    int input = in.nextInt();
    in.nextLine();
    return input;
}
```

The method uses the query hasNextInt to "guard" the invocation of nextInt, since nextInt will fail if the next token in the input stream does not have the format of an optionally signed integer literal. In fact, nextInt throws a *java.util.InputMismatchException* if there is not a well-formed integer in the input stream.

Modify this method so that, rather than guarding nextInt with hasNextInt, it catches the *InputMismatchException*. When the exception is caught, the method informs the user that an integer must be keyed, and "tries again" by prompting the user.

SELF-STUDY EXERCISE SOLUTIONS

15.1   A failure is the inability of a system, at run-time, to accomplish its intended purpose. An exception is the occurrence of a detectable, abnormal situation that may lead to system failure.

15.2   *a.*   11

      b.   21 (An *ArithmeticException* is a *RuntimeException*.)

      c.   It will not return a value; it will propagate the exception to its caller.

      d.   It will not return a value; it will propagate the error to its caller.

      e.   2

15.3   A method fails when it is not able to satisfy its contract, even though the client has satisfied all of the preconditions. It reports failure by throwing an exception.

15.4   Only options *a* and *e* are legitimate. The method may not return a value to the client if it fails, and the method has no business at all doing output.

15.5   It can attempt to correct the situation that caused the problem, and try again.

CHAPTER 16   **Stream i/o**

In this chapter, we take a closer look at Java's stream i/o. We were introduced to streams in Chapter 7, and, to this point, have used streams for all of our input and output needs. Now we'll examine the organization of the standard Java library that supports stream i/o. In the next chapter, we'll consider the standard library for graphical, event driven i/o.

The chapter is unusual in that it is organized around a particular set of standard classes and their use. It is a somewhat technical in nature, and can be treated as a reference or supplement. While we see some further examples of standard class organizational patterns, we really do not deal with software design issues here. Basically, we're interested in exploring the structure and features of a fundamental, commonly used library.

We start with a review of data streams, and an overview of the java.io library. We then survey the principal classes in the four basic stream categories: input byte streams, input character streams, output byte streams, and output character streams.

We discuss the basic organization and primary functionality of the stream i/o classes. Our presentation is neither comprehensive nor in depth. It should be adequate, though, for needed details to be easily obtained from standard reference documents.

Objectives

After studying this chapter you should understand the following:

- byte streams and character streams, and the class structure of the standard libraries for manipulating these streams;
- how to use the standard libraries to construct utility i/o classes.

Also, you should be able to:

- use standard Java stream classes to read and write bytes and characters;
- define input classes designed for specific purposes.

16.1   Data Streams

Data streams for input and output were introduced in Chapter 7. Now we want to take a closer look at Java's facilities for manipulating data streams.

Recall that a data stream is essentially a sequence of bytes. If the stream is a source of data for an application, it is an *input stream*. If it is a destination (or "sink"), it is an *output stream*. An application *reads* data, removing it from an input stream, and *writes* data, appending it to an output stream.

The source of the data in an input stream might be a user's keyboard, a file, another program, a network connection, an external device, *etc*. The destination of an output stream could be a terminal window, a file, another program, a network connection, and so on.

A data stream can be finite, for instance, if the source of an input stream is a file, or conceptually unbounded, for instance, if the source is a sensor that continually reports temperature every ten seconds. An application generally has a way of determining that an input stream is exhausted—that all the data has been read and no more data will appear in the stream—and a way of indicating that an output stream is complete.

The bytes that comprise a data stream can be interpreted in many ways. If they are to be interpreted as characters, the stream is usually referred to as a character stream. Otherwise, the stream is a binary stream. For example, if the source of an input stream is a text file, the stream is a character stream. If the source is a file in which each group of four bytes is a two's complement binary integer, the stream is a binary stream.

We need to be a little careful with our terminology in regard to Java. Specifically, Java represents characters with a 16-bit Unicode encoding. In Java, the term *character stream* refers to a data stream whose elements are to be interpreted as Unicode characters. Any other data stream, even one whose elements are ordinary 8-bit ASCII characters, is a *byte stream*.

16.2   The *java.io* library

The standard package java.io contains the basic predefined facilities for reading and writing data streams. In the previous chapters, we've used one of these classes extensively for textual output: System.out is a *java.io.PrintStream*. However, when we needed to read textual data, we used instances of the class *java.util.Scanner*, since java.io does not provide an easy mechanism for reading and parsing textual input.

The package java.io is a menagerie containing, at last count, twelve interfaces, fifty classes, and sixteen exceptions. The functionality can be categorized as

- facilities for reading and writing data streams;
- facilities for manipulating files;
- facilities for serializing objects.

File manipulation facilities include the class *File*, which models a file in the local file system, and the class *RandomAccessFile*, which includes mechanisms for reading and writing a file in a nonsequential manner. Object serialization provides a means for writing objects to a byte stream, and later recreating the objects from the byte stream. We will not cover serialization in this book.

The classes that support reading and writing from data streams can be organized into four categories:

- *InputStream* classes for reading byte streams;
- *OutputStream* classes for writing byte streams;
- *Reader* classes for reading character streams;
- *Writer* classes for writing character streams.

Each category has an abstract class at the top of its hierarchy: *InputStream* and *OutputStream* for byte streams, and *Reader* and *Writer* for character streams.[1] Other classes in the hierarchies extend the functionality of the base classes in two ways: some add functionality by extending the base classes; others add functionality by wrapping an instance of another class. (Wrapping and extension were discussed in Section 11.3.3.)

16.3   Input streams

16.3.1 Input byte streams

Abstract class InputStream

The top of the hierarchy is the abstract class *InputStream*. Fundamental methods for reading a stream are specified in this class, including:

public abstract int read () **throws** IOException
> Read and return the next byte of data from the input stream. Return –1 if the end of the stream is encountered (the stream is exhausted).
>
> **ensure:**
> ```
> (0 <= this.read() && this.read() <= 255) ||
> this.read() == -1
> ```

public void close () **throws** IOException
> Close the input stream and release associated resources.

Note that the method read is neither a proper command nor a proper query. It changes the state of the stream *and* returns a value. Most of the java.io input methods are of this flavor. There are several overloaded versions of read for reading either one

---

1. The character stream classes were developed after the byte stream classes. So although there are similarities, byte stream and character stream classes are not entirely symmetric.

byte or a sequence of bytes. However, the method `read` specified above is the only abstract method in the class. Other `read` variants are implemented in terms of this one. Thus a concrete subclass need only implement a single method that provides the next byte of input.

The method `read` can throw a *java.io.IOException*. As this exception is a checked exception (*i.e.*, not a *RuntimeException*), a client method that invokes `read` must either catch the exception (with a try-catch) or include a throws clause in its header.

Standard input

In Section 7.2, we were introduced to the stream *standard input*. Standard input is an input byte stream generally available in every program. The default source of bytes for this stream is the keyboard, although the source can be redirected by the operating system when an application is run,

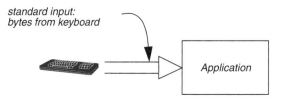

standard input:
bytes from keyboard

Application

Figure 16.1 Standard input is an input byte stream.

The bytes encode the characters keyed in, using the system's default encoding scheme, ASCII for instance.

Standard input can be accessed by means of the constant `in` defined in the class *java.lang.System*:

```
public static final InputStream in; // standard input
```

Thus we can read a byte from standard input by writing

```
int b = System.in.read();
```

Class FileInputStream

FileInputStream is a straightforward concrete extension of *InputStream*.

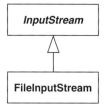

InputStream

FileInputStream

FileInputStream specifies a file as the source of the input stream, but otherwise adds no functionality to that specified by *InputStream*. A *FileInputStream* is generally wrapped with a *BufferedInputStream*, an *InputStreamReader*, or a *DataInputStream*, to provide a richer interface to the input stream.

The file is identified—either with a *String* file name, a *File* object, or a system-specific file descriptor—in the *FileInputStream* constructor. The file is implicitly opened when the *FileInputStream* instance is created. The constructors are:

```
public FileInputStream (String name)
    throws FileNotFoundException, SecurityException

public FileInputStream (File file)
    throws FileNotFoundException, SecurityException

public FileInputStream (FileDescriptor fd)
    throws FileNotFoundException, SecurityException
```

The *String* name is a system-dependent file name. For example, the expression

```
new FileInputStream("/home/fred/willow.jpg")
```

will create a *FileInputStream* by opening a connection to a file in a Unix environment named /home/fred/willow.jpg. If the file does not exist, is a directory rather than an ordinary file, or for some other reason cannot be opened for reading, a *FileNotFoundException* will be thrown. (A *SecurityException* is thrown by a *SecurityManager*. Discussion of security managers is beyond the scope of this text.)

A *File* is an abstract, system-independent representation of a pathname. A *FileDescriptor* is a handle to the underlying machine-specific structure representing an open file or other byte source. We won't discuss *FileDescriptors* further.

A method processing a *FileInputStream* byte by byte will look something like this:

```
public void processFile (String fileName)
    throws IOException {
    FileInputStream in = new FileInputStream(fileName);
    int b;
    while ((b = in.read()) != -1) {
        process b
    }
    in.close();
}
```

The *FileInputStream* constructor, read method, and the close method can all throw *IOExceptions*. Thus the method processFile must either include a throws clause in its header or must catch the exceptions.

Note that an *assignment expression* b = in.read() is used in the while condition. (See Section 2.7 for details on assignment expressions.) The value of this expression is the value of the right operand of the assignment operator, in.read() in this case. When the expression is evaluated, the next byte of the input stream is read, its value stored in b, and the value is compared to −1. So here we have an expression with two side effects: the state of the input stream is changed (since a byte has been read) and the variable b is changed. Such expressions should generally be avoided, but it is common practice to write a read loop as shown above.

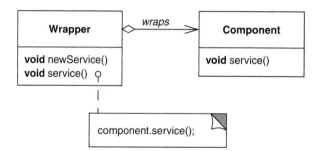

Figure 16.2 **A wrapper can add new functionality to a class.**

Class FilterInputStream

We saw in Chapter 11 that functionality can be added to a class by composition. A wrapper class adds functionality and forwards requests for some services to its component. One advantage of this approach is that the component need not be fixed until runtime.

FilterInputStream provides no additional functionality, but serves as a base class for *InputStream* wrappers that add functionality.

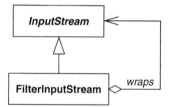

A *FilterInputStream* simply forwards all service requests to its component *InputStream*. Note that *FilterInputStream* is also a subclass of *InputStream*. This allows one *FilterInputStream* to wrap another *FilterInputStream*.

Two commonly used subclasses of *FilterInputStream* are *DataInputStream* and *BufferedInputStream*.

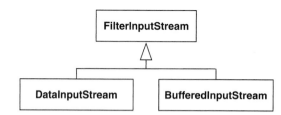

DataInputStream provides methods for reading values of primitive Java data types from the input stream in a machine-independent way. Functions provided by a *DataInputStream* include:

public boolean readBoolean () **throws** IOException
        Read one byte and return *true* if the byte is nonzero, *false* if the byte is zero.

public char readChar () **throws** IOException
>   Read two bytes and return the value as a Unicode character.

public double readDouble () **throws** IOException
>   Read eight bytes and return the value as a **double**.

public int readInt () **throws** IOException
>   Read four bytes and return the value as an **int**.

public byte readByte () **throws** IOException
>   Read and return one input byte. The byte is treated as a signed value in
>   the range –128 through 127, inclusive.

Note that these methods do *not* read character representation of the values, but binary representations generated by Java's *DataOutputStream* routines. An application uses a *DataOutputStream* to write data that can later be read by a *DataInputStream*. In fact, a *DataInputStream* should *only* be used to read data generated by a *DataOutputStream*.

These methods throw a *java.io.EOFException* if the end of the input stream is encountered during the read attempt. *EOFException* is a subclass of *java.io.IOException*.

A *BufferedInputStream* uses an in-memory buffer to store input from the stream. That is, a large number of bytes are read from the input stream and stored in an internal buffer. Bytes are then read directly from the internal buffer. When the buffer is exhausted, it is filled again with another chunk of data from the input stream. Of course, the operating system also buffers input data in memory if possible. Using a *BufferedInputStream*, however, reduces the number of calls to the operating system. The operating system need only be accessed occasionally to fill the buffer.

As we've said, these subclasses of *FilterInputStream* wrap an *InputStream*. The *InputStream* component is provided as a constructor argument:

public DataInputStream (InputStream in)
>   Create a *DataInputStream* that reads from the given *InputStream*.

public BufferedInputStream (InputStream in)
>   Create a *BufferedInputStream* that buffers input from the given
>   *InputStream* in a buffer with the default size of 2048 bytes.

Suppose the file noise.dat contains a sequence of 32-bit integer values written by a *DataOutputStream*. Since *FileInputStream* is a subclass on *InputStream*, the file can be opened and wrapped with a *DataInputStream* as follows:

```
FileInputStream in = new FileInputStream("noise.dat");
DataInputStream data = new DataInputStream(in);
```

The integer values can be read by using the *DataInputStream* method readInt:

```
int i;
try {
   while (true) {
      i = data.readInt();
      process(i);
   }
```

```
    } catch (EOFException e) {
      data.close();
    }
```

Note that we have deliberately written an infinite loop here. When all the data in the file has been read, the next invocation of readInt will throw an *EOFException*. The loop will terminate and the exception will be caught with the catch clause. We are using the exception mechanism as part of the "normal" execution of the method. We certainly expect the *EOFException* to be thrown! As we explained in Section 15.2, this is really a misuse of the exception mechanism. But we have little choice, since *DataInputStream* offers no direct way of testing for end of file.

We mentioned that since *FilterInputStream* is a subclass of *InputStream*, one *FilterInputStream* can wrap another. If we wanted to buffer input from the above file, we could first wrap the *FileInputStream* in *BufferedInputStream*:

```
FileInputStream in = new FileInputStream("noise.dat");
BufferedInputStream bf = new BufferedInputStream(in);
DataInputStream data = new DataInputStream(bf);
```

Note what we are doing here. We start with a *FileInputStream*, which is an *InputStream*, and wrap it in a *BufferedInputStream* to get in-memory buffering. Then we wrap the *BufferedInputStream*, which is also an *InputStream*, in a *DataInputStream* to get the methods for reading primitive data values.

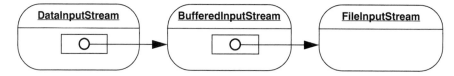

When the *DataInputStream*'s readInt method is invoked, the *DataInputStream* invokes the *BufferedInputStream*'s read method four times to get the four bytes that comprise the integer value. When the *BufferedInputStream*'s read method is invoked, it retrieves a byte from its buffer. If the buffer is empty, it invokes the *FileInputStream*'s read method to fill the buffer.

There is really no need to name all these instances. We could just as easily write:

```
DataInputStream data =
    new DataInputStream(
        new BufferedInputStream(
            new FileInputStream("noise.dat")));
```

16.3.2 Input character streams

Abstract class Reader

The top level of the input character stream hierarchy is the abstract class *Reader*. *Reader* is similar in purpose and structure to *InputStream*. *Reader* reads a stream of Unicode characters rather than bytes. Its simplest `read` method is specified as follows:

> **public int** `read () ` **throws** `IOException`
>> Read and return the next character of data from the input stream. The character is returned as an integer in the range 0 to 65535 (0 to $2^{16}-1$). Return -1 if the end of the stream is encountered (the stream is exhausted).
>
>> **ensure:**
>>> `(0 <= this.read() && this.read() <= 65535) ||`
>>> `this.read() == -1`

Note that the method returns a value of type **int**, not of type **char**. (Why? So that there is a convenient "noncharacter" value that can be returned if the end of the stream has been reached.) The postcondition guarantees that the **int** can be safely cast to a **char**:

```
int i = reader.read();
if (i != -1)
    char c = (char)i;
```

Abstract class FilterReader

FilterReader has the same relationship to *Reader* as *FilterInputStream* has to *InputStream*. That is, it provides no additional functionality, but serves as a base class for *Reader* wrappers that will add functionality. However, *FilterReader* is abstract while *FilterInputStream* is not.

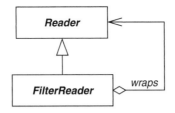

Class BufferedReader

BufferedReader buffers character stream input in much the same way that *BufferedInputStream* is used to buffer byte stream input.

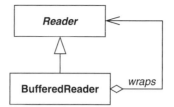

BufferedReader has a handy method for reading a line of input:

public String readLine () **throws** IOException
> Read and return a line of text. Return *null* if the end of the stream is encountered. Line terminating characters are not included in the *String*.

Class InputStreamReader

InputStreamReader is an adapter class that wraps an *InputStream* and provides the functionality of a *Reader*.

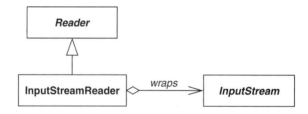

The *InputStreamReader* converts each byte of the *InputStream* to a Unicode character using an encoding scheme that can be specified when the *InputStreamReader* is created. If no encoding scheme is specified, a system default is used.[1]

public InputStreamReader (InputStream in)
> Create an *InputStreamReader* that reads from the given *InputStream* and translates bytes to characters using the system default encoding.

public InputStreamReader (InputStream in, String enc)
throws UnsupportedEncodingException
> Create an *InputStreamReader* that reads from the given *InputStream* and translates bytes to characters using the specified encoding.

To improve efficiency, an *InputStreamReader* is often wrapped in a *BufferedReader:*

```
BufferedReader in = new BufferedReader(
    new inputStreamReader(System.in));
```

---

1. A typical default is ISO-8859-1 (Latin 1). This is an 8-bit character set that covers most Western European languages. The first 128 characters (characters 0 to 127) are identical to ASCII. It is denoted in Java by the *String* "ISO8859_1".

Class FileReader

FileReader extends *InputStreamReader*. In effect, a *FileReader* is an *InputStreamReader* using the system default encoding and wrapped around a *FileInputStream*.

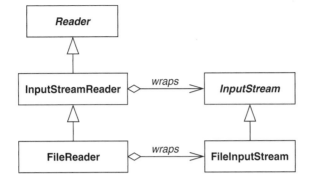

The constructors are similar to those of *FileInputStream*:

```
public FileReader (String name)
    throws FileNotFoundException, SecurityException

public FileReader (File file)
    throws FileNotFoundException, SecurityException

public FileReader (FileDescriptor fd)
    throws FileNotFoundException, SecurityException
```

Writing

```
FileReader in = new FileReader(fileName);
```

is essentially the same as writing

```
InputStreamReader in = new InputStreamReader(
    new FileInputStream(fileName));
```

16.3.3 Input examples

Reading byte streams

Let's develop a few examples that illustrate how to use Java's input facilities. First we write a method that reads a binary file and writes out the bytes, as two hexadecimal digits, to standard output. (The value returned by *InputStream*'s read is an **int** in the range 0 – 255: in hexadecimal, 0 – ff.)

We've already seen the basic structure of such a method. We use a *BufferedInput-Stream* to gain efficiency and to illustrate how wrapping is done.

```
public void displayBinaryFile (String fileName)
    throws IOException {
```

```
            BufferedInputStream in =
                new BufferedInputStream(
                    new FileInputStream(fileName));
            int b;
            while ((b = in.read()) != -1) {
                write out hex representation of b
            }
            in.close();
        }
```

We can get a *String* containing the hexadecimal representation of an integer with one of *Integer*'s toString methods:

> **public static** String toString (**int** i, **int** radix)
> A *String* representation of the first argument in the radix specified by the second argument.

The only thing remaining is to add a leading zero if the integer is less than 16, that is, if the *String* consists of only one character.

```
            public void displayBinaryFile (String fileName)
                throws IOException {
                BufferedInputStream in =
                    new BufferedInputStream(
                        new FileInputStream(fileName));
                int b;
                while ((b = in.read()) != -1) {
                    String hex = Integer.toString(b,16);
                    if (hex.length() == 1)
                        hex = '0' + hex;
                    System.out.println(hex);
                }
                in.close();
            }
```

Next, let's write a method that reads a file containing a sequence of 32-bit integer values written by a *DataOutputStream*. Again, we've already seen the format. This time, we wrap the *InputStream* in a *DataInputStream* so that we can use the readInt method.

```
            public void displayIntFile (String fileName)
                throws IOException {
                DataInputStream in =
                    new DataInputStream(
                        new BufferedInputStream(
                            new FileInputStream(fileName)));
                try {
                    int i;
                    while (true) {
```

```
            i = in.readInt();
            System.out.println(i);
        }
    } catch (EOFException e) {
        in.close();
    }
}
```

Reading character streams

We next write a method that reads an ordinary text file, and counts the number of occurrences of a given character in the file.

```
/**
 * The number of occurrences of the specified
 * character in the named file.
 */
public int charCount (char c, String fileName)
    throws IOException {
    FileReader in = new FileReader(fileName);
    int count = 0;
    int charRead;
    while ((charRead = in.read()) != -1)
        if ((char)charRead == c)
            count = count + 1;
    in.close();
    return count;
}
```

Remember that a *FileReader* is an *InputStreamReader*. Executing the read method will read a single byte of input, and convert that byte to a **char** using the system default encoding.

The first 128 Unicode characters are the same as the ASCII characters. (See Section 1.2.1 and Appendix iii.) Thus if the text file is an ASCII file, "converting the byte to a **char**" is simply adding high order 0's. In this case, we could have used a *FileInputStream* rather than a *FileReader*. The result of the read command would be the same in either case.

Let's modify the problem a bit and write a method that counts the number of lines that begin with the specified character. Here, we'll wrap the *FileReader* with a *BufferedReader* to take advantage of *BufferedReader*'s readLine method.

```
/**
 * The number of lines beginning with the specified
 * character in the named file.
 */
public int charCount (char c, String fileName)
```

```
    throws IOException {
    BufferedReader in =
        new BufferedReader(
            new FileReader(fileName));
    int count = 0;
    String line;
    while ((line = in.readLine()) != null)
        if (line.charAt(0) == c)
            count = count + 1;
    in.close();
    return count;
}
```

Reading String representations of primitive values

We've mentioned that the input classes in `java.io` do not include facilities for easily parsing character sequences that represent primitive values such as numbers. As a result, we use classes such as *java.util.Scanner* to read and parse input character sequences. Let's take a look at how such a class might be built.

To start with, let's construct a set of methods that allow us to read representations of integers and doubles from standard input. Specifically, we'll design a class containing the following methods:

> **public class** `SimpleInput`
> > A simple class that prompts to standard output and reads from standard input.
>
> **public static int** `readInt (String message)`
> > Write the prompt message to standard output, and return user's response from standard input. User's response must have the format of an integer.
>
> **public static double** `readDouble (String message)`
> > Write the prompt message to standard output, and return user's response from standard input. User's response must have the format of a double.
>
> **public static char** `readChar (String message)`
> > Write the prompt message to standard output, and return first character of user's response from standard input. User's response must be at least one character long. Subsequent characters are ignored.
>
> **public static** `String readString (String message)`
> > Write the prompt message to standard output, and return user's response from standard input.

A client will invoke a method something like this:

```
int age = SimpleInput.readInt("Enter your age: ");
```

The user will see the prompt, and key in an integer,

```
Enter your age: 32
```

which will be assigned to the variable `age`. Of course, what the user actually keys is a sequence of characters that must be converted to an **int** value.

The only difficulty is converting *Strings* to **int** and **double** values. Fortunately, the classes *Integer* and *Double* have what we need. *Integer* has a method specified as

public static int parseInt (String s)
> The integer value of the *String*, considered as a signed decimal integer. The characters in the *String* must all be decimal digits, except that the first character may be a minus sign '−'.

and *Double* has a method

public static double parseDouble (String s)
> The double value represented by the *String*. Leading and trailing white space characters are ignored. The remainder of the *String* must have the form of an optionally signed floating point literal.

Both of these methods throw a *NumberFormatException* if the *String* does not have the proper format. (Although a *NumberFormatException* is a *RuntimeException*, we include it in the throws clauses below to emphasize that the method can throw this exception.)

We can now define the class, without comments, as follows:

```
public class SimpleInput {

    private static BufferedReader in =
        new BufferedReader(
            new InputStreamReader(System.in));

    public static int readInt (String message)
        throws IOException, NumberFormatException {
        prompt(message);
        return Integer.parseInt(in.readLine());
    }

    public static double readDouble (String message)
        throws IOException, NumberFormatException {
        prompt(message);
        return Double.parseDouble(in.readLine());
    }

    public static char readChar (String message)
        throws IOException {
        prompt(message);
        return in.readLine().charAt(0);
    }
```

```
        public static String readString (String message)
          throws IOException {
          prompt(message);
          return in.readLine();
        }

        private static void prompt (String message) {
          System.out.print(message);
          System.out.flush();
        }
    }
```

Although this class is quite straightforward, it suffers from several deficiencies.

- Input can only be read from standard input.

- Only one value per line can be read.

- Double values can begin with a '+' or '–' and can be preceded and followed by blanks (white space); integer values, however, cannot be preceded by a '+' and cannot be preceded or followed by blanks.

- The public methods are neither proper queries nor proper commands. They change the state of the input stream like commands, but return values like queries.

Let's next sketch a class with a bit more flexibility. We call the class *SimpleScanner*, and provide two constructors, one reading from standard input and one reading from a named file:

> **public** SimpleScanner ()
>> Create a *SimpleScanner* attached to standard input.

> **public** SimpleScanner (String fileName)
>> Create a *SimpleScanner* attached to the named file.

Rather than define state-modifying value-returning methods as in *java.util.Scanner*, we separate methods into proper queries and proper commands. For instance, the command readInt reads an integer from the input stream and the query lastInt returns the most recent integer read. A client invokes the command readInt to instruct the *SimpleScanner* to read input (and change state), and then invokes the query lastInt to determine the integer most recently read. Since lastInt does not change the *Simple-Scanner*'s state, successive calls to lastInt will return the same value until the *Simple-Scanner*'s state is changed by an invocation of readInt. The pair of statements

```
        input.readInt();
        int n = input.lastInt;
```

where input is a *SimpleScanner*, is roughly equivalent to the statement

```
        int n = input.nextInt()
```

where input is a *java.util.Scanner*.

The command `readInt` skips white space, reads an optionally signed decimal integer, and leaves the character following the integer at the head of the input stream. For example, if the input stream contains

> •••+12345abc••↵

where "•" represents a space and "↵" represents the line termination character(s), then after `readInt` is invoked the input stream will contain

> abc••↵

and `lastInt` will return 12345. Note that this is not the same behavior as that of the *java.util.Scanner* method `nextInt`. That method insists that the next *token* have the format of an integer. Given the input above, `nextInt` would fail, since the token +12345abc does not have the proper format. We can presume similar methods for reading doubles, booleans, and so on.

To get an idea of how *SimpleScanner* can be constructed, we'll build the method `readInt`. Assume the class has an instance variable `lastInt` that contains the value of the most recently read integer:

```
private int lastInt;
```

The method `lastInt` simply returns the value of this instance variable:

```
public int lastInt () {
    return this.lastInt;
}
```

Now what must the method `readInt` do? It must

- skip any leading white space in the input stream;
- check for a sign;
- read the digits and store the value denoted in `lastInt`.

One problem we must deal with is that `readInt` must do a one character "look ahead" to determine that all the digits have been read. The code to read the digits will look something like this:

```
int inchar = input.read();
while (isDigit(inchar)) {
    process inchar
    inchar = input.read();
}
```

Notice that the character *after* the digit string must be read before we know that we've read all the digits. In the example above, the character 'a' following the digit '5' will be read to stop the loop. We must have some way of "peeking ahead" at the next character before it's read or of "putting back" a character after it's read.

There are several ways of handling this situation. Probably the most straightforward is to use the wrapper class *PushbackReader*. A *PushbackReader* allows characters to be "pushed back" into the input stream.

```
public class PushbackReader extends FilterReader
```
A character-stream reader that allows characters to be pushed back into the stream.

There are two constructors:

```
public PushbackReader (Reader in)
```
Create a new *PushbackReader* with a one-character pushback buffer.

```
public PushbackReader (Reader in, int size)
```
Create a new *PushbackReader* with a pushback buffer of the given size.

The basic method for pushing back a character is `unread`:

```
public void unread (int c) throws IOException
```
Push back a single character.

If we wrap a *PushbackReader* around the input stream in the *SimpleScanner* constructors, we will be able to put a character back onto the input stream.

```
public SimpleScanner (String fileName) throws
    java.io.FileNotFoundException {
    input = new PushbackReader(
            new BufferedReader(
                new FileReader(fileName)));
    ...
}

public SimpleScanner () {
    input = new PushbackReader(
            new BufferedReader(
                new InputStreamReader(System.in)));
    ...
}
```

where `input` is an instance variable

```
private PushbackReader input;
```

Since the *FileReader* constructor can throw a *java.io.FileNotFoundException*, the first *SimpleScanner* constructor must either catch this exception or include a throws clause.

The class *java.lang.Character* defines several methods useful in writing `readInt`:

```
public static boolean isWhitespace (char ch)
```
The specified character is white space.

```
public static boolean isDigit (char ch)
```
The specified character is a digit.

```
public static int digit (char ch, int radix)
```
The numeric value of the character in the specified radix.

For example, `Character.digit('5',10)` returns the **int** value 5.

Before completing `readInt`, we write an auxiliary method that skips over blanks and other whitespace and returns the first "nonwhite" character in the input stream:

```
private int skipSpace () throws java.io.IOException {
    int inchar = in.read();
    while (Character.isWhitespace((char)inchar)) {
        inchar = in.read();
    }
    return inchar;
}
```

The complete implementation of `readInt` is shown in Listing 16.1. Note the following.

- Both the methods `read` and `unread` might throw *java.io.IOExcpetions*. Thus the readInt must include a throws clause in its header.

- If a digit is not found after the initial white space and optional sign, an *InputFormatException* is thrown. We assume this exception class is defined in the same package as *SimpleScanner*.

- Digits are read left to right. Thus as each new digit is read, the previous value of `lastInt` is multiplied by 10, and the value of the new digit added.

- The nondigit character that terminates the while loop is "pushed back" onto the input stream.

Finally, we should mention that the class *java.util.Scanner* is substantially more complex than our example. While our `readInt` method requires a single character look ahead, *Scanner* methods such as `hasNextInt` require an arbitrary amount of look ahead. Thus *Scanner* must be prepared to buffer an arbitrary about of input in memory, and then "read" from the buffer. Additionally, since *Scanner* is tailorable in several ways, it makes use of the `java.util.regex` classes *Pattern* and *Matcher* to recognize tokens. Discussion of these classes is beyond the scope of this text.

Listing 16.1 **The method *readInt***

```
public void readInt () throws java.io.Exception {
    int sign = 1;
    int inchar = skipSpace();

    if ((char)inchar == '-')
        sign = -1;
    if ((char)inchar == '+' || (char)inchar == '-')
        inchar = input.read();
```

continued

Listing 16.1 **The method *readInt* (cont'd)**

```
if (inchar == -1)
    throw new java.io.EOFException(
            "Encountered EOF; expected digit");
else if (!Character.isDigit((char)inchar)) {
    input.unread(inchar);
    throw new InputFormatException(
        "Encountered " + inchar + "; expected digit");
    }

lastInt = 0;
while (Character.isDigit((char)inchar)) {
    lastInt =
        10*lastInt + Character.digit((char)inchar,10);
    inchar = input.read();
}
lastInt = lastInt*sign;
if (inchar != -1)
    input.unread(inchar);

}
```

16.4   Output streams

The output stream classes mirror the input classes. We briefly introduce them below.

16.4.1 Output byte streams

Abstract class OutputStream

At the top of the output byte stream hierarchy is the abstract class *OutputStream*. Fundamental methods are:

> **public abstract void** write (**int** b) **throws** IOException
>> Write the specified byte (low order 8 bits of the **int** provided) to the output stream.

> **public void** close () **throws** IOException
>> Close the output stream and release any associated resources.

> **public void** flush () **throws** IOException
>> Write any buffered bytes to the output stream.

Class *FileOutputStream*

FileOutputStream extends *OutputStream* by allowing a file to be specified as the destination of the output, in much the same way that *FileInputStream* extends *InputStream*.

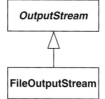

Constructors are:

public FileOutputStream (String name)
    throws FileNotFoundException, SecurityException
        Create a *FileOutputStream* to write to the file with the specified name.

public FileOutputStream (String name, **boolean** append)
    throws FileNotFoundException, SecurityException
        Create a *FileOutputStream* to write to the file with the specified name. If the second argument is true, then bytes will be written to the end of the file rather than the beginning.

public FileOutputStream (File file)
    throws FileNotFoundException, SecurityException
        Create a *FileOutputStream* to write to the file represented by the specified *File* object.

public FileOutputStream (File file, **boolean** append)
    throws FileNotFoundException, SecurityException
        Create a *FileOutputStream* to write to the file represented by the specified *File* object. If the second argument is true, then bytes will be written to the end of the file rather than the beginning.

public FileOutputStream (FileDescriptor fd)
    throws FileNotFoundException, SecurityException
        Create a *FileOutputStream* to write to the specified file descriptor.

Notice that a *FileOutputStream* can be created that appends to an existing file rather than overwriting the file. Otherwise, the file specified in the constructor is created if it does not already exist.

Classes *FilterOutputStream*, *BufferedOutputStream*, and *DataOutputStream*

FilterOutputStream provides a base class for *OutputStream* wrappers, again in a way similar to its input counterpart, *FilterInputStream*. *BufferedOutputStream* and *DataOutputStream* extend *FilterOutputStream*, and provide functionality symmetric with their input stream counterparts.

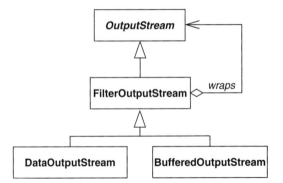

In particular, *DataOutputStream* contains the following methods.

public void writeBoolean (**boolean** v)
>   Write a **boolean** to the underlying output stream as a 1-byte value.

public void writeByte (**int** v)
>   Write a byte to the underlying output stream as a 1-byte value.

public void writeBytes (String s)
>   Write the *String* to the underlying output stream as a sequence of bytes.

public void writeChar (**int** v)
>   Write a **char** to the underlying output stream as a 2-byte value, high byte first.

public void writeChars (String s)
>   Write a *String* to the underlying output stream as a sequence of characters.

public void writeDouble **double** v)
>   Write a **double** to the underlying output stream as an 8-byte quantity.

public void writeInt (**int** v)
>   Write an **int** to the underlying output stream as four bytes.

Further details about these classes can be obtained from the standard documentation.

Class PrintStream: standard output and standard error

The class *PrintStream* also extends *FilterOutputStream*. However, *PrintWriter*, discussed below, should be used instead of *PrintStream*.

There are, however, two *PrintStreams* that are commonly used. They are *standard output* and *standard error*, introduced in Section 7.2. These are output byte streams, generally available to every program. The default destination for these streams is the display window in which the program is being run. Error messages should be directed to standard error and never to standard output. The reason is that standard output can be redirected to some other destination by the operating system when the program is run. Standard error is rarely redirected.

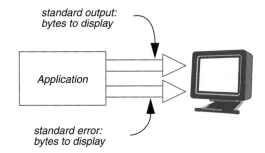

standard output:
bytes to display

Application

standard error:
bytes to display

Figure 16.3 **Standard output and standard error are output byte streams.**

Standard output and standard error can be accessed by means of the constants defined in the class *java.lang.System*:

```
public static final PrintStream out;// standard output
public static final PrintStream err;// standard error
```

PrintStream methods are very similar to those defined by *PrintWriter* described below.

16.4.2 Output character streams

Abstract class Writer

The abstract class *Writer* is at the top of the output character stream hierarchy. It is similar in functionality to *OutputStream*, but of course its `write` method writes a Unicode character rather than a byte.

```
public abstract void write (int c) throws IOException
```
           Write a character consisting of the low order 16 bits of the **int** provided to the output stream.

Classes BufferedWriter, OutputStreamWriter, and FileWriter

The wrapper class *BufferedWriter* extends *Writer*, and is symmetric to the *Reader* class *BufferedReader*.

    OutputStreamWriter adapts an *OutputStream* to a *Writer*, and is symmetric to *InputStreamReader*. *FileWriter* extends *OutputStreamWriter* in a manner similar to *FileReader*'s extension of *InputStreamReader*.

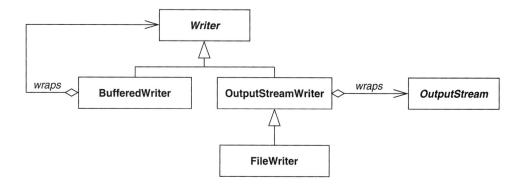

Class PrintWriter:

The class *PrintWriter* is one of the most useful output stream classes. *PrintWriter* extends and wraps a *Writer*, and provides functionality for writing string representations of primitive values and objects.

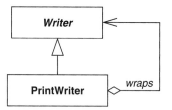

The four constructors are specified as follows:

public PrintWriter (OutputStream out)
> Create a *PrintWriter* that sends output to the specified *OutputStream*. An intermediate *OutputStreamWriter* that converts characters to bytes using the system default encoding is also constructed.

public PrintWriter (OutputStream out,
  boolean autoFlush)
> Create a *PrintWriter* that sends output to the specified *OutputStream*. An intermediate *OutputStreamWriter* that converts characters to bytes using the system default encoding is also constructed.
>
> If autoFlush is true, the *PrintWriter* calls its flush method after every invocation of println.

public PrintWriter (Writer out)
> Create a *PrintWriter* that sends output to the specified *Writer*.

public PrintWriter (Writer out, **boolean** autoFlush)
> Create a *PrintWriter* that sends output to the specified *Writer*.
>
> If autoFlush is true, the *PrintWriter* calls its flush method after every invocation of println.

Notice that a *PrintWriter* constructor can be given an *OutputStream* as argument. In this case, an *OutputStreamWriter* wrapping the *OutputStream* is automatically created. Characters are converted to bytes using the system default encoding scheme. Thus writing

```
new PrintWriter(someOutputStream)
```

is equivalent to writing

```
new PrintWriter(
    new OutputStreamWriter(someOutputStream))
```

Among the methods provided by *PrintWriter* are the following.

public void print (**boolean** b)
    Write "true" or "false" to the output stream depending on the value specified.

public void print (**char** c)
    Write the specified character to the output stream.

public void print (**int** i)
    Write a string representation of the specified **int** to the output stream.

public void print (**double** d)
    Write a string representation of the specified **double** to the output stream.

public void print (Object obj)
    Write a string representation of the specified *Object* to the output stream, using the *Object*'s toString method.

public void print (String s)
    Write the specified *String* to the output stream.

For each of the above print methods, there is a corresponding **println** method that appends a line separator. For instance,

public void println (**int** i)
    Write a string representation of the specified **int** to the output stream, followed by a line separator.

DrJava: character streams and byte streams

This exercise will involve creating files. On most systems, the files will be created in the directory from which *DrJava* was started.

Open the file Exercise.java, located in exercise, in ch16, in nhText. This class contains four static utility methods for the exercise.

It will be somewhat easier to deal with *File* object rather than file names.

1.   Create a *File* object for a file named "temp":

```
> import ch16.exercise.*;
> import java.io.*;
> File f = new File("temp");
```

Look at the method `printOut`. This method writes to an *OutputStream*. First it writes a single byte containing the value 51 with the `write` command. Then it writes a representation of the number 51, as a sequence of ASCII (probably, but dependent on your system) characters, with the `print` command.

2.   Create a file using the method `printOut`. Check its size and contents.

```
> Exercise.printOut(f);
> f.length()
> Exercise.displayFile(f);
```

The method `displayFile` writes out the contents of a file, byte by byte, showing each byte as a decimal number.

Is there any special "end of file" byte in your file, or just the three(?) bytes that you have written?

What is the ASCII encoding of the character '5'? You would expect the encoding of the character '1' to be four less. Is it?

Look at the method `writeOut`. Recall that an *OutputStreamWriter* serves as a bridge between a character stream (produced by a *Writer*) and a byte stream (modeled with an *OutputStream*). When the *OutputStreamWriter* is created, a method of encoding 16-bit **char** values to bytes is specified.

The *OutputStreamWriter* `out1` uses the system default encoding. Typically, this encoding will simply convert the **char** to an equivalent ASCII character. (What if there is no equivalent ASCII character? Experiment!) The *OutputStreamWriter* `out2` specifies that a 16-bit char is to be written as two bytes, high order to low order.

3.   Create two files using the method `printOut`. Compare their sizes and contents.

```
> File f1 = new File("temp1");
> File f2 = new File("temp2");
> Exercise.writeOut(f1,f2);
> f1.length()
> f2.length()
> Exercise.displayFile(f1);
> Exercise.displayFile(f2);
```

Finally, look at the method `printLine`. This method creates a file containing two lines of three characters each. Using `displayFile`, you can see any "line termination" characters.

4.   Create a file using `printLine`. Examine its size and contents.

```
> Exercise.printLine(f);
> f.length()
> Exercise.displayFile(f);
```

5.   Clean up the files that you have created.

```
> f.delete();
> f1.delete();
> f2.delete();
```

✳ 16.5   The class *File*

The class *File* abstracts the representation of file and directory pathnames in a system independent fashion. An abstract pathname has two components:

1. an optional system-dependent *prefix* string, such as a disk-drive specifier, "/" for the UNIX root directory, or "\\" for a Microsoft Windows UNC pathname, and

2. a sequence of zero or more string *names*.

Each name in an abstract pathname except the last denotes a directory; the last name may denote either a directory or a file. The conversion of an abstract pathname to or from a *String* is inherently system-dependent.

A pathname may be either *absolute* or *relative*. An absolute pathname is complete in that no other information is required to locate the file that it denotes. A relative pathname, however, must be interpreted in terms of some other pathname. By default `java.io` classes interpret relative pathnames with respect to the directory from which the program was run.

Constructors include:

> **public** File (String pathname)
>> Create a new *File* instance by converting the given *String* into an abstract pathname

> **public** File (String parent, String child)
>> Create a new *File* instance from a parent pathname *String* and a child pathname *String*. The parent *String* is taken to denote a directory. The child *String* is taken to denote either a directory or file.

> **public** File (File parent, String child)
>> Create a new *File* instance from a parent abstract pathname and a child pathname *String*. The parent abstract pathname is taken to denote a directory. The child *String* is taken to denote either a directory or file.

Note that creating a *File* instance does not create an actual file in file system. A *File* instance models the path name for a file or directory. An actual file is created, for instance, by invoking a *FileOutputStream* or *FileWriter* constructor.

Among the methods defined by *File* are the following.

> **public boolean** canRead ()
>> The application can read the file denoted by this abstract pathname.

> **public boolean** canWrite ()
>> The application can modify to the file denoted by this abstract pathname.

> **public boolean** exists ()
>> The file or directory denoted by this abstract pathname exists.

> **public boolean** isDirectory ()
>> The file denoted by this abstract pathname is a directory.

public boolean isFile ()

The file denoted by this abstract pathname is a normal file and not a directory.

public boolean createNewFile () **throws** IOException

Create a new, empty file named by this abstract pathname if and only if a file with this name does not yet exist. Returns *true* if the named file does not exist and was successfully created; *false* if the named file already exists.

public boolean delete ()

Delete the file or directory denoted by this abstract pathname. If this pathname denotes a directory, then the directory must be empty in order to be deleted. Returns *true* if and only if the file or directory is successfully deleted; *false* otherwise.

As with many of the methods in the java.io library, createNewFile and delete are neither proper commands nor proper queries. They change the state of the system like commands, but return values like queries.

16.6 Summary

We have looked at the basic classes in the java.io stream library. Specifically, there are four root classes, one for each category of stream: *InputStream* models input byte streams, *Reader* models input character streams, *OutputStream* models output byte stream, and *Writer* models output character streams. Character streams in Java represent characters with a 16-bit Unicode encoding. Any other stream is considered a byte stream.

Classes add functionality to the root classes by extension and composition. Each root class has a corresponding *Filter* class that serves as a basis for extension:

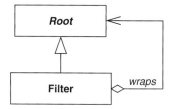

The *Filter* both extends and wraps the root class. It adds no new functionality, but simply forwards all requests to the component root class instance. Functionality is added by extending the *Filter*. Since the *Filer* is a subclass of the root, functionality can be accumulated by having one *Filter* wrap another.

The classes *InputStreamReader* and *OutputStreamWriter* are *Reader* and *Writer* subclasses that wrap an *InputStream* and *OutputStream* respectively. An *InputStreamReader* converts each byte of input to a 16-bit character using a system default or specified encoding. *OutputStreamWriter* converts each 16-bit character to a byte, again using a system default or specified encoding.

FileInputStream, *FileOutputStream*, *FileReader*, and *FileWriter* allow a file to be specified as stream source or destination. The file can be specified by name, with a *File* object, or with a file descriptor.

There are three standard predefined streams available to every application: `System.in`, `System.out`, and `System.err`. `System.in` is an *InputStream*. `System.out` and `System.err` are *PrintStreams*. A *PrintStream* is a *FilterOutputStream* with a number of useful methods for writing out character representations of values.

A particularly useful output class is *PrintWriter*. A *PrintWriter* is a *Writer* with methods similar to *PrintStream*'s for converting values to character strings. The characters are converted to bytes using a system default encoding before being written to an *OutputStream*.

SELF-STUDY EXERCISES

16.1   Indicate whether each of the following statements is true or false:

   a.   In Java, an input stream containing ASCII characters is considered a byte stream and not a character stream.

   b.   An input stream whose source is a file is necessarily finite.

   c.   Java's standard i/o library provides easy to use methods for reading and parsing textual input, but not for generating textual output.

   d.   The *InputStream* method read throws an *EOFException* if the end of stream is encountered.

   e.   Standard input, as accessed through the variable `System.in`, is a byte stream.

16.2   A *DataInputStream* is an *InputStream*, and so inherits *InputStream*'s read method. What are the differences between *DataInputStream*'s readByte and read methods?

16.3   *FilterInputStream* extends *InputStream*. *InputStream* is abstract, but *FilterInputStream* is not. Thus *FilterInputStream* must implement the abstract method read inherited from *InputStream*. How does *FilterInputStream* do this, if it "adds no new functionality" to *InputStream*?

16.4   Why bother with *FilterInputStream* if it adds no new functionality? Why not simply let classes like *DataInputStream* and *BufferedInputStream* extend *InputStream* and inherit *InputStream*'s functionality?

16.5   Suppose we want a *Reader* to read from a file named `"foo.bar"` where the translation from bytes to characters is done by an encoding named `"UTF-16BE"`. Write the definition of a *Reader* named `input` to do this.

16.6   Suppose that `out` is an *OutputStream*. How will the following "translate" a character to a byte?

```
char c = ...
out.write((byte)c);
```

16.7 If the file `foo.bar` does not exist, what will the statement

```
FileOutputStream out =
    new FileOutputStream("foo.bar");
```

do?

16.8 If the file `foo.bar` exists, what will the statements

```
FileOutputStream out =
    new FileOutputStream("foo.bar");

FileOutputStream out =
    new FileOutputStream("foo.bar",true);
```

do?

16.9 Why should error messages be directed to `System.err` rather than `System.out`?

✳ 16.10 Suppose the file `foo.bar` does not exits. Assuming no errors, which of the following statements creates the file?

(a)   `File f = new File("foo.bar");`

(b)   `FileOutputStream output = new FileOutputStream(f);`

EXERCISES

16.1 Write a method `nullCount` that takes an *InputStream* as argument, and returns the number of null (0) bytes contained in the stream.

16.2 Write a method compress that takes a *Reader* and a *Writer* as arguments. The method reads from the *Reader*, until end of stream is encountered, and writes to the *Writer*. Multiple spaces in the input stream are replaced with a single space in the output stream.

16.3 Write a method `replace` that takes two *String* arguments, `match` and `subst`. The method reads from standard input and writes to standard out. All occurrences of the *String* `match` in the input stream are replaced with the *String* `subst` in the output stream. Be careful when matching a *String* like `"aab"` against input `:b`.

16.4 Using a web browser, access the Java API documentation for the class *java.lang.String-Buffer*. A *StringBuffer* implements a mutable string of characters. That is, a *StringBuffer* is like a *String* that can be modified. When a string of characters must be constructed one by one, it is generally more efficient to fill a *StringBuffer* than to use *String* concatenation.

Rewrite the method `readInt` of Listing 16.1. Rather than multiplying `lastInt` by 10 and adding each digit, store the digit characters in a *StringBuffer*, and then use the *Integer* method `parseInt` to convert to an int.

16.5 Define a class *SimpleInput* that extends *BufferedReader*. *SimpleInput* should have methods similar to those specified for the class *SimpleInput* on page 646, but the methods will not have a prompt and will not be static. For example,

public int readInt ()
>   Read a single line of input and return the value of the integer represented on the line. The characters on the line must be all decimal digits, except that the first character may be a minus sign '–'.

16.6   Define a class *SimpleInput* that extends *PushbackReader*. *SimpleInput* should have one additional method:

public int readInt ()
>   Read an **int**. The digit string is interpreted as a decimal integer.
>
>   **require:**
>>   leading characters in the input stream must consist of:
>>>   zero or more white space characters, followed by
>>>   an optional sign, followed by
>>>   one or more decimal digits.

16.7   Write a method writeList that takes a *List<Integer>* and a *DataOutputStream* as argument, and writes the contents of the list to the output stream.

>   Write a companion method readList that takes a *DataInputStream* as argument. The *DataInputStream* should contain a sequence of 32-bit integers written by a *DataOutputStream*. The method should read the input stream and return a *List<Integer>* containing the values.

16.8   Write a method saveCard that takes a *PlayingCard* (Section 2.6) and a *String* file name as arguments, and appends a representation of the *PlayingCard* to the file.

>   Write a companion method restoreCardList that takes a *String* file name as argument, and returns a *List<PlayingCard>*. The file should contain a sequence of *PlayingCard* representations produced by the method saveCard.

16.9   Write a method saveGame to be included in the class *Game* of Chapter 8. The method should take a *String* argument, and save a representation of the same in the file named by the *String*. You may include similar methods in the classes *Player* and *Pile* if you wish.

16.10   Write a static method restoreGame that rebuilds the nim game saved by the saveGame method of the previous exercise. The method should take a *String* argument, the name of the file to read, and return a *Game*.

SELF-STUDY EXERCISE SOLUTIONS

16.1   *a.*   True.
>   *b.*   True.
>   *c.*   False.
>   *d.*   False.
>   *e.*   True.

16.2 `readByte` returns a **byte**, in the range –128 through 127, and throws an *EOFException* if end of stream is encountered.

read returns an **int**, in the range 0 through 255, or returns –1 if end of stream is encountered.

16.3 *FilterInputStream* has an *InputStream* component. (It wraps an *InputStream*.) *FilterInputStream* simply forwards the responsibility to its component:

```
public int read() throws IOException {
    return in.read();
}
```

where

```
private InputStream in;
```

is the component variable.

16.4 By using composition, we can dynamically build a class adding whatever functionality is needed. For instance, we can get the benefits of buffering and the functionality of a *DataInputStream* by wrapping a *BufferedInputStream* in a *DataInputStream*. If we used extension alone, we'd need to define a new class for every possible set of functionality.

16.5 ```
Reader input = new InputStreamReader(
    new FileInputStream("foo.bar"),"UTF-16BE"));
```

16.6 By "throwing away" the high order eight bits of c.

16.7 It will create the file, or throw a *FileNotFoundException* (a form of *IOException*) if this cannot be done.

16.8 The first will overwrite the existing file. The second will append to the existing file. In either case, a *FIleNotFoundException* will be thrown if the file cannot be opened for writing.

16.9 `System.out` is sometimes redirected away from the terminal window when an application is run. `System.err` almost never is.

16.10 Statement *(b)* creates the file.
```

CHAPTER 17

Building a graphical user interface

In this chapter, we look at the fundamental classes used for implementing a graphical user interface. In Java, these classes are provided primarily in a user interface library know as *Swing*. Swing is an enhancement of a library called the *Abstract Window Toolkit*, or *AWT*. The AWT has been available as long as the language itself and has undergone substantial evolution since its original design. Swing is an extension of the AWT, intended to provide the functionality and flexibility necessary to develop substantial commercial applications.

The Java user interface libraries are large and complex, containing several hundred classes and interfaces. This complexity is probably unavoidable in any set of tools capable of supporting the degree of customization required in building sophisticated, portable, extensible graphical user interfaces. Furthermore, the Swing components are built as an extension of previous AWT library elements. The designers likely had in mind maintaining some degree of compatibility between Swing and existing applications built with the AWT and providing a relatively straightforward path for upgrading applications to Swing. Maintaining compatibility between versions of a software system almost inevitably leads to increased complexity in the later versions.

A comprehensive discussion of the Swing components and their use would require thousands of pages and is clearly beyond the scope of this text. Our intention is not to develop proficiency in designing user interfaces with Swing. Rather, we want to understand some of the more fundamental concepts and take a brief look at a few of the most central classes. This will serve our purpose, which is to see how an event-driven, window-based application is structured. Furthermore, as our goal in this chapter is to understand the user interface, we will keep the model component of our examples as simple as possible.

Swing will also serve as a case study of how a large library is organized. However, many Swing design decisions were influenced both by the existing AWT libraries and by the need to provide a degree of flexibility well beyond the scope of this discussion. As a result, we cannot always offer a convincing justification for the underlying structures of the user interface libraries. Fortunately, there are several good reference texts available to the reader who needs detailed information regarding Swing and its use.

Objectives

After studying this chapter you should understand the following:

- the idea of an event driven interface;
- Java's Swing component and container structure;
- the use of layout managers to manage component positioning and sizing;
- handling events occurring in a component.

Also, you should be able to:

- build a simple display from graphical components;
- write event handlers that listen for high-level events;
- build a simple graphical user interface for an application.

17.1   Event-driven interfaces

We have seen that the *interface* and the *model* are two of the principal components of a software system. The model is the basic problem representation and problem-solving component; the interface handles interaction with the external world. When the external world is a person, we refer to the interface as a *user interface*. We have concentrated previously on design and implementation of the model. Now we take a closer look at the user interface.

There are two fundamental patterns describing how an application interacts with its environment, that we'll call *algorithm-driven* and *event-driven*. An application's structure substantially depends on the approach adopted. In an algorithm-driven approach, the application determines exactly what information it needs from the environment, and when to get it. The text-based interfaces that we designed in Chapters 7 and 8 are algorithm driven.

While the application is active in an algorithm-driven interface, it is passive in an event-driven system. In an event-driven system, the application waits for something to happen in the environment. That is, it waits for an *event*. When an event occurs, the application responds to the event, and then waits for the next event. Applications with a graphical, window-based user interface (usually called simply a *graphical user interface*, or *GUI*) are almost always event driven.

> **event-driven:** an input-output model in which the application waits for an event to occur, responds to the event, and waits for the next event.

An application with a window-based interface provides the user with a graphical "control panel" containing a range of options. There may be menus, buttons, text fields, *etc.* After displaying the interface, the application waits for the user to do something. The

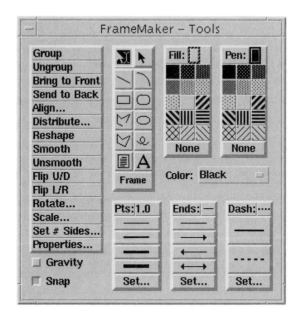

Figure 17.1 **A graphical user interface window, offering a number of options.**

user can press a button, choose a menu item, enter text in a text field, or exercise any other
option provided. When the user performs an action, the application responds to this event,
and then waits for the next user action.

In a window-based system, there is a native windowing system (such as Windows XP
or X Windows) that manages the display and detects events like mouse clicks, mouse
movement, key strokes, *etc*. A Java application interacts with the native windowing system
through AWT components. The application communicates with the native windowing system to create a display. Then events occurring in the display are detected by the native
windowing system and *delivered* to the application. The application performs some action
in response to the event (possibly changing the display), and then waits for notification of
the next event.

17.2   An introduction to Swing

17.2.1 Components

A graphical user interface is made up of *components* (sometimes called *widgets)*. Components are things like windows, buttons, checkboxes, menus, scroll bars, text fields, labels,

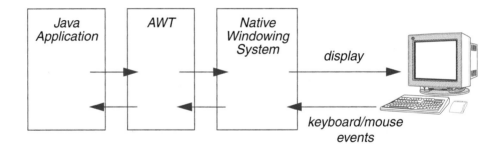

Figure 17.2 **Java applications interact with the native widowing system through the AWT.**

and so on. A component occupies display screen real estate: it has location, size, shape, color, *etc*.

There are two fundamental types of components.

- *Basic* components, sometimes called "atomic" components, are self-contained entities that present information to or get information from the user. A basic component can be a very simple thing like a button or label, or a complex structure like an editor pane (a text area for entering, displaying, and editing various kinds of textual content) or a combo box (a component that combines a button or editable field with a drop-down list).

- *Containers* are components whose function is to hold and position other components. A *top-level container* contains all of the visual components of an application's graphical user interface, and provides the screen real estate used by the application. The window in which an application is run, such as the window labeled *Components* in Figure 17.3, is a top-level container. Other containers, called *intermediate containers*, are used to simplify the organization and positioning of basic graphical components.

Some elementary component attributes

The Java Swing components are defined in the package `javax.swing` and its subpackages. An application uses these classes to build and manage a graphical user interface. One of the fundamental classes in `javax.swing` is the abstract class *JComponent*. Most of the components created by an application are instances of some *JComponent* subclass

JComponent is a subclass of the older *AWT* class *java.awt.Component*, and inherits many of its most obvious properties from that class. Component properties include foreground and background colors, location, size, and font. We'll see more as we go along. The values of these properties can be obtained with queries:

```
public Color getForeground ();
public Color getBackground ();
public Point getLocation ();
public Dimension getSize ();
public Font getFont ();
```

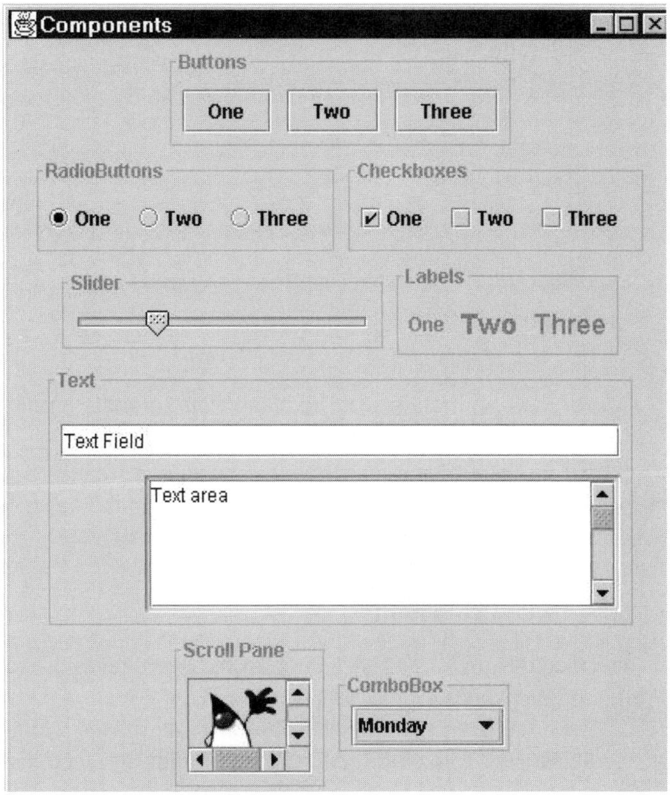

Figure 17.3 **Some Swing** *components.*

and can be set with methods:

```
public void setForeground (Color fg);
public void setBackground (Color bg);
public void setLocation (Point p);
public void setSize (Dimension d);
public void setFont (Font f);
```

Many of the methods are overloaded. For instance, there are versions of setLocation and setSize that take two **int** arguments rather than a *Point* or *Dimension*.

Color, Point, Dimension, and *Font* are AWT classes (defined in the package java.awt) that model the obvious notions. Instances of the class *Color* are immutable: once the instance is created, it cannot be changed. The class *Color* defines a number of constant references, such as Color.red, Color.blue, Color.green.

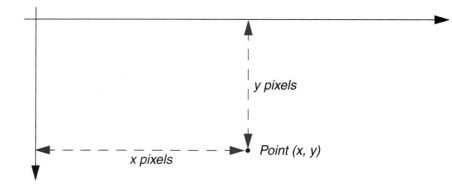

Figure 17.4 **An instance of the class *Point* models a point on the display screen.**

An instance of the class *Point* represents a (relative) position in an *x-y* coordinate space. Units are pixels,[1] and the origin (0,0) is in the upper left. Attributes of a *Point* can be accessed through *public*(!) instance variables x and y:

```
public int x;
public int y;
```

(The methods getX and getY return the coordinates as **double**s. There are no setX and setY methods.)

An instance of the class *Dimension* encapsulates width and height, again in pixels. Attributes are accessed directly through public instance variables as was the case with *Point*:

```
public int height;
public int width;
```

(As with *Point*, methods getHeight and getWidth return the values of the attributes as **double**s.)

Instances of the class *Font* represent text fonts. A font provides information needed to render text in a visible way. Working with fonts is a rather complex business. We touch briefly on fonts later in the chapter.

Basic components

As we mentioned, basic or "atomic" components present information to or get information from the user. We briefly describe some of common components below. Some are illustrated in Figures 17.3 and 17.5. These components are defined in javax.swing, and are subclasses of *JComponent*.

The following are used primarily to get input from the user.

---

1. A pixel is the smallest dot that can be independently colored on a display screen.

JButton	a simple push button that can be "pushed" with a mouse click.
JCheckBox	a button that can be toggled on or off, and displays its state to the user.
JRadioButton	a button that can be toggled on or off, and displays its state to the user. Only one radio button in a group can be on.
JComboBox	a drop-down list with an optional editable text field. The user can either key in a value or select a value from the drop-down list.
JList	a component that allows a user to select one or more items from a list.
JMenu	a popup list of items from which the user can select. Menus either appear on a "menu bar" or as "pop-ups" associated with a user action such as pressing the right mouse button.
JSlider	a component that lets the user graphically select a value by sliding a knob within a bounded interval.
JTextField	an area for entering a single line of input.

These components are used to provide information to the user.

JLabel	a component containing a short text string, an image, or both.
JProgressBar	a component that communicates the progress of some work by displaying its percentage of completion and possibly a textual display of this percentage.
JToolTip	a small window that describes another component.

The remaining atomic components provide formatted information and a way of editing it.

First Name	Last Name	Position	Averange	Number
Johnny	Damon	cf	.261	18
Todd	Walker	2b	.282	12
Nomar	Garciaparra	ss	.322	5
Manny	Ramirez	lf	.312	24
David	Ortiz	dh	.291	34

```
☐ Computer Science
  ╿ ☐ Software Engineering
      ┝ ▢ The Art of Software Architecture: Design Methods and Techniques
      ┝ ▢ Software Engineering: An Object-Oriented Perspective
      ┝ ▢ Software Engineering: An Engineering Approach
      └ ▢ Software Engineering: An Engineering Approach
  ╿ ☐ Data Communications
      ┝ ▢ Principles of Network and System Administration
      └ ▢ LAN Management with SNMP and RMON
```

Figure 17.5 **Some complex components: Table and Tree.**

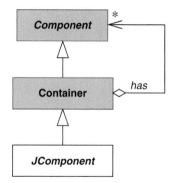

Figure 17.6 **A** *JComponent* **is-a** *Container* **is-a** *Component.*

JTree	a component that displays hierarchical data in outline form.
JTable	a component user to edit and display data in a two-dimensional grid.

Classes *JTextArea*, *JTextPane*, and *JEditorPane* define multiline areas for displaying, entering, and editing text.

17.2.2 Containers

An object that contains components is a *container*. Containers are modeled by the `java.awt` abstract class *Container*. An important simplifying aspect of the library structure is that a *Container* is just another kind of component. That is, the class *Container* is a subclass of the class *Component*. This means that a *Container* can contain another *Container*. Furthermore, the Swing class *JComponent* is a subclass of *Container*. This relationship is illustrated in Figure 17.6. In this and subsequent figures, shaded rectangles denote AWT classes, and unshaded rectangles Swing classes.

Since *JComponent* is a subclass of *Container*, any *JComponent*, even a basic component, can contain other components. However, basic components are generally not used to hold other components.

> **component:** a distinct element of a graphical user interface, such as a button, text field, and so on.
>
> **container:** a graphical user interface component that can contain other components.

Since a *Container* can hold another *Container*, a user interface has a *hierarchical containment strucutre*.

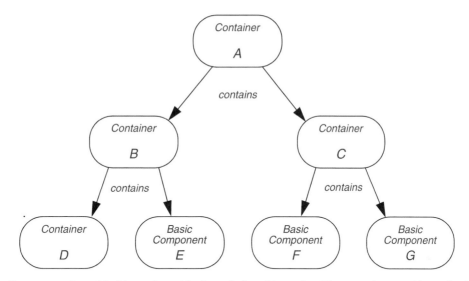

Do not confuse this hierarchy with the subclass hierarchy. The containment hierarchy is defined by a relation between objects: one object *contains* another.

We often use "genealogical" terminology when referring to objects in the hierarch: if *A* contains *B*, we say "*A* is the *parent* of *B*" and "*B* is the *child* of *A*." Terms like *ancestor*, *descendent, etc.* have the obvious meanings. In the above illustration, *A* is parent of *B* and an ancestor of *D*. *F* is a child of *C* and a descendent of *A*.

The class *Container* defines an extensive set of methods for adding components and manipulating its contents, including five overloaded version of the method `add`. But containers in a user interface tend to be stable. Once they are built and populated with components, there is rarely much need to add to, remove from, or rearrange their contents.

Intermediate containers

Intermediate containers are used to organize and position other components. The simplest, garden-variety, no-frills intermediate container is a *JPanel*. A *JPanel* is generally used just as a place for collecting other components. For instance, the following creates a *JPanel* and adds two buttons, labeled "on" and "off."

```
JPanel p = new JPanel();
p.add(new JButton("on"));
p.add(new JButton("off"));
```

Some other intermediate containers are:

JScrollPane   provides a "scrollable" view of another component, that is, a view with scroll bars (see Figure 17.3);

JSplitPane   divides two components graphically; the components can be interactively resized by the user;

JTabbedPane	lets the user switch between a group of components by clicking on a labeled tab;
JToolBar	is useful for displaying a set of commonly used controls.

Top-level containers

A *top-level container* is one that is not contained in any other container. Top-level containers provide a screen area where other components can display themselves. Instances of Swing classes *JApplet*, *JDialog*, *JFrame*, and *JWindow* are commonly used as top-level containers. The standard top-level container for an application's user interface is a *JFrame*. We concentrate our attention on *JFrames*.

A *JFrame* is a window with title and border. It can be moved, resized, iconified, *etc.* like any other native system window. A *JFrame* can also have a menu bar. There are two things to note about the class *JFrame*. First, though it is a subclass of *java.awt.Container*, it is not a subclass of *JComponent*. Second, it delegates the responsibility of managing its components to another object.

The detailed structure of a *JFrame* need not concern us at the moment. We can consider a *JFrame* to have a component called a *content pane*[1]. This is the working area of the *JFrame*, excluding the title, border, and menu. The content pane is generally a *JPanel*. If we want to add a component to a *JFrame*, we actually add it to the *JFrame*'s content pane. The content pane can be obtained with the method `getContentPane`, which returns a *Container*. We add a button to a *JFrame* like this:

```
JFrame f = new JFrame("A Frame");
JButton b = new JButton("Press");
Container cp = f.getContentPane();
cp.add(b);
```

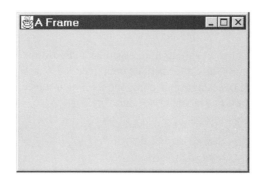

Figure 17.7   A JFrame is a top-level application window.

---

1. A *JFrame* has a *JRootPane*, which has a *JLayeredPane,* which actually contains the content pane and an optional *JMenuBar*.

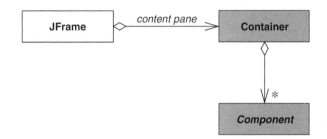

Figure 17.8 A *JFrame* delegates responsibility for managing components.

Heavyweight components and component peers

Instances of the classes *JApplet*, *JDialog*, *JFrame*, and *JWindow* are called *heavyweight* components. Other Swing components, in particular instances of *JComponent* subclasses, are *lightweight* components. When a heavyweight component is created, an associated native GUI component called a *peer* is also created. For instance, if the application creates a *JFrame*, a frame peer will also be created. The peer is part of the native windowing system, and does the actual work of capturing user input and managing the screen area in which the component is displayed. You will notice that the label bar and window control buttons in some figures differ from those in other figures. (Compare Figure 17.7 and Figure 17.20.) This is because the windows were created with two different native windowing systems, each with its own default "look and feel.".

Lightweight components, on the other hand, are completely implemented by Java. They are not associated with peer objects in the native windowing system. Lightweight components are essentially drawn on the space provided by their heavyweight parent containers. Lightweight components are more efficient and flexible than heavyweight components.

Since all the underlying details are handled behind the scenes by AWT-related classes, we don't usually need to worry about peer objects.

17.3   Creating a display

17.3.1 The top-level frame

The implementation of a Java application with a graphical user interface involves the use of a *JFrame* to display application output, gather user input, and provide access to the application's functionality. Creating and displaying a frame is relatively simple. Let's start with a trivial program that creates an empty display. For simplicity, we do everything at first in the method `main`. In an actual system, of course, building and managing the display is the job of the user interface.

First, we need to create a *JFrame* instance:

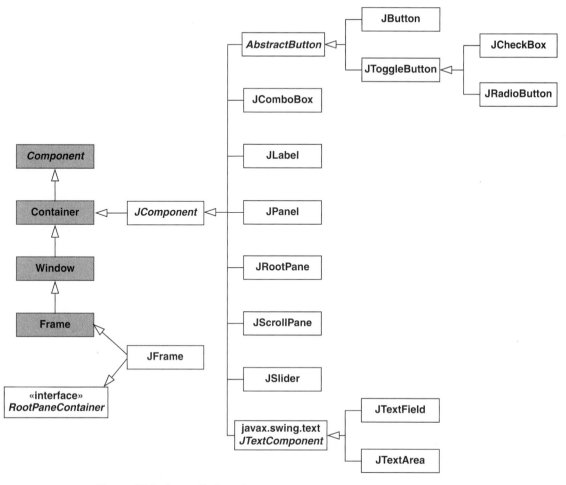

Figure 17.9 **Some Swing classes.**

```
import javax.swing.*;

public class DisplayFrame {

    public static void main (String[] args) {
        JFrame f = new JFrame("A Frame");
        ...
```

The *String* argument to the *JFrame* constructor gives the frame a title, and can be omitted.
The *JFrame* instance has an initial width and height of 0 when created. We'll set its
size a little bigger, to make it easier to deal with:[1]

1. How a 0×0 window actually looks is system dependent.

```
f.setSize(300,200);
```

This sets the width of the *JFrame* to 300 pixels and the height to 200. The exact physical size of the *JFrame* and how much display real estate it will occupy depend on the size and resolution of the display screen.

If we look up the class *JFrame* in the Swing documentation, we won't find the method `setSize`. *JFrame* inherits `setSize` from *Component*.

The *JFrame* has been created and sized, but is not yet visible on the display screen. In effect, the native windowing system which actually manages the display knows nothing about the *JFrame*. To show the *JFrame*, we must set its *visible* property to *true*:

```
f.setVisible(true);
```

This command does considerably more than change the state of the object. A peer is created, and the *JFrame* is displayed on the screen, as shown in Figure 17.7.

17.3.2 The event dispatching thread

Suppose we complete the program from the previous section,

```
import javax.swing.*;

public class DisplayFrame {

    public static void main (String[] args) {
        JFrame f = new JFrame("A Frame");
        f.setSize(300,200);
        f.setVisible(true);
    }
}
```

and run it. A window similar to that pictured in Figure 17.7 is displayed on the screen. Simple enough. But something odd is happening. Look at the method `main`. It consists of three statements. When the program is run, the method `main` is executed. The three statements comprising `main` are executed, and the method terminates. The variable `f`, local to `main`, is deallocated. But the application has not terminated, even though the method `main` has completed execution. The *JFrame* remains on the screen. You can resize, move, and iconify the *JFrame*, just as with any other native GUI window.

Choosing *"Close"* from the *JFrame* window menu will likely close the window, but not terminate the application. As things are now, the only way that you can terminate the application is by an explicit signal from the operating system. (`Control-C` works on many systems, but if you don't know how to get the operating system to kill a process, don't run this application!)

The reason the application does not terminate when `main` is finished is that a second *thread*, called the *event dispatching thread*, is created when the *JFrame* is set visible. A *thread* is essentially a sequence of instructions being executed by the processor.

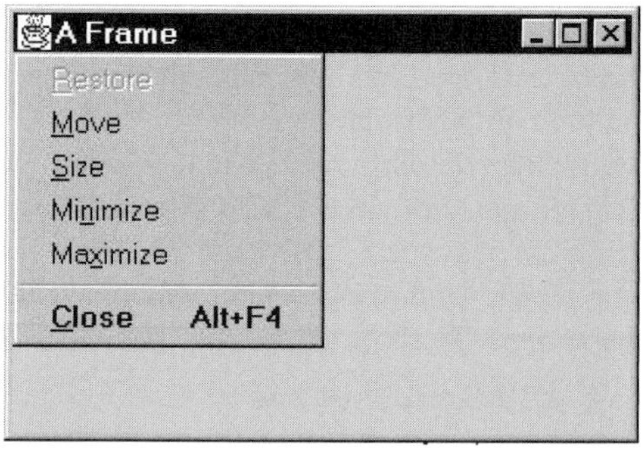

Figure 17.10   **Closing the top-level frame does not automatically terminate the application.**

So far, all of our programs have consisted of a single thread, called the *main* thread. This is the sequence of actions initiated by the `main` method. But a program can contain several threads. That is, there can be several independent sequences of actions being carried out simultaneously in the program. If there is a single processor executing the program, these actions are not, in fact, happening at the same time. The processor will execute a few instructions from one thread and then execute a few instructions from another. But in general, we cannot determine whether a particular statement in one thread will be executed before or after a particular statement in another thread.

Managing threads is a complex and demanding business, as it is easy to introduce subtle errors into the code. The details of coordinating and synchronizing interacting threads is well beyond the scope of this text. However, you should understand that all the code that involves repainting components and handling events executes in the event dispatching thread. After the *JFrame* has been made visible, the main thread should not, in general, perform actions that affect or depend on the state of the user interface.[1]

17.3.3 Adding components: layout

Containers are used to contain other components. These components are added to the container using one of the `add` methods mentioned earlier. But as you might guess, it is not enough simply to add a component. We want to control how a component will be positioned in the container when the container is painted on the screen.

---

1. In fact, invoking `setVisible` from the main thread is not entirely thread safe and is not recommended practice in production systems. The event dispatching thread can be active before `setVisible` completes. A detailed discussion of the problem and possible solutions is well beyond the scope of this text.
   See `http://java.sun.com/docs/books/tutorial/uiswing/misc/threads.html` for more information.

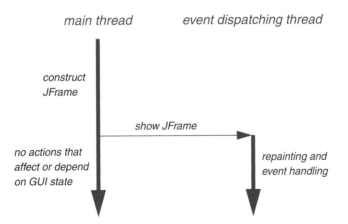

Figure 17.11 **GUI component repainting and event handling occurs in the event dispatching thread.**

To handle this problem, each container is equipped with a *layout manager*. A layout manager is an object with the responsibility of positioning and sizing components in a container. The container delegates these responsibilities to its layout manager. We control the positioning of components by setting the container's layout manager and by telling the layout manager how to position components as they are added to the container.

A layout manager must implement the interface *java.awt.LayoutManager*. This interface specifies the methods all layout managers must provide. Some layout managers implement the interface *java.awt.LayoutManager2*, which extends *LayoutManager*. A *Container* has query `getLayout` and command `setLayout` for accessing and setting its layout manager:

```
public LayoutManager getLayout();
public void setLayout (LayoutManager manager);
```

Java provides several classes that implement *LayoutManager*, including *FlowLayout*, *BorderLayout*, *GridLayout*, *CardLayout*, *GridBagLayout*, *BoxLayout*, and *OverlayLayout*. *BoxLayout* and *OverlayLayout* are defined in the package `javax.swing`. The others are defined in `java.awt`. You can, of course, implement your own layout manager. Some layout manager classes are designed so that a single layout manager instance can manage the layout of several containers. In other cases, each container requires its own layout manager instance.

Discussing layout in detail is well beyond the scope of this chapter. We briefly summarize the standard layout managers.

FlowLayout   lays out components left to right, top to bottom. *FlowLayout* is the default layout of a *JPanel*.

BorderLayout   lays out up to five components, positioned "north," "south," "east," "west," and "center." *BorderLayout* is the default layout of a *JFrame*'s content pane.

GridLayout	lays out components in a two-dimensional grid.
CardLayout	displays components one at a time from a preset deck of components.
GridBagLayout	lays out components vertically and horizontally according to a specified set of constraints; the most complex and flexible of the Java-provided layout managers.
BoxLayout	lays out components in either a single horizontal row or single vertical column. *BoxLayout* is the default layout for the Swing lightweight container *Box*.
OverlayLayout	lays out components so that specified component alignment points are all in the same place. Thus components are laid out on top of each other.

The default layout manager of a *JPanel* is a *FlowLayout*. However, a *JFrame*'s content pane is a *JPanel* with a *BorderLayout*. A *FlowLayout* simply lays out components in the order in which they are added to the container. With a *BorderLayout*, a component's position is specified by a second argument to the add method when the component is added to the container. For instance, if pane is a container with a *BorderLayout*,

```
pane.add(new JButton("Push"), BorderLayout.NORTH);
```

adds a *JButton* to the container to be positioned "north," that is, at the top of the container. Figures 17.7 and 17.7 illustrate containers with *FlowLayout* and *BorderLayout* respectively.

Container validity

We mention one further *Container* property before moving on to events. A *Container* is *valid* if it does not need to be laid out. That is, if its size is known to the system, and its

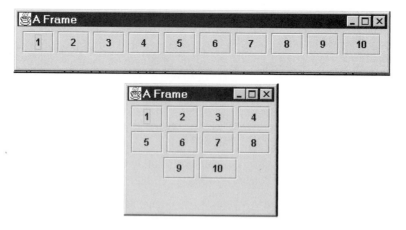

Figure 17.12 Two instances of a *JFrame* laid out with *FlowLayout*.

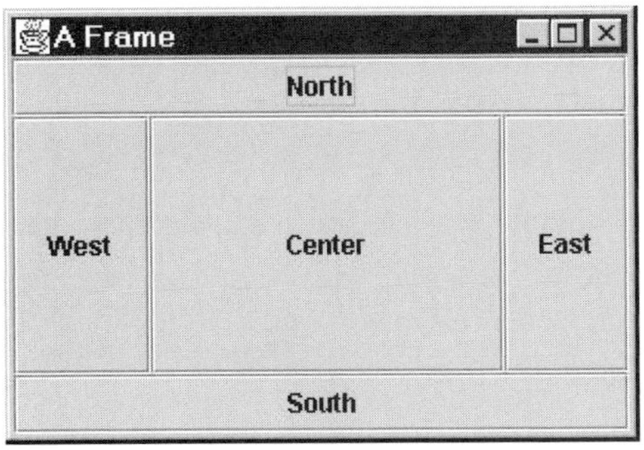

Figure 17.13 **A *JFrame* laid out with *BorderLayout*.**

layout manager knows about all of its components and has laid them out properly. A *Container* is invalid if its state is inconsistent with its appearance. Adding a component to a *Container* does not automatically cause the *Container* to be laid out again. The layout manager determines when to layout the *Container*. A *Container* to which a component has been added after it was last laid out is invalid.

Any number of things can cause a layout manager to lay out a *Container*. Layout managers typically notice a change in *Container* size, for example, and lay out the *Container* again if the user resizes the *Container*. The command `validate` explicitly sets the *Container's valid* property to *true* and instructs the layout manager to lay out the *container*. The query `isValid` returns the value of this property. The features are specified (for the class *Component*) as follows:

```
public boolean isValid ();
public void validate ();
```

DrJava: layout managers

The purpose of this exercise is to see how layout managers position and size components. Open the file `BorderExample1.java`, located in directory `layout`, in `ch17`, in `nhText`. This file contains a program that generates a *JFrame* containing a single button. The button is positioned north by a *BorderLayout*.

1. In the *Interactions* pane, run the program `BorderExample1`.

    ```
    > java ch17.layout.BorderExample1
    ```

    Resize the window and note how the layout manager resizes the button. The height of the button remains fixed, but the width expands and shrinks as the window is resized. To exit the program, close the window.

2. Modify the program so that the button is positioned west rather than north. Save and recompile.

3. Run the program again and notice how this button is resized as you resize the window.

Open the file `BorderExample2,java`. This program generates a *JFrame* containing five buttons positioned by a *BorderLayout*.

4.   Run the program `BorderExample2`.

> `java ch17.layout.BorderExample2`

Resize the window and note how the layout manager resizes the buttons.

Open the file `FlowExample.java`. This program generates a *JFrame* containing ten buttons positioned by a *FlowLayout*.

5.   Run the program `FlowExample`:

> `java ch17.layout.FlowExample`

Resize the window and note how the layout manager positions the buttons.

Open the file `GridExample.java`. This program generates a *JFrame* containing six buttons positioned by a *GridLayout*.

6.   Run the program `GridExample`:

> `java ch17.layout.GridExample`

Resize the window and note how the layout manager positions and resizes the buttons.

7.   Edit the program so that ten buttons are produced rather than six. Do not change the specification of the grid. Save, compile, and run the program. Note how the ten buttons are positioned.

17.4   Events: programming the user interface

An event-driven system waits for and responds to external events. In a system with a window-based graphical user interface, external events are user actions such as moving the mouse, pressing a key, *etc*. Programming the user interface reduces to capturing and handling these events.

Some events are low level: pressing or releasing a key on the keyboard, moving the mouse, pressing or releasing a mouse button. Other events are high-level: selecting an item from a menu, pressing a button, entering text in a field. Note that a high-level event usually involves one or more low-level events: to enter text in a text field, the user moves the mouse cursor, clicks a mouse button, and presses and releases several keyboard keys.

We summarize some events categories below. We limit our attention in the examples, however, to high-level events. (See Table 17.1 on page 684 for a more comprehensive list of components and the events they can generate.)

key event: keyboard key has been pressed or released.

mouse event: mouse button has been pressed or released; mouse has been moved or dragged; mouse cursor has entered or left component.

component event: component has been hidden, shown, resized, or moved.

container event: component has been added to or removed from a container.

window event: window has been opened, closed, iconified, deiconified, activated, deactivated.

focus event: component has gained or lost focus.

The following are high-level events.

action event: component-defined action has occurred (*e.g.*, a button has been pressed, a checkbox selected, *Return/Enter* pressed in a *JTextField*).

adjustment event: scrollbar has been moved.

item event: user has selected a checkbox or list item.

document event: content has changed in a *TextComponent*.

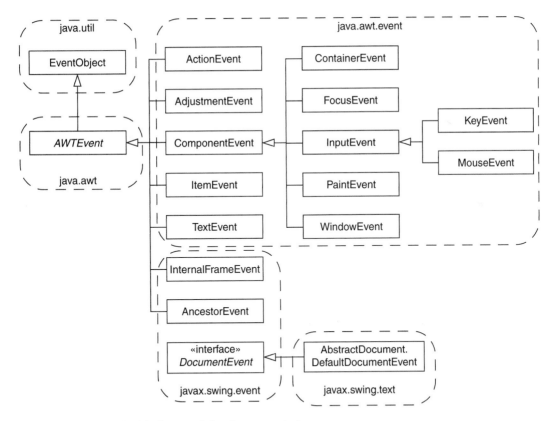

Figure 17.14 **Some of the Java event classes.**

Table 17.1   **Components and generated events**

Component	Event Generated	Meaning
Button	*ActionEvent*	User clicked button
CheckBox	*ItemEvent*	User selected or deselected item
CheckBoxMenuItem	*ItemEvent*	User selected or deselected item
Choice	*ItemEvent*	User selected or deselected item
Component	*ComponentEvent*	Component moved, resized, hidden or shown
	FocusEvent	Component gained or lost focus
	KeyEvent	User pressed or released key
	MouseEvent	User pressed or released mouse button, mouse entered or exited component, user moved or dragged mouse
Container	*ContainerEvent*	Component added or removed
List	*ActionEvent*	User doubled-clicked list item
	ItemEvent	User selected or deselected list item
MenuItem	*ActionEvent*	User selected menu item
Scrollbar	*AdjustmentEvent*	User moved scrollbar
TextComponent	*TextEvent*	User changed text
TextField	*ActionEvent*	User finished editing text
Window	*WindowEvent*	Window opened, closed, iconified, deiconified, or requested close

An important aspect of *Components* is that they are the *source* of events: events occur within *Components*. The *Component* in which an event occurs is said to *generate* the event, or to be the *source* of the event.

Events are, surprise, represented by objects. Many events are modeled by subclasses of the abstract class *java.awt.AWTEvent*, which is itself a subclass of *java.util.Event-Object*. (See Figure 17.14.)

An event object knows the event source and other relevant information about the event. We can determine the source of an event with the query `getSource`, defined on the class *EventObject*:

```
public Object getSource();
```

Note that the method returns an *Object*. If we know that the source is, say, a *JButton*, and want to treat it as such, we must cast the returned value to *JButton*. We'll see examples below.

An object that is interested in knowing when an event occurs is called a *listener*, or *event handler*. To be notified of an event, a listener must *register* with the event's source,

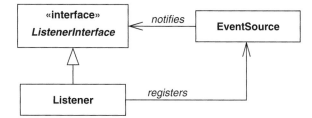

Figure 17.15 **An event listener is notified when an even occurs.**

that is with the component that will generate the event. A component can have any number of listeners, and a listener can register with any number of components. When an event occurs, each listener registered with the event's source is *notified* by having a specific listener method invoked. The relation between a listener and an event source is the same as that between an *InteractiveController* and *InteractivePlayer*, defined in Section 9.5.3.

Each kind of event is associated with an interface, called the *event listener interface*. This interface specifies the methods that must be implemented by a handler for that kind of event. Programming a handler for an event consists of implementing the interface associated with the event type (See Figure 17.17, and Table 17.2 on page 690 for a list of events, their listener interfaces, and the methods specified by the interfaces.).

---

event: the occurrence of an action, typically external to the system, that the system is aware of and must respond to.

17.4.1 An example

Let's develop a simple example to get an idea of how this works. We program an application that displays a button. When the button is pressed, its foreground and background colors are swapped.

First, we create a *JFrame* containing a single large button with black foreground and white background. Since it's the only component, we add it to the center of the content pane. The *BorderLayout* manager allocates any extra space to the button. Thus the button occupies the entire content pane, as shown in Figure 17.16.

```
import java.awt.*;
import javax.swing.*;
import java.awt.event.*;

class OnOffSwitch extends JFrame {

    public OnOffSwitch () {
        super("On/Off Switch"); // frame title
```

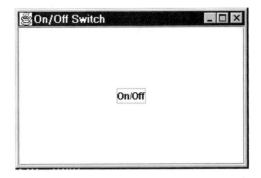

Figure 17.16 OnOffSwitch: a big *JButton* in a *JFrame*.

```
                    // create button and set its colors
                    JButton button = new JButton("On/Off");
                    button.setForeground(Color.black);
                    button.setBackground(Color.white);

                    // add button to JFrame's content pane:
                    this.getContentPane().add(
                        button, BorderLayout.CENTER);
                }
            }

        public class OnOffTest {
            public static void main (String[] args) {
                OnOffSwitch frame = new OnOffSwitch();
                frame.setSize(300,200);
                frame.setVisible(true);
            }
        }
```

We've organized things a little differently this time. Specifically, we've extended the class *JFrame* with *OnOffSwitch*, and given its constructor the responsibility for building the frame.

If we execute the program, pressing the button will have no effect at all. This is not surprising. When the button is pressed, it generates an *ActionEvent*. (Actually, pressing the button generates a number of events, such as *mouse pressed, mouse released, etc.* We are concerned only with the high-level *ActionEvent*.) But we have not yet written any listeners that will do anything about the event. We have not "programmed" the user interface.

Programming the GUI: adding an ActionListener for the JButton

If the user presses the button, the *JButton* object generates an *ActionEvent*. Let's implement a listener that will handle this event.

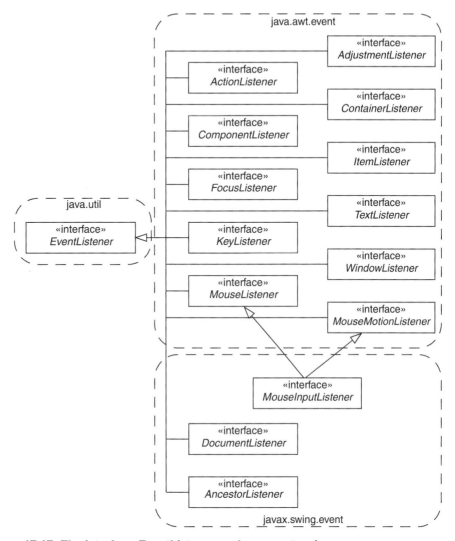

Figure 17.17 **The interface *EventListener*, and some extensions.**

First, the listener—we'll call it a *Switcher*—must implement the interface *java.awt.event.ActionListener*. As we've said, Java defines an interface for each category of event, and an object interested in being notified of a particular kind of event must implement the appropriate interface. This ensures that the listener object defines the methods that will be called when an event occurs.

There is only one method specified in the interface *ActionListener*:

```
public void actionPerformed (ActionEvent e);
```

This method is invoked to inform the listener that an event has occurred. A minimal implementation of the *Switcher* class looks like this:

```
class Switcher implements ActionListener {

    public void actionPerformed (ActionEvent e) {
    }
}
```

Of course with this implementation, a *Switcher* does nothing about the event after being informed of it. We'll take care of that in a bit. First, though, let's add code to create a listener and register it with the *JButton* component:

```
public OnOffSwitch () {
    super("On/Off Switch"); // frame title

    // create button and set its colors
    JButton button = new JButton("On/Off");
    button.setForeground(Color.black);
    button.setBackground(Color.white);

    // create and register button's listener:
    button.addActionListener(new Switcher());

    // add button to JFrame's content pane:
    this.getContentPane().add(
        button, BorderLayout.CENTER);
}
```

We create a new *Switcher* instance and register it with the *JButton* component by calling the *JButton*'s addActionListener method. This tells button that the listener wants to be informed of any *ActionEvents* it generates.

Finally, let's make the *Switcher* do something in response to the event. As we said above, we'll have it invert the foreground and background colors of the button.

```
class Switcher implements ActionListener {

    public void actionPerformed (ActionEvent e) {
        Component source = (Component)e.getSource();
        Color oldForeground = source.getForeground();
        source.setForeground(source.getBackground());
        source.setBackground(oldForeground);
    }
}
```

Note that we query the event to determine the source. Since the query getSource returns an *Object*, we must cast the result to a *Component* in order to invoke *Component* methods getForeground, setForeground, and setBackground.

Let's review this program before moving on. There are three objects involved: the top-level *OnOffSwitch* (a *JFrame*); a component *JButton*; and an event handler, the *ActionListener Switcher*. The main method creates the top-level *OnOffSwitch,* sizes it, makes it vis-

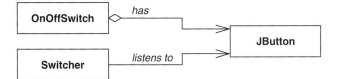

Figure 17.18 **Container, Component, and Listener.**

ible, and exits. The *OnOffSwitch* constructor creates a *JButton* and then registers a *Switcher* with the *JButton* so that any *ActionEvents* generated by the *JButton* will be delivered to the *Switcher*. Finally, the *OnOffSwitch* adds the *JButton* to itself as a component (by adding the *JButton* to its content pane).

When the user presses the button, an *ActionEvent* is generated by the button. This event is delivered to all of the button's *ActionListeners*, by means of an invocation of their `actionPerformed` method. In this case, there is only one listener and its `actionPerformed` method inverts the button's foreground and background colors.

Programming the GUI: adding a WindowListener for the JFrame

Next, let's look at how we can terminate the application cleanly, without explicitly requesting the operating system to kill it.

We would like to terminate the application when the user selects the "*Close*" option from the top-level window menu. Selecting "*Close*" generates a *WindowEvent* in the *JFrame*, specifically a window-closing event. So we must first create a listener for *WindowEvents*. The *WindowListener* interface is a bit more complicated than the *ActionListener* interface. *WindowListener* specifies seven methods, while *ActionListener* specifies only one. Each of these methods handles a different kind of *WindowEvent*. Specifically, *WindowListener* specifies the methods:

> **void** `windowActivated (WindowEvent e)`
>> Invoked when the window is set to be the user's active window, which means the window (or one of its subcomponents) will receive keyboard events.

> **void** `windowClosed (WindowEvent e)`
>> Invoked when a window has been closed as the result of calling dispose on the window.

> **void** `windowClosing (WindowEvent e)`
>> Invoked when the user attempts to close the window from the window's system menu.

> **void** `windowDeactivated (WindowEvent e)`
>> Invoked when a window is no longer the user's active window, which means that keyboard events will no longer be delivered to the window or its subcomponents.

Table 17.2   **Generated events and corresponding listener interfaces**

Event Generated	Listener Interface	Listener Methods
ActionEvent	*ActionListener*	`actionPerformed()`
AdjustmentEvent	*AdjustmentListener*	`adjustmentValueChanged()`
ComponentEvent	*ComponentListener*	`componentHidden()`
		`componentMoved()`
		`componentResized()`
		`componentShown()`
ContainerEvent	*ContainerListener*	`componentAdded()`
		`componentRemoved()`
FocusEvent	*FocusListener*	`focusGained()`
		`focusLost()`
ItemEvent	*ItemListener*	`ItemStateChanged()`
KeyEvent	*KeyListener*	`keyPressed()`
		`keyReleased()`
		`keyTyped()`
MouseEvent	*MouseListener*	`mouseClicked()`
		`mouseEntered()`
		`mouseExited()`
		`mousePressed()`
		`mouseReleased()`
	MouseMotionListener	`mouseDragged()`
		`mouseMoved()`
TextEvent	*TextListener*	`textValueChanged()`
WindowEvent	*WindowListener*	`windowActivated()`
		`windowClosed()`
		`windowClosing()`
		`windowDeactivated()`
		`windowDeiconified()`
		`windowIconified()`
		`windowOpened()`

void windowDeiconified (WindowEvent e)
Invoked when a window is changed from a minimized to a normal state.

void windowIconified (WindowEvent e)
Invoked when a window is changed from a normal to a minimized state.

void windowOpened (WindowEvent e)
Invoked the first time a window is made visible.

We are not interested in most of these *WindowEvents*. We're only interested in events associated with the user closing the window. To simplify implementation of listeners, Java provides a collection of abstract *event adapter classes*. These adapter classes (see Figure 17.19) implement listener interfaces with empty, do-nothing methods. To implement a listener class, we can extend one of the adapter classes and override only the methods we are interested in.

We'll call our *WindowListener* class *Terminator*. It extends the adapter class *WindowAdapter*.

```
class Terminator extends WindowAdapter {
    ...
}
```

The class *WindowAdapter* implements *WindowListener*, and since *Terminator* is a subclass of *WindowAdapter*, it also implements *WindowListener*. *Terminator* inherits the seven *WindowListener* methods from *WindowAdapter*. These are all null "do-nothing" methods. We must override the methods relating to the events we're interested in: namely, the events that are generated when the user tries to close the window.

A *window-closing event* occurs when the user attempts to close the window. This event results in an invocation of the listener's windowClosing method. Thus we must override windowClosing:

```
class Terminator extends WindowAdapter {
    public void windowClosing(WindowEvent e) {
        ...
    }
}
```

What should we do when a window-closing event is delivered? We could simply terminate the application. But there is a slightly better approach, since in general we do not know if there are other listeners also interested in this event. What we'll do is release the window's resources, close it, and remove its peer. This is accomplished by the *Window* method dispose:

```
class Terminator extends WindowAdapter {
    public void windowClosing(WindowEvent e) {
        Window w = e.getWindow();
        w.dispose();
    }
}
```

The *WindowEvent* method `getWindow` is essentially the same as the *EventObject* method `getSource`, except that it returns a *Window* rather than an *Object*. Thus we are saved the trouble of casting the result.

Disposing of the window causes it to generate one more event, a *window-closed event*. We handle this event with the method `windowClosed`, and here is where we finally terminate the application:

```
class Terminator extends WindowAdapter {

    public void windowClosing(WindowEvent e) {
        Window w = e.getWindow();
        w.dispose();
    }

    public void windowClosed(WindowEvent e) {
        System.exit(0);
    }
}
```

The call to `System.exit` causes the application to terminate. By convention, an argument of 0 indicates normal termination, and a nonzero argument indicates abnormal termination, typically because of some error condition.

Of course, we still must create a *Terminator* instance and register it with the top-level *JFrame*. This is straightforward:

```
public OnOffSwitch () {
    super("On/Off Switch");
    ...
    this.addWindowListener(new Terminator());
    ...
}
```

Since we only need one instance of the *WindowListener*, rather than explicitly defining a class like *Terminator*, we typically use an anonymous class (see Section 14.2.4):

```
this.addWindowListener(
    new WindowAdapter() {
        public void windowClosing(WindowEvent e) {
            Window w = e.getWindow();
            w.dispose();
        }
        public void windowClosed(WindowEvent e) {
            System.exit(0);
        }
    }
);
```

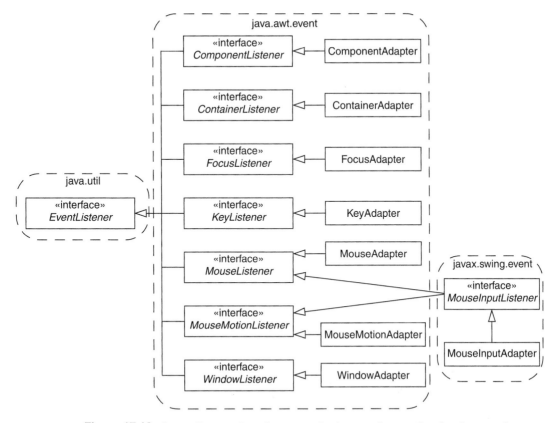

Figure 17.19 **Some listener interfaces, and adaptor classes that implement them.**

The application is now complete, and consists of the classes *OnOffSwitch*, *Switcher*, and *Terminator* (or anonymous *WindowListener*).

This introductory example illustrates only graphical user interface design and implementation. We have no model component at all. In a complete application, the user interface event handlers interact with the model, and changes in the model generally require the interface to be updated.

Sizing components

In the example just completed, we set the size of the *JFrame* but not the size of the *JButton*. In general, the size of a component is controlled by the layout manager of the container holding the component. The *JFrame* is a top-level container, and so is not contained in any other container. Therefore its size is not controlled by a layout manager. The size of the *JButton*, on the other hand, is determined by the *BorderLayout* manager of the *JFrame*'s content pane.

For components controlled by a layout manager, the best we can do is to provide suggestions, or "hints," about their size to the layout manager. This is done by overriding a

JComponent's `getMinimumSize`, `getMaximumSize`, and `getPreferredSize` methods.[1] Exactly how the layout manager uses this information is up to the layout manager. Some layout managers, such as *FlowLayout* and *GridBagLayout*, invoke these methods to determine how to size a component. *BorderLayout*, on the other hand, gives the north and south components their preferred height, and the east and west components their preferred width. North and south components are stretched or squashed horizontally, and east and west components are stretched or squashed vertically, depending on the container size. The center component gets whatever space is left over. In particular, if you resize the window containing the *OnOffSwitch*'s button, the button will be resized as well.

Let's sketch a simple approach for having the button remain the same size, regardless of how the user resizes the window. First, we extend *JButton*, overriding the methods `getPreferredSize` and `getMinimumSize` so that they return the size we want:

```
class OnOffButton extends JButton {

    public OnOffButton (String label) {
        super(label);
    }

    public Dimension getPreferredSize () {
        // make the width 50 pixels, height 100
        return new Dimension(100,50);
    }

    public Dimension getMinimumSize () {
        return this.getPreferredSize();
    }
}
```

Rather than creating a *JButton* in the *OnOffSwitch* constructor, we create an *OnOffButton*:

```
public OnOffSwitch () extends JFrame {
    super("On/Off Switch"); // frame title

    // create button and set its colors
    OnOffButton button = new OnOffButton("On/Off");
    ...
}
```

Finally, we change the content pane's layout manager to a *FlowLayout*:

```
public OnOffSwitch () extends {
    ...
    // use FlowLayout and add button to JFrame's
    // content pane:
```

---

1. Most standard layout managers ignore maximum size.

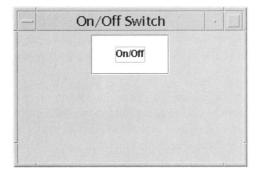

Figure 17.20 *OnOffSwitch* using a *FlowLayout*.

```
    this.getContentPane().setLayout(new FlowLayout());
    this.getContentPane().add(button);
}
```

As shown in Figure 17.20, *FlowLayout* will use the *JButton's* preferred size and keep it centered horizontally, regardless of how the window is resized. The button, however, will be at the top of the pane. If we want the button to remain centered vertically as well as horizontally, we would use a more flexible (but more complicated) layout manager like *GridBagLayout*. (We'll see an example using *GridBagLayout* in the next chapter.)

Event handling happens in the event dispatching thread

Remember that all component repainting and event handling is done in the event dispatching thread. Suppose we put a delay in the action event handling method:

```
public void actionPerformed (ActionEvent e) {
    Component source = (Component)e.getSource();
    Color oldForeground = source.getForeground();
    source.setForeground(source.getBackground());
    source.setBackground(oldForeground);
    // wait 10 seconds:
    nhUtilities.utilites.Control.sleep(10);
}
```

(Recall from Section 8.3.5 that the *nhUtilities.utilites.Control* method `sleep` causes the program—actually the thread—to pause for a specified number of seconds.)

If we run the program now, we will notice that there is about a 10 second delay between the time we press the button and the time it changes color. Furthermore, the application will seem "frozen" during this period. The reason is that the button is *scheduled* to be repainted, but is not repainted until *after* the action event handling is complete. In fact, no repainting or other event handling will be done until processing this event is complete. This implies that event handling methods should do their work quickly. If the response to an event requires an lengthy, time-consuming action, a new thread should be created to perform the action. Creating and managing threads, however, is beyond the scope of our discussion.

DrJava: threads

Open the file `DelayExample.java`, located in `threads`, in `ch17`, in `nhText`. This application generates a *JFrame* containing two buttons and two text fields. The text fields display how many times each button has been pressed.

Note that the *ButtonPanel* constructor has an int parameter, `delay`. If the value of the argument is positive, the button's action listener will sleep for the specified number of seconds before returning.

1. In the *Interactions* pane, run the application `DelayExample` and note its behavior.

   ```
   > java ch17.threads.DelayExample
   ```

   Exit the program by closing the window.

2. Modify the program so that the west *ButtonPanel* is created with a five second delay in its event handler:

   ```
   pane.add(new ButtonPanel(5),BorderLayout.WEST);
   ```

3. Run the program again. Note that the text field is not repainted until after the delay. Also notice that the application appears to "freeze" during the delay. This is because repainting and event handling is all done in the same thread. Repainting is not done until handling the button press event is complete.

17.5   A more complex example

We next develop a little more complex user interface. In this section, we just build the display and show how to use a few more components. We won't bother completely programming the event handlers.

The interface, pictured in Figure 17.21, is for an application that gathers some miscellaneous student data. It is consists of five areas: the top, occupied by a text field used to enter age; the left, containing a combo box used to enter college; the center, consisting of two buttons for sex; the right, containing check boxes for miscellaneous information,; and the bottom, consisting of a "finished" button. With this structure, it seems natural to use a *BorderLayout*.

Rather than adding components directly to the top-level frame's content pane, we'll build a *JPanel* and add the *JPanel* to the content pane. This is a standard technique. It gives us a bit more flexibility in that the *JPanel* can be easily incorporated into other structures if we need to expand or modify the application. Thus the `main` method will look like this

```
public static void main (String[] args) {
    JFrame top = new JFrame("Student survey");
    top.getContentPane().add(
```

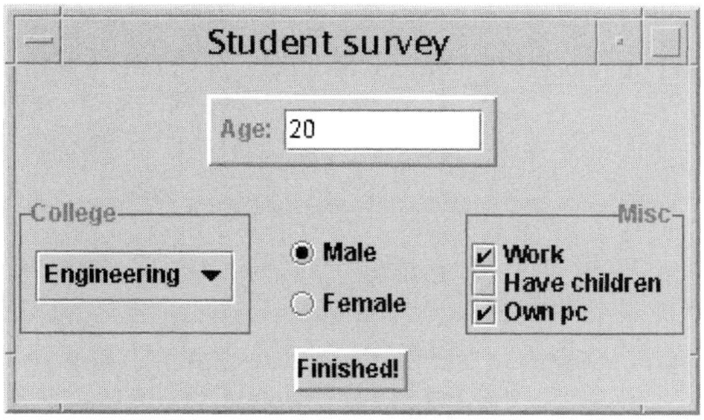

Figure 17.21 **Student survey user interface.**

```
        new StudentSurveyPanel(), BorderLayout.CENTER);
    ...
}
```

where

```
class StudentSurveyPanel extends JPanel {

    public StudentSurveyPanel () {
        setLayout(new BorderLayout());
        ...
```

is the *JPanel* that contains the graphical structure. Note that we must explicitly set the *JPanel*'s layout manager to *BorderLayout*. The default *JPanel* manager is *FlowLayout*.

We construct each section in its own *JPanel*, and add them to the *StudentSurveyPanel*. For each section, we write a method that creates and returns the *JPanel*:

```
public StudentSurveyPanel () {
    setLayout(new BorderLayout());
    add(agePanel(), BorderLayout.NORTH);
    add(collegePanel(), BorderLayout.WEST);
    add(sexPanel(), BorderLayout.CENTER);
    add(miscPanel(), BorderLayout.EAST);
    add(finishedPanel(), BorderLayout.SOUTH);
    ...
```

Now all that remains is to write the five methods that construct the panels.

The button panel

Let's start with the "finished" panel. It contains only a single button, and we've already seen how to use buttons. You'll notice from the figure that this button has a raised, three-dimensional look to it. That's because we've put a border around it. The *JComponent* method

```
public void setBorder (Border border)
```

is used to put a decorative border around a component. Standard borders are obtained from the class *javax.swing.BorderFactory*. The particular border used here is a "raised bevel border," generated with the factory method

```
public static Border createRaisedBevelBorder ()
```

We also add an *ActionListener* for the button, but as we mentioned above, we won't program the *ActionListener*.

```
private JPanel finishedPanel () {
    JButton button = new JButton("Finished!");
    button.setBorder(
        BorderFactory.createRaisedBevelBorder());
    button.addActionListener(new DoneListener());
    JPanel finishedPanel = new JPanel();
    finishedPanel.add(button);
    return finishedPanel;
}
```

The *JPanel*'s default *FlowLayout* respects the preferred size of the button. If the window is resized by the user, the button will remain the same size and the *JPanel* that contains it will be stretched or compressed as necessary.

The text field panel

The methods that create the other panels will have similar structures to `finished-Panel`. But constructing them is a bit more complex.

In the age panel, there is a label and a text field contained in a panel with a border. We can build it like this:

```
JLabel agePrompt = new JLabel("Age: ");
JTextField ageField = new JTextField(10);
ageField.addActionListener(new AgeListener());
JPanel innerPanel = new JPanel();
innerPanel.add(agePrompt);
innerPanel.add(ageField);
innerPanel.setBorder(
    BorderFactory.createRaisedBevelBorder());
```

The integer argument passed to the *JTextField* constructor, 10 in the example, indicates the number of "columns" in the field. This number is used along with size of the field's font to determine the field's preferred width. It does not limit the number of characters the user can enter.

An *ActionEvent* is generated in a *JTextField* when the user presses the *Return/Enter* key in the field. An *ActionListener* can get the text in the field as a *String* using the *JText-Field*'s `getText` method.

We need to be able to access the text field after it is constructed, other than from the listener. Specifically, we want to clear the text field as part of a "reset" operation. Therefore, rather than making the variable ageField local as shown above, we make it an instance variable of the *StudentSurveyPanel*:

```
private JTextField ageField;
```

We can add the innerPanel to a *JPanel*, just as we did with the button, so the innerPanel won't expand or contract if the window is resized.

```
JPanel agePanel = new JPanel();
agePanel.add(innerPanel);
```

If the window is resized, the innerPanel remains the same size while the agePanel expands or contracts as necessary.

Remember that a *FlowLayout* manager will keep the contents of its container centered right to left, but at the top of the container. To separate the innerPanel from the top of the window and from the sections below it, we add an empty 10-pixel border to the agePanel. The complete method can now be written. (Yes, yes, the literals should really be named constants.)

```
private JPanel agePanel () {
    JLabel agePrompt = new JLabel("Age: ");
    ageField = new JTextField(10);
    ageField.addActionListener(new AgeListener());
    JPanel innerPanel = new JPanel();
    innerPanel.add(agePrompt);
    innerPanel.add(ageField);
    innerPanel.setBorder(
        BorderFactory.createRaisedBevelBorder());
    JPanel agePanel = new JPanel();
    agePanel.add(innerPanel);
    agePanel.setBorder(
        BorderFactory.createEmptyBorder(10,10,10,10));
    return agePanel;
}
```

The combo box panel

The college panel contains a simple combo box: a pull-down list of options from which the user chooses one. To make the combo box, we simply add items to the pull-down list. Like the age text field, we want the combo box to be available to a "reset" operation. So we define it as a *StudentSurveyPanel* instance variable:

```
private JComboBox collegeChooser;
```

The panel is decorated with a named border, using *BorderFactory*'s method

```
public static TitledBorder createTitledBorder (
    Border border, String title)
```

The collegePanel method can be written as follows:

```
private JPanel collegePanel () {
    collegeChooser = new JComboBox();
    collegeChooser.addItem("Sciences");
    collegeChooser.addItem("Liberal Arts");
    collegeChooser.addItem("Engineering");
    collegeChooser.addItem("Fine Arts");
    collegeChooser.addActionListener(
        new CollegeListener());

    JPanel collegePanel = new JPanel();
    collegePanel.add(collegeChooser);
    collegePanel.setBorder(
        BorderFactory.createTitledBorder(
            BorderFactory.createLineBorder(Color.red),
            "College"));
    return collegePanel;
}
```

The *JComboBox* generates an *ActionEvent* when the user selects an item from the list. The *ActionListener* can determine which item was selected by invoking the *JComboBox* method getSelectedItem or getSelectedIndex. For example, if the user chooses the option "Sciences" from the above list, getSelectedItem returns the *String* "Sciences", and getSelectedIndex returns the integer 0. (The method getSelectedItem is defined as returning an *Object*, so the result must be cast before it can be treated as a *String*.)

The check box panel

The "miscellaneous" panel contains a set of check boxes in a bordered panel. The check boxes themselves are independent of each other, and are instances of *JCheckBox*. Again, we make the check boxes instance variables so they can be reset.

```
private JCheckBox worksBox;
private JCheckBox hasKidsBox;
private JCheckBox ownsPCBox;
```

A check box is a form of button (both *JButton* and *JCheckBox* are subclasses of *JAbstractButton*), and we can handle them much as we do a button. But let's use an *ItemListener* instead of an *ActionListener*, and rather than creating a separate listener for each check box, let's create one listener for the group.

First, we define a class *MiscellaneousListener* to implement *ItemListener*. We introduced inner classes in Section 10.5. We can make the listener classes private inner classes of *StudentSurveyPanel*. In particular, we define

```
private class MiscellaneousListener
    implements ItemListener ...
```

in the class *StudentSurveyPanel*, and create an instance of this class:

```
MiscellaneousListener miscListener =
    new MiscellaneousListener();
```

We can create a simple labeled check box and add the listener as follows:

```
worksBox = new JCheckBox("Work");
worksBox.addItemListener(miscListener());
```

When the state of the check box changes, that is, when it is selected or deselected, the *ItemListener*'s itemStateChanged method is invoked:

```
private class MiscellaneousListener
    implements ItemListener {

    public void itemStateChanged (ItemEvent e) {
        ...
```

The *ItemEvent* method getItemSelectable tells which check box originated the event. The method getStateChange returns either the **int** value ItemEvent.SELECTED or the **int** value ItemEvent.DESELECTED, so the listener can determine whether the check box is being selected or deselected. The listener code will look like this:

```
private class miscellaneousListener
    implements ItemListener {

    public void itemStateChanged (ItemEvent e) {
        JCheckBox box =
            (JCheckBox)(e.getItemSelectable());
        if (box == worksBox)
            if (e.getStateChange() == ItemEvent.SELECTED)
                ...
```

Notice that the body of the method will end up involving six cases: three boxes, two possible state changes for each box. As we noted in Section 11.2, this is not the kind of structure we are happy to see in object-oriented code. But we'll leave the code unimproved for now, having noted a slight smell.

We want to add the combo box boxes in a column to a *JPanel*. An easy way to do this is to equip the *JPanel* with a *GridLayout*. A *GridLayout* manager lays out the components in a rectangular grid of equal sized rectangles, as shown in Figure 17.22. The number of rows and columns is specified when the *GridLayout* is created.

```
JPanel miscPanel = new JPanel();
miscPanel.setLayout(new GridLayout(3,1));
miscPanel.add(worksBox);
miscPanel.add(hasKidsBox);
miscPanel.add(ownsPCBox);
```

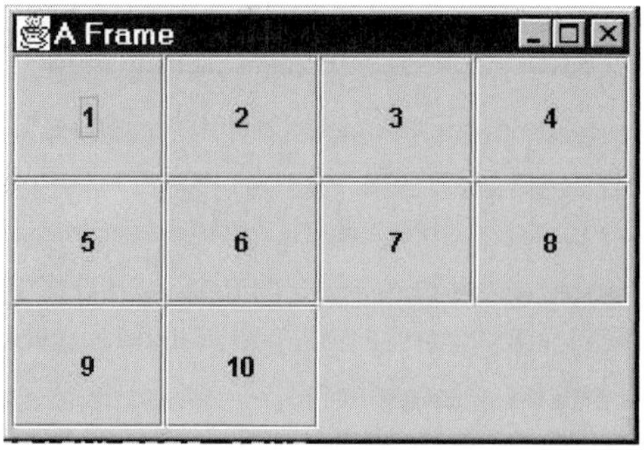

Figure 17.22   A *JFrame* laid out with *GridLayout*.

Finally, it takes a bit more effort to create the border, since the default position of the label is top left. In this case we, want it to be top right. The completed method is given below.

```java
private JPanel miscPanel () {
    MiscellaneousListener miscListener =
        new MiscellaneousListener();

    worksBox = new JCheckBox("Work");
    worksBox.addItemListener(miscListener);
    hasKidsBox = new JCheckBox("Have children");
    hasKidsBox.addItemListener(miscListener);
    ownsPCBox = new JCheckBox("Own pc");
    ownsPCBox.addItemListener(miscListener);

    JPanel miscPanel = new JPanel();
    miscPanel.setLayout(new GridLayout(3,1));
    miscPanel.add(worksBox);
    miscPanel.add(hasKidsBox);
    miscPanel.add(ownsPCBox);
    miscPanel.setBorder(
        BorderFactory.createTitledBorder(
            BorderFactory.createLineBorder(Color.red),
            "Misc",
            TitledBorder.RIGHT,
            TitledBorder.TOP));

    return miscPanel;
}
```

The radio button panel

The final panel consists of two radio buttons for selecting sex. Radio buttons are different from check boxes in that exactly one of a group will always be selected.

As with the check boxes, we make the radio buttons *StudentSurveyPanel* instance variables.

```
private JRadioButton maleButton;
private JRadioButton femaleButton;
```

After the buttons are created, they are added to a group. One of the buttons is initially selected.

```
maleButton = new JRadioButton("Male");
femaleButton = new JRadioButton("Female");
femaleButton.setSelected(true);
ButtonGroup sexGroup = new ButtonGroup();
sexGroup.add(maleButton);
sexGroup.add(femaleButton);
```

Each time the user presses a button, one or two *ItemEvents* (one for the deselected button, one for the selected button) and one *ActionEvent* (for the selected button) are generated. We generally handle radio buttons with an *ActionEventListener*.

Again. let's have a single handler for both buttons, which we'll call a *SexListener*:

```
private class SexListener implements ActionListener {

    public void ActionPerformed (ActionEvent e) ...
```

We'll use a slightly different technique than we used with the check boxes to determine which button has been selected. *ActionEvents* contain a *String* called an "action command." This *String* is set by the component generating the event, and can be accessed by the *ActionEvent* getActionCommand method. We'll have the buttons set specific action commands in the *ActionEvent* they generate:

```
maleButton = new JRadioButton("Male");
maleButton.setActionCommand("male");
femaleButton = new JRadioButton("Female");
femaleButton.setActionCommand("female");
```

and the listener determine which button was selected by examining the action command:

```
public void ActionPerformed (ActionEvent e) {
    if (e.getActionCommand().equals("male") ...
```

(Once again, we admit that all these *String* literals should really be named constants.)

We add the buttons to a *JPanel* with a *GridLayout*, and to keep them centered, add this to a *JPanel* with *FlowLayout*. (Yes, there are other ways of doing this!) The complete method:

```
private JPanel sexPanel () {
    SexListener sexListener = new SexListener();
    maleButton = new JRadioButton("Male");
    maleButton.setActionCommand("male");
    maleButton.addActionListener(sexListener);
    femaleButton = new JRadioButton("Female");
    femaleButton.setActionCommand("female");
    femaleButton.addActionListener(sexListener);
    femaleButton.setSelected(true);

    ButtonGroup sexGroup = new ButtonGroup();
    sexGroup.add(maleButton);
    sexGroup.add(femaleButton);

    JPanel innerPanel = new JPanel();
    innerPanel.setLayout(new GridLayout(2,1));
    innerPanel.add(maleButton);
    innerPanel.add(femaleButton);
    JPanel sexPanel = new JPanel();
    sexPanel.add(innerPanel);
    return sexPanel;
}
```

The reset method

We've mentioned a "reset" method several times. This method puts the display in a standard, initial configuration. It sets the data collection widgets to their initial states, and requests focus for the text field.

```
private void resetView () {
    ageField.setText("");
    ageField.requestFocus();
    collegeChooser.setSelectedIndex(0);
    worksBox.setSelected(false);
    hasKidsBox.setSelected(false);
    ownsPCBox.setSelected(false);
    femaleButton.setSelected(true);
}
```

The complete class definition is rather lengthy, so we won't repeat it in the text. It is available in the directory studentSurvey, located in ch17, in nhText.

✳ 17.6   Menus, dialogs, fonts, and graphics

In this section, we briefly introduce a few additional graphical user interface topics. As usual, details can be obtained from the standard Java API specifications.

17.6.1 Menus and menu bars

A *menu* offers a number of options from which the user may choose. Menus are not generally placed with other components in the user interface. Instead, a menu usually appears either in a *menu bar* or as a *popup menu*. A menu bar contains one or more menus and is usually located at the top of the application window. A popup menu is invisible until the user performs a specific action, such as pressing the right mouse button, over a popup-enabled component. The popup menu then appears under the cursor.

A *JFrame* often has a menu bar. A menu bar can be added to a *JFrame* with the method setJMenuBar:

```
JFrame window = new JFrame("Some Application");
JMenuBar menuBar = new JMenuBar();
window.setJMenuBar(menuBar);
```

As shown in Figure 17.23, a menu bar can hold several menus, and each menu can offer a number of menu choices. Menus are created as *JMenu* instances and added to the menu bar:

```
JMenu batter = new JMenu("Batter");
menuBar.add(batter);
```

Menu choices are modeled with the class *JMenuItem*, and are added to the menu:

```
JMenuItem swing = new JMenuItem("Swing");
JMenuItem take = new JMenuItem("Take");
JMenuItem bunt = new JMenuItem("Bunt");
batter.add(swing);
batter.add(take);
batter.add(bunt);
```

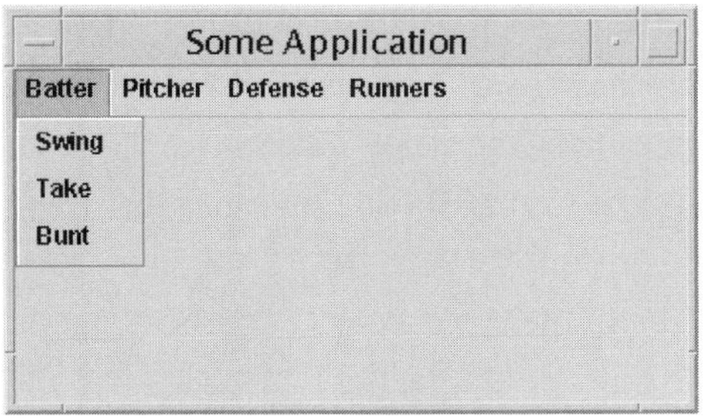

Figure 17.23   *JFrame* containing a menubar.

When the user selects an item, the *JMenuItem* selected generates an *ActionEvent*. To program menu events, implement an *ActionListener* for each *JMenuItem*.

17.6.2 Basic dialogs

A *dialog* is a window generated by an application as necessary to present information to or gather input from the user. Since dialogs are explicitly created by the application when input or output is needed, their use manifests more of an application-driven style than an event-driven style. Be conservative in your use of dialogs. Excessive dialog use generally implies a poorly designed interface.

Swing provides a library of easy to use dialog windows, as well as classes for building complex dialogs. The classes *JOptionPane*, *JFileChooser*, and *JColorChooser* can be used to create simple, standard dialogues, while *JDialog* is used to tailor custom dialogs.

Every dialog is dependent on a frame, called its *owner*. A dialog is destroyed if its owner is destroyed, and disappears from the screen while its owner is iconified.

The dialogs we consider are called *modal* dialogues. User input to all other windows of a program is blocked when a modal dialog is visible. To create non-modal dialogs, you must use *JDialog*.

The JOptionPane method showMessageDialog

The class *JOptionPane* is used to create simple, standard dialogues. The simplest are created with the method `showMessageDialog`. (There are actually three overloaded methods with this name.) The method displays a simple, one-button, informational dialog window. The most general `showMessageDialog` specification is:

```
public static void showMessageDialog (
    Component parentComponent, Object message,
    String title, int messageType, Icon icon)
```

The parameters are as follows.

- `parentComponent` – determines the frame on which the dialog depends. The frame containing the parent component (or the parent component, if it is a frame) is the frame owner for the dialog. Its screen coordinates are used to determine the placement of the dialog window. If the argument is null, a default frame is used as owner, in which case the dialog window is usually centered in the screen.

- `message` – the message to be displayed in the dialog window, typically a *String*.

- `title` – the title of the dialog window.

- `messageType` – an **int** value indicating the style of message. Possible values are

  -- `JOptionPane.ERROR_MESSAGE`

  -- `JOptionPane.INFORMATION_MESSAGE`

  -- `JOptionPane.WARNING_MESSAGE`

  -- `JOptionPane.QUESTION_MESSAGE`

  -- `JOptionPane.PLAIN_MESSAGE`

- icon – the icon to be displayed in the dialog.

Two variants of the method use default arguments:

```
public static void showMessageDialog (
        Component parentComponent, Object message)
```

produces an information message titled "Message," and

```
public static void showMessageDialog (
        Component parentComponent, Object message,
        String title, int messageType)
```

uses a default icon determined by the message type.

Figure 17.24 shows sample message dialog windows, and the code that created them.

```
JOptionPane.showMessageDialog(frame,
    "He went galumphing back",
    "Important", JOptionPane.INFORMATION_MESSAGE);


JOptionPane.showMessageDialog(frame,
    "Beware the Jabberwock, my son!",
    "Important", JOptionPane.WARNING_MESSAGE);


JOptionPane.showMessageDialog(frame,
    "The vorpal blade went snicker-snack!",
    "Important", JOptionPane.ERROR_MESSAGE);


JOptionPane.showMessageDialog(frame,
    "And, has thou slain the Jabberwock?",
    "Important", JOptionPane.QUESTION_MESSAGE);


JOptionPane.showMessageDialog(frame,
    "Twas brillig, and the slithy toves",
    "Important", JOptionPane.PLAIN_MESSAGE);
```

Figure 17.24 **Message dialog windows.**

```
JOptionPane.showInputDialog(frame,
    "Message Type");
```

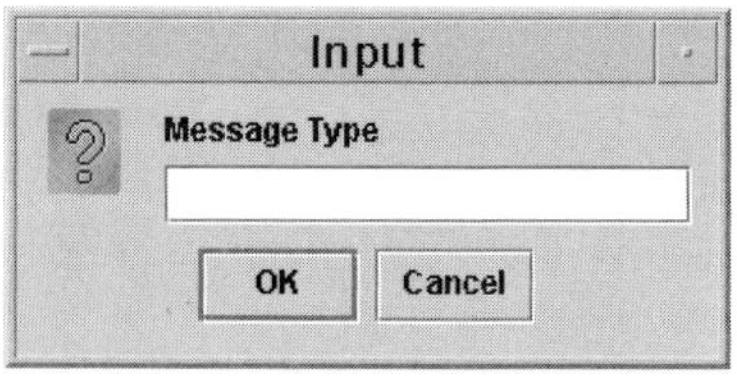

Figure 17.25 **Input dialog window.**

The JOptionPane method showInputDialog

The method `showInputDialog` is used to get input from the user. (Again, the method is overloaded; there are six `showInputDialog` methods.) This method gets a *String* from the user, using either a text field or a combo box.

One of the simpler variants of the method is specified as

> **public static** String showInputDialog (
>   Component parentComponent, Object message)

The parameters are the same as in `showMessageDialog`. Figure 17.25 shows a typical dialog window produced by the method.

Other variants allow window title, message type, icon, initial value, and combo box options to be specified.

When the user presses the "OK" button, the contents of the text field (or selected item if a combo box is used) is returned. A null value is returned if the user presses "Cancel" or closes the window.

Note the contents are returned as a *String*. If you request a number from the user, you must validate the format and convert the *String* to the appropriate type of value. For example,

```
int count;
try {
   count = Integer.parseInt(
       JOptionPane.showInputDialog(frame,"Count:"));
} catch (NumberFormatException e) {
   // user did not key in an integer
   ...
}
```

The JOptionPane method showConfirmDialog

The `showConfirmDialog` (there are four variants) generates a two or three button window. The two button window provides "Yes" and "No" buttons or 'OK" and "Cancel" buttons; the three button window, "Yes," "No," and "Cancel" buttons. Sample invocations are shown in Figure 17.26.

```
JOptionPane.showConfirmDialog(frame,
    "Take over the world?",
    "The Brain",
    JOptionPane.YES_NO_OPTION);
```

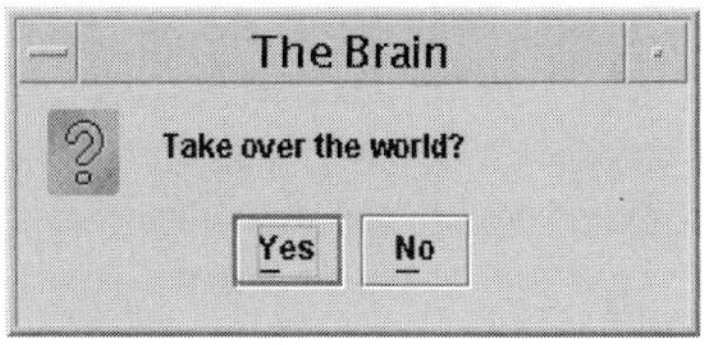

```
JOptionPane.showConfirmDialog(frame,
    "Take over the world?",
    "The Brain",
    JOptionPane.YES_NO_CANCEL_OPTION);
```

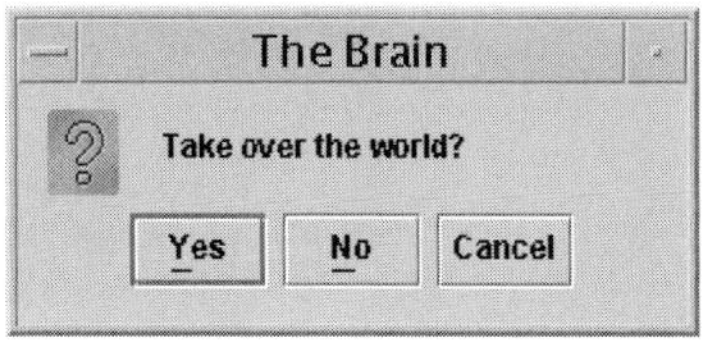

Figure 17.26 **Confirm dialog windows.**

The method returns an **int** indicating the user's response. Possible return values include JOptionPane.YES_OPTION, JOptionPane.OK_OPTION, JOption-Pane.NO_OPTION, JOptionPane.CANCEL_OPTION, and, if the user closes the window, JOptionPane.CLOSED_OPTION.

The JOptionPane method showOptionDialog

The showOptionDialog generates a two or three button dialog window, similar to a confirm dialog, but with customized buttons. A sample window is shown in Figure 17.27.

The first three parameters of the showOptionDialog method are familiar: parent component, message, and window title.

The fourth parameter is option type, just as for the confirm window. This value determines whether a two or three button window will be displayed.

The fifth parameter, message type, determines the default icon for the dialog.

The sixth parameter indicates the icon to be used. Since it is null in this example, the default "question message" icon is used.

The next parameter is an array that determines the button labels. Finally, the last parameter indicates the initialized choice.

The method returns an **int** value just like a confirm window. It does not matter what the buttons have been labeled. The value returned will be either JOptionPane.YES_OPTION, JOptionPane.NO_OPTION, JOptionPane.CANCEL_OPTION, or JOptionPane.CLOSED_OPTION.

JFileChooser and JColorChooser

Two other standard dialogs are defined by the classes *JFileChooser* and *JColorChooser*. *JColorChooser* presents a pane of controls that allow a user to select and manipulate a

```
Object[] options =
   {"Of course!","Sorry, no.","Say what?"};

JOptionPane.showOptionDialog(frame,
   "Have you completed all the exercises?",
   "Done Check",
   JOptionPane.YES_NO_CANCEL_OPTION,
   JOptionPane.QUESTION_MESSAGE,
   null, options, options[0]);
```

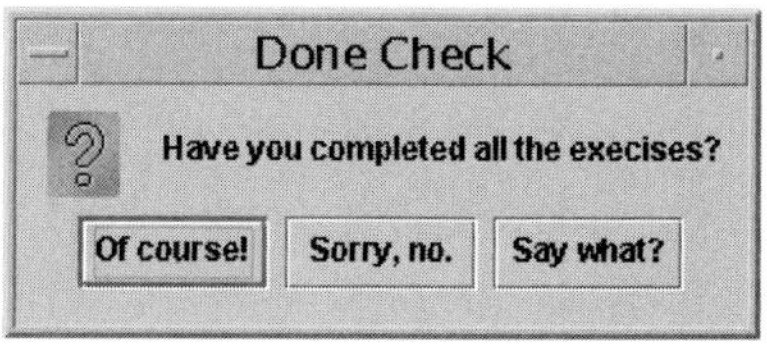

Figure 17.27 Option dialog window.

color. *JFileChooser* is provides a simple mechanism for a user to select a file. (See Figure 17.28.) We briefly look at *JFileChooser*.

A directory can be specified, either as a *String* or as a *File*, when the a *JFileChooser* is constructed. Three of the constructors are:

> **public** JFileChooser ()
> **public** JFileChooser (String currentDirectoryPath)
> **public** JFileChooser (File currentDirectory)

If no directory is specified, or if the argument is null, a system dependent default directory is used. This is typically the user's home directory in a Unix environment, or the "My Documents" folder in Windows.

The simplest way to display a dialog is to use one of these methods:

> **public int** showOpenDialog (Component parent)
> **public int** showSaveDialog (Component parent)

The argument in each case determines the dialog's owner. The first pops up a "save file" dialog; the second, an "open file" dialog. Each dialog has two buttons: "save" and "cancel" buttons in the first case, "open" and "cancel" buttons in the second. The methods return one of the following three integers:

- JFileChooser.APPROVE_OPTION if the "save" or "open" button is pressed;
- JFileChooser.CANCEL_OPTION if the "cancel" button is pressed;
- JFileCHooser.ERROR_OPTION if an error occurs or the dialog is dismissed.

The file chosen can be determined by the method

> **public** File getSelectedFile ()

The *JFileChooser* can be tailored in any number of ways. Details can be found in the standard documentation.

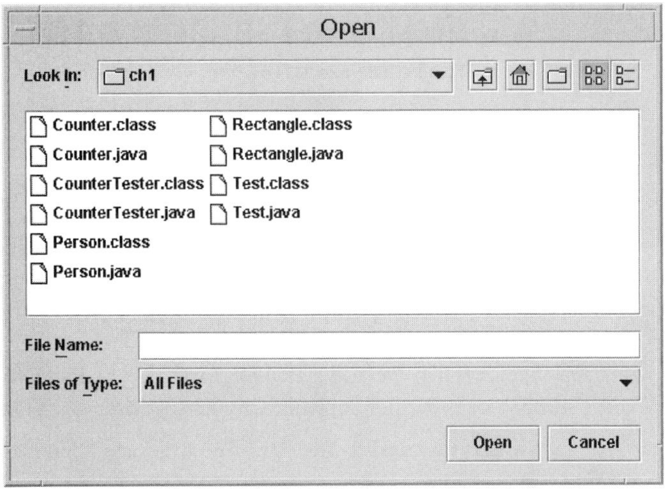

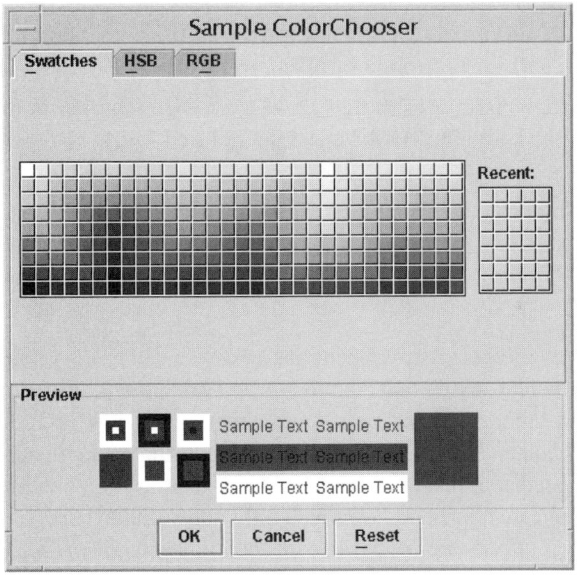

Figure 17.28 **JFileChooser** and **JColorChooser** dialogs

The JDialog class

The *JDialog* class is used to create custom dialog windows. A *JDialog* is a top-level window very much like a *JFrame*. However, a *JDialog* doesn't have caption bar controls allowing the user to iconify or maximize the window. Like a *JOptionPane*, a *JDialog* has an owner, generally a frame, but possibly another dialog. The *JDialog* always appears in front of its owner. If you try to move the owner over the *JDialog*, the owner moves behind instead. A *JDialog* is iconified and deiconified with its owner.

A typical constructor (there are eleven) is specified as follows:

```
public JDialog (Frame owner, String title,
    boolean modal)
```

The third argument specifies whether the *JDialog* is modal or non-modal. As we mentioned above, input to all other windows is blocked when a modal dialog is visible.

Like a *JFrame*, a *JDialog* delegates management of its components to a content pane. A *JDialog* is constructed in the same way that a *JFrame* is, by adding components to its content pane and adding component listeners to detect user input. A *JDialog* is displayed by invoking its setVisible method with an argument of **true**, and is hidden by invoking its setVisible method with an argument of **false**.

It is almost always the case that we want to catch or prevent a user's attempt to close a *JDialog*. Generally, we add a *WindowListener* to handle window closing event. The *JDialog*'s behavior is further controlled by its setDefaultCloseOperation method:

```
public void setDefaultCloseOperation (int operation)
```

The argument is one of three possible values:

* JDialog.DO_NOTHING_ON_CLOSE – the close attempt is handled by the window-Closing method of a *WindowListener*.

* JDialog.HIDE_ON_CLOSE – the *JDialog* is hidden (isVisible(**false**) is invoked) after any listeners are notified.

* JDialog.DISPOSE_ON_CLOSE – the *JDialog* is hidden and disposed of (dispose() is invoked) after any listeners are notified.

17.6.3 Fonts

Every Swing component has an associated *font*. A font provides the information needed to display text in that component. A *character* is an abstract representation of an item such as a letter, digit, or punctuation mark. A *glyph* is a shape used to render a character or sequence of characters. A font encapsulates a collection of glyphs and other information needed to render a particular set of characters. Fonts and text rendering can be a very complicated business. We touch only a few points here.

Fonts are modeled with the class *java.awt.Font*. Every component has an associated *Font*, which can be set or retrieved with the methods

```
public void setFont (Font font)
public Font getFont ()
```

Java distinguishes between *physical* fonts and *logical* fonts. Physical fonts are the actual libraries containing the information necessary to map sequences of characters to sequences of glyphs. The set of available physical fonts is system and implementation dependent.

There are five logical font families supported by Java: *Serif*, *SansSerif*, *Monospaced*, *Dialog*, and *DialogInput*. Logical font names are mapped to physical fonts by the Java runtime environment. The mapping is system and implementation dependent.

A Serif font

A SansSerif font

A Monospaced font

Figure 17.29 **Three font styles.**

The simplest *Font* constructor requires font name, style, and point size as arguments:

```
public Font (String name, int style, int size)
```

The parameters are:

- `name` – either a logical font name, such as `"SansSerif"` or a font face name, such as `"Helvetica"`;
- `style` – `Font.PLAIN`, `Font.BOLD`, `Font.ITALIC`, or `Font.BOLD + Font.ITALIC`;
- `size` – the point size of the font.

For example, we can set the *Font* to be used to render a button's label as follows:

```
JButton button = new JButton("Help!");
button.setFont(new Font("SansSerif", Font.BOLD, 14);
```

17.6.4 Graphics

Every component has a *graphics context* that gives access to the display space occupied by the component. The graphics context is modeled by an instance of the abstract class *java.awt.Graphics*. Since this is an abstract class, it can't be instantiated. The only way we can get an instance is from a component.

The *Graphics* object provides a large number of methods for drawing text, images, and geometrical figures on components. The methods have names like `drawLine`, `drawImage`, `drawRect`, `drawString`, `fillRect`, *etc.*

The state of the *Graphics* object includes the current painting color, current font, drawing area, and paint mode. (The paint mode determines how pixels painted in a graphics operation interact with those already drawn.)

To see how this works, let's draw a triangle on a *JPanel*. (A *JPanel* is a convenient blank canvas on which to draw.) The *JPanel* defines an integer coordinate system with coordinates ranging from (0,0) in the upper left to (*width*-1, *height*-1) in the lower right. Units are pixels.

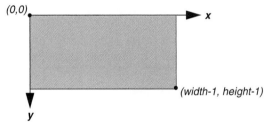

To draw on a *JPanel*, we override the method `painComponent`:[1]

```
class TrianglePanel extends JPanel {
    ...
    public void paintComponent (Graphics g) ...
```

This method is invoked in the event dispatching thread to allow the component to update its display.

Note that a *Graphics* object is passed to the method. This *Graphics* object will allow us to paint on the *JPanel*. The *Graphics* object is initialized to the font and foreground color of the *JPanel*. The drawing area is the entire *JPanel*. The default paint mode simply overwrites with the current color. All of these properties can be set by invoking appropriate *Graphics* methods.

Let's draw a right triangle with a 100 pixel base and 70 pixel height. We'll leave a 10 pixels above and to the left o the triangle. We need to draw three lines connecting the points illustrated below.

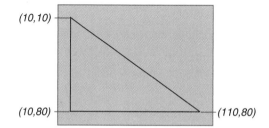

The method can be written as follows.

```
public void paintComponent (Graphics g) {
    super.paintComponent(g);
    g.drawLine(10,10,10,80);
    g.drawLine(10,80,110,80);
    g.drawLine(110,80,10,10);
}
```

The first statement invokes *JPanel*'s `paintComponent` implementation, which paints in the background. The next three statements draw the lines.

Finally, we should override `getPreferredSize` and `getMinimumSize` to make sure that *JPanel* is large enough to display the triangle.

```
public Dimension getPreferredSize () {
    return new Dimension(120,90);
}

public Dimension getMinimumSize () {
    return this.getPreferredSize();
}
```

---

1. `paintComponent` is inherited from *JComponent*.

✳ 17.7   Some class features

We conclude this chapter by summarizing a few additional features of the classes we have been studying. There is no attempt at completeness. Recall that all the Swing component classes are extensions of the java.awt classes *Component* and *Container*, and that *JFrame* is a subclass of the java.awt classes *Window* and *Frame*.

17.7.1 *Component*

Parent

The *Container* that contains the *Component*. The method getParent returns *null* if the *Component* is a top-level window:

```
public Container getParent ()
```

Enabled

If the *Component* is enabled, the user can interact with it and it can generate events. If it is disabled, the user cannot interact with it:

```
public boolean isEnabled ()
public void setEnabled (boolean enabled)
```

Valid

The *Component* is valid if the system knows its size, and in the case of a *Container*, if it's properly laid out. If the size of the *Component* has changed since it was last displayed, the *Component* is invalid. A *Container* is also invalid if one of its *Components* is invalid, or if a *Component* has been added or removed since the *Container* was last laid out. A layout manager typically notices an event such as *Container* resizing, and lays out the *Container* again.

Invoking a *Container*'s validate method will cause the *Container* to lay out its subcomponents again. Invoking a *Component*'s invalidate method marks the *Component* and all its ancestors as needing to be laid out.

```
public boolean isValid ()
public void validate ()
public void invalidate ()
```

Visible and Showing

Visible and *showing* can be somewhat confusing. A *Component* is *showing* if the user can find it on the display screen. It does not matter if the *Component* or window containing the *Component* is iconified or hidden behind another window.

If a *Component* is *visible*, then it should be showing when its parent is. A *Component* can be *visible* without appearing on the display screen. For a *Component* to be *showing*, it must be *visible* and be contained in a *Container* that is *visible* and *showing*. It is possible for *visible* to be *true*, and *showing* to be *false*, but not *vice versa*.

A top-level window is either *showing* and *visible*, or *not showing* and *not visible*. That is, the *visible* and *showing* properties for a top-level window always have the same value. Top-level windows are not visible when created. They must be explicitly made visible. Other *Components* are *visible* when they are created.

(There must certainly be a reason behind this distinction, but we admit to being at a loss.)

```
public boolean isVisible ()
public boolean isShowing ()
public void setVisible (boolean visible)
```

17.7.2 *Container*

Component Manipulation

The number of Components in the *Container*:

```
public int getComponentCount ()
```

The *Component* at the specified position. (Note: the first *Component* is at position 0.)

```
public Component getComponent (int position)
    require:
        0 <= position <= this.getComponentCount() - 1
```

The *Component* containing a given point. These methods return the *Container* itself if the point is in the *Container*, but not in any of the *Container*'s *Components*. They return *null* if the point is not in the *Container*:

```
public Component getComponentAt (int x, int y)
public Component getComponentAt (Point p)
```

Remove a *Component* from a *Container*:

```
public void remove (Component component)
public void remove (int position)
```

17.7.3 *Window*

The following are some general *Window* commands.
Resize the *Window* to the preferred size of its *Components*, and validate it.

```
public void pack ()
```

Bring the *Window* to the display foreground.

```
public void toFront ()
```

Send the *Window* to the display background.

```
public void toBack ()
```

Release a *Window*'s resources, and remove its peer.

```
public void dispose ()
```

17.7.4 *Frame*

Title

```
public String getTitle ()
public void setTitle (String title)
```

Resizable

The *resizable* attribute determines whether or not the user can resize the Frame. It muse be set before the Frame's peer is created and the Frame made visible.

```
public boolean isResizable ()
public void setResizable (boolean resizable)
```

17.7.5 *JComponent*

JComponent overrides many *Component* methods, but with the same basic functionality. Some additional features provided by *JComponent* include the following.

Ancestors

Get the *JRootPane* ancestor for the component, or the top-level ancestor of the component:

```
public JRootPane getRootPane ()
public Container getTopLevelAncestor ()
```

Transparency

A component is opaque if its background will be filled with the background color. Otherwise, it its transparent:

```
public void setOpaque (boolean isOpaque)
public boolean isOpaque()
```

17.7.6 *JFrame*

Default close operation

When a user attempts to close a window representing a *JFrame*, after the WINDOW_CLOSING event has been delivered to any listeners, the *JFrame* may hide or dispose of itself on its own accord. The default action is that the *JFrame* will hide itself: that is, it will become *not visible*. In this case, the program could later make the frame *visible* again.

The default response taken by a *JFrame* to a close action can be determined or set with these methods:

```
public int getDefaultCloseOperaton ()
public void setDefaultCloseOperation (int operation)
```

The argument passed to setDefaultCloseOperation must be one of the following constants:

```
JFrame.DO_NOTHING_ON_CLOSE
JFrame.HIDE_ON_CLOSE
JFrame.DISPOAE_ON_CLOSE
JFrame.EXIT_ON_CLOSE
```

17.8   Summary

In this chapter, we took a first look at Java's facilities for building an event-driven, graphical user interface. A graphical user interface is constructed from *components*, such as buttons, text fields, and so on. After displaying the graphical image, an event-driven application waits for an external "event" such as the user pressing a button or entering text in a text field. The application responds to the event, and then waits for the next event.

The graphical components that make up the user interface not only deliver information to the user, but are the *sources* of the user-generated events that provide input. When the user performs an action such as pressing a button, the component in which the action takes place *generates* an event. An *event listener* is an object that responds to or handles a particular kind of event. The event listener registers with the component, and is subsequently informed when the component generates an applicable event. The listener responds by performing some appropriate action.

There are two kinds of components, basic components and containers. Basic, or atomic, components are self contained entities, that furnish information to or gather input from the user. Buttons and text fields are examples. Containers, on the other hand, hold and position other components. Since containers are themselves components, a container can be a component of another container. Each container has a layout manager to which the container delegates the responsibility for arranging and sizing its components.

The top-level container in a Java application is a *JFrame*. A *JFrame* is a window in which the application interacts with the user. A *JFrame* delegates responsibility for managing its components to its content pane. The graphical display is created by adding components to the *JFrame*'s content pane.

Event handling and updating the appearance of the graphical interface take place in a separate thread called the event dispatching thread. This thread is created when the top-level *JFrame* is set visible, and is independent of the main thread, in which the method main is executed.

We have introduced several kinds of components and layout managers, and have examined a number of component features. We've seen how to associate event listeners with basic components to handle events generated by the components. It should be obvious that building a graphical user interface is a complex and tedious business. We have touched on only a small fraction of the functionality available in the standard libraries, and have concentrated on the user interface ignoring the model for the most part. In the next chapter, we address issues involved in putting the interface and the model together.

SELF-STUDY EXERCISES

17.1 Indicate whether each of the following statements is true or false:

a. Every Java *Container* is a Java *Component*.

b. Every Java *JComponent* is a Java *Container*.

c. Saying that a *JPanel* is the parent of a *JButton* means that *JButton* is a subclass of *JPanel*.

d. A *JFrame* is a *JComponent*.

e. To say that a component is "lightweight" means that it does not contain other components.

f. Event handling happens in the event dispatching thread, while component repainting happens in the main thread.

17.2 Write an expression to compute the area (in pixels) of a *Component* c.

17.3 Suppose that frame is a *JFrame*. The following code is intended to set *JFrame*'s layout manager to a *FlowLayout*, and add a *JButton* to the *JFrame*:

```
frame.setLayout(new FlowLayout());
frame.add(new JButton("Press me"));
```

Is this correct?

17.4 Write code to create a black *JFrame*, 200 pixels wide and 200 pixels high, titled "Black hole."

17.5 Write code to define a class *BlackButton* implementing a black button, 50 pixels wide and 50 pixels high.

17.6   If a *BlackButton* is added to a container, will it always be 50 pixels by 50 pixels? Why or why not?

17.7   Write code that will create a *JFrame* 200 pixels wide and 200 pixels high containing a 50 by 50 *BlackButton*.

17.8   Assume `button` is a *JButton*. Write code that creates an anonymous *ActionListener* and registers it with the button. The *ActionListener* should write out the message "The button has been pressed!" to standard output whenever the button is pressed.

17.9   Why do we extend *WindowAdapter* rather than implementing *WindowListener* directly? Can we extended *WindowListener* directly, or must we use *WindowAdapter*?

17.10 Suppose two threads are executing similar code and access the same variable x:

	thread A		*thread B*
a1.	`assert x >= 0;`	*b1.*	`assert x >= 0;`
a2.	`if (x > 0)`	*b2.*	`if (x > 0)`
a3.	`    x = x - 1;`	*b3.*	`    x = x - 1;`
a4.	`assert x >= 0;`	*b4.*	`assert x >= 0;`

Assume that the variable x is initially 1. One processor executes the threads, alternating between them. Give a possible execution sequence that will cause the assert of line *a4* to succeed, but the assert of line *b4* to fail.

✳ 17.11 Look at the code on page 708 for reading an integer from an input dialog. Complete the code so that it will continue to show the input dialog until the user keys an integer.

EXERCISES

17.1   Using a web browser, read the Java API documentation for the *JFrame* method `pack` (hint: it's not defined in *JFrame*, it's inherited), the *JComponent* method `setBorder`, and the *BorderFactory* method `createRaisedBevelBorder`. These classes are all defined in `javax.swing`. Modify the *OnOffSwitch* so that the button has a preferred size of 100 pixels by 100 pixels, and has a raised bevel border. Pack the *JFrame* rather than explicitly setting its size.

17.2   Create a *JFrame* with two buttons, labeled "One" and "Two." Create a single *ActionListener* to listen to both buttons. When a button is pressed, the *ActionListener* should write "Button one pressed" or "Button two pressed" to standard output.

17.3   Create a *JFrame* containing a single text field. When the user enters text into the text field and presses *Return/Enter*, the text filed is cleared and the text is written to standard output.

17.4   Create a JFrame similar to that in the previous exercise, but containing a text field and a button. When the user pressed the button, whatever was in the text field is written to standard output, and the text field is cleared.

17.5 Create a *JFrame* containing a single black button that stays in the center as the *JFrame* is resized. To do this, use a *GridBagLayout*. Create a *GridBagConstraints* object, and set its `gridx`, `gridy`, `anchor`, and `insets` properties. Note that these are public *instance variables*. Set `gridx` and `gridy` to 0, and set `anchor` to `GridBagConstraints.CENTER`. (Which of these are default values?) The value of `insets` specifies the external padding of the component. Set 50 pixels of pad as follows, were `constraints` is assumed to be the *GridBagConstraints* object:

```
constraints.insets = new Insets(50,50,50,50);
```

When you add the button, provide the *GridBagConstraints* object as second argument to the `add` command.

17.6 Create a *JFrame* with a 100 pixel by 100 pixel black button in the center, as described in the previous exercise. Create an *ActionListener* for the button. Whenever the button is pressed, the *ActionListener* reduces the button's preferred (and minimum) size by two pixels.

The trick is to get the button redrawn. One way to do this is to have the *ActionListener* invalidate the button (by invoking the button's `invalidate` method). This marks the button and all its ancestors as needing to be laid out. Then the *ActionListener* invokes the button's parent's `validate` method. This will cause the layout manager to layout the container again.

The next sequence of exercises involves building a simple accumulator that lets users add numbers to a running total. The application interface will a simple window that looks something like the following:

The user enters a summand by keying into the text field and pressing *Return/Enter*. Pressing the button labeled "+" adds the summand to a running sum, which is displayed in the text field after the button is pressed.

17.7 First, we will build the model for the application. The model is a very simple class specified as follows:

> **class** Accumulator
> A simple object that maintains a running integer sum.
>
> > **public** Accumulator ()
> > Create a new *Accumulator*, with sum and summand set to 0.

> **public int** sum ()
>> The running sum.
>
> **public int** summand ()
>> The value to be added to the sum.
>
> **public void** add ()
>> Add summand to sum.
>
> **public void** setSummand (**int** val)
>> Set the value of the summand.
>
> **public void** reset ()
>> Set the value of the sum and summand to 0.

Implement and test this class.

17.8   The interface will be defined by a class *SimpleAccumulatorUI*. This class will extend *JFrame*. It contains a *JLabel*, *JTextField*, and *JButton* A *SimpleAccumulatorUI* will be given a model instance as a constructor argument. The main method creates an *Accumulator* instance, creates a *SimpleAccumulatorUI* instance passing the *Accumulator* as argument, and sets the *SimpleAccumulatorUI* visible.

Implement the class *SimpleAccumulatorUI* and the top-level class containing the main method. Include a *WindowListener* to terminate the application, but no other listeners. Make the reference to text field an instance variable, so that it will be able to be accessed other than from its listener. The application should run and display the user interface, but of course nothing happens when you enter data or press the button.

17.9   Add *ActionListeners* for the *JButton* and the *JTextField*.

The button listener should do the following when the button generates an *ActionEvent*.

a.   Command the model to do an addition.

b.   Query the model for the current sum.

c.   Display the current sum in the text field.

   The *Integer* method toString can be used to convert an **int** value to a *String*, and the *JTextField* method setText to set the text in the text field.

The text field listener should do the following when the text field generates an *ActionEvent*.

a.   Get the number entered by the user in the text field.

   The *JTextField* method getText can be used to read the contents of the text field, and the *Integer* method parseInt to convert the *String* to an **int**.

b.   Set the summand in the model to the value entered by the user.

17.10   Suppose that the text field listener in the above exercise responds to *TextEvents* rather than *ActionEvents*. How will the behavior of the application change?

17.11 The interface above is not particularly "user friendly." For instance, the user must press *Return/Enter* before pressing the "+" button. (What happens if a user keys a number into the text field, doesn't press *Enter*, and presses the "+" button?)

Without changing the model, design a better interface, with the following properties:

a. The interface has two text fields, one for input and one for output. The field used for output is not enabled.

b. The user need only press the "+" button after entering a number. The *Return/Enter* key need not be pressed.

c. A "Reset" button is provided to reset the accumulator.

d. An informational dialog is displayed if the user attempts to enter text that is not a decimal integer.

SELF-STUDY EXERCISE SOLUTIONS

17.1 *a.* True.
b. True.
c. False.
d. False.
e. False.
f. False.

17.2 `c.height * c.width`

17.3 No, a *JFrame* delegates responsibility for managing its components to its content pane. The proper code would be

```
(frame.getContentPane()).setLayout(new FlowLayout());
(Frame.getContentPane()).add(new JButton("Press me"));
```

17.4
```
JFrame frame = new JFrame("Black hole");
(frame.getContentPane()).setBackground(Color.black);
frame.setSize(200,200);
```

17.5
```
class BlackButton extends JButton {

    public BlackButton() {
        super();
        this.setBackground(Color.black);
    }

    public Dimension getPreferredSize () {
        return new Dimension(50,50);
    }
}
```

```
        public Dimension getMinimumSize () {
           return this.preferredSize();
        }
     }
```

17.6   It will not always be 50 pixels by 50 pixels. Its size depends on the layout manager.

17.7   Either change the layout manager of the *JFrame*'s content pane as in self study exercise
       17.3, or add the button to a *JPanel* which is then added to the content pane. For instance:

```
        JFrame frame = new JFrame("The button");
        JPanel panel = new JPanel();
        panel.add(new BlackButton());
        (frame.getContentPane()).add(
           panel,BorderLayout.CENTER);
        frame.setSize(200,200);
```

17.8   button.addActionListener(
          new ActionListener() {
             public void actionPerformed (ActionEvent e) {
                System.out.println("The button has been pressed!");
             }
          });

17.9   We use *WindowAdapter* because it avoids our having to explicitly implement all seven
       WindowListener methods. We could implement *WindowListener* directly, if we are will-
       ing to implement all seven methods.

17.10 1.   *a1* and *a2* of thread *A* are executed; since x is positive, the if condition is true.

       2.   *b1* and *b2* of thread *B* are executed; since x is positive, the if condition is true.

       3.   *a3* is executed, changing x to 0.

       4.   *a4* is executed; the assert condition holds.

       5.   *b3* is executed, changing x to -1.

       6.   *b4* is executed; the assert condition fails.

17.11 int count;
       boolean failure = true;
       while (failure)
          try {
             count = Integer.parseInt(
                JOptionPane.showInputDialog(frame,"Count:"));
             failure = false;
          } catch (NumberFormatException e) {}

CHAPTER 18

Integrating user interface and model: the Model-View-Controller pattern

The *Model-View-Controller* (*MVC*) pattern is often used to structure graphical user interfaces. In this approach, the interface or an interface element is partitioned into two components, view and controller. The view is responsible for displaying some aspect of the model, and the controller is responsible for capturing input events and effecting appropriate state changes in the model.

In this chapter, we consider MVC and how to implement it in Java. In the process, we will see the standard Java library facilities for implementing the *observes* relation. As examples of the MVC pattern, we build several interfaces for a simple right triangle, and put a graphical user interface on our nim game.

Finally, we will see that the basic Swing components we encountered in the last chapter are themselves structured along the lines of the MVC pattern.

Objectives

After studying this chapter you should understand the following:

- the Model-View-Controller pattern: components and their roles;
- the observer pattern, as realized by the class *Observable* and interface *Observer*, and its use in the MVC pattern.

Also, you should be able to:

- write a graphical user interface for a simple application using the MVC architecture.

18.1   Model-View-Controller

The *Model-View-Controller* (MVC) pattern is commonly used in designing event-driven, window-based applications. With this approach, graphical user interface components are partitioned into *views* and *controllers*. An application is composed of

- *model components*: the objects that model and solve the problem at hand;
- *view components*: the objects that determine the manner in which the model components are to be displayed; and
- *controller components*: the objects that handle user input.

    The advantages of this structure are rather obvious:

- input processing is separated from output processing;
- controllers can be interchanged, allowing different user interaction modes (expert or novice, for instance);
- multiple views of the model can be easily supported.

    Views and controllers are often paired. But in some applications, several views might share the same controller, or there might be views with no controllers.

    The fundamental relationship between components is shown in Figure 18.1. The view and controller explicitly know about the model, but the model does not require details of the other components. The model need not know how it is being displayed, or precisely how the user interacts with the application. While the controllers and views directly depend on the model, the model does not depend in any essential way on the views and controllers. Thus the model can be readily retrofitted with a new look and feel.

    The view must ensure that the display accurately reflects the current state of the model. Thus the view must be *notified* when the model's state changes. We've seen this relation before. It's called the *observer* relation, and it's the relationship between a listener

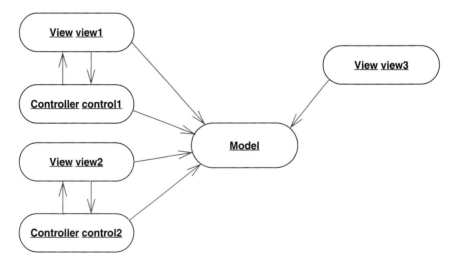

*Figure 18.1 **Model-View-Controller** components.*

and event-generating component that we saw in Section 17.4, and the relationship between *InteractiveController* and *InteractivePlayer* that we saw in Section 9.5.3. An *observer* must know of state changes in a *target*, but the target should remain independent of the observer. The observer *registers* with the target, and the target *informs* the observer (by invoking a particular observer method) when it (the target) changes state.

The controller must effect changes in the model as determined by user input. The controller is simply a client of the model.

The controller defines how the view responds to user input. A view essentially uses a controller to implement a particular response strategy. The relation between view and controller is often *has-as-strategy* as discussed in Section 11.3.1. The controller, on the other hand, generally captures events generated by view components. Thus the controller typically *listens to* the view or its components.

Finally, we note that a view is often a composite built of simpler views. For instance, a complex control panel might be composed of views of the individual controls, or a maze view in a maze game might be composed of views of the maze rooms and passages. The structure exhibited here is identical to the *Component-Container* structure seen in the previous chapter.

18.2   Implementing MVC in Java

To see how we might implement the MVC pattern in Java, we'll consider a simple example in which the model is a right triangle. We develop three different views of the triangle and one controller. One view describes the triangle by displaying the lengths of its three sides. A second view displays the triangle graphically. Finally, a third view logs changes in the triangle state to a file.

The controller is associated with the first view, and allows a user to modify the sides of the triangle.

18.2.1 The model

The model is a very simple class modeling a right triangle, as shown in Listing 18.1. We permit the lengths of two of the sides, called the *base* and the *height*, to be modified. The length of the third side, the *hypotenuse*, is determined by the lengths of the base and the height.

The methods `round` and `sqrt` are static functions defined in *java.lang.Math*. They perform the obvious operations of rounding a double to an integer, and computing the square root of a number.

18.2.2 The class *Observable* and interface *Observer*

To support the observes relation, Java provides a class *Observable* and an interface *Observer* in the package `java.util`. The *Observer* is client and the *Observable* is

---

Listing 18.1   The model class *RightTriangle*

```java
/**
 * A right triangle. Units assumed to be pixels.
 */
public class RightTriangle {

   // the sides of the triangle
   private int base;
   private int height;
   private int hypotenuse;

   /**
    * Create a right triangle with the specified base
    * and height.
    * @require    base >= 0 && height >= 0
    */
   public RightTriangle (int base, int height) {
      this.base = base;
      this.height = height;
      setHypotenuse();
   }

   /**
    * The base.
    * @ensure     result >= 0
    */
   public int base () {
      return this.base;
   }

   /**
    * The height.
    * @ensure     result >= 0
    */
   public int height () {
      return this.height;
   }

   /**
    * The hypotenuse.
    * @ensure     result >= 0
    */
```

continued

Listing 18.1   The model class *RightTriangle* (cont'd)

```java
    public int hypotenuse () {
        return this.hypotenuse;
    }

    /**
     * Change base.
     * @require    newBase >= 0
     */
    public void setBase (int newBase) {
        this.base = newBase;
        setHypotenuse();
    }

    /**
     * Change height.
     * @require    newHeight >= 0
     */
    public void setHeight (int newHeight) {
        this.height = newHeight;
        setHypotenuse();
    }

    /*
     * Adjust hypotenuse.
     */
    private void setHypotenuse () {
        this.hypotenuse = (int) Math.round(
            Math.sqrt(base*base + height*height));
    }
}
```

server. The *Observer* registers with the *Observable*, and the *Observable* informs the *Observer* when it (the *Observable*) changes state.(See Figure 18.2.)

The most important methods provided by the class *Observable* are

```java
public void addObserver (Observer o);
protected void setChanged ();
public void notifyObservers ();
public void notifyObservers (Object arg);
```

An *Observer* invokes `addObserver` to register with an *Observable*, in much the same way that an *ActionListener* invokes `addActionListener` to register with a

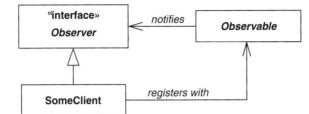

Figure 18.2 **The *Observer* pattern in Java.**

Component. The remaining three are used by an *Observable* to notify all the registered observers that it has changed state.

To be specific, the method `setChanged` sets the *Observable*'s `hasChanged` attribute to true. When `notifyObservers` is called, if `hasChanged` is true, all of the registered observers are notified, and `hasChanged` is reset to false. Thus an object takes note of the fact that it has changed and it must notify its observers by setting its `hasChanged` attribute. It then actually notifies observers by calling one of its `notify-Observers` methods.

An *Observable* can provide information to its observers by supplying an argument to `notifyObservers`. This argument typically includes details about exactly what changed in the *Observable*, so that the observers can conduct their response more efficiently.

To continue our example, we make the class *RightTriangle* an extension of *Observable*:

> **public class** RightTriangle **extends** Observable ...

A client registers as an observer by calling the method `addObserver`. For instance, if a client (perhaps a view) wants to register with a *RightTriangle* `rt`, it executes the call

> `rt.addObserver(`**this**`);`

When the *RightTriangle* changes state, it calls its methods `setChanged` and `notifyObservers`:

> `setChanged();`
> `notifyObservers();`

to notify all the registered observers of the event.

A *RightTriangle* changes state only in response to a `setBase` or `setHeight` command. Therefore, observers should be informed when these commands are executed:

```
public void setBase (int newBase) {
    this.base = newBase;
    setHypotenuse();
    setChanged();
    notifyObservers();
}
```

```
public void setHeight (int newHeight) {
    this.height = newHeight;
    setHypotenuse();
    setChanged();
    notifyObservers();
}
```

Since the state of the model is so simple, we simply inform observers that something has changed without providing additional information in the form of an argument to the notifyObservers method.

We are finished with the model. Note that the model is independent of its observers: it does not need to know who its observers are, or what they intend to do about changes in its state.

18.2.3 An *Observer*

Let's take a look at how an observer is structured. We sketch a class *RTObserver* that implements the interface *Observer*, and observes a *RightTriangle*.

```
/**
 * RightTriangle observer.
 */
class RTObserver implements Observer {

    private RightTriangle target;

    /**
     * Create an observer of RightTriangle rt.
     */
    public RTObserver (RightTriangle rt) {
        target = rt;
        target.addObserver(this);
    }
    ...
}
```

An observer must know the target object. In this case, the observer is told about the target *RightTriangle* when it, the observer, is created. The observer then registers itself with the target. The fact that the target extends *Observable* ensures that it will support an addObserver method.

The interface *Observer* specifies only one method:

```
void update (Observable o, Object arg);
```

This is the method that is invoked when the target notifies the observer of a state change. The first parameter references the target object reporting the change, and the second is the notifyObservers argument. That is, if a target object invokes the method

```
notifyObservers(info);
```

the `update` method of each of its observers will be called, with a reference to the target as first argument, and `info` as second. If a target invokes

```
notifyObservers();
```

with no argument, the `update` method of each of its observers will be called, with a reference to the target as first argument, and a null value as second argument.

The observer implements the method `update`, defining what it wants to do about the target state change.

```
public void update (Observable o, Object arg) {
    do something about o's state change.
}
```

To summarize, an *Observable* has a property `hasChanged` and maintains a list of *Observers*. The method `addObserver` adds an object to the list. The method `notify-Observers` calls the `update` method of each *Observer* on the list. We could implement our own minimal version of *Observable* as follows:

```
public abstract class Observable {

    private boolean hasChanged;
    private List<Observer> observers;

    protected Observable () {
        observers = new DefaultList<Observer>();
        hasChanged = false;
    }

    public void addObserver (Observer o) {
        observers.add(o);
    }

    public void setChanged () {
        hasChanged = true;
    }

    public void notifyObservers (Object arg) {
        if (hasChanged) {
            for (int i = 0; i < observers.size(); i = i+1)
                ((Observer)observers.get(i)).update(
                    this, arg);
            hasChanged = false;
        }
    }

    public void notifyObservers () {
        this.notifyObservers(null);
    }
}
```

✳ 18.2.4 Observer, Observable, and subtyping

It should be obvious that an observer and its target are closely related. In particular, an observer knows considerably more about its target than simply that the target extends *Observable*. Similarly, the target often has some idea of what its observers are interested in. If the target passes hints about its state change as an argument to `notifyObservers`, the target and observer must agree on the format of the information passed.

The interface *Observer* defines a type, and any class that implements the interface defines a subtype. The same is true for the abstract class *Observable*. The fundamental rule of subtyping (Chapter 9) states that an instance of a subtype can be provided in any context requiring an instance of the supertype. But the rule clearly does not apply here. For example, the class *RightTriangle* inherits the method

public void addObserver (Observer o)

from *Observable*. According to the subtyping rule, this method can be invoked with an instance of *any* class that implements *Observer* as an argument. While the compiler will allow this, it is clearly nonsense to provide a client that does not expect to be observing a *RightTriangle*.

In particular, we should consider the abstract class *Observable* as a convenience, intended simply to capture common functionality and not properly to define a type.

18.2.5 A simple view and controller

Now that we've seen how an observer is structured, let's build a simple user interface for a *RightTriangle*. We opt for simplicity over flexibility and elegance in constructing the GUI.

The model is an instance of the class *RightTriangle* given above. We build a view that shows the three components of the triangle in text fields, as shown in Figure 18.3.

A controller will capture input from the text fields labeled *Base* and *Height*, and modify the state of the *RightTriangle* appropriately. (We won't let the user change *Hypotenuse*.)

For simplicity, we put everything in the same package.

The view

The view extends *JPanel* and implements *Observer*. We'll add the *JPanel* to the content pane of a top level *JFrame*. The *RightTriangle* to display is provided as a constructor argument:

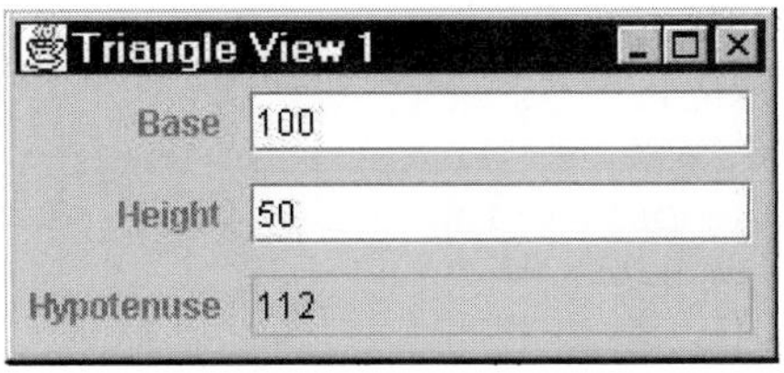

Figure 18.3 **View of a RightTriangle.**

```
class TextView extends JPanel implements Observer {

    public TextView (RightTriangle model) {
        super();
        ...
```

The fundamental components of the view are the three text fields. They will be referenced by instance variables and created in the *TextView* constructor. We'll see how to handle the layout later. The text fields are created to be FIELD_SIZE characters wide, and are each assigned an *action command*. The *action command* is incorporated in any *Action-Event* generated by the text field. By looking at the *action command* of an *ActionEvent*, we can determine which text field generated the *ActionEvent*. (See page 703 for an example using an action command.) The *editable* property of the hypotenuse text field is set to *false*, so that it cannot be changed by the user. Since hypotenuse will not generate any *ActionEvents*, its *action command* need not be set:

```
class TextView extends JPanel implements Observer {

    private final static int FIELD_SIZE = 16;
    private JTextField base;
    private JTextField height;
    private JTextField hypotenuse;

    public TextView (RightTriangle model) {
        super();
        ...
        base = new JTextField(FIELD_SIZE);
        base.setActionCommand("Base");
        ...
        height = new JTextField(FIELD_SIZE);
        height.setActionCommand("Height");
        ...
        hypotenuse = new JTextField(FIELD_SIZE);
        hypotenuse.setEditable(false);
        ...
    }
    ...
}
```

Since *TextView* implements *Observer*, it must implement the method update specified by the interface. As we've seen, this method is invoked by the model whenever it changes state. When the model changes state, the text fields must be updated with new model state information. Thus update queries the model for the new state information, and writes it to the text fields:

```
public void update (Observable model, Object arg) {
    int side;
    RightTriangle rt = (RightTriangle)model;
    side = rt.base();
    base.setText(String.valueOf(side));
    side = rt.height();
    height.setText(String.valueOf(side));
    side = rt.hypotenuse();
    hypotenuse.setText(String.valueOf(side));
}
```

Note that since the *RightTriangle* invokes the `notifyObservers` method with no arguments, the second argument to `update (arg)` will be null. The *JTextField* method `setText` writes a text string into the text field. The *String* method `valueOf` with an **int** argument returns a *String* representation of the integer value.

The controller

We're not quite finished with the view, but let's now look at the controller. The controller captures input from the `base` and `height` text fields, and updates the model. It must therefore know about both the view's text fields, and the *RightTriangle* the view is displaying.

The controller and the view are very closely related. Because of this tight coupling, and to simplify the design, we make the controller class a private inner class of *TextView*. That is, we define the controller class, which we call *TVController*, inside *TextView*. The controller will then have direct access to the view's text field components. We'll provide a reference to the model when the controller is constructed.

The controller needs to know when the user enters a value in the `base` or `height` text fields. Specifically, it must respond to *ActionEvents* generated by these text fields. (A text field generates an *ActionEvent* when the user presses *Return/Enter* in the text field.) To respond to the appropriate *ActionEvents*, the controller must be an *ActionListener* and must be added as a listener to the `base` and `height` text fields of the view. As an *ActionListener*, it must implement the method `actionPerformed`.

```
private class TVController implements ActionListener {

    private RightTriangle model;

    /**
     * Create a new controller for this TextView of the
     * specified RightTriangle.
     */
    public TVController (RightTriangle model) {
        this.model = model;
        TextView.this.base.addActionListener(this);
        TextView.this.height.addActionListener(this);
    }
```

❶

```
/**
 * Update the model in response to user input.
 */
public void actionPerformed (ActionEvent e) {
    do something when user has entered text in a
    text field
}
}
```

The notation TextView.**this**.base, seen in line **❶**, was introduced in Section 10.5.3. It specifies that base is a feature of the *TextView* associated with this *TVController*, that is, of the *TextView* instance enclosing the definition of this *TVController*. We could just as easily have written

```
base.addActionListener(this);
```

but the additional syntax emphasizes that base is a *TextView* component.

When the user enters text, the controller gets the value of the text field and instructs the model to update the appropriate component, either *base* or *height*. As we've seen, *ActionEvents* generated by the text fields have an *action command* property. By examining this property, the controller can determine which text field generated the event.

The actionPerformed method can be written as follows:

```
         /**
          * Update the model in response to user input.
          */
         public void actionPerformed (ActionEvent e) {
❶           JTextField tf = (JTextField)e.getSource();
            try {
❷               int i = Integer.parseInt(tf.getText());
❸               if (i < 0) throw new NumberFormatException();
❹               String which = e.getActionCommand();
                if (which.equals("Base"))
                    model.setBase(i);
```

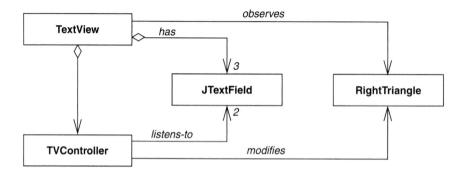

Figure 18.4 View, controller, and model.

```
                 else
                     model.setHeight(i);
❺           } catch (NumberFormatException ex) {
                 TextView.this.update(model, null);
            }
        }
```

A few notes on the implementation.

❶ The *ActionEvent* query `getSource` returns a reference to the *Object* that was the source of the event.

❷ The *JTextField* query `getText` returns the text in the text field, as a *String*. The method `parseInt` of the class *Integer* converts the *String* to the **int** that it denotes. This method will throw a *NumberFormatException* if its argument does not consist of a sequence of decimal digits.

❸ A negative number is treated the same way as if it were not a number. A *Number-FormatException* is explicitly thrown, and caught in the catch clause.

❹ The *ActionEvent* query `getActionCommand` returns action command of the event. In this case, either `"Base"` or `"Height"`.

❺ If the user keys gibberish, we catch the *NumberFormatException* and explicitly tell the view to update itself. This results in the view getting the current state of the model and updating the display, replacing the gibberish keyed by the user with correct values from the model.

View layout

Now let's finish the view by seeing how to do the layout. The view will be composed of three labels and three text fields. The components will be laid out in a 3×2 grid, using a *GridBagLayout* layout manager.

GridBagLayout is a flexible, but somewhat complicated, layout manager. Complete details are beyond the scope of our presentation. We only remark on features necessary for the example.

A *GridBagLayout* layout manager uses a *GridBagConstraints* object to position each component. The constraints object specifies things like which grid cells the component is

cell (0,0)	*cell (1,0)*
cell (0,1)	*cell (1,1)*
cell (0,2)	*cell (1,2)*

Figure 18.5 **Components are laid out in a 3 × 2 grid of cells.**

to occupy, how the component should be positioned in its cell or cells, how extra space is to be allocated to the cells, and so on.

We set the layout manager for the *TextView* to *GridBagLayout*, and create a *GridBagConstraints* instance. (We can use the same constraint instance to position each component.)

```
public TextView (RightTriangle model) {
    super();
    setLayout(new GridBagLayout());
    GridBagConstraints constraints =
        new GridBagConstraints();
```

The *GridBagConstraints* object has a number of public instance variables. Positioning of the component is determined by the values of these variables. First we set the attributes of the constraints object to position the labels. The labels all appear in column (gridx) 0. We set the row (gridy) to the special value RELATIVE. The effect of this is to place each component below the previous one.

```
constraints.gridx = 0;
constraints.gridy = GridBagConstraints.RELATIVE;
```

We set the anchor attribute so that the labels are right-justified in their cells.

```
constraints.anchor = GridBagConstraints.EAST;
```

Finally, we use an *Insets* instance to place a 5-pixel border around the label.

```
constraints.insets = new Insets(5,5,5,5);
```

Now that the constraints object has been created and set, it can be used to position the labels.

```
add(new JLabel("Base"),constraints);
add(new JLabel("Height"),constraints);
add(new JLabel("Hypotenuse"),constraints);
```

Note that we use the version of add that requires two arguments. In this case, the component is the first argument, and the constraints object is the second.

If we change the column position to 1, we can use the same constraints object for positioning the text fields that we used for the labels:

```
constraints.gridx = 1;

base = new JTextField(FIELD_SIZE);
base.setActionCommand("Base");
add(base,constraints);

height = new JTextField(FIELD_SIZE);
height.setActionCommand("Height");
add(height,constraints);
```

```
        hypotenuse = new JTextField(FIELD_SIZE);
        hypotenuse.setEditable(false);
        add(hypotenuse,constraints);
```

We conclude the constructor by registering with the model, creating a controller, and getting the initial model state.

```
        model.addObserver(this);
        controller = new TVController(model);
        update(model,null);
    }
```

The complete definition, including the top-level class, is given in Listing 18.2.

Listing 18.2 **The class *TextView***

```
import java.util.*;
import java.awt.*;
import java.awt.event.*;
import javax.swing.*;

/**
 * View for a RightTriangle, as three text fields.
 */
class TextView extends JPanel implements Observer {

    private final static int FIELD_SIZE = 16;
    private TVController controller;
    private JTextField base;
    private JTextField height;
    private JTextField hypotenuse;

    /**
     * Create a view for the specified RightTriangle.
     */
    public TextView (RightTriangle model) {
        super();
        setLayout(new GridBagLayout());
        GridBagConstraints constraints =
            new GridBagConstraints();

        constraints.gridx = 0;
        constraints.gridy = GridBagConstraints.RELATIVE;
        constraints.anchor = GridBagConstraints.EAST;
        constraints.insets = new Insets(5,5,5,5);
```

continued

Listing 18.2   The class *TextView* (cont'd)

```java
        add(new JLabel("Base"),constraints);
        add(new JLabel("Height"),constraints);
        add(new JLabel("Hypotenuse"),constraints);

        constraints.gridx = 1;

        base = new JTextField(FIELD_SIZE);
        base.setActionCommand("Base");
        add(base,constraints);

        height = new JTextField(FIELD_SIZE);
        height.setActionCommand("Height");
        add(height,constraints);

        hypotenuse = new JTextField(FIELD_SIZE);
        hypotenuse.setEditable(false);
        add(hypotenuse,constraints);
        model.addObserver(this);
        controller = new TVController(model);
        update(model,null);
    }

    /**
     * Update the view with current model state.
     */
    public void update(Observable model, Object arg) {
        int side;
        RightTriangle rt = (RightTriangle)model;
        side = rt.base();
        base.setText(String.valueOf(side));
        side = rt.height();
        height.setText(String.valueOf(side));
        side = rt.hypotenuse();
        hypotenuse.setText(String.valueOf(side));
    }
```

continued

Listing 18.2   The class *TextView* (cont'd)

```java
/**
 * RightTriangle controller for a TextView.
 */
private class TVController implements ActionListener {

    private RightTriangle model;

    /**
     * Create a new controller for the specified TextView
     * of the specified RightTriangle.
     */
    public TVController (RightTriangle model) {
        this.model = model;
        TextView.this.base.addActionListener(this);
        TextView.this.height.addActionListener(this);
    }

    /**
     * Update the model in response to user input.
     */
    public void actionPerformed (ActionEvent e) {
        JTextField tf = (JTextField)e.getSource();
        try {
            int i = Integer.parseInt(tf.getText());
            if (i < 0) throw new NumberFormatException();
            String which = e.getActionCommand();
            if (which.equals("Base"))
                model.setBase(i);
            else
                model.setHeight(i);
        } catch (NumberFormatException ex) {
            TextView.this.update(model, null);
        }
    }
} // end of class TVController

} // end of class TextView
```

continued

Listing 18.2   **The class *TextView* (cont'd)**

```
/**
 * Create an editable RightTriangle and View it.
 */
public class RightTriangleViewer {

    public static void main (String[] args) {
        JFrame f = new JFrame("Triangle View 1");
        RightTriangle model = new RightTriangle(1,1);
        TextView view = new TextView(model);
        f.getContentPane().add(view, BorderLayout.CENTER);
        f.addWindowListener(
            new WindowAdapter() {
                public void windowClosing(WindowEvent e) {
                    e.getWindow().dispose();
                }

                public void windowClosed(WindowEvent e) {
                    System.exit(0);
                }
            }
        );
        f.pack();
        f.setVisible(true);
    }
}
```

18.2.6 A graphic view

We implement another view of the *RightTriangle*, this one without a controller. This view simply shows a graphic rendition of the triangle. The basic structure is the same as the previous view. We define the view as an extension of *JPanel* that we can pack into a top-level frame. For convenience, we include a local method for retrieving the current model state:

```
/**
 * Graphical view for a RightTriangle.
 */
class GraphicView extends JPanel implements Observer {

    private int modelBase;
    private int modelHeight;
```

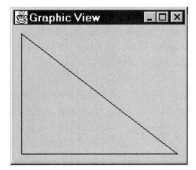

Figure 18.6 **Graphic View of a *RightTriangle*.**

```
/**
 * Create a graphic view for the specified
 * RightTriangle.
 */
public GraphicView (RightTriangle model) {
    super();
    model.addObserver(this);
    update(model, null);
}

/**
 * Update the view with current model state.
 */
public void update (Observable model, Object arg) {
    ...
}

/*
 * Get the properties of the model.
 */
private void getModelState (RightTriangle model) {
    modelBase = model.base();
    modelHeight = model.height();
}
}
```

We use the *JPanel* as a blank canvas on which to draw the triangle. We've seen how to do this in Section 17.6.4, and you might want to review that section. The simplest way to draw on a *JPanel* is to override its paintComponent method. This method is invoked in the event dispatching thread to allow the component to update its display. The method gets a *Graphics* object as argument, that gives access to the displace space occupied by the component.

We define `paintComponent` as follows:

```
public void paintComponent (Graphics g) {
    super.paintComponent(g);
    g.drawLine(
        BASE_X,BASE_Y+modelHeight,
        BASE_X+modelBase,BASE_Y+modelHeight);
    g.drawLine(
        BASE_X,BASE_Y,
        BASE_X,BASE_Y+modelHeight);
    g.drawLine(
        BASE_X,BASE_Y,
        BASE_X+modelBase,BASE_Y+modelHeight);
}
```

The first statement of the method calls the *JPanel* `paintComponent`, which paints the background. The final three statements draw the three lines of the triangle. The constants BASE_X and BASE_Y are offsets from the left and top edges of the panel:

```
private final static int BASE_X = 10;
// offset of drawing from left edge of panel (pixels)
private final static int BASE_Y = 10;
// offset of drawing from top of panel (pixels)
```

We override these `getPreferredSize` and `getMinimumSize` to make sure that the panel is big enough to contain the drawing of the triangle and the 10-pixel border.

```
/*
 * Define preferred and minimum size so that the
 * triangle fits.
 */
public Dimension getPreferredSize () {
    return new Dimension(
        2*BASE_X+modelBase, 2*BASE_Y+modelHeight);
}

public Dimension getMinimumSize () {
    return getPreferredSize();
}
```

Finally, we implement `update`:

```
/**
 * Update the view with current model state.
 */
public void update (Observable model, Object arg) {
    getModelState((RightTriangle)model);
    repaint();
    Container w = getTopLevelAncestor();
```

```
    if (w instanceof Window)
        ((Window)w).pack();
}
```

This method first gets the current state of the model. The invocation of repaint causes the component to be redrawn as soon as possible. This method is invoked when we want the component to be redrawn. Finally, we force the top-level window containing the *JPanel* to be resized to fit the preferred size of the *JPanel*. The complete class definition is given in Listing 18.3.

Listing 18.3 **The class *GraphicView***

```
/**
 * Graphical view for a RightTriangle.
 */
class GraphicView extends JPanel implements Observer {

    private int modelBase;          // base of model (pixels)
    private int modelHeight;        // height of model (pixels)
    private final static int BASE_X = 10;
        // offset of drawing from left edge of panel (pixels)
    private final static int BASE_Y = 10;
        // offset of drawing from top of panel (pixels)

    /**
     * Create a graphic view for the specified RightTriangle.
     */
    public GraphicView (RightTriangle model) {
        super();
        model.addObserver(this);
        update(model,null);
    }

    /**
     * Update the view with current model state.
     */

    public void update (Observable model, Object arg) {
        getModelState((RightTriangle)model);
        repaint();
        Container w = getTopLevelAncestor();
        if (w instanceof Window)
            ((Window)w).pack();
    }
```

continued

Listing 18.3   **The class *GraphicView* (cont'd)**

```java
/**
 * Draw the triangle on this JPanel.
 */
public void paintComponent(Graphics g) {
    super.paintComponent(g);
    g.setColor(getForeground());
    g.drawLine(
        BASE_X, BASE_Y+modelHeight,

        BASE_X+modelBase, BASE_Y+modelHeight);
    g.drawLine(
        BASE_X, BASE_Y,
        BASE_X, BASE_Y+modelHeight);

    g.drawLine(
        BASE_X, BASE_Y,
        BASE_X+modelBase, BASE_Y+modelHeight);
}

/*
 * Define preferred and minimum size so that the triangle
 * fits.
 */
public Dimension getPreferredSize () {
    return new Dimension(
        2*BASE_X+modelBase, 2*BASE_Y+modelHeight);
}

public Dimension getMinimumSize () {
    return getPreferredSize();
}

/*
 * Get the properties of the model.
 */

private void getModelState (RightTriangle model) {
    modelBase = model.base();
    modelHeight = model.height();
}
}
```

18.2.7 A logger as a view

We give one more example of a view, to illustrate that a view need not be part of a graphical interface. This view simply logs changes in the model's state to a file. It is straightforward, and shown in Listing 18.4.

There is only one item of note in the logger. When the application terminates, the log file must be closed. We assume that the top-level window will be closed when the application terminates. Thus the logger catches the window closing event and closes the log file. We can see here why it is useful to distinguish between "window closing" and "window closed" events. If the application terminated on the window closing event, the logger would not have a chance to close the log file.

Listing 18.4   **The class *RTLogger***

```java
import java.util.*;
import java.io.*;
import java.awt.*;
import java.awt.event.*;

/**
 * RTLogger logs changes in a RightTriangle to a file.
 */
class RTLogger implements Observer {

    private PrintWriter logFile;
    private int modelBase;
    private int modelHeight;

    /**
     * Create a RightTriangle logger, to log changes in the
     * specified model to the specified log file.
     */
    public RTLogger (RightTriangle model, String fileName,
        Window application) throws java.io.IOException {
        logFile = new PrintWriter(
            new FileOutputStream(fileName));
        application.addWindowListener(
            new WindowAdapter() {
                public void windowClosing (WindowEvent e) {
                    logFile.close();
                }
            });
        getModelState(model);
        logFile.println(modelBase + " " + modelHeight);
        model.addObserver(this);
    }
```

continued

Listing 18.4   **The class *RTLogger* (cont'd)**

```
/**
 * Close the log file.
 */
public void close () {
   logFile.close();
}

/**
 * Log when model changes state.
 */
public void update (Observable model, Object arg) {
   getModelState((RightTriangle)model);
   logFile.println(modelBase + " " + modelHeight);
}

/*
 * Get the properties of the model.
 */
private void getModelState (RightTriangle model) {
   modelBase = model.base();
   modelHeight = model.height();
}
}
```

✳ 18.3   Adding a graphical interface to the nim game

In Chapters 8 and 9, we developed the simple nim game with a text-based user interface. Let's see how a graphical user interface for that application might be structured using MVC. Since the code for a graphical interface tends to be substantial without being particularly illuminating, we only sketch an approach.

The model for the game involves several classes, as shown in Figure 18.7. We assume two concrete *Player* classes, *InteractivePlayer* and *IndependentPlayer*. An *InteractivePlayer* gets its moves from the user. An *IndependentPlayer* determines its moves algorithmically.

We constructed a text-based user interface in Chapter 8, and in Chapter 9 built a text-based controller for an *InteractivePlayer*. (See Figure 18.8.) There are two aspects of that design to recall. First, the responsibility of getting moves from the user and giving them to the *InteractivePlayer* was allocated to the *TUIController*. The *TUIController* registers with the *InteractivePlayer*, and when the *InteractivePlayer* is about to make a move, it

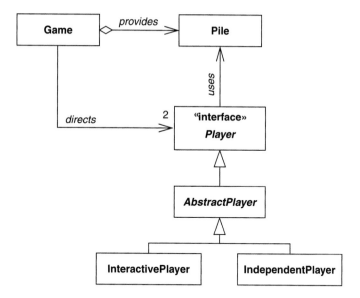

Figure 18.7 **Nim game model classes.**

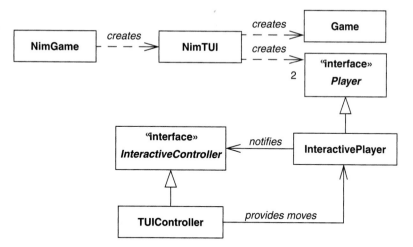

Figure 18.8 **Text-based user interface classes for the nim game.**

informs its controller. The controller then prompts the user for a move, reads the user's input, and tells the *InteractivePlayer*. (The case is illustrated in Figure 9.5.)

Second, we located the play loop,

```
while (!game.gameOver())
    game.play();
```

in the user interface. We noted at the time that the "looping" in an event driven system is not explicitly written in the code, but results from the user repeatedly performing some action. We will modify both these decisions in designing the graphical interface.

The view

We create a simple graphical display as illustrated in Figure 18.9. The display is composed of four panels: a panel to display the number of sticks remaining in the game, two panels each containing a text field to report the plays of a player, and a panel containing buttons for the user to make a move.

An instance of the class *NimInterface* builds the display, and observes the *Game*:

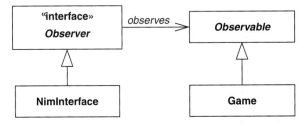

When the *Game* completes a play, it notifies its *Observers*.

```
public void play () {
    if (!gameOver()) {
        nextPlayer.takeTurn(pile,MAX_ON_A_TURN);
        previousPlayer = nextPlayer;
        nextPlayer = otherPlayer(nextPlayer);
        setChanged();
        notifyObservers();
    }
}
```

The *NimInterface* then queries the *Game* and updates the display.

We make the *NimInterface* responsible for displaying the number of sticks remaining in the game and for reporting the winner when the game is over. (An informational option pane is used to report the winner.) Rather than having the *NimInterface* directly responsible for reporting *Player* moves, we define an inner class *PlayerView* with this responsibility. A *PlayerView* observes a *Player*, and updates the text field when the *Player* takes a turn. (Some designers would prefer to have all interactions between view and model filtered through the *Game*. We want to illustrate that there can be any number of view objects, each responsible for monitoring some aspect of the model.)

To give a visual hint as to who's turn it is, we black out the move-reporting text field for the player who is to play next. Figure 18.9, for instance, shows that it is the user's turn. The buttons are enabled only during the user's turn.

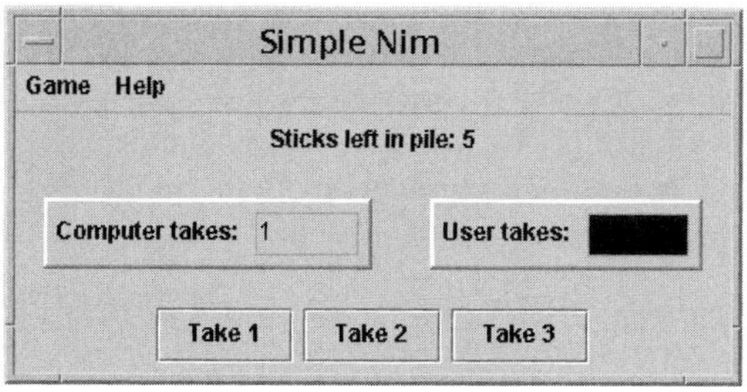

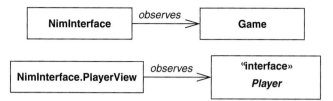

Figure 18.9 **Graphical display for Simple Nim.**

NimInterface — observes → Game

NimInterface.PlayerView — observes → «interface» Player

Figure 18.10 **Simple Nim view objects.**

The controller

The *NimInterface* class *NimController* is responsible for getting input from the user and controlling the game. *NimController* listens to the buttons in the display. When the user presses a button indicating the number of sticks to take, the *NimController* informs the *InteractivePlayer* by invoking its setNumberToTake method. The *NimController* then twice invokes the *Game*'s play method, once for the *InteractivePlayer* and once for the *IndependentPlayer*.

Notice that there is no longer any need for a "play loop." Play continues because the user continues to take turns (by pressing a button) until the game is over. Also notice that the *InteractivePlayer* no longer needs to inform a controller that it needs a move. The button-pressing event results in the *NimController* giving the *InteractivePlayer* its move, followed by the *InteractivePlayer* and the *IndependentPlayer* each taking a turn.

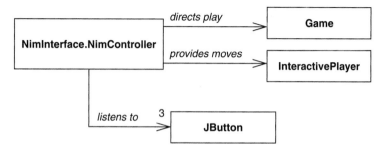

Figure 18.11 **Simple Nim controller.**

It might seem that the knowledge that there are two plays in a "round" properly belongs in the *Game* and not in the *NimController*. We could add a method `playRound` to the *Game*, and have the *NimController* give the *Game* the command `playRound` rather than twice giving the *Game* the command `play`. But the *NimController* must still make sure that a round begins with the *InteractivePlayer*. That is, the sequence of actions after the user presses a button must be

> `setNumberToTake` invoked for *InteractivePlayer*;
> *InteractivePlayer* takes a turn;
> *IndependentPlayer* takes a turn;

and not

> `setNumberToTake` invoked for *InteractivePlayer*;
> *IndependentPlayer* takes a turn;
> *InteractivePlayer* takes a turn;

In the latter case, the user would be forced to choose a move before knowing what the other player will do. In particular, if the *IndependentPlayer* is to play first in the game, the *NimController* must "prime" the system by giving the *Game* the `play` command for the first move before listening for user input. Furthermore, as we'll see later, we want to treat the *IndependentPlayer*'s turn a little differently from the *InteractivePlayer*'s. Any distinction between *IndependentPlayer* and *InteractivePlayer* is inappropriate in the *Game*: the *Game* is written in terms of the interface *Player*, and does not depend on the concrete classes of the participating *Players*. Thus it seems we have little choice but to put some knowledge in the *NimController*.

Initialization and model creation

Initialization is by means of a *JDialog* displayed by the *NimController*. The user selects the "New Game" menu item from the "Game" menu displayed in the top-level *JFrame*'s menu bar. The menu item listener invokes the *NimController*'s `initializeGame` method. This method displays a *JDialog*, gets initialization data from the user, and creates a *Game*.

We let the *NimInterface* create the *Players* in its constructor. In a more fully developed system, this function would probably also be done by the *NimController* in response to some user menu selection.

Delaying the IndependentPlayer

There is one other aspect of the *NimController* that is not entirely obvious. We would like some delay to occur between the user selecting a move and the *IndependentPlayer* making a move. Otherwise, both moves will appear to happen simultaneously. The game will have a better "feel" if there is a noticeable delay between moves.

To delay the *InteractivePlayer*, we might be tempted simply to put a delay between the two invocations of `play` in the *NimController*:

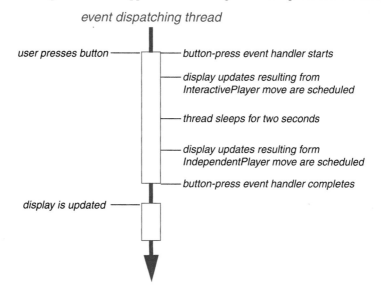

Figure 18.12 **Nim configuration dialogue.**

```
public void actionPerformed (ActionEvent e) {
    ...
    user.setNumberToTake(number);
    game.play();            // InteractivePlayer
    nhUtilities.utilities.Control.sleep(2);
                            // sleep 2 seconds
    game.play();            // IndependentPlayer
    ...
}
```

The problem is that the *NimController* is executing in the event dispatching thread as a result of the button-pressing event. (See Section 17.3.2.) Changes in the display that result from the player moves are scheduled to take place in the event dispatching thread as well. But these updates don't happen until handling the button press event is complete.

event dispatching thread

user presses button —— button-press event handler starts

—— display updates resulting from InteractivePlayer move are scheduled

—— thread sleeps for two seconds

—— display updates resulting form IndependentPlayer move are scheduled

—— button-press event handler completes

display is updated ——

Thus even though the application will pause for several seconds, both moves still appear to take place at the same time. To avoid this problem, the *NimController* does not give the *Game* two consecutive `play` commands. Rather, the *NimController* uses a *javax.swing.Timer* to schedule the second invocation of the *Game*'s `play` command several seconds after the first. Thus the *IndependentPlayer*'s move occurs after the button-press event handling is complete:

Implementation code is much too large to show here. It is available in the directory `nim`, located in `ch18`, in `nhText`.

✳ 18.4   The MVC pattern and Swing components

Up to now we've treated Swing components as if they were monolithic entities. In fact, the components themselves are structured along the Model-View-Controller pattern. Though a detailed discussion is well beyond the scope of the text, we can get at least an elementary idea as to how Swing components are built.

The model

Each Swing *JComponent* has an associated model object that is responsible for maintaining the component's state. A *JButton* or *JCheckBox* has a *ButtonModel*, for instance, while a *JTextArea* or *JTextField* has a *Document*. *ButtonModel* and *Document* are interfaces defined in `javax.swing` and `javax.swing.text` respectively.

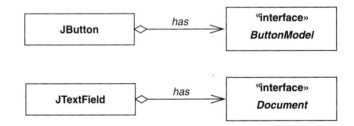

Figure 18.13   *JComponents* have models.

The state of a button is rather simple. It can be *enabled* (only an enabled button can be pressed), it can be *pressed*, and, in the case of a check box or radio button, it can be *selected*. (There are a few more aspects of a button's state that we'll ignore.) Different states of the button are typically reflected in the view. A button that is not enabled might be grayed-out, for instance. The *ButtonModel* is responsible for managing the button state; the interface specifies methods for setting and getting the button's state. For example

public boolean isPressed()
  This button is pressed.

public boolean isEnabled()
  This button can be pressed or selected by an input device.

```
public void setPressed (boolean b)
```
Set this button to pressed or unpressed.

```
public void setEnabled (boolean b)
```
Enable or disable this button.

The state information maintained by a *Document* is much more complex. It includes the actual text of the document plus structural information about the text. Support is provided for editing the text and manipulating text attributes, and for notifying listeners when changes are made to the *Document*.

In the case of an ordinary button, the model is usually provided by an instance of the javax.swing class *DefaultButtonModel*. Applications don't generally interact directly with the model. Rather, the component itself provides methods that manipulate the model. For example, the class *JButton* has methods isEnabled and setEnabled that simply invoke the corresponding *ButtonModel* methods.

In the case of a *JTextField*, an instance of the javax.swing.text class *Plain-Document* is the default model. A *JTextField* can be customized by changing or extending the model. For example, the *Document* method insertString inserts characters into the *Document*. In particular, it is invoked every time the user enters a character into the text field. If we want the text field to ignore any characters that are not digits, for example, we can extend the model overriding the insertString method.

```
/**
 * A PlainDocument that will contain only digits.
 */
class NumberDocument extends PlainDocument {

    public void insertString (int offset, String str,
        AttributeSet a) throws BadLocationException {
        if (str.length() > 0)
            if (Character.isDigit(str.charAt(0)))
                super.insertString(offset,str,a);
    }
}
```

A text field equipped with this model will only accept digits keyed as input. For instance, if base and height are *JTextFields*, we can restrict input to digits as follows:

```
base.setDocument(new NumberDocument());
height.setDocument(new NumberDocument());
```

The UI delegate

Since the view and controller for a component are very closely related, they are combined into one object for many Swing components. The component delegates the view and control responsibilities to its *UI delegate*. The package javax.swing.plaf ("pluggable look-and-feel") contains an abstract delegate class for each Swing component. For instance the abstract class *ButtonUI* provides the "look-and-feel" interface for a button.

Allocating the view and controller responsibilities to a UI delegate makes it possible to change the look-and-feel of the component, and even define a custom look-and-feel. The package `javax.swing.plaf.basic` contains a set of classes that can be used as the basis for building custom look-and-feel components. The class *BasicButtonUI* in the package `javax.swing.plaf.basic`, for instance, extends *ButtonUI* and provides a basic button drawing facility. Other subpackages of `javax.swing.plaf` provide sets of classes defining specific look-and-feel implementations. For example, the package `javax.swing.plaf.metal` contains a custom look-and-feel designed to give a Java application the same appearance across all platforms. For a button, the `javax.swing.plaf.metal` class *MetalButtonUI* extends *BasicButtonUI* and draws a button with the standard Java "metal" look.

A Swing component such as a *JButton* has several constituents. In the case of a *JButton*, the standard look-and-feel implementations separate view and controller functions into different classes. Thus a standard *JButton* implementation consists of:

- a model, that implements the interface *ButtonModel* and is usually a *DefaultButtonModel*;

- a look-and-feel specific view element that knows how to draw the button; for instance, a *MetalBasicButtonUI*;

- an element that responds to user input, and functions as a controller. This is generally an instance of the `javax.swing.plaf.basic` class *BasicButtonListener*.

(A button also has an object responsible for drawing its border: an instance of the `javax.swing.plaf.metal` class *MetalButtonBorder*, for example.)

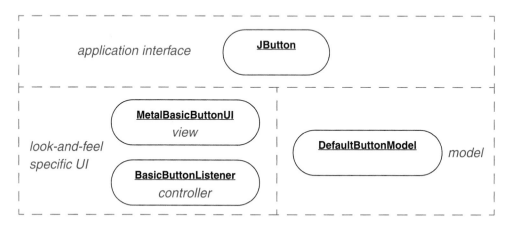

Figure 18.14 **Fundamental elements of a *JButton*.**

DrJava: pluggable look-and-feel

Open the file StudentSurvey.java, located in lookAndFeel, in ch18, in nhText. This file contains the interface for the "Student survey" example of the previous chapter.

1. Run the application.

    > java ch18.lookAndFeel.StudentSurvey

    The application does nothing, but displays a dialog when the 'Finished!" button is pressed.

2. Remove comments from the four lines at the start of the main method. Save, compile, and run the application again. (Be sure to press the "Finished!" button.) This should give a different "look" to the interface.

3. Replace the argument to the method UIManager.setLookAndFeel with each of the following in turn. In each case, save, compile, and run the application. (Your system may not support all of these "looks.")

    *   "javax.swing.plaf.metal.MetalLookAndFeel"
    *   "com.sun.java.swing.plaf.gtk.GTKLookAndFeel"
    *   "com.sun.java.swing.plaf.windows.WindowsLookAndFeel"
    *   UIManager.getCrossPlatformLookAndFeelClassName()
    *   UIManager.getSystemLookAndFeelClassName()

18.5   Summary

In this chapter, we saw the basic format of the *Model-View-Controller* pattern, commonly used to structure event-driven graphical user interfaces. With MVC, interface responsibilities are partitioned into two segments: the *view* has display responsibilities, while the *controller* modifies the model in accordance with user input.

As an example, we developed three views of a right triangle. In the process, we noted the facilities provided by the standard Java library for implementing the *observes* relationship. The fundamental relationship between the view and the model is *observes*, and can be easily implemented by making the model object an extension of the class *Observed*, and having the view implement the interface *Observer*. We also added a graphical user interface to the nim game, using the MVC pattern.

Finally, we discovered that the Swing components are themselves structured along the lines of MVC. Each Swing component has an associated model object that is responsible for maintaining the component's state. It also has a UI delegate, to which view and control responsibilities are delegated. One advantage of this structure is that it is possible to change the look-and-feel of an application in a system-independent way.

SELF-STUDY EXERCISES

18.1   Indicate whether each of the following statements is true or false:

    a.   One goal of the MVC pattern is to keep the model as independent as possible of the user interface.

    b.   In MVC, the controller is independent of the view.

    c.   Every view must have a controller.

    d.   The goal of the observer relation is to keep the observable independent of the observer.

18.2   Look at the class *Counter*, defined in Listing 2.2 on page 80. What modifications must be made to this class to make it an *Observable*?

18.3   What must the class *CounterView* do in order to observe a *Counter*?

18.4   Write the *CounterView* method `update`. The *CounterView* should write the *Counter's* current count to standard output whenever the count changes.

18.5   What would happen if a *CounterView* registered as an observer of a *RightTriangle*?

18.6   Suppose the *Counter* invokes `notifyObservers` with an *Integer* argument containing the current count:

```
notifyObservers(new Integer(tally));
```

Rewrite the *CounterView* `update` method so that it does not query the *Counter*.

18.7   Suggest a modification of *TextView* that would not require the model being passed as an argument to the *TVController* constructor.

18.8   The *TVController*'s `update` method throws a *NumberFormatException* if the user enters a negative value for base or height (❸ on page 736). Why is the method incorrect if this line is removed?

18.9   What would happen if *GraphicView*'s `update` method did not invoke its top level ancestor's `pack` method?

EXERCISES

18.1   Exercises 17.7 through 17.11 developed a graphical user interface for a simple accumulator. Modify the interface to conform to the MVC structure.

18.2   Using MVC, create a graphical user interface that will work with either a "modulus counter" (Exercises 2.2 and 2.13) or a "step" counter (Listing 2.2, page 80).

18.3   Create a graphical user interface for the "balls and strikes" counter of Exercises 2.1 and 4.8.

18.4   Create a graphical user interface for the "dollars and cents" counter of Exercise 4.9.

18.5   Create a graphical user interlace for the digit-by-digit lock of Chapter 4 (Listing 4.4).

18.6   Create a graphical view for the class *Circle*. The view should allow the user to enter the radius of the circle in a text field, and should display an image of the circle in a *JPanel*.

18.7   Using MVC, create a graphical user interface for the *TrafficSignal* class of Chapter 2 (Listing 2.4). How will a version in which the *TrafficSignal* invokes `notifyObservers` with no arguments differ from a version in which the *TrafficSignal* passes its current light (as an *Integer*) as a `notifyObservers` argument?

18.8   Create a graphical user interface for the *Elevator* of Exercise 11.8.

18.9   Look at the maze crawl game of Exercise 8.9. Assume that the rooms are uniform in size, and are laid out in a cartesian grid. For instance, a maze of five rooms might look like this:

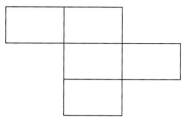

Create a class *RoomView* to display a room. A *RoomView* will display a different color if it is occupied.

Create a class *MazeView* to display a maze. A *MazeView* will be composed of several *RoomViews*. (The maze structure can be "hard coded.")

Develop a user interface that allows the user to move the *Explorer* through the maze. The "occupied room" should be displayed in a different color from an unoccupied room. Attempting to move in an illegal direction should raise an informational dialog.

Feel free to modify the model classes to support the user interface.

SELF-STUDY EXERCISE SOLUTIONS

18.1   *a.*   True.
       b.   False.
       c.   False.
       d.   True.

18.2   ```
public class Counter extends Observable {
   ...
   public void incrementCount () {
      tally = tally + 1;
      setChanged();
      notifyObservers();
   }
```
```

```
...
    public void reset () {
        tally = 0;
        setChanged();
        notifyObservers();
    }
    ...
}
```

18.3   It must implement the interface *java.util.Observer*, register with the *Counter* by invoking the *Counter*'s addObserver method, and implement the method update.

18.4
```
public void update (Observable target, Object arg) {
    int count = ((Counter)target).currentCount();
    System.out.println(count);
}
```

18.5   When the *RightTriangle* changed state, the *CounterView*'s update method would be invoked with a reference to the *RightTriangle* as first argument. The cast to *Counter* would then fail.

18.6
```
public void update (Observable target, Object arg) {
    System.out.println((Integer)arg);
}
```

18.7   One possibility is to make model an instance variable of *TextView*. Then *TVController*, as an inner class, could access it. *TextView* could also register controller as a listener for the text fields. (But *TVController*'s actionPerformed method still needs access to the model.)

18.8   *RightTriangle*'s setBase and setHeight methods both require their argument to be non-negative.

18.9   The top-level window would remain its original size, regardless of the size of the drawn triangle.

CHAPTER 19　　　　Recursion

In this chapter, we examine an algorithmic technique know as *recursion*. As in Chapter 14, we are primarily concerned here with algorithm design.

Recursion is a technique related to iteration. It is a powerful tool that can be effectively used by following a few simple guidelines. Every programming language must provide facilities for at least one of these two techniques. Most languages, of course, offer both. A recursive algorithm solves a problem by repeatedly reducing the problem to simpler and simpler cases. This "unwinding" process continues until a trivial case is reached. The trivial case is solved directly, and the process "rewinds" building the solution for each more complex case from the just-obtained solution of the simpler case.

Writing a recursive algorithm is much more straight-forward than tracing the solution process. A recursive algorithm need only provide a direct solution for a trivial case of the problem, and describe how the general case is reduced to a slightly simpler one.

In this chapter, we'll look at several examples of recursive algorithms, including a very efficient sorting algorithm known as *quicksort*. We also look at indirect recursion, a process in which several mutually recursive methods work together to solve a problem, and backtracking, a technique for situations in which a large number of alternatives must be examined to find a problem solution. We conclude with an example of object recursion, a process in which the problem solution is developed using class structure to control the recursion.

Objectives

After studying this chapter you should understand the following:

- recursion, and the relationship between recursive and iterative algorithms;
- the design of the quick sort algorithm;
- indirect recursion;
- backtracking and the class of problems it solves;
- object recursion and its class structure.

Also, you should be able to:

- write simple recursive algorithms;
- use backtracking in the solution to problems;
- structure class definitions to use object recursion.

19.1   Recursion and iteration

19.1.1 Iteration

Recursion is an algorithmic technique closely related to iteration. When we develop an iterative solution to a problem, we describe a single step toward the solution. We then repeat the step until the problem is solved. If we consider selection sort or bubble sort of Chapter 14, a single step is "put one element of the list in its proper position." This action is repeated until all the elements are in position:

```
while ( elements left to position )
     put one element of the list in its proper position
```

The sorts differ in which element they choose to position and how the element is determined. Selection sort can be described as

```
first = 0;
last = list.size()-1;
while (first < last) {
     find the smallest of elements first through last,
     and put it in position with index first
     first = first+1;
}
```

while bubble sort can be expressed as:

```
last = list.size()-1;
while (last > 0) {
     bubble the largest of elements 0 through last into
     position with index last
     last = last-1;
}
```

Both are clearly iterative. The algorithm specifies a step in the solution process that is to be repeated or iterated. After each iteration, we are measurably closer to the desired solution, and we are certain that we will reach the solution after a finite number of iterations.

19.1.2 Recursion

With recursion, the idea is to solve a trivial, basic case of the problem, and then design a solution to the general case by showing how to "reduce" the general case to one that is a step closer to the basic case. The solution is built on a strategy for reducing the general case of the problem so that repeated reduction ultimately ends with the basic case.

Reducing the general case to a slightly easier case roughly corresponds to a single step in the iterative approach. Reaching the base case stops the recursion in much the same way that exit condition stops the iteration. In an iterative solution, we step toward the solution until the while condition becomes false. In a recursive solution, we continually reduce or "unwind" the problem until we reach a trivial case that can be easily solved. With an iterative solution, we explicitly drive the repetition with a loop. In the recursive solution however, we need only write a solution for the base case and the reduction step. The form of a recursive solution is

```
if ( trivial case )
    solve directly
else
    solve in terms of a slightly easier case
```

If we consider the problem of sorting a list, the case in which the size of the list is one or zero is the trivial case. The case in which the list has $n > 1$ elements is the general case. The "slightly easier" problem we reduce the general case to is to sort a list with one fewer element:

```
if ( list is empty or has one element )
    solution is easy: do nothing
else
    sort the list, assuming a way of sorting a list
    with one fewer element is available
```

A recursive algorithm is implemented so that it handles the trivial case of the problem directly. Given an instance of the general case, the algorithm *invokes itself* to solve a slightly reduced case. The solution of the general case is constructed from the solution of the slightly reduced case. Executing the algorithm results in a chain of self-calls, each with a slightly easier problem to solve than the previous. Ultimately the method is invoked with the trivial case, for which there is a direct solution. To ensure correctness, we must guarantee that the general case will eventually reduce to the basic case.

19.1.3 Some simple examples

Exponentiation

We begin with a few simple problems in order to understand the basic solution process and underlying mechanism. Suppose we want to write a method that raises an integer to a power. We require the power to be a non-negative integer.

Essential design of a recursive algorithm:

- Find one or more base cases for which there is a direct solution.
- Give a solution to the general case in terms of a slightly simpler case, that is, in terms of a case slightly closer to a base case.

Figure 19.1 **Structure of a recursive algorithm.**

```
public static int power (int number, int exponent)
```
The specified number raised to the specified power.

require:
```
exponent >= 0
```

We can write a straightforward iterative solution:

```
public static int power (int number, int exponent) {
    int result = 1;
    int count = 0;
    while (count != exponent) {
        result = number * result;
        count = count + 1;
    }
    return result;
}
```

As the iteration proceeds, result takes on the values $number^0$, $number^1$, $number^2$, *etc.* The invariant is result equals number raised to the count power. The fact that exponent is required to be non-negative ensures that the iteration will terminate.

Now let's consider a recursive solution. First we need to separate the problem instances into base and general cases. What is the base case? If exponent is 0, we have no work to do at all. We know the answer is 1. So we can consider an exponent of 0 to be a base case, and an exponent of $n > 0$ to be the general case.

- *Base cases*: raise an integer to the power 0.

- *General case*: raise an integer to the power n, where n is an integer and $n > 0$.

Next we need to reduce the general problem to one that is slightly closer to the base case. That is, we describe a solution to the general problem in terms of a slightly simpler problem. What is slightly simpler than raising a number to the power n? Clearly raising a number to the power $n - 1$. So we need to describe how to compute number to the power n, *assuming we have already computed* number *to the power n - 1*. That is, we reduce the problem of computing $number^n$ to the problem of computing $number^{n-1}$.

If we have $number^{n-1}$, we simply multiply this value by number to get $number^n$. Thus the algorithm looks like this:

```
public static int power (int number, int exponent) {
    int result;
    if (exponent == 0)
        result = 1;
    else
        result =
            number * number to the power exponent-1;
    return result;
}
```

All that is necessary is to compute `number` to the power `exponent-1`. But we have a method to do this—the one we're writing. So we invoke the method itself:

```
/**
 * The specified number raised to the specified power.
 * @require    exponent >= 0
 */
public static int power (int number, int exponent) {
    int result;
    if (exponent == 0)
        result = 1;
    else
        result = number * power(number,exponent-1);
    return result;
}
```

At first glace, it may seem that we're cheating. But notice that the method works by the exact strategy described above. In the trivial case, the method simply returns 1. In the general case, the method invokes itself with a slightly simpler case. The solution to the general case is built by reducing the problem to one that is a step closer to the trivial case.

We are sure that the precondition holds in the recursive invocation: the value of `exponent` must be positive to reach the recursive call. (Why?)

Verification of correctness can be done with a straightforward induction. The base case of the induction is obviously the base case of the algorithm. The general case of the induction handles the general case of the algorithm.

We'll trace an example to illustrate the underlying mechanism. But you should understand that you do not consciously step through a trace when you write a recursive solution.

Suppose the method is invoked with arguments 2 and 3. Method variables are allocated for the parameters, and initialized with the argument values. (The arrow shows the next step to be performed.)

Since `exponent` is not 0, the else option is done:

Now the method `power` is invoked again, with the same first argument but with the second argument reduced by 1. The mechanism is exactly the same as in the original method invocation: method variables are created, and the parameters are initialized with the argument values.

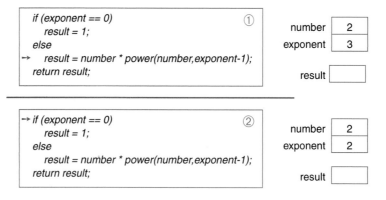

All that has happened here is ordinary method invocation. The fact that the method being invoked happens to be the one that is executing is irrelevant. We now have two sets of method variables, one for each invocation of the method `power`. This is no different than if we had invoked two different methods. The first invocation has not yet completed, so its method variables have not yet been deallocated. But the second invocation of the method is completely independent of these variables: they are method variables for the first invocation.

Again `exponent` is not 0, and the else branch is taken.

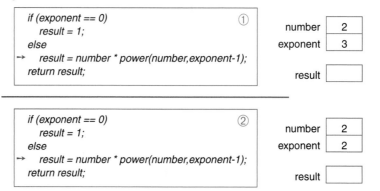

The method `power` is invoked again, this time with 1 as the second argument

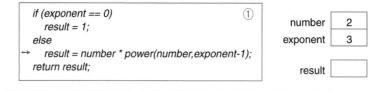

```
if (exponent == 0)                              ②
    result = 1;
else
→   result = number * power(number,exponent-1);
return result;
```

number	2
exponent	2
result	

```
→ if (exponent == 0)                            ③
    result = 1;
else
    result = number * power(number,exponent-1);
return result;
```

number	2
exponent	1
result	

Again the else part of the conditional is done.

```
if (exponent == 0)                              ①
    result = 1;
else
→   result = number * power(number,exponent-1);
return result;
```

number	2
exponent	3
result	

```
if (exponent == 0)                              ②
    result = 1;
else
→   result = number * power(number,exponent-1);
return result;
```

number	2
exponent	2
result	

```
if (exponent == 0)                              ③
    result = 1;
else
→   result = number * power(number,exponent-1);
return result;
```

number	2
exponent	1
result	

and `power` is invoked one final time, now with 0 as second argument.

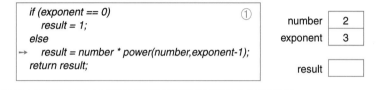

```
if (exponent == 0)                              ①
    result = 1;
else
→   result = number * power(number,exponent-1);
return result;
```

number	2
exponent	3
result	

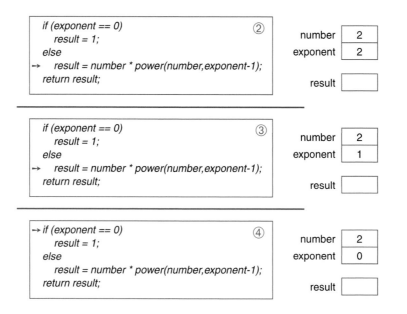

```
if (exponent == 0)                                    ②
    result = 1;
else
→   result = number * power(number,exponent-1);
    return result;
```

number [2]
exponent [2]

result [   ]

```
if (exponent == 0)                                    ③
    result = 1;
else
→   result = number * power(number,exponent-1);
    return result;
```

number [2]
exponent [1]

result [   ]

```
→ if (exponent == 0)                                  ④
      result = 1;
  else
      result = number * power(number,exponent-1);
      return result;
```

number [2]
exponent [0]

result [   ]

We have now reduced the problem to the base case, which assigns a value to
`result`:

```
if (exponent == 0)                                    ①
    result = 1;
else
→   result = number * power(number,exponent-1);
    return result;
```

number [2]
exponent [3]

result [   ]

```
if (exponent == 0)                                    ②
    result = 1;
else
→   result = number * power(number,exponent-1);
    return result;
```

number [2]
exponent [2]

result [   ]

```
if (exponent == 0)                                    ③
    result = 1;
else
→   result = number * power(number,exponent-1);
    return result;
```

number [2]
exponent [1]

result [   ]

```
if (exponent == 0)                                    ④
→   result = 1;
else
    result = number * power(number,exponent-1);
    return result;
```

number [2]
exponent [0]

result [   ]

The last invocation of the method can now return the value stored in `result`.

```
if (exponent == 0)                              ①        number    2
    result = 1;
else                                                     exponent  3
→   result = number * power(number,exponent-1);
    return result;                                       result
```

```
if (exponent == 0)                              ②        number    2
    result = 1;
else                                                     exponent  2
→   result = number * power(number,exponent-1);
    return result;                                       result
```

```
if (exponent == 0)                              ③        number    2
    result = 1;
else                                                     exponent  1
→   result = number * power(number,exponent-1);
    return result;                                       result
```

```
if (exponent == 0)                              ④        number    2
    result = 1;
else                                                     exponent  0
    result = number * power(number,exponent-1);
→   return result;                                       result    1
```

When the method returns, all method variables allocated for that particular invocation of the method are freed. The assignment statement in the previous invocation can be competed, by multiplying `number` times the value returned and storing the result in `result`.

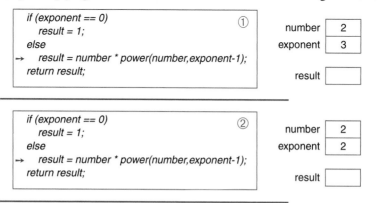

```
if (exponent == 0)                              ①        number    2
    result = 1;
else                                                     exponent  3
→   result = number * power(number,exponent-1);
    return result;                                       result
```

```
if (exponent == 0)                              ②        number    2
    result = 1;
else                                                     exponent  2
→   result = number * power(number,exponent-1);
    return result;                                       result
```

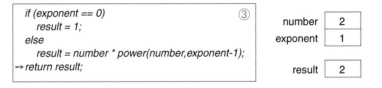

This method invocation can now complete, returning the result to its caller.

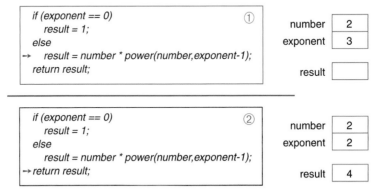

One more return leaves only the initial invocation active.

And the final result is returned to the original client.

We've presented this trace of the algorithm to make the mechanism clear and explicit. But note that there is nothing but ordinary method invocation happening here. There is no special "recursive mechanism." Also, as we've said, when you write recursive methods, you do not think in terms of traces. You simply solve the base case and write code that reduces the general case to a case closer to the base case.

A few other observations are in order before we leave this example. We have identified the case in which `exponent` is 0 as the trivial base case. The computation is also trivial if `exponent` is 1, and isn't so hard if `exponent` is 2. We can include as many base cases as we want. For instance, we could write

```java
public static int power (int number, int exponent) {
    int result;
    if (exponent == 0)
        result = 1;
    else if (exponent == 1)
        result = number;
```

```
    else
        result = number * power(number,exponent-1);
    return result;
}
```

There is really nothing wrong with this, but the extra cases are unnecessary and complicate the code. The case where `exponent` is 1 reduces perfectly well to the case where `exponent` is 0. It is preferable to keep the code as clean and simple as possible, and avoid extraneous cases.

Second, suppose we decide to reduce the general case of computing a number to the power *n* to the easier case of computing a number to the power *n* −2:

```
/**
 * The specified number raised to the specified power.
 * @require    exponent >= 0
 */
public static int power (int number, int exponent) {
    int result;
    if (exponent == 0)
        result = 1;
    else
        result = number*number*power(number,exponent-2);
    return result;
}
```

The problem is that this strategy reduces the case in which `exponent` is 1 to the case in which `exponent` is −1. But the precondition on `power` requires that its second argument be non-negative. When the recursive call is reached, we can only be sure that `exponent` > 0. (The precondition guarantees that `exponent` >= 0, and the true branch of the if statement takes care of 0.) We cannot guarantee that `exponent-2` >= 0, as required to make the recursive call legal. If `exponent` is 1, the recursive call is not valid since the precondition does not hold. In fact, if we invoke the method with an odd value for `exponent`, the base case will never be reached. Such an error is sometimes called an "infinite recursion."

DrJava: watching recursion

Open the file `Example.java`, located in directory `exponent`, in `ch19`, in `nhText`. This utility class contains the method `power` described above.

1. Turn on debugging mode, and set breakpoints at the if statement and the return statement.

2. In the *Watches* pane, enter `exponent` and `result` as the names of variables to watch.

3. In the *Interactions* pane, invoke the method `power` with 3 and 3 as arguments.

```
> import ch19.exponent.*;
> Example.power(3,3)
```

4. Note that when the first breakpoint is reached, `exponent` has a value of 3.

5. Press *Resume*. This time, the first breakpoint is reached and `exponent` has a value of 2. You should realize that there are two different automatic variables named `exponent`. One contains 3 and one contains 2. The debugger shows only the variables accessible from the "active" invocation.

6. Press *Resume* two more times. This results in two more invocations of the method `power`. There are now four active invocations of the method `power`, each with its own set of automatic variables. If you look at the pane tabbed *Stack*, you will see the method `ch19.exponent.Example.power` listed four times. This means that there are four active invocations of the method.

7. Press *Resume* again. Now we reach the second breakpoint without invoking the method again. (We are handling the trivial case. Note that `result` is now 1.)

8. Press *Resume* again. We are at the second breakpoint in the invocation in which `exponent` is 1. Note that the method `power` now appears only three times in the *Stack* pane. The fourth invocation has terminated.

9. Press *Resume* twice more. We have completed all but the original invocation of `power`.

10. Pressing *Resume* once more completes the invocation and returns the result to the *Interactions* pane.

Finding the minimum element

In Section 12.5.3, we wrote an iterative method to find the minimum value on a list. Specifically, we wrote a method to find the minimum grade for a list of *Students*:

> **public int** minFinalExam (List<Student> students)
> The lowest final exam grades of the specified *Students*.
>
> **require:**
> students.size() > 0

Let's rewrite this method recursively. Again, we must separate the problem into base and general cases. An obvious base case is the case in which there is only one *Student* on the list. (We can't have an empty list as argument.)

- *Base case*: find the smallest element on a list that contains only a single element.

    The general case, then, is a list with more than one element.

- *General case*: find the smallest element on a list containing n elements, where $n > 1$.

    We express the problem in terms of the number of elements on the list because that is the basis by which we separate the problem into base and general cases.

    Next we need to reduce the general problem to one slightly closer to the base case. What is slightly simpler than finding the smallest of n elements? Finding the smallest of fewer elements: specifically, of $n-1$ elements. So we need to describe how to find the smallest of n elements, assuming we know how to find the smallest of $n-1$ elements. We can do this as follows:

1. Find the smallest of the $n-1$ elements following the first.
2. Find the smaller of this and the first.

Thinking about the problem a bit, it is clear that we are dealing with a single list. The "$n-1$ elements following the first" is simply a segment of this list. Rather than thinking in terms of "the smallest element on a list," it will be helpful to think of the problem as "the smallest on a segment of a list." We can use an argument to specify the portion of the list we are concerned with, just as we did when writing binary search in Chapter 14. We specify the method as follows:

```
private int minFinalExam (List<Student> students,
    int first)
```
>   The lowest final exam grades of *Students* on the list with indexes greater than or equal to `first`.
>
>   **require:**
>   ```
>   0 <= first && first < students.size()
>   ```

This recursive method is an auxiliary method, hence the private designation. The method we actually want is public and invokes the private recursive method with 0 as a first argument:

```
public int minFinalExam (List<Student> students) {
    return minFinalExam(students,0);
}
```

The private and public methods will be in the same class. Recall that it is legal to have two methods with the same name (overloading) as long as the methods differ in number and/or type of parameters. It is not uncommon to build auxiliary methods with additional parameters when using recursion.

Now let's write the method. As before, an if-then-else will distinguish cases.

```
private int minFinalExam (List<Student> students,
    int first) {
    int smallest;
    int gradeOfFirst = students.get(first).finalExam();
    if (first == students.size()-1)
        // the base case: only one item to consider
        smallest = gradeOfFirst;
    else {
        // the general case:
        int minOfRest = minFinalExam(students,first+1);
        if (minOfRest < gradeOfFirst)
            smallest = minOfRest;
        else
            smallest = gradeOfFirst;
    }
    return smallest;
}
```

Each time we invoke the method recursively, the second argument is increased by one. Calling the method with a second argument of zero results in the method being called with an argument of one, which results in the method being called with an argument of two, and so forth. Ultimately, we reach the base case where the second argument indexes the last element of the list, and we have only one element to consider. The recursion then "rewinds" with each invocation in turn getting the value of the following invocation, and using it to compute its return value.

Assume a client invokes the public method `minFinalExam` with a list of three *Students*, having final grades 63, 78, 67. The public method invokes the auxiliary recursive method with a second argument of 0. We trace key steps in the recursion below.

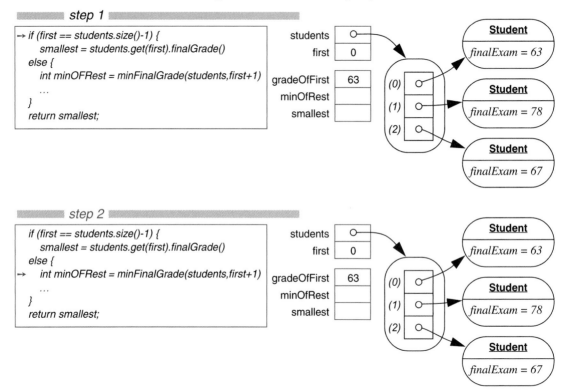

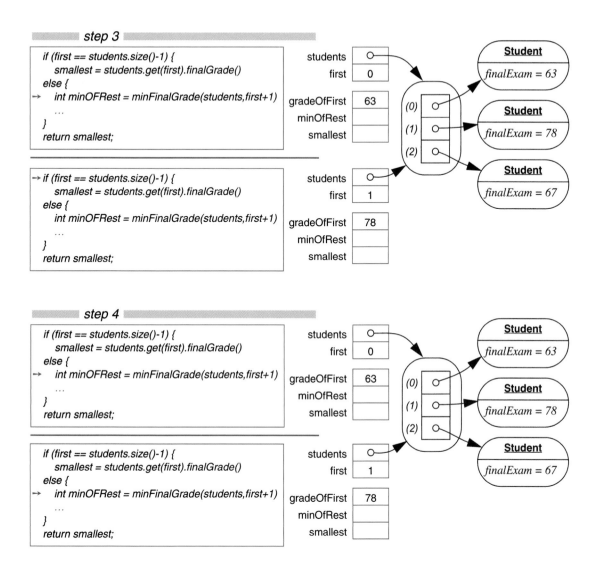

step 3

```
if (first == students.size()-1) {
    smallest = students.get(first).finalGrade()
else {
→   int minOFRest = minFinalGrade(students,first+1)
    ...
}
return smallest;
```

```
→ if (first == students.size()-1) {
    smallest = students.get(first).finalGrade()
else {
    int minOFRest = minFinalGrade(students,first+1)
    ...
}
return smallest;
```

step 4

```
if (first == students.size()-1) {
    smallest = students.get(first).finalGrade()
else {
→   int minOFRest = minFinalGrade(students,first+1)
    ...
}
return smallest;
```

```
if (first == students.size()-1) {
    smallest = students.get(first).finalGrade()
else {
→   int minOFRest = minFinalGrade(students,first+1)
    ...
}
return smallest;
```

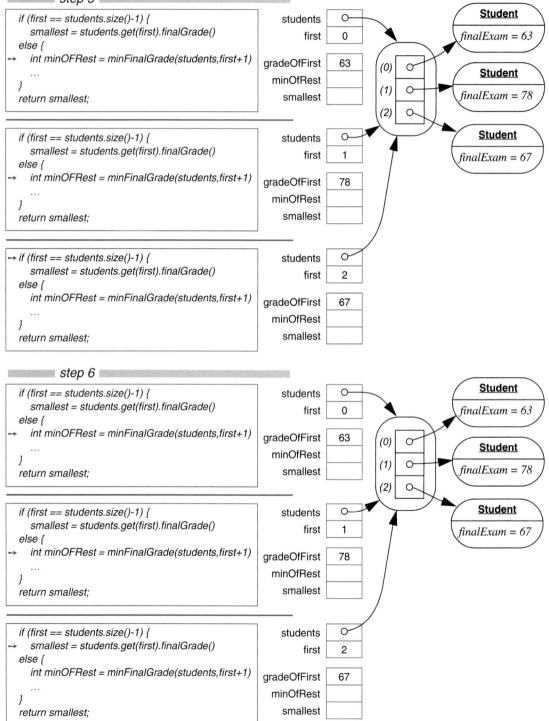

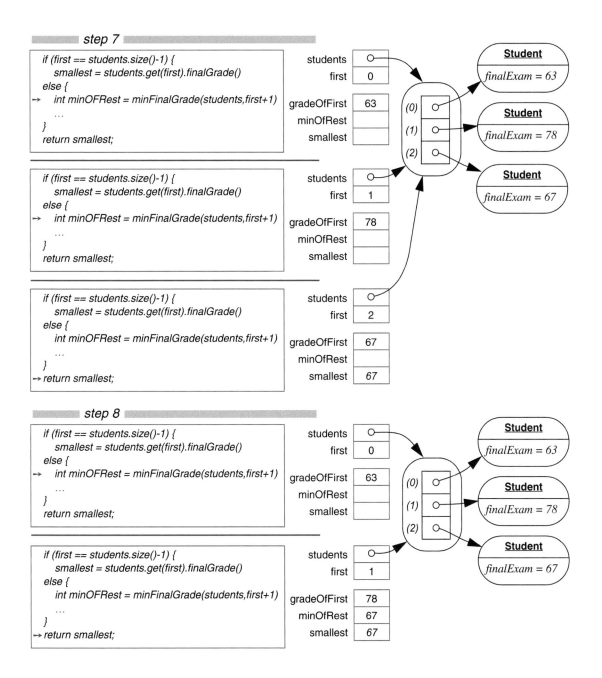

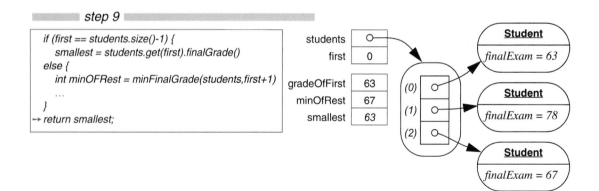

step 9

```
if (first == students.size()-1) {
    smallest = students.get(first).finalGrade()
else {
    int minOFRest = minFinalGrade(students,first+1)
        ...
}
→ return smallest;
```

students
first   0

gradeOfFirst   63
minOfRest   67
smallest   63

(0)
(1)
(2)

Student
finalExam = 63

Student
finalExam = 78

Student
finalExam = 67

Selection sort

As a final example, let's consider a recursive version of selection sort. Again, we first separate the problem into trivial and nontrivial instances. What are the trivial cases? If the list to be sorted is empty or contains only a single element, sorting is certainly easy. We need, in fact, do nothing at all. This gives us base cases.

- *Base cases*: sort a list that is empty or contains only a single element.

The general case is to sort a nontrivial list. That is, sort a list not covered by the base case:

- *General case*: sort a list containing n elements, where $n > 1$.

Note that we have included both the empty list and the one element list as base cases. We could have chosen just the empty list as the base case. But since no action is required with either the empty list or the one element list, we include both.

Next we need to reduce the general case. What is slightly simpler than sorting a list of n elements? Sorting a list with fewer elements: specifically, sorting a list of $n-1$ elements. So we need to describe how to sort a list of n elements, assuming we know how to sort a list of $n-1$ elements.

Basically, there are two steps: (1) get one element in position, and (2) sort the remaining elements. Different sorts result depending on the order in which we do these steps, the element we choose to position, and the manner in which we position it. If we're thinking in terms of selection sort, the first step is to find the smallest element and put it first. Thus the solution to the general case for selection sort can be described as follows.

1. Find the smallest element and put it first.
2. Sort the remaining $n-1$ elements.

Again, we're dealing with a single list, and the step "sort the remaining $n-1$ elements" refers to a segment of the list. As in the previous example, it will be useful to make the recursive method an auxiliary method that solves the problem of sorting a segment of a list. We write a static generic version, with the order as a parameter (see page 587).

```
    private static <Element> void selectionSort (
        List<Element> list, int first, Order<Element> order)
```
Sort *List<Element>* from index `first` through the end of the list
according to the specified *Order*.

First, we must distinguish cases. A simple if statement will serve, since we need do
nothing at all in the base case:

```
    private static <Element> void selectionSort (
        List<Element> list, int first, Order<Element> order) {
        if (first < list.size()) {
            find the smallest element and put it first;
            sort the remaining n-1 elements
        }
    }
```

We know how to find the smallest element and put it first. This was a well-defined
step of selection sort (see page 587):

```
    private static <Element> void selectionSort (
        List<Element> list, int first, Order<Element> order) {
        if (first < list.size()) {
            int small =
                smallestOf(list,first,list.size()-1,order);
            interchange(list,first,small);
            sort the remaining n-1 elements
        }
    }
```

All that is left is to sort the remaining *n* –1 elements: that is, sort the elements
`list.get(first+1)` through `list.get(list.size()-1)`. To do this, we
recursively invoke the method itself:

```
    private static <Element> void selectionSort (
        List<Element> list, int first, Order<Element> order) {
        if (first < list.size()) {
            int small =
                smallestOf(list,first,list.size()-1,order);
            interchange(list,first,small);
            selectionSort(list,first+1,order);
        }
    }
```

The public method that we want to define calls the recursive auxiliary method with a
second parameter of 0:

```
    public static <Element> void selectionSort (
        List<Element> list, Order<Element> order) {
        selectionSort(list,0,order);
    }
```

19.2   Example: the tower puzzle

The recursive methods we've seen so far illustrate a simple form of recursion: there is a single recursive call and the recursive and iterative versions of the algorithm are essentially identical. But there are many problems for which the recursive solution is conceptually simpler, as we shall see next.

Let's look at a well-known example, called the "tower puzzle." The puzzle consists of a set of disks of different sizes and three pegs. The disks are stacked on one of the pegs in order of size, with the largest disk on the bottom, as illustrated in Figure 19.2.

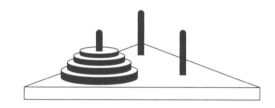

Figure 19.2 **A four-disk tower puzzle.**

The point is to move the stack of disks from the starting peg to one of the other pegs. The disks are moved one at a time, and a disk can never be placed on top of a smaller one.

For instance, the following sequence of moves will move a stack of three disks. We label the pegs 1, 2, and 3 for easy reference.

Assume the disks start on peg 1, and we want to move them to peg 2.

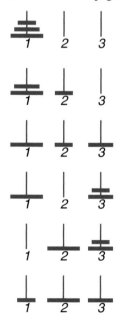

1.   Move a disk from peg 1 to peg 2.

2.   Move a disk from peg 1 to peg 3.

3.   Move a disk from peg 2 to peg 3.

4.   Move a disk from peg 1 to peg 2.

5.   Move a disk from peg 3 to peg 1.

6.   Move a disk from peg 3 to peg 2.

7.   Move a disk from peg 1 to peg 2.

So far in this chapter, we've been looking at methods without paying much attention to where the methods live. We want to write a method that solves the tower puzzle, something like this:

public void moveTower **(int** n, **int** from, **int** to)
> Move a tower of the specified number of disks from the specified starting peg to the specified destination peg.
>
> **require:**
> ```
> n >= 1 &&
> 1 <= from && from <= 3 &&
> 1 <= to && to <= 3 &&
> from != to
> ```

We put this method in a class *PuzzleSolver*. A *PuzzleSolver* is an object that knows how to solve the tower problem.

But what exactly do we expect the *PuzzleSolver* to do? We expect it to provide a sequence of moves similar to those given above that indicate how to move a tower of a specified size. A *PuzzleSolver* is rather clearly a model object. It's not part of the user interface, and shouldn't be doing any output. In fact, at this point we have no idea of what form the output will take. Let's specify a method for making one move that will somehow interact with the user interface. We'll deal with its definition later:

private void moveDisk **(int** from, **int** to)
> Move a single disk from the specified peg to the specified destination.
>
> **require:**
> ```
> 1 <= from && from <= 3 &&
> 1 <= to && to <= 3 &&
> from != to
> ```

Now we can develop a recursive solution to the puzzle. First, we must separate the problem into base case and general case. The situation in which we have only one disk to move is clearly trivial, and will serve as the base case. Since there is only one disk to move, we invoke the method moveDisk:

```
public void moveTower (int n, int from, int to) {
    if (n == 1)
        moveDisk(from,to);
    else {
        handle the general case
    }
}
```

The general case requires us to move a stack of n disks, where $n > 1$. Moving a stack of one fewer disks is a bit simpler—a step closer to the base case. Thus we need to describe how to move a stack of n disks, assuming we know how to move a stack of $n - 1$ disks.

Notice that if we have a stack of n disks, we can ignore the largest disk on the bottom of the tower when considering the $n - 1$ smaller disks. The largest disk won't get in the way when moving the others. Hence we can reduce the problem of moving n disks to the problem of moving $n - 1$ as follows.

1. Move $n - 1$ disks from the starting peg to the "other" peg.

2. Move a disk from the starting peg to the destination peg.

3. Move $n - 1$ disks from the "other" peg to the destination peg.

The "other" peg can easily be determined by subtracting source peg number (`from`) and target peg number (`to`) from 6 ($= 1 + 2 + 3$).

```java
public void moveTower (int n, int from, int to) {
    if (n == 1) {
        moveDisk(from, to);
    } else {
        int other = 6-from-to;   // not from or to
        moveTower(n-1, from, other);
        moveDisk(from, to);
        moveTower(n-1, other, to);
    }
}
```

In this algorithm, we invoke the method recursively twice. Each time we are closer to the base case. We know that the preconditions of the method are met: n is guaranteed to be positive, and the case where n is 1 is explicitly handled in the if statement. Thus we are sure that n will be greater than 1, and $n - 1$ will therefore be greater than 0, when the recursive calls are done.

Now let's return to the `moveDisk` method. We could simply have this method write a move to standard output:

```java
private void moveDisk (int from, int to) {
    System.out.println(
        "Move a disk from peg " + from +
        " to peg " + to + '.');
}
```

But this is not very satisfactory. The class *PuzzleSolver* is a model class and should be independent of the user interface. Model classes have no business writing to standard output. In fact, from the point of view of the model, the actual destination of bytes written to standard output is not specified.

Thus we postulate some user interface client that is responsible for actually displaying the moves to the user. The method `moveDisk` must communicate the move to the user interface. How does the method report the move to the user interface? The client (the user interface) needs to know when the server (the *PuzzleSolver*) has determined the next move. But we want to keep the server as independent of the client as possible. This is exactly the kind of situation for using the *Observer* pattern, seen in the previous chapter. Recall that with the observer pattern, a client (an *Observer*) defines a method named update. The client registers with a server (an *Observable*) by invoking the server's addObserver method. The server lets its client know that something has happened by invoking its notifyObservers method. This results in the update method of each *Observer* being invoked.

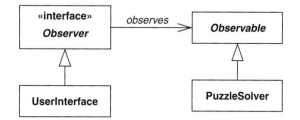

Figure 19.3 **User interface observes *PuzzleSolver*.**

Furthermore, the server can pass an argument to the client. If the sever invokes notifyObservers with an argument, this argument is passed to the client's update method. In the case at hand, the server should pass a move to the client. We take a straight-forward approach and model a move as a class instance. Since the top disk on a peg is the only one that can be moved, a move is completely characterized by the peg the disk is moved from and the peg the disk is moved to.

public class Move
>A move in the tower puzzle. Pegs are numbered 1, 2, 3.

public Move (**int** from, **int** to)
>Create a move of a disk from the peg from to the peg to.

public int from ()
>Peg the disk is moved from.

public int to ()
>Peg the disk is moved to.

We can now complete the moveDisk method. It need only notify any observers of the move to make.

```
private void moveDisk (int from, int to) {
    setChanged();
    notifyObservers(new Move(from, to));
}
```

Unlike the previous examples, this algorithm is considerably more complex and less intuitive if we attempt to write it iteratively.

19.3   Quick sort

For our next example, we return to the sort problem and present a classic algorithm called *quick sort*. Quick sort's advantage over those previously seen is efficiency. While selection sort and bubble sort take on the order of n^2 steps to sort a list of n elements, quick sort typically takes on the order of $n \cdot \log_2 n$ steps.

n	n^2	$n \cdot \log_2 n$
10	100	33
100	10,000	664
1,000	1,000,000	9,966
10,000	100,000,000	132,877
100,000	10,000,000,000	1,660,964
1,000,000	1,000,000,000,000	19,931,569

Like bubble sort and selection sort, quick sort starts by putting one element into position. But rather than positioning the largest or smallest element, quick sort puts an arbitrary element in proper position, with smaller elements below and larger elements above. The two sublists—the elements below the positioned element and the elements above it— are then (recursively) sorted. The algorithm is essentially the following:

1. Put an element in its proper sorted position, with smaller elements below and larger elements above. (The positioned element is referred to as the "pivot element," and can be any element on the list.)

2. Sort the sublist of smaller elements below the positioned element.

3. Sort the sublist of larger elements above the positioned element.

Since we reduce the problem of sorting a list to the problem of sorting a shorter list, the approach is clearly recursive.

As with recursive selection sort, we implement a private method to sort a list segment. The public `sort` simply calls this method with the entire list:

```
/**
 * Sort specified List<Element>, using quick sort.
 */
public static <Element> void quickSort (
    List<Element> list, Order<Element> order) {
    quickSort(list, 0, list.size()-1, order);
}

/**
 * Sort list elements indexed first through last.
 * @require    0 <= first && last < list.size()
 */
private static <Element> void quickSort (
    List<Element> list, int first, int last,
    Order<Element> order) { ...
}
```

The base case is the same as for recursive selection sort: an empty list or a list with a single element. The general case is handled by the three steps described above. The only complexity is in the first step, sometimes called the *pivot step*. We separate this step out into a private method called `partition`. This method positions an element (the *pivot element*) as described in step 1 above, and reports where the element was placed.

Like several other auxiliary methods we've seen, the method is neither a proper command nor a proper query. It changes the state of the list like a command, and returns a value like a query. Since this is an ancillary method and not a public feature, we are not too concerned.

```
private static <Element> int partition (
    List<Element> list, int first, int last,
    Order<Element> order)
```

Suppose `list` is the list shown below, `order` is numeric "less than," and the method `partition` is called with second and third arguments of 0 and 14.

```
partition(list,0,14,compare)
```

61	41	45	12	55	1	46	28	23	3	18	73	19	30	56
(0)	(1)	(2)	(3)	(4)	(5)	(6)	(7)	(8)	(9)	(10)	(11)	(12)	(13)	(14)

The method can position any of the 15 elements of the list. Suppose the element 28 is chosen to be positioned. (This is the pivot element.) The proper position for this element in the list is position 6. (There are 6 elements smaller than 28, 8 elements larger.) The method will put 28 in the sixth position, with the smaller 6 elements, in any order, in positions 0 through 5, and the larger 8 elements, again in any order, in positions 7 through 14. For instance, as a result of partitioning the list might be rearranged as follows.

12	1	23	3	18	19	**28**	56	45	61	55	73	41	30	46
(0)	(1)	(2)	(3)	(4)	(5)	(6)	(7)	(8)	(9)	(10)	(11)	(12)	(13)	(14)

The method returns the value 6, the index of the pivot element.

Using the method `partition`, we can easily implement quick sort:

```
private static <Element> void quickSort (
    List<Element> list, int first, int last,
    Order<Element> order) {
    if (first < last) {
        int position;   // the pivot index
        position = partition(list,first,last,order);
        quickSort(list,first,position-1,order);
        quickSort(list,position+1,last,order);
    }
}
```

We need only write the method `partition` and we are done. While there are many possible approaches, we must make sure that the method makes only one pass through the list to maintain the efficiency of quick sort. We adopt an approach that is straightforward, though perhaps not the most efficient.

We choose the middle element of the sublist as pivot element. For instance, if we are to partition all 15 elements in the following list, we choose the seventh element, 28, as pivot element.

61	41	45	12	55	1	46	**28**	23	3	18	73	19	30	56
(0)	*(1)*	*(2)*	*(3)*	*(4)*	*(5)*	*(6)*	*(7)*	*(8)*	*(9)*	*(10)*	*(11)*	*(12)*	*(13)*	*(14)*

First, we move the pivot element into the last position to "get it out of the way," interchanging it with the last element:

61	41	45	12	55	1	46	56	23	3	18	73	19	30	**28**
(0)	*(1)*	*(2)*	*(3)*	*(4)*	*(5)*	*(6)*	*(7)*	*(8)*	*(9)*	*(10)*	*(11)*	*(12)*	*(13)*	*(14)*

Then we examine each element of the list, shuffling smaller elements to the front. To do this, we keep two indexes into the list. The first index, `i`, simply steps through the list, identifying each element in turn to be examined. The second index, `pi`, separates elements found to be smaller than the pivot element from those found to be larger. For instance, as illustrated below, if `i` is 8, then the first eight elements (items 0 through 7) have already been examined and the next element to examine is item 8. If `pi` is 3, then elements indexed 0 through 2 are less than the pivot element, and elements indexed 3 through 7 are greater than or equal to the pivot element.

s	s	s	L	L	L	L	L	?	?	?	?	?	?	**28**
(0)	*(1)*	*(2)*	*(3)*	*(4)*	*(5)*	*(6)*	*(7)*	*(8)*	*(9)*	*(10)*	*(11)*	*(12)*	*(13)*	*(14)*

↑ pi ↑ i

In the partition operation, both indexes start at the element 0.

61	41	45	12	55	1	46	56	23	3	18	73	19	30	**28**
(0)	*(1)*	*(2)*	*(3)*	*(4)*	*(5)*	*(6)*	*(7)*	*(8)*	*(9)*	*(10)*	*(11)*	*(12)*	*(13)*	*(14)*

↑ pi ↑ i

Elements are examined until one is found that is smaller than the pivot element.

61	41	45	12	55	1	46	56	23	3	18	73	19	30	**28**
(0)	*(1)*	*(2)*	*(3)*	*(4)*	*(5)*	*(6)*	*(7)*	*(8)*	*(9)*	*(10)*	*(11)*	*(12)*	*(13)*	*(15)*

↑ pi ↑ i

The items at the two indexes are interchanged, the smaller one moving down and the larger one up

12	41	45	61	55	1	46	56	23	3	18	73	19	30	28

(0) (1) (2) (3) (4) (5) (6) (7) (8) (9) (10) (11) (12) (13) (14)

↑pi   ↑i

and the indexes are incremented.

12	41	45	61	55	1	46	56	23	3	18	73	19	30	28

(0) (1) (2) (3) (4) (5) (6) (7) (8) (9) (10) (11) (12) (13) (14)

    ↑pi   ↑i

Note that the elements below `pi` are less than the pivot element, and the elements from `pi` up to (but not including) `i` are greater than or equal to the pivot element.

The process is repeated, until all the elements have been examined.

Find next element smaller than pivot

12	41	45	61	55	1	46	56	23	3	18	73	19	30	28

(0) (1) (2) (3) (4) (5) (6) (7) (8) (9) (10) (11) (12) (13) (14)

    ↑pi   ↑i

Interchange elements

12	1	45	61	55	41	46	56	23	3	18	73	19	30	28

(0) (1) (2) (3) (4) (5) (6) (7) (8) (190)(10) (11) (12) (13) (14)

    ↑pi   ↑i

Increment indexes

12	1	45	61	55	41	46	56	23	3	18	73	19	30	28

(0) (1) (2) (3) (4) (5) (6) (7) (8) (9) (10) (11) (12) (13) (14)

       ↑pi   ↑i

Find next element smaller than pivot

12	1	45	61	55	41	46	56	23	3	18	73	19	30	28

(0) (1) (2) (3) (4) (5) (6) (7) (8) (9) (10) (11) (12) (13) (14)

       ↑pi   ↑i

Interchange elements

12	1	23	61	55	41	46	56	45	3	18	73	19	30	28

(0) (1) (2) (3) (4) (5) (6) (7) (8) (9) (10) (11) (12) (13) (14)

       ↑pi   ↑i

Increment indexes

12	1	23	61	55	41	46	56	45	3	18	73	19	30	**28**
(0)	(1)	(2)	(3)	(4)	(5)	(6)	(7)	(8)	(9)	(10)	(11)	(12)	(13)	(14)

↑pi (3)   ↑i (9)

Find next element smaller than pivot

12	1	23	61	55	41	46	56	45	3	18	73	19	30	**28**
(0)	(1)	(2)	(3)	(4)	(5)	(6)	(7)	(8)	(9)	(10)	(11)	(12)	(13)	(14)

↑pi (3)   ↑i (9)

Interchange elements

12	1	23	3	55	41	46	56	45	61	18	73	19	30	**28**
(0)	(1)	(2)	(3)	(4)	(5)	(6)	(7)	(8)	(9)	(10)	(11)	(12)	(13)	(14)

↑pi (3)   ↑i (9)

Increment indexes

12	1	23	3	55	41	46	56	45	61	18	73	19	30	**28**
(0)	(1)	(2)	(3)	(4)	(5)	(6)	(7)	(8)	(9)	(10)	(11)	(12)	(13)	(14)

↑pi (4)   ↑i (10)

Find next element smaller than pivot

12	1	23	3	55	41	46	56	45	61	18	73	19	30	**28**
(0)	(1)	(2)	(3)	(4)	(5)	(6)	(7)	(8)	(9)	(10)	(11)	(12)	(13)	(14)

↑pi (4)   ↑i (10)

Interchange elements

12	1	23	3	18	41	46	56	45	61	55	73	19	30	**28**
(0)	(1)	(2)	(3)	(4)	(5)	(6)	(7)	(8)	(9)	(10)	(11)	(12)	(13)	(14)

↑pi (4)   ↑i (10)

Increment indexes

12	1	23	3	18	41	46	56	45	61	55	73	19	30	**28**
(0)	(1)	(2)	(3)	(4)	(5)	(6)	(7)	(8)	(9)	(10)	(11)	(12)	(13)	(14)

↑pi (5)   ↑i (12)

Find next element smaller than pivot

12	1	23	3	18	41	46	56	45	61	55	73	19	30	**28**
(0)	(1)	(2)	(3)	(4)	(5)	(6)	(7)	(8)	(9)	(10)	(11)	(12)	(13)	(14)

↑pi (5)   ↑i (12)

12	1	23	3	18	19	46	56	45	61	55	73	41	30	**28**
(0)	(1)	(2)	(3)	(4)	(5)	(6)	(7)	(8)	(9)	(10)	(11)	(12)	(13)	(14)

Interchange elements

↑ pi (at index 5)   ↑ i (at index 13)

12	1	23	3	18	19	46	56	45	61	55	73	41	30	**28**
(0)	(1)	(2)	(3)	(4)	(5)	(6)	(7)	(8)	(9)	(10)	(11)	(12)	(13)	(14)

Increment indexes

↑ pi (at index 6)   ↑ i (at index 14)

Now there are no more elements less than the pivot element. The last step is to put the pivot element into position by swapping it with the element at `pi`.

12	1	23	3	18	19	**28**	56	45	61	55	73	41	30	46
(0)	(1)	(2)	(3)	(4)	(5)	(6)	(7)	(8)	(9)	(10)	(11)	(12)	(13)	(14)

Increment indexes

↑ pi (at index 6)

The index `pi` identifies the proper location of the pivot element.

(You should note that this operation takes *n* steps if there are *n* element in the sublist to be partitioned. Each element in the sublist is examined once.)

We can now write the implementation. Basically, we want a loop that pushes `i` from `first` to `last`, maintaining the invariant that all the items with indexes less that `pi` are "smaller" than the pivot element, and all the items with indexes greater than or equal to `pi` but less than `i` are "greater than or equal to" the pivot element:

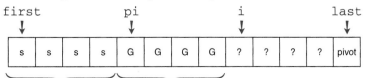

these are smaller than pivot   these are not

```
private static <Element> int partition (
    List<Element> list, int first, int last,
    Order<Element> order) {

    int pi;        // pivot index
    int i;         // index of the next to examine

    Element pivot; // pivot item
    int mid = (first+last)/2;
    pivot = list.get(mid);

    // put pivot item at end of list for now
    interchange(list,mid,last);
```

```
                    pi = first;
                    i = first;      // haven't examined anything yet

❶                   /* loop invariant:
                     *     for all j: first <= j && j < pi implies
                     *         order.inOrder(list.get(j),pivot)
                     *     for all j: pi <= j && j < i implies
                     *         !order.inOrder(list.get(j),pivot)
                     */
❷                   while (i != last) { // list.get(last) is pivot item
                       if (order.inOrder(list.get(i),pivot)) {
                       interchange(list,pi,i);
                       pi = pi+1;
                     }
                     i = i+1;
                   }
                   interchange(list,pi,last); // put pivot item in
                                              // place
                   return pi;
                 }
```

A few observations are in order:

- The key loop invariant is given at ❶. It says that smaller items will be in positions first ... pi-1, and larger elements will be in positions pi ... i-1.

  Note that when line ❷ is reached for the first time, the clauses of the invariant are vacuously true. Since first == pi == i, there is no value j such that first <= j && j < pi, and there is no value j such that pi <= j && j < i.

- When the loop terminates, i == last, all the elements have been examined, pi points at the first element greater than or equal to the pivot, and the pivot item is at position last.

  We should mention why we choose the middle element of the sublist as pivot, rather than, say, the last element. After all, the algorithm will work regardless of which element we choose as pivot. As noted above, quick sort takes about $n \cdot \log_2 n$ steps to sort a list of n elements in almost all cases. There are, however, a few pathological cases for which the algorithm requires n^2 steps. Essentially, these are situations where each partition operation leaves the pivot element at one end or the other of the sublist. If we choose the last (or first) element as pivot, then situations that might well occur in practice, such as a list that is already ordered, can require n^2 steps. The pathological cases that occur if we choose the middle element as pivot are much less likely to be actually encountered.

DrJava: counting quick sort steps

Open the file SortUtilities.java in the directory quickSort, in ch19, in nhText. This file contains versions of quick sort and selection sort, similar to *SortUtili-*

ties of the exercise on page 771. The directory also includes a file `Exercise.java`, containing a method `generateList` for generating lists of *Integers* and a definition of an *Order* `increasing` on *Integers*, again similar to the exercise on page 771.

1. Sort a list of 10,000 *Integers* using quick sort, and note the number of steps required.

```
> import ch19.quickSort.*;
> SortUtilities.quickSort(
        Exercise.generateList(10000,7),
        Exercise.increasing);
```

2. Sort the same list using selection sort, and note the number of steps required.

```
> SortUtilities.selectionSort(
        Exercise.generateList(10000,7),
        Exercise.increasing);
```

Was there a discernible difference is actual response time in the two cases?

19.4 An inefficient algorithm

While recursion is a powerful problem solving tool, we need to be a little careful in analyzing the work required by a recursive algorithm. For example, the Fibonacci numbers can be defined as the sequence of integers beginning with 0 and 1, and in which each successive number is the sum of the previous two:

0, 1, 1, 2, 3, 5, 8, 13, 21, 34, …

We can write a very straightforward recursive algorithm to compute the *n*th Fibonacci number. (We consider 0 to be the "0-th" number in the sequence.)

```
/**
 * The nth Fibonacci number.
 *      require:
 *          n >= 0
 */
public static int fib (int n) {
    if (n == 0)
        return 0;
    else if (n == 1)
        return 1;
    else
        return fib(n-1)+fib(n-2);
}
```

The problem with this algorithm is that it is notoriously inefficient. Each level of the recursion essentially duplicates work done at the previous level. For instance, computing *fib*(6) requires computing *fib*(5) and *fib*(4). But the computation of *fib*(5) also computes *fib*(4), repeating the work of the previous level. In fact, since the work required to compute *fib(n)* is the sum of the work required to compute *fib(n-1)* and the work required to compute *fib(n-2)*, it is not difficult to see that time required to compute *fib(n)* is roughly proportional to *fib(n)*! A simple iterative approach solves the problem in computational time proportional to *n*.

Of course, one can write an efficient recursive algorithm to compute the Fibonacci numbers, and inefficiencies due to unnecessarily repeated work can be found in iterative algorithms as well. But the inefficiency is often more obvious in an iterative algorithm, since we control the steps in an iterative process more directly than in a recursive process.

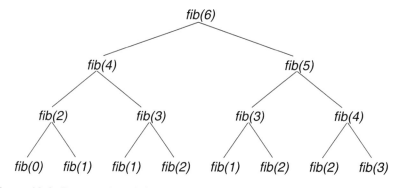

Figure 19.4   Repeated work in the simple Fibonacci algorithm.

✳ 19.5   Indirect recursion

The previous examples have all involved a method invoking itself: direct recursion. A method can also invoke itself *indirectly*: for instance, method m_1 invokes m_2 which invokes m_3 ... which invokes m_n which invokes m_1. We consider a rather contrived example to see how this works.

Assume we have two methods head and tail, each requiring a nonempty *String* as argument. head gives us the first character of the argument, and tail returns a *String* that is equal to the argument with the first character removed:

> **public char** head (String s)
> The first character of the specified nonempty *String*.

> **public** String tail (String s)
> A *String* equal to the specified nonempty *String* with its first character removed.

For instance, head("abc") produces the character 'a', and tail("abc") produces the *String* "bc".

Now let's write a recursive method removeSet that gets a balanced string of parentheses as argument and removes the first balanced substring from the front. The first balanced substring in each of the following is shown in blue.

```
" ( ) "
" ( ) ( ) ( ) ( ) "
" ( ( ( ) ) ) "
" ( ( ) ( ) ( ( ) ( ) ) ) ( ) ( ( ) ) "
```

The method returns the indicated result when applied to each of these *Strings*:

```
removeSet ( " ( ) " )  ⇒  " "
removeSet ( " ( ) ( ) ( ) ( ) " )  ⇒  " ( ) ( ) ( ) "
removeSet ( " ( ( ( ) ) ) " )  ⇒  " "
removeSet ( " ( ( ) ( ) ( ( ) ( ) ) ) ( ) ( ( ) ) " )  ⇒  " ( ) ( ( ) ) "
```

(Clearly we could do this in a straightforward, nonrecursive manner!)

We specify the method as:

> **public** String removeSet (String s)
>> A *String* equal to the specified *String* with the first balanced substring of parenthesis removed.
>
>> **require:**
>>> s is a nonempty balanced string of parentheses.

Now clearly the argument *String* must contain at least two characters and must begin with an open parenthesis. We need to find the closed parenthesis that matches the first open parenthesis.

If we remove the first parenthesis, we have a shorter *String*. And we must now remove the first substring of this *String* that has an extra close parenthsis.

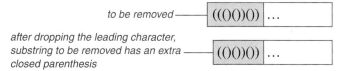

We specify an auxiliary method to do this:

> **private** String reduceClosed (String s)
>> A *String* equal to the specified *String* with the first substring containing one more closed parenthesis than open parenthesis removed.
>
>> **require:**
>>> s is a string of parentheses that would be balanced if an open parenthesis were appended to the front; in particular, s contains one more closed parentheses than open parentheses.

For example,

```
reduceClosed ( " ) " )  ⇒  " "
reduceClosed ( " ) ( ) ( ) " )  ⇒  " ( ) ( ) "
reduceClosed ( " ( ( ) ) ) ) ( ( ) )  ⇒  " ( ( ) ) "
reduceClosed ( " ( ) ( ) ( ( ) ( ) ) ) ( ) ( ( ) ) " )  ⇒  " ( ) ( ( ) ) "
```

The implementation of `removeSet` calls this method after chopping off the leading open parenthesis:

```
        public String removeSet (String s) {
            return reduceClosed(tail(s));
        }
```

Now let's think recursively about the implementation of `reduceClosed`. Is there a trivial case? Yes, if the first character in `s` is a closed parenthesis, we remove it and we're done. That is, we return the tail of `s`:

```
        private String reduceClosed (String s) {
            if (head(s) == ')')
                return tail(s);
            else
                ...
```

So the general case must be the case in which the first character of `s` is an open parenthesis. This means that there is a balanced substring at the beginning of `s`. We must remove the balanced substring, and recursively apply the method to what's left. But how to remove a balanced substring from the beginning of a *String*? Well, that's exactly what `removeSet` does! We can implement the method as follows:

```
        private String reduceClosed (String s) {
            if (head(s) == ')')
                return tail(s);
            else
                // head(s) == '('; first remove a balanced set
                return reduceClosed(removeSet(s));
        }
```

An invocation of `removeSet` calls `reduceClosed`, which may again call `removeSet`. This is an example of *indirect recursion*. Indirect recursion typically involves a set of mutually recursive methods, as is the case here.

✳ 19.6   Backtracking

Backtracking is an algorithmic technique for solving problems that cannot be solved directly. Backtracking is used when a large set of possible solutions must be examined to find an actual solution to the problem.

For backtracking to be an appropriate technique, the problem solution must be:

- a composite, made up of parts;
- constructible in a series of steps, with each step adding a piece to the solution.

At each step there will be several possible ways of extending the partial solution of the previous step. Some of these alternatives will lead to a solution, others will not.

As an example, suppose we have a maze consisting of a set of rooms connected by passages. Each room is connected to one or more passages. A passage may lead to another room, or may lead to the maze exit. For instance, a maze with seven rooms might look like this, where the rooms are lettered and the doors are labelled north, south, east, west:

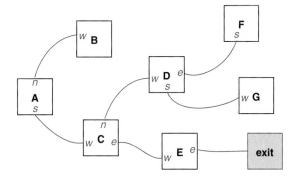

The problem is to find a path from a given room to the exit. Note that the solution to the problem is composite: "to reach the exit from room F, go south to room D, west to room C, east to room E, east to the exit." The path can be constructed in a series of steps, each step adding a component to the partial solution built in the previous step. At each step, there may be several alternatives. For example, the first step in the above solution is "go south to room D." This partial solution can be extended in two ways: "go west to room C" or "go south to room G." The first option leads to a solution, while the second does not. Room G is a dead end.

Backtracking works by repeatedly extending a partial solution until a solution is found or a "dead end" is reached. (A dead end is simply a state that cannot be further extended.) If a dead end is reached, the algorithm "backs up" to the most recent point at which untried possibilities exist, and tries one.

To see how this works, suppose we are trying to reach the exit from room A in the above maze. The algorithm might go through the following steps:

> *room a:*
>> go north to *room B*:
>>> dead end; back up to room A.
>> go south to *room C*:
>>> go north to *room D*:
>>>> go east to *room F*
>>>>> dead end; back up to room D.
>>>> go south to *room G*
>>>>> dead end; back up to room D.
>>>> no more choices (dead end); back up to room C
>>> go east to *room E*:
>>>> go east to exit.

Implementing a backtracking algorithm

Let's implement a backtracking algorithm for the maze traversal problem. A *Maze* is composed of a number of *Rooms*, with each *Room* connected to a number of other *Rooms*.

Rather than identifying connections as north, south, east, west, we'll index connections with integers. Thus a *Room* will have properties:

public List<Room> connections ()
    The list of *Rooms* this *Room* is connected to.

public boolean isExit ()
    This *Room* is a maze exit.

A *PathPoint* consists of a *Room* and a connection:

public class PathPoint
    A *Room* and a connection from the *Room*.

    public PathPoint (Room room, **int** connection)
        Create a new *PathPoint*.

      require:
        0 <= connection &&
        connection < room.connections().size()

A *path* is a list of *PathPoints* modeling a sequence of connected *Rooms*. If *PathPoint* [B,*j*] follows [A,*i*] on the list, then connection *i* from *Room* A leads to *Room* B. That is, A.connections(*i*) == B. For instance, the figure below shows the same maze as above, but with connections indexed.

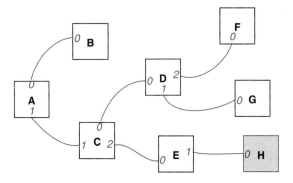

The path from *Room* A to *Room* H is given by the list

[(A,1),(C,2),(E,1)]

We further require that a *Room* appear on a path no more than once. First, it's pointless for a *Room* to appear more than once on an exit path, and second, if we allow it, our algorithm could get stuck in an infinite cycle:

[(A,0),(B,0),(A,0),(B,0),...]

(For a different problem, say find a path that visits all the *Rooms* in the maze, we might very well allow a *Room* to appear more than once on a path.)

We want to write a method that will produce an exit path from a specified *Room*:

```
public List<PathPoint> exitPathFrom (Room room)
        A path leading from the specified Room to an exit; returns null if no
        path exists.
```

We use an auxiliary method that takes a partial solution and extends it. The auxiliary method specified as

```
private List<PathPoint> extendedPathFrom (
    Room room, List<PathPoint> path)
        The specified path extended from the specified Room to an exit. Returns
        null if the path cannot be extended to an exit. The specified path must be
        empty or lead to the specified Room.
```

The public method calls the auxiliary method with an empty initial path:

```
public List<PathPoint> exitPathFrom (Room room) {
    return extendedPathFrom(
        room, new DefaultList<PathPoint>());
}
```

Now we must implement the auxiliary method. The second argument is a path that leads from the original starting Room to the Room given as the first argument. If the first argument is an exit, we are done:

```
private List<PathPoint> extendedPathFrom (
    Room room, List<PathPoint> path) {
    if (room.isExit())
        return path;
    else
        ...
}
```

Otherwise, we try each connection from room until we find one that leads to an exit. If none lead to an exit, we fail and return null.

```
private List<PathPoint> extendedPathFrom (
    Room room, List<PathPoint> path) {
    if (room.isExit())
        return path;
    else {
        boolean found = false;
        List<PathPoint> solution = null;
        int i = 0;
❶      while (i < room.connections().size() && !found) {
            // get a Room to extend the path
            Room nextRoom = room.connections().get(i);
❷          if (!pathContains(path, nextRoom)) {
❸              List<PathPoint> extendedPath = path.copy();
                extendedPath.add(new PathPoint(room,i));
```

```
                           solution = extendedPathFrom(
                                        nextRoom,extendedPath);
                           found = solution != null;
                       }
                       i = i+1;
                   }
                   return solution;
               }
           }
```

There are a few points to note about the algorithm.

- First, the loop in line ❶ has two exit conditions: a path to the exit has been found, or all the connections have been tried without success.

- Second, the if statement in line ❷ makes sure that nextRoom is not already on the path before attempting the connection. This is to avoid the infinite cycle problem mentioned above. (We assume that pathContains is some auxiliary method that determines whether or not a *Room* is on a path.)

- Finally we extend a *copy* of the path at line ❸ before making the recursive call. The reason is that we want to extend the same path at each iteration of the loop, and the add operation changes the state of the list object. If we didn't use a copy, we'd have to remove any failed extensions:

```
           solution = extendedPathFrom(
               nextRoom,path.add(new pathPoint(room,i)));
           found = solution != null;
           if (!found) path.remove(path.size()-1);
```

This method finds a solution if one exits. It is sometimes necessary to find all solutions. To do this, the method must record a solution when one is found, but continue as if a solution was not found.

Summarizing, backtracking is an algorithm design technique that can be used when the solution consists of components. At each step in constructing a solution, the algorithm tries to extend a partial solution from a set of alternatives. When a partial solution cannot be extended, the algorithm "backtracks" to a previous partial solution with remaining untried extensions. If no previous partial solution with untried extension exists, a solution cannot be found.

Backtracking can be described as a "brute force" solution process: it tries all possible solutions until an actual solution is found. As such, it is not very efficient and cannot generally be applied to very large problems without modification. For instance, it may be possible to "direct" the search for a solution in "promising" directions. It is, nonetheless, an important strategy and one that you must sometimes resort to.

✳ 19.7   Object recursion

The previous examples have all involved algorithms implemented by recursive methods, that is, methods that invoked themselves, directly or indirectly. In this section, we examine another form of recursion, called *structural recursion* or *object recursion*. Structural recursion uses object structure in a recursive manner to derive problem solutions.

With algorithmic recursion, a recursive method invokes itself to solve a simpler version of the problem. With object recursion, an object tasked with solving a problem gets assistance from a similar object that solves a simpler instance of the problem. The object constructs a solution by extending the solution of the simpler problem. Structurally, the similar object that provides the solution to the simpler problem is a component of the original object:

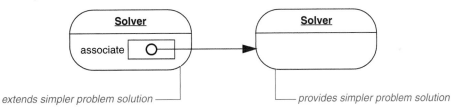

With algorithmic recursion, we separate the problem into base and general cases. In object recursion, we have two flavors of solver objects: one is the general problem solver, and the other is the trivial problem solver. We make these children of a common abstract parent:

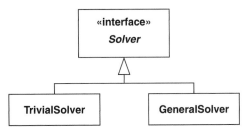

Since we want to concentrate on the structure of the objects, we'll develop a rather trivial example. Suppose we want to construct an odometer-like counter consisting of a sequence of digits. A digit turning over from 9 to 0 causes its left neighbor to increment.

A *solution* is simply a stable state of the counter, one in which all digits are set. We can tell the counter to find the first solution, that is, reset all digits to 0. And we can tell the counter to find the next solution, that is, increment the counter by 1. There is a final solution, in which all digits are 9. We specify that attempting to find the next solution after the final state will fail. That is, a counter that is all 9s will not turn over to all 0s.

Figure 19.5 **Five-digit counter.**

The general solver class will be named *Digit*, and the trivial solver class *NullDigit*. Each *Digit* instance is responsible for a single digit of the solution. Each *Digit* has an *associate*, the *Digit* to its left. A *Digit* will extend the solution provided by its associate. Thus the *Digits* are "linked together" to form the counter. The high-order (left-most) *Digit* has a *NullDigit* as its associate. The high-order *Digit* really needs no associate. The logic in the *NullDigit* simply ends the recursion. We have the following fundamental class structure:

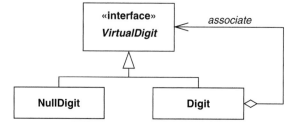

A *Digit* that is right-most in a three-digit number, for example, has an associate that is right-most in a two-digit number. The three-digit number is built by extending the two-digit number. (See Figure 19.6.) Notice that the right-most *Digit* in a one-digit number has a *NullDigit* as associate.

Now let's see how this all works. If we want a three-digit counter, we need to create three *Digit* instances and one *NullDigit*, structured as shown in Figure 19.6. Notice that a *Digit* and its associate component have the same structure, hence the term "structural recursion." We call the top-level object that contains the structure a *DigitCounter*.

We introduced the idea of a member class or inner class in Section 10.5. We make *VirtualDigit* a private inner interface and *Digit* and *NullDigit* private inner classes of the *DigitCounter*.

When we build the *DigitCounter*, we start with a *NullDigit*, and create one *Digit* instance for each digit in the counter.

```
/**
 * A counter containing the specified number of
 * digits.
 */
public class DigitCounter {

    private VirtualDigit lowDigit; // right-most digit
```

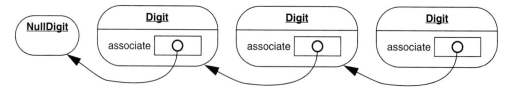

Figure 19.6   Objects comprising a three-digit counter.

```
/**
 * Create a new DigitCounter with the specified
 * number of digits.
 * @require    digits >= 1
 */
public DigitCounter (int digits) {
    VirtualDigit d = new NullDigit();
    for (int i = 1; i <= digits; i = i+1)
        d = new Digit(d);
    lowDigit = d;
}
...

private interface VirtualDigit {

    ...
} // end of interface VirtualDigit

private class NullDigit implements VirtualDigit {

    ...
} // end of class NullDigit

private class Digit implements VirtualDigit {

    // high order neighbor:
    private VirtualDigit associate;

    public Digit (VirtualDigit associate) {
        this.associate = associate;
        ...
    }
    ...
} // end of class Digit

} // end of class DigitCounter
```

Pay particular attention to the loop body in the *DigtCounter* constructor:

```
d = new Digit(d);
```

The constructor for *Digit* gets an associate as argument. The statement creates a new *Digit* with the previously created *Digit* as associate. A reference to the newly created *Digit* is then stored in d. It becomes the associate of the *Digit* created on the next iteration of the loop.

What features should *DigitCounter* have? It should have commands for finding the first solution and for finding the next. That is, the command first sets the counter to all 0s, and the command next increments the counter. The counter is used by giving it the command `first`, and then repeatedly giving it the command `next`. It has a query `solved` to determine whether a solution was found. We expect `solved` to return *false* initially, and then return *true* after we have given the command `first`. It should continue to return *true* until we try to increment a counter consisting of all 9s. Finally, the `toString` method returns the value of the counter as a *String*. For example, a two-digit counter would behave as follows:

command:	solved():	toString():
—	*false*	—
first()	*true*	00
next()	*true*	01
next()	*true*	02
...		
next()	*true*	99
next()	*false*	—

The *DigitCounter* methods simply forward the service request to the right-most digit of the counter, `lowDigit`. Omitting documentation, we have:

```java
public class DigitCounter {

    private VirtualDigit lowDigit;// right-most digit

    public DigitCounter (int digits) ...

    public void first () {
        lowDigit.first();
    }

    public void next () {
        lowDigit.next();
    }

    public boolean solved () {
        return lowDigit.solved();
    }

    public String toString () {
        return lowDigit.toString();
    }

    private interface VirtualDigit {
        public boolean solved ();
        public void first ();
        public void next ();
        public String toString ();
    }
    ...
}
```

How does a *Digit* work? When given the command `first`, it instructs its left neighbor to find the first number, and then tacks on its own 0. When given the command `next`, it increments its digit if it's not 9. If its digit is 9, it instructs its left neighbor to increment, and then tacks on a 0. In each case, it checks to make sure that the neighbor was successful. Again omitting documentation, *Digit* is defined as follows:

```java
private class Digit implements VirtualDigit {

    private VirtualDigit associate;   // left neighbor
    private boolean solved;           // a valid number
    private int digit;                // my digit

    public Digit (VirtualDigit associate) {
        this.associate = associate;
        this.digit = 0;
        this.solved = false;
    }

    public boolean solved () {
        return solved;
    }

    public void first () {
        associate.first();
        if (associate.solved()) {
            digit = 0;
            solved = true;
        } else
            solved = false;
    }

    public void next () {
        if (digit < 9) {
            digit = digit + 1;
            solved = true;
        } else {
            associate.next();
            if (associate.solved()) {
                digit = 0;
                solved = true;
            } else
                solved = false;
        }
    }

    public String toString () {
        if (solved)
```

```
            return associate.toString() + digit;
        else
            return "No solution";
    }
}
```

A little analysis will show the test in `first` and many of the assignments to `solved` are unnecessary. Still, we include them to give the flavor of the general approach. Notice how the recursive nature of the solution is evident from object recursion. The digit structure is traversed, with each object delegating the job to its associate. This logic is particularly clear in the method `toString`, where an object delegates building the *String* representation to its associate, and then adds its digit. We can also see this logic in the methods `first` and `next`, where the object is delegating responsibility to its associate.

We have only to complete the definition of *NullDigit*. Remember that `first` and `next` are called by an element's right neighbor. `first` is called when the right neighbor has its initial piece of the solution, and needs only to get the first solution from its associate. On the other hand, `next` is called when the right neighbor can no longer extend the current partial solution on its own and needs a new partial solution from its associate. *NullDigit* represents the solution to the empty problem. It always solves the problem vacuously, and therefore has a "first" solution; but does not have a "next" solution. *NullDigit* should be built as follows:

```
private class NullDigit implements VirtualDigit {

    private boolean solved;

    public NullDigit () {
        this.solved = false;
    }

    public boolean solved () {
        return solved;
    }

    public void first () {
        solved = true;
    }

    public void next () {
        solved = false;
    }

    public String toString () {
        if (solved)
            return "";
        else
            return "No solution";
    }
}
```

Structurally we do not need the class *NullDigit*. Its purpose is to permit all object entries in the structure to be treated uniformly. If we do not give the left-most *Digit* an associate, the methods of the *Digit* class will be polluted with tests to determine whether or not the *Digit* is left-most, that is, whether or not its associate is *null*. Thus every *Digit* instance is given a non-*null* associate. What kind of associate should the left-most *Digit* be given? An instance of *NullDigit*, a class whose method logic is straightforward. By making the type of the associate component *VirtualDigit*, a *Digit* can be equipped with a *Digit* or *NullDigit* as an associate. Polymorphism distinguishes the two classes, allowing us to write simpler methods for the class *Digit*. The complete class is shown in Listing 19.1.

Listing 19.1 **The class *DigitCounter***

```
/**
 * A counter containing the specified number of digits.
 */
public class DigitCounter {

    private VirtualDigit lowDigit;    // right-most digit

    /**
     * Create a new DigitCounter with the specified number of
     * digits.
     * @require    digits >= 1
     */
    public DigitCounter (int digits) {
        VirtualDigit d = new NullDigit();
        for (int i = 1; i <= digits; i = i+1)
            d = new Digit(d);
        lowDigit = d;
    }

    /**
     * Find the first number: i.e., set this DigitCounter
     * to all 0.
     */
    public void first () {
        lowDigit.first();
    }

    /**
     * Find the next number: i.e., increment this
     * DigitCounter by 1 if possible.
     */
    public void next () {
        lowDigit.next();
    }
```

continued

Listing 19.1   **The class *DigitCounter* (cont'd)**

```
/**
 * This DigitCounter contains a legitimate count. That
 * is, first() or next()
 * has been successfully performed.
 */
public boolean solved () {
   return lowDigit.solved();
}

/**
 * The number contained in this DigitCounter.
 */
public String toString () {
   return lowDigit.toString();
}

/**
 * A single digit in the DigitCounter. A "solution" is a
 * legal count.
 */
private interface VirtualDigit {

   /**
    * (Partial) solution ending with this Digit has been
    * found.
    */
   public boolean solved ();

   /**
    * Get the first (partial) solution ending with this
    * Digit.
    */
   public void first ();

   /**
    * Get the next (partial) solution ending with this
    * Digit, if one exists.
    */
   public void next ();

   /**
    * String representation of the (partial) solution
    * ending with this Digit.
    */
```

continued

Listing 19.1 **The class *DigitCounter* (cont'd)**

```java
    public String toString ();

} // end of interface VirtualDigit

/**
 * An actual digit in the DigitCounter.
 */
private class Digit implements VirtualDigit {

    private VirtualDigit associate;   // left neighbor
    private boolean solved;           // a valid number
    private int digit;                // my digit

    /**
     * Create a new Digit with the specified higher-order
     * neighbor. associate is the next higher order Digit
     * in the counter.
     */
    public Digit (VirtualDigit associate) {
        this.associate = associate;
        this.digit = 0;
        this.solved = false;
    }

    /**
     * (Partial) solution ending with this Digit has been
     * found.
     */
    public boolean solved () {
        return solved;
    }

    /**
     * Get the first (partial) solution ending with this
     * Digit.
     */
    public void first () {
        associate.first();
        if (associate.solved()) {
            digit = 0;
            solved = true;
        } else
            solved = false;
    }
```

continued

Listing 19.1   **The class *DigitCounter* (cont'd)**

```java
/**
 * Get the next (partial) solution ending with this
 * Digit.
 */
public void next () {
    if (digit < 9) {
        digit = digit + 1;
        solved = true;
    } else {
        associate.next();
        if (associate.solved()) {
            digit = 0;
            solved = true;
        } else
            solved = false;
    }
}

/**
 * String representation of the (partial) solution
 * ending with this Digit.
 */
public String toString () {
    if (solved)
        return associate.toString() + digit;
    else
        return "No solution";
}
} // end of class Digit

/**
 * A NullDigit represents the 0-digit counter. It sits
 * to the left of the high-order digit in a
 * DigitCounter.
 */
private class NullDigit implements VirtualDigit {

    private boolean solved;

    /**
     * (Partial) solution ending with this Digit has been
     * found.
     */
```

continued

Listing 19.1 **The class *DigitCounter* (cont'd)**

```
        public boolean solved () {
            return solved;
        }

        /**
         * First solution is OK.
         */
        public void first () {
            solved = true;
        }

        /**
         * Can't advance a NullDigit.
         */
        public void next () {
            solved = false;
        }

        /**
         * String representation of the 0-digit counter.
         */
        public String toString () {
            if (solved)
                return "";
            else
                return "No solution";
        }
    } // end of class NullDigit

} // end of class DigitCounter
```

19.8   Summary

In this chapter, we introduced the problem solving technique of recursion. We've seen two forms of recursive computation: *algorithmic recursion*, in which a method invokes itself directly or indirectly, and *object recursion*, based on the creation of composite object structure in which the structure of a component is the same as that of the composite object.

With direct algorithmic recursion, the solution logic depends on identifying simple base cases that can be easily solved directly, and on describing how to reduce the general case to one that is slightly simpler, that is, slightly closer to a base case. The method that actualizes this logic invokes itself to solve the slightly simpler case to which the general case is reduced.

A well-known algorithm using direct recursion is quick sort. Quick sort is much more efficient than the selection and bubble sorts seen in Chapter 14, generally requiring on the order of $n \cdot \log_2 n$ steps to sort a list of n elements. Quick sort works by positioning an arbitrary element, with smaller elements below and larger elements above. The list segments containing the smaller elements and the larger elements are then recursively sorted.

With indirect recursion, a method is invoked before it returns through a sequence of other method invocations. That is, method m_1 invokes m_2 which invokes m_3 ... which invokes m_n which invokes m_1. When indirect recursion is used, we generally set a collection of mutually recursive methods.

Backtracking is an algorithmic technique for examining a set of possible solutions to a problem in an organized way in order to find an actual solution. The solution to the problem is a composite, made up of several pieces. Each step in a backtracking algorithm attempts to extend the partial solution produced by the previous step. If it is not possible to extend the partial solution, the algorithm "backs up" to find another partial solution to extend.

Using object recursion, a solver object is structured with a similar solver object as an associate. The solver object delegates the responsibility of solving a simpler version of the problem to its associate, and then extends the solution provided by the associate. The recursive nature of the approach is seen here as well: a solution to the general case is found by using a solution to a simpler case given by the associate.

SELF-STUDY EXERCISES

19.1   The *factorial* function (written !) can be defined for non-negative integers as follows:

$$0! = 1$$
$$n! = 1 \times 2 \times 3 \times \dots \times n, \text{ for } n \geq 1.$$

What is the base case? What is the general case? How can the general case be expressed in terms of a slightly simpler case?

19.2   Write a recursive method that computes the factorial of a non-negative integer.

19.3   The version of `power` on page 765 that reduces computing a number to the power n to the easier problem of computing a number to the power $n - 2$ is incorrect. Would it be correct if it included `exponent` values of both 0 and 1 as base cases? That is,

```
public static int power (int number, int exponent) {
    int result;
    if (exponent == 0)
        result = 1;
    else if (exponent == 1)
        result = number;
    else
```

```
            result = number*number*power(number,exponent-2);
        return result;
    }
```

19.4 Consider the following specification:

> **private static int** sum (List<Integer> list, **int** start)
> The sum of list.get(start) through
> list.get(list.size()-1), as an **int**.
>
> **require:**
> 0 <= start && start <= list.size()

The method is to be written recursively. What is the base case? What is the general case?

19.5 Implement the method sum specified above, using direct recursion. Then using this method as an auxiliary method, implement a method sum that sums the elements on a *List<Integer>*.

19.6 Can the tower puzzle moveTower method be written as follows? Why or why not?

```
public void moveTower (int n, int from, int to) {
    if (n == 1) {
        moveDisk(from,to);
    } else {
        int other = 6-from-to;    // not from or to
        moveDisk(from,other);
        moveTower(n-1,from,to);
        moveDisk(other,to);
    }
}
```

19.7 Given the list below, trace the quick sort partition method. Assume the order is "less than" and that the entire list is to be partition. What value is returned? What does the list look like after partitioning?

15	3	2	7	14	4	1
(0)	(1)	(2)	(3)	(4)	(5)	(6)

19.8 Again assume the order is "less than" and that the entire list is to be partition. Suppose that the quick sort partition method chooses the last element of the segment to position, rather than the choosing the middle element and swapping it with the last element. What value will be returned and what will the list look like after partitioning if the list is originally

1	2	3	4	7	14	15
(0)	(1)	(2)	(3)	(4)	(5)	(6)

19.9 Write a simple iterative implementation of the Fibonacci function, fib.

19.10 The class *Pair* models a pair of integers:

> **public class** Pair
> > A pair of **int**'s.
>
> > **public** Pair (**int** first, **int** second)
> > > Create a new *Pair*.
> >
> > **public int** first ()
> > > The first element of this *Pair*.
> >
> > **public int** second ()
> > > The second element of this *Pair*.

Consider the method

> **private static** Pair fibPair (**int** n)
> > A *Pair* consisting of the (*n*–1)-st Fibonacci number and the *n*-th
> > Fibonacci number.
> >
> > **require:**
> > > n > 0

Write a recursive implementation of fibPair. Using this method as an auxiliary, write an implementation of fib. Is this implementation more efficient than the one given on page 791?

EXERCISES

19.1 Write a recursive version of the binary search algorithm of Section 14.4.

19.2 Write a recursive version of insertion sort as described in Exercise 14.5.

19.3 Recall from Exercise 14.4 that a *merge* operation takes two similarly sorted lists and combines them into a single sorted list. *Merge sort* can be described informally as follows:

a. Break the list into two halves.

b. Sort each half.

c. Merge the two sorted halves into a sorted list.

Implement merge sort.

19.4 Write a recursive method reverse that takes a *String* argument and produces a *String* that is the reverse of the argument as result. For instance, reverse("abc") should produce the *String* "cba".

19.5 Write a recursive method reverse that takes a *List<Element>* as argument and produces a *List<Element>* that is the reverse of the argument as result.

19.6 Write a recursive method palindrome that takes a *String* argument, and determines whether or not the *Sting* is a palindrome. (A *palindrome* is a sting that reads the same forward and backward: for instance "amanaplanacanalpanama.")

19.7 Write a simple user interface for the tower puzzle. The user interface should read the number of disks as input, and write the moves to standard output. You might want to sleep for a second or so before writing each move so the moves don't all appear at once. Test with only a small number of disks. The number of moves increases exponentially with the number of disks.

19.8 An *integer expression* is either an integer, a unary operator and operand, or a binary operator and left and right operands. Unary operators are + and −. Binary operators are +, −, *, and /. An operand is another integer expression.

Design a class to model integer expressions. The class should include a method `evaluate` that returns the integer value of the expression.

∗ 19.9 In the game of chess, a queen can move vertically, horizontally, or diagonally. Thus the queen shown can move into any square covered by the arrows.

The *queens problem* is to place *n* queens on an *n* × *n* chessboard in such a way that no queen can capture any other in one move. The problem is trivial if *n* is 1, and has no solution if *n* is 2 or 3. A solution for *n* = 4 is shown below.

Implement a solution to the queens problem using backtracking. Clearly there must be exactly one queen in each row (and in each column) of a solution. A partial solution will have *m* queens placed in the first *m* rows. A step in constructing the solution is to add a queen to the next row.

∗ 19.10 Implement a solution to the queens problem of the previous exercise using object recursion. The value for *n* is specified when the problem instance is created. If the problem cannot be solved, `solved` will return *false* after the method `first` is invoked. Otherwise, first produces a solution and successive invocations of next produce successive solutions to the problem.

Consider creating a *Solver* instance for each row of the board. A *Solver* instance is responsible for extending the partial solution provided by its neighbor by adding a queen to its row.

SELF-STUDY EXERCISE SOLUTIONS

19.1   Base case: find the factorial of 0.

General case: find the factorial of n, for $n > 0$.

Reduce general case to slightly simpler: for $n > 0$, $n! = n \cdot (n-1)!$

19.2
```
public static int factorial (int n) {
    if (n == 0)
        return 1;
    else
        return n*factorial(n-1);
}
```

19.3   Yes, this is correct. Invocations with an even exponent reduce to the 0 case; invocations with an odd exponent reduce to the 1 case.

19.4   The base case is start == list.size()-1. The general case is start < list.size()-1.

19.5
```
public static int sum (List<Integer> list, int start) {
    if (start == list.size())
        return 0;
    else
        return list.get(start).intValue()+sum(list,start+1);
}

public static int sum (List<Integer> list) {
    return sum(list,0);
}
```

19.6   No it cannot. The problem of moving n disks cannot be reduced to the problem of moving $n-1$ disks with a smaller one on one of the pegs. If we put the smallest disk on the other peg, we can't "ignore it" when moving the remaining $n-1$ disks.

19.7   The value returned is 4. The list will be

3	2	1	4	7	15	14
(0)	(1)	(2)	(3)	(4)	(5)	(6)

19.8   The value returned will be 6. The list will be unchanged.

19.9
```java
public static int fib (int n) {
    if (n == 0)
        return 1;
    else {
        int count = 1;
        int first = 0;      // (count-1)st fib
        int second = 1;     // (count)th fib
        while (count != n) {
            int next = first+second;
            first = second;
            second = next;
            count = count + 1;
        }
        return second;
    }
}
```

19.10
```java
private static Pair fibPair (int n) {
    if (n == 1)
        return new Pair(0,1);
    else {
        Pair p = fibPair(n-1);
        return new Pair(p.second(),p.first()+p.second());
    }
}

public static int fib (int n) {
    return fibPair(n).second();
}
```

This method is much more efficient. It makes only *n* recursive calls to compute the *n*-th Fibonacci number.

CHAPTER 20

Implementing lists: linked implementations

In Chapter 13, we saw how to implement a *List* using arrays. In this chapter, we explore a number of linked implementations. With an array, the list structure is derived from the sequential relationship between the array elements. With a linked implementation, the structure is explicitly built through object references. Linked implementations can be used in a natural way to implement structures more complex than a simple sequence.

Objectives

After studying this chapter you should understand the following:

- the design and structure of linked list implementations;
- variations in designs for linked lists, including doubly linked lists;
- advantages and disadvantages of linked *vs.* array-based implementations.

Also, you should be able to:

- write algorithms for linked-based structures;
- define classes implemented with linked-based structures.

20.1 A linked *List* implementation

A list has a particularly simple structure. The elements are arranged in a linear sequence. If the list is not empty, there is a first element and a last element; every element (except the last) has one following it; and every element (except the first) has one preceding it. In an array implementation, the sequential structure of the list is modeled with the sequential structure of memory. Variables referencing successive list elements occupy successive areas of memory. A reference to the first list element is stored first in memory, followed by

Array implementation

node

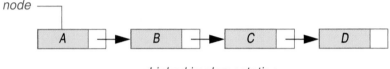

Linked implementation

Figure 20.1   Alternate list implementations.

a reference to the second list element, *etc.* In a linked implementation, a structure is explicitly built from a collection of *nodes* that reference each other. A node contains a variable referencing a list element, and one or more variables referencing other nodes in the structure. In our first implementation, each node will reference the node containing the next list element. That is, each node references the next one in sequence. The list structure is explicitly constructed by "gluing" nodes together.

We name the list class *LinkedList<Element>*,[1] and define a class *Node* to model the nodes that comprise a list. Since the node structure is purely implementation detail, the class *Node* is local to *LinkedList*.

The structure of a *Node* is straightforward. A *Node* has two responsibilities: it must know an element of the *List*, and it must know the next *Node* in sequence. Hence a *Node* has two data components, the list element, and the next *Node*. Since *Node* is a private inner class of *LinkedList<Element>*, we omit methods for accessing and setting these variables, and manipulate them directly.

```
public class LinkedList<Element>
    extends AbstractList<Element> {
    ...
private class Node {

    private Element element;
    private Node next;

    /**
     * Create a Node containing the specified
     * element.
     */
    public Node (Element element) {
```

---

1. The standard library package java.util includes a concrete class *LinkedList<E>*.

```
            this.element = element;
            this.next = null;
        }
    } // end of class Node
} // end of class LinkedList
```

A *LinkedList* instance contains an instance variable `size`, and an instance variable `first` that references the first *Node* of the list, as illustrated in Figure 20.2.

```
public class LinkedList<Element>
    extends AbstractList<Element> {

    private int size;
    private Node first;

    /**
     * Create an empty LinkedList<Element>.
     */
    public LinkedList () {
        size = 0;
        first = null;
    }
    ...
}
```

Note that the `next` variable of the last *Node* is null, and the *LinkedList* variable `first` is null if the list is empty. An empty list is shown in Figure 20.3.

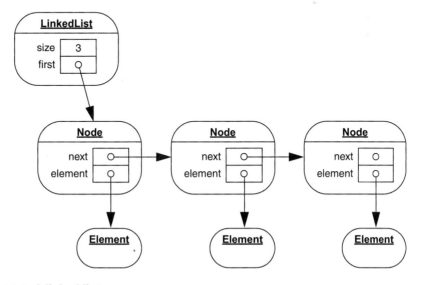

Figure 20.2 **A linked list.**

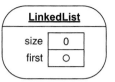

Figure 20.3 **An empty list.**

20.1.1 Implementing *LinkedList* methods

Let's take a look at some of the methods that depend on the linked structure. In particular, we'll look at get, remove, and add. Each of these methods requires traversing the list to find the *i*-th node, for an arbitrary value *i*. So we start by writing an auxiliary method to do that:

```
/**
 * The i-th node of this LinkedList.
 * The LinkedList must be non-empty.
 * @require    0 <= i && i < this.size()
 */
private Node getNode (int i) {
    Node p = first;
    int pos = 0;    // p is the pos-th Node
    while (pos != i) {
        p = p.next;
        pos = pos + 1;
    }
    return p;
}
```

Carefully examine how this method works. In particular, note the relationship between the variables p and pos. The variable p is initialized with a reference to the 0-*th* *Node* of the list:

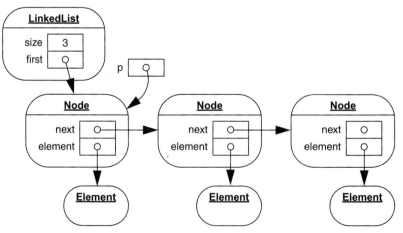

Each iteration of the loop assigns p a reference to the next element of the list, and increments pos. For instance, after one iteration, p references the *Node* with index 1:

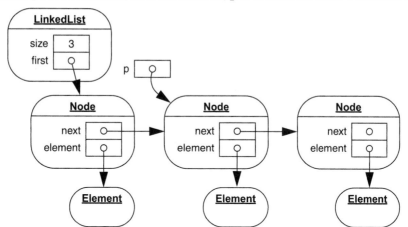

In particular, the fact that p references the *Node* containing the element with index pos is an invariant of the loop. When the loop terminates, pos == i, and p references the *Node* we are looking for.

get

Using the auxiliary method, the implementation of get is straight forward.

```
public Element get (int index) {
    Node p = getNode(index);
    return p.element;
}
```

remove(int)

Next let's look at the method to remove an element with a specified index. To remove a *Node*, we need to find the *Node* in front of it. That is, we need to find a *Node* p such that p.next is the *Node* to be removed. Assuming index is the index of the element to be deleted, we find the *Node* in front with the auxiliary method:

```
Node p = getNode(index-1);
```

For instance, if index is 2, p will reference the element with index 1:

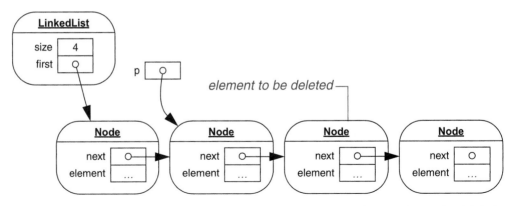

Now we must make index 1 *Node's* next component reference the *Node* with index 3, effectively eliminating the element with index 2 from the list:

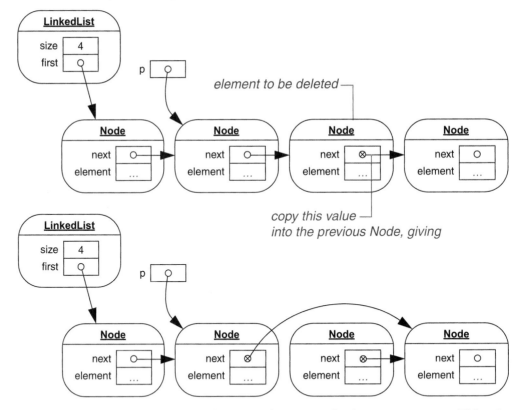

The value we need to copy is next of p.next, that is, p.next.next. This value should be set to the next component of the *Node* referenced by p:

```
p.next = p.next.next;
```

Note that since p.next is the *Node* to be deleted, p.next cannot be null. Thus the reference p.next.next is legal.

This operation may seem confusing at first, and you should make sure that you understand what is happening. Such operations are very typical of linked structure manipulation.

We must be a bit more careful, though. Recall that getNode requires its argument to be greater than or equal to 0. The precondition of remove guarantees index >= 0. If index is 0, the statement

```
Node p = getNode(index-1);
```

is not legal. We must treat removing the element with index 0 as a special case. In this case, the instance variable first of the *LinkedList* object must be modified. The complete method can be written as follows:

```
public void remove (int index) {
    if (index == 0)
        first = first.next;
    else {
        Node p = getNode(index-1);
        p.next = p.next.next;
    }
    size = size - 1;
}
```

add(int,Element)

As with remove, if we want to add an element at the *i*-th position, we must find the element with index *i*–1. And as with remove, we have a special case to consider when *i* is 0.

We can write the method as follows (see next page):

```
public void add (int index, Element element) {
    Node newNode = new Node(element);
    if (index == 0) {
        newNode.next = first;
        first = newNode;
    } else {
        Node p = getNode(index-1);
        newNode.next = p.next;
        p.next = newNode;
    }
    size = size + 1;
}
```

The add variant that appends an element to the end of the list can be written in terms of this method, as we have done before.

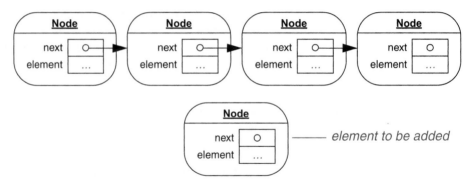

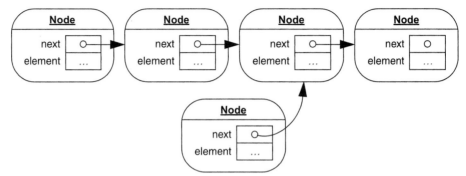

to add a new element with index 2,
the new Node must be made to reference
the old Node with index 2

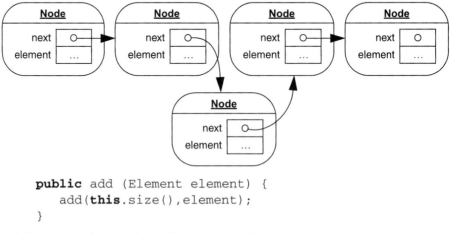

and the Node with index 1 must
be made to reference the new Node

```
public add (Element element) {
    add(this.size(),element);
}
```

A few observations on the implementation so far.

- get, remove, and add all require linear time on average. We expect to traverse half the list to find the *Node* we're looking for, so the time required grows in proportion to the length of the list. Deleting the first element and inserting a new first element, however, are constant time operations. Traversing the list is not required in these cases.

- We must be particularly careful of "boundary" cases: cases involving the empty list, a list with one element, the first or last element of a list. These may well require explicit handling.

20.2 Linked list variations

A simple change to our model will allow adding to the end of a list in constant time. If we keep references to both the first and last elements in the *LinkedList<Element>*, we don't need to traverse the list in order to add to the end.

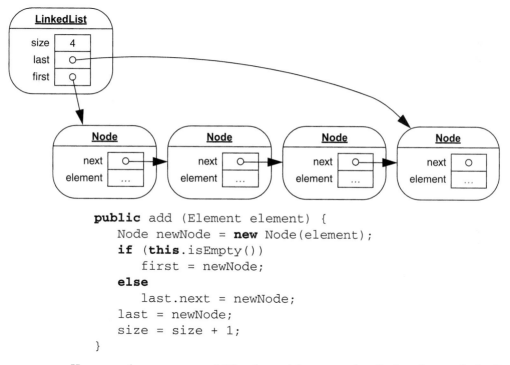

```
public add (Element element) {
    Node newNode = new Node(element);
    if (this.isEmpty())
        first = newNode;
    else
        last.next = newNode;
    last = newNode;
    size = size + 1;
}
```

However, there are now additional special cases to handle in other methods. For instance, remove must explicitly check for the case in which the last element is deleted:

```
public void remove (int index) {
    if (size == 1) {
        // remove the only element
        first = null;
        last = null;
    }else if (index == 0) {
```

```
            // remove the first element
            first = first.next;
      }else {
            Node p = getNode(index-1);
            p.next = p.next.next;
            if (index == size-1)
                // last element removed
                last = p;
      }
      size = size - 1;
}
```

We could also make adding to the end of a list constant time by having the *LinkedList*
object reference the last *Node* in the list, and each *Node* reference the *preceding Node*
rather than next. We leave this as an exercise.

Header nodes

One way to eliminate special cases in list algorithms is to employ a *header* node. This is a
"dummy" node that contains no element, but is always present at the front of the list. The
instance variable `first` always references the header node, and is never null. In particular, the empty list contains only a header.

We extend the class *Node* to produce headers:

```
private class Header extends Node {
      public Header () {
            super(null);
      }
}
```

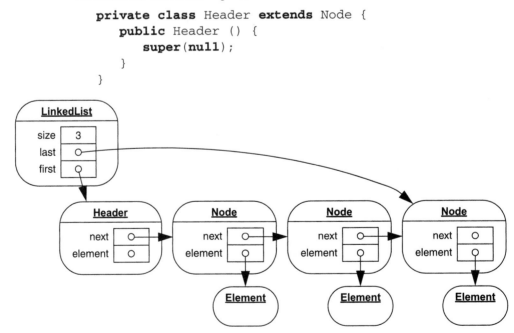

Figure 20.4 **A linked list with header.**

The *LinkedList* constructor creates the header:

```
public LinkedList () {
    size = 0;
    first = new Header();
    last = first;
}
```

Note how this simplifies many methods. The method add, for instance, need not explicitly check for the empty list:

```
public add (Element element) {
    Node newNode = new Node(element);
    last.next = newNode;
    last = newNode;
    size = size + 1;
}
```

Circular lists

There are many variations on the linked list theme. In a circular linked list, for instance, the la*st node* references the first. We show a circular list without header in Figure 20.5, though of course a header could also be used.

An advantage of a circular list is that it is possible to traverse the entire list starting from any node. (Clearly care must be taken with this kind of structure to avoid infinite iterations or recursions.) This additional structure would not be of particular advantage in implementing the functionality we have defined for the interface *List<Element>*. But we can easily imagine other abstractions where such a structure would prove useful. We won't consider details here.

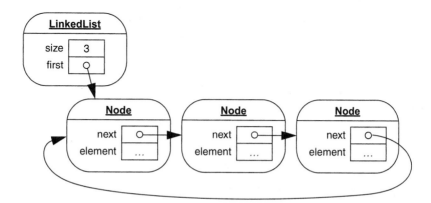

Figure 20.5 **A circular linked list without header.**

20.3   Doubly-linked lists

A common linked list variation is a *doubly-linked list*. In this structure, each node references the preceding as well as the following node. We sketch the construction of a class *DoublyLinkedList<Element>*, whose instances are doubly-linked circular lists with headers. Such a structure is illustrated in Figure 20.6:

A *Node* in a doubly-linked lists contains three components: the list element, and references to its two neighbor *Nodes*. The *DoublyLinkedList* object has a size and a reference to the header *Node*. As was the case with the class *LinkedList*, we make the *Node* class local to the class *DoublyLinkedList*.

```
public class DoublyLinkedList<Element>
    extends AbstractList<Element> {

    private int size;
    private Node header;
    ...

    private class Node {

        Element element;
        Node next;
        Node previous;

        public Node (Element element) {
            this.element = element;
            this.next = null;
            this.previous = null;
        }
    } // end of class Node
}
```

Assuming that *Header* extends *Node* as before, the *DoublyLinkedList* constructor creates the header *Node*, and links it to itself.

```
public DoublyLinkedList () {
    size = 0;
    header = new Header();
    header.next = header;
    header.previous = header;
}
```

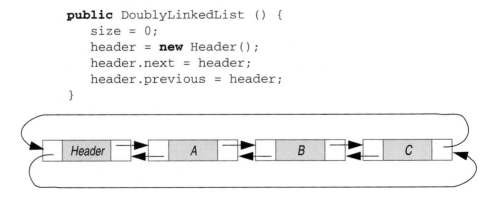

Figure 20.6 **Doubly-linked circular list with header.**

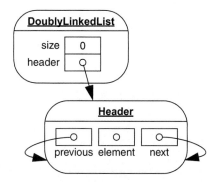

Figure 20.7 **An empty *DoublyLinkedList*.**

Note that, as shown in Figure 20.7, the empty list contains only the header, which references itself:

Operations on a *DoublyLinkedList* are a bit more complicated since we have two references in each *Node* to deal with. But the combination of a circular structure and a header eliminate the need for handling most boundary cases explicitly.

Let's consider the add(Element) method for this structure. The variable previous of the header references the last element in the list, and the variable next of the last element references the header.

As illustrated in Figure 20.8, to append a new element, we must set:

(1) the variable previous of the new *Node* to reference the old last *Node*;

(2) the variable next of the new *Node* to reference the header;

(3) the variable previous of the header to reference the new *Node*;

(4) the variable next of the old last node to reference the new *Node*.

Note that no special test is required to handle the empty list. The method can be written as follows.

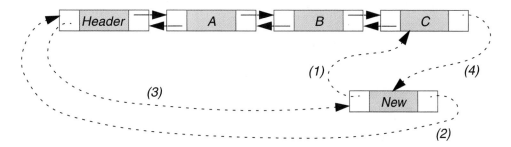

Figure 20.8 **Adding a new *Node* to the end of a *DoublyLinkedList*.**

```
public void add (Element element) {
    Node newNode = new Node(element);
    Node last = header.previous;
    newNode.previous = last;
    newNode.next = header;
    header.previous = newNode;
    last.next = newNode;
    size = size + 1;
}
```

20.4   Limitations of linked structures

The principal disadvantage of a linked implementation compared to an array-based implementation is that accessing elements by index requires linear time. That is, the average
number of steps required to access an element increases in proportion to the length of the
list. To execute the method get for a linked list requires that we traverse about half the
list. In an array based implementation, get requires constant time, regardless of the size
of the list. Thus we would not likely use a linked implementation if the primary operation
is to access elements randomly by index.

To this point we have used indexes as our primary means for accessing list elements.
For instance, to determine if an element is on a list, we obtain each element of the list by
means of its index:

```
public int indexOf (Element element) {
    int i = 0;
    while (i < this.size() &&
              !this.get(i).equals(element))
        i = i+1;
    if (i < this.size())
        return i;
    else
        return -1;
}
```

If the element is not on the list and the list contains n elements, the iteration requires n
steps since each element of the list must be examined. If the element is on the list, we
expect, on average, to need to look at half the elements. This is not so bad if we have an
array based implementation, where get requires a fixed amount of time independent of the
list length.

But look at what happens with a linked implementation. The method get uses get-
Node as shown on page 820. To get a *Node*, this method starts at the beginning of the list
and traverses the list. It requires i steps to get the *Node* with index i. If the element is not
on the list, we must execute get n times, with values 0 through $n-1$:

value of i: 0 1 2 ... $n-1$
steps of get(i):   0 1 2 ... $n-1$

We can compute the total number of steps required by adding up the number of steps required by each invocation of get. This happens to be a well-known sum:

$$0 + 1 + 2 + \ldots + (n-1) = (n^2 - n)/2.$$

This is not so good. The method is quadratic. That is, we expect the time required to grow proportional to the *square* of the size of the list.

The only reason we use item indexes in the above method is to obtain each element of the list successively. We can do this for a linked list without invoking the method get. For instance, the following linear method determines if a given object is on a *LinkedList*:

```
public int indexOf (Element element) {
    Node p = first;
    int pos = 0;
    while (p != null && !element.equals(p.element)) {
        p = p.next;
        pos = pos+1;
    }
    if (p == null)
        return -1;
    else
        return pos;
}
```

Of course, the above method uses private members of the class *LinkedList*. It could only be legally written within the definition of *LinkedList*. We'll see how to develop a more general solution to this problem in the next chapter, by means of objects called *iterators*.

DrJava: linked list access time

Open the file ListTest.java, located in exercise, in ch20, in nhText. The class contains two utility methods for building a *List<Integer>*. One adds elements at the front of the list (at index 0), the other adds to the rear of the list. It also contains a method that accesses each list element by index to determine if a particular element is on the list.

(1) Create two *LinkedList<Integer>* instances.

```
> import nhUtilities.containers.*;
> import ch20.exercise.*;
> List<Integer> l1 = new LinkedList<Integer>();
> List<Integer> l2 = new LinkedList<Integer>();
```

(2) Load one from the front and the other from the rear.

```
> ListTest.buildFromFront(l1,20000);
> ListTest.buildFromRear(l2,20000);
```

Do you notice a significant time difference in the two method executions? Can you explain why?

(3) Now search for an element using the method indexOf as implemented in *LinkedList*, and the method contains from *ListTest*.

```
> l1.indexOf(new Integer(-1))
> ListTest.contains(l1,new Integer(-1));
```

Again, you should notice a significant difference in the time required. Make sure that you understand why.

(4) Repeat the experiments with *BoundedList* and *DefaultList*.

✳ 20.5   Dynamic storage allocation

Though details are beyond the scope of this text, we briefly review issues of storage allocation and deallocation. Recall that memory space for method variables—parameters and local variables—is allocated when the method is invoked, and reclaimed ("deallocated") when the method completes. This is sometimes called *automatic* allocation and deallocation. Space for an object's instance variables is allocated when the object is created. This is sometimes called *dynamic* allocation.

In an array-based list implementation, memory space for the array elements is allocated when the array is created, that is, when the list object is created. In a linked implementation, space required for a node is allocated when the node is created, that is, whenever an item is added to the list. But when is this space deallocated?

The Java run-time system or interpreter implements a facility called *garbage collection*. Dynamically allocated space that can no longer be accessed is termed *garbage*. If we create an object and then lose all references to the object, the memory space occupied by the object becomes garbage. For instance, a node deleted from a linked list is garbage.

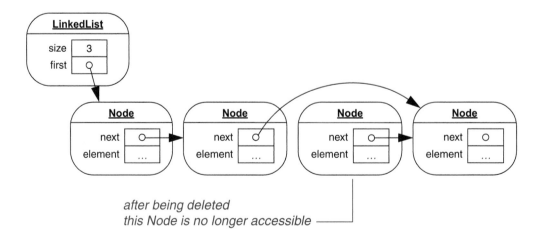

The run-time system continuously looks for garbage and reclaims the space—"collects the garbage." Of course there is some overhead involved, but this is generally not a problem unless we are writing an extremely time-critical, real-time application.

Many programming languages do not include garbage collection as part of their run-time systems. These languages require programs to *explicitly deallocate* dynamically allocated space. The problem with this is that it is often difficult to know when an object is no longer accessible and can be safely deallocated. Subtle errors can easily lead to some garbage not being recognized and reclaimed (sometime called a "memory leak"), or to space that is still accessible being mistakenly reclaimed as garbage. A reference to space that has been mistakenly reclaimed is called a *dangling reference*. Dangling references result in errors that are often extremely difficult to track down. The effect is that memory space still being used for an accessible object is reclaimed and used for something else. Thus two independent objects end up using the same memory space for unrelated purposes.

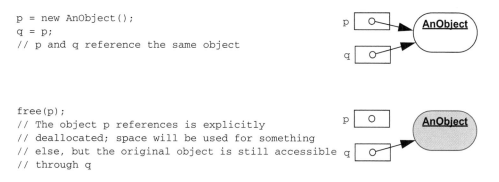

```
p = new AnObject();
q = p;
// p and q reference the same object
```

```
free(p);
// The object p references is explicitly
// deallocated; space will be used for something
// else, but the original object is still accessible
// through q
```

Figure 20.9 **A dangling reference.**

20.6 Summary

With linked structures, structural relationships between objects in a container are explicitly modeled by references between nodes that contain the objects. In this chapter, we saw several approaches to implementing lists with linked structures. In the simplest approach, each node contains an element of the list and references the node containing the next element. We noted that the addition of a header node simplifies the implementation by eliminating some of the special cases that must otherwise be handled explicitly.

We considered several variations including a doubly-linked circular list with header. In this structure, each node references both the preceding and the following node. The structure is circular: the header follows the last node in the list, and the last node in the list precedes the header.

One shortcoming of the linked list implementations we constructed is that get, remove, and add are all linear. In each case, we must start at the beginning of the list and traverse the list to locate the node with a particular index. This becomes a problem when we need to iteratively examine each element of a list. We will see how to overcome this difficulty in the next chapter.

Finally, we briefly considered dynamic storage allocation. In Java, the run-time system recognizes when an object is no longer accessible and reclaims the storage space used by that object. This mechanism is called garbage collection. In some programming languages, the application must explicitly free storage space that is no longer needed. This can lead to subtle errors in a program. On the one hand, space might become inaccessible without being explicitly freed; on the other, space might be freed which is still accessible.

SELF-STUDY EXERCISES

20.1   Trace the methods `remove` and `add` as implemented on page 823, verifying that `remove` correctly removes the last element from a list and `add` correctly adds the first element to a list.

20.2   What happens if the method `getNode` shown on page 820 is invoked with **this**.size as argument?

20.3   What happens if the method `getNode` shown on page 820 is invoked with an argument greater than **this**.size?

20.4   Implement the method `set` for the class *LinkedList<Element>*.

20.5   Implement the method `clear` that removes all elements of a list for the class *LinkedList<Element>*. This method should work directly, in constant time, and not simply invoke `remove` for each element.

20.6   Modify the method `getNode` of page 820 so that it works for a list with header as shown in Figure 20.4.

20.7   Using `getNode` from the previous exercise, implement `remove(`**int**`)` for a list with header as shown in Figure 20.4.

20.8   Look at the circular list structure shown in Figure 20.5. Suppose p is a variable referencing one of the *Nodes* on the list. How could you test whether p was referencing the last *Node* on the list?

20.9   Trace the method `add` for doubly linked lists, implemented on page 830. Verify that it works correctly when adding an element to the empty list.

20.10 Implement the method `clear` that removes all elements of a list for the class *DoublyLinkedList<Element>*. This method should work directly, in constant time, and not simply invoke `remove` for each element.

EXERCISES

20.1   Write a *LinkedList<Element>* method that will reverse a list by "reversing" the nodes. The method should not create any new nodes, and should not change the element a particular node contains.

20.2   Consider a *LinkedList<Element>* implementation in which the *LinkedList* object references the last element of the list, and each *Node* references the preceding *Node*, rather than the following *Node*. Implement the methods `add(Element)` and `remove(int)` for this structure.

20.3   Implement the method `add(Element)` for a circular list without header.

20.4   Implement methods `remove(int)` and `add(int,Element)` for the class *DoublyLinkedList<Element>*.

20.5   Define a linked implementation of the class *IntVector* described in Exercise 10.6.

The class is specified as follows.

> **public class** IntVector
> > A finite, possibly empty, sequence of integers.
>
> **public** IntVector ()
> > Create a new empty *IntVector*.
> >
> > **ensure:**
> > > this.isEmpty()
>
> **public boolean** isEmpty ()
> > This *IntVector* is empty.
>
> **public** IntVector prefix (**int** i)
> > A new *IntVector*, constructed by prefixing the specified int to this *IntVector*.
> >
> > **ensure:**
> > > !(this.prefix(i)).isEmpty()
>
> **public** int head ()
> > The first element of this *IntVector*.
> >
> > **require:**
> > > !this.isEmpty()
>
> **public** IntVector tail ()
> > An *IntVector* equal to this *IntVector* with the first element removed.
> >
> > **require:**
> > > !this.isEmpty()
>
> **public boolean** equals (Object obj)
> > The argument is an *IntVector*, and represents the same sequence of integers as this *IntVector*.

public String toString ()
A *String* representation of this *IntVector.*

20.6   Implement the *LinkedList<Element>* method

private Node find (Element element)

that returns the *Node* immediately before the first occurrence of the specified *Element*. If the specified *Element* is first on the list, or is not contained on the list, the method returns *null.*

Implement a version of the method find for linked lists with headers. If the specified *Element* is first on the list, the method returns the header.

20.7   Use the method find from Exercise 20.6 to implement the method

public void remove (Element element)

which removes the first occurrence of the specified *Element* from a list.

20.8   Implement the method

public void removeAll (Element element)

which removes all occurrences of the specified *Element* from a *LinkedList.*

20.9   Consider the abstraction *CircularList.* A *CircularList* is a finite collection of elements, one of which is designated the "current element." A *CircularList* has a feature get for accessing the current element, and a feature next for changing the current element to the "next" element in the list. If the *CircularList* has *n* elements, then performing next *n* times will iterate "current" through all elements, and leave the current element the same as when the process began. Note that there is no notion of "first" or "last" element.

A *CircularList* should also have features for adding and removing elements.

Write a complete specification for the class *CircularList.* Define two implementations, one based on an array and the other on a linked structure.

20.10 Consider a recursive list implementation as follows. The class *RecursiveList<Element>* has a *ListState* component, to which it forwards all service requests.

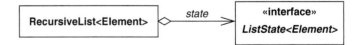

ListState<Element> is implemented by classes *EmptyList* and *NonEmptyList. EmptyList* has no components. *NonEmptyList* has components *head* and *tail: head* is the first element on the nonempty list; *tail* is the *ListState<Element>* denoting the "rest" of the list.

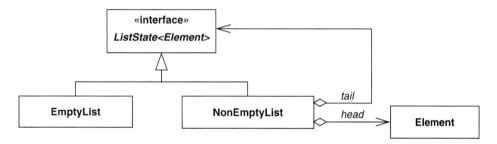

RecursiveList<Element> provides the following functionality, with the obvious semantics:

```
public boolean isEmpty ()
public int size ()
public Element get (int index)
public int indexOf (Element element)
public void add (Element element)
public void set (int index, Element element)
public void add (int index, Element element)
public void remove (int index)
```

As mentioned above, *RecursiveList* simply forwards all responsibility to its *state* component. For example, size is implemented as:

```
public int size () {
    return state.size();
}
```

The interface *ListState<Element>* specifies the following methods:

```
boolean isEmpty ()
int size ()
Element get (int index)
int indexOf (Element element)
void set (int index, Element element)
ListState<Element> add (int index, Element element)
ListState<Element> remove (int index)
```

The methods add and remove return a modified state.

The implementation of these methods for *EmptyList* is straightforward. For instance, size simply returns 0, while set throws an exception.

A *NonEmptyList* generally must decide whether to handle the request itself, or forward the request to its *tail*. For example, *NonEmptyList* might implement set as follows:

```
public void set (int index, Element element) {
    if (index == 0)
        head = element;
```

```
        else
            tail.set(index-1,element);
    }
```

Complete the implementation of *RecursiveList<Element>*.

Why would it not be a good idea to eliminate the class *RecursiveList*, and make *ListState* directly available to clients?

SELF-STUDY EXERCISE SOLUTIONS

20.1   remove executes the true branch of the if, and assigns null to `first`. `add` also executes the true branch of the if, and assigns null to `newNode.next`.

20.2   When `i` is `size-1`, p references the last *Node* and `p.next` is null. The next iteration assigns null to p. The loop terminates, and null is returned.

20.3   As in the previous question, p is eventually assigned null. But the loop does not terminate at this point. The next iteration attempts to access `p.next`, with p null. This causes a *NullPointerException* to be thrown.

20.4
```java
public void set (int index, Element element) {
    Node p = getNode(index);
    p.element = element;
}
```

20.5
```java
public void clear () {
    first = null;
    size = 0;
}
```

20.6
```java
/**
 * The i-th node of this LinkedList.
 * Returns the header if i is -1.
 * @require    -1 <= i && i < this.size()
 */
private Node getNode (int i) {
    Node p = first;
    int pos = -1;
    while (pos != i) {
        p = p.next;
        pos = pos + 1;
    }
    return p;
}
```

This will prove more useful than initializing p to `first.next` and initializing pos to 0.

20.7
```
public void remove (int index) {
    Node p = getNode(index-1);
    p.next = p.next.next;
    if (index == size-1)
        last = p;
    size = size - 1;
}
```

20.8
```
p.next == first
```

20.9 `last` will reference the header node, so that both the `next` and `previous` variables of the header will be set to reference the new *Node*.

20.10
```
public void clear () {
    header.next = header;
    header.previous = header;
    size = 0;
}
```

Iterators

In previous chapters, we have seen several list implementations, both link structured and array based. We noted that accessing the elements of a linked list by index does not always result in optimal code. We now introduce the notion of an *iterator*: an object that allows us to access the elements of a list efficiently regardless of its structure.

We conclude the chapter with a brief look at the standard Java library interface *Collection*, and some of its related classes.

Objectives

After studying this chapter you should understand the following:

- the role of iterators in container classes;
- various implementations of the *Iterator* interface;
- iterators as an abstraction of indexes in list operations;
- the notion of an internal iterator;
- the basic structure of the `java.util.Collection` hierarchy.

Also, you should be able to:

- use iterators in algorithms dealing with lists;
- define a class that provides a new implement of the *Iterator* interface.

21.1 Iterators

In the introduction to containers in Chapter 12, we included "performing some specific operation on each item in the container" as a basic container operation. We've subsequently seen many situations in which we need to access each element of a list. To this point, the only way we have of accessing each element of a list is by index. As noted in the previous chapter, accessing by index is fine for array-based implementations, but not entirely satisfactory for linked implementations. The reason is that `get(i)` is linear for linked implementations: to find the *i*-th element, the method starts at the beginning of the list and steps through the list. The result is that a loop like

```
for (int i = 0; i < list.size(); i = i+1)
    do something with list.get(i);
```

is quadratic: the number of steps required is proportional to the square of the length of the list.

Furthermore, we locate an element in a container so that we can do something with it: delete it, copy it, modify it, insert another element in front of it, *etc*. If we write

```
int i = list.indexOf(element);
list.remove(i);
```

both statements are linear for a linked implementation. In the first statement, we search the list sequentially to find the element. Then, having obtained its index, we invoke `list.remove(i)` which starts at the beginning of the list and counts through the list elements to locate the *i*-th element. This seems particularly pointless, since we're needlessly doing the same work twice.

(Both statements are linear for an array-based implementation as well, but for a different reason. The `remove` method is linear for an array-based implementation since elements need to be "shuffled" up in the array.)

The problems of examining each element of a container and of obtaining a "handle" on a particular container element are very general. The element's index is the only way we have, so far, for accessing a list element. But as we have seen, this is not always satisfactory.

An *iterator* is an object associated with a particular container that provides a means of sequentially accessing each element in the container. We specify the following interface for iterators.[1]

public interface Iterator<Element> **extends** Cloneable
    Iterator for accessing and traversing elements of a container.

public void reset ()
    Initialize this *Iterator* to reference the first element.

public void advance ()
    Advance this *Iterator* to the next element.
    require:
        !this.done()

public boolean done ()
    No more elements to traverse in the container.

public Element get ()
    Element this *Iterator* currently references.
    require:
        !this.done()

---

1. The package `nhUtilities.containers2` contains the classes described here. The standard package `java.util` includes a different interface also named *Iterator<E>*.

public boolean equals (Object obj)
> The specified *Object* is an *Iterator* of the same class as this, and references the same relative element of the same container.

public boolean traverses (Object container)
> This *Iterator* traverses the specified container.

public Object clone ()
> A copy of this *Iterator*.

public void setEqualTo (Iterator<Element> other)
> Set this *Iterator* to reference the same container element as the specified *Iterator*. Both *Iterators* must traverse the same container.
>
> **require:**
> ```
> this.traverses(container) implies
> other.traverses(container)
> ```
>
> **ensure:**
> ```
> this.equals(other)
> ```

Assuming that c is a container of some sort and i an iterator associated with it, we can access each element in the container as follows:

```
i.reset();
while (!i.done()) {
    do something with i.get();
    i.advance();
}
```

For instance, we can see if element is in the container:

```
i.reset();
while (!i.done() && !i.get().equals(element))
    i.advance();
```

If i.done() is true when this loop terminates, element is not in the container. If i.done() is false, the iterator i references element.

An **int** variable used to index a list is a simple form of iterator. It is reset by assigning it 0 and advanced by incrementing. It is done when it equals the length of the list.

Note that for two *Iterators* to be equal, they must reference the same relative element of the same container. This implies that equal *Iterators* remain equal if each is advanced. Suppose the same object appears more than once on a *List*, perhaps with indexes 3 and 5. An *Iterator* that references the element with index 3, would not be equal to an *Iterator* that references the element with index 5, even though the two *Iterators* in fact happen to reference the same object.

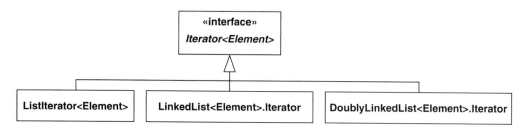

Figure 21.1   Iterator classes for *Lists.*

21.1.1 Iterator classes

If an iterator is to traverse a container efficiently, it must utilize the container's implementation. Thus we define an appropriate iterator class for each different list implementation.

The class *ListIterator* uses an **int** index value to reference a list element, and is adequate for array-based implementations. Classes *LinkedList* and *DoublyLinkedList* define their own iterators for traversing *LinkedList* and *DoublyLinkedList* structures respectively. These will be private inner classes, defined in the relevant list class

First look at the class *ListIterator<Element>*, given in Listing 21.1. A *ListIterator* is given a reference to the *List* it will traverse when it is created. The "current element" referenced by the iterator is represented simply as an integer index. Since indexing is efficient for arrays, we use this class to provide iterators for array-based implementations.

Listing 21.1   The class *ListIterator<Element>*

```
public class ListIterator<Element>
    implements Iterator<Element> {

    private int current; // index into theList
    private List<Element> theList;
            // the List this Iterator references

    /**
     * Create a new iterator for the specified List.
     */
    public ListIterator (List<Element> list) {
        theList = list;
        current = 0;
    }

    /**
     * Initialize this Iterator to reference the first
     * element.
     */
```

continued

Listing 21.1   **The class *ListIterator<Element>* (cont'd)**

```
public void reset () {
   current = 0;
}

/**
 * Advance this Iterator to next element.
 * @require    !this.done()
 */
public void advance () {
   current = current + 1;
}

/**
 * No more elements to traverse in the container.
 */
public boolean done () {
   return current >= theList.size();
}

/**
 * Container element this Iterator currently references.
 * @require    !this.done()
 */
public Element get () {
   return theList.get(current);
}

/**
 * The specified Object is an Iterator of the same class
 * as this, and references the same relative element of
 * the same container.
 */
public boolean equals (Object obj) {
   if (obj instanceof ListIterator<Element>) {
      ListIterator<Element> other =
         (ListIterator<Element>)obj;
      return this.current == other.current &&
             this.theList == other.theList;
   } else
      return false;
}
```

continued

Listing 21.1   The class *ListIterator<Element>* (cont'd)

```
/**
 * This Iterator traverses the specified container.
 */
public boolean traverses (Object container) {
   return container == theList;
}

/**
 * A copy of this Iterator.
 */
public Object clone () {
   try {
      return super.clone();
   } catch (CloneNotSupportedException e) {
      return null;
   }
}

/**
 * Set this Iterator to reference the same container
 * element as the specified Iterator. Both Iterators must
 * traverse the same container.
 * @require    this.traverses(container) implies
 *                    other.traverses(container)
 * @ensure     this.equals(other)
 */
public void setEqualTo (Iterator<Element> other) {
   this.current = ((ListIterator<Element>)other).current;
}
}
```

Advancing an integer index, though, is not an efficient way to traverse a *LinkedList*. It is preferable to keep a reference to a *Node*, which can be efficiently advanced to reference the next *Node* in the list. To do this, the iterator must have access to the implementation structure of the *LinkedList*. That is, it must be tightly coupled to the class *LinkedList<Element>*. As mentioned above, we define an iterator class for *LinkedList<Element>* as a private inner class. An iterator can then directly access the implementation structure both of the *LinkedList* and of the component *Nodes*. It simply keeps a reference to the *Node* containing the current element. The class is given in Listing 21.2.

A few points should be noted.

❶ The private inner class *Iterator* does not have a generic parameter. The containing class *LinkedList<Element>* is defined with the generic paramenter *Element*.

❷ Since the interface and the inner class have the same name, references to the interface *Iterator* must be fully qualified.

❸ The expression LinkedList.**this** refers to the *LinkedList* instance that the class is a memeber of. (See Section 10.5.3.) Since there is no name conflict, this line could have been written

```
current = first;
```

The syntax is required, however, at ❺.

❹ If the two *Iterators* reference the same *Node*, clearly they reference the same element of the same container.

Listing 21.2 **The *LinkedList<Element>* class *Iterator***

```
❶   private class Iterator
❷       implements nhUtilities.containers2.Iterator<Element> {

        private Node current;
        /**
         * Create a new Iterator for this LinkedList.
         */
        public Iterator () {
            reset();
        }

        /**
         * Initialize this Iterator to reference the first
         * element.
         */
        public void reset () {
❸           current = LinkedList.this.first;
        }

        /**
         * Advance this Iterator to next element.
         * @require    !this.done()
         */
        public void advance () {
            current = current.next;
        }
```

continued

Listing 21.2   The *LinkedList<Element>* class *Iterator* (cont'd)

```java
    /**
     * No more elements to traverse in the container.
     */
    public boolean done () {
        return current == null;
    }

    /**
     * Container element this Iterator currently references.
     * @require    !this.done()
     */
    public Element get () {
        return current.element;
    }

    /**
     * The specified Object is an Iterator of the same class
     * as this, and references the same relative element of
     * the same container.
     */
    public boolean equals (Object obj) {
        if (obj instanceof Iterator)
            return this.current == ((Iterator)obj).current;
        else
            return false;
    }

    /**
     * This Iterator traverses the specified container.
     */
    public boolean traverses (Object container) {
        return container == LinkedList.this;
    }

    /**
     * A copy of this Iterator.
     */
    public Object clone () {
        try {
            return super.clone();
        } catch (CloneNotSupportedException e) {
            return null;
        }
    }
```

❹

❺

continued

Listing 21.2   The *LinkedList<Element>* class *Iterator* (cont'd)

```
    /**
     * Set this Iterator to reference the same container
     * element as the specified Iterator. Both Iterators must
     * traverse the same container.
     * @require    this.traverses(container) implies
     *                     other.traverses(container)
     * @ensure     this.equals(other)
     */
    public void setEqualTo (
        nhUtilities.containers2.Iterator<Element> other) {
        this.current = ((Iterator)other).current;
    }
}
```

21.1.2 Creating an iterator

Since an iterator is tightly bound to the container it is traversing, we add functionality for creating an iterator to the interface *List<Element>*.

```
public interface List<Element>
    A finite list of Elements.

    public Iterator<Element> iterator ()
        Create a new Iterator for this List.
```

While the interface defines an abstract method for creating an object, the exact kind of object to be created is determined by the implementing subclass. For instance, the class *AbstractList<Element>* creates a *ListIterator<Element>*:

```
public abstract class AbstractList<Element> implements
    List<Element> {
    ...
    public Iterator<Element> iterator () {
        return new ListIterator<Element>(this);
    }
    ...
}
```

Since this is adequate for array-based implementations, classes like *DefaultList<Element>* need not override the implementation.

The class *LinkedList<Element>*, on the other hand, overrides the method and returns a *LinkedList<Element>.Iterator*:

```
public class LinkedList<Element> implements
    List<Element> {
    ...
    public nhUtilities.containers2.Iterator<Element>
        iterator () {
        return new Iterator();
    }
    ...
    private class Iterator implements
        nhUtilities.containers2.Iterator<Element> {
        ...
    }
}
```

This situation in which an abstract class or interface specifies a method for creating an object, while letting each implementing subclass determine an appropriate class to instantiate, is not uncommon. Such a method is sometimes called an *abstract constructor* or *factory method*.

To obtain an iterator for a *List<Element>*, a client invokes the *List<Element>* method iterator. The list object creates the appropriate kind of iterator, and returns it to the client. If the concrete object is a *LinkedList<Element>*, a *LinkedList<Element>.Iterator* is created and returned to the client. If the concrete object is a *DefaultList<Element>*, a *ListIterator<Element>* is created.

The iterator references the concrete list object, and has access to the underlying structure of the implementation. The client can use the iterator to traverse the list efficiently, without concern for the implementation structure.

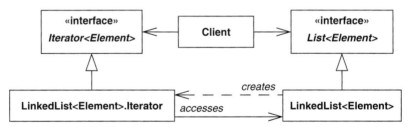

The events in creation and use of an iterator are summarized in the following interaction diagram.

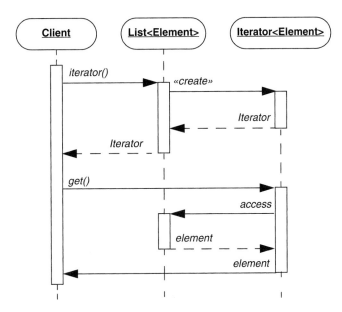

DrJava: list access with Iterators

Open the file `Exercise.java`, located in `exercise`, in `ch21`, in `nhText`. This class contains methods to construct a *LinkedList<Integer>* and a *DefaultList<Integer>*. It also contains methods to search a list by index and by iterator. Note that the file imports `nhUtilities.containers2`. This package defines lists with iterators, as described in this chapter.

1. Create a *DefaultList<Integer>* and a *LinkedList<Integer>* of reasonable size.

   ```
   > import nhUtilities.containers2.*;
   > import ch21.exercise.*;
   > List<Integer> def = Exercise.generateDefault(20000);
   > List<Integer> link = Exercise.generateLinked(20000);
   ```

2. Search each list by index and by iterator.

   ```
   > Exercise.contains1(def,new Integer(-1))
   > Exercise.contains2(def,new Integer(-1))
   > Exercise.contains1(link,new Integer(-1))
   > Exercise.contains2(link,new Integer(-1))
   ```

Which method takes the longest? Why?

21.2   *List<Element>* methods with iterators as arguments

We'd like to use iterators in much the same ways we've been using integer indexes. Like an index, an iterator identifies a particular element of a list. We'd like to be able to delete the element identified by an iterator, change it, insert an element in front of it, *etc.*

To do this, we overload the *List<Element>* methods that take index arguments with methods taking iterator arguments. In particular, we add the following methods to *List<Element>*.

public Element get (Iterator<Element> iterator)
The *Element* referenced by the specified *Iterator*.

require:
```
iterator.traverses(this)
!iterator.done()
```

public Iterator<Element> iteratorAt (Element element)
An *Iterator* referencing the first occurrence of the specified *Element* in this *List<Element>*; *Iterator<Element>* is done if this *List<Element>* does not contain the specified *Element*.

require:
```
element != null
```

ensure:
if element equals no element of this *List* then
    iteratorAt(element).done()
else
    element.equals(iteratorAt(element).get()),
    and iteratorAt(element) references the first position in
    a traversal for which this is true

public void add (
    Iterator<Element> iterator, Element element)
Insert the specified *Element* at the specified position. The *Iterator* will reference the newly added *Element*.

require:
```
iterator.traverses(this)
!iterator.done()
element != null
```

ensure:
```
this.size() == old.size() + 1
iterator.get().equals(element)
(iterator.advance(); iterator.get()).equals(
    old.iterator.get())
```

public void remove (Iterator<Element> iterator)
Remove the *Element* at the specified position. The *Iterator* will reference the *Element* following the removed *Element*. If no *Element* follows

the removed *Element* (*i.e.*, the removed *Element* was last in this *List*), `iterator.done()` is true.

require:

```
iterator.traverses(this)
!iterator.done()
```

ensure:

```
this.size() == old.size() - 1
if !iterator.done()
    iterator.get().equals(
        (old.iterator.advance();
        old.iterator.get()))
```

public void set (
    `Iterator<Element> iterator, Element element)`

Replace the element at the specified position with the specified *Element*.

require:

```
iterator.traverses(this)
!iterator.done()
element != null
```

ensure:

```
this.get(iterator).equals(element)
```

The final postconditions for `add` and `remove` indicate a sequence of method calls. The `add` postcondition

```
(iterator.advance(); iterator.get()).equals(
    old.iterator.get())
```

states that advancing the iterator followed by a `get` gives the same element `get` would have returned before the `add`. That is, the new element is added in front of the old current element, and the iterator references the new element. Note that this is the same behavior as that exhibited by an integer index.

The `remove` postcondition

```
iterator.get().equals((old.iterator.advance();
    old.iterator.get()))
```

indicates that the element referenced by the iterator after the `remove` is the one following the element that was removed.

The implementation of these methods is straightforward. The `get` operation can be forwarded to the *Iterator<Element>*:

```
public Element get (Iterator<Element> iterator) {
    assert iterator.traverses(this);
    return iterator.get();
}
```

Most other operations depend on the implementation structure, and are implemented in the concrete classes.

21.2.1 Improving *LinkedListIterator<Element>*

In Section 21.1.1, we defined a *LinkedList<Element>.Iterator* that referenced the "current" node of a *LinkedList<Element>*:

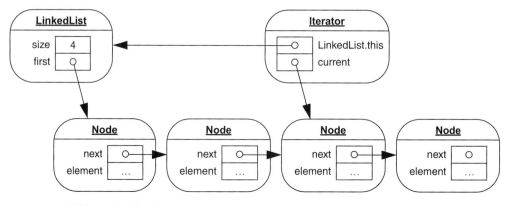

This works fine for `get` and `set`. But when we try to implement `remove` and `add`, we notice that we need a reference to the *Node preceding* the current *Node*. We are forced to traverse the list again to find the *Node* that we need.

This problem can be avoided in a number of ways. We could keep a pair of references in the iterator, one to the current *Node* and one to the preceding *Node*. Or we could just keep a reference to the *Node* preceding the current one. In either case, it will simplify things if a *LinkedList<Element>* has a header.

21.2.2 *Iterator* extensions

If we look at the implementation of the class *DoublyLinkedList<Element>*, we see that since each node contains both forward and backward pointing references, it is possible to move forward or backward through the list. This suggests that we extend the capabilities of iterators that traverse this class.

We can define an *Iterator<Element>* extension that permits forward and backward traversal of a list, and ensure that a *DoublyLinkedList<Element>* creates such an iterator:

public interface BiDirectionalIterator<Element>
    extends Iterator<Element>
        An *Iterator* that can move to previous as well as next element.
        offRight is *true* if the *Iterator* has been advanced past the last element, or if the container is empty. offLeft is *true* if the *Iterator* has been backed up past the first element, or if the container is empty.
        done is equivalent to offRight.

public boolean done ()
        This *Iterator* has been advanced past the last element, backed up past the first element, or the container is empty. Equivalent to offRight().

public boolean offRight ()

> This *Iterator* has been advanced past the last element, or the container is empty.

public boolean offLeft ()

> This *Iterator* has been backed up past the first element, or the container is empty.

public void advance ()

> Move this *Iterator* forward to the next element.
> If this.offLeft() and the container is not empty, move to the first element.
>
> **require**
>> !this.offRight()

public void backup ()

> Move this *Iterator* back to the previous element.
> If this.offRight() and the container is not empty, move to the last element.
>
> **require**
>> !this.offLeft()

public class DoublyLinkedList<Element>

> ...

public Iterator<Element> iterator ()

> Create a new *Iterator* for this *DoublyLinkedList*.
>
> **ensure:**
>> this.iterator() instanceof
>> *BiDirectionalIterator<Element>*.

Furthermore, the implementation of *DoublyLinkedList* is "circular," and allows easy traversal from the first element to the last, and from the last to the first. We could further extend *Iterator* for a *DoublyLinkedList* so that advancing from the last element leaves us at the first, and backing up from the first leaves us at the last. In designing such a circular iterator, we must be careful in specifying the behavior of offLeft and offRight. The precondition for get only requires that the list not be empty. We leave details to the reader.

21.2.3 Iterators and list modification

We now have two ways of modifying a list: by specifying an index and by using an *Iterator*. Furthermore, more than one *Iterator* can be traversing the same list. We must be explicit about how an *Iterator* behaves when the *List* it is traversing is modified.

Suppose an *Iterator* i is referencing a particular element of a *List<Element>* list, the element with index 2 for instance:

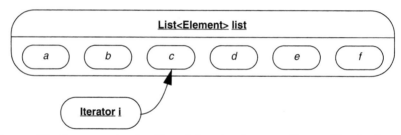

The specifications promise that if we delete the element referenced by the *Iterator*, the *Iterator* will reference the next element. That is, after

```
list.remove(i);
```

the *List* will look like this:

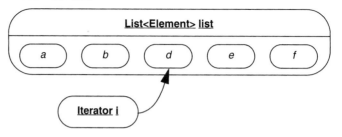

The specifications also promise that if we next do

```
list.add(i, x);
```

for some *Element* x, the *List* will be modified as shown:

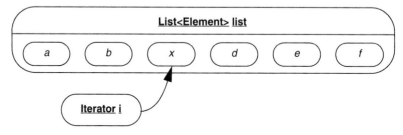

The question arises as to how an *Iterator* behaves if the *List* is modified by means of another *Iterator*, or by means of an index. For instance, suppose i and j are distinct *Iterator* instances referencing the same element:

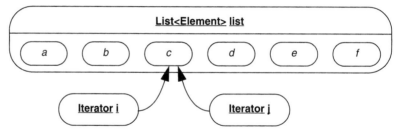

If we do

```
list.remove(j);
```

or

```
list.remove(2);
```

what will the state of i be? The specifications don't tell us. In fact, the result depends on the iterator implementation. If i is a *ListIterator* that keeps track of the referenced element by index, i will reference the (new) element with index 2: *d* in the above picture, after *c* is removed. On the other hand, if i is a *DoublyLinkedList<Element>.Iterator*, i will continue to reference the removed node containing *c*.

We could build *Iterators* that are *Observers* of an *Observable List*. The *Iterators* register with the *List*, and the *List* informs all its *Iterators* whenever it is structurally modified. In this case, the specifications could clearly promise how the *Iterators* behave in the event of *List* modification.

Rather than add this additional structure, we simply assume that if a *List* is modified by index, all *Iterators* that reference the *List* become invalid. Furthermore, if a *List* is modified by an *Iterator*, all other *Iterators* that reference the *List* become invalid. Specifically, we specify:

Except when an *Iterator*'s behavior is explicitly defined, an *Iterator* becomes undefined when the *List* is modified by add or remove.

This may seem a very limiting assumption—in particular, it appears to make method verification difficult, since we generally can't account for all the possible objects that might be referencing a given object. In practice, iterators typically have very local scope and short lifetimes, so the assumption does not present serious practical problems.

We might decide to add methods to the class *List<Element>* that take several *Iterators* as arguments. For instance, we could define a method that deletes all the elements between two given *Iterators*:

```
public void remove (
    Iterator<Element> i1, Iterator<Element> i2)
```
> Delete all the elements of this *List* from the element specified by the first *Iterator* through the element specified by the second, inclusive.

In such a case, the method postconditions would describe the state of the *Iterators* after the method is executed.

✳ 21.2.4 Internal iterators: *forEachDo*

With the iterator mechanism we have defined, a client is responsible for controlling the iteration. That is, a client obtains an iterator for a list and explicitly steps the iterator through the list. There is another flavor of iterator, sometimes called an *internal* or *passive* iterator, that shifts this responsibility from the client to the iterator. Using a passive iterator, a client provides an operation and the iterator applies the operation to each element of the container.

At this point we could develop a collection of interfaces and classes to implement the notion of internal iterator. But justifying the reasonableness of such structures would require a substantial number of examples illustrating a distinctive programming style. As an alternative, we simple show how to add a `forEachDo` method to the *List* interface.

Recall that in Section 12.1, we included "performing some specific operation on each item in the container" as one of the basic container operations. But we have no method in the class *List* for accomplishing list. We consider adding such a method:

```
public interface List<Element> {
    ...
    /**
     * Perform the specified Operation on each element
     * of this List.
     */
    public void forEachDo ( ... );
    ...
```

The operation to be performed should clearly be provided as a method argument, and so must be encapsulated in an object, in much the same way as we encapsulated orderings in Section 14.2.4. We define an interface to model an operation:

public interface Operation<Element>
> An operation that can be performed on an *Element*.

public void execute (Element element)
> The operation.

The method `forEachDo` has an *Operation* parameter:

```
/**
 * Perform the specified Operation on each element
 * of this List.
 */
public void forEachDo (Operation<Element> operation);
```

The method can be implemented in *AbstractList<Element>* using an *Iterator*:

```
public void forEachDo (Operation<Element> operation) {
    Iterator<Element> iterator = this.iterator();
    iterator.reset();
    while (!iterator.done()) {
        operator.execute(iterator.get());
        iterator.advance();
    }
}
```

For example, suppose `roll` is a *List<Student>* and we want to add ten points to each *Student*'s grade. We might write:

```
roll.forEachDo(
    new Operation<Student> () {
        public void execute(Student element) {
            element.setGrade(element.getGrade() + 10);
        }
    });
```

The method as we have written it is somewhat limited. It allows us only to perform an operation on each list element. It does not, for example, allow us to replace elements. Furthermore, we often want to query the list for some value that requires querying each element. For example, we might want the highest grade or average grade from a list of *Students*. The method we have written does not lend itself to such tasks.

One difficulty with a list transaction that is a query is that there must be some way of accumulating "intermediate" results. For instance, if we need the average grade of a list of *Students*, we must be able to incrementally accumulate a sum. Handling such problems requires substantially more structure than we are prepared to consider here.

21.3   Comparing implementations

We summarize the time required by features of array-based and linked *List<Element>* implementations in the following table.

Table 21.1   **Complexity of *List* features**

feature	array-based	linked
get(**int**)	constant	linear
get(Iterator)	constant	constant
indexOf(Element)	linear	linear
iteratorAt(Element)	linear	linear
add(Element)	constant	constant
add(**int**, Element)	linear	linear
add(Iterator, Element)	linear	constant
remove(**int**)	linear	linear
remove(Iterator)	linear	constant
set(**int**, Element)	constant	linear
set(Iterator, Element)	constant	constant

21.4   The java.util *Collection<Element>* hierarchy

The standard Java package `java.util` defines a set of interfaces and classes rooted at the interface *Collection<Element>*, and referred to as the *collection hierarchy*. This hierarchy contains a number of members closely related to the classes and interfaces described in this chapter. While a detailed presentation is beyond the scope of this text, we briefly introduce some of the fundamental members. This library has been available since the release of the Java version 1.2, and has been retrofitted for type parameters in version 5.0. For simplicity of notation, we refer to the interfaces and classes of this generic library without explicit use of the type parameter *<Element>*.

The interface *Collection* models a rather generalized container. Some *Collections* allow duplicate elements, while others do not. Some *Collections* impose an ordering on the elements; some are unordered. Principal methods specified by the interface include:

> **public boolean** contains (Element e)
> > This collection contains the specified element.

> **pubic boolean** isEmpty()
> > This collection contains no elements.

> **public int** size ()
> > The number of elements in this collection.

> **public** java.util.Iterator iterator()
> > An iterator over the elements in this collection.

Operations to add and remove elements are "optional." An implementing class can choose to support them or not. For instance, the method `add` is specified as follows:

> **public boolean** add (Element element) **throws**
> > UnsupportedOperationException,
> > ClassCastException,
> > IllegalArgumentException

Note that the method returns a **boolean**. It returns *true* if the specified element is successfully added to the *Collection*, and returns *false* if the element is already in the *Collection* and the *Collection* does not allow duplicates. That is, the **boolean** result indicates whether or not the *Collection* has changed state as a result of the operation.

If the operation `add` is not supported by the implementing class, an *UnsupportedOperationException* is thrown. A *Collection* client cannot, therefore, assume that method `add` is available for a *Collection*—which may cause the reader to wonder why it is specified here.

The method `add` can also throw a *ClassCastException* or *IllegalArgumentException*. This warns a *Collection* client that a specific implementing class may not be willing to add an arbitrary *element*. If the class of the argument prevents it from being added to the *Collection*, a *ClassCastException* is thrown. If any aspect of the element other than its class prevents it from being added to the *Collection*, an *IllegalArgumentException* is thrown.

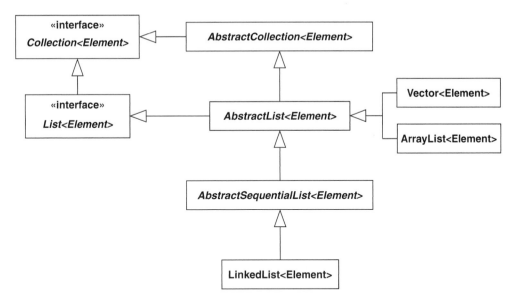

Figure 21.2 **Lineage of *java.util.LinkedList*, *java.util.ArrayList*, and *java.util.Vector*.**

In `java.util`, *List* is an interface that extends *Collection*. This interface models a sequential collection in which elements can be accessed by index. The interface *List* specifies, for example, the familiar method `get`:

>**public** Element get (**int** index)
>
>The element at the specified position in this *List*.

A *List* can contain duplicate elements, but operations to add and remove elements are still specified as optional. The interface *java.util.Set*, on the other hand, extends *Collection* and specifies a *Collection* that does not contain duplicate elements.

Corresponding to the interfaces *Collection*, *List*, and *Set* are abstract classes *Abstract-Collection*, *AbstractList*, and *AbstractSet*. These classes provide skeletal implementations of the interfaces. *AbstractList*, for instance, extends *AbstractCollection* and implements *List*.

Concrete implementation classes typically extend these abstract classes. Array-based list implementations such as *java.util.ArrayList* and *java.util.Vector* extend *AbstractList* directly. Linked implementations, such as *java.util.LinkedList*, extend the abstract class *AbstractSequentialList*, which extends *AbstractList*. Like *Vector*, *ArrayList* replaces its array component with a larger one when necessary. *LinkedList* is implemented as a doubly-linked list.

Iterators

The `java.util` interface *Iterator<Element>* specifies three methods:

>**public boolean** hasNext ()
>
>The iteration has more elements.next

```
public Element next () throws NoSuchElementException
```
The next element in the iteration. Throws *NoSuchElementException* if `hasNext()` is *false*.

```
public void remove () throws
   UnsupportedOperationException,
   IllegalStateException
```
Removes from the underlying collection the last element returned by the iterator (optional operation). This method can be called only once per call to `next`.

The query `hasNext` is essentially the converse of our *Iterator* method `done`. Note that the method `next` is not a proper query since it changes the state of the iterator. We could implement `next` by accessing the current element and then advancing the iterator:

```
public Element next () {
   Element temp = this.get();
   this.advance();
   return temp;
}
```

The `java.util` interface *ListIterator<Element>* extends *Iterator<Element>*. Using a *ListIterator*, it is possible to traverse a list in either direction, and modify the list during iteration. It includes a method `previous` that serves as a companion to `next`, and optional methods for adding, removing, and setting list elements.

✳ 21.4.1 Implementing *for each*

The "for each" variant of the for statement was introduced in Section 12.6. Recall that the format is

```
for (type identifier : container)
   bodyStatement
```

where *type* is the type of the container elements. The body of the loop is executed for each container element, with the variable named by the identifier referencing a different container element on each iteration. For instance, if `names` is a *List<String>*, the following will write each *String* on the list to standard output:

```
for (String name : names)
   System.out.println(name);
```

The container specified in the statement must either be an array or must implement or extend the interface *java.lang.Iterable*. This interface specifies only a single method:

```
public interface Iterable<Type>
```
Implementing this interface allows an object to be the target of a "for each" statement.

```
public java.util.Iterator<Type> iterator()
```
An iterator over a collection of elements of type *Type*.

The implementation of the for statement shown above is effectively the following.

```
Iterator<type> iterator = container.iterator();
while (iterator.hasNext()) {
    type identifier = iterator.next();
    bodyStatement;
}
```

21.5 Summary

Providing both array-based and linked implementations for *List* raises the question of method performance. While elements in an array-based implementation can be accessed by index in constant time, accessing an element of a linked implementation by index requires linear time. Thus simple operations that iterate through each *List* element become quadratic for linked implementations when elements are accessed by index. Abstracting the notion of index, we introduced iterators. Iterators allow us to iterate through each element of a *List* in linear time, regardless of the implementing structure. The iterator abstraction provides the operations for traversing a *List* while examining each *List* element in turn. The structure of each *List* implementation dictates the algorithms used to traverse it; thus iterator implementations are tightly coupled to the structure they traverse. Having noted this, we provide each implementation with an inner class that implements an appropriate iterator. The client of the *List* abstraction is provided with a factory method to create iterators suitable for a chosen implementation.

List operations that take an index can be overloaded with operations that take *Iterator* instances, providing a richer *List* abstraction. Care must be taken in specifying *Iterator* behavior with regard to *List* modification. We chose to mimic the behavior of indexes as closely as possible. For instance, deleting an element with a given index "moves" the next element of the *List* up to that index position. We similarly define deletion with an iterator: after the deletion, the iterator references the "next" *List* element.

We must also be careful when modifying a *List* referenced by an *Iterator* by a means other than with the *Iterator*. For instance, if we delete a *List* element by index, we assume that any *Iterators* referencing the *List* become invalid.

Iterators give rise to the internal iterator abstraction, where the implementor is in full control of the traversal. As an example, we defined a *List* method `forEachDo` that performed an operation provided as an argument on each element of the *List*.

We concluded the chapter with a short tour of the *Collection<Element>* interfaces and abstractions found in the standard Java package `java.util`. The *Collection* interface provides a very rich abstraction with several implementations. *List* is an interface that extends *Collection* and models a sequential collection in which elements can be accessed by index. The package `java.util` also provides iterators for *Collections*.

SELF-STUDY EXERCISES

21.1   Write a method that counts the number of negative values in a *List<Integer>* using an *Iterator*.

21.2   Look at the definition of *ListIterator* in Listing 21.1. Suppose two *ListIterators* reference the same element of the same *DefaultList*:

```
DefaultList<Integer> list = ...;
Iterator<Integer> i1 = list.iterator();
Iterator<Integer> i2 = list.iterator();
```

An element is added to the list using i1:

```
list.add(i1, new Integer(1));
```

Will i2 equal i1 after the add operation? Which element will i1 reference? Which element will i2 reference?

21.3   Suppose the class *Iterator.LinkedList<Element>* is implemented as shown in Listing 21.2. As in the previous exercise, two *Iterators* reference the same element in the same *LinkedList*, and an element is added to the list using i1:

```
LinkedList<Integer> list = ...;
Iterator<Integer> i1 = list.iterator();
Iterator<Integer> i2 = list.iterator();
list.add(i1, new Integer(1));
```

Will i2 equal i1 after the add operation? Which element will i1 reference? Which element will i2 reference?

21.4   Suppose that, as suggested in Section 21.2.1, a *LinkedList<Element>.Iterator* keeps a reference to the *Node* preceding the *Node* containing the current *Element* in the variable current, rather than a reference to the *Node* containing the current *Element*. Assume that a *LinkedList* has a header. Implement the *Iterator* method get for this structure.

21.5   Assuming the structure of the previous exercise, write the *LinkedList* method add(Iterator, Element).

21.6   Using the structure described in Exercise 21.4, answer the question of Exercise 21.3.

21.7   Suppose that, as suggested in Section 21.2.1, a *LinkedList<Element>.Iterator* keeps a references to both the *Node* containing the current *Element* and the *Node* preceding the current *Element*. Assume that a LinkedList has a header. Under these assumptions, answer the question of Exercise 21.3.

21.8   Using an *Iterator*, write a method that will remove all the negative values from a *List<Integer>*.

EXERCISES

21.1 Rewrite the bubble sort and selection sort of Chapter 14 using iterators.

21.2 Using *BiDirectionalIterators*, write a method that reverses a *DoublyLinkedList*. Don't create a new *List*.

21.3 Implement the merge operation, described in Exercise 14.4, using iterators.

21.4 Write a method `concatenate` that takes two *List<Element>*'s as arguments and returns a new *List<Element>* in which the elements of the second *List* appear after the elements of the first *List*.

21.5 Implement the class *DoublyLinkedList<Element>.Iterator*.

21.6 A *List<Element>* is a *palindrome* if it appears to be the same when traversed in either direction. Using a *BiDirectionalIterator*, write a method that determines whether or not a *DoublyLinkedList* is a palindrome.

21.7 Extend the interface *Iterator<Element>* by defining operations for removing, adding, and setting the underlying container directly with the *Iterator*.

21.8 A *RobustIterator<Element>* *observes* the *List* it is referencing, and maintains a well-defined state when the *List* is modified.

Specify reasonable behavior for a *RobustIterator* when the *List* is modified by an `add` or `remove`.

When the *List* is modified, it must notify observers of the modifying operation (`add` or `remove`) and of the index or *Iterator* used in the modification. A *RobustIterator* must remember the index of the element it is referencing. For some *List* implementation, modify the implementation and the iterator to provide *RobustIterators*.

SELF-STUDY EXERCISE SOLUTIONS

21.1
```java
public static int negativeCount (List<Integer> list) {
    int count = 0;
    Iterator<Integer> i = list.iterator();
    i.reset();
    while (!i.done()) {
        if (i.get().intValue() < 0)
            count = count + 1;
        i.advance();
    }
    return count;
}
```

21.2 Since *ListIterators* identify an element by index, both `i1` and `i2` will reference the newly added 0-th element.

21.3   The *Iterators* each contain a reference to the "current" *Node*. After adding, i1 will reference the newly added *Node*, while i2 will reference the *Node* that was previously first. They will not be equal.

21.4
```
public Element get () {
    return current.next.element;
}
```

21.5
```
public void add (
    Iterator<Element> iterator, Element element) {
    Iterator i = (Iterator)iterator;
    Node newNode = new Node(element);
    newNode.next = i.current.next;
    i.current.next = newNode;
}
```

21.6   After the add, both *Iterators* will contain references to the *Node* preceding the newly added *Node*. They will be equal.

21.7   After the add, i2 will be inconsistent. It will contain two references to *Nodes* that should follow each other on the list. But the *Nodes* will no longer follow each other. A new *Node* will have been inserted in between.

21.8
```
public static void removeNegatives (List<Integer> list) {
    Iterator<Integer> i = list.iterator();
    i.reset();
    while (!i.done()) {
        if (i.get().intValue() < 0)
            list.remove(i);
        i.advance();
    }
    return count;
}
```

SUPPLEMENT A   Systems and software

In order to understand the computation described by a program, we need a model of the underlying computing system on which our software will run. In this section, we sketch a simple operational model of a computing system; in the next section we describe some software tools essential for system development.

a.1   A model of a computer system

We view a computer system as composed of four functional components: input/output, processor, memory, and file system.

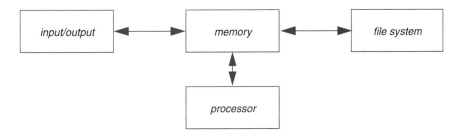

Figure a.1 **Simple model of a computer system.**

Input/output

Input and *output devices* are the means by which the system communicates with the outside world. There are many possible ways for a system to interact with users and other devices. A system intended for use by a person typically has at least a keyboard and mouse for input and a monitor for output. A system used to control some other device, such as an antilock braking system controlling brakes on a vehicle, may have only simple environmental sensors for input and control signals to the other device for output. Other common input devices include cameras, microphones, digitizing pads, *etc.* Output devices include speakers, printers, and so on.

Processor

The *processor* is the component of the system that actually performs the actions of a computation. A processor has a set of actions that it can perform, a set of instructions it can carry out. This set of instructions is called the *instruction set* or the *machine language* of the processor. These instructions are generally very simple: "add two numbers," for example. The power of the processor comes from the fact that it can perform millions of these very simple instructions each second.

The instructions for a processor are encoded as sequences of *bits*, that is, sequences of *binary digits*, zeros and ones. For example, the instructions for Sun Microsystems' SPARC processor are sequences of 32 bits. Each action the processor can perform has its own unique representation as a string of 32 zeros and ones. These bit strings are what the processor actually understands.

Note that different kinds of processors have very different instruction sets. Instructions for Intel's Pentium processor, for instance, bear little resemblance to those for a SPARC processor. The SPARC instruction for, say, adding two numbers looks quite different from a Pentium instruction. It would be senseless to give a Pentium processor instructions coded for a SPARC processor, or *vice versa*.

Memory

The *memory*, sometimes called the store, main memory, or RAM, is where the data and algorithm the system is currently using reside. The algorithm is expressed in machine language, in terms of the instruction set of the processor. The processor can understand nothing else. The data must also be encoded as sequences of bits so that it can be stored in the system's memory.

Different kinds of data are encoded using different encoding schemes. But while there is considerable difference in the instruction sets of different machines, there is substantial uniformity in the manner in which data is encoded. Textual data—the letters, digits, punctuation marks that you key from a keyboard and are displayed on your monitor screen—are often represented as eight-bit sequences using the ASCII (American Standard Code for Information Interchange) code. That is, each character is assigned a unique eight-bit sequence: the letter *A*, for example, is represented by the sequence 01000001. When you key an uppercase letter *A* on the keyboard, this sequence of bits is sent to processor and stored in memory. It's also what gets sent as output to the monitor and displayed on the screen as the letter *A*. Numbers that are to be used in arithmetic operations are stored in a different way. Details are beyond the scope of this discussion.

The memory is divided into a number of fixed size (typically eight bit) storage locations. Each location has a unique numeric *address* associated with it. The processor is able to access a data value or instruction stored in memory by knowing its address and its size. The processor repeatedly fetches instructions of the algorithm from memory, decodes and performs them. If we took a snapshot of the system, we would see the data values and algorithm stored in memory. Two successive snapshots might look something like what is shown in Figure a.2. (Of course, everything would actually be encoded as bit sequences.) The figure shows a data value (the number 17) stored in the location with address 100. An instruction, which we assume to be 32 bits long, is stored in (four) locations 500 through 503. The processor knows the location and size of the next instruction it is to execute. The processor simply reads the 32-bit instruction from memory, and performs the action specified. Usually instructions are simply fetched one after the other from memory. So if one 32-bit instruction were located at address 500, the next one would be at location 504.

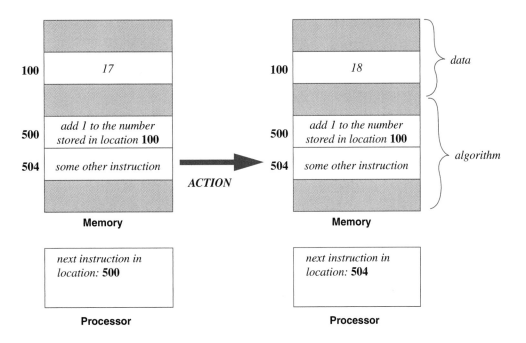

Figure a.2 **Successive snapshots of a machine.**

As the processor successively executes the instructions of the algorithm, the data values stored in memory are changed. The algorithm, however, remains fixed during the computation.

File system

The *file system*, sometimes called secondary storage, is similar to the memory in that it stores data values and algorithms. However, while the contents of the memory are volatile and change constantly—the memory contains the data and algorithm the system is using *at the moment*—the contents of the file system are relatively stable. Algorithms and data remain in the file system whether the system is operational or not. To use a student records system as an example, if the machine is in the process of producing a transcript for a particular student, data relevant to that student and the algorithm for producing a transcript are in memory. Data for other students, and algorithms for other functions, remain in the file system.

The file system is organized into a collection of *named files*, in which data and algorithms are stored. A file might contain a program expressed in the processor's machine language, data for a program, results from running a program, text such as this book chapter, *etc.* Exactly what a file name looks like depends on the particular computer system we are using. In general, though, one tries to give a file a name that is descriptive of its contents. For example, the file containing the text of the first chapter of this text is named *Chapter1.fm*. (The software used to create and format the text is called FrameMaker. The suffix "*.fm*" gives a clue that the file is intended to be used with this software.) File systems are generally implemented on magnetic disks.

Network

Finally, we conclude by hooking our computer to a *network*. We can view a network simply as a wire to which a number of computers and other devices are connected, permitting them to communicate with each other and share resources. (If we want to, we can view the network connection simply as a special input/output device.)

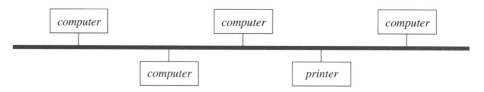

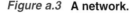
Figure a.3 **A network.**

The description of a computer system we have given is, admittedly, rather abstract. Though we have ignored many details in this sketch, it should provide an adequate model for understanding program execution.

a.2   Software tools

Operating systems

The basic hardware computer, as described in the previous section, is a rather tiresome beast. To make it usable, software called an *operating system* is almost always included as part of the system. Examples of operating systems include MS-DOS, Windows XP, and various flavors of UNIX such as Solaris, Linux, Mac OS X, and HP-UX. The operating system is the fundamental hardware-resource management software. Some portion of the operating system is always resident in the computer's memory. It performs functions such as verifying user name and password on a multiuser system, deciding exactly where in memory a program will be loaded, loading programs from disk into the machine's memory and starting their execution, managing the file system by allocating and freeing disk space for files. When a program needs to read data from or write data to an i/o device or the file system, the program actually makes a request of the operating system. The operating system handles all the low level details of moving the data between memory and the device or the disk. In some cases, the operating system is also responsible for managing the graphical user interface or windowing system through which the user interacts with the system. In other cases, the windowing system is a separate software component, independent of the operating system.

Programming languages

The data descriptions and algorithms that define a software system must at some point be expressed in a formal notation called a *programming language*. Unlike the machine languages discussed in the previous section, programming languages are intended to be written and read by people. They are designed to assist a programmer in structuring and building a problem solution in a natural way. That is, they are intended to be "problem oriented" rather than "machine oriented": the problem solution can be expressed in terms appropriate to the problem rather than in terms specific to some computing system. If we are developing a student record system, for instance, the programming language should allow us to write in terms of students and courses rather than in terms of bits and bytes. Programming languages are independent of the peculiarities of any particular processor or computing system.

Programming languages are defined in terms of a *syntax* and *semantics*. The syntax is the set of grammatical and punctuation rules for the language. The syntactic rules tell us how to write legal constructs. The semantics of the language is the set of rules that specify the meaning of syntactically legal constructs. A programming language is much more rigorous in both syntax and semantics than a natural language like English. Whether we punctuate an English sentence with a comma or semicolon isn't likely to affect its understandability. In a programming language, however, using a comma rather than a semicolon may make a construct invalid or completely change its meaning. Furthermore, most sentences in English have some degree of ambiguity: different readers construe slightly (or in some cases, seriously) different meanings from the same sentence. In a programming language, a construct has one unique meaning. This necessity for absolute precision is sometimes difficult for beginning programmers to grasp.

Many program languages have been designed and implemented during the past forty or so years. We use Sun Microsystems' Java™ language in this text.

Editors

Using the notation provided by the language, the programmer defines the data and algorithms appropriate for solving the problem. An essential tool for this activity is a *text editor*, a program which allows the user to create and modify text files in the computer's file system. If we're lucky, our editor is *language sensitive*. This means the editor has some understanding of the syntax of the language we're using, and can help by providing templates for common constructs, immediately identifying syntactic errors, and so on. Text files that contain data descriptions and algorithms expressed in a programming language are called *source files*. The text that makes up a program is often simply referred to as *code*.

Translators

It is all well and good to express our solution in a readable programming language. The difficulty is that the machine that is actually going to solve the problem doesn't understand our programming language: it only understands its own machine language. What to do? We need to *translate* our program from the *programming language* into something the machine we're going to run the program on can understand. A program that performs this translation is called a *compiler*. A compiler reads our source file as input and produces a version of the program translated into something more like machine language.

There are a number of different approaches that can be taken in this translation process. In the most straightforward approach, called compilation and linking, the program is translated into the actual machine language of the computer on which it's to be run. This is usually done in several steps, to make it easier to combine several modules, perhaps written at different times in different programming languages, into a single machine language program.

The language we use in this text is Java. The first implementations of this language were *interpreted*. In this approach, rather than producing a machine language version of the program, the compiler translates the program into a *machine independent* intermediate language, called "byte-code" in a Java implementation. The Java byte-code "language" consists of low-level instructions, similar to machine language. However, the language is not tied to the architecture of any particular type of machine. Another program called an *interpreter* reads and executes the program after it has been translated into this intermediate language. Figure a.4 shows a Java program being compiled on a SPARC workstation, and Figure a.5 shows the program being interpreted on a Pentium PC.

Figure a.4 **Translation to an intermediate language.**

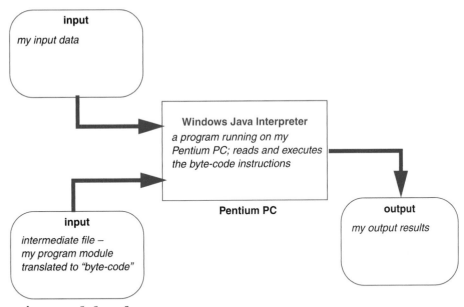

my_java_module.class

Figure a.5 **Interpretation.**

Note that with compilation and linking, a program is translated to the machine language of the computer on which it is to run. When the program is run, the machine language translation is loaded into the computer's memory and executed. With an interpreted implementation, as shown in Figure a.5, when a program is run, the *interpreter* is loaded into the computer's memory and executed. The interpreter reads and executes the byte-code one step at a time. The principal disadvantage of an interpreter is efficiency. It is not surprising to find that an interpreted program runs 10 to 20 times slower than a similar compiled and linked program.

The reason that Java was initially implemented this way is that Java programs are intended to be executed across a network. That is, a program can be written, compiled, and reside on one machine and be executed on a completely different kind of machine. Since there is no way of telling when a program is compiled what kind of machine will ultimately execute the program, it is not possible to translate the program into a specific machine language.

> **compiler:** a program that translates programs written in a specific programming language into a language more like machine language.

There are other hybrid approaches, called "Just in Time (JIT) compilers," in which the "interpreter" translates the byte-code into machine language as it executes it. This provides the advantages of an interpreter, but with a less severe efficiency penalty. Details are well beyond our present discussion.

SUPPLEMENT B   Programming errors

b.1   Errors in the programming process

In this section, we briefly consider the kinds of errors that can arise in the programming process. On one hand, we tend to think of computers as extremely reliable systems. We even tend to attribute a degree of infallibility to computer produced output. (If your check-book balance doesn't agree with your bank statement, where do you assume the error lies?) On the other hand, we've all heard stories of credit cards and million dollar water bills addressed to the family pet. The culprit in these cases is usually identified as "the computer." This dichotomy is not entirely surprising. A computer can perform millions of additions in a second flawlessly. But the systems we build are so incredibly complex that it is almost inconceivable that they are completely correct.

We should, at this point, distinguish between *errors* and *failures*. An *error* is a mistake on the part of a system designer, programmer, or user that prevents a system from functioning properly. A *failure* is the inability of a system or system component to perform its intended function. If you forget to replace the oil pan drain plug when changing your car's oil, you have made an error. When the engine seizes because of a lack of oil pressure, the system has failed. Simply put, errors cause failures. Of course, a system failure might not be directly attributable to an error on the part of the user, designer, or builder. Your car's oil pump may break, for instance, even though it is well-designed, properly built, and you have meticulously and accurately followed the maintenance schedule.

Computer systems fail to function as expected because of *conceptual errors*, *data errors*, *hardware failures*, and *software errors*. A conceptual error is a misunderstanding on the part of the user of the function of the system or of how to use the system. The result can hardly be considered a system failure. Even a completely correct, flawlessly designed system can fail to meet a user's expectations if the user expects the wrong thing. (This is not quite as trivial as it may seem; probably more dissatisfaction with computing systems arises from conceptual errors than any other cause.)

Data errors are obvious: if the price for a can of beans is incorrectly entered into my grocer's data base, my bill won't be correct when I buy beans. We might expect the software to detect gross errors—if the price of beans were entered as $59 per can rather than $0.59. But if the correctness of the data could be completely determined by the software, there would be no need to enter the data at all.

Though there have been a few very well-publicized exceptions, hardware components are very carefully designed to ensure their correct functioning. Hardware components are usually considerably simpler in design than large software systems, and the quantity in which they are produced justifies the expense of rigorously verifying design correctness. Hardware can, of course, fail during use. Fortunately such failures are usually easy to detect: rather than producing incorrect results, the system simply doesn't function at all.

As system designer, we are concerned primarily with software errors. The simplest errors to deal with are *syntactic errors*, sometimes called *compilation errors*. A syntactic error occurs when what we write is not legal in the programming language we are using. We use a comma where a period is required for instance, or misspell the word "begin" as "beign." Though syntactic errors often cause us aggravation when we're first leaning a new programming language, they're easy to detect: the compiler (or even the editor) will point them out. Now we might need to be a bit ingenious to understand what the compiler tells us. The compiler will know what we've entered is not legal, but may not know exactly why. We can't expect the compiler to understand our intentions, after all. Nevertheless, there's never any danger of someone using a syntactically incorrect program: it won't compile much less run.

Since syntactic errors are easy to detect, programming languages are designed so that some key aspects of a program's correctness are built into the language syntax. For instance, a common programming error is attempting to perform an inappropriate operation on a data value. Suppose you're mixing pastry dough, and I hand you a jar of powdered sugar. If you mistakenly use it as flour, the resulting product is not likely to be satisfactory. You've performed the "add three cups of flour" operation, an inappropriate operation to perform with the sugar jar. The *type structure* of the language is intended to allow the compiler to detect this kind of error. For instance if a variable is typed as **boolean**, then the operations that can be performed on the variable's value are known at compile time. An attempt to add one to the value of the variable will be detected as an error by the compiler.

Of course a software component can be syntactically correct, that is, legal in the programming language, and still not do what it's supposed to do. For example, a component generating an invoice might compute sales tax before applying a discount, when tax should be computed properly only on the discounted balance. Or a programmer may forget to take into account the possibility that a player can have zero at bats when writing a program to compute batting average. In these cases, the component is said to contain *logical errors*. Logical errors can be very difficult to detect. A logically incorrect program may produce results that appear reasonable but are in fact quite erroneous.

Logical errors can cause a program or component to experience *run-time failure*, that is, fail during execution. Exactly how a run-time failure appears to the user depends on many circumstances, but for the moment we can imagine a message popping up during program execution saying something like "General system failure." Run-time failure can also result from the inability of the operating system to provide some essential resource to the program. For instance, the program may attempt to access a file that has been locked by another user. Dealing with failures is discussed extensively in Chapter 15.

SUPPLEMENT C   **Applets**

c.1   Applets

We have been concerned in this text with the development of independent software applications and the libraries to support them. Java is also used to write *applets*. Applets are
small programs intended to be run by another program, typically a web browser such as
Netscape Navigator. In a typical scenario, a compiled applet is downloaded by a browser
as part of an HTML[1] document, and executed by the client system.

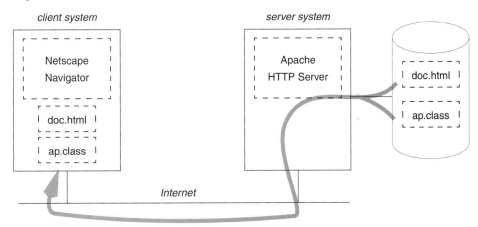

The HTML document identifies an applet to be loaded with either an `<applet>` tag[2]
or an `<object>` tag. Though a discussion of HTML is well beyond the scope of this text,
a minimal HTML document that loads an applet `Hello.class` might look like this:

```
<html>
<head>
<title>Simple HTML document</title>
</head>
<body>
```

---

1. H*yper*T*ext* M*arkup* L*anguage*, the standard notation for writing Web documents.
2. Deprecated in HTML 4.0.

```
<applet code="Hello.class" height=100 width=300>
</applet>
</body>
```

After downloading and displaying the HTML document, the browser downloads and executes the applet. Execution of the applet continues until the applet code terminates or the user stops viewing the document containing the applet. The browser sets aside a region in the document display space for the applet, exactly as it would for an in-line image. The size and position of the display area is controlled by the browser and the HTML code. The applet controls what is displayed inside the area. A single document can contain several applets, in which case they are run in parallel, and can communicate with each other.

The contextual structure and run-time environment required for executing the applet is provided by the browser. For obvious security reasons, an applet's access to the client computing system is restricted. Applets can get user input through the mouse and keyboard, and can read and write data on the originating server system. However, the browser will generally prevent the applet from accessing files on the client system or connecting to other "third party" systems.

Applets can be used for more than simple web page decoration. One can build a web-based user interface for an application, in which the interface is presented by a browser. Applets running as part of the interface can communicate across a network with an application running on a server, sending and receiving data. A discussion of web-based applications, however, is beyond the scope of this supplement.

c.1.1 The class *JApplet*

Applets are instances of *javax.swing.JApplet*, a Swing class with a lengthy lineage. *JApplet* extends *java.applet.Applet*, which extends *java.awt.Panel*, which extends *java.awt.Container*. We were introduced to *Container* in Chapter 17.

JApplet has the same structure as *JFrame* (Section 17.2.2), and serves as the "top-level" container for an applet in much the same way that a *JFrame* serves as the top-level container for an application's user interface.

JApplet inherits some fundamental methods from *java.applet.Applet*. In particular, there are four methods invoked by the browser that control overall execution of the applet. These methods are commonly overridden in classes that extend *JApplet*.

public void init ()
> Called once by the browser after the applet has been first loaded. It should be used for initialization functions that need to be done only once. Subclasses of *JApplet* generally do not provide a constructor. Functions that would otherwise be performed in a constructor are done in init.

public void start ()
> Called after init and each time the browser revisits the page containing the applet. May be called when the browser is deiconified. This is the "main" method of the applet.

public void stop ()
>
> Called whenever the browser leaves the page containing the applet, and just before the applet is to be destroyed. May be called when the browser is iconified. This method should stop or suspend everything the applet is doing.

public void destroy ()
>
> Called when the browser determines it will no longer keep the applet in its cache. The applet should release any resources it has allocated. In practice, most applets don't need to override destroy.

Here's an example of a very simple applet.

```java
import javax.swing.*;
import java.awt.*;

public class Hello extends JApplet {

    public void start () {
        Container cp = getContentPane();
        cp.add(new JLabel("Hello, World."));
    }

}
```

This applet can be tested by loading the HTML file shown on page 877 with the Java Development Kit *appletviewer*. If the HTML file is named Hello.html, the command is

```
appletviewer Hello.html
```

and the resulting display looks like this:

Just as with a *JFrame* (Chapter 17), a *JApplet*'s content pane is a *JPanel* with *Boarder-Layout*. Every time the applet is started, the label "Hello, World" is added to the *JPanel*'s "center" component, replacing any previous center component.

Since this applet is completely static, we could achieve the same effect by adding the label in the init method rather than overriding the start method:

```
import javax.swing.*;
import java.awt.*;

public class Hello extends JApplet {

    public void init () {
        Container cp = getContentPane();
        cp.add(new JLabel("Hello, World."));
    }
}
```

We can get a better picture of what's happening by giving the content pane a *Flow-Layout*. With a FlowLayout, add will append the new label rather than replace the previous one. With the applet defined as follows,

```
import javax.swing.*;
import java.awt.*;

public class Hello extends JApplet {

    private Container cp; // the content pane

    public void init () {
        cp = getContentPane();
        cp.setLayout(new FlowLayout());
        cp.add(new JLabel("init."));
    }

    public void start () {
        cp.add(new JLabel("start."));
    }
}
```

the display looks like this after the *appletviewer* has been iconified and deiconified twice.

c.1.2 Applets as applications

There are a number of ways of writing an applet so that it can either execute from within a browser or run as a stand-alone application. (We must admit that it is not clear *why* one would want to do this.) In particular, an applet can be equipped with a main method. A browser ignores this method when it runs the applet. The main method can create a *JFrame* to display the applet, and invoke the applet methods init, start, stop, and destroy just as a browser would.

As an example, we show how the applet Hello can be written to run as an application in Listing c.1. Note the following:

- A main method has been added to the applet class. This method creates a *JFrame* to contain the applet.

- The *JFrame* constructor creates an instance of the applet, and adds it to its content pane.

- The *JFrame* constructor initializes and starts the applet, in much the same way that a browser does.

- The *JFrame WindowListener* stops and starts the applet as appropriate. After restarting the applet, the *JFrame*'s layout manager is prompted (validate) to layout the *JFrame* again.

Listing c.1   The class *Hello*

```java
import javax.swing.*;
import java.awt.*;
import java.awt.event.*;

public class Hello extends JApplet {

    private Container cp;

    public static void main (String[] args) {
        AppletAppFrame f =
            new AppletAppFrame("Hello, World.");
    }

    public void init () {
        cp = getContentPane();
        cp.setLayout(new FlowLayout());
        cp.add(new JLabel("init."));
    }

    public void start () {
        cp.add(new JLabel("start."));
    }
} // end of class Hello
```

continued

Listing c.1   **The class *Hello* (cont'd)**

===

```java
class AppletAppFrame extends JFrame {

    private Hello applet;

    public AppletAppFrame (String title) {
        super(title);
        applet = new Hello();
        this.getContentPane().add(applet);
        this.setSize(300,100);
        applet.init();
        applet.start();
        this.setVisible(true);

        this.addWindowListener(
            new WindowAdapter() {

                public void windowClosing(WindowEvent e) {
                    e.getWindow().dispose();
                }

                public void windowClosed(WindowEvent e) {
                    applet.destroy();
                    System.exit(0);
                }


                public void windowIconified(WindowEvent e) {
                    applet.stop();
                }

                public void windowDeiconified(WindowEvent e) {
                    applet.start();
                    AppletAppFrame.this.validate();
                }
            });
    }
} // end of class AppletAppFrame
```

---

c.1.3 An example: a simple clock

As an example of a dynamic applet, we illustrate a simple clock. The applet uses a text field to display the current time. Approximately every thirty seconds, the applet gets the current time and updates the text field.

If we run the applet from an HTML document similar to that shown on page 877, the display will appear as follows:

As with most dynamic applets, this applet creates a new *thread*. A thread is an independent sequence of actions. Creating a new thread specifies a sequence of statements that can be executed in parallel with, and independently of, the original sequence of statements. A detailed discussion of threads is beyond the scope of this supplement.

The code for the applet is given (without comments) in Listing c.2. Note the following.

- The method `init` adds the text field to the content pane. The text field needs to be at least eight characters wide to display the time.

- The method `start` creates and starts a new thread. This thread will actually get and write the time. The argument "`this`" to the *Thread* constructor specifies that the new thread will execute the `run` method of the current object.

- The method `run` contains the sequence of statements that will be executed by the timer thread. *Date* and *SimpleDateFormat* are classes defined in `java.util`. A *Date* object represents an instant in time, with millisecond precision. The *SimpleDateFormat* can produce a *String* representation of a *Date*. The constructor argument specifies that the format will be "hours:minuites AM/PM".

- The body of the infinite loop in the method `run` first creates a new *Date* object containing the current time. The formatter converts this to a *String* in the specified format. This *String* is written to the text field. Finally, the thread waits for about 30 seconds before continuing.

Listing c.2   The class *SimpleClock*

```
import javax.swing.*;
import java.awt.*;
import java.util.*;
import java.text.*;

public class SimpleClock extends JApplet
    implements Runnable {
```

continued

Listing c.2   The class *SimpleClock* (cont'd)

```java
private final static int TEXT_SIZE = 8;
private final static int DELAY = 30*1000;// milliseconds
private Container cp;
private JTextField clock;
private Thread timer;

public void init () {
    cp = getContentPane();
    clock = new JTextField(TEXT_SIZE);
    cp.add(clock);
}

public void start () {
    timer = new Thread(this);
    timer.start();
}

public void stop () {
    timer = null;
}

public void run () {
    Date currentTime;
    SimpleDateFormat formatter =
        new SimpleDateFormat("h:mm a");
    while (true) {
        currentTime = new Date();
        clock.setText(formatter.format(currentTime));
        try {
            Thread.currentThread().sleep(DELAY);
        } catch (InterruptedException e) {}
    }
}
```

---

c.1.4 An example: an animated box

We conclude with one final example. In this applet, a box moves randomly around the display. A snapshot of the running applet looks something like this:

A *timer* is used to control the animation. A timer is a thread that periodically generates action events. Each time the timer generates an event, the applet randomly computes a new position for the box and redraws the display. The code (again, without documentation) is shown in Listing c.3.

Note the following.

- The class *Timer* is defined in the package `javax.swing`. The constructor requires two arguments: a delay *d* (milliseconds) and an action listener. The *Timer* notifies its listener (by generating an action event) every *d* milliseconds.

- The class *Random* is defined in `java.util`. An instance is used to produce a stream of pseudorandom numbers. A method invocation such as

      `random.nextInt(MAX_MOVE)`

  produces a non-negative pseudorandom integer that is less than `MAX_MOVE`. The method invocation

      `random.nextBoolean()`

  produces a pseudorandom `boolean` value.

- The *JPanel* method `repaint` invokes the method `paintComponent`, providing it with a graphics context. `paintComponent` is overridden in *Canvas* to draw the box and fill it with the color red.

Readers who would like more examples of applets are referred to Sun's Java tutorial. The tutorial can be found at

      `http://java.sun.com/docs/books/tutorial/`

A list of applets can be found at

```
http://java.sun.com/docs/books/tutorial/
listofapplets.html#swing
```

Listing c.3   The class *Jumpy*

```java
import java.awt.*;
import java.util.*;
import java.awt.event.*;

public class Jumpy extends JApplet
   implements ActionListener {

   private final static int REC_WIDTH = 50;
                            // width of the rectangle
   private final static int REC_HEIGHT = 50;
                            // height of the rectangle
   private final static int DELAY = 1000;
                               // elapsed time between timer
                               // events (microseconds)
   private final static int MAX_MOVE = 20;
                               // max pixels the rectangle
                               // will move in either direction
                               // on one move

   private Timer timer;     // generates action events
   private Canvas canvas;   // JPanel in which the action
                            // takes place
   private Random random;   // pseudo random number generator
   private int x,y;         // coordinates of upper left
                            // corner of the rectangle

   public void init () {
      Container cp = getContentPane();
      canvas = new Canvas();
      cp.add(canvas);
      cp.validate();    // so we can get width and height of
                        // canvas
      random = new Random();
      timer = new Timer(DELAY,this);

      // Start the rectangle in the middle of the canvas.
      x = (canvas.getWidth()-REC_WIDTH)/2;
      y = (canvas.getHeight()-REC_HEIGHT)/2;
      canvas.repaint();
   }
```

continued

Listing c.3   **The class *Jumpy* (cont'd)**

```java
public void start() {
   timer.start();
}

public void stop() {
   timer.stop();
}

public void actionPerformed (ActionEvent e) {
   // When the timer clicks, randomly update rectangle
   // coordinates and repaint the canvas.
   if (random.nextBoolean())
      x = x+random.nextInt(MAX_MOVE);
   else
      x = x-random.nextInt(MAX_MOVE);
   if (random.nextBoolean())
      y = y+random.nextInt(MAX_MOVE);
   else
      y = y-random.nextInt(MAX_MOVE);
   canvas.repaint();
}

private class Canvas extends JPanel {

   public void paintComponent(Graphics g) {
      super.paintComponent(g); // paint background
      g.drawRect(x, y, REC_WIDTH-1, REC_HEIGHT-1);
      g.setColor(Color.red);
      g.fillRect(x+1, y+1, REC_WIDTH-2, REC_HEIGHT-2);
   }

}

}
```

SUPPLEMENT D

Generics and enumerations: the rest of the story

Java 2 Software Edition 5.0 introduced several new features to the language, including generic structures and enumeration types. Generic structures were introduced in Section 12.2.2, enumerations in Section 5.4. In this supplement, we take a closer look at these two features.

d.1 Generics

As we have seen in Chapter 12, genericity allows us to define classes, interfaces, and methods with type parameters. There are two additional aspects of generic structures we should mention.

- Generic structures can have more than one type parameter.

Consider the class *KeyValueTable* defined in Listing d.1. The class is defined with two type parameters, `Key` and `Value`. Instantiating the generic class requires two type arguments. For example,

```
KeyValueTable<String, Integer> grades =
    new KeyValueTable<String, Integer>();
```

The method `grades.add` requires a *String* and an *Integer* as arguments, and the method `grades.lookUp` requires a *String* argument and returns an *Integer*:

```
grades.add("Henry", new Integer(97));
Integer henrysGrade = grades.lookUp("Henry");
```

- Type parameters can be "bounded" by another type.

Suppose *Keyed* is an interface defined as

```
public interface Keyed {
    public String getKey ();
}
```

Listing d.1   **The class *KeyValueTable***

===

```
/**
 * A simple (key, value) table.
 */
public class KeyValueTable<Key, Value> {

    private List<Key> keys;        // the keys
    private List<Value> values;    // the values

    /**
     * Create a new empty table.
     */
    public KeyValueTable () {
        keys = new DefaultList<Key>();
        values = new DefaultList<Value>();
    }

    /**
     * Add the specified (key, value) to this table. If the
     * key is already in the table, replace the associated
     * value with the one specified.
     */
    public void add (Key key, Value value) {
        int i = keys.indexOf(key);
        if (i = -1) {
            keys.add(key);
            values.add(value);
        } else
            values.set(i,value);
    }

    /**
     * The value associated with the specified key. Returns
     * null if the key is not in the table.
     */
    public Value lookUp (Key key) {
        int i = keys.indexOf(key);
        if (i != -1)
            return values.get(i);
        else
            return null;
    }
}
```

Then the following version of the generic class *KeyValueTable* requires its argument to be a subtype of *Keyed*.

```
public class KeyValueTable<Entry extends Keyed> {

    private List<String> keys;
    private List<Entry> entries;
    ...
    public void add (Entry entry) {
       String key = entry.getKey();
       ...
    }

    public Entry lookUp (String key) {
       ...
    }
}
```

Note that the keyword for bounding a type is **extends**, regardless of whether the bounding type is defined by an interface or by a class.

The add method takes advantage of the fact that a generic argument will be a subtype of *Keyed*, and thus define the method getKey. If *Student* implements *Keyed*,

```
public class Student implements Keyed ...
```

we can instantiate the generic class with *Student* as argument:

```
KeyValueTable<Student> grades =
    new KeyValueTable<Student>();
Student henry = ...;
grades.add(henry);
```

Since henry is a *Student*, and *Student* implements *Keyed*, henry supports the method getKey.

Now suppose *Keyed* is a generic interface:

```
public interface Keyed<Key> {
    public Key getKey ();
}
```

The following version has two type parameters, the second depending on the first.

```
public class KeyValueTable
    <Key, Entry extends Keyed<Key>> {

    private List<Key> keys;
    private List<Entry> entries;
    ...
    public void add (Entry entry) {
       Key key = entry.getKey();
       ...
    }
```

```
public Entry lookUp (Key key) {
    ...
}
}
```

If the first generic argument is *String*, for example, the second must be a subtype of *Keyed<String>*. Assuming that *Student* implements *Keyed<String>*, and so defines a method `String getKey()`, we can instantiate the generic class as follows.

```
KeyValueTable<String, Student> grades =
    new KeyValueTable<String, Student>();
Student henry = ...;
grades.add(henry);
```

d.1.1 Wildcard types

Generics and subtyping, revisited

We have seen in Section 9.2.3 that the fundamental rule of subtyping states that if *A* is a subtype of *B*, then an *A* value can be provided wherever a *B* value is required. For instance, the *Object* method `equals` requires an *Object* argument:

```
public boolean equals (Object obj) ...
```

Since *Student* is a subtype of *Object*, we can invoke the method with a *Student* as argument:

```
if (someObject.equals(henry)) ...
```

In Section 12.2.2 we learned that *A* being a subtype of *B* does not imply that *List<A>* is a subtype of *List<B>*. If it were, the fundamental rule of subtyping would be violated. For instance, we could write a method that adds a *String* to a *List<Object>*,

```
public void addString (List<Object> list) {
    list.add("end"); // OK: String a subtype of Object
}
```

and then invoke the method with a *List<Integer>* as argument:

```
List<Integer> numbers = new DefaultList<Integer>();
addString(numbers);
    // OK if List<Integer> is a subtype of List<Object>!
```

The rule is true in general for generic types: if *T<E>* is a generic type (with parameter *E*), then *A* being a subtype of *B* does not imply that *T<A>* is a subtype of *T<B>*.

An example

Suppose we have an interface *ClosedFigure* that specifies a method for computing area:

```
public interface ClosedFigure
```
A regular closed two-dimensional geometric figure.

```
public double area ()
```
The area of this figure.

We can write a method that takes a *List<ClosedFigure>* and produces the total area of the elements of the list.

```
public double totalArea (List<ClosedFigure> list) {
    double sum = 0.0;
    for (int i = 0; i < list.size(); i = i+1)
        sum = sum + list.get(i).area();
    return sum;
}
```

If a *Circle* is a *ClosedFigure*, we should be able to invoke the method with a *List<Circle>* as argument. All the method does is query each list element for its area, and certainly a *Circle* can be queried for its area. But if hoops is a *List<Circle>*, the invocation

```
totalArea(hoops)
```

fails to compile because *List<Circle>* is not a subtype of *List<ClosedFigure>*.

Wildcards

Wildcards are an extension to the type system intended to improve the flexibility of generic structures. Syntactically, a wildcard is an expression of the form ?, ? **extends** *T*, or ? **super** *T*, where *T* is a type. Wildcards denote types, and can be read as follows:

?	—	"some type"
? **extends** *T*	—	"*T* or some subtype of *T*"
? **super** *T*	—	"*T* or some super type of *T*"

The first form is called an "unbounded wildcard" and is essentially equivalent to ? **extends** Object.

Wildcards can only be used as type arguments in generic instantiations. For example, we can write variable declarations like these

```
List<?> list;
List<? extends Exception> exceptionList;
```

but not like these:

```
? something;
? extends Exception someException;
```

Consider the simple generic class shown in Listing d.2. The expression Item<?> denotes "*Item<some type>*," while Item<? **extends** Exception> denotes "*Item<some type of Exception>*." For example, the parameter of the following method

---

Listing d.2   The class *Item*

```
public class Item<Element> {

    private Element value;

    public Item (Element value) {
        this.value = value;
    }

    public Element value () {
        return value;
    }

    public void setValue (Element value) {
        this.value = value;
    }
}
```

(I)
```
public Object getItemValue (Item<?> item) {
    return item.value();
}
```

specifies that the argument must be "an *Item* of some type." The method can be invoked
with any kind of *Item* as argument, for example

```
Item<String> i1 = new Item<String>("hello");
Item<Integer> i2 = new Item<Integer>(new Integer(2));
Object o1 = getItemValue(i1);
Object o2 = getItemValue(i2);
```

Since the argument of getItemValue can be any type of *Item*, the only thing we
can conclude about the value returned by item.value() is that it is an *Object*. Thus the
method getItemValue is specified as returning an *Object*.

Now consider the method

```
public String getString (
    Item<? extends Exception> item) {
    return item.value().getMessage();
}
```

We can be sure that the argument supplied to this method will be an *Item<T>*, where *T* is
some type of *Exception*. Thus the value returned by item.value() is an *Exception* and
has a method getMessage that returns a *String*.

Finally, consider the method

```
public boolean sameValue (Item<?> one, Item<?> two) {
    return one.value().equals(two.value());
}
```

The first argument must be an *Item* of some type and the second argument must be an *Item* of some type. But there is no requirement that the types of the *Items* are the same. That is, we cannot assert that `one.value()` and `two.value()` have the same type. The method can be invoked, for instance, with an *Item<String>* first argument and an *Item<Integer>* second argument.

By now, you probably wonder what we have bought with all this new syntax. Why could we not just write

(II)

```
public Object getItemValue (Item<Object> item) {
    return item.value();
}

public String getString (Item<Exception> item) { ...
    return item.value().getMessage();
}
```

and so on. To see the difference consider the invocation of the `getItemValue` shown above:

```
Item<String> i1 = new Item<String>("hello");
Object o1 = getItemValue(i1);
```

If `getItemValue` is defined as *(II)*, this invocation will not compile because *Item<String>* is not a subtype of *Item<Object>*. If it were, we could write a method

```
public void setNumber (Item<Object> item) {
    Integer integer = new Integer(1);
    item.setValue(integer);
}
```

and invoke it with

```
Item<String> i1 = new Item<String>("hello");
setString(i1);
```

But we have seen that if `getItemValue` is defined as *(I)*, the invocation

```
Object o1 = getItemValue(i1);
```

succeeds, where `i1` is an *Item<String>*. So *Item<String>* must be a subtype of *Item<?>*, even though it is not a subtype of *Item<Object>*.

What if we write

```
public void setNumber (Item<?> item) {
    item.setValue(new Integer(1));
}
```

This method will not compile. Since `item` is of type *Item<?>*, all we know is that `item.setValue` requires "some type" of argument. We cannot conclude that *Integer* is an appropriate type. That is, inside `setNumber`, the signature if `item.setValue` is essentially **void** setValue(?). There are no (proper) subtypes of *?*.

On the other hand, suppose we define

```
public void setRTE (Item<? super Exception> item) {
    item.setValue(new RuntimeException());
}
```

Now we can be sure that the argument supplied to setRTE is of type *Item<T>* where *T* is *Exception* or a supertype of *Exception*. Thus item.setValue will require an argument of type *T*, where *T* is *Exception* or an *Exception* supertype. Now *RuntimeException* is a subtype of *Exception*, and so a subtype of any *Exception* supertype. Hence *RuntimeException* is a subtype of whatever type item.setValue expects, and the invocation is legal. Inside setNumber, the signature of item.setValue is **void** setValue(? **super** Exception). *Exception* and its subtypes are subtypes of *? super Exception*.

Figure 4.1 illustrates the subtype relationship between wildcard types. In the figure, *T* is a type, *SubT* is a subtype of *T*, and *SuperT* is a supertype of *T*. Remember that wildcard type expressions, such as ? and ? **extends** T, can only be written as type arguments for generic types.

Returning to the *ClosedFigure* example, the solution is to use a wildcard type in the definition of totalArea:

```
public double totalArea (
    List<? extends ClosedFigure> list) {
    double sum = 0.0;
    for (int i = 0; i < list.size(); i = i+1)
        sum = sum + list.get(i).area();
    return sum;
}
```

Since *Circle* is a subtype of *ClosedFigure*, *List<Circle>* is a subtype of *List<? extends ClosedFigure>*. The invocation totalArea(hoops), where hoops is a *List<Circle>*, is legal.

Finally, we should mention that a wildcard type can be the type of a variable. For example, suppose we wanted to keep a list of all the *Item* instances ever created. (Don't ask why.) We can write the following

```
public class Item<Element> {

    private Element value;
    public static List<Item<?>> items =
        new DefaultList<Item<?>>();

    public Item (Element value) {
        this.value = value;
        items.add(this);
    }

    ...
```

The static variable items is of type *List<Item<?>>*. This means that an *Item* of any type can be added to the list.

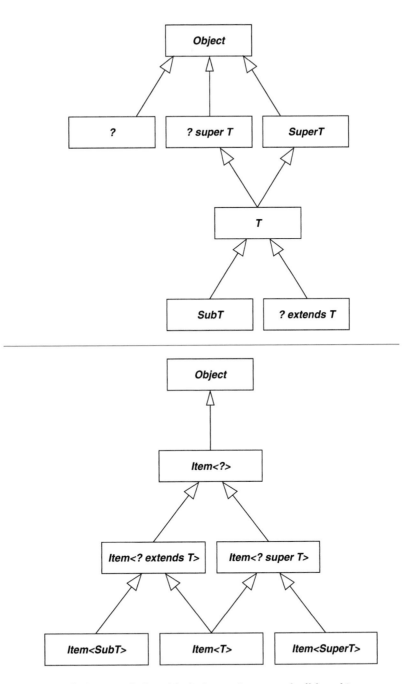

Figure 4.1 **Subtype relationship between types and wildcard types.**

Wildcards and generic methods

Some of the methods written above with wildcards could have been written as generic methods. For example,

```
public <Type> Object getItemValue (Item<Type> item) {
    return item.value();
}

public <Type extends Exception> String getString (
    Item<Type> item) {
    return item.value().getMessage();
}

public <Type1, Type2> boolean sameValue (
    Item<Type1> one, Item<Type2> two) {
    return one.value().equals(two.value());
}

public <Type extends ClosedFigure> double totalArea (
    List<Type> list) {
    double sum = 0.0;
    for (int i = 0; i < list.size(); i = i+1)
        sum = sum + list.get(i).area();
    return sum;
}
```

(We cannot write setRTE as a generic method.)

When should we use wildcard types and when should we write generic methods? Wildcards are considered clearer and easier to understand than generic methods. The general guideline is to use wildcards if we want to express polymorphism. That is, we want to express the fact that the method can be invoked with different argument types. If we want to express dependencies between arguments, or between arguments and return type, we write a generic method. For example, we can write a tighter version of getItemValue as a generic method:

```
public <Type> Type getItemValue (Item<Type> item) {
    return item.value();
}
```

Here we have expressed a dependency between the argument type and the return type. With the argument type expressed as a wildcard, the most we can say about the returned value is that it is an *Object*.

Similarly, we can use a generic method to require that the arguments of sameValue be of the same type. If we write

```
public <Type> boolean sameValue (
    Item<Type> one, Item<Type> two) {
    return one.value().equals(two.value());
}
```

then `sameValue` cannot be invoked, for instance, with an *Item<String>* first argument and an *Item<Integer>* second argument.

Opening wildcards

Occasionally we want to use a wildcard parameter for purposes of expression, but need a name for the type in the implementation. For example, suppose we are writing a method that swaps two items of a list. It is natural to express the method with a wildcard list type:

```
public void swap (List<?> list, int i, int j)
```
>   Swap the elements with indexes i and j.

But when we implement the method, we find that we need to name the list element type:

✗
```
public void swap (List<?> list, int i, int j) {
    ? temp = list.get(i);   // whoops! Can't do this
    list.set(i, list.get(j));
    list.set(j, temp);
}
```

One approach is to define the public method with a wildcard, and have it call a private generic version. The generic version, which must have a different name, "captures" the list element type with a name.

```
public void swap (List<?> list, int i, int j) {
    swapImp(list, i, j);
}

private <Type> void swapImp (
    List<Type> list, int i, int j) {
    Type temp = list.get(i);
    list.set(i, list.get(j));
    list.set(j, temp);
}
```

d.2 Enumeration types

Enumeration types (the *enum facility*) were introduced in Section 5.4. We saw that an enumeration types provides a convenient way for defining a class that has a small fixed number of instances. For example, the class *PlayingCard* can be defined with enumeration types modeling suit and rank:

```
public class PlayingCard {

    public enum Suit {clubs, diamonds, hearts, spades}
    public enum Rank {two, three, four, five, six,
```

```
                    seven, eight, nine, ten, jack, queen, king,
                    ace}
        ...
```

Now the *PlayingCard* constructor, for instance, can be defined with parameters of type *Suit* and *Rank*,

```
        public PlayingCard (Suit suit, Rank rank) ...
```

and the compiler can verify that a client provides arguments of the correct type.

An enum declaration defines a public, static, member class. For example, the definition of *Suit* in *PlayingCard* defines a member class with four instances, referenced by named constants clubs, diamonds, hearts, and spades. The definition is roughly equivalent to the following:

```
        public static class Suit {

            private final String name;

            public static final Suit clubs =
                new Suit("clubs");
            public static final Suit diamonds =
                new Suit("diamonds");
            public static final Suit hearts =
                new Suit("hearts");
            public static final Suit spades =
                new Suit("spades");

            private Suit (String name) {
                this.name = name;
            }

            public String toString () {
                return this.name;
            }
        }
```

PlayingCard.Suit is a class, and clubs is a named constant defined in the class and referencing one of the four instances of the class. PlayingCard.Suit.clubs references an instance of *PlayingCard.Suit*. Since the constructor for *PlayingCard.Suit* is private, a client cannot create new *Suit* instances.

As suggested above, the method toString returns the name of the constant. For instance,

```
        PlayingCard.Suit.clubs.toString ()  ⇒  "clubs"
```

Other methods defined for an enum class include

public int compareTo (*EnumClass* obj)
> Compare this enum constant with the specified object for order. Returns a negative integer, zero, or a positive integer as this object is less than,

equal to, or greater than the specified object. Enum constants are comparable only to other enum constants of the same enum class. The natural order implemented by this method is the order in which the constants are declared.

public final int ordinal ()

The ordinal of this enumeration constant (its position in its enum declaration, where the initial constant is assigned an ordinal of zero).

public static final *EnumClass*[] values ()

An array containing the elements of the enum type in the order in which they were declared.

For example,

```
Suit.clubs.compareTo(Suit.hearts) ⟹ a negative value
Suit.clubs.compareTo(Suit.clubs)  ⟹ 0
Suit.hearts.compareTo(Suit.clubs) ⟹ a positive values
Suit.clubs.ordinal()                  ⟹ 0
Suit.spades.ordinal()                 ⟹ 3
Suit.values[0]                        ⟹ clubs
Suit.values[3]                        ⟹ spades
```

The array returned by values can be used to iterate through the elements of an enum class. For example,

```
List<PlayingCard> deck =
    new DefaultList<PlayingCard>();
for (int i = 0; i < Suit.values().length; i = i+1)
    for (int j = 0; j < Rank.values().length; j = j+1)
        deck.add(new PlayingCard(Suit.values()[i],
            Rank.values()[j]));
```

or, using the "for each" construct,

```
for (Suit suit : Suit.values())
    for (Rank rank : Rank.values())
        deck.add(new PlayingCard(suit,rank));
```

Adding features to an enum type

An enum declaration defines a class with a set of predefined features. However, it is possible to define additional features for the class. For example, suppose we want a class that models coins. We might define an enum class as

```
public enum Coin {penny, nickel, dime, quarter, half}
```

But suppose we want the *Coin* objects to know their monetary value. We can create an enum class with additional features:

```
public enum Coin {
    penny(1),
    nickle(5),
    dime(10),
    quarter(25),
    half(50);

    private int monetaryValue;
    private Coin (int monetaryValue) {
        this.monetaryValue = monetaryValue;
    }

    public int monetaryValue () {
        return monetaryValue;
    }
}
```

A *Coin* now has a private instance variable monetaryValue, and a public query with the same name. We have also explicitly defined a constructor requiring an **int** argument. The numbers in the definition of the enum constants, 10 in dime(10) for instance, are constructor arguments. For example,

Coin.dime.monetaryValue() ⟹ 10

Modifying the behavior of enum instances

Let's take a look at the class *TrafficSignal*, specified in Listing 2.3. Recall that this class defines three named constants,

```
public static final int GREEN = 0;
public static final int YELLOW = 1;
public static final int RED = 2;
```

It includes a query for the current light and a command to change to the next light.

public int light ()
> The light currently on.

> **ensure:**
> ```
> this.light() == TrafficSignal.GREEN ||
> this.light() == TrafficSignal.YELLOW ||
> this.light() == TrafficSignal.RED.
> ```

public void change ()
> Change to the next light.

Clearly we can use an enum type rather than **int** constants to define the lights:

```
public enum Light {green, yellow, red}
...
/**
 * The Light currently on.
 */
public Light light () ...
```

Rather than implementing the method `change` as a cascade of if statements (see Section 4.3), we can produce a cleaner solution if we let each *Light* instance know which *Light* follows it. We add this functionality to the class *Light*:

```
public enum Light {
    green, yellow, red;

    private Light next () {
        return values()[this.ordinal()+1];
    }
}
```

When queried for `next`, a *Light* returns the next *Light* in the enumeration. Thus

```
Light.green.next()  ⇒  Light.yellow
Light.yellow.next() ⇒  Light.red
```

But if we query `red` for `next`, we generate an *ArrayIndexOutOfBoundsException*, since `Light.red.ordinal()` is 2, and `Light.values()` contains only three elements, with indexes 0, 1, and 2. There is no enum value with index 3.

We want the next method for `red` to return the first enum value, `green`. We accomplish this by making `red` an instance of an anonymous *Light* subclass that overrides the implementation of `next`. The enum syntax makes this easy:

```
public enum Light {
    green,
    yellow,
    red {
        protected Light next () {
            return values()[0];
        }
    };

    protected Light next () {
        return values()[this.ordinal()+1];
    }
}
```

The method `next` cannot now be private, since it is to be overridden in the anonymous subclass of `red`. The complete implementation of *TrafficSignal* is shown in Listing d.3.

Listing d.3   The class *TrafficSignal*

```java
public class TrafficSignal {
    private Light current; // The Light currently on.
    /**
     * The signal lights.
     */
    public enum Light {
        green,
        yellow,
        red {
            protected Light next () {
                return values()[0];
            }
        };
        /**
         * The light that comes on after this one.
         */
        protected Light next () {
            return values()[this.ordinal()+1];
        }
    }
    /**
     * Create a new TrafficSignal, initially green.
     * @ensure     this.light() == Light.green
     */
    public TrafficSignal () {
        current = Light.green;
    }
    /**
     * The light currently on.
     */
    public Light light () {
        return current;
    }
    /**
     * Change to the next light.
     */
    public void change () {
        current = current.next();
    }
}
```

APPENDIX I

Compiling, executing, and documenting

i.1 Compiling and running an application

How you compile and run a program depends on the computing environment you are using. We describe compiling and running a program from the command line interface in a simple UNIX or Windows environment, in which packages are stored in the file system. We use UNIX syntax for specifying files in the examples.

i.1.1 Compilation units

The program source is contained in files called *compilation units*. In standard implementations, a compilation unit is nothing more than a file containing your class definitions. A compilation unit can contain one or more class definitions, subject to the following constraints:

- all classes in a compilation unit must belong to the same package;
- only one class in a compilation can be referenced from outside the compilation unit; in particular, only one class in a compilation unit can be public;
- a compilation unit must be named with the name of the externally referencable class followed by ".java"; in particular, if a compilation unit contains a public class, it must be named with the name of the public class followed by ".java".

For instance, a source file containing the definition of the public class Counter must be named Counter.java. Note that case is significant. The file cannot be named COUNTER.JAVA for example.

i.1.2 Package name and directory hierarchy

Files, both source ".java" files and bytecode ".class" files, are located in directories (*i.e.*, folders) according to package. For example, the definition of the public class counters.Counter, that is, the class Counter in the package counters, must be in a file named Counter.java in a directory counters.

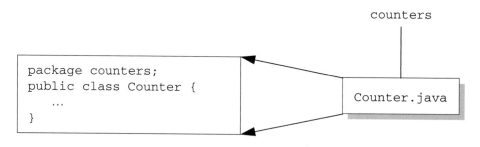

Though there is no semantic significance, a package can be a member of another package. For instance, suppose the package mazeGame contains the package maze which contains the public class Room. The complete name of the package containing the class Room is mazeGame.maze, and the fully qualified name of the class is maze-Game.maze.Room. The definition of this class must be in a file Room.java, which is in a directory named maze, which is in a directory named mazeGame.

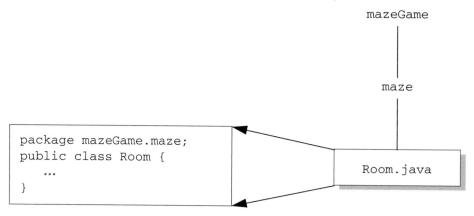

Assuming the UNIX file name separator slash (/), mazeGame/maze/Room.java is a relative path name for the file containing the definition of the class mazeGame.maze.Room.

i.1.3 The environment variable *CLASSPATH*

The package and class name determine a *relative* path name for a file containing the class definition or bytecode. The process environment variable CLASSPATH determines where the compiler or interpreter looks to locate a file.

CLASSPATH is an environment variable that is part of the process state. The compiler or interpreter process generally inherits the variable from its parent process. Details of processes and process state are beyond the scope of this presentation. But in effect, changing the value of CLASSPATH in a command window will only affect processes run in that window.

The value of the variables is a colon separated (UNIX) or semicolon separated (Windows) sequence of directories. You can examine the value of the variable by keying the command line

```
echo $CLASSPATH
```

in a UNIX environment, or

```
echo %CLASSPATH%
```

in a Windows environment. For example, keying "echo $CLASSPATH" in a UNIX environment might display something like

```
/apps/java:/home/fred/Java
```

The equivalent command in a Windows environment will display something like

```
C:\apps\java;E:\home\fred\Java
```

How to set the value of this variable is beyond the scope of this discussion.

When the compiler or interpreter needs to find a file containing a class, it searches the directories listed in the CLASSPATH in the order in which they are listed. For example, assuming the CLASSPATH given above, if the interpreter needed to locate a file containing the bytecode for the class

```
mazeGame.maze.Room
```

it would first look for the file

```
mazeGame/maze/Room.class
```

in the directory /apps/java, then in the directory /home/fred/Java. That is, it would look first for the file

```
/apps/java/mazeGame/maze/Room.class
```

and if that file did not exits, it would look for the file

```
/home/fred/Java/mazeGame/maze/Room.class
```

i.1.4 Compiling and running

Compiling

The compiler, javac, expects one or more *files* as command line arguments. For instance, suppose that the file /apps/java/mazeGame/maze/Room.java contains the definition of the class mazeGame.maze.Room. If the working directory is /apps/java/mazeGame/maze, we can compile the class by keying the command

```
javac Room.java
```

If the working directory is /apps/java, we can compile by keying

```
javac mazeGame/maze/Room.java
```

If the compiler needs other classes in order to compile the specified file, it uses the CLASSPATH to locate them. For instance, assuming the CLASSPATH above, if the class Room referenced the class mazeGame.items.Scroll, the compiler would search for mazeGame/items/Scroll.class or mazeGame/items/Scroll.java first in /apps/java and then in /home/fred/Java.

Running

The interpreter, java, expects a fully qualified **class name** as argument. For example, keying

```
java -ea mazeGame.Game
```

runs the main method in the class mazeGame.Game. The interpreter searches the directories in the CLASSPATH looking for a file mazeGame/Game.class, containing the executable bytecode.

The option "-ea" is required to enable assertions. The default behavior is for the interpreter to ignore assert commands.

i.2   Generating documentation

The standard tool for generating documentation is javadoc. javadoc produces a set of HTML documents from the doc comments in a collection of source files. Source files can be named explicitly in the command line, or can be referenced through their package. For instance, the command

```
javadoc Room.java Passage.java
```

produces documentation for the classes defined in the files Room.java and Passage.java. (These files would have to be in the current directory.) The command

```
javadoc /home/fred/Java/*.java
```

generates documentation for all the files ending "*.java" in the directory /home/fred/Java.

Classes to be documented can also be specified by package. For instance, the command

```
javadoc mazeGame mazeGame.maze
```

generates documentation for all classes in the mazeGame and mazeGame.maze packages. In this case, the environment variable CLASSPATH is used to locate the packages, just as with the interpreter. Subpackages are not automatically included in the documentation. To include subpackages, the option -subpackages must be used. For example,

```
javadoc -subpackages mazeGame
```

produces documentation including the package mazeGame and all its subpackages. Several packages can be specified with this option, separated by semicolons.

```
javadoc -subpackages mazeGame.maze:mazeGame.items
```

documents packages mazeGame.maze and mazeGame.items, and all their subpackages.

Destination

Generally, we do not want to put the HTML files in the same directories as the source or executables. The option -d allows us to specify the destination directory in which javadoc places the generated HTML files. For example,

```
javadoc -d /home/docs/mazeGame -subpackages mazeGame
```

specifies that the generated HTML files are to be placed in the directory /home/docs/mazeGame.

Require and ensure tags

By convention, we identify preconditions in a method or constructor specification with a @require tag, and postconditions with an @ensure tag. We want preconditions and postconditions to be setoff visually in the documentation. To do this, we use the -tag option. Consider the command line

```
javadoc -tag require -tag ensure Room.java
```

javadoc will produce documentation for the source file Room.java, labeling preconditions "**Require:**" and postconditions "**Ensure:**". For instance, a comment line like

```
@require    this.isEmpty()
```

will produce output something like this:

> **Require:**
>> this.isEmpty()

HTML tags in doc comments

Doc comments can include HTML tags. In particular, it is conventional to wrap Java syntax used in a comment in <code> ... </code> tags. For example, we might write the doc comment for the query stamina as follows:

```
/**
 * Damage (hit points) required to defeat
 * this <code>Explorer</code>.
 *
 * @ensure   <code>this.stamina() >= 0</code>
 */
public int stamina () { ...
```

The generated documentation will look something like this:

stamina

```
public int stamina ()
```

Damage (hit points) required to defeat this `Explorer`.

Ensure:

```
this.stamina() >= 0
```

APPENDIX II   **DrJava**

DrJava is an easy to use software development environment for writing Java programs. It was created by the Computer Science Department at Rice University, and is currently being developed by the JavaPLT group at Rice. DrJava is designed primarily for students, and provides an interactive facility for evaluating Java code. It includes an editor and debugger, and incorporates the JUnit testing framework and javadoc documentation generating tool. The jar[1] file can be downloaded from

```
http://drjava.sourceforge.net/
```

To complete the DrJava exercises in the text, you will also need the package nhUtilities. This can be downloaded from

```
http://www.cs.uno.edu/~fred/nhText/Utilities or
http://wakko.cs.uno.edu/nhText/Utilities
```

Since DrJava is still being actively developed, we cannot give a definitive set of instructions for installing and configuring the environment. The version you are running will almost certainly differ in some details from what is described here.

To run DrJava, supply the jar file to the Java interpreter using the -jar option. For example, assuming the jar file is named drjava-20040331-0037.jar and is located in a directory named /apps/java in a Unix environment, you would key

```
java -jar /apps/java/drjava-20040331-0037.jar
```

DrJava will open a window containing three primary panes, as shown in Figure ii.1. The large *Definitions Pane* is the main subwindow. It is used for displaying and editing the active source file. The editor provides features such as syntax coloring, automatic indention, and brace matching. The pane to the left of the *Definitions Pane* lists all currently open files.

The *Interactions Pane* is one of the tabbed panes at the bottom of the display. You can dynamically enter and evaluate Java statements and expressions in the *Interactions Pane*.

Details can be found by choosing the *Help* option from the *Help* menu.

The package root directory of any class opened in the *Definitions Pane* is added to the Classpath for *Interactions Pane*. To view the Classpath, display the *Interactions Pane* con-

---

1. A "jar" file is a *Java Archive* File. A jar file bundles multiple files, typically the class files for an application, into a single archive.

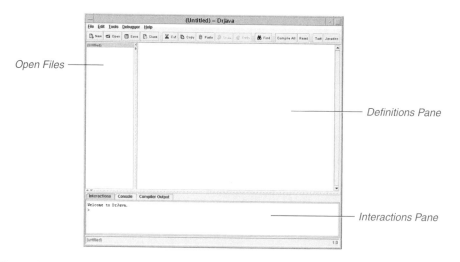

Open Files

Definitions Pane

Interactions Pane

Figure ii.1 **DrJava window.**

text menu by right-clicking in the pane. (Mac users use *Ctrl*+Click or *Option*+Click.) Then choose "View Interactions Classpath" from the context menu. Alternatively, you can choose "View Interactions Classpath" from the *Tools* pull-down menu.

To configure DrJava, choose the *Preferences* option from the *Edit* pull-down menu. Choose the "Resource Locations" category and add the directory *containing* the package `nhUtilities` to the "Extra Classpath" text area. To do this, you must use the *Add* button, and select the directory with the file chooser. Be careful and read what you've added. It's easy to create a nonsense path with the chooser.

Depending on your environment and the version of DrJava you are using, you might also need to identify other "Resource Locations." The *Help* facility will provide details.

Press the *Apply* button at the bottom of the window to apply these changes.

You might also want to customize Javadoc to recognize `@require` and `@ensure` tags. To do this, choose the "Javadoc" category from the *Preferences* window. Add the following to "Custom Javadoc Parameters":

```
-tag require -tag ensure
```

Press *Apply* and *Ok* to exit the *Preferences* window.

APPENDIX III

Controls and basic Latin: the first 128 Unicode characters

The first 128 Unicode characters are the same as the familiar ASCII characters set.

Controls

0	*NULL*	16	*DATA LINK ESCAPE*
1	*START OF HEADING*	17	*DEVICE CONTROL ONE*
2	*START OF TEXT*	18	*DEVICE CONTROL TWO*
3	*END OF TEXT*	19	*DEVICE CONTROL THREE*
4	*END OF TRANSMISSION*	20	*DEVICE CONTROL FOUR*
5	*ENQUIRY*	21	*NEGATIVE ACKNOWLEDGE*
6	*ACKNOWLEDGE*	22	*SYNCHRONOUS IDLE*
7	*BELL*	23	*END OF TRANSMISSION BLOCK*
8	*BACKSPACE*	24	*CANCEL*
9	*HORIZONTAL TABLULATION*	25	*END OF MEDIUM*
10	*LINE FEED*	26	*SUBSTITUTE*
11	*VERTICAL TABULATION*	27	*ESCAPE*
12	*FORM FEED*	28	*FILE SEPARATOR*
13	*CARRIAGE RETURN*	29	*GROUP SEPARATOR*
14	*SHIFT OUT*	30	*RECORD SEPARATOR*
15	*SHIFT IN*	31	*UNIT SEPARATOR*

ASCII characters

32	*SPACE*	33	!	34	"	35	#	36	$	37	%
38	&	39	`	40	(	41	)	42	*	43	+
44	,	45	–	46	.	47	/	48	0	49	1
50	2	51	3	52	4	53	5	54	6	55	7
56	8	57	9	58	:	59	;	60	<	61	=
62	>	63	?	64	@	65	A	66	B	67	C

68	D	69	E	70	F	71	G	72	H	73	I
74	J	75	K	76	L	77	M	78	N	79	O
80	P	81	Q	82	R	83	S	84	T	85	U
86	V	87	W	88	X	89	Y	90	Z	91	[
92	\	93	]	94	^	95	_	96	`	97	a
98	b	99	c	199	d	191	e	101	f	103	g
104	h	105	i	106	j	107	k	108	l	109	m
110	n	111	o	112	p	113	q	114	r	115	s
116	t	117	u	118	v	119	w	120	x	121	y
122	z	123	{	124	|	125	}	126	~	127	*DELETE*

GLOSSARY

abstract class: a class that can contain abstract methods and can't be instantiated. The purpose of an abstract class is to serve as a foundation on which to build subclasses.

abstract constructor: an abstract method for creating objects defined in an abstract class or interface. Subclasses implement the method and determine which actual concrete class to instantiate.

abstract method: a method specification in an interface. The method is specified but no implementation is provided.

abstraction: the process of ignoring irrelevant details and emphasizing essential ones. To abstract is to disregard certain differentiating details.

adapter: a wrapper.

adapter pattern: the structure consisting of a wrapped class and its wrapper, used to adapt the wrapper class to the needed specification.

address: a number uniquely identifying a particular location in memory.

algorithm: a set of instructions describing a pattern of behavior guaranteed to achieve a specific goal.

anonymous class: a nameless class that is defined and instantiated in the same expression.

antisymmetric relation: a relation that satisfies the property that *x* related to *y* implies *y* not related to *x*, for all values *x* and *y* for which the relation is defined.

application: a program or software system that is not part of the "system management" software. Specifically, a program not associated with the operating system.

application-driven: an input-output model in which the application explicitly determines when to get input and when to produce output.

applied occurrence: an occurrence of an identifier that is not a defining occurrence. The identifier is being used to refer to some entity (*e.g.*, method, variable) that it names.

architectural class: class that helps form the underlying structure of the solution.

argument: a value provided by a client when invoking a method or constructor specified with a parameter. The client must provide an argument of the appropriate type for each parameter appearing in the method or constructor definition.

arithmetic expression: an expression that produces an integer or floating point value when evaluated.

array: a structure composed of a contiguous sequence of variables, all of the same type.

assert statement: a statement that predicates the truth of a boolean condition. If the condition is true, the statement has no effect. If the condition is false, the statement causes an error exception which will terminate the program.

assignment statement: a statement that instructs the processor to compute a value and store it in a variable.

associativity rule: a rule that specifies the order in which unparenthesized operators of equal precedence are applied in the evaluation of an expression.

atomic component: a *basic component.*

automatic allocation: variable allocation strategy in which space for variables is allocated when a method is invoked, and deallocated when the method completes.

backtracking: an algorithmic technique when a composite solution must be found from a number of alternatives. The process consists of a number of steps, each step adding a piece of the solution to the partial solution produced by the previous step. At each step, there are several possible ways of extending the partial solution, some of which will lead to a solution and some of which will not. When a "dead end" is reached, the process "backtracks" to the previous partial solution with untried extensions.

base class: a class that is extended to define a subclass.

basic component: a self-contained component used to present information to or get information from the user.

binary operator: an operator that requires two operands, that is, computes a value from two given values. Also called a *dyadic* operator.

binary search: a search algorithm that locates an item on a sorted list of n elements in $\log_2 n$ steps. On each step, half of the remaining list elements are eliminated from consideration until only one remains.

black box test: a test designed by considering only the expected behavior of a system, without regard for the internal implementation structure of the system.

block: a compound statement.

boolean expression: an expression that yields a value of type **boolean** (*i.e.*, *true* or *false*) when evaluated.

boolean operator: a unary or binary operator that requires **boolean** operands and evaluates to a `boolean` value.

break statement: a statement that can be used to terminate a switch statement at an arbitrary point.

bridge pattern: a design structure for uncoupling two hierarchies with the same root. The two hierarchies can then be independently developed. For instance, the set of implementations of a class can be separated into an implementation hierarchy. The class is equipped with an implementation by means of composition.

bubble sort: a simple sort algorithm that "bubbles" each element into position. On each pass, pairs of successive elements are compared and interchanged if they are out of order.

byte stream: in Java, any stream in which the bytes are not interpreted as an encoding of the Unicode characters.

case sensitive: a method of comparing identifiers in which identifiers that differ in the case (upper or lower) of the constituent letters are considered to be different identifiers. The identifiers ABC, Abc, and abc are all different in a case-sensitive language, all the same in a language that is not case sensitive.

cast: an operation in which a value of one type is explicitly converted into a value of a different type. A reference-valued expression can be cast to a supertype or a subtype.

catch clause: a syntactic part of a *try-catch* statement that handles one class of exceptions.

character stream: a data stream in which the bytes are interpreted as characters using some encoding scheme; in Java, a stream in which the bytes are interpreted as an encoding of the Unicode characters.

checked exception: an exception that is not an instance of *RuntimeException* or of one of its subclasses. Methods that can throw checked exceptions must document this face with a *throws* clause in the method heading.

circular list: a list structure in which the node containing the last element references the first node of the list.

class: a collection of similar objects. Objects that are members of the same class have the same set of features.

class declaration: the Java construct used to define a class. The class declaration includes both the specification and implementation of the class.

class invariant: an invariant regarding properties of class instances, that is, a condition that will always be true for all instances of a class.

class method: a method associated with a class rather than with instances of the class. See *static feature*.

client: in reference to a given object, a client is another object which uses the given object. The given object is called the server. The client accesses the features of the server, that is, it invokes the server's methods.

clone: a copy of an object that is distinct from the original object, equals the original object, and is of the same class as the original object.

collaborator: an object that assists another object in carrying out its responsibilities. Often a component of a composite object.

command: a constituent (feature) of an object used to instruct the object to perform some action which typically results in a change of the object's state.

comment: text included in a program purely for the benefit of a human reader. Comments are ignored by the compiler.

compilation error: a syntactic error.

compilation unit: a text file ("source file") containing the definitions of one or more classes of a package.

compiler: a program that translates programs written in a high-level programming language into a language closer to machine language.

component: **1:** a well-defined part of a system. **2:** a class from which another composite class is constructed, or an instance of such a class used in building a composite object. (See *composition.*) **3:** a distinct element of a graphical user interface, such as a button, text field, and so on.

composed class: a class that is structured from other component classes; a composite class.

composite: a class, or instance of a class, constructed from other component classes. (See *composition.*)

composition: **1:** the process of building a system using simpler components. **2:** the process of defining a new class by putting together existing classes. An instance of the new class, the composite, references instances of the existing classes, its components.

compositional process: a procedure for building an entity by combining simpler pieces.

compound statement: a sequence of statements grouped syntactically to form a single statement. The constituent statements are executed in the order in which they are written.

computation: a sequence of goal-directed actions performed by a processor.

concatenation: an operation in which two *Strings* are joined together to form a longer *String*.

conceptual error: a misunderstanding on the part of the user of the function of the system or of how to use the system.

concrete class: a class that contains a complete implementation, and is instantiated to provide run-time objects that participate in the problem solution.

condition: a boolean expression.

conditional statement: a composite statement that describes a number of alternative processor actions. The action performed by the processor depends on the value of a boolean expression (a condition) included as part of the statement. (See *if-then* and *if-then-else* statements.)

constructor: a mechanism used to create a new object.

container: **1:** an object whose main purpose is to contain other objects. **2:** a graphical user interface component that can contain other components.

contract: part of a method specification that explicitly states the responsibility of the client and the responsibility of the server.

core class: a class used as a component of a composed class.

dangling reference: an erroneous situation arising from reclaiming storage that is still accessible.

data: the information a program deals with.

data description: a description of the kind of data a program requires.

data error: an error caused by incorrect data being provided to a program.

data management: the subsystem responsible for managing persistent data.

data stream: a sequence of bytes to which an application can append data (an output stream) or from which an application can read data (an input stream).

deep copy: a copy of an object in which component objects of the original object are copied.

defensive programming: a programming style in which the server assumes responsibility to check the validity of any arguments provided by the client.

defining occurrence: an occurrence of an identifier in a variable definition, method definition, or parameter specification, in which it is introduced as the name of a method or variable.

dialog: an informational or data gathering window displayed by an application as needed.

direct recursion: an algorithmic technique in which a method directly invokes itself.

dispatching: see *polymorphism.*

distributed system: a collection of networked systems that share resources, and in some ways function as a single system.

do loop: a do statement.

do statement: a statement that specifies an action to be repeated until a condition becomes false. The condition is evaluated after the action is performed.

doc comment: a specially formatted comment that is recognized by system documentation-producing tools.

doubly linked list: a linked list structure in which nodes reference both the following and preceding nodes.

dynamic allocation: variable allocation strategy in which space is explicitly allocated, for instance when an object is created.

dynamic binding: see *polymorphism.*

editor: a program that allows the user to create and modify text files in a computer's file system.

empty: the state of a container that has no elements: an empty container contains 0 elements.

enumeration: a class having a small number of fixed, named, instances.

equivalency group: a set of cases that are expected to behave identically for a test. If one member of an equivalency group passes a given test, all members should pass the test.

error: a mistake by a system designer or user that prevents a system from functioning properly. Errors cause failures.

event: the occurrence of an action, typically external to the system, that the system is aware of and must respond to.

event handler: an *event listener.*

event listener: an object that will be notified when a particular event occurs in a particular component, and that will then take appropriate action in response to the event.

event-driven: an input-output model in which the application waits for an external event, such as mouse click, button press, menu choice *etc.*, to occur, responds to the event, and waits for the next event

exception: the occurrence of a detectable, abnormal situation that may lead to system failure. Also, an instance of the class *Exception* that carries information about the cause of an abnormal situation.

expression: a language construct that specifies how to compute a particular value.

extends: the relationship of a class to a more abstract class, or of an interface to a more abstract interface. Also called *is-a.*

extension: the language mechanism for implementing abstraction.

external interface: the subsystem responsible for communicating with the external world. See *user interface.*

factory method: an abstract constructor.

failure: the inability of a system or method to accomplish its intended purpose at run-time.

feature: a query or command to which an object responds.

file: a named collection of information stored in a machine's file system.

file system: the collection of files, containing programs and data, that a machine has access to; usually stored on disk.

final feature: a component or parameter that cannot be changed after it is given a value.

font: an entity that encapsulates a collection of glyphs and other information necessary to render a set of characters.

for statement: a loop statement in which the initialization, test, and update parts are combined in the loop heading.

function object: an object whose only purpose is to carry some functionality. Typically, a function object has no state.

functional specification: a description of the functionality required of a system. (See *system specification.*)

functional test: a test to determine if a system meets customer specifications.

functionality: the actions a program is expected to perform, or the purpose it is expected to satisfy.

garbage collection: memory reclamation strategy in which the run-time system notes when variables are no longer accessible and reclaims the allocated storage space.

generalization: the relationship of a class or interface to a more concrete class or interface.

generic instantiation: defining an interface, class, or method from a generic structure by providing "type arguments" for the type parameters.

generic method: a method having type parameters.

generic structure: an interface, class, or method that has one or more "type parameters."

glyph: a shape used to render a character or sequence of characters.

gray box test: a test in which specification of the component classes is used to develop test cases.

guard: a boolean expression associated with a statement, that prevents or allows the statement to be executed. A guarded statement will be executed only if its guard evaluates to *true.* (See *if-then* statement.)

hardware failure: the failure of a system due to hardware malfunction.

header: a node that does not carry an element, but serves the purpose of always being present even in an empty list.

heavyweight component: a graphical user interface component that has a corresponding (peer) component in the native windowing system of the machine.

hierarchy: the structure of relationships that results from reiterated abstraction or extension.

identifier: a sequence of characters that can be used to name entities in a program. A Java identifier can contain letters, digits, underscores, and dollar signs. It must not begin with a digit.

identifier literal: a sequence of characters that conforms to the rules for an identifier, but is in fact a literal. Identifier literals cannot be used as identifiers. `true`, `false`, and `null` are identifier literals in Java.

if-then statement: a conditional statement that specifies an action that is to be performed only if a stipulated condition is true.

if-then-else statement: a conditional statement that specifies two alternative actions, one to be performed if a stipulated condition is true, the other if the condition is false.

immutable object: an object that does not change state after it is created.

implementation: the actual internal details that support the specification of an object.

implementation class: class that supports the algorithmic implementation of the system.

implementation driven testing: a testing strategy in which the structure of the implementation is used to design the tests. See *white box testing*.

import statement: a statement that permits a class to be referred to with its simple name rather than with its fully qualified name.

index: position of a list element relative to the beginning of the list: the first element on a list is at index 0, the second element is at index 1, and so on. Same as *offset*.

indirect recursion: an algorithmic technique in which a method calls another method, resulting in a chain of calls that ultimately includes a call to the original method.

infinite loop: a loop for which the continuation condition remains true. An infinite loop, theoretically, never terminates.

inheritance: the mechanism by which a class or interface automatically gets all of the non-private features of its superclass or superinterface.

inner class: a nested class that is not a static member class.

input stream: a data stream from which an application can read data.

input/output device: a mechanism by which a computer system communicates with the outside world.

instance: an object. An object that is a member of a class is called an "instance of the class."

instance variable: a variable that contains data stored as part of an object's state. An instance variable is a permanent part of an object; memory space for the variable is allocated when the object is created.

instanceof: an operator that determines, at run-time, whether or not a reference value is of a specified type.

instruction: a description of an action to be performed by a processor.

instruction set: the set of instructions that a particular processor can understand.

interaction diagram: a diagram that shows the order in which requests between objects are performed.

interface: **1:** a language structure that specifies functionality without any hint at implementation. An interface contains method specifications but no method implementations. It defines the functionality required by a client of a server. **2:** the collection of features of an object as seen by its clients. Also called the specification of the object.

intermediate container: a container whose purpose is to simplify the organization and positioning of basic graphical components.

internal iterator: an object that will perform a specified operation with each element of a container. Traversal of the container is controlled by the iterator implementation rather than by the client.

interpreter: a program which reads and executes, step by step, another program that typically has been translated into an intermediate language.

invariant: a condition that always holds.

irreflexive relation: a relation in which no value is related to itself.

is-a: the relationship of a class or interface to a more abstract class or interface. Also called *extends*.

iteration: a process in which an operation is performed several times. More precisely, a problem solving technique in which the solution is obtained in a series of similar "steps," each step building on the partial solution provided by the previous step.

iterative process: a procedure for solving a problem by repeated steps.

iterator: an object used to access each element in a container.

keyword: a sequence of characters that conforms to the rules for an identifier, but is used for a special syntactic purpose, and cannot be used as an identifier.

layout manager: an object responsible for positioning and sizing components in a container.

lightweight component: graphical user interface component that is implemented entirely in Java. It has not corresponding (peer) component in the native windowing system of the machine.

linear search: a search algorithm that locates an item on a list by examining each list item in sequence. Same as *sequential search*.

linked list: a list implementation in which the sequential relationship between list elements is explicitly modeled by references between nodes.

list: a container in which the elements are kept in sequence: there is a first element, a second, and so on, depending on the number of elements in the container.

literal: a sequence of characters used in a program to denote a particular value.

local class: a named class defined in the body of a method or constructor.

local variable: a method variable created as part of a method execution, used to hold intermediate results needed during the computation.

logical error: an error in a program which causes it to produce incorrect results, even though the program is syntactically legal. A program containing logical errors is legal in the programming language, but does not produce the intended results.

loop: an iteration. More precisely, a programming language mechanism for carrying out an iterative solution.

loop invariant: a condition that is true no matter how many times the body of the loop is executed. In particular, the invariant is true when the loop is started, and is still true when the loop terminates.

machine language: the instruction set of a particular processor.

main method: the top-level method that initiates execution of the system.

member class: a nested class that is defined directly in the containing class. It is a feature of the containing class.

memory leak: an erroneous situation resulting from inaccessible storage not being reclaimed.

memory: a computer system component in which data and algorithm reside when the processor is using them.

menu: a pull-down or pop-up list of options from which the user may choose.

menu bar: an area, typically at the top of a window, containing one or more menus.

method: the Java construct used to specify and implement queries and commands.

method body: the sequence of statements that comprise the implementation of a method. When the method is invoked, the processor executes the statements that make up the method body.

method invocation: the action of a client that causes an object to execute a method.

method variable: a variable that is created when a method is invoked, and deallocated when the method is completed.

modal dialog: a dialog that blocks interaction with all other application windows while it is visible.

model: the subsystem responsible for representing and actually solving the problem at hand. Also known as the problem domain subsystem.

model class: class that directly models an aspect of the external system.

Model-View-Controller: a pattern for structuring a graphical user interface or graphical user interface component, in which display responsibilities for a model are delegated to a separate *view*, and input responsibilities are delegated to a separate *controller*.

multiple inheritance: the ability of a class to implement more than one interface, or of an interface to extend more than one interface.

mutable object: an object that can change state after it is created.

named constant: a value that has an identifier (a name) associated with it; the associated identifier can be used to refer to the value.

nested class: a class whose definition is contained in the body of another class.

nested loops: two (or more) loops, where one of the loops is contained in the body of the other.

network: a number of computers and other devices connected together so that they can communicate with each other and share resources.

node: a member of a linked structure that carries an element of the structure, and references other nodes of the structure.

null reference: a unique reference value that doesn't denote any object.

numeric promotion: the automatic conversion of a numeric value of one type to an equivalent value of a different type, as required by context.

object: a software abstraction representing some data component to be manipulated by the system.

object-oriented: a method of software development in which the system is organized around data objects.

object recursion: a recursive technique in which an object builds a solution by obtaining a solution to a simpler version of the problem from a component that is similar to itself.

observer pattern: a structural pattern by which a server informs a client that it (the server) has reached some particular state.

offset: position of a list element relative to the beginning of the list; same as *index*.

operand: a value given to an operator and used in the computation of another value.

operating system: the fundamental resource management software of a computer system.

operator: a symbol denoting an operation to be performed on one or more values, producing another value as result.

operator precedence rules: rules that specify the order in which operators are applied in the evaluation of an expression.

ordering: an antisymmetric, transitive relation on a class.

output stream: a data stream to which an application can append output.

overloading: providing a class with several distinct methods having the same name.

overriding: redefining the implementation of a method that a class inherits from its superclass.

package: a set of related class definitions. A package is the fundamental structural unit of a Java application.

package private: attribute of a feature that makes it accessible to all class members of same package.

package statement: the Java construct used to state the package to which a source file belongs.

parameter: a method variable defined in a method or constructor specification, that is initialized with a client-supplied argument when the method or constructor is invoked.

partial correctness: the assertion that a loop is correct if it terminates.

passive iterator: an internal iterator.

peer: a native windowing system component, associated with a (heavyweight) Java component.

persistent data: data that must be maintained whether the system is running or not.

polymorphism: dynamic behavior by which the algorithm performed as the result of a call to an overridden method is determined by the run-time class of the object executing the method. Also referred to as *dispatching* or *dynamic binding.*

postcondition: a condition the implementor of a method guarantees will hold when the method completes execution.

precondition: a condition the client of a method must make sure holds when the method is invoked.

primitive type: a type provided as an integral part of the language. Java's built-in types include **byte**, **short**, **int**, **long**, **float**, **double**, **char**, and **boolean**.

problem analysis: a thorough examination of the problem to be solved, resulting in a *system specification.*

problem domain subsystem: See *model.*

processor: the component of the system that actually performs the actions of a computation.

program: a collection of data descriptions and algorithms, expressed in a programming language, designed to solve a problem. A program is usually considered to be a self-contained piece of software that solves a particular, static, well-defined problem.

programming by contract: a programming style in which the invocation of a method is viewed as a contract between client and server, with each having explicitly stated responsibilities.

programming language: a formal notation in which data descriptions and algorithms are expressed.

programming language: a formal notation in which data descriptions and algorithms are expressed.

property: a characteristic of an object. A value is associated with each property of an object.

protected: attribute of a features that makes it accessible in subclasses.

public class: a class that is accessible from the entire software system. A class not identified as public is accessible only from within its package.

query: a constituent (feature) of an object used to obtain some data value from the object. A query might simply provide the value associated with some property, or might require the object to perform a computation to produce the value.

quick sort: an efficient recursive sorting algorithm that first partitions a list into elements smaller than a selected pivot element, the pivot element in proper position, and elements larger than the pivot elements. The sublists of smaller and larger elements are then recursively quick sorted.

recursion: a problem solving technique in which a general case problem solution is built from a solution to a slightly simpler version of the problem.

reference value: a value which denotes or refers to an object.

reflexive relation: a relation in which each reference value is related to itself. If $\approx$ is a reflexive relation, then $x \approx x$ is true for every reference value x.

relational expression: an expression composed of two arithmetic expressions joined with a relational or equality operator.

return statement: a statement that specifies the value to be delivered to the client. A return statement is the last statement executed in a query method.

run-time failure: a failure that occurs while a program is executing (running).

scope: the section of program text in which applied occurrences of an identifier refers to the identifier introduced by a particular definition.

scoping rules: language rules that associate applied identifier occurrences with defining occurrences.

selection sort: a sort algorithm that operates by repeatedly finding the smallest item not yet positioned, and putting it in its proper position.

semantic error: a logical error.

semantics: the set of rules that specify the meaning of a syntactically legal construct in a programming language.

sequential search: a search algorithm that locates an item on a list by examining each list item in sequence. Same as *linear search*.

serialization: a mechanism for writing objects to a byte stream, and later recreating the objects from the byte stream.

server: in reference to a given object, a server is another object, which provides a service to the given object. The given object is called the *client*. The client accesses the features of the server, that is, it invokes the server's methods.

shallow copy: a copy of an object in which instance variable values of the original object are copied.

single inheritance: the restriction that requires each class to have exactly one parent class.

software error: a syntactic or logical error in a program.

software life cycle: phases a software system undergoes from its inception to its retirement.

software system: a collection of data descriptions and algorithms, expressed in a programming language, designed to solve a particular problem or set of related problems.

sort: an algorithm arranges the elements of a list according to some ordering.

source file: a text file containing data descriptions and algorithms expressed in a programming language.

specification: the collection of features of an object as seen by its clients. Also called the *interface* of the object.

standard error: a standard output stream used for writing error messages. The default destination of standard error is the terminal window from which the program is run.

standard input: a standard input stream available to an application. The default source of standard input is the keyboard.

standard output: a standard output stream available to an application. The default destination of standard output is the terminal window from which the program is run.

state: the set of properties of an object and their current values.

statement: a language construct that describes an action for the processor to perform.

static diagram: a diagram showing classes and their relation to each other.

static feature: a feature associated with a class rather than with instances of the class. See *class method.*

strategy pattern: a structural pattern by which an object is provided with a changeable component to which it delegates certain functionality.

stream: a data stream.

structural recursion: a structure in which an object has a component of the same class as itself.

subclass: the relationship of a class to the class it extends. The more concrete class is a *subclass* of the more abstract class.

subtype: a type whose constituent values are also members of another (super) type. If A is a subtype of B, then an expression of type A can be written in any context requiring a value of type B.

superclass: the relationship of a class to a class that extends it. The more abstract class is a *superclass* of the more concrete class.

supertype: a type that contains the values of another (sub) type. (See *subtype.*)

Swing: a particular collection of library classes and interfaces used to build graphical user interfaces in Java.

switch statement: a statement in which the value of an integer or character expression is used to determine where to begin a sequence of component statements.

symmetric relation: a relation that satisfies the property that $x \approx y$ implies $y \approx x$, for all reference values x and y.

syntactic error: an error resulting from not adhering to the grammatical rules of a programming language. A program containing syntactic errors is not a legal program in the language in which it is written.

syntax: the set of grammatical and punctuation rules for a programming language.

system design: defining a collection of classes and their interactions that will satisfy the system specifications.

system functionality: the set of tasks a system is required to be able to perform.

system implementation: constructing the (software) modules that will make up the system, using programming languages and other software development tools.

system maintenance: modifying a system to meet changing requirements and correcting problems detected after the system is put into production.

system specification: a description of the functionality required of a system. (See *functional specification*.)

test driven implementation: an implementation strategy in which tests for a feature are written before the feature is implemented.

test fixture: a set of objects on which a test is to be performed.

test plan: a document that details how a system or system component will be tested.

testing: an activity whose goal is to determine whether or not an implementation functions as intended, according to specification.

text-based user interface: a user interface in which input is in the form of text keyed by the user, and output is in the form of text displayed in the window in which the program is run.

thread: an independent sequence of instructions being executed by the processor.

top-level class: a class that is not a nested class.

top-level container: a graphical user interface container that is not an element of any other container.

transitive relation: a relation that satisfies the property that x related to y and y related to z implies x related to z, for all values x, y, and z for which the relation is defined.

try block: the syntactic part of a *try-catch* statement that defines the "normal" execution of the statement.

try-catch statement: a Java statement used to detect and handle exceptions.

type: a set of similar values along with the operations that can be performed with them.

unary operator: an operator that requires one operand; that is, computes a value from one given value. Also called a *monadic* operator.

unchecked exception: an exception that is an instance of *RuntimeException* or of one of its subclasses. Unchecked exceptions can occur almost anywhere in a program.

unit test: a test to determine if a class is correctly implemented.

user interface: the subsystem responsible for interacting with the human user of a system. See *external interface.*

value: a fundamental piece of information manipulated in a program.

variable: a portion of memory reserved to hold a single value.

variable declaration: a language construct that causes a variable with specified type and name to be allocated.

variable definition: a variable declaration.[1]

while loop: a while statement.

while statement: a statement that specifies an action to be repeated until a condition becomes false. The condition is evaluated before the action is performed.

white box test: a test designed by taking into account the implementation of the system of the component being tested.

wrapper: A class, or instance of a class, that modifies the specification of an existing class. The wrapper has the wrapped class as a component, and forwards requests for service to the component.

---

1. In some programming languages, there is a technical distinction between a definition and a declaration. However, there is no consistency in the distinction. What one language calls a "declaration" another calls a "definition" and *vice versa*. The *Java Language Specification* [Joy 00] uses the term "declaration" exclusively. We use the two terms as synonyms.

REFERENCES

[Arnold 00]
Ken Arnold, James Gosling and David Holmes. *The Java Programming Language, Third Edition*. Addison-Wesley, 2000.

[Beck 03]
Kent Beck. *Test-Driven Development By Example*. Addison-Wesley, 2003.

[Booch 01]
Grady Booch, Robert Martin, and James W. Newkirk. *Object-Oriented Analysis and Design with Applications, Third Edition*. Addison-Wesley, 2001.

[Budd 02]
Timothy Budd. *An Introduction to Object-Oriented Programming, Third Edition*. Addison-Wesley, 2002.

[Coad 99]
Peter Coad, Mark Mayfield, and Jonathan Kern. *Java Design: Building Better Apps and Applets. Second Edition*. Prentice Hall, 1999.

[Cooper 00]
James W. Cooper. *Java Design Patterns: A Tutorial*. Addison-Wesley, 2000.

[Deitel 03]
H. M. Deitel and P. J. Deitel. *Java How to Program, Fifth Edition*. Prentice Hall, 2003.

[Gamma 95]
Erich Gamma, Richard Helm, Ralph Johnson, and John Vlissides. *Design Patterns: Elements of Reusable Object-Oriented Software*. Addison-Wesley, 1995.

[Goodrich 03]
Michael T. Goodrich, Roberto Tamassia. *Data Structures and Algorithms in Java, Third Edition*. John Wiley & Sons, 2003.

[Horstmann 01]
Cay Horstmann. *Big Java: Programming and Practice*. John Wiley & Sons, 2001.

[Jia 02]

Xiaoping Jia. *Object Oriented Software Development Using Java, Second Edition.* Addison-Wesley, 2002.

[Joy 00]

Bill Joy, Guy Steele, Jar Gosling, and Gilad Bracha. *The Java Language Specification, Second Edition.* Addison-Wesley, 2000.

[Larman 01]

Craig Larman. *Applying UML and Patterns: An Introduction to Object-Oriented Analysis and Design, Second Edition.* Prentice Hall, 2001.

[Lazslo 02]

Michael J. Laszlo. *Object Oriented Programming featuring Graphical Applications in Java.* Addison-Wesley, 2002.

[Meyer 88]

Bertrand Meyer. *Object-Oriented Software Construction.* Prentice Hall, 1988.

[Meyer 97]

Bertrand Meyer. *Object-Oriented Software Construction, Second Edition.* Prentice Hall, 1997.

[Topley 00]

Kim Topley. *Core Swing: Advanced Programming.* Prentice Hall, 2000.

[Topley 02]

Kim Topley. *Core Java Foundation Classes, Second Edition.* Prentice Hall, 2002.

[Warren 99]

Nigel Warren and Philip Bishop. *Java in Practice: Design Styles and Idioms for Effective Java.* Addison-Wesley, 1999.

[Wirth 75]

Niklaus Wirth. *Algorithms + Data Structures = Programs.* Prentice-Hall, 1975.

INDEX